The Psychology of
Language,
Thought,
and Instruction

The Psychology of

Language,

Thought,

and Instruction

READINGS

JOHN P. DE CECCO

San Francisco State College

46040

HOLT, RINEHART AND WINSTON, INC.

New York · Chicago · San Francisco · Toronto · London

Library of Congress Catalog Card Number: 66–13293
2558658
Printed in the United States of America
2   3   4   5   6   7   8   9

To My Colleagues in Education and Psychology

Preface

We need a book on how to teach language and thought. This book does *not* satisfy that need. Nor does any book. Inspection of the available research literature reveals this sobering state of affairs: we have little basic knowledge in the three areas, language, thought, and teaching, and even less knowledge of their interrelations. If the student wants to pursue the madness of asking how we should conduct instruction in conceptual thought and linguistic behavior, he soon finds himself perusing the basic research even though his chief interests are more practical than theoretical.

Yet, more than ever before, we need to know. American education has renewed its pledge to teach the children of the poor and the rich all the basic skills and subject matter. In a highly verbal culture there are obvious advantages for all children to speak, read, and write well. In a scientific culture all children must learn the type of conceptual thinking we associate with science and mathematics. What were once educational objectives reserved only for the "gifted" or the middle and upper classes are now serious commitments for all American children. Teaching methodology now enjoys popular discussion because we are discovering that we have too little knowledge of how to teach language and thought, especially to the children of the poor.

In addressing himself to the problem of instruction in language and thought, the editor found it necessary to cross many disciplines and attend to their interrelations. He has borrowed theory and fact from linguistics, psycholinguistics, the psychology of cognition and verbal learning, developmental psychology, anthropology, sociology, and education. In this collection none of these areas can stand alone. The risk that an interdisciplinary book must take is the profound disappointment it causes the disciplinary scholar, who feels that his field is somehow misrepresented. The purpose of the book, however, is not to represent each discipline separately but only within the framework of the general objective—greater knowledge and understanding of instruction in language and thought.

The fulfillment of this objective, as we have stated, required excursions into many disciplines. One of these disciplines is linguistics. In maturity of technique and theory and wealth of data the science of linguistics rivals the science of psychology. Linguistics describes the state or nature of the language. It is the study of messages once they are "on the air" [Chapter 1]. Descriptive linguistics includes the study of phonology, morphology, and syntax. Linguistics assumes that languages are codes that can be described without reference to meaning and that the spoken language has primacy over the written language. Beyond descriptive linguistics is generative or transformational grammar, which tries to explain why the native speaker is able to understand and produce an infinity of novel sentences.

Psycholinguistics, itself an interdisciplinary field with which this anthology is seriously concerned, explores the relation between messages and the encoding and decoding processes of the human beings who select and interpret them [Chapter 1]. Therefore, although the linguist studies messages, the psycholinguist studies communicators. The psycholinguist uses language to study thought. Psycholinguistic research has found Chomsky's transformational grammar a fruitful theoretical base because transformations are a combined product of linguistic structure and psychological processes within the speaker. The relation between language mastery and various intellectual processes is explored in articles in Chapter 1.

There is also the interdisciplinary field of anthropological linguistics—sometimes called linguistic relativity and ethnolinguistics [Chapter 2]. This field is the study of the relation of language and thought to culture. While education embraces the children of divergent cultural backgrounds we must build anthropological variables into our educational research. Franz Boas, and Edward Sapir [Chapter 2], both of whom helped to establish the primacy of the phoneme, are the "fathers" of anthropological linguistics.

The current lively interest in the relation of language and thought to social class differences is a direct reflection of our present concern for the education of the "culturally disadvantaged." In Chapter 3 we see that a major disadvantage of the underprivileged is their verbal and cognitive underdevelopment. Unfortunately, in education and psychology we sometimes substitute a limp compassion, sentimentality, and romanticism of lower-class values for the serious business of teaching underprivileged children what they need to know. We are not demeaning the poor when we study their linguistic and cognitive deficiencies. It is also patently absurd to masque these deficiencies as cultural "differences." Knowledge of the linguistic and cognitive habits of the underprivileged will enable us to devise appropriate instruction. The articles in Chapter 3 attempt to identify social class differences in linguistic and cognitive behavior.

Several chapters represent the discipline of psychology. In Chapter 4 we raise the thorny question of the meaning of meaning and how meaning is acquired. We see how semantic theory must supplement grammatical theory to explain the ability of native speakers to interpret sentences. About four of the chapters deal with various aspects of the relation of language and cognition. Chapter 6 discusses how thought is studied. Chapter 7 concerns the development of language and thought. Chapter 8 discusses how language is acquired. Finally, Chapter 9 considers the relation of language and problem solving. An underlying issue in these four chapters is the differences in the theoretical models, terminology, and, to some lesser extent, the research techniques of the behavioral and cognitive theorists. In the tradition of S-R learning theory and methodology, the behaviorists use horizontal models that relate antecedent stimulus conditions to consequent response events [Chapter 6]. The cognitive theorists use vertical hierarchies in which lower-level operations, patterns, meaning, strategies, and so on, are subsumed under higher-level functions. On the surface it appears that no two conceptualizations of thought or behavior could be more divergent. It all looks like an exciting controversy made venerable by the tradition that opposed Gestalt and behaviorist psychology. However, the coalescing of the two points of view, which in substance may chiefly reflect the personal preferences of researchers for various models and terminology, may be even more exciting and fruitful. In any event, the neo-behaviorists are developing and using more intervening variables, such as response hierarchies and verbal mediators; and the cognitive theorists, such as Piaget, are paying more attention than ever before to the specification and control of independent stimulus and dependent response variables. As Kendler observes, however [Chapter 6], we may discover that as the stimulus-response unit shifts from the nonsense syllable and single word to the phrase or sentence we may be in for more theoretical surprises than we now anticipate. The editor joins Kendler in the hope that there can be a greater rapprochement between learning and developmental psychologists in their investigations of the acquisition of language and thought.

Two chapters are directly concerned with instruction in language and thought. Chapter 5 concerns instruction in reading, for which there is a vast polemical and empirical literature. The research is frequently basic, as in the study of grapheme-phoneme correspondence (Gibson and associates [Chapter 5]), or it is applied, as in comparing the use of i.t.a. and traditional orthography. Chapter 10 largely concerns research on instruction in conceptual thinking. The issue that this research must resolve is the relative merits of deductive and inductive teaching for various levels of student aptitude and subject matter and for available classroom time. Inductive instructional models are now the most popular in the research literature (but not necessarily in the schools), but there is little published research that can help teachers decide under what conditions an inductive approach is preferable to a deductive approach. Chapter 10 also deals with research on the teaching of English and foreign languages. Linguistics has made "audio-lingual" approaches popular in the teaching of grammar and in the language laboratories, but it is hard to see what additional *direct* contributions to instructional methodology linguistics can make at this time. The editor believes that modern linguistics will make its chief contributions to psycholinguistics in the study of human encoding and decoding processes. The findings of psycholinguistics, in turn, may become a fruitful base for research on teaching.

Only recently, in fact, has research on teaching seriously undertaken the development of models and theory. In discussing research on the teaching of reading, language, mathematics, and so on, we often forget that we have little or no basic research on teaching methodology. Under federal grants at several major universities this research is now seriously under way. Until we know a little more about teaching in general it will be difficult if not impossible to discover much of consequence in teaching various subject matter and intellectual skills.

To avoid a book of unmanageable length it has been necessary to exclude many excellent articles that deal with specialized aspects of topics (for example, intra-dimensional shifts as an aspect of the study of reversal and nonreversal shifts) or with different but related topics (such as perception and language). We have not included articles on the neurological aspects of language and thought, although we list and discuss a few of the important references [Chapters 2 and 7]. With the exception of the Whorf thesis we have excluded articles that specifically explore the relation of perception and language, particularly as this study is reflected in the work of Roger Brown, Harry Helson, Eric Lenneberg, Leo Postman, and Mark Rosenzweig. We should have liked to include some of the studies of cognitive style, as exemplified in the research of Jerome Kagan and H. A. Moss. The work of Allen Newell, Earl Hunt, and their associates on the computer simulation of thought or problem-solving processes deserves more note than we have given to it. Experimental tests of Piaget's theories and hypotheses by British and American psychologists required more space than we could provide. And there is a growing field of experimental anthropology which may considerably add to our understanding of language and thought.

The editor's introductions to each chapter are designed for two purposes: (1) to point up questions and issues that the relevant research has raised or answered and (2) to provide a theoretical background for the various articles in the chapters. The introductions include the discussion of more articles than appear in this collection. The references following the introductions list articles discussed but not included in this book. Students who wish to read more extensively in the current literature will find these lists useful.

At one point the editor considered the inclusion of a glossary. However, because meanings of technical terms vary over time and from author to author, it was decided to index the various definitions rather than favor one definition over another or define a term so generally that it means very little. The index will indicate pages in the text that define technical terms.

The editor gratefully acknowledges the authors and publishers who have generously consented either to the reprinting or original publication of their articles. He is deeply indebted to those who reviewed the various drafts of the prospectus, suggested inclusion and deletion of various articles, and commented on the drafts of his introductory materials: Professors Roger Brown and John Carroll of Harvard University, Professor Dale Harris of the Pennsylvania State University, Professor Arthur Jensen of the University of California at Berkeley, Professor William Kesson of Yale University, and Professor Jerome Podell of San Francisco State College. The editor wishes to thank his colleagues in the Department of Psychology and the Center for Interdisciplinary Studies in Education at San Francisco State College for their help and encouragement. He also wishes to thank Professor Eric Hamp of The University of Chicago for the revision of his paper on linguistics.

For their loyal and patient help in attending to the many details in the final preparation of the manuscript, the editor owes his appreciation to Professor Ann Paterson (an editor in her own right), Miss Patricia Quance, Mr. Howard Lloyd Kelley, and to Miss Yvette Gagnon, a graduate student in psychology at San Francisco State College.

J. P. DE C.

San Francisco
November 1966

Contents

The Psychology of

Language,

Thought,

and Instruction

The Study of Language: In the Beginning Was the Sound

_____ *1*

INTRODUCTION

Language has been with us a long time and, like other familiar phenomena, to single it out for special attention always appears somewhat artificial. In education we pay due respect to its importance even if we do not always understand its nature. In psychology, beginning with Ebbinghaus, the study of verbal learning and verbal behavior has a long tradition and a promising future. The fear of "verbalism" in both education and psychotherapy, the use of words without meaning for the user, has occasionally prompted the educator and the therapist to decry the use of language and, perhaps more whimsically than seriously, to entertain the possibility of carrying on treatment and instruction without the use of words. Also, some educators speak about "verbal intelligence" and almost suggest that it is an idiosyncracy of the middle class which the education of underprivileged children should disavow. Even in psychology the study of language as the most distinctive aspect of human, as opposed to animal, behavior has received modest attention [Miller, Chapters 1, 8].[1] In textbooks on general and educational psychology, language, as a topic, receives cursory attention, considered either as an extension of animal learning or an aspect of social psychology and communication.

In both education and psychology there are strong indications of renewed interest in language as a subject matter in its own right and as an important domain of human behavior. Beyond the application of linguistics to the teaching of grammar, reading, and foreign language, there are investigations of language and thought in European, American, and Soviet psychology and education that may considerably improve our

[1] References in brackets are to passages in this anthology; those in parentheses are to the lists at the ends of the introductions and selections.

1

knowledge of how language is acquired and how it relates to thought. For example, although operant conditioning enjoys considerable favor in American psychology, the cognitive theorists with their interest in brain function and central processes are enjoying equal if not greater favor. Even the behaviorists find invisible mediating processes fruitful explanations of stimulus-response relations [Kendler, Chapter 9]. Some are even attempting to provide a neo-behavioristic framework for investigating the relation of motivation to thinking (Berlyne, 1965). We should like to prophesy that the empiricism of the cognitive theorist, as indicated by his interest in brain function and the computer, and the mediational processes of the behaviorist may herald a belated rapprochement, but investigators of both schools still find their differences much more important than their similarities [Skinner, Miller, Chapter 8].

The scientific study of language is called linguistics. More properly, linguistics is the study of messages once they are "on the air" (Osgood and Sebeok, 1965, page 3). The linguist determines the *code* of the message, the characteristics that distinguish one message from another. Psycholinguistics, an area of research with which this anthology is concerned, concerns the relation between messages and the characteristics of the persons who select and interpret them. The psycholinguist studies the *encoding* and *decoding* processes of human individuals. In summary, just as the linguist studies messages, the psycholinguist studies communicators. The study of communicators, moreover, combines the study of language and thought.

Eric Hamp, in an article in this chapter, describes the two basic assumptions of linguistics: (1) that language as a set of signs or as a code can be described quite apart from meaning or what the signs or codes refer to in the objective, personal, or social world; and (2) that the spoken language (the sounds of the language) precedes and is more fundamental in the description of the language than are the peculiar characteristics of the written language. Hamp's discussion introduces key linguistic terms. There is the *phoneme*, which describes the range of sound a native speaker distinguishes or fails to distinguish. The native speaker, of course, distinguishes an infinitely small number of all possible vocal sounds. Although he contrasts a few sounds, the phonemes of his language, he conveniently lumps all other vocal sounds into relatively few pigeonholes. There are about forty-five phonemes in the English language. *Morphemes* are considerably more difficult to define and identify. Hamp develops the idea of morphemes in connection with meaning, although some modern linguists prefer to avoid the subject of meaning just as many psychologists of learning prefer to avoid the discussion of motivation and perception. Morphemes at least refer to form. Any form that cannot be divided into two or more forms is a morpheme (Carroll, 1964). Take the words "lighthouse," "redbook," and "unreconstructed." The morphemes are as follows: *light, house, red, book, un-, re-, construct,* and *-ed.* Note that *con* could be a morpheme except that *struct* cannot stand alone as an independent form. Morphemes are almost words, but Hamp points out how "word" is an ill-defined concept. He also distinguishes between different types of morphemes—free forms and bound forms.

The notion that people speak ungrammatically does not make good linguistic sense. They are more likely to write ungrammatically if their writing somehow is divorced from their speech practices. Certain modes of speaking may have particular snob or esthetic value, but they do not have greater linguistic justification. Since the linguists have been asserting with ideological conviction the primacy of speech, there have been sharp debates of what is good English, with the "purists" insisting on resisting change and the erosion of traditional standards, and the linguistic "liberals" sometimes espousing that "anything you hear is right." Most teachers of English must define for themselves and their students a position between these extremes. In the meantime most writers will at least occasionally split an infinitive.

Hamp also discusses how different languages cause their native speakers to "slice their universe" in different ways and to express or fail to express and to have knowledge of some objects and experiences. The dozen genders of the Bantu languages, as compared with the two genders in French, give gender in these languages considerably more refinement. This assumption is based on the Whorf thesis, which is discussed in Chapter 2.

Beyond descriptive linguistics, the description of the language code, there is the generative or transformational grammar of Chomsky and his followers (Chomsky, 1957). Transformational grammar is the attempt to explain why the native speaker is able to understand and produce sentences that may have never been written or spoken before. Its basic assumption is that language is a system of rules which can be variously arranged to form and understand new sentences. Knowledge of a language is based on intuitive mastery of the rules. There are two important concepts in transformational grammar, the *kernel sentences* and *transforms*. Kernel sentences are the basic stuff of language. Chomsky describes them as the underlying structures which express all the syntactical relations and functions that appear in any sentence (Chomsky, 1964, page xiii). The article by Henry Gleason demonstrates how these transformations are made. Gleason also uses "noun phrase" and "verb phrase." In the sentence, "The boy hit the ball," the noun phrase is "the boy," and "hit the ball" is the verb phrase. In many kernel sentences the noun phrase can be more familiarly identified as the subject and the verb phrase as the predicate. However, in the transforms the relation between these phrases may be quite different from the one described by the subject-predicate relation. Recently Postal has used the concept of *phrase makers* to describe underlying linguistic structure (Postal, 1964). Phrase makers describe the parts of this structure, how these parts are grouped together into significant sequences, and what type of grouping each is.

Chomsky's transformational grammar is of major importance in the study of the relation of language and thought, or psycholinguistics. The transformations to which he refers are a combined product of linguistic structure and psychological processes within the speaker. For example, attempts have been made to study the relation of grammatical transformations to the recall of English sentences (Mehler, 1963). Miller, in an article in this chapter, is interested in studying human encoding and decoding processes, which he describes as the "combinatorial power" to arrange grammatical rules to form new and useful sentences. As a psychologist, Miller is concerned less with explaining language structure than with the human intellectual processes that underlie language mastery. Miller uses the notion of syntactic categories (roughly equivalent to parts of speech) to raise some interesting questions: (1) what is the relation to our memory of words and syntactic categories? and (2) what is the relation of these categories to our understanding of a sentence? The research he describes suggests how at least certain aspects of transformational processes may be investigated. In effect, Miller is using modern linguistic theory to study the functions of the human mind. As he indicates, "mind" is a four-letter word that American psychologists need no longer avoid.

Vygotsky, in the following article, proposes a functional interrelation of language and thought. Vygotsky criticizes atomistic and behavioristic studies of verbal learning that essentially separate thought and word, sound and meaning. He suggests that a more fruitful way to pursue the study of language and thought is to use a "unit of analysis" comparable to the molecule in the physical sciences and to the cell in biology. This unit, he proposes, is *word meaning*.

It is far too early to predict how useful linguistic theory and the linguistic description of language will be for the study of human thought. We can report only that the use of language to study thought processes has produced some interesting experimentation and that the results of this research could make important contributions to the theory and practice of instruction. One psychologist has suggested several possible relations between linguistics and education (Carroll, 1953).

REFERENCES

Berlyne, D. E. *Structure and direction in thinking.* New York: Wiley, 1965.

Carroll, J. B. *Language and thought.* Englewood Cliffs, N.J.: Prentice-Hall, 1964.

———. *The study of language: A survey of linguistics and related disciplines in America.* New York: Cambridge, 1953.

Chomsky, N. *Syntactic structures.* 's-Gavenhage, Holland: Mouton, 1957.

———. Introduction. In *P. Roberts, English syntax: Alternate edition.* New York: Harcourt, 1964.

Mehler, J. Some effects of grammatical transformations on the recall of English sentences, *J. verb. Learn. verb. Behav.*, 1963, **2**, 346–351.

Osgood, C. E., and T. E. Sebeok. *Psycholinguistics: A survey of theory and research prob-lems.* This includes A. R. Diebold, Jr., *A survey of psycholinguistic research 1954–1964.* Bloomington: Indiana University Press, 1965.

Postal, P. M. Underlying and superficial linguistic structure, *Harvard Educ. Rev.*, 1964, 34, No. 2, 246–266.

Saporta, S. (Ed.) *Psycholinguistics: A book of readings.* New York: Holt, Rinehart and Winston, 1961.

Language in a Few Words: With Notes on a Rereading, 1966

ERIC P. HAMP

The fundamental aim of scholarship is to advance knowledge. For this purpose it is necessary for the specialist to make use of terms and methods some of which are technically very complex. But the fruits of scholarship will be barren indeed, if from time to time they are not made intelligible to educated men at large in such a form that the nonspecialist may increase his understanding without being expected to retrace all the steps laboriously trodden in the first place by the specialist.

The fact that there is no comparable understanding of the advance of knowledge of such a familiar phenomenon as language seems hard to understand. [This situation has happily changed somewhat since these words were written, though with two reservations: (1) Recent knowledge has still not really percolated to the level of the average newspaper reader. (2) Attention to linguistics in the schools has not of late been entirely happy; in its new burst of popularity it threatens often to be more modish than informed.]° Recent, but quite fundamental, findings concerning language have scarcely emerged from the snug covers of learned journals, indigestible dissertations,

° Material within brackets are the notes of the rereading in 1966.

and formidable monographs concerned with elusive minutiae. From time to time attempts are made to quicken the body; yet they all have failed. Think, for example, of the expert who starts with remarks to the effect that language is usually thought to be a dull subject and then get no further than promising to inspect a few of the fascinating byways of this "absorbing discipline," as he proceeds to unfurl tiresome, and often irrelevant, periphrastic expressions of the passive voice in English or Eskimo. Then there is the bombardier who opens a barrage of countless languages or the museum director who sets out to guide you through a picture gallery of languages. "Just look at all those words that resemble one another," says he. The intelligent reader, who is probably plagued every day with sufficient chaos of detail, is by now reaching for the string on the bed lamp. [To these there has been added in the last decade a new blight: the term-swapper. In this era of extravagant awe for chromium-plated scientism, authors frequently increase and impress their audiences, thinking to enrich and enhance their

Reprinted with the permission of the author and the publisher (and revised by the author) from the *Journal of General Education*, 1951, **5**, No. 4, 286–302.

own scholarly precision, by parading very old and tired notions under technical-sounding names. Thus, sounds or letters become "phonemes"; parts of speech lose their old names and become numbers; old-style commas and the spaces after simple phrases get replaced by single- and double-bars with superscript numerals peppered about; and in this guise a jargonish brand of pseudo-reasoning and would-be data begin to sound as if they really meant something and led somewhere.]

Another subject concerned with language has come to the fore in recent years, an ingredient that in many ways only beclouds the issue precisely because of its validity as a province of knowledge in its own right, namely, that worrisome and sometimes popular topic, semantics. Semantics certainly has its proper place in any consideration of human communication; it is unfortunate that at present both controls and methods for observing and sifting semantic data are embarrassingly undeveloped. Just how are we to draw the lines defining how people "feel" about the connotations of linguistic expression? And to say—what seems to be a widespread notion—that when we have dealt with semantics we have explained a basic portion of the nature of language is simply not true. [Semantics is still a troubled subject. But in the past several years, with the advent of generative grammatical theory, a healthy attention has once again turned to it, and notable hypotheses, if not yet solutions, are being developed.]

Under the rubric of semantics there is also the question of the expression that logical categories and functions find in language. But, as long as discussion is restricted to these considerations of logic, the crucial question of language remains untouched. Languages are garments that clothe and enhance, or at times detract from, what we assume to be the mental processes of human beings. To use a gross simile, a tailor who restricts his study to anatomy will not learn what a good suit of clothes consists

of; the success of Christian Dior does not rest on mere measurements of the configurations shared by all women. And, like good Chinese *couture*, the waist of a Paris mode in a given year has no necessary relationship to that slender middle part of a woman's body that finds quite different expression in the terms of a physical anthropologist or of the average man with an eye for beauty. Let me illustrate this with two English sentences: *There is no democracy where there is ruthless subjection of the peace-loving masses by the few* and *There are no whelps in that pigsty*. The first statement offers certain difficulties which it would be highly desirable to define. With the aid, if necessary, of an expert in animal husbandry, the second statement offers no problems at all of the same order.

Now if the equivalent of the first statement were found in *Pravda*, it might be alleged that the form of "subjection" has a different coverage in the realm of ideas from that usually found, for example, in the *New York Times*. But that does not prevent the *Pravda* version from occurring in English in the *Daily Worker*. An analysis of this discrepancy does not necessarily tell us anything about the difference between the Russian *language* and English. On the other hand, among the various *linguistic* differences which we should find in the two versions would be the absence of any feature in the Russian to express our English form *the*. This does not mean that a Russian is unaware of such a distinction; in a given instance we can know nothing about such an alleged awareness, since we cannot crawl into his mind to find out. The important *linguistic* fact is that Russian simply puts a speaker under no compulsion to express this distinction at every turn, just as we do not have to change the form of a noun after a negative verb (a Russian does). [This discussion ignores the fact that there are also equally *linguistic*, but semantic, differences which could now be more fruitfully tackled in light of recent theoretical developments: e.g., *no* (contrasted with the Russian equivalent in such a sentence, where *there is* is negated), or *whelps* (which is compatible only with an interesting range of animals).]

Now let us regard these statements from the point of view of language. Both are statements in English, and both have essentially the same structure. That is to say, both make use of a great many of the same fundamental building blocks and also put them together in similar patterns. To point out a few characteristic English features, we notice that there are certain units of sound which occur in these statements: voiced *th* in *there*, voiceless *th* in *ruthless;* a voiceless rush of breath through the lips (if you speak one of certain forms of Standard English other than my own) for the *wh* of *whelps.* Unless you grew up speaking a language other than English, you can detect an audible rush of breath immediately after the *p* in *peace;* this does not occur after *p* in *whelps.* We find combinations of sounds such as *thl* (*ruthless*), *bj* (*subjection*), *lps* (*whelps*), *gst* (*pigsty*); we shall never find these at the beginning of an English word, as we may with *fy* in *few* (contrast *feud* and *food*). [Current theory now lays stress on the occurrence and non-occurrence of sound sequences such as these; but they are, of course, still features of the language, even if rather superficial ones.]

I have picked out a few striking phonological features of English. Among European languages, phonological systems that use two *th*-sounds are found only in Welsh, Greek, Icelandic, and Albanian; Castilian Spanish has the voiceless *th* (I am, of course, referring throughout to *sounds,* and not spelling, which is merely an imperfect and often, as in the case of English, a grossly inadequate symbolism). [Linguistic theory has taken in recent years a much more active concern with graphic representations of language in their own right and their accounting within an adequate framework.] The *wh* is a *significant contrast* (note, for example, *which* beside *witch*) is shared by no other standard European language.

Now when we say "significant contrast,"

we have struck at the heart of sound-systems in language. Certain other linguistic groups can be heard to pronounce our *wh*, but for them it may be simply a nonsignificant variation of one of their sound units. Manx, the language of the Isle of Man and now practically extinct, [It *is* now extinct.] employed the voiced *th* sound in the middle of a word between vowels. This was, however, not a distinctive sound, since it varied from time to time and from person to person with *z* in the selfsame forms. In other words, it made no difference to a Manxman which of these two sounds he produced in that position. If we say the word *peace* immediately after we have taken a drink of water (opening our vocal chords with a snap), we are likely to produce what a phonetician would call a "glottalized" *p*. That will not bother us at all (so long as the water went down the right way), since this is not a significant distinction in our language. Tzeltal speakers in southern Mexico might be misunderstood in a similar circumstance. *Their* sound-pattern is such that they distinguish glottalized consonants clearly and significantly from the nonglottalized variety. To us some consonants merely sound "funny." This sort of inattention to sounds which are not significant in the language of the observer is one of the principal inadequacies of the earlier grammars written by Europeans of so-called "primitive" languages.

It is probable that no speaker produces precisely the same acoustical sound twice in succession. As yet, no absolute phonetic criteria have been established on an acoustic basis.

All the illustrations which we have just noticed have the point in common that in a given position one sound unit of a language may occur indiscriminately with varying qualities, as measured either in terms of physiological production or of the acoustic result which the observer hears; *within a limited range,* no matter what sound occurs, the result is still perfectly intelligible to a native speaker. Not only is it quite intelligible, it doesn't even sound the least bit "funny." To put the point another way, the interior economy of the linguistic pattern is not disturbed by these variations. It would appear that compounds are "pigeonholed" and associated by the hearer by means of a complex psychological process not yet understood by competent investigators. [It appears increasingly likely that sentences (and, in turn, their sounds) are "heard" by listeners through the medium of a vicarious unspoken (hence inaudible and non-obvious) imitation of the total grammatical process which was inferred to have gone into producing the model sentence, and then by mental comparison of the sub-liminal output of the imitation with the original perceived stimulus. In this sense, one's range of tolerance for "hearing" is a function of one's range of articulatory production coupled with one's perception of an individual acoustical instance embedded in a set of abstract grammatical rules thought to apply to a guessed sentence or discourse.] When we have to deal with different languages, the criterion of intelligibility, or of contrast within the sound-pattern, is contained in the fact that for different "sounds" different linguistic groups have varying ranges of tolerance. We may call the haphazard occurrence of an articulatory complex or "sound" within this range of tolerance in a given language FREE VARIATION.

To return to the *th* sounds found in European languages, it was noted above that, whereas various linguistic groups of Europe boasted both voiced and voiceless *th's*, Spanish has only the voiceless variety. Anyone who knows Spanish will no doubt have already remarked that you can hear voiced *th's* in great number in many dialects of Spanish. Although this is true as a phonetic or, if you will, acoustical fact, this phenomenon has no significance for the present-day patterning of the language. [That is, more accurately, for the basic abstract forms of words.] For, if our Spanish-speaking reader will think again, he will realize that he has never heard a clear *d*, in

which the breath is stopped as it is in the English *d*, in the middle or at the end of a word in such Spanish dialects in positions where this voiced *th* sound occurs. In other words, in standard Spanish we have one sound unit *d*, which in initial position sounds to us like a *d* but, in most positions, medially and finally sounds to us like a voiced *th*.[1] Let us now look at English along the same lines as an Oregon Takelma Indian might. He would notice that English has a breathed *p* initially in words such as our word *peace* noted above; an unbreathed *p* in words such as *spit* or *span;* an unexploded *p* very often in a word like *cup*, where, once they have been closed, the lips are not opened until the next sound is produced; and a "glottalized" *p*, as when a Scotsman snaps his vocal chords after he has puffed a *p* with his lips.

We have found, now, that certain acoustic features occur in a given language only in certain positions and environments. If we tabulate all acoustic differences for any language, we shall discover whole categories of sounds whose members may vary enormously within a category, in their phonetic or absolute acoustic quality, but never occur in the same environment. To put it another way, they never offer a distinctive contrast; they are environmentally conditioned. By grouping these mutually exclusive sounds together, we arrive at the significant sound units of the language which we are inspecting. As is not surprising, these units, most conveniently so grouped, turn out to share a goodly number of phonetic, or acoustic, features. Linguists call a "bundle" of such mutually exclusive sounds a PHONEME. We are then in a position to say that English, for example, has such-and-such phonemes, including the phoneme *p*, which, in turn, has such-and-such positional variants in the stated environments—and then we must enumerate the various positional phonetic values that *p* has in all the environ-

[1]Plus a unit *th*, which is generally voiceless, but which gets voiced to a different sort of *th* in certain combinations (e.g., *hazlo*, "do it!").

ments in which it may occur, some of which we took note of above. It does not surprise us that all these variants of *p* share the feature of double-lip closure. The reason we must go through this lengthy procedure to arrive at a statement which no doubt seems quite obvious to any speaker of English is that different linguistic groups, as pointed out above, have very different habits as to what constitutes a significant contrast. [Enormous changes in our view of the organization of the sounds of language have come about in the past decade. Many linguists now deny the utility of the notion of *phoneme,* and claim that, by concentrating one's attention on trivial or even technically misguided aspects, it has distracted us from the important and explanatory aspects of grammatical organization. Nevertheless, this change does not vitiate the important point of arbitrary distinctiveness, range of fluctuation and systematic variation in context which are specific to the sounds of a given language.]

When we say above that phonemes have varying values in all positions in which they *may* occur, we have implied a limitation on the number of combinations or clusters of phonemes that may be found in a given language. This brings us to another fundamental feature of the interior economy or patterning that is found in all languages. Everybody, including radio announcers, found out during the war that Russians not only give their babies and cities unconscionably long names but also do their best to make them unpronounceable. One might recall Pskov, Dniepropetrovsk, or the late Mr. Zhdanov as a few random examples. In the way of everyday words the Russians produce with ease such specimens as *vstrechátsya,* "to meet one another"; *vverkhú,* "upstairs"; *éto mne ne nrávitsya,* "I don't like that." Georgian, "Uncle Joe's" native language (not at all related to Russian), furnishes us with a verb *vhmtsqsi,* "I pasture my flock" (the sounds I write as *ts* and *q* here involve features difficult to explain briefly to an English speaker). Alba-

nians find no trouble with *mpshtiell,* "to wrap"; nor do the Czechs with *čtvrt,* "one quarter" (the *r* is here vocalic). Examples can be multiplied indefinitely. The thing that strikes us forcibly, as English speakers, is the "outrageousness" of some of the combinations that these languages permit, particularly in the case of initial consonant clusters which always seem to be more noticeable. [To us. Our final consonant clusters bother and amaze a Serb.] These clusters, although employing individual sounds units or phonemes many of which are not at all foreign to us, involve combinations which we in our language do not happen to permit. In isolation, every sound in the above Albanian word occurs in English; *sh* represents the first sound in our word "show," and the whole word rimes with *peal.* But, to look at English from a Russian point of view, one finds equally inconceivable clusters in such words as "si*xths,*" "be*tw*ixt," or even the diphthong in our word *know* (Russian has practically no diphthongs; we have scarcely any nondiphthongized long syllables).

Every language has a clear-cut pattern in the combinations which it will or will not employ. It so happens that in some languages the range of permitted clusters is much greater than for others. In the matter of consonants, for example, permitted clusters in Japanese and Malay are extremely restricted; in the Bannack Shoshone (American Indian) language, only one consonant occurs in clusters with others. Many Bantu languages (spoken over enormous areas of Africa roughly south of the Equator), on the other hand, reject many clusters which seem quite reasonable to us, yet employ other combinations which we regard as singular, to say the least. That is the main reason that the names of the beplumed chieftains who arrive in London for conferences seem so incongruous to us. In turn, the patterning of "pidgin" languages encountered by many Americans, for example, in the South Pacific during the recent war, is to a large extent accounted for by the fact that English patterning seemed "funny" to those people; so they, as we do in everyday speech with Russian names, "tidied up" our language for us and made it look like something civilized.

The story has presumably been the same as long as men have been talking. We read in Tacitus (*Hist. ii.* 22) that the Romans, whose language many of us in the classroom have not always regarded with unqualified approval, found some of our Germanic fore-bears on the banks of the Rhone singing "harsh songs." One need go no farther than the pages of *King Henry* V to find out what Englishmen have thought about the pat-terning of Welsh.

The usual statements made about other people's languages are almost universally based on a misconception of this phonologi-cal patterning. German is regularly referred to as a "guttural" language. What has really been noticed by such an observer is the presence of a pattern strikingly different from English (such combinations as *shl, tst, mt* in forms like *schlange, jetzt, amt*) and the use of *one* phoneme in particular (*ch*) which sounds bizarre to English ears. Many have the mistaken impression that good standard German is produced by a liberal seasoning with *ch*'s. But the *ch* actually has two dis-tinct positional variants in forms such as *doch* and *nicht;* in the latter type, that is, after a front vowel, the *ch* more closely approximates our English *sh,* where the closure is surely far removed from the throat. In short, "guttural" seems to refer in a vague, impressionistic fashion to real phenomena, but as a scientific term it is misleading and meaningless. When Italian is referred to as a "singing" or "lilting" lan-guage, presumably what has been noticed is the prominent vocalic pattern, the falling pitch on stressed syllables, a more restricted pattern (than in English) for consonant clusters, and the presence of doubled con-sonants (that is consonants held for twice their normal length), e.g., in *fratello, madonna, fato,* "fate," but *fatto* "deed." We tend particularly to notice the last fea-ture, because English has no double conso-

nants, except when chance brings two forms together, e.g., *night-table;* the difference between *later* and *latter* is not in the con-sonants; it is the vowels spelled *a.*

In the course of defining our sound units, or phonemes, it was pointed out that the deciding factor is the feature of significant contrast. There are many languages in the world which employ tone, or relative pitch of the voice, as the sole feature of contrast between many forms. Chinese is the lan-guage most familiar to Westerners which displays this characteristic. Since we do not use such features to distinguish individual words, the whole concept is somewhat strange to us; that is, it is outside our phono-logical pattern, and, just as in the case of glottalized consonants, whispered vowels, clicks, and the like, it is hard for us to hear these distinctions. To be sure, we make use of pitch in one fashion over long segments of speech, as when we use a rising inflection to denote an attitude of doubt or inconclu-siveness, or over shorter segments to give semantically vague subjective overtones to an expression (e.g., *well, ah, yes*). But these are features of a different order. Tone in Chinese distinguishes one item of vocabu-lary from another; we may say it has a "lexical" value (i.e., the dictionary must show it). In Ibo, a language spoken in West Africa, a verb is made negative merely by changing the tone. In Mazatec, a language spoken in southern Mexico, a change in the subject of the verb often involves a change in tone. We may say that tone here has a grammatical value; it is as much a part of the grammar as is the change in endings on a Latin verb or the addition of an ending to an English noun to make it plural. These features are certainly elements of phonemic contrast.

All language flows within a framework of time. I cannot utter an expression, how-ever short, without finishing later than I began it. The sound contrasts which were discussed when we set up such phonemes as *p* are linear segments in a continuum of time; that is, they are distinctive features that occur one after the other (roughly speaking; this is imprecise in strict acoustic terms). These we may call "segmental" or "linear" phonemes. [Nowadays, in the framework of generative grammar, we do better to refer not to phonemes in this fashion, but to segments that come one after the other and that are each marked with a limited number of non-predictable distinctive features.] We have seen, however, that we must also take into account such things as tone. Now tone (in languages I know of) never occupies an interval of time when nothing else, equally distinctive, is going on, and sometimes overlaps several segmental phonemes. Tone, therefore, might be called a "simultaneous" phoneme. Stress, such as we employ in English, where one syllable of most words is spoken more forcibly than another, is also an example of a simultaneous phoneme. [If we state the structure of lexical and grammatical elements in terms of segments marked by sets of distinctive features which are themselves simultaneous bundles, then such things as tone are simply distinctive features no different in this respect from the others.] Once again, the occurrence of a feature may not mean that it is significant; Czech has a marked stress accent, but it always occurs on the initial syllable of the word. Therefore, it never offers a contrast and hence is not a phoneme in Czech.

We have now established another fundamental feature of language: that we do not necessarily have to slice time laterally in order to find all significant wound contrasts. [*Note A:* When this paper was written the field of linguistics was dominated by an insistance on the methods of discovering and arriving at the entities isolated in a grammatical statement. Such methods were supposed to be overt and automatically reproduceable, so that a machine with no intuition could arrive at the same results. This in turn led to an emphasis on means of slicing up, and assigning to recoverable classes, the acoustical stream (i.e., sentences) that was supposed to be composed of such segments. That is, the grammar was imagined to be discoverable from the purely superficial configurations of the stream of sound that we hear when speech occurs; this contention is now generally agreed to have been wrong and misleading.]

We see, therefore, that one of the fundamental things that gives any language its own particular quality is its rigid adherence to a closed pattern of sound units, which permits variation only within strikingly limited ranges of tolerance. From the enormous number of sounds the human organism can produce, every language selects a surprisingly limited stock. All languages thus far adequately described employ phonemes numbering roughly between twenty and fifty. [In these terms, a more accurate typology would be ca. a dozen (Hawaiian or Wichita, a North American Plains language of the Caddoan family) to over eighty (Oubykh, belonging to the family spoken on the northwest slope of the Caucasus mountains). But expressed in distinctive features, the range is much less drastic: somewhere between a half-dozen and a dozen.] Indeed, there is reason to suspect the validity of an analysis that yields a number of phonemes in the upper span of this range, though as yet there is no reason to assume any absolute number as a ceiling. These units are then combined in well-defined patterns, much like chessmen on a board. To break the rule is to sacrifice intelligibility.

We have now not only considered structural patterning of the sound units of languages; we have also taken a brief glance at some of the ways whereby we may discover these units [see Note A above]. When we do this, how do we know that we have arrived at a valid or "right" analysis? How does the physicist know he has a valid analysis when he posits subatomic particles which he has not yet seen or measured? The criterion for "rightness" in matters of analysis and description is empirically faithful economy. The best descriptions is that which explains all observed phenomena with a minimum of assumptions and statements. The best description of a language is the most economical description.

Up to this point we have been talking exclusively about the sounds of languages. But the chief use of language is to communicate meaning. The sounds have no intrinsic meaning of their own; they are merely the smallest contrasted units that can be isolated in the stream of speech. They may be likened to bricks which, though each has its own color, consistency, and character, may be put together to build a wall, a sewer, a well, or even a statue. But what of the resultant meaningful combinations of these linguistic bricks? The question sometimes arises, when we put a hyphen between two forms, whether the result is one word or two. This demands, in the first place, a definition of a "word." We usually regard *light* as a word, and similarly *house*. One supposes that *lighthouse* is also a word; we seem so sure of this that we write the two parts together. On the other hand, we seem equally sure that a *light house* is two words. The criterion would seem to be whether you write them together or leave a space between. If this space between the two words is valid, then it should correspond to something in our stream of speech. Certainly this blank space becomes a tenuous quantity when we say *a light house* in rapid speech. We must search for something else more capable of measurements. [The point is poorly made here. While there is some truth in what is said, much of the technical arguments surrounding "juncture" (which admittedly is often not audible, even in adjacent sounds) would be needed to refine these statements. But that would go beyond the scope and aim of this nontechnical paper.]

We found that one of our linguistic bricks in English is the phoneme of strong stress. Now we have a real distinction. In *lighthouse*, *light* receives a strong stress accent, whereas *house* receives less stress; in *light house* both forms may receive strong stress. That seems to answer the question:

an English word can be defined as a segment of speech which bears only one loud stress.

We have been able to make a statement describing an English word, but we are interested in language in general. When we use the same technique with French (nonvulgar Parisian), a different situation develops. In French stress is not a phoneme; in fact, French stress is extremely weak, and the feature which occurs simultaneously with this weak stress, a rising tone inflection, is by far the more predominant. The French stress-tone feature occurs automatically on the last syllable of all phrase-groups; for this reason it never serves as a feature of contrast and hence is not phonemic. We are, therefore, deprived of this criterion in an attempt to isolate words in the expression *je ne l'ai pas fait*. Or, on the other hand, we must say that a French word equals a phrase-group, however long. There is naturally nothing wrong with such a statement, except for the fact that we have now merely renamed something we had already isolated. But we had set out to find some more manageable, more "minimal," unit. If we were to proceed from language to language, we should find similar obstacles in our way whenever we attempted to establish a general criterion for defining a "word." It will be remembered that the criteria established for recognizing a phoneme can be stated in such a way as to apply to any language. It is precisely such general features and criteria which are necessary for an understanding of the nature of language as such. But if our observations and analysis are correct, wherever we do not find such general criteria we are presumably faced with phenomena which are not universal characteristics of language. A "word," then, as we know it, is not a universal phenomenon.

A stream of speech consists of a succession not only of units of sound but also of units which convey meaning to the speakers of the language. How do we know they contain meaning, and how can we test for meaning? The only way we can test with absolute assurance is by collecting large quantities of specimens of continuous speech from a speaker of a given language.

As we collect our specimens from the speaker, we also find out what his utterances mean. As we collect more and more specimens we find increasingly large numbers of segments of varying lengths that differ only by small fractions: *the house, the red house, the big red house, the big red house where my brother lives, my sister's big red book,* and so on. These expressions, your native from New York informs you, mean different things in his language. Putting these segments side by side in all possible combinations, we can isolate minimum segments of meaning by finding pairs that differ by one feature only. The value of this simple technique is the fact that it can be applied to any language. Linguists call these segments MORPHEMES.

Such morphemes may turn out to contain any number of phonemes, as few as one. In the word *zone* or *ozone* the *z* is merely a phoneme; it means nothing of itself; it is merely the feature of contrast, without unitary meaning, between, e.g., *zone, bone,* and *loan.* This observation is substantiated by the fact that the remaining segment *-one* in these words has no common feature of meaning. The *z* which we hear at the end of the word *boys* is likewise a phoneme, but it is at the same time a morpheme because it is the sole feature by which we distinguish this plural form from a singular *boy* and because it occurs affixed to hosts of other English forms (*maid, leg, valley, train*), always with the same meaning, viz., "more than one." [More accurately (and this applies to this entire paragraph), it always has the same grammatical role. On the other hand, *z* in *zone* or *ozone* never plays any grammatical role.]

Just as morphemes are built up from phonemes, we next observe that all longer segments of language are built up from morphemes. [*Note B:* Contrary to what is said here, current theory claims that grammars are concerned not with concatenated aggregates that make segments of sentence length, but rather with the rules that explain how sentences and their parts are related to one another. This, of course, diminishes the emphasis on a search for basic units.] These are the two basic units of all languages; in fact, these are at present the only basic units that may safely be posited for all languages. With these units, grammars and dictionaries for every known language can be compiled.

There is reason to believe, with certain reservations, that morphemes can be extracted on a still more objective basis. If we had an immense amount of English text all transcribed in phonemes, we would find the combination ksθbr,[2] which occurs in such segments as "si*xth* *br*ick" or "si*xth* *br*idge," extremely rare in occurrence. Such frequencies could be computed by tabulating clusters of phonemes in a running text one at a time, two at a time, . . . *n* at a time. One *might* find a discrete break in the frequency curve between sequences that mean something and clusters of the type just cited. In other words, morphemes are bound to recur with some degree of frequency in a language because people normally intend to make sense. Clusters such as the last-mentioned occur only as random results of the juxtaposition of morphemes.

This approach is a purely theoretical matter [see Note A above]. It illustrates, however, by the hypotheses underlying it, two fundamental characteristics of language: first, the strikingly mechanical way in which linguistic structures behave and, second, the vast gulf, from a descriptive point of view, that lies between language as a structure and the semantic content which this structure conveys.

Just as in the case of phonemes, so we find that linguistic patterns emerge again on the morpheme level. One of the striking characteristics of phonemes is the fact that languages restrict themselves to a very

---

[2] θ represents the *th*-sound in a word like thing (θiŋ).

limited stock. This is not quite so true in the case of morphemes. All languages make use of immensely larger numbers of morphemes than of phonemes. Though most speakers actively employ only a small fraction of the total roster and passively understand or recognize a somewhat larger number, the total stock of morphemes in a given language at a given time runs well into the thousands. This number, moreover, cannot be fixed with exactitude, that is to say, the "approximate exactitude" that we were able to state for phonemes. Even if we could suppose that it were possible to collect all English morphemes in use on a given day, the number is subject to change the next day—for instance, on those days on which *simonize, bowdlerize, chauvinism, GI,* or *jilet,* which is Turkish for "safety razor," first came into use. In this fashion it is apparent that an exact ceiling cannot be presumed for the number of morphemes in a language. There is a very good reason for this: morphemes, unlike phonemes, have meaning, and the world of experience is vast and can be catalogued endlessly; for that is precisely what speakers set out to do with their morphemes.

If that is so, why don't languages have an infinite number of morphemes? Obviously because no one could remember or use them all, and communication would be impaired. Even though the numerical ceiling is hazy, the prominent linguistic feature of selection once again asserts itself. But how, with a limited number of units, can men set out to catalogue the universe? Primarily by two methods: omission and combination. We shall take up the second of these first, since it leads us back to a statement which we seem in some degree to have vitiated. It was implied above that there are parallels between the roles of phonemes and those of morphemes. By operating with limited, but still fairly large, numbers of morphemes, languages combine these units according to rigidly enforced patterns. Just as phoneme clusters are strictly regulated, so the order of morphemes in a given lan-

guage is closely policed. In English we may not tack our plural endings onto the beginning of nouns (*zboy* does not occur); *John hits Bill* and *Bill hits John* both occur, but mean different things. Within the framework of these patterns, combinations are made of varying numbers of morphemes so that the "covering power" of the original number of units is vastly increased. These combinations may involve morphemes which can be found along in other contexts; for example, in German one combines *Hand* and *Schuh* to make *Handschuh,* that is, a "glove." Some morphemes are never found standing alone, such as the plural *-z* in *boys* or the unstressed *the* in *the house.*

It is convenient to give a name to those forms which may stand alone (for example, in a brief answer to a question); we therefore call *Hand, Schuh,* and *Handschuh* "free forms"; *fish gold, boy, goldfish,* and *boys* are likewise free forms. Contrariwise, *-z* is a "bound form"; it never occurs in normal unstudied speech without some accompanying form; quotations of such bound forms in technical discussions among linguists have about the same frequency and special syntactical occurrence as citations of hoot owls among ornithologists.

Having established the notion of a free form, we have returned in a measure to our point of departure on the matter of a "word"; indeed, if it were not for the likelihood of confusion in terms, a free form might be called a "word." It happens that most of our conventional "words" are free forms; but some "words" are not free forms: e.g., *the;* and, vice versa, some free forms are not single "words": e.g., *the house.* To return to the problem with French, free forms may be isolated as follows: *je ne l'ai pas fait* (zənle pa fe, or colloquial Parisian, žle pa fe), *pas du tout* (pa dytu), *rien du tout* (rjē dytu), *du tout* (dytu, also means "not at all"), *rien* (rjē), etc. Note in these examples how free forms have been separated by finding parts of sequences successively standing alone. Note also that we have written *pas* (pas) as a free form, even though we have not found it alone. This is justified by its close parallelism in structural usage to such forms as *rien, personne, plus,* etc., which we do find standing alone, it is further justified by the serious disturbances caused in the whole pattern by the contrary assumption, in which case we should have to regard it as a suffix in *je ne le fais pas,* as a prefix in *pas mal,* and as a prefix in a very queer construction in *pas du tout.* On the other hand, though *tout* (tu) occurs alone, *du,* (dy-) never does, nor does it structurally parallel anything else that does; then again, its occurrence parallels perfectly sundry "prepositions" and the "definite article," all of which are bound prefixed in modern French.

But, though in a great many cases we find that free forms correspond to "words," we saw quickly that "words" are a quicksand to build on, while free forms can be established on a solid basis for any language. We may reasonably ask, then, what it was that prompted us to expect that a system and general approach could be based on "words." And the answer appears to be: purely a traditional regard for the spaces we are accustomed to reading and writing between forms, reinforced by the fact that in many cases these spaces happen to be valid. But the placing of these spaces is an accident of history. When the Greeks, the Romans, and early Germans (in this case, Englishmen), and sundry others each in turn learned how to write, they divided their lines of letters in the course of time into groups which the intuitively regarded as free forms. Like many things done by people using their heads and having no cause for stale superstition, these divisions doubtless had a high degree of validity when first employed in each language. As time went by, changes in the language occurred: many free forms remained just that, and thus we find this illusory faith in "words"; but some forms have suffered radical change of status —yet we write *the* separately because the article was so treated in Old English; the French do the same for *je* because in Latin

ego could stand alone. We tack our plurals on the end because that is what the Romans and early Germanic people did. If history by chance had brought writing to these people about three thousand years earlier, it is possible that today we might be writing a "word" *s* after a noun to make it plural. Had we mastered writing only fifty years ago, apéyj əvíngliš máyt præps bimɔ̄r làyk ðís. Tradition is pleasant, but we must recognize the traps.

It so happens that these morphemes which never stand alone almost invariably occur with far higher frequency than do the independent type. Some languages have great numbers of them (Latin or Greek, for example); other languages have fewer of them, as is the case with English. All languages seem to have some. Because of the frequency of these dependent forms, the combinations into which they will enter, their individual meanings, and the meaning of resultant combinations are of great importance for the purpose of describing an individual language. For this reason the statements concerning these elements of high frequency are made separately from those appertaining to the less frequent elements. This treatment not only reflects the structural state of affairs in a language; it is of practical value to treat the elements in this twofold fashion, for, from the point of view of a prospective learner of the language or of the theoretical linguist, the most frequent elements must be known before anything can be done with, or said about, that particular language. The enumeration of these elements of high frequency and the statements of rules governing their combination are therefore assembled into what we call "grammars." The less frequent elements, which generally have far fewer limitations placed upon the combinations into which they will enter, are assembled and identified in the dictionary or lexicon. [Current theory sees a very different relation between lexical entries and the grammar—but that would require another essay. See Note C below.]

Is the dictionary always right? If it is a good dictionary, generally speaking, yes, in the sense that it records current usage of these items. But, since the occurrence of these items is of much lower frequency than that of other units of the language and since individual men must gather the data, there is considerable room for omission or inadequacy of statement. The compilers could not conceivably have heard and read every statement made in that language during the period they set out to cover. But he is a bad grammarian indeed who makes mistakes of a similar nature in writing his grammar, for 99 per cent of his material can be verified over and over again in the course of a single day's listening to native speakers.

How, then, can there be bad grammars and good grammars if the compilers have such splendid opportunities to excel? In the case of the better-known languages there are rarely errors of observation in any grammar. Roughly speaking, the individual elements are always reasonably well identified. The inadequacies of a grammar are usually those of arrangement, a failure to observe and present clearly the patterning of the units, whether they do phonemes or morphemes. This does not refer to pedagogical arrangement, which involves factors other than those of linguistic structure. The inadequacies of most grammars stem to a large extent from a confusion of phonemes with orthography. That is why so much stress was laid above on the recognition of phonemes and the criteria for determining them.

A grammar may likewise prove inadequate in the analysis and presentation of the morphemes of a language and their combinations (combinations are often conveniently shown by means of paradigms, e.g., Latin noun declensions and verb conjugations). As we have discovered, the real, significant contrasts in a language are revealed by stripping all forms off, layer by layer, as we place contrasted segments side by side. We shall not find such forms by setting out with the plan of uncovering pre- conceived categories which we have decided ought to be there. Or again, on this basis we may claim to have found anything we want to look for. By putting certain words together, we define concepts which have been called "pluperfect" and "conditional perfect." But these constructs are not of the same order as, for example, the past tense. English, shocking as it may seem has at most only four primary categories of verb inflection, and only two of these are tenses (if we wish to keep a useful term for identifying the category of time). The other two involve derivation which transfers the verb to another form-class, that is, adjective or noun. [Changes in current theory would of course alter the detail of this account of the verb, but the essential point remains.] If you leave the verb stem bare or, if you will (since it is a significant contrast), add zero, the result is "present"; if you add -d, -ed, -t (a few verbs like *cut, hit* add zero), or change the interior vowel (*sing: sang*), the result is "past"; if you add -d, -ed, -t, -n, -en, or again alter the vowel (*sung*), the result is an adjective-participial form (without context one cannot tell which); finally, if you add -ing, the result is an adjective of a different sort from the last or a verbal noun. The only other thing that can be done, on this level of construction, to all English verbs is to inflect them for person and number—not six forms, as many a grammar will say, but three, if we wish to include the archaic "thou"-form: "second singular," "third singular," and "all other persons." For if we are to insist on six, which happens to be the Latin pattern, we must immediately expand that to include forms for the dual (two of a kind), a category which was universally distinguished in earlier classical Greek, Sanskrit, Gothic, Old Church Slavonic; was still preserved in the personal pronouns of our own Old English; and is still in use in certain dialects of Lithuanian and Slovene. Then we must further increase our number of imagined contrasts to include for the first person an exclusive form ("the other fellow and I"), a limited inclusive ("you and I"), and a general inclusive ("you and I and the other fellows"), for this distinction is made by the Popolucas of Veracruz in southern Mexico. On the other hand, for the second and third persons the question of number or inclusiveness never troubles a Popoluca speaker.

What is to be done, then, with such a form as *I had worked?* It obviously has a clear place in English grammar: *I had worked too hard* is very different from *I am worked too hard.* It is a construct on a higher level than that of *I worked.* It must be treated and described under phrase-formation as we might call it, along with *I had a book, the book is read, the book is red.* [Such an analysis, which is now to be rejected, illustrates the error of grouping together superficial resemblances in the shape of strings that make up sentences. This is one implication of what is referred to in notes A and B above.]

Why, then, have grammarians written about pluperfect tenses in English? Presumably because there is a pluperfect in Latin and Greek, two languages that for a long time were considered indispensable in education. A grammar of a language must confine itself to those categories that are really present in that language and to the patterns within which these categories are framed. To set up the vast forest of categories found in other languages,[3] not to mention the limitless jungle that can be imagined *in abstracto,* is not only to burden the reader or learner with useless repetition and alleged refinements; it is simply tampering with and obscuring the pattern of the language—tampering with the very thing that makes that language what it is. For pedagogical purposes it is often useful to point out to the learner what the other language lacks. But that is not part of the grammar of that language; it is a combined

[3] A negative conjugation for English verbs, for example (Japanese has one); or a "definite" declension for English nouns (Albanian has one); or a conjugation for English verbs following a particle (Old Irish had one).

commentary on the features which the learner's own language does happen to have and on the disparity of treatment among languages on how the universe is to be divided.

The foregoing remarks, therefore, make it plain that much of the existing grammatical literature is inadequate and misguided. This is as it should be; scholarship would be a poor thing if we did not make advances. It happens that the inadequacies of earlier work are sometimes striking merely because our advances have recently been rather rapid. This is good reason to rejoice; but it is not reason to disparage and carp at our predecessors with learned hindsight. Indeed, it is largely through the efforts of our predecessors that we have reached the degree of technical skill we now pride ourselves on, incomplete as those efforts may now appear in their own right. Our job is rather to take honest note of the advances made, profit by them, and push things further. Time spent in crowing over past ignorance is time lost to building our future reputations; good manners often make good sense.

Since the grammarian's millennium has not yet arrived and since most existing collections of past research are framed in "traditional" treatments, the serious student cannot yet escape mastering the older terminologies and systems; in fact, he must be able to transpose, where possible, from any one system to another. Otherwise, he will be unable to get at much valuable material and will also be at a loss to distinguish what is enduring from what is superseded, and validity from nonsense.

We have discussed the question of combinations of morphemes, their analysis and the statement of them in grammars, and the ways in which grammars, found on accurate observation, sometimes succeed in obscuring the real distinctions which these combinations express. It was noted earlier that the morphemes themselves must be listed and identified in a dictionary and that there are thousands of them. Is that what makes

Webster's New International[4] so fat? Certainly not. Dictionaries are usually regarded as being of a very different breed from grammars. In actual fact, the dividing line is very vague; it is merely one of convenience. [*Note C:* More recently a much more precise and satisfactory notion of what the dictionary is has been developed. In brief, the dictionary (or lexicon) may be said to comprise those parts of all grammatical rules which consist of lists characterized, for each form, in terms of segments marked by sets of distinctive sound features and in terms of semantic markers for the form as a whole. In other words, the dictionary is not amorphous and indeterminate in the fashion implied in this context; it is just much more fine-grained than the syntactic parts of the grammar. Hence, decisions on this aspect should not be arbitrary.] The dictionary is the grammarian's scrap basket, into which go all the forms that do not so much defy analysis as require so many statements and lists as would make the grammar unwieldy. In short, there is a borderline area of linguistic formations that can go either way; either you may write more rules, or you may put the pieces back together and pop the form into the lexicon, which will be lengthy in any event. The decision is quite arbitrary in many cases. Sometimes the sum of the parts does not equal the whole: *un-bend, through-out.* Some cases are clear-cut: there is no advantage in saving one dictionary entry, or even twenty, at the price of five grammatical statements. In terms of the speaker of the language, this sort of instance probably means you have weeded out elements which he does not take apart and recombine in his daily speech.

English dictionaries use as their norm, in so far as they pretend to apply any strict norm, the stress feature of English—that is, if we ignore such encyclopedic information as weights and measures, coins, flags of all nations, the fine points of heraldry and armor, steam engines, dog breeding, and antiquated classifications of the languages of the world. In general, forms that receive one main stress get in; if you want to sell more copies over the drugstore counter you hold the gate open a bit longer. Historically, in general, dictionaries have simply grown, later works being compiled on the skeletons of earlier works. The men responsible were never much troubled about the definition of a word, free form, etc.; they simply explained what they thought not to be self-explanatory, whatever that is. This accounts for the somewhat sprawling nature of most dictionaries—and for their astonishing gaps.

The criterion of scope for a dictionary is best decided on the basis of the language under consideration. Mongolian, being a pleasant, tidy affair, can be well accommodated by listing little more than the morphemes; wholes rarely fail to equal sums of their parts. Old Irish perhaps wins the prize at the other end of the scale. Not only do the same problems arise that crop up in English; several hundred of the most common verbs are irregular, some so much so that several dozen forms must be quoted for certain verbs (the verb *to go* builds its forms from six recognizably different stems). [Here the complexity has been attributed to the wrong part of the grammar. In a gross fashion, Old Irish probably has no more dictionary entries than Mongolian—or any other language selected at random. Rather, it may well have more, or more complicated, rules which modify the shape of dictionary elements as they enter into various combinations.]

I have stated above that, in his linguistic attempt to catalogue the universe, man uses two principal methods, omission and combination. We have glanced at the process of combination, whereby the basic building   blocks—morphemes—may   be

---

[4] I pass over that monument of scholarship, the *New* (or *Oxford*) *English Dictionary*, because it tells one not only what the words *mean*, but what they *have meant* at different times in voluminous citations of literature culled from the Old English period on. It further gives the dates of occurrences and abundant quotations. As its subtitle demurely states, it is a historical dictionary. Never was a title more modest.

combined to express extensions in various directions of a nuclear idea. I use the term "omission" as a label to characterize the directions which these extensions of the nucleus may take. To subdivide the universe into all thinkable categories would be an endless and hopeless job for any language. Consequently, by the simple process of omission, different languages select particular directions for overt grammatical expression. This point was briefly touched upon when we considered the ways in which a grammarian might write a bad grammar. It was suggested that the bad grammarian, in his eagerness to force English into the mold of Latin and Greek, had overlooked all manner of further possibilities which Latin and Greek do not happen to display. In other words, Latin and Greek, like all other languages, have their own idiosyncrasies on the subject of how the universe is overtly to be divided.

To simplify the argument at the time, I purposely restricted my illustrations to categories that are readily understandable to an English speaker, even though his own language does not happen to treat them in the same way, if at all. It was noted that Japanese has a negative category in its system of verb conjugation. Any English speaker knows what a negative form is and uses negative phrasal inflection with present and past verbs (*I don't go, I didn't go*) and he may wonder why one can say that English does not have this grammatical category throughout its constructions. In English the form *not* in verb phrases other than those just mentioned is a purely lexical item; that is, it belongs to a class of English forms that may optionally occur in certain combinations and positions in a sentence. [In detail, this assertion, as stated, can now be said to be wrong. Negatives are an important part of basic English sentence syntax. But the general point being made still stands.] It is parallel in many ways to the word *already*, for we may substitute one form for the other in statements of the type *I have not gone, I have already gone.* The grammatical process of substitution in this case is no different

from the process displayed by a contrasting pair, such as *that is a white horse, that is a black horse.* In other words, to express negativity in such expressions, an English speaker merely extracts the item *not* from his bag of morphemes if he wishes to use it, just as he adds the item *white* to the sentence when he wishes to be specific about the color of the horse. There are several classes of constructions into which *not* may enter: *I have not gone, It is white, not black, Not that I wish to intrude,* etc. But when a Japanese negates a verb he inflects the verb itself in a special way, much as we do to express a past tense.

Thus in Japanese it is impossible to utter a verb form without showing implicitly whether the action is positive or negative. That is why I referred above to *overtly* expressed categories. The real categories in a language are those which may never be left unexpressed in any utterance containing a form to which such categories apply.

Now that we have defined the nature of categories and how they may be recognized, it is of interest to see how different linguistic groups have sliced the universe and what slices certain groups may never leave unexpressed. To start from home ground we may mention a few from English: number, person, tense, case (genitive and nongenitive, the latter split into subject and object for *he, she, who,* and the restricted number of nouns for which these pronouns may be substituted[5]): contrary to widespread opinion, English chooses a rather small number

---

[5] For example: *Father$_1$ ate an apple. The apple made father$_2$ sick. Father$_1$* and *father$_2$* do not differ in form (as do Lithuanian *t'évas: t'évq*), but they differ grammatically in the substitutes which they demand. *He ate it. It made him sick.* A word like *apple,* on the other hand, shows no such distinction, whereas Lithuanian would have *óbuoli: obuolỹs,* respectively, with change of ending and of accent. Likewise, there is no distinction in *Make your father (him) happy: Give your father (him) an apple;* here Lithuanian would have, respectively, *t'évq (jī̃): t'évui (jám).* [Actually, there is a distinction in the English, too, of a deep-seated sort. For the last sentence may, unlike the preceding one, have an equivalent *Give an apple to your father.*]

with which to slice its universe. On the basis of naïve arguments often heard, English must then be a singularly poor language. Nevertheless, we seem to get along; later on, we shall return to this question of how we manage. Sanskrit employs a much wider range of categories, but most of them are things with which we are familiar from the Latin and Greek tradition in our education. To mention a few: case (eight of them), number (singular, dual, and plural), person, tense, mode, infinitive form, voice, gender. A fairly full supply, it would seem, but in the view of some speakers, as we shall see, a rather biased view of the universe. Most of the Slavonic languages show a range similar to that of Sanskrit, and for a very good reason, since they have simply preserved categories found in the common Indo-European parent-language. Slavonic, however, shows a striking development of another category, that of aspect. It is impossible for a Russian, Pole, Czech, Serb, or Bulgarian to utter a verb form without specifying whether the action is regarded as finished and done with or as in process of development. Thus, for the equivalent of any English verb, one must select in Russian one of two verb forms.

When we mention gender, we usually think in terms of masculine, feminine, and neuter. We are familiar with this feature from German, Russian, Sanskrit, Latin, and so forth. French, Spanish, and Italian limit the gender category to masculine and feminine. This often has nothing whatever to do with biological sex: a French table is feminine, a Spanish hat is masculine, a German young lady is neuter. In view of such disparities, it would perhaps seem better to label genders with A, B, C, or something of the sort.

The independence of sex and gender becomes more striking when we find that the Bantu languages in Africa normally distinguish about a dozen genders. In all the branches of this great linguistic family, all nouns belong to one or another of these gender classes. For most classes there is a corresponding plural form, but there is often no correlation between the semantic value of the noun and the class to which it belongs. Unlike European languages, these gender markers appear in the form of prefixes. Thus in the Zulu language the stem *-ntu* means "person"; *umuntu* means "man"; plural *abantu* means "people." It is from this form, which has cognates in all these languages, that the name of the whole family is taken.

It is convenient here to point out that any alleged connections between the so-called "primitive" cultures of some peoples and the kinds of languages they speak are quite groundless. There seems to be a tendency to attribute to the languages of primitive peoples naïve inarticulate simplicity or, contrariwise, exuberant complexity, owing to an inability to generalize. The latter point might seem superficially to apply to Bantu. Hosts of languages of the world, including modern English, remain to be described according to principles now considered valid. Yet with the data at hand it is crystal clear that there is no reason whatever to infer that there is any connection between cultural level, accomplishments of civilization, and linguistic structure.

Many groups in the world have no categories of tense, which seems so important if we think only of European languages. They simply specify, if they feel the need, "yesterday," "tomorrow," or "many long years ago," much as we do for the color of horses or for the matted mess the moths have made of Grandpa's old uniform—Sierra Popoluca of Veracruz, which ignores tense, has an affix for nouns to denote old, used or unwanted objects. We, who feed regularly of pronouncements that so often begin "I have it on good authority that . . . ," "Competent observers . . . ," "I am instructed to inform you that the records of this office disclose that . . . ," tend to overlook the presence within our own borders of many a native language that neatly covers all events not directly observed by casting the verb in a quotative mode. Some of those languages boast double quotatives, inflections that inform the hearer that the quoted source in turn had it secondhand. This is no more a matter of meticulous intellectual honesty or scholarly acumen than it is in our case when we say "houses" on seeing more than one of them. A dubitative mode for English could relieve much of the stylistic tedium of a Ph.D. thesis or a foreign correspondent's communiqué.

Thus we discover by inspecting sundry languages radically different from our own that the number of ways in which the universe may be sliced or the number of segments that may simply be omitted is varied in the extreme. To be sure, certain concepts, such as plurality, time, location, and direction, find frequent overt expression in grammar. But if we cast aside the limited and arbitrary preconceptions with which we have linguistically lived all our lives, the complete relativity of categories emerges in its true perspective as a cardinal feature of language. When one considers *in abstracto* the vast range of possibilities that exists, it becomes obvious that no one language might reasonably be expected to display a complete roster of all conceivable categories. Such would only defeat the purpose of language.

If we could afford the mnemonic overhead of vast numbers of categories, most sentences could be turned out in the form of concise, highly organized, unitary words. Some languages are famous for their apparent approach to this state of affairs. In the last century Max Müller, discussing the causes of the Crimean War, said that a Turk could explain the whole difficulty in a single word: "because of their not having been able to be made mutually to love one another."[6] Many complete statements may be found in Eskimo in the form of a single marathon word. But then again, many a Turkish statement can be found that to our way of thinking is extremely wordy.

In the case of various languages employ-

ing complex and highly inflected forms of expression, it has been my experience that this apparent ability to embrace a large number of concepts in a single unified form is not a characteristic of combined complexity and brevity of an order foreign to, e.g., English or French. It is merely a function of structural emphasis on concepts which we recognize every day of our lives but which we are under no structural compulsion to express in every utterance. We simply specify such things by ising more words when the occasion demands it. Contrariwise, many languages entirely ignore certain things which we could never leave unexpressed.

Classical Mongolian is a good example of this difference in emphasis. It paid strict attention to sundry combinations of time and completeness of a verbal action and had an elaborate way of turning verb forms into nouns, with the result that a subordinate clause may be said not to have existed in classical Mongolian. Yet distinctions for singular and plural nouns and third person subject pronouns did not exist in this language; if there were two or three or lots of something or if there was a possible ambiguity as to who was doing what, a Mongol simply stated such details by using more words. "What you lose on the swings you gain on the roundabouts"; and we might add that English, viewed through Mongol eyes, would seem just as queer.

We have seen that, of the vast range of sounds the human mechanism can produce, each language selects a very limited number and that many languages differ considerably in their choice. All languages agree in using a comparatively small number of meaningful building blocks, when we consider the complexity of the world inhabited

---

[6] *sevistirilemediklerinden*. A Sanskrit drama opens with the word *parya'nkagranthibandhad-viguṇitabhujagāślesasamvītajānorantahprānāvaro-dhavyuparatasakalajñānaruddhendriyasya*, "of him who squats with a knotted girdle wound between his knees, like the embrace of a twice-folded serpent, and with his breath checked, all his consciousness ceased, and his sense-perception

dormant." This form is, however, very different from the Turkish example, since it is a huge compound of elements that could just as well be rephrased as I have done in the English translation and since it has only one inflexional morpheme—the *-asya* on the end, which makes the entire noun genitive singular masculine. This sort of thing became a literary trick in Sanskrit.

alike by Wall Street brokers, Buddhist pundits, and Hottentot cowherds. Individual languages differ strikingly in the combinations they permit and the categories they choose in order to expand the scope of these individual units and to link the isolated forms into chains of fruitful and relatively unambiguous utterances. Above all, it is clear that the possession or lack of particular categories is no hindrance to free communication in a linguistic community.

We are now in a position to make some general statements on subjects relating to language that are frequently misunderstood. It is often remarked that some people speak their language poorly, or ungrammatically, or that most people in such and such a place do so. I have arranged these allegations in ascending order of asininity. Many people prefer Mr. Churchill, E. B. White, or Faulkner to the London cabby or the Brooklyn soda jerker. That is a matter of taste and style, conditioned partly by considerations of prestige, environment, and individual temper. Stylistically—that is to say, in matters of arrangement of *optional* sequences—certain ir.dividuals excel; some people tell jokes very badly. Linguistically, all native speakers handle their own dialect neither poorly nor well; they simply speak it, if we discount slips of the tongue.

To say that people speak "ungrammatically," if by that one means "without a grammatical system," is pure rubbish.[7] All normal human beings learn at an early age to make themselves understood within the framework of the patterns obtaining in their own linguistic society. People frequently lack adroitness in finding the happy expression; many people are diffuse or insufficiently specific in their choice of terms in a complicated discussion. If a person speaks ungrammatically, he can probably best be

[7]We must recognize that "ungrammatically" also seems to mean "in a linguistic fashion I don't like"; to move direct from this meaning to the one suggested above would be the same as my insisting that all rubbish is homogeneous because I have just called it "pure."

located in an institution or under a grave marker. Most human beings seem to enjoy playing ball. Some play cricket, others football. Regardless of whether you aspire to be a star, if you don't obey the rules the game breaks up.

The notion that most people speak incorrectly is a pure contradiction in terms. Such a statement can be reinterpreted in three ways. To maintain that most people can behave in a nonstandard fashion requires somewhat better logic than Messrs. Aristotle, Russell, Carnap, or Quine can supply.

To say that most people are now speaking differently from the way they did some time ago is a platitude that supports no judgment one way or another. Of course they are; this has been happening continuously at varying rates in different groups from the inception of our earliest records of language. If the past is any indication of the future, dialects will continue to mushroom though perhaps with new divergences and less speed than could have been foreseen before the age of *Life, Look,* and the radio.

The third possible interpretation hinges on the word "correct" or "proper"; and it is on this point that an enormous and disproportionate amount of confusion has arisen and been perpetuated in the province of normative grammar—that branch of linguistics that concerns itself with what people "ought" to say. Effective or colorless *style* is possible within any given dialect, in its own terms; that is not the point at issue here. Forms such as *ain't* and *he don't* are the prevailing forms in any American dialects. From a purely linguistic point of view these are the "correct" forms in these dialects, in the sense that that is what those people normally say. However, in the sense that these forms are not admired and acceptable in certain groups, they are not "correct" for purposes of finding favor with such groups. But this is a very different sort of "correctness," and the two must not be confused. When a German speaker says *He has gone already home,* he has made an "incorrect" construction, not because it is socially unacceptable but because it is not English; a native English speaker does not make this sort of "error." It is "correct" to wear coats and trousers (but not kilts) to keep from catching cold and to avoid entanglements with the law of indecent exposure; but if you want to cut a figure at a swank club, it behooves you to look to the cut and quality of the tweed. The conventions of human society are inescapable, and anyone looking for a job or wanting to hobnob with the "right" people must conform to a degree. Whether this is a good thing is not for a linguist to say; it is simply a fact. It is, however, the duty of a linguist not to confuse the criteria involved in these linguistic situations.

The honest way to handle this sort of "correctness" is to label it something like "Linguistic Recipes for Swank Speakers." That is really what most of our normative grammar is, and thus it should be subject to just as exact analysis as anything else. There is, of course, nothing wrong with all this,

so long as we know what we are doing and recognize it for what it is.

Some people express aesthetic preferences or, more commonly, revulsion for certain languages. I hope that I have been able to show a few of the many ways in which speakers of different languages manage to say practically everything they ever need to. It should be obvious, then, that, since all linguistic mediums seem to be equally adequate and at the same time equally arbitrary, a question of choice is irrelevant. People who grow up eating corned beef and cabbage or curdled goats' milk think them splendid foods. There is, to be sure, a somewhat greater mastery and ease of control to be enjoyed in the use of a language than in the eating of foods. But, again, the language which every man handles most easily is his own language. On that basis the choice should be simple. Some people may like French because it reminds them of that extravagant winter down near the Pyrenees. Such a preference is extra-linguistic.

*Transformations**

H. A. GLEASON, JR.

12.1   A favorite exercise in public school English has been the changing of sentences from one form to another. Thus from a sentence like

John is writing a letter.

may be formed, among others, the following:

John isn't writing a letter.
Is John writing a letter?
A letter is being written by John.

* For the sake of clarity, the original format has been retained in this selection.

Reprinted with the permission of the author and the publisher from *An Introduction to Descriptive Linguistics.* (2d ed.) New York: Holt, Rinehart and Winston, Inc., 1955, Chap. 12.

Very little is ordinarily given by way of clearly formulated rules for these processes, yet students seem to learn the technique more or less readily. Given the same sentence to start with, and the same rather simple instructions (e.g., "Make this negative."), there will be a very high degree of agreement in the answer. All this would suggest that such exercises must reflect some significant structural relationships in the English language. If so, they are worth careful investigation and formal statement.

When such changes are discussed at all, it is generally in terms of the meanings of the sentences. But this cannot be very exact, and is seldom very helpful. For example, it is easy enough to label *Is John writing a letter?* as a question. But what is the meaning of a question? Indeed, we cannot even give a good definition of the word "question." There is, of course, nothing unusual in finding difficulties in describing meanings, or in making clear statements about language on the basis of meaning. But with questions, it seems particularly difficult and unsatisfactory.

On the other hand, a little examination will show that changes of the sorts illustrated above can be described structurally—that is, in terms of the addition of elements, the rearranging of elements, or the altering of the form of elements. What specific portions of the sentence are involved, and how, can be very exactly stated. This is done, not in terms of their meanings, but on the basis of their structural position within the sentence. Moreover, the descriptions so arrived at have very wide applicability. For example, almost any English sentence not already negative, may be made into a negative sentence in a way very similar to that shown. This can then be formulated into a rule of considerable power, precisely the kind of rule that we desire in grammars.

12.2 Not all changes are of this sort. Thus the same sentence might be altered to

John is penning an epistle.

Native speakers of English will recognize a very significant relationship between this sentence and its prototype. But they also sense that the relationship here is of an entirely different sort. The sentence structure is not changed; substitutions are made within the same structural framework. From a structural point of view

Mary is baking a cake.

is just as closely related to the original. There is a difference, of course. It lies in the fact that *penning* is a "synonym" of *writing*, whereas *baking* is not. Synonymy is not a precisely definable concept, nor indeed a structural concept. Changes of this sort are therefore not structurally describable. Moreover, they are of much more restricted scope. Clearly, not all operations of altering sentences to related sentences have the same linguistic interest. The ones involving structural changes stand apart from all the others. They will be called transformations.

12.3 A **transformation** is a statement of the structural relation of a pair of constructions which treats that relation as though it were a process. Hence, it is normally stated in the form of rules which may be applied to one of the pair—an **input**—altering it to produce the other—an **output.** Note that transformations are directional. Some can be described in either direction, though practically we must choose one. Others can be described effectively only in one way.

12.4 As an example we might consider the following set of sentence pairs. These are obviously a sample from a very much larger number.

1. *John is writing a letter.*   *John isn't writing a letter.*
2. *Jim has been trying to do it.*   *Jim hasn't been trying to do it.*
3. *James will come tomorrow.*   *James won't come tomorrow.*

4. *Ruth was a beautiful girl.*   *Ruth wasn't a beautiful girl.*
5. *Mary could have been there.*   *Mary couldn't have been there.*
6. *His father walked home.*   *His father didn't walk home.*
7. *My friends like chess.*   *My friends don't like chess.*
8. *The car runs well.*   *The car doesn't run well.*
9. *Sam started running immediately.* *Sam didn't start running immediately.*

If we can find a single clearly statable rule to cover all of these, we may describe these nine sentence pairs as examples of a single transformation. The sentences seem to fall into two groups. For sentences 1 to 5 a simple rule is immediately evident: *-n't* is added as a suffix to the first word in the verb phrase. This is true whether the verb phrase consists of a single word as in 4, or several as in 2 and 5. There is a minor complication in 3: *will* + *-n't* yields *won't*. We can easily show that this is quite regular, a fact about the language which would have to be described in any case. Pairs 6 to 9 seem to follow a different rule. Before the *-n't* is added, *walked* is changed to *did walk* and comparable changes are made in the other cases. If we try applying the pattern of the first five pairs without this intermediate step we get such very strange outputs as

His father walkedn't home.

These two rules may be combined into one, if certain conditions can be met. The first of these is that we find a clear conditioning which determines which applies. This we can do: *-n't* is never added to words like *walked*. Which of the two rules applies is determined by whether or not the first word is one of the small list (*is, are, was, has, can, might*—an English-speaking student can easily complete the list) to which *-n't* can be added. If not, it is changed to a verb phrase which starts with *did, do, does*. A second condition which must be met is to find a clear statement as to how this change, *walked* to *did walk*, etc., is to be described.

12.5 The following sentence pairs may help with this problem:

10. *The boy ran away.*   *The boy didn't run away.*
11. *The boy did run away.*   *The boy didn't run away.*

These present no difficulty for the rules just mentioned for the negative transformation. In 11 the verb phrase begins with *did*, and *-n't* is added directly. In 10 *ran* is a word to which *-n't* cannot be added; it is therefore changed to *did run*. The interesting feature is that the outputs in the two pairs SEEM to be identical. Actually this is something of an illusion. There are a number of different pronunciations for a writing like *The boy didn't run away.* Only one factor, the position of the sentence stress, needs to be noted here. There are at least the following pairs:

10. a. *The boy ran awáy.*   *The boy didn't run awáy.*
    b. *The boy rán away.*   *The boy didn't rún away.*
    c. *The bóy ran away.*   *The bóy didn't run away.*
11.   *The boy díd run away.*   *The boy dídn't run away.*

This seems clearly the natural way to match them up. The sentences in each pair have the sentence stress in the same place. *Did run* occurs in the input only when the sentence stress falls on *did*. (A sentence like *The boy did run awáy.* sounds at best extremely archaic, and certainly cannot be considered normal modern English.) It follows, then, that *did* occurs in such sentences ONLY either when *-n't* is suffixed or when it receives the sentence stress. There are other uses of *did*, but most of them fit into the same pattern. The auxiliary *did* occurs in English only where sentence structure demands it. It is never required by the meaning, and it never means anything at all. The difference between *The boy ran awáy.* and *The boy díd run away.* is not a matter of the presence or absence of *did*, only of the stress position. *Did* is there only to provide a meaningless carrier for that stress in the required position. If anything else were available, *did* would not occur. Compare

The boy will run awáy.   *The boy wíll run away.*

Did, do, does, done (the verb *do* in all its forms) as auxiliaries are always completely meaningless—mere position makers. *Do* may also occur as a main verb, in which case it does have meaning: *I díd do my homework.*

The morphemes $\{-Z_3\}$ and $\{-D_1\}$ can occur only in the first word of a verb phrase. If that word ceases to be first by addition of $\{do\}$, these morphemes must shift to the new first word. Thus

walked $(= \{walk\} + \{-D_1\})$ becomes *did walk* $(= \{do\} + \{-D_1\} + \{walk\})$
like $(= \{like\})$ becomes *do like* $(= \{do\} + \{like\})$
runs $(= \{run\} \; + \{-Z_3\})$ becomes *does run* $(= \{do\} + \{-Z_3\} + \{run\})$

Both these rules (addition of *do* and position of $\{-Z_3\}$ and $\{-D_1\}$) are ones that will be needed anyway. They are not proposed merely to facilitate the definition of the negative transformation. This is, of course, the best possible recommendation of the result so far: All the rules are quite general. All the sentence pairs we have discussed can then be subsumed under one rule—the negative transformation—plus in some cases the operation of certain other rules, but these are also quite general.

12.6 We cannot speak of "the question transformation" in English, since there are a number of different ones, no one of which has any clear pre-eminence. But we can readily describe each of this rather heterogeneous family of transformations. Some are of considerable interest. Among them are

12. *John is writing a letter.*   *Who is writing a letter?*
13.   *Is John writing a letter?*
14.   *What is John writing?*
15.   *John is writing a letter, isn't he?*

Of these, number 12 seems the simplest. A question word (*who* or *what*) is merely substituted for the subject of the sentence. The intonation remains the same. This is a simple example of a transformation which can be described in only one direction. *Mary is writing a letter.*, *That old man over there is writing a letter.*, and many other input sentences all yield this same output. If the process is reversed, taking the question to be the input, how is the proper output to be selected from the multitude of sentences which are paired with it?

Number 13 is more complex. The first word in the verb phrase is transposed to the first position in the sentence. It must be one of the same list of forms as was found taking the suffix *-n't*. If it isn't, the verb phrase is first altered by the addition of a *do*, thus:

John wrote a létter. → °
John did write a létter. →
Did John write a létter?

The intermediate stage is marked with ° because it does not occur in that form in normal use. In pronunciation there is, of course, also a change in intonation. Commonly it is from /231↘/ to /233↗/.

Number 14 is also best described as involving a series of changes. First, the first word in the verb phrase is moved, as in number 13. Then a question word is substituted for some sentence element, and this is transposed to the initial position:

> *John is writing a letter.* →
> *Is John writing a letter?* →
> *Is John writing what?* →
> *What is John writing?*

This illustrates another very common characteristic of transformations. When two or more apply in one sentence, it is usually easier to describe them in one fixed order; sometimes it is extremely difficult or impossible to use another order. Almost always the form in which the rules are stated must be changed if they are not applied in the same order.

Number 15 involves both change of the intonation (commonly to /232→/) and the addition of a second clause. This consists of only two words. The first is identical with the first word in the input's verb phrase, except that only one of the two must have the suffix *-n't*. The other word is the proper pronoun to substitute for the subject. This is pronounced with the intonation /233↗/.

12.7 Describing various types of questions in this way does not merely elucidate their structure. It also provides a good basis for understanding some of the dialectal or stylistic variations which occur. The following two outputs from a single input will illustrate:

16. *John is writing to his mother.*   *To whom is John writing?*
17.   *Who is John writing to?*

Examined as they stand, these two results have quite different sentence structure. But looked at in terms of transformations, they are seen to be very much more similar. The intermediate steps are something like the following:

> *John is writing to his mother.* → *Is John writing to his mother?*
> → *Is John writing to* $\begin{cases} whom \\ who \end{cases}$ → $\begin{cases} \textit{To whom is John writing?} \\ \textit{Who is John writing to?} \end{cases}$

In the last stage they differ as to how much of the sentence is transposed. The transposition of a whole phrase, *to whom,* is found almost exclusively in literary and quite formal English. Colloquial usage very seldom transposes more than a single word. (Colloquial usage, including informal writing, is also much more likely to use *who* than *whom,* particularly when separated from its conditioning context.) The result is sentences with final prepositions and various other "errors." As is often the case, these "errors" are not the result of "loose grammar," but of very rigid and explicit patterns. Most colloquial English usage calls for transposition of the single question word, result what may.

In this discussion there is no desire to evaluate either pattern. The intention is rather to point out that much of our prescriptive grammar, and equally much of the rebellion against it, is vitiated by bad diagnosis. Linguistic description is neutral in such questions. Its task is to give a clear and significant description of usages which actually occur, and when usages differ, to make clear and significant statement as to how they differ. That is, descriptive linguistics can provide the diagnosis on the basis of which an evaluation can be made. Every thoughtful speaker must evaluate conflicting usages; he will do so more effectively with a clearer understanding of the facts. One of the strengths of a transformational description of this type of question is the clarity with which it sets forth this particular difference in usage.

12.8 In the process of operating these transformations we find that not only are words shifted around in sentences, but even affixes are moved from one word to another. Not infrequently this causes rather complex changes in forms. For example, applying two of the transformations we have just discussed in succession:

John will go. → *John won't go.* →
John won't go, will he?

With the addition of *-n't*, the form of *will* was changed. Then in the second operation the *-n't* had to be removed, restoring the original form of *will*. This constant shifting of forms is awkward and wasteful. As long as every stage in our description is plagued with these operations, many of them only to be later undone, transformational description is unnecessarily complex.

One way around this difficulty is to operate not with sentences but with "strings" of morphemes, leaving the adjustment to the proper form to the last:

{John} {will} {go} → /²ĵâʜn⁺wìl⁺³gów¹↘/ *John will go.*
  ↓

{John} {will} {–n't} {go} → /²ĵâʜn⁺wòwnt⁺³gów¹↘/ *John won't go.*
  ↓

{John} {will} {–n't} {go} {will} {he}
  → /²ĵâʜn⁺wòwnt⁺³gów² → ²wíliy³↗/ *John won't go, will he?*

So described, there are two quite distinct sets of operations. The vertical arrows indicate transformations. They carry one string of morphemes into another. The horizontal arrows represent **morphophonemic** operations. They give any string of morphemes a phonemic shape. (Or, if a written language is being described, a comparable set of operations gives it a graphic shape.) Morphophonemic operations are described as applying only after all transformations have been completed. This, of course, will require some restatement of the transformational rules discussed above. It will also require a slight redefinition of transformation, since transformations do not alter one sentence into another, but one string of morphemes into another. These strings may be said to underlie the sentences which we used in the presentation above.

12.9   The word "string" might easily be misleading. We must certainly mean more than merely some assortment of morphemes arranged in some linear order. Several reasons for this should be apparent from the discussion above. Many of the transformations must be stated in terms of an operation performed on a certain element in a certain position in the string. For example, many of these we have discussed involve the first word in the verb phrase. But if a string were merely a sequence of elements in linear order, the only position we might define would be something like "second element" or "third from the end." Some of the question transformations involve substitution of a question word for a constituent. This might consist of a single morpheme, or of a considerable number. If transformations are to apply to strings, strings must be assemblages of elements having constituent structure. When used in description in terms of transformations, "string" must mean a special sort of sequence of elements, which, because it is characterized by a constituent structure may be called a **structured string**.

Since transformations operate on structured strings, a grammar which is to describe transformations must first describe the construction of a set of structured strings. This can best be done in terms of very much the same concepts as have been described in Chapter 10.

12.10   When carried out consistently, the ideas just sketched result in a grammar quite characteristic in its organization and form of statement. Such a description is called a **transformational grammar**. It is claimed by some linguists that this type of statement can attain to a degree of precision, completeness, and conciseness not possible in any other way—in fact, that this technique can overcome certain limitations which are inherent in any other known form of description. Needless to say, these claims are not universally accepted. Both the technique and the claims imply a certain distinctive general theory of linguistics. This differs from other descriptive linguistic theories in certain ways that produce characteristic features in grammatical statements. Certain of these should be pointed out:

1. A transformational grammar is organized in three sections. The first of these describes certain strings of comparatively simple structure. The basic theory here is similar to that underlying all descriptions in terms of immediate constituents. For this reason, it is called the **constituent structure,** or by others, the **phrase structure,** segment of the grammar. The second, or **transformational** section, describes all the transformations by which the output strings of the first section of the grammar are carried into **terminal strings,** sufficient in number to underlie all of the sentences of the language. The third is the **morphophonemic** section. Here are described all of the processes by which terminal strings are given shapes which can be identified as utterances or portions of utterances. Any transformational grammar must have all three, but some individual sentences may involve no transformations. That is to say, the transformational section may be by-passed in some sentences; the other two cannot.

2. Since in such a scheme, no matter of phonemic (or orthographic) form comes in until the third, morphophonemic, portion of the grammar, the greater part of the statement, is properly in terms of quite abstract symbols. If the symbols used should have a form reminiscent of a familiar spelling or of a phonemic transcription, this is of no particular significance. In most instances the symbols are more or less arbitrary letters representing classes of structures, often with subscripts representing subclasses. Some of these symbols bear no obvious meaning, being selected merely for convenience. The use of such abstract symbols gives a thoroughgoing transformational grammar an algebraic appearance. This is often enhanced by the fact that the terminology and phraseology used in such grammars has been strongly influenced by that of mathematics. However, a transformational grammar is not properly any more mathematical than any other type of grammar in its basic features.

3. The statement is largely in the form of a set of rules. These are of two kinds. The first is of the form "X → Y + Z." This should be read as "X is to be rewritten as Y + Z." Such rules are referred to as **rewrite rules.** They have the effect of changing a symbolization, generally in the direction of making it more specific and explicit. For example, in one formulation of English grammar the starting point is the symbol S, roughly to be read as "sentence." The first rule is S → NP + VP. This substitutes for the very general representation, S, the more specific and explicit representation, NP + VP, roughly to be interpreted as "noun phrase plus verb phrase." This is not a statement that a sentence CONSISTS OF a noun phrase and a verb phrase. Many do, of course, but not all: e.g., *Come here!* lacks the noun phrase. Rather it is a statement that all sentences (or only one set if there is another rewrite rule that starts from S) must be DESCRIBED IN TERMS OF a noun phrase and a verb phrase. Subsequent rules may have the effect of cutting out some of these structures.

The rewrite rule applies to any string wherein the proper symbols are found. The second type of rule, the **transformational rule,** is similar in many respects, but operates only on certain symbols in certain places within a constituent structure. Thus a rewrite rule applying to NP, will apply to any NP. But a transformational rule may apply to certain NPs only. For example, a transformation involving the moving of an NP in object position relates the following pair of sentences:

    18. *I saw John*   *John I saw*
          yesterday.   *yesterday.*

But cannot apply to an NP in some other position:

> 19. *I gave the money to the man*
> *with John.*
>
> *John I gave the money*
> *to the man with.*

4. Transformational grammars are generally very explicit about the conditions under which any given rule can be applied. Careful attention is given to the order of application of rules. An effort is made to distinguish clearly between **optional** and **obligatory** rules, and between **recursive** rules (ones that can be applied repeatedly) and **non-recursive** rules. Properly, this is not a peculiarity of transformational grammars as such, but of all grammars which attempt to be thoroughly rigorous in their description.

5. A key word in all transformational grammar is **generate**. This is used in a sense taken from mathematics.

$$(x - a)^2 + (y - b)^2 = c^2$$

may be said to generate a set of circles in a plane defined by x and y. That means that for any given a, b, and c this equation defines one specific circle. For all possible values of a, b, and c it defines all possible circles in the plane concerned. In the same way, a transformational grammar consists of a set of statements which generate all possible sentences in a given language. Depending on the choices made wherever a choice is possible (whether to apply a certain optional rule, or which alternative to select when several are offered), it defines each specific sentence. In this sense, a particular running through of the grammar is not to be considered as CREATING a sentence, but more nearly as SELECTING a sentence from a pre-existing stock (the language) of all possible sentences. Thus the grammar might start with the symbol S and in a particular application of it end with /²jâʜn⁺wìl⁺³gów¹↘/. But the last expression does not represent anything not represented by the first. Rather S stands for ALL sentences in the language, and thus represents, among others, /²jâʜn⁺wìl⁺³gów¹↘/. The process of running through the grammar and making the required choices is a matter of singling out a specific sentence to replace the general symbol S. Nothing is created, increased, or added to; the meaning is instead very much narrowed. In much the same way $(x - 2)^2 + (y - 5)^2 = 3^2$ represents nothing not already completely covered by $(x - a)^2 + (y - b)^2 = c^2$, but only one specific instance out of the total set of circles. The selection is made by choosing values 2, 5, and 3 for a, b, and c.

12.11 At the beginning of this chapter a few transformations were described in terms of familiarly spelled sentences. Later it was shown that it would be preferable to work, not with sentences, but with structured strings. In the last section it was suggested that a transformational grammar, when formally stated would be quite different from the nonrigorous description above. Here will be given a more formal description of the pair of sentences with which the discussion began. Not all alternatives are stated at every step, but some are mentioned so that it will be clear where choices must be made and how it is that more than one sentence might come out. At each step the rule being applied is listed at the left and the form resulting from its application at the right. Braces around morpheme symbols have been omitted.

The description starts, of course, with the general expression for a sentence.

STEP 1.   S

The first rewrite rule is generally described as obligatory, that is, there is no other choice at this step:

STEP 2. S → NP + VP   NP + VP

There are a variety of ways in which the VP might be developed leading to a variety of sentence patterns: . . . *ran.*, . . . *is good* . . . *saw him.*, etc. At this point a choice of rewrite rules will determine which type, in the broadest sense, will result.

STEP 3. VP → Verb + NP   NP + Verb + NP

At the next step there are two alternatives, between which a choice must be made. In such a case a rewrite rule giving the alternatives can be stated in the following form:

STEP 4. NP → $\begin{Bmatrix} NP_{sing} \\ NP_{pl} \end{Bmatrix}$ NP_{sing} + Verb + NP

The import of this rule is to demand a choice between singular and plural for each NP. It must be applied twice, since there are two occurrences of NP in the form resulting from step 3. These must be considered as two separate steps, since they are quite independent of each other. Moreover, one basic principle of this sort of grammar is that each rewrite in the constituent structure must replace just one symbol.

STEP 5. NP_{sing} + Verb + NP_{sing}

STEP 6. Verb → Aux + V NP_{sing} + Aux + V + NP_{sing}

STEP 7. Aux → C(M) + (have + en) + (be + ing)
                        NP_{sing} + C + be + ing + V + NP_{sing}

The parentheses in this rule mean that a choice may be made. C must be used, M (which stands for *can, may, shall,* etc.) may be omitted, have + en and be + ing can be omitted. Of the optional elements only be + ing was selected. The next rule also presents some choices, but these are partly controlled by the context.

STEP 8. C → $\begin{Bmatrix} Z_3 \text{ in the context } NP_{sing} \\ \o \text{ in the context } NP_{pl} \\ \text{past in any context} \end{Bmatrix}$
                        NP_{sing} + Z_3 + be + ing + V + NP_{sing}

Next there are several alternatives for the rewriting of NP_{sing}, of which only two are listed here.

STEP 9. NP_{sing} → $\begin{Bmatrix} D + N + \o \\ N_{prop} \\ \text{etc.} \end{Bmatrix}$
                        N_{prop} + Z_3 + be + ing + V + NP_{sing}

STEP 10. N_{prop} + Z_3
+ be + ing + V + D + N + ø

The ø in the last rule points out the lack of an inflectional suffix in contrast to NP_{pl} → D + N + Z_1. The result of step 10 is an expression consisting of some symbols for specific morphemes, either affixes like Z_3 or stems of function words like *be*, and some symbols standing for classes of stems or words. The next four steps consist of substituting an actual member of the class for each class symbol.

STEP 11. N_{prop} → Mary, John, Henry, . . .
                John + Z_3 + be + ing + V + D + N + ø

STEP 12. V   → write, read, take, . . .
                John + Z_3 + be + ing + write + D + N + ø

STEP 13. D   → the, this, a, . . .

$$\text{John} + Z_3 + \text{be} + \text{ing} + \text{write} + a + N + \emptyset$$

STEP 14. N   → ball, man, letter, . . .

$$\text{John} + Z_3 + \text{be} + \text{ing} + \text{write} + a + \text{letter} + \emptyset$$

The result of step 14 is a possible terminal string. Two courses of further development are open. We may apply certain transformations, or we may pass to the morphophonemic section of the grammar immediately. In the latter case there will be a variety of rules which must be applied, and no attempt will be made to give them in detail here. However, one type needs to be noticed. Certain affixes will regularly be combined with the following verbal element. In spelling the effect is as follows:

$$\text{John} + \underbrace{Z_3 + \text{be}} + \underbrace{\text{ing} + \text{write}} + a + \underbrace{\text{letter} + \emptyset}$$

John   is   writing   a   letter.

Or we may apply to the result of step 14 a transformation:

STEP 15. $NP + C + \begin{bmatrix} M \\ have \\ be \end{bmatrix} \ldots \rightarrow C + \begin{bmatrix} M \\ have \\ be \end{bmatrix} + NP \ldots$

$$\underbrace{Z_3 + \text{be}} + \text{John} + \underbrace{\text{ing} + \text{write}} + a + \underbrace{\text{letter} + \emptyset}$$

Is   John   writing   a   letter?

Again, the morphophonemic steps are not given in detail, but only suggested by showing the final result in spelling. Much the same set of rules applies, however, as did above.

12.12   At first reading, the last section seems to be a very elaborate and complex way of describing a pair of quite simple sentences. But such an evaluation is not entirely appropriate. To be sure a very much more simple description is possible: In *John is writing a letter.*, the first word is *John,* the second word is *is,* the third word is *writing,* . . . . But such a description tells us very little if anything about the sentence. It might be possible to make a somewhat more sophisticated description of the same anecdotal sort, but however detailed this might be, it would tell nothing whatever about the grammar of the sentence. A sentence has a grammar only as it stands in relation to other sentences as part of a language. Any speaker of English immediately sees something of the grammar in a sentence like *John is writing a letter.* This is only possible because he knows the language, and can fit this sentence into its place within the language. The sentence *apko kya cahīye,* "What do you want?" is just as grammatical, but the grammar is inaccessible to most readers of this book, simply because they cannot relate it to other sentences in Hindi. A grammatical description must place any given sentence in a framework which can be used to describe any sentence in the language, even though this requires making some statements which do not seem, superficially, to be of any great pertinence to the sentence at hand. Many features of the statement in the last section are not demanded by anything in the sentences being discussed, but by things in other (perhaps very many other) English sentences. At every point where a choice was presented, these two sentences were related to, and set off from, a host of other sentences. The statement did not merely describe the sentences in themselves, but rather put the two sentences into their place within the whole structure of the English language. The English language is an immensely complex thing, ramifying in many directions, and a description which does actually relate a single sentence to this complex structure cannot be very simple. One of the marvelous things about language is that any statement as short as that just given could in fact approach adequacy in relating these two sentences to the billions of billions of other sentences in the language.

In a statement of this sort, given with just two sentences in focus, the reasons for some of the features of the statement could not be made clear. To understand them, it would be necessary to trace out some of the consequences of other alternatives. An excerpt from a grammar cannot be as meaningful as a full grammar. To have given a full grammar of English, even if very much lacking in detail, would have been impossible here. What was given is a little like a full recounting of all the moves of the king's bishop in a championship chess game, mentioning the other pieces only when they fall directly in the path of the bishop.

There is another very important reason why the statement may seem unduly cumbersome. It attempted to state explicitly a number of things which are quite easily taken for granted. Every grammar leaves a great deal unsaid which the user must supply somehow from his "common sense" or "Sprachgefühl" or some other undefinable source. Much of this seems so obvious that to state it seems gratuitous. But research consists very largely of attempting to state the phenomena as explicitly as possible. Thus, Newton's law is traditionally said to have been found through dissatisfaction with treating the fall of an apple as simple and obvious, and was nothing more than an attempt to explain explicitly how it falls. Progress in linguistics must come largely by raising questions about the unstated phenomena, probing into them and attempting to make explicit statements in places where it had not previously been done. An explicit statement is not necessarily an acceptable statement. But it is often a testable statement. It always calls the attention of investigators to the question, and often provides a starting point toward a better formulation. Work on a transformational grammar of English has forced explicit statement at some points in the structure of the language and in general linguistic theory which had previously been passed by.

12.13 The introductory sections of this chapter centered around a small selection of sentence pairs related through a few transformations. The rules were not explicitly stated. Indeed, it would have been rather pointless to have given an explicit statement of the transformations without building this on an explicit statement of the underlying constituent structure. It should be pointed out, however, that a formal statement is possible. None of the sentences discussed would require the use of any very complex rules, and most of the rules would be quite general in application. Indeed, a proper writing of the rules might lead to a further step in generalization. For example, pairs 12 and 14 were described differently. But this is not necessary. Instead, the same sequence of transformational rules can be applied to produce both. The first fifteen steps in the generation are identical with that described in 12.11. Step 14 gives the string which, if taken directly through the morphophonemic rules, would give *John is writing a letter*. In the same way, the product of step 15 would yield *Is John writing a letter?*. As a string it is of the form:

STEP 15. Z_3 + be + John + ing + write + a + letter + ø

The next step replaces an NP by a question word. There are two NPs in this string, *John*, and *a letter*. They belong to different classes, one which requires *who* as a substitute, and one that requires *what*.

STEP 16. Z_3 + be + who + ing + write + a + letter + ø

OR Z_3 + be + John + ing + write + what

This is followed by an obligatory transformation which shifts any such question word to the initial position:

STEP 17.   who + Z_3 + be +   ing + write + a + letter + ø
what + Z_3 + be + John + ing + write

To these the same morphophonemic rules would apply. They would have the effect of taking them into a phonemic form familiarly associated with the spellings of examples 12 and 14:

Who   is   writing   a letter?
What   is   John   writing?

The other transformations discussed can be formally stated in much the same way.

A complete transformational grammar of English would, of course, list many more transformations than this small sample. Some of them would be rather different in general form and effect. In the following sections a few more will be mentioned in order to show the range of possibilities. All are, of course, capable of formal statement. But for the present purpose, it will be better to revert to the less rigorous style of discussion in which sentences are compared rather than strings, and in which only certain outstanding features are mentioned.

12.14   One type of transformation uses two or more inputs, combining them into one output. A very simple case is the following:

20. *The car stopped suddenly.*   }   *The car stopped suddenly and I*
I was thrown against the   *was thrown against the wind-*
windshield.   *shield.*

This particular transformation can be described in terms of nothing more than concatenation, the addition of a marker *and,* and appropriate adjustment of the intonation (or in writing of the punctuation). But the situation can be more complex:

21. *You have some bananas.*   }   *If you have any bananas, I*
I would like about a dozen.   *would like about a dozen.*

At first sight, sentence 21 would seem to come from ° *You have any bananas.* and *I would like about a dozen.* But the first of these two sentences seems quite unnatural. A little investigation will show that there is a very special relation between *any* and *some.* The one occurs in certain types of sentences, the other in other types. An adequate set of transformational rules will have to include a rule which has the effect of substituting *any* for *some* to produce sentences like that in 21. This is not as special a rule as it might seem. Very much the same relationship is seen in other pairs of sentences, so that the same rule can be applied in the series of transformations which connect them.

22. *I have some bananas.*   *I haven't any bananas.*
23. *You have some bananas.*   *Have you any bananas?*

Another somewhat similar phenomenon is illustrated in the following:

24. *I will come.*   *He said he would come.*

Only one of the two input sentences is shown here; the other will be discussed in 12.15. There is a change of *will* to *would,* and of *I* to *he.* These changes are conditioned by the occurrence of *said* and *he* in the first part of the sentence, as may be seen by comparing the set of sentences in 25, all having the same input:

25. *I will come.*   *He says he will come.*
I said I would come.
I say I will come.

Transformations which have the effect of putting two or more inputs together into one output involve a number of rules. There is the addition of various construction markers, *and, either . . . or, because, therefore, if . . . then,* etc. There may be changes of certain specific items, *some → any, sometime → ever,* etc. Verb forms may be changed to bring them into the proper relationship. (Traditional grammar gives a partial treatment of these phenomena under the rules of "sequence of tenses.") Pronouns may undergo various changes. As all of these can be structurally defined, they belong in a grammar and can be formulated in transformational rules.

12.15   Example 24 illustrates another feature of some transformations. The other underlying sentence cannot easily be *He said.* Such a sentence does occur, but rather infrequently, and in a quite specialized situation. Rather it must come from something like *He said it.* In the transformation, *it* is replaced by *he would come.* This sort of transformation does not merely connect strings; it inserts one into another so that it becomes an element in the structure of the other. In doing so it removes and replaces some element. Sometimes it is fairly obvious what this replaced element must be. In other cases it is not clear from the final result what such an element should be considered to have been in the input. In this respect, such a transformation is exactly like some of the question transformations. In example 12, the transformation involved the substituting of *who* for *John.* Looking at the output alone, it would not be clear what nominal was involved. It might have been *Mary, the man, my neighbor who grows daffodils,* or innumerable other possibilities. But it could not be *the pen* or *that typewriter,* or many others, which would require the substitution of *what* rather than *who.* Perhaps it is just this uncertainty which lies behind calling a sentence like *Who is writing a letter?* a question. It is not possible to go from the output sentence backward and reconstruct in detail every step of the generation. But it is possible to know that *who* substitutes for an NP, and equally to know that *he would come* must substitute for an NP.

Another type of transformation which inserts one input into another is exemplified by the following two sentences:

26.   *The man who drives the yellow Cadillac hit a lamppost yesterday.*

27.   *The man who hit a lamppost yesterday drives the yellow Cadillac.*

Both these sentences can be generated from the same pair of inputs.

The man hit a lamppost yesterday.
The man drives the yellow Cadillac.

To be usable in this transformation, the two inputs must have some part in common, in this case, *the man.* For this constituent in one input may be substituted *who* or *which,* whereby the whole S becomes attributive to the matching noun in the other, and is inserted in the position after the noun. When the NP replaced by *who* or *which* is not initial, then additional changes have to be specified.

By means of various transformations of these types, it is possible to take care of all those sentence types which are traditionally labeled as "compound" or "complex." So conceived, the phrase structure sector of the grammar generates certain clauses, and the transformational sector unites these into sentences. In the light of this, it is not, strictly speaking, correct to read the symbol S at the start of 12.11 as meaning "sentence" as used in traditional grammar. Nor indeed is it necessarily much better to read it as meaning "clause" in the sense of traditional grammar, since some transformations will carry an S into some structure other than what is traditionally called either a "clause" or a "sentence." But this does not mean that S does not designate some real and significant unit, only that it is not a unit identical with any one of those defined in traditional grammar. It is better to consider S as a designation for a unit which is basic to English grammatical patterns as described by a transformational grammar. If read as "sentence" it means only "sentence" as understood in this kind of grammar. It should not be expected to match precisely any unit in any other statement of English grammar. A transformational grammar is not merely a restatement of, or a minor amendment to, a traditional grammar or an immediate constituent grammar, but a basically different approach to language structure. It must find different units.

12.16 Once it is recognized that transformations can be applied to a pair of input strings to reduce one to the status of an element within the other, a vast panorama of possibilities opens up. Certain types of what are traditionally labeled "phrases" seem quite similar in important ways to "subordinate clauses" and suggest that a similar treatment is possible. As examples the following sentences will serve:

> 28. *His coming and going*
> *like that gives me the willies.*
>
>   from   *He comes and goes*
>   *like that.*
>
> 29. *His continual drumming*
> *on the table makes me*
> *nervous.*
>
>   from   *He continually*
>   *drums on the table.*

These both have a great deal of the underlying sentence pattern still remaining, and therefore have a great deal that commends such treatment.

If it is permissible with sentences like 28 and 29, why not also with similar phrases with less of the sentence elements preserved? The following all seem to be related in some way to example 29, and should perhaps be treated as having the same origin:

> 30. *His continual drumming   makes me nervous.*
>   *His   drumming on the table makes me nervous.*
>   *Continual drumming on the table makes me nervous.*
>   *His   drumming   makes me nervous.*
>   *Continual drumming   makes me nervous.*
>   *Drumming on the table makes me nervous.*
>   *Drumming   makes me nervous.*

but not

>   *His continual   on the table makes me nervous.*, etc.

All of these differ from 29 only in the omission of certain parts. Any element or combination of elements can be omitted except *drumming*. They might accordingly be described in terms of a special type of transformation which merely deletes certain statable constituents.

This sort of transformation has a very wide usefulness, but it requires caution. It would be quite possible to generate 29 by a series of deletions from something like:

31. *His continual drumming*
 on the table with his knife
 and fork while the toast-
 master is introducing the
 speaker of the evening makes
 me nervous.

But this is quite unnecessary. There seems to be no reason to start from the longer sentence. *He continually drums on the table.* is sufficient as an input. But if so, why not merely *He continually drums.* for the first sentence in 30? In this case a deletion transformation would be unnecessary. But this is not true of all these sentences. The input may be *He continually drums.*, or *He drums on the table.*, or simply *He drums.*, but it must have *he* or some other NP in the subject position. Those sentences in 30 without *his* must be derived by the use of a deletion transformation if the *drumming* is to be gotten from the VP of an S. Unnecessary deletions are not justifiable, but some deletions are necessary in a transformational grammar of English.

12.17 One of the commonest criticisms of traditional school grammar has been directed at the use of "understood" sentence parts. For example, an imperative sentence like *Come here!* is commonly described as having as subject "*you* understood." *You* in such sentences is quite rare and exceptional. Some linguists reject the use of such "understood" elements in a grammatical statement. Here, as in many other instances, a transformational grammar parallels traditional grammar in some respects. This sentence can be derived by the same first rewrite rule as used in 12.11, S → NP + VP. If so, at a later point in the grammar, a deletion transformation must remove the NP. The question is, then, is it necessary to have the NP in the derivation? There is some evidence that it is. *Myself* occurs, generally speaking, only in sentences in which *I* occurs in subject position. *Yourself* occurs commonly in two kinds of sentences, those with *you* for the subject, and imperatives. All these facts can be brought under one rule if *you* could be the subject of imperative sentences at the point in their generation at which the rules introducing *yourself* apply. That is, if something like *You go chase yourself!* were one stage in the generation of the imperative sentence *Go chase yourself!*

Within the framework of a transformational grammar deletion transformations seem to have a place when they are required to explain existing patterns. Unnecessary deletion transformations have no such place—no unnecessary rule of any kind can be tolerated. In other types of grammars the use of "understood" elements may be less easily justified, and whether they will be used or not is a decision which the linguist must make, just as he must decide which of several possible forms of statement he will follow. There is, however, one special danger in "understood" elements which explains, and at least partly justifies, the condemnation of many linguists. This is the use of "understood" elements in field linguistics. It requires a very profound knowledge of a language to be able to assess when such a device is justified by the structure of the language itself. The temptation in preliminary stages is to supply "understood" elements in order to bring the structure into line with that of some other language. For example, in Hebrew /ṭóob haaʔíiš/ 'The man is good.,' /ṭóob/ means 'good' and /haaʔíiš/ means 'the man.' There is no direct equivalent to 'is,' though of course the sentence structure as a whole is in some way equivalent to the structure of the English sentence as a whole. Some grammarians have stated that 'is' is understood, or even that /haayáa/ is understood. (This is glossed in some dictionaries as meaning, among other things, 'to be.') But it is difficult to see how /haayáa/ can be "restored" to this sentence without utterly changing it. In no instance can there be any justification for "understood" elements or deletion transformations except in the STRUCTURE of the language. That "the meaning requires"—or the exigencies of translation, or any other non-structural indication, real or imaginary—is totally irrelevant.

12.18   If individual words can be introduced into a sentence by means of a transformation combining two structured strings, it would seem possible to give a similar treatment to a great deal more of what has in the past been taken care of in the IC structure, or handled by traditional grammatical devices of various kinds. For example, it has been proposed that attributive adjectives can be introduced into noun phrases by this means.

> 32. *I see the house.* ⎫
>   *The house is red.* ⎬   *I see the red house.*

In favor of this suggestion is the fact that *I see the red house.* does seem to be related in some way to *I see the house which is red.* The latter clearly can be gotten from the inputs of 32. It is claimed that this procedure does result in a considerable simplification of description, but some linguists are less convinced of the value of such transformations than of those described earlier in this chapter.

Such a proposal seems to be pointing in the direction of making all of sentence structure a matter of transformations. But this is not the case. While it is easy enough to derive *red house* from an input *The house is red.*, it does not seem possible to generate *the house* in this way. Certainly it cannot be done in a strictly parallel way, since there is no sentence of the form *House is the.* In any case, it would seem that there must be at least a small collection of sentences in the derivation of which no transformations are applied. Nevertheless, one of the important issues in regard to transformational grammars is determining the proper apportionment of the task of description between the phrase structure sector and the transformational sector of the description. Some would push the use of transformational description much farther than others.

The use of transformations in grammar, in any rigorous sense, has been a new development in the decade of the 1950's. Involving as it does a reorientation of linguistic theory and a significantly different technique of description, it has necessarily been the center of a vigorous controversy. At the time of writing, several of the issues are not as yet clearly defined. Not enough has been published in the way of transformational grammars of a variety of languages. It is, therefore, not yet possible to evaluate its potentialities adequately. It may be expected, however, that the theory will continue to play a significant role in the development of linguistics by virtue of having raised some important, previously overlooked issues, and perhaps by contributing to their solution.

Some Psychological Studies
of Grammar

GEORGE A. MILLER

Language is a topic that psychologists have long discussed from many points of view. We have treated it as a system of cognitive categories, as a medium for self-expression or for persuasion, therapy, and education, as a tool for ordering and controlling our other mental operations, and in

Reprinted with the permission of the author and the publisher from the article of the same title, *American Psychologist*, 1962, **17**, 748–762.

many other ways. The approach I want to take here, however, is to regard language as an extremely complicated human skill. My aspiration is to examine that skill in detail in the hope of learning something more about what it consists of and how it functions.

When psychologists talk about language as a skill they frequently emphasize problems of *meaning*. Learning what different utterances mean is, of course, a fundamental skill that any user of a language must acquire. But meaning is too large a problem to solve all at once; we are forced to analyze it into more manageable parts. Consequently, there is in psychology a long tradition of defining meaning in terms of *reference*—in terms of an arbitrary association between some referent and a vocal utterance—and then reducing reference in turn to a simple matter of *conditioning*. In that way many difficult problems of human language are transformed into simpler processes that can be studied in lower animals as well as in man, so the general similarities, rather than the specific differences between linguistic and other skills are emphasized.

I have no quarrel with that approach as long as we recognize that it treats only the simplest 1% of the psycholinguistic problem, and that our crucially important human skill in arranging symbols in novel and useful combinations is largely ignored by the successive reduction of language to meaning to reference to conditioning.

Our combinatorial power, which is so characteristically human, provides the psychological foundation for something that linguists usually call "grammar." I use the term defiantly, for I am fully aware that it is a grim and forbidding subject. It still reeks of the medieval trivium of grammar, logic, and rhetoric; it still reminds us vividly of all those endless and incomprehensible rules that our teachers tried to drum into us in grammar school. I wish I could gloss over it with some euphemism about "communication theory" or "verbal behavior," but, alas, I have no honest alternative but to admit that it is grammar that concerns me. It is grammar that is so significantly human,

so specific to our species, so important for psychologists to understand more clearly. I do not in any sense wish to criticize psychological studies of the referential process, or of the intricate associative network that supports the referential process. My goal is rather to persuade psychologists, by argument and illustration, that there is much more to our linguistic skills than *just* the referential process. I do not see how we are going to describe language as a skill unless we find some satisfactory way to deal with grammar and with the combinatorial processes that grammar entails.

In order to illustrate what our linguistic skills are, I need to draw on certain basic concepts of modern linguistics. Fortunately, modern linguists have a somewhat different conception of grammar—a more scientific conception—than your English teacher had years ago. If I can communicate this newer conception of grammar well enough, perhaps it will revive some spark of interest that you may still have.

Consider a brief sample of the scientific approach to grammar. Let us choose a sentence so simple that we can have no trouble in analyzing it or in understanding the principles of analysis that are being used. Interesting sentences are much more complicated, of course, but the same principles are involved.

Take the sentence *Bill hit the ball*. To native speakers of English it is intuitively obvious that this sequence of words has a kind of structure, that some pairs of adjacent words are more closely related than others. For instance, *the ball* feels like a more natural unit than, say, *hit the*. One way to express that fact is to say that it is very easy to substitute a single word for *the ball*, but it is difficult to think of a single word for *hit the* that would not change the underlying structure of the sentence.

On the first line at the top of Table 1-1 is the original sentence, *Bill hit the ball*. On line 2 is the derived sentence, *Bill hit it*, which is formed by substituting *it* for *the ball*. On line 3 there is another substitution —*acted* instead of *hit it*—and so we obtain the sentence *Bill acted*.

TABLE 1-1

Illustrating Constituent Analysis of a
Simple Sentence

1	Bill	hit	the	ball
2	Bill	hit	it	
3	Bill	acted		

Bill	hit	the *T*	ball *N*
	V	*NP₂*	
NP₁	*VP*		

This process, in one form or another, is called "constituent analysis" by modern linguists (Harris, 1946; Nida, 1948; Pike, 1943; Wells, 1947). As described so far, it may sound as though it depends on your perseverence in searching for alternative words to substitute for each constituent. We can generalize the procedure, however, by introducing specific names for the various kinds of constituent units. Such a use of names is indicated in the lower half of the table. *The* is an article (symbolized *T*) and *ball* is a noun (symbolized *N*); together they form a noun phrase (symbolized *NP*). The verb *hit* combines with the noun phrase to form a verb phrase (symbolized *VP*). And,

finally, the initial noun phrase *Bill* combines with the verb phrase to form a grammatical sentence. Thus each type of constituent has its own name.

As soon as we try to deal abstractly with grammatical sentences, we become involved with these kinds of structured patterns. Obviously, we need some formal system to keep track of them. Several theoretical possibilities are currently available.

One way to deal with the constituent structure of a sentence is to use what linguists have come to call a *generative grammar* (Chomsky, 1956). The central idea was first developed for combinatorial systems in the study of formal logic (Post, 1936, 1944). Starting from a basic axiom, we apply rules of formation that permit us to rewrite the axiom in certain acceptable ways until we have finally derived the desired sentence. If the rules are formulated properly, only the grammatical sentences will be derivable; all other sentences will be ungrammatical.

Figure 1-1 illustrates how a small fragment of English grammar might be expressed in this manner. The basic axiom is S. The rewriting rules F1–7 permit us to form the sentence *Bill hit the ball* in a sequence of steps. First S is rewritten as *NP + VP*, according to rule F1. Then we can rewrite *NP* as *Bill* according to rule F4. Since there is not any rule available for rewriting *Bill*, we are forced to stop at this point. We can, however, rewrite *VP* according to rule F3, thus getting *Bill + V + NP*. In this way we can proceed as indicated by

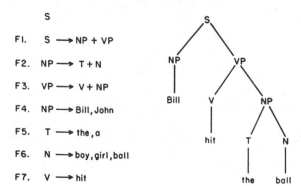

S

F1.   S ⟶ NP + VP

F2.   NP ⟶ T + N

F3.   VP ⟶ V + NP

F4.   NP ⟶ Bill, John

F5.   T ⟶ the, a

F6.   N ⟶ boy, girl, ball

F7.   V ⟶ hit

FIGURE 1-1. *A fragment of English grammar, phrased in terms of rewriting rules, illustrating a generative grammar.*

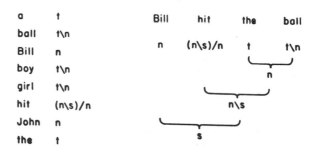

a	t
ball	t\n
Bill	n
boy	t\n
girl	t\n
hit	(n\s)/n
John	n
the	t

FIGURE 1-2. *A fragment of English grammar, phrased in terms of rules of cancellation, illustrating a categorial grammar.*

the tree graph on the right until the desired sentence is derived. Note that the diagram of the derivation corresponds to the constituent structure that we saw in Table 1-1.

The set of rewriting rules on the left of Figure 1-1 can be conveniently referred to as the grammar, and the set of sentences that the grammar generates defines the language. It is an important feature of this kind of grammar that there are terminal symbols, symbols that cannot be rewritten, and these comprise what we ordinarily recognize as the vocabulary of the language. According to this way of representing it, the vocabulary is included in the grammar.

Most people, when they encounter a generative grammar for the first time, get an impression that it means we must always form our sentences from axiom to terminal symbols, that we must always decide what phrases we want before we can decide what words we want to use. That is not a necessary assumption, however. These rules of formation, and the trees that represent the structures of the grammatical sentences, are purely formal devices for representing word groupings. How a sentence is actually manufactured or understood by users of the language—what particular cognitive processes he performs—is not a linguistic problem, but a psychological one.

Just to suggest how the same structural properties can be formalized in a different manner, therefore, consider briefly something that linguists have come to call a *categorial grammar* (Bar-Hillel, 1953; Lambek, 1958). This alternative was also borrowed from symbolic logic. (Cf. Ajdukiewicz, 1935.) According to this way of

thinking about grammar, all the words and constituents must be classified into syntactic categories—corresponding roughly to what you may once have learned to call *parts of speech*—that, like chemical elements, are characterized by the ways they can combine with each other. I can make the reasoning clear most quickly, I think, by an example. In Figure 1-2 on the left is a small segment of the English vocabulary, alphabetized as it would be in any proper dictionary. Listed after each entry are a set of symbols that indicate the syntactic categories that the word belongs to. In order to use those category markers you must understand a simple fact about the way they cancel, namely, that left and right cancellation are distinct. The word *ball* belongs to the category $t\backslash n$ (read "t under n") and has the characteristic that when a member of t is placed to its left, the ts cancel, much as in ordinary algebra, leaving simply n. According to this way of representing the grammar, each word in the sentence is first replaced by its category symbol, then the category symbols are combined by left and right cancellation in all possible ways. If any result includes the single symbol s, then we know that we are dealing with a grammatical sentence; the order of cancellations indicates its underlying constituent structure. In the case of *Bill hit the ball*, the successive cancellations are shown on the right half of Figure 1-2.

There are obvious differences between categorial grammars and generative grammars. A categorial grammar starts with the words and works toward a single symbol that represents a grammatical sentence; a generative grammar seems to move in the opposite direction. Notice also that the categorial system seems to have all its grammatical rules included in the dictionary, whereas the generative system does just the opposite and includes the dictionary in its grammatical rules. In spite of these superficial differences, however, it has been possible to show—by stating each type of system precisely and studying its formal properties—that they are equivalent in the range of languages that they are capable of characterizing (Bar-Hillel, Gaifman, and Shamir, 1960).

That is enough grammatical theory for the moment. It is time now to stop and ask whether there are any psychological implications to all this. Are these systems of rules nothing more than a convenient way to summarize linguistic data, or do they also have some relevance for the psychological processes involved? If human speech is a skilled act whose component parts are related to one another in the general manner that the linguists have been describing, what measurable consequences can we expect to find? What measurable effects would such skills have on our other psychological processes?

First, we might ask if there is any solid empirical evidence for the psychological reality of syntactic categories. One clear implication of these linguistic hypotheses would be that we must have our memory for the words of our language organized according to syntactic categories. Is there any evidence that such an organization exists? There is, of course. For example, psychologists who work with word associations have always claimed—although until recently they have done relatively little to explore the claim—that responses from adult subjects on a word-association test have a marked tendency to be members of the same syntactic category as are the stimuli that evoke them (Ervin, 1961). Certainly there is *some* lawful relation between the syntactic category of the stimulus word and the syntactic category of the response word, but exactly what the relation is may not be

quite as simple as originally advertised. James Deese has recently begun to study the syntactic dimensions of word associations in considerable detail; in a few years we may be in a much better position to discuss these relations.

As further evidence for the psychological reality of syntactic categories, recall that our syntactic categories affect the way we memorize and remember new verbal materials. Here again everybody knows this relation exists, but few studies have tried to exploit it. One example should indicate what I have in mind. Murray Glanzer (1962) has shown that in learning paired associates it is clearly easier for us to learn associations between nonsense syllables and content words (nouns, verbs, adjectives, adverbs) than it is to learn associations between nonsense syllables and function words (pronouns, prepositions, conjunctions). That is to say, YIG-FOOD and MEF-THINK can be associated more readily than TAH-OF and KEX-AND, etc.

Of particular interest in Glanzer's studies, however, was the fact that function words become easier to learn when they are placed in contexts that seem more suitable to them. For instance, when triplets consisting of syllable-word-syllable were used, then TAH-OF-ZUM and KEX-AND-WOJ are learned faster than are YIG-FOOD-SEB and MEF-THINK-JAT. The point, of course, is that in the triplet context the function words are more readily bound to the nonsense syllables because they seem to form natural syntactic constituents in that context.

Where do syntactic categories come from? The development of these categories is currently a matter of great concern and excitement to several psychologists. Here again I will mention only one example, just to indicate the sort of thing that is going on. In an effort to discover how children learn the syntactic categories, Martin Braine (1963) has recently used very simple artificial languages to explore a process he calls "contextual generalization." Contextual generalization resembles stimulus generalization, where the verbal context plays the role of the stimulus. Will a verbal response learned in one context generalize to other contexts? If so, the process might help to explain how children learn the syntactic categories. Braine has his subjects learn a few of the nonsense sentences in the artificial language, then tests generalization to other sentences that the learners have not seen before.

There are limits to what we can explain with a notion such as contextual generalization. Some of its inadequacies may become apparent below when we consider transformational aspects of grammar. However, this is not the time and I am not the person to review Braine's work in detail. I mention it merely to persuade you that the psychological problems posed by these simple grammatical concepts are indeed well defined and that with a little patience and ingenuity it is even possible to coax them into the psychological laboratory.

One unavoidable fact about nonsense materials, however, is that they are nonsense; and artificial languages are inescapably artificial. I believe that the case for the psychological reality of these grammatical conventions might be strengthened if we would focus on the process of comprehension, rather than on the process of learning and memory. In order to phrase the matter in a strong form, consider the following proposition: *We cannot understand a sentence until we are able to assign a constituent structure to it.*

Perhaps the simplest way to illustrate what I have in mind is to examine a sentence that is syntactically ambiguous. In Figure 1-3 we have an example of the sort that linguists like to consider: *They are eating apples* is really two sentences, even though both of them consist of exactly the

same sequence of words. The sentence on the left would answer the question, *What are your friends doing?* The one on the right would answer the question, *Are those apples better for eating or for cooking?* On the basis of the linear sequence of words alone, however, we cannot tell which meaning is intended. Somehow, from the context, we must decide which syntactic structure is appropriate. Until we have decided on its structure, however, the sentence is ambiguous and we cannot completely understand its meaning. Thus, the proper functioning of our syntactic skill is an essential ingredient in the process of understanding a sentence. Again I emphasize that the problem of meaning involves a great deal more than the matter of reference.

For still another example of the psychological significance of syntactic structure let me draw on some of my own research on the perception of speech. Several years ago I participated in an experimental study showing that words can be perceived more accurately when they are heard in the context of a sentence than when they are pronounced separately as individual items on a list of test words (Miller, Heise, and Lichten, 1951). Those results are shown graphically in Figure 1-4, where the percentage of the words that were heard correctly is plotted as a function of the signal-to-noise ratio. As you can see, the same words were heard more accurately in sentences than in isolation.

In 1951 when we first reported this observation we argued that a sentence context serves to narrow down the set of alternative words that the listener expects, and so makes the perceptual task of recognition just that much easier. I still believe that our original explanation was correct, as far as it went. But it did not go far enough. It left

FIGURE 1-3. *Syntactic ambiguity arises when two different sentences are expressed by the same string of words.*

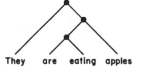
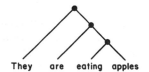

They   are   eating apples   They   are   eating apples

open the psychologically crucial question of exactly *how* the sentence context reduced the variety of alternatives.

Words in sentences are often slurred and pronounced carelessly, yet we found they were more accurately perceived; an explanation in terms of reduced alternatives might account for that, of course. But words in sentences also run together. A listener must segment the ongoing flow of sound in order to discover the word units, yet this extra operation seemed to be no burden; the explanation in terms of reduced alternatives says nothing at all about this extra operation of segmentation. And, perhaps, worst of all, the explanation seemed to imply that a listener makes separate, successive decisions about the identity of the separate, successive words he is hearing in the sentence. Since words can be spoken at a rate of two or three per second, the rate at which successive sets of alternative words must be conjured up, recognized, and replaced by the listener is really quite remarkable. In short, the more I thought about how the sentence context exerts its helpful influence, the more complicated it seemed.

In order to explore the matter further, therefore, we performed the following experiment (Miller, 1962): First, we drew up a list of 25 monosyllabic English words

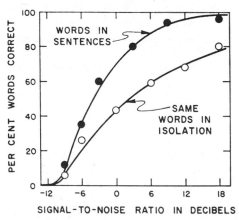

FIGURE 1-4. *The effect of sentence context on the intelligibility of words (from Miller, Heise, and Lichten, 1951).*

and divided it into five sublists of five words each, as shown in Table 1-2. These sublists are constructed in such a way that if you chose any words successively from sublists 1, 2, 3, 4, and 5, they will form a grammatical English sentence. The subjects in this experiment spent an entire summer with me—four afternoons a week—listening to these 25 words in the presence of a masking noise. To say they knew the lists perfectly is a gross understatement; before the summer was over we all were thoroughly sick of them.

TABLE 1-2

Five Subvocabularies Used to Explore the Perceptual Effects of Grammatical Context

1	2	3	4	5
Don	Brought	His	Black	Bread
He	Has	More	Cheap	Sheep
Red	Left	No	Good	Shoes
Slim	Loves	Some	Wet	Socks
Who	Took	The	Wrong	Things

We tested four separate conditions. The first two conditions provided a kind of control. In one case, successive words were selected from the entire set of 25 words in random order. In the second case, successive words were selected in random order from one of the five sublists of five words. The words were spoken in groups of five and heard by the listeners against a background of random masking noise. The listeners' responses were spoken aloud and individually recorded, so the tests did not need to be delayed in order to allow time for the listeners to write down their responses. As we had expected, the words were easier to recognize when they occurred as one of 5 alternatives than when they were one of 25 alternatives. Those two control conditions provided the calibration we needed for the two remaining experimental conditions.

In the third test condition, words were chosen from the subgroups successively so as to form grammatical sentences: *Don has no wet things,* for example. And in the fourth test condition, the order of the subgroups was reversed, so that the sequence of words was not grammatical: *things wet no has Don,* for example. Since these backward strings were based on exactly the same sublists of alternatives as were the sentences, we called them pseudosentences.

Our question, of course, was whether there would be any difference between the intelligibility of the sentences and the intelligibility of the pseudosentences. The answer was both yes and no. When we paused between successive strings of five words and gave the listeners a chance to think about what they had just heard, there was no difference; sentences and pseudosentences gave the same results, and both were the same as the results for the 5-word sublists.

When the test was speeded up, however, by eliminating the pauses between successive sentences, a difference appeared. Under time pressure we got the results shown in Figure 1-5. On the left the word intelligibility scores are plotted as a function of the signal-to-noise ratio for all four test conditions. The sentences and the 5-word vocabularies give one function; the pseudosentences and the 25-word vocabularies give another. On the right are the corresponding

functions obtained when the scoring unit was the entire sentence, rather than the individual words.

The results with pseudosentences demonstrated that when time is short and words do not follow a familiar grammatical pattern, subjects are unable to exploit a narrower range of alternatives. They do not have time to hear each word separately, decide what it was, then anticipate the next set of alternatives, listen to the next word, etc. At slow speeds they had time to make separate decisions about each word, but not at the more rapid speeds that would be characteristic of normal, conversational speech. All they could do with the rapid pseudosentences was to treat the successive words as if they were chosen randomly from the larger set of 25 alternatives.

Thus it is possible to show that the sentence context does indeed serve to narrow the range of alternative words, but the mechanism involved seems to be more complicated than we had originally imagined. In addition to reducing the variety of competing alternatives, the sentence context also enables us to organize the flow of sound into decision units larger than individual words—perhaps into units similar to the linguist's constituents—and so to make

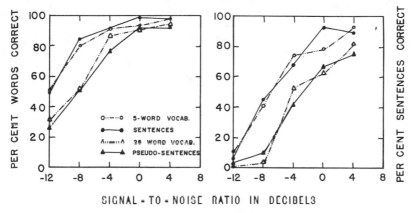

FIGURE 1-5. *Word intelligibility (left) and sentence intelligibility (right) scores indicate that under time pressure grammatical contexts facilitate speech perception and ungrammatical contexts do not, even though the number of different words involved is not altered by the context (after Miller, 1962).*

our perceptual decisions about what we are hearing at a slower and more comfortable rate.

In short, I am arguing that in ordinary conversation the functional unit of speech perception is usually larger than a single word or a single morpheme and more nearly the size and shape of a syntactic constituent. As long as we studied speech perception by using lists of words spoken in isolation, the existence of those larger units was not apparent. As soon as we begin to combine words into continuous sequences, however, we discover that the familiar grammatical sequences form unique and distinctive patterns of words. And that, of course, is just what a linguistic theory of syntactic structures would lead us to expect.

The experiment I have just described argues for the existence of perceptual units larger than a single word. It does not, however, argue in favor of any particular type of structure underlying those larger units. That is, it does not show that some form of grammatical structure must be preferred to, say, a Markovian structure of the kind that communication theorists talk about (Shannon, 1948, 1951).

In order to illustrate the psychological reality of these syntactic structures, we must consider the critical feature that these grammatical systems admit, but that Marko-

vian structures do not—namely, the possibility of unlimited self-embedding (Chomsky, 1959). Again I will draw upon my own research, but now in the field of verbal learning and verbal memory.

One important feature of the grammatical rules that linguists have proposed is that they are recursive. That is to say, there is no limit to the number of times that the same rule can be applied in the derivation of a sentence. In general, three different kinds of recursiveness are permitted by our grammatical rules. In Figure 1-6 we see syntactic structures illustrating each of the three types: left-recursive, right-recursive, and self-embedding. All three are characterized by the fact that a given type of constituent—labeled "A" in this figure—can appear as a part of itself; where it appears —at the left end, at the right end, or in the middle—determines the type of recursiveness. In English, for example, a left-recursive construction would be *The obviously not very well dressed man is here,* or *John's father's car's roof's color is red.* Right-recursive structures can be strung out at great length; a famous example is *This is the cow with the crumpled horn that tossed the dog that worried the cat that killed the rat that ate the malt that lay in the house that Jack built.* This same sentence can be rephrased, however, to illustrate a self-

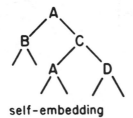

self-embedding

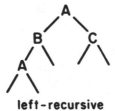

left-recursive

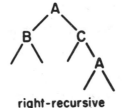

right-recursive

FIGURE 1-6. *Illustrating three types of recursive rules that permit an element of type A to be part of an element of type A.*

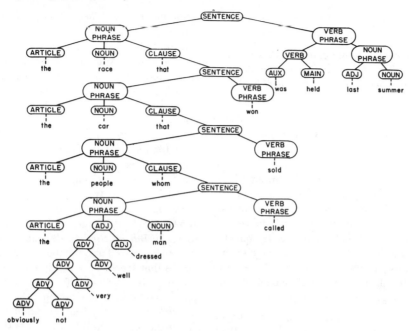

FIGURE 1-7. *Syntactic structure of the self-embedded sentence, "The race that the car that the people whom the obviously not very well dressed man called sold won was held last summer."*

embedded construction. We can build up the self-embedded version step by step:

> *The rat ate the malt,*
> *The rat that the cat killed ate the malt,*
> *The rat that the cat that the dog worried killed ate the malt,*
> *The rat that the cat that the dog that the cow tossed worried killed ate the malt, etc.*

It is fairly clear that even though the self-embedded version is perfectly grammatical, it is far more complicated psychologically —harder to understand and to remember— than the right-recursive version.

There are some relatively profound reasons why this should be the case. A language that could be characterized entirely in terms of right-recursive rules could be described in terms of a Markov process (Chomsky, 1956; Chomsky and Miller, 1958). The possibility of unlimited self-embedding, however, means that a Markov system is too simple to serve as a grammar for a natural language. Of more practical significance, however, is the fact that self-embedding by its very nature places heavier demands on the temporary storage capacity of any device that attempts to cope with it —far heavier than do either left-recursive or right-recursive constructions. And, since our temporary memory is quite limited, we can experience great difficulty following grammatical rules in this type of syntactic structure.

In order to explore this matter we can take some sentences with very complicated syntactic structure and ask people to repeat them. For example, one sentence I have worked with is diagramed in Figure 1-7:

> *The race that the car that the people whom the obviously not very well dressed man called sold won was held last summer.*

Then, as a control, the same words were arranged in a right-branching structure:

> *The obviously not very well dressed man called the people who sold the car that won the race that was held last summer.*

I read such sentences as these to college students who tried to repeat them as accurately as possible.

As you would expect, on the basis of almost any theory of verbal learning that I can imagine, right-recursive sentences are easier for English-speaking people to repeat and to memorize than are self-embedded sentences. I will not summarize the quantitative results, but I think that some of the qualitative results are amusing. For example, after hearing the self-embedded sentence only once, subject may say:

> *The race—that the car—that the clearly not so well dressed man—saw—sold one—last summer?*

The subjects who respond in this way are quite interesting; their intonation is characteristic of the recitation of a list of unrelated phrases, not the utterance of a sentence. And I was also interested to note that the number of items on the list would usually be about six or seven, close to the span of immediate memory for those subjects (Miller, 1956).

The second time such a subject hears the same sentence he may still recite it as though it were a list, but with somewhat more accurate recall of the individual items. By the second or third time through, however, there may be an "Aha!" experience, and from then on he tries to give it a normal, sentence intonation.

These examples should indicate why I believe that sentences are not just arbitrary chains of vocal responses, but that they have a complex inner structure of their own. How we perceive them, understand them, and remember them depends upon what we decide about their structure. Just as we induce a three-dimensional space underlying the two-dimensional pattern on the retina, so we must induce a syntactic structure underlying the linear string of sounds in a sentence. And just as the student of space perception must have a good understanding of projective geometry, so a student of psycholinguistics must have a good understanding of grammar.

There is much more to grammar, however, than just the system of syntactic categories and constituent structure. Let me lapse once again into linguistics long enough to introduce the transformational rules of grammar (Chomsky, 1956, 1957; Harris, 1952a, 1952b, 1957). Go back to the simple sentence *Bill hit the ball.* But now observe that there are a large number of other sentences that seem to be closely related to it: the negative, *Bill didn't hit the ball;* the passive, *The ball was hit by Bill;* various interrogative forms, *Did Bill hit the ball?, What did Bill hit?, Who hit the ball?,* and so on.

Linguists disagree about the best way to describe these different kinds of relations among sentences. One opinion is that we learn "sentence frames" that we keep filed away in a sort of sentence-frame dictionary. The declarative, interrogative, affirmative, negative, active, passive, compound, complex, etc., sentence frames are all supposed to be learned separately and to have no intrinsic relation to one another. A second opinion agrees with the first in seeing no intrinsic relations among the various types of sentences, but argues that there are too many different frames to learn them all separately. The advocates of this second view say that there must be rules, similar to those we have just been discussing, that the talker can use actively to manufacture a grammatical frame as it is needed. But, according to this view, there is one set of rules for manufacturing active, declarative, affirmative sentences, another set of rules for manufacturing passive, declarative, affirmative sentences, etc.

On the other side of the argument are linguists who wish to describe the relations among these sentences in terms of explicit rules of transformation. One version of this view, which I favor, says that we do indeed have a scheme for manufacturing simple, active, declarative sentences, but we can apply rules of transformation to change them from active to passive, or from declarative to interrogative, or from affirmative to negative, or to combine them, etc. This transformational scheme shortens the statement of a grammar considerably, since many rules need be stated only once and need not be repeated for each separate type of sentence. And once you have admitted such rules to your grammar you quickly discover many uses for them.

Transformational rules are both complicated and powerful, however, so many linguists are reluctant to use them. There has been some esthetic disagreement about which kind of simplicity is more desirable in a linguistic theory. Is it better to have a long list of short rules, or a short list of long rules?

The arguments among linguists—who seem to rely heavily on their linguistic intuitions, on logical counterexamples, and on appeals to the economy and elegance of simplicity—can get rather bitter at times. And it is by no means obvious a priori that the most economical and efficient formal description of the linguistic data will necessarily describe the psychological process involved when we actually utter or understand a grammatical sentence. In the hope of providing a more experimental foundation to the argument, therefore, we have recently begun to test some of the psychological implications of a transformational linguistic theory. Our efforts to explore this aspect of linguistic skill are still tentative, however, so the two examples to be mentioned below are still in the enthusiastic stage and subject to revision as more data accumulate. But they will serve to support the main point, that an experimental approach to these matters is both possible and (potentially) rewarding.

Perhaps the simplest way to study grammatical transformations experimentally would be to tell a person what transformation to perform, then give him a sentence, and measure how long it takes him to make the transformation. We intend to explore the transformation process in just that way, but at the moment we are not prepared to report on the results. Instead, therefore, let me tell you about a more indirect method —a sentence-matching test—that Kathryn Ojemann McKean, Dan Slobin, and I have been using.

Our first assumption is that the more complicated a grammatical transformation is, the longer it will take people to perform it. The purpose of the test is to give subjects a set of sentences to transform and to see how many of them they can complete in a fixed interval of time. Of course, there is much more that we would like to know about the transformation than just how long it takes, but at least this is one way to begin.

One form of the test that we have used contains 18 basic, or kernel sentences: all of the sentences that can be formed by taking *Jane, Joe,* or *John* as the first word, *liked* or *warned* as the second word, and *the small boy, the old woman,* or *the young man* as the final phrase. In addition, we used the corresponding sets of 18 sentences that can be produced from those kernels by negative, passive, and passive-negative transformations. Thus, for example, *Joe liked the small boy* appears in the set of kernels; *Joe didn't like the small boy* appears in the set of negatives; *The small boy was liked by Joe* appears in the set of passives; and *The small boy wasn't liked by Joe* appears in the set of passive-negatives.

A test is constructed by taking two of these four sets of 18 sentences and asking people to pair them off. Take as an example the test that requires people to match passive sentences with their corresponding passive-negative forms. The test sheet looks something like Table 1-3. Half of the pairs are arranged with the passive sentences on the left, half with the passive-negative sen-

TABLE 1-3

Example of a Sentence-Matching to Study Transformations
between Affirmative-Passive and Negative-Passive Sentences

_____ The old woman was warned by Joe	1. The small boy wasn't warned by John
_____ The small boy wasn't liked by Joe	2. The old woman wasn't warned by Jane
_____ The young man was liked by John	3. The young man was warned by Jane
_____ The old woman wasn't liked by Joe	4. The old woman wasn't warned by Joe
_____ The young man wasn't warned by Jane	5. The old woman was liked by John
_____ The small boy was liked by Jane	6. The small boy wasn't liked by John
_____ The young man wasn't liked by Jane	7. The young man wasn't warned by John
_____ The old woman was warned by Jane	8. The old woman was warned by John
_____ The small boy wasn't warned by Joe	9. The young man wasn't warned by Joe
_____ The small boy was warned by John	10. The small boy was warned by Jane
_____ The young man was warned by John	11. The small boy was warned by Joe
_____ The small boy wasn't warned by Jane	12. The small boy wasn't liked by Jane
_____ The small boy was liked by John	13. The young man wasn't liked by John
_____ The young man wasn't liked by Joe	14. The young man was liked by Jane
_____ The young man was warned by Joe	15. The old woman was liked by Joe
_____ The old woman was liked by Jane	16. The old woman wasn't liked by Jane
_____ The old woman wasn't liked by John	17. The small boy was liked by Joe
_____ The old woman wasn't warned by John	18. The young man was liked by Joe

tences on the left. This produces two lists, a left-hand list and a right-hand list, which are presented to the subject. Similar tests can be constructed for all the other pairs of sentence types.

Before the two lists of sentences are presented, the subject studies a sample pair of sentences that illustrates the desired transformation, and he prepares himself to perform the same transformation (or its inverse) on the test sentences. When the signal is given to start, he begins with the first sentence at the top of the left column, identifies its type and decides whether the transformation or its inverse is called for, performs the indicated transformation (or its inverse), searches for the transformed sentence in the right-hand column, then places the number of the transformed sentence to the left of the original sentence in the left-hand column. He continues in this way down the left-hand list until, at the end of one minute, he is instructed to stop. This general strategy is shown in Figure 1-8 by a flow chart.

As a control condition, six further tests required no transformations at all; the sentences in the left column were simply matched with the identical sentences in the right column (where the right column was the same one used in the corresponding experimental test). From these measurements on the identity transformation, therefore, we could estimate how long subjects required to read down the right-hand column, find the sentence they wanted, and write its number in the appropriate space. We assume that on these control tests the subject's strategy is just the same as on the experimental tests, except that the steps enclosed in dotted lines in Figure 1-8—the transformational steps—can be omitted. Therefore, we can subtract the time spent searching and writing from the total time, and so can obtain an estimate of the time required to recognize, analyze, and transform the sentences.

We knew, of course, that subtracting reaction times involves some of the oldest pitfalls in psychology, and we would not have been terribly surprised if the results had been meaningless. Fortunately, we got fairly large and (we believe) sensible differences for the various kinds of transformations.

Consider what you might expect to get

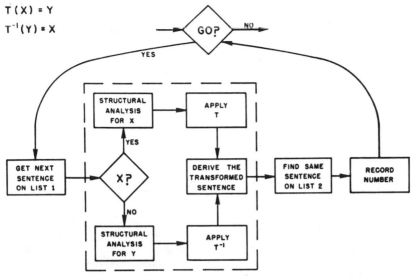

$$T(X) = Y$$
$$T^{-1}(Y) = X$$

FIGURE 1-8. *Flow chart for strategy used in sentence-matching test. (On the control tests—identity transform—the operations inside the dashed line could presumably be omitted.)*

on the basis of various theories that grammarians have talked about. Linguists who look upon the four different sentence types as four separate, coordinate, and independent sentence frames would probably expect that moving between any two of them should be about as difficult as moving between any other two. This line of reasoning is depicted in Figure 1-9, where the letters indicate the various kinds of sentences—kernels, negatives, passives, and passive-negatives—and the lines between them indicate all the possible relations between them. A grammatical theory that says that all sentence frames are coordinate would assign the same difficulty to every one of those connecting lines. It is just one step from any type of sentence to any other type of sentence.

On the other hand, a transformational theorist would like to reduce those six direct relations to a pair of transformations, one for the affirmative-negative aspect and one for the active-passive aspect. This line of reasoning leads to Figure 1-10, where the lines indicate the direct results of applying a grammatical transformation. In this view of things, two steps are required to go between

kernels and passive-negative sentences, or between passives and negatives. Therefore, a transformational theory leads us to expect that these diagonal relations will take longer to perform than the simpler, one-step relations.

Some data are given in Table 1-4. For each type of test, Table 1-4 gives the average number of sentences that our 60 subjects were able to transform and/or locate in one minute. The reciprocals give the time per sentence for the average subject. And in

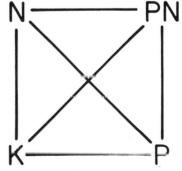

FIGURE 1-9. *Graph indicating six pairs of sentence types that can be formed with kernel sentences (K), negatives (N), passives (P), and passive-negatives (PN).*

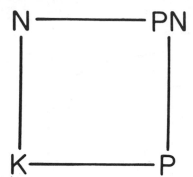

FIGURE 1-10. *Graph indicating one-step transformations.*

the right-hand column is the result we are looking for—the estimates (in seconds) of the time it took to perform the grammatical transformations.

It is apparent that some tests were easier than others. Look at the pattern: the top two of these estimated times involve only a negative transformation or its inverse; they seem to occur rather quickly. The second pair of these estimated times involves only the passive transformation or its inverse; these are slightly longer, which would agree with one's intuitive impression that the passive is a more complicated transformation. And, finally, the bottom two estimated

times involve both the negative and the passive transformations; on the average, they are the slowest of all.

In their gross outline, therefore, these data support the transformational theorists. In their fine detail, however, they raise several interesting questions. Before we spend too much effort answering them, however, we had better make sure the data are correct. At the present time, therefore, we are trying to perfect our measuring instrument in order to obtain results accurate enough to test in detail some of the available linguistic theories about the transformational process.

There are, of course, many other psychological methods that we might use to test the validity of a transformational theory of grammar. One that I believe holds considerable promise has been proposed by Jacques Mehler; he has only begun to explore it, but already the results look interesting. His idea was to present a list of sentences for people to learn and to score the results in terms of the syntactic errors that they made. For example,

The typist has copied the paper is a kernel sentence;

TABLE 1-4

**The Mean Number of Sentences Matched Correctly in One Minute,
with Transformations (Exper.) and Without (Contr.), is Used to
Estimate the Average Transformation
Time per Sentence
(N = 60)**

Test condition	Mean number of sentences correct		Time for average subject (secs.)		Estimated transformation times (secs.)
	Exper.	Contr.	Exper.	Contr.	
K:N	7.5	8.7	8.0	6.9	1.1
P:PN	5.5	6.4	10.5	9.3	1.2.
K:P	8.1	10.1	7.4	5.9	1.5
PN:N	6.7	8.5	8.9	7.1	1.8
K:PN	6.9	10.0	8.7	6.0	2.7
N:P	5.6	8.4	10.7	7.2	3.5

The student hasn't written the essay is a
  negative sentence;

*The photograph has been made by the
  boy* is a passive sentence;

Has the train hit the car? is a query;

*The passenger hasn't been carried by the
  airplane* is a passive-negative sentence;

Hasn't the girl worn the jewel? is a negative query;

*Has the discovery been made by the biol-
  ogist?* is a passive query; and

*Hasn't the house been bought by the
  man?* is a passive-negative query.

Other sets of sentences can easily be generated, of course, by permuting the kernels
with the various transformations.

Mehler presents such a list of sentences
—without the syntactic comments, of
course—to his subjects, who then try to
write them out word for word. He gives
them five trials, scrambling the order on
each trial.

The first question, of course, is whether
or not subjects make any syntactic errors in
this situation. Mehler's preliminary results
are shown in Figure 1-11. Errors have been
grouped into three main classes: (*a*) errors of
omission, (*b*) syntactic errors, and (*c*) other
types of errors (which includes the introduction of extraneous words and the confusion of two different sentences). As you can
see from the figure, the probability that a
sentence will be completely missing in recall
decreases very rapidly, and the probability
of semantic confusion is low and relatively
constant. The bulk of the errors that people
make on this task are of a syntactic nature
—they recall the sentence, but they alter
its syntactic form.

For several years now I have held rather
stubbornly to the opinion that there is an
operation called "recoding" that frequently
plays an important role in remembering verbal materials. Let me develop this opinion
into a specific hypothesis about Mehler's
experiment.

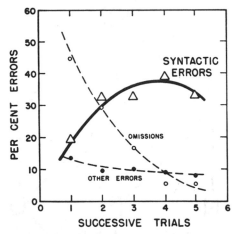

FIGURE 1-11. *Syntactic errors can be relatively common in the free recall of sentences
that are of different types.*

The hypothesis is that what people
remember is the kernel sentence, but that
when you ask them to recite the original
sentence exactly, they supplement their
memory of the kernel with a footnote about
the syntactic structure. This variant of
Woodworth's "schema-plus-correction"
method of recoding turns *Hasn't the girl
worn the jewel?* into the kernel sentence *The
girl has worn the jewel,* plus some kind of
implicit code that—if remembered correctly—enables the subject to make the
necessary grammatical transformations
when he is called upon to recite the original
sentence.

The relations among the eight types of
sentences that Mehler uses are indicated in
Figure 1-12. The lines connect the types of
sentences that would become confused if
the subject remembered incorrectly just one
of the three transformations that he has to
keep track of. If my recoding hypothesis was
correct, of course, I would expect most of
the syntactic errors to involve just one of the
three transformations, and two and three
step errors would be relatively less frequent.

Before Mehler's data were analyzed I
had expected to find a strong shift toward
the recall of kernels. There is some tendency

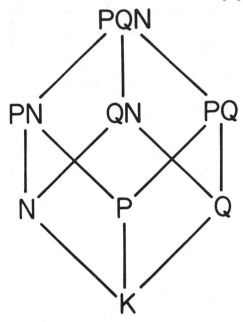

FIGURE 1-12. *Graph indicating relations among eight types of sentences formed by negative (N), passive (P), and interrogative (Q) transformations.*

for people to favor kernel sentences when they recall, but it is insignificant and probably would not have been noticed at all if we had not been looking for it. What seems to happen, however, is actually simpler than I had expected. The subjects quickly get the impression that about half the sentences are negative, half are passives, half are questions; in recall, therefore, they try a little probability matching. If a transformation is forgotten, it is not simply omitted; instead, a guess is made, based upon the overall impression of how often each transformation should be applied.

The upshot of this argument was that I constructed a very simple hypothesis, based on this kernel-plus-code idea, plus an absurd but convenient assumption that each of the four elements necessary for correct recall— that is to say, the kernel and the three transforms—was recalled independently of the other three. Thus the probability of a

correct recall would be simply the product of the probabilities of recalling each of the four components, and the probability of one syntactic error would be the product of the probability of recalling the kernel and the probability of getting two transformations right and one wrong, and so forth. The simple result of this line of reasoning is the following equation. Given these definitions: k = probability of recalling the kernel; $p = 1 - q$ = probability of recalling transform; m = number of transforms to be recalled; P_i = probability of recall with i syntactic errors; then, on the assumption of independent recall of the kernels and the several transformations, we have:

$$P_i = k \binom{m}{m - i} p^{m-i} q^i.$$

Now by lumping together all of Mehler's 15 subjects on all trials for all sentences, we can estimate the necessary probabilities and then see if the assumption of independence will predict the observed distribution of errors. The results are shown in Table 1-5. The estimated probability of recalling the kernel was 0.66. The estimated probabilities for getting each of the transformations correct were all very close to 0.80, so that a single value was used for all three. And when we put these parameter values into the equation for P_i, we obtain fairly good agreement between data and hypothesis. Or to state the matter more carefully, on the basis of Mehler's preliminary evidence, we cannot reject the hypothesis that sentences were recoded and that each of the four components of the kernel-plus-code was remembered correctly or

TABLE 1-5

Distribution of Syntactic Errors in Free Recall of Sentences

Errors: i	0	1	2	3
Calculated P_i	0.34	0.25	0.06	0.01
Obtained P_i	0.36	0.20	0.09	0.01

incorrectly independently of the others.

Here again our work has only begun and so my report of it is still colored by all the natural enthusiasm and prejudices that seem to accompany every programmatic statement. My colleagues and I now see syntactic structure as an important variable to explore. The logicians and linguists are currently defining the theoretical issues with great precision, so that the full range of our experimental and psychometric methods can be brought to bear. I am enthusiastically convinced that such studies have an important contribution to make to the science of psychology.

In the course of this work I seem to have become a very old-fashioned kind of psychol-ogist. I now believe that mind is something more than a four-letter, Anglo-Saxon word —human minds exist and it is our job as psychologists to study them. Moreover, I believe that one of the best ways to study a human mind is by studying the verbal systems that it uses. But what I want most to communicate here is my strong conviction that such a program is not only important, but that it is also possible, even now, with the relatively crude and limited empirical weapons that we have already developed. In the years ahead I hope we will see an increasing flow of new and exciting research as more psychologists discover the opportunities and the challenge of psycholinguistic theory and research.

REFERENCES

Ajdukiewicz, K. Die syntaktische Konnexität. *Stud. phil.*, 1935, **1**, 1–27.

Bar-Hillel, Y. A quasiarithmetical notation for syntactic description. *Language*, 1953, **29**, 47–58.

———, C. Gaifman, and E. Shamir. On categorial and phrase-structure grammars. *Bull. Res. Council Israel*, 1960, **9F**, 1–16.

Braine, M. D. S. On learning the grammatical order of words. *Psychol. Rev.*, 1963, **70**, 323–348.

Chomsky, N. Three methods for the description of language. *IRE Trans. Inform. Theory*, 1956, **IT-2**, 113–124.

———. *Syntactic structures.* 's-Gravenhage: Mouton, 1957.

———. On certain formal properties of grammars. *Inform. Control*, 1959, **2**, 137–167.

———, and G. A. Miller. Finite state languages. *Inform. Control*, 1958, **1**, 91–112.

Ervin, S. M. Changes with age in the verbal determinants of word-association. *Amer. J. Psychol.*, 1961, **74**, 361–372.

Glanzer, M. Grammatical category: A rote learning and word association analysis. *J. verbal Learn. verbal Behav.*, 1962, **1**, 31–41.

Harris, Z. S. From morpheme to utterance. *Language*, 1946, **22**, 161–183.

———. Discourse analysis. *Language*, 1952a, **28**, 1–30.

———. Discourse analysis: A sample text. *Language*, 1952b, **28**, 474–494.

———. Co-occurrence and transformation in linguistic structure. *Language*, 1957, **33**, 283–340.

Lambek, J. The mathematics of sentence structure. *Amer. math. Mon.*, 1958, **65**, 154–169.

Miller, G. A. The magical number seven, plus or minus two. *Psychol. Rev.*, 1956, **63**, 81–97.

———. Decision units in the perception of speech. *IRE Trans. Inform. Theory*, 1962, **IT-8**, 81–83.

———, G. A. Heise, and W. Lichten. The intelligibility of speech as a function of the context of the test materials. *J. exp. Psychol.*, 1951, **41**, 329–335.

Nida, E. A. The analysis of immediate constituents. *Language*, 1948, **24**, 168–177.

Pike, K. L. Taxemes and immediate constituents. *Language*, 1943, **19**, 65–82.

Post, E. L. Finite combinatory processes: Formulation I. *J. symb. Logic*, 1936, **1**, 103–105.

———. Recursively enumerable sets of positive integers and their decision problems. *Bull. Amer. Math. Soc.*, 1944, **50**, 284–316.

Shannon, C. E. A mathematical theory of communication. *Bell Sys. tech. J.*, 1948, **27**, 379–423.

———. Prediction and entropy of printed English. *Bell Sys. tech. J.*, 1951, **30**, 50–64.

Wells, R. S. Immediate constituents. *Language*, 1947, **23**, 81–117.

Language and Thought:
The Problem and the Approach

L. S. VYGOTSKY

The study of thought and language is one of the areas of psychology in which a clear understanding of interfunctional relations is particularly important. As long as we do not understand the interrelation of thought and word, we cannot answer, or even correctly pose, any of the more specific questions in this area. Strange as it may seem, psychology has never investigated the relationship systematically and in detail. Interfunctional relations in general have not as yet received the attention they merit. The atomistic and functional modes of analysis prevalent during the past decade treated psychic processes in isolation. Methods of research were developed and perfected with a view to studying separate functions, while their interdependence and their organization in the structure of consciousness as a whole remained outside the field of investigation.

The unity of consciousness and the interrelation of all psychological functions were, it is true, accepted by all; the single functions were assumed to operate inseparably, in an uninterrupted connection with one another. But in the old psychology the unchallengeable premise of unity was combined with a set of tacit assumptions that nullified it for all practical purposes. It was taken for granted that the relation between two given functions never varied; that perception, for example, was always connected in an identical way with attention, memory with perception, thought with memory. As constants, these relationships could be, and were, factored out and ignored in the study of the separate functions. Because the rela-

tionships remained in fact inconsequential, the development of consciousness was seen as determined by the autonomous development of the single functions. Yet all that is known about psychic development indicates that its very essence lies in the change of the interfunctional structure of consciousness. Psychology must make these relations and their developmental changes the main problem, the focus of study, instead of merely postulating the general interrelation of all functions. This shift in approach is imperative for the productive study of language and thought.

A look at the results of former investigations of thought and language will show that all the theories offered from antiquity to our time range between *identification,* or *fusion,* of thought and speech on the one hand, and their equally absolute, almost metaphysical *disjunction* and *segregation* on the other. Whether expressing one of these extremes in pure form or combining them, that is, taking an intermediate position but always somewhere along the axis between the two poles, all the various theories on thought and language stay within the confining circle.

We can trace the idea of identity of thought and speech from the speculation of psychological linguistics that thought is "speech minus sound" to the theories of modern American psychologists and reflexologists who consider thought a reflex inhibited in its motor part. In all these theories the question of the relationship between thought and speech loses meaning. If they are one and the same thing, no relationship between them can arise. Those who identify thought with speech simply close the door on the problem. At first glance, the adherents of the opposite view seem to be in a better position. In regarding speech as the outward manifestation, the mere vestment, of thought, and in trying (as does the Wuerzburg school) to free thought from all sensory components including words, they not only pose but in their own way attempt to solve the problem of the relationship between the two functions. Actually, however, they are unable to pose it in a manner that would permit a real solution. Having made thought and speech independent and "pure," and having studied each apart from the other, they are forced to see the relationship between them merely as a mechanical, external connection between two distinct processes. The analysis of verbal thinking into two separate, basically different elements precludes any study of the intrinsic relations between language and thought.

The fault thus lies in the *methods of analysis* adopted by previous investigators. To cope successfully with the problem of the relationship between thought and language, we must ask ourselves first of all what method of analysis is most likely to ensure its solution.

Two essentially different modes of analysis are possible in the study of psychological structures. It seems to us that one of them is responsible for all the failures that have beset former investigators of the old problem, which we are about to tackle in our turn, and that the other is the only correct way to approach it.

The first method analyzes complex psychological wholes into *elements*. It may be compared to the chemical analysis of water into hydrogen and oxygen, neither of which possesses the properties of the whole and each of which possesses properties not present in the whole. The student applying this method in looking for the explanation of some property of water—why it extinguishes fire, for example—will find to his surprise that hydrogen burns and oxygen sustains fire. These discoveries will not help him much in solving the problem. Psychology winds up in the same kind of dead end when it analyzes verbal thought into its components, thought and word, and studies them in isolation from each other. In the course of analysis, the original properties of verbal thought have disappeared. Nothing is left to the investigator but to search out the mechanical interaction of the two elements in the hope of reconstructing, in a purely speculative way, the vanished properties of the whole.

This type of analysis shifts the issue to a level of greater generality; it provides no adequate basis for the study of the multiform concrete relations between thought and language that arise in the course of the development and functioning of verbal thought in its various aspects. Instead of enabling us to examine and explain specific instances and phases, and to determine concrete regularities in the course of events, this method produces generalities pertaining to all speech and all thought. It leads us, moreover, into serious errors by ignoring the unitary nature of the process under study. The living union of sound and meaning that we call word is broken up into two parts, which are assumed to be held together merely by mechanical associative connections.

The view that sound and meaning in words are separate elements leading separate lives has done much harm to the study of both the phonetic and the semantic aspects of language. The most thorough study of speech sounds merely as sounds, apart from their connection with thought, has little bearing on their function as human speech since it does not bring out the physical and psychological properties peculiar to speech but only the properties common to all sounds existing in nature. In the same way, meaning divorced from speech sounds can only be studied as a pure act of thought, changing and developing independently of its material vehicle. This separation of sound and meaning is largely responsible for the barrenness of classical phonetics and semantics. In child psychology, likewise, the phonetic and the semantic aspects of speech development have been studied separately. The phonetic development has been studied in great detail, yet all the accumulated data contribute little to our understanding of linguistic development as such and remain essentially unrelated to the findings concerning the development of thinking.

In our opinion the right course to follow is to use the other type of analysis, which may be called *analysis into units*.

By *unit* we mean a product of analysis which, unlike elements, retains all the basic properties of the whole and which cannot be further divided without losing them. Not the chemical composition of water but its molecules and their behavior are the key to the understanding of the properties of water. The true unit of biological analysis is the living cell, possessing the basic properties of the living organism.

What is the unit of verbal thought that meets these requirements? We believe that it can be found in the internal aspect of the word, in *word meaning*. Few investigations of this internal aspect of speech have been undertaken so far, and psychology can tell us little about word meaning that would not apply in equal measure to all other images and acts of thought. The nature of meaning as such is not clear. Yet it is in word meaning that thought and speech unite into verbal thought. In meaning, then, the answers to our questions about the relationship between thought and speech can be found.

Our experimental investigation, as well as theoretical analysis, suggest that both

Gestalt and association psychology have been looking for the intrinsic nature of word meaning in the wrong directions. A word does not refer to a single object but to a group or to a class of objects. Each word is therefore already a generalization. Generalization is a verbal act of thought and reflects reality in quite another way than sensation and perception reflect it. Such a qualitative difference is implied in the proposition that there is a dialectic leap not only between total absence of consciousness (in inanimate matter) and sensation but also between sensation and thought. There is every reason to suppose that the qualitative distinction between sensation and thought is the presence in the latter of a *generalized* reflection of reality, which is also the essence of word meaning; and consequently that meaning is an act of thought in the full sense of the term. But at the same time, meaning is an inalienable part of word as such, and thus it belongs in the realm of language as much as in the realm of thought. A word without meaning is an empty sound, no longer a part of human speech. Since word meaning is both thought and speech, we find in it the unit of verbal thought we are looking for. Clearly, then, the method to follow in our exploration of the nature of verbal thought is semantic analysis—the study of the development, the functioning, and the structure of this unit, which contains thought and speech interrelated.

This method combines the advantages of analysis and synthesis, and it permits adequate study of complex wholes. As an illustration, let us take yet another aspect of our subject, also largely neglected in the past. The primary function of speech is communication, social intercourse. When language was studied through analysis into elements, this function, too, was dissociated from the intellectual function of speech. The two were treated as though they were separate, if parallel, functions, without attention to their structural and developmental interrelation. Yet word meaning is a unit of both these functions of speech. That understanding between minds is impossible without some mediating expression is an axiom for scientific psychology. In the absence of a system of signs, linguistic or other, only the most primitive and limited type of communication is possible. Communication by means of expressive movements, observed mainly among animals, is not so much communication as a spread of affect. A frightened goose suddenly aware of danger and rousing the whole flock with its cries does not tell the others what it has seen but rather contaminates them with its fear.

Rational, intentional conveying of experience and thought to others requires a mediating system, the prototype of which is human speech born of the need of intercourse during work. In accordance with the dominant trend, psychology has until recently depicted the matter in an oversimplified way. It was assumed that the means of communication was the sign (the word or sound); that through simultaneous occurrence a sound could become associated with the content of any experience and then serve to convey the same content to other human beings.

Closer study of the development of understanding and communication in childhood, however, has led to the conclusion that real communication requires meaning —i.e., generalization—as much as signs. According to Edward Sapir's penetrating description, the world of experience must be greatly simplified and generalized before it can be translated into symbols. Only in this way does communication become possible, for the individual's experience resides only in his own consciousness and is, strictly speaking, not communicable. To become communicable it must be included in a certain category which, by tacit convention, human society regards as a unit.

Thus, true human communication presupposes a generalizing attitude, which is an advanced stage in the development of word meanings. The higher forms of human intercourse are possible only because man's thought reflects conceptualized actuality. That is why certain thoughts cannot be communicated to children even if they are familiar with the necessary words. The adequately generalized concept that alone ensures full understanding may still be lacking. Tolstoy, in his educational writings, says that children often have difficulty in learning a new word not because of its sound but because of the concept to which the word refers. There is a word available nearly always when the concept has matured.

The conception of word meaning as a unit of both generalizing thought and social interchange is of incalculable value for the study of thought and language. It permits true casual-genetic analysis, systematic study of the relations between the growth of the child's thinking ability and his social development. The interrelation of generalization and communication may be considered a secondary focus of our study.

It may be well to mention here some of the problems in the area of language that were not specifically explored in our studies. Foremost among them is the relation of the phonetic aspect of speech to meaning. We believe that the recent important advances in linguistics are largely due to the changes in the method of analysis employed in the study of speech. Traditional linguistics, with its conception of sound as an independent element of speech, used the single sound as the unit of analysis. As a result, it concentrated on the physiology and the acoustics rather than the psychology of speech. Modern linguistics uses the phoneme, the smallest indivisible phonetic unit affecting meaning and thus characteristic of human speech as distinguished from other sounds. Its introduction as the unit of analysis has benefited psychology as well as linguistics. The concrete gains achieved by the application of this method conclusively prove its value. Essentially, it is identical with the method of analysis into units, as distinguished from elements, used in our own investigation.

The fruitfulness of our method may be demonstrated also in other questions concerning relations between functions or between consciousness as a whole and its parts. A brief reference to at least one of these questions will indicate a direction our future studies may take, and point up the import of the present study. We have in mind the relation between intellect and affect. Their separation as subjects of study as a major weakness of traditional psychology since it makes the thought process appear as an autonomous flow of "thoughts thinking themselves," segregated from the fullness of life, from the personal needs and interests, the inclinations and impulses, of the thinker. Such segregated thought must be viewed either as a meaningless epiphenomenon incapable of changing anything in the life or conduct of a person or else as some kind of primeval force exerting an influence on personal life in an inexplicable, mysterious way. The door is closed on the issue of the causation and origin of our thoughts, since deterministic analysis would require clarification of the motive forces that direct thought into this or that channel. By the same token, the old approach precludes any fruitful study of the reverse process, the influence of thought on affect and volition.

Unit analysis points the way to the solution of these vitally important problems. It demonstrates the existence of a dynamic system of meaning in which the affective and the intellectual unite. It shows that every idea contains a transmuted affective attitude toward the bit of reality to which it refers. It further permits us to trace the path from a person's needs and impulses to the specific direction taken by his thoughts, and the reverse path from his thoughts to his behavior and activity. This example should suffice to show that the method used in this study of thought and language is also a promising tool for investigating the relation of verbal thought to consciousness as a whole and to its other essential functions.

Language, Thought, and Culture: Linguistic Trickery

_____ 2

INTRODUCTION

The study of the relation of language and culture is not new on the academic scene. Recently the topic has acquired new labels that often reflect the theoretical proclivities of their authors. Saporta refers to "linguistic relativity" (1961), Olmsted to "ethnolinguistics" (1950), and Hymes to "anthropological linguistics" (1964). According to Diebold (1965), their major proposition is that "language and thought are interdependent and that the structural particulars of one are necessarily replicated in the other." The possible fruitfulness of combining linguistic, psychological, and anthropological efforts in the study of language and thought is indicated in the articles in this chapter.

Orr and Cappannari discuss the relation of an *external domain* of culture, ecology, behavior, and stimulus, all of which provide sound, and an *internal domain* of neuron, synapse, symbol, dream, and adaptive capacity, all of these latter linked to nerve impulse. This formulation suggests that the study of language and thought must include neurophysiology. Language, these authors contend, would not be possible if it lacked either man's inner biological trappings or the necessary environmental interaction (it would not be enough to be able to speak to oneself) In considering the external and internal domains, the authors discuss relations that could be productively studied: the neurological discontinuity between speaking and hearing; the neurological proximity between finger movements and motor speech; and the importance of neurological inhibition (not excitation) in the emergence of language.

The famous Whorf thesis, described by its author in the second article, would seem to stress the importance of the internal over the external domain. Whorf and fellow relativists are suggesting, according to Carroll (1956), that "all of one's life one has been tricked, all unaware, by the structure of language into a certain way of perceiving reality, with the implication that awareness of this trickery will enable one to see the world with fresh insight" (Carroll, 1956, page 7). It has been pointed out that the Whorf thesis is not really original with Americans like Sapir and Whorf but that it owes much to the Neo-Humboldtians of Europe, such as Ernst Cassirer (Diebold, 1965, page 260). Fearing (1954) believes that Whorf's emphasis on language shaping thought probably undervalues the importance of thought shaping language. As we discover more about the biological substratum of cognition and the universal characteristics of language and thought we shall know in more precise form the degree of overstatement of linguistic relativity in the Whorf thesis. Carroll, in reviewing the available evidence, believes that the linguistic-relativity hypothesis has little empirical support. He states, "Our best guess at present is that the effects of language structure will be found to be limited and localized (Carroll, 1964, page 110).

Communication can have either a private or public meaning. It can refer to thinking, or communicating with oneself, or to conveying thoughts, feelings, and facts to others. Sapir discusses communication in the public or social sense. He was one of the earliest American anthropologists to see language as a major means of enculturation—inducting the child into the ways of his culture. In the article here he adopts a broad definition of communication to include communication at several "levels," gesture and imitation as well as language. The inclusion of gesture recalls the conclusion of Orr and Cappannari, which indicates the neurological proximity between finger movements and motor speech. Psychotherapists are often trained to observe the "language" of gesture as well as the spoken words of their clients. One of Sapir's most interesting speculations is how technological advances in communication, by increasing the size of the audience, has not been an unmixed blessing in the development of constructive personal, social, and international relations.

D. H. Hymes has given considerable leadership to the field of anthropological linguistics (Hymes, 1964). In the excerpt in this chapter Hymes explores the relation of speech and personality development, which, he contends, varies considerably from society to society. Central to this discussion is the concept of *behavior settings*. These settings are the various occasions when speech must occur, when it occurs only at the option of the speaker, or when it must not occur. According to Hymes, these behavior settings differ from society to society, and these social variations produce differences in personality. The Hymes thesis is almost an extension of Whorf's in that language or speech determines not only cognition but also personality. By learning to respond appropriately to the various behavior settings of his society the child becomes a member of his community. He must, of course, as Chomsky has indicated, also master the rules and the basic structure of his language.

Unless there are some well-defined and measurable aspects of all behavior settings, the thesis of Hymes would be difficult to translate into careful research. Psychologists who are trained in the experimental method find "personality" even more than "mind" a difficult dependent variable. Often, however, experimental psychologists have used the term "stimulus" or "stimulus situation" to cover as much and even more than Hymes included in behavior settings. That behavior settings refer to speech customs makes their objective description and manipulation possible. In any event, these behavior settings may become an interesting intersection of anthropological, psychological, and linguistic investigation.

REFERENCES

Anisfield, M., N. Bogo, and W. E. Lambert. Evaluational reactions to accented English speech. *J. abnorm. soc. Psychol.*, 1962, **65**, 223–231.

Carroll, J. B. (Ed.) *Language, thought, and reality: Selected writings of Benjamin Lee Whorf.* Cambridge, Mass.: Technology Press, 1956.

Diebold, R., Jr. A survey of psycholinguistic research, 1954–1964. In C. E. Osgood and T. A. Sebeok (Eds.), *Psycholinguistics.* Bloomington: Indiana University Press, 1965.

Fearing, F. An examination of the conceptions of Benjamin Whorf in the light of theories of perception and cognition. In H. Hoijer (Ed.), *Language in culture.* Chicago: University of Chicago, 1954, 47–81.

Hymes, D. H. (Ed.) *Language in culture and society: A reader in linguistics and anthropology.* New York: Harper, 1964.

Olmsted, D. L., Ethnolinguistics so far. In *Studies in linguistics*, Occasional Papers, No. 2. Norman: University of Oklahoma, 1950.

Saporta, S. (Ed.) *Psycholinguistics: A book of readings.* New York: Holt, Rinehart and Winston, 1961.

The Emergence of Language[1]

WILLIAM F. ORR

STEPHEN C. CAPPANNARI

Pared to its most basic components, the problem of the emergence of language may be divided into two elements: (1) a study of the evolution of the human brain to the point where it can integrate the functions of the diaphragm, larynx, lips, tongue to emit sounds for speech and decipher and store these stimuli when they are applied to the ear; (2) the elucidation of those methods (such as "learning") of transmission of these acquisitions which are more rapid, flexible, and cumulative than is permitted by genetic inheritance.

Reprinted with the permission of the authors and the publishers, from the article of the same title, *American Anthropologist*, **66** (1964), No. 2, 318–324.

[1] This is a revised version of our paper which was read at the 61st Annual Meeting of the American Anthropological Association in Chicago, 1962.

Though both of these elements are of equal importance and mutually interdependent, regrettably they fall into two distinct fields of study with few academic ties: we have the area of psycholinguistics; we do not as yet have neuro-anthropology.

If we postulate that the extensive studies on living primates (Gavan, 1944; W. N. and I. A. Kellogg, 1953; Kortlandt, 1962; Spuhler, 1959; Washburn, 1960, 1961) have relevance to social organization of early Hominidae, it would appear that offspring matured slowly, lived in small groups, used signal vocalization, and employed tools. In the neuro-biological area this implies he had both acute hearing, ability to vocalize, and a useful hand.

Before considering the development of the core aspects of language (facility in speaking and hearing) we wish to point out that the *relationship* between these two abilities is channeled through extraorganismic (environmental) channels rather than through neuro-anatomical connections. Not only are the organs associated with these functions (the cochlea and larynx respectively) separate and distinct, but also there are minimal internal neuro-anatomical pathways between speaking and hearing, and those which do exist are not unique to man.

Since the relationship between speech and hearing does not depend solely upon internal neuro-anatomical connections, let us for a moment look at local-auditory speech as a circular function with the receptor, the ear, at one pole, and the emitting structures (larynx, lips, tongue, lungs, etc.) at the other. As we go between these poles we first traverse the outside world of sound and people, of ecology and culture and of environmental stimulus. If we complete our circle from the ear back to the voice we travel through the domain of nerve impulses and synapse, dream and symbol and adaptive capacity, Figure 2-1. It is obvious that language is a creature of both of these worlds; the spoken word is the external aspect of the internal dream and symbol. It is equally obvious that to understand the foundations of speech we must look not only at both of these domains but also examine the fundamental relationships between the two.

We view symbolism in this context as that facility of the human mind which allows it to internalize and store images (coded neurological patterns) of an external world. This permits a functional inter-communication between the neurological systems (speech and hearing) and thus frees man from complete dependence upon an external world for its continuous operation —i.e., he can be alone and talk to himself without uttering a sound.

LANGUAGE

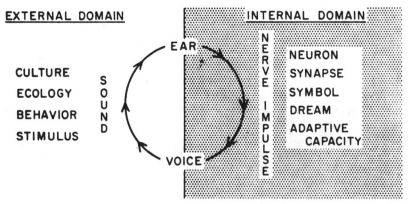

FIGURE 2-1.

The relationship between speech and hearing may be illustrated best by an analogy; the former (speech) being compared to a radio receiver which is able to decode electromagnetic waves and recode them as *sound.* The latter (hearing) in similar manner is analogous to the radio transmitter in being able to translate sound into electromagnetic waves.

The system of sound reception and sound emission in the human is as externally and internally independent as the radio receiver and the transmitter (which may be built in different factories) and is connected only as a result of stimulus and response to stimulus. Man's capacity for language thus depends on a walkie-talkie system built in different locations (frontal and temporal lobes), but housed in the same container (the skull) as a joint solution to an environmental pressure. Thus by suggesting parallel evolution of these systems we imply the gradual selection of a population of similar genetic patterns based upon proto-man's ability to use sound.

As an example, suppose some 500,000 years ago an absurdly improbable mutation occurred; an infant was born with genetic structure identical to yours, and suppose this creature survived; it would have the internal neurological configurations necessary for dream and symbol, but it could not have language because there would be no one with whom it could talk. The symbolic interaction within the social process, so ably described by George Herbert Mead, could not occur (1934).

The reverse of this relationship between internal and external speech may be viewed in a less fantastic manner. We refer to the failure to teach the more "intelligent" primates to have language (Hayes, 1951, Chapter 8). Thus even in a world containing language, a brain with neuronal patternings permitting symbol formation is necessary for it.

One of the properties essential to language and unique to man has been called "duality" by Hockett. He refers to the nec-

essary relationship between the meaning of words and relative position of constituent sounds which are themselves meaningless, as in "meat" and "team," or "tack," "cat" and "act" (1960, pages 4–5).

Experimental animals, a rat for example, may be taught to perform a series of responses in an arbitrary sequence not originally in his repertoire. This behavior may be homologous to duality as described by Hockett (Skinner, 1938, pages 339–340).

Another essential feature of language is its arbitrariness, i.e., phonemes and morphemes do not have inherent meaning. For language to be arbitrary implies, among other things, that close contact and sharing between members of a group must have been present for it to have evolved.

A prerequisite to an explanation of the beginning of language is a description of a method by which an acquired or conditioned "duality" and "arbitrariness" may be socially transmitted to succeeding generations. Not only must the social relationships which allow these subtleties to be imparted be intimate and intense, they must also be prolonged. Further, the transmitting organism must be essentially unchanging, and the receiving organism quite susceptible to change during this period.

Such a situation exists during the long period of infant helplessness and slow maturation of the human young. Each individual's psycho-biology is incomplete for so long that unique environmental effects may be built into it before change-resisting maturity, and each person thus becomes in turn a relatively stable reservoir for the accumulated techniques of past generations.

Thus, duality would be taught to the animal during the prolonged period of immaturity. It seems unlikely that a quality as abstract as the principle of duality could confer survival value and therefore be selected for in the absence of a learned language!

This implies that socially organized groups, using vocalizations, were already highly operative *before* the internal neurological arrangements evolved which permitted phonologically symbolic speech.

In this frame of reference first one aspect of language, the social, for example, took the lead until genetic mutations produced a neurological framework which could be advantageously selected, and this allowed a second advance, perhaps for better communication, problem solving, ability to speculate, and so forth.

Some of the genetic changes prerequisite to speech, such as slowly maturing young, ability to conceptualize, duality, etc., conveyed so little adaptational advantage until he developed speech that the wonder is that man did not become extinct. These changes presaged what was to come when viewed retrospectively, but, until their full maturation, they did not allow him to exploit the implicit advantages. If this is true, we are no longer required to believe that the early foundations of language conferred adaptive advantages to prehumans, but simply that they did not militate against his survival. Viewed in this fashion, it may well be that language was a corollary or epiphenomenon implicit in other evolutionary change. For example, the growth of the cortical control of fine movements of the fingers was most certainly selectively advantageous. We believe this was accomplished by a complex system of suppressor and inhibitory networks involving also the lips, tongue, larynx, because of the already present basic intrinsic patterns of neuronal arrangements (Brock, 1953, pages 312–313). The latter change, which was the precursor of articulate speech, may have had no evident survival value at that time.

It is this fact—the hand with its precise, complex, highly-integrated faculties evolved concomitantly with the marked expansion of the cerebral cortex in size and complexity and both of these apparently parallel the development of language—that is so challenging.

Unlike hearing and speech which are anatomically quite distantly related, the cortical motor-speech area is intimately related to a similar representation of the hand. Not only are they juxtaposed in related cortical gyri, but are of highly similar neuronal type (Ransom and Clark, 1959, pages 304–305).

Not only does much remain to be learned about the neurological basis of speech, but also there should be greater understanding and application of what is known. More and more evidence points to the fact that the cortical control of articulate speech is an inhibitory rather than excitatory phenomenon. Penfield, after many hundreds of careful experiments electrically stimulating the cerebral cortex in conscious individuals, has never caused a subject to utter a word, nor has anyone else for that matter. Stimuli applied at various well defined areas on the cortex may produce any number and variety of movements, sensations, even complex fantasies, dreams, but never words. Stimulation of Broadmann's area 44 (more commonly known as Broca's area—the prime center of motor speech) while the subject is speaking produces cessation of speech and the inability to "think" of words (Penfield and Roberts, 1959). Yet, if this same area is destroyed by trauma, tumor, or removed surgically, the patient becomes aphasic, can neither speak nor have adequate comprehension of what is said to him (Brock, 1953, pages 287–292; Nielsen, 1947, pages 21, 31). It would appear from this that the center is concerned more with the suppression of extraneous impulses than with the emission or integration of pertinent ones.[2]

This is in accord with known facts about human speech. The vocalizing infant emits many more different phones than the loquacious adult and in no recorded lan-

[2] Penfield and Roberts discuss at length the cortical representation of speech to relationship to thalamic representation. They end this discussion with the following sentence: "It is proposed, as a speech hypothesis, that the functions of all three cortical speech areas in man are coordinated by projections of each to parts of the thalamus, and that by means of these circuits the elaboration of speech is *somehow* (italics ours) carried out" (1959, pp. 207–208). We feel that evidence strongly indicates the "somehow" is through suppressive and inhibitory mechanisms.

guage do adults utilize more than a small percentage of possible phones (McCarthy, 1946, pages 477–581). (It is interesting that this principle of neurological inhibition is equally applicable to other abilities unique to man, the precise movements of the fingers, for example.)

It seems probable that the cortical evolution which led to language involved more the development of restrictive and constraining neurophysiological mechanisms (extinction, inhibition and suppression) rather than the addition of new (efferent) motor pathways. Man is able to select a few out of many potential sounds for articulate speech only because he can selectively inhibit the emission of irrelevant noise.[3]

Man, like other organisms, retains many primitive features, but these are overlayed and selectively suppressed by those higher in the evolutionary hierarchy. In the child's maturation, grasping is reflexive for several months and his ability to perform voluntary release is not fully established until the close of the first year (Gesell, 1940, pages 82–83). It is significant that speech begins in the child concomitantly with his ability to inhibit his grasp reflex. Herbert Spencer wrote almost a hundred years ago: "—it is not improbable that, in the course of nerve

[3] The literature in this field is extensive, both on theoretical and mechanistic levels. See: Bremer 1959:1241–43; Eccles 1959:59–74; French 1959: 1391–2; Hines 1936:76; Magoun & Rheni 1946: 165; Towe 1961:410.

evolution, centers that were once the highest are *supplanted* by others in which *co-ordination is carried a stage further,* and which thereupon became the places of feeling while the centers before predominant became automatic" (Jackson, 1931, page 107).

Indirect evidence for this process in which language has supplanted ejaculation and not evolved from it is found in observations that have been made of individuals who suffered injury to Broca's area, could not say more than a few words, but retained the ability to curse and utter exclamations such as "Hallelujah" (Nielsen, 1947, *ibid.*).

SUMMARY

We have outlined a scheme in which man established a relationship between the inner and outer world and noted that speech and hearing are in the main disconnected neurological systems.

We have attempted to explain how the ever increasing prolongation of maturity became functionally related to the transmission of language. We stressed the neurological proximity of manipulative skills and motor speech, suggested that these evolved concomitantly, and that the latter may be regarded as an epiphenomenon. Language appears to have been made possible by a process of inhibition and suppression from the most recently evolved cortical centers.

REFERENCES

Bremer, F. Central regulatory mechanism. In John Field, N. W. Magoun, and Victor E. Hall (Eds.), *Handbook of physiology-neurophysiology*. Washington, D.C.: American Physiological Society, 1959. Vol. 2, pp. 1241–1243.

Brock, Samuel. *The basis of clinical neurology.* Baltimore: Williams & Wilkins, 1953.

Eccles, I. C. *Neuron physiology.* In John Fields, N. W. Magoun, and Victor E. Hall (Eds.), *Handbook of physiology-neurophysiology.* Washington, D.C.: American Physiological Society, 1959. Vol. 1, pp. 59–74.

French, I. P. The reticular formation. In John Field, N. W. Magoun, and Victor E. Hall (Eds.), *Handbook of physiology-neurophysiology.* Washington, D.C.: American Physiological Society, 1959. Vol. 2.

Gavan, James A. (Arranged by). *The non-human primates and human evolution.* Detroit: Wayne State University Press, 1944.

Gesell, Arnold. *The first five years of life.* New York: Harper, 1940.

Hayes, Cathy. *The ape in our house.* New York: Harper, 1951.

Hines, Marion. The anterior border of the monkey's (*Macaca mulatta*) motor cortex and the production of spasticity. *Amer. J. Physiol.*, 1936, **116**, 76.

Hockett, Charles F. The origin of speech. *Sci. Amer.*, September 1960, **203**, 89–96.

Jackson, John Hughlings. *The selected writings of Dr. John Hughlings Jackson.* James Taylor (Ed.) London: Hodder, 1931.

Kellogg, W. N., and I. A. Kellogg. *The ape and the child.* New York: McGraw-Hill, 1953.

Kortlandt, Adrian. Chimpanzees in the wild. *Sci. Amer.*, May 1962, **206**, 128–139.

McCarthy, Dorothea. Language development in children. In Leonard Carmichael (Ed.), *Manual of child psychology.* New York: Wiley, 1946.

Magoun, N. W., and R. Rheni. Bulbar reticular inhibition mechanisms. In John Field, N. W. Magoun, and Victor E. Hall (Eds.), *Handbook of physiology-neurophysiology.* Washington, D.C.: American Physiological Society, 1946.

Mead, George H. *Mind, self and society.* Chicago: University of Chicago Press, 1934.

Nielson, J. M. *Agnosia, apraxia, aphasia—their value in cerebral localization.* New York: Hoeber, 1947.

Penfield, Wilder, and Lamar Roberts. *Speech and brain-mechanisms.* Princeton, N.J.: Princeton University Press, 1959.

Ransom, Stephen S., and Sam L. Clark. *The anatomy of the nervous system.* Philadelphia: Saunders, 1959.

Skinner, B. F. *The behavior of organisms: An experimental analysis.* New York: Appleton, 1938.

Spuhler, J. N. *The evolution of man's capacity for culture.* Six essays arranged by J. N. Spuhler. Detroit: Wayne State University Press, 1959.

Towe, A. L. Inhibition and occlusion in cortical neurons. In Ernst Florey (Ed.), *International symposium on nervous inhibition* (held at Friday Harbor in 1960). New York: Pergamon, 1961.

Washburn, Sherwood. Tools and human evolution. *Sci. Amer.*, September 1960.

———. *Social life of early man.* Viking Fund Publications in Anthropology, No. 31, Wenner-Gren Foundation for Anthropological Research, Inc., 1961.

Science and Linguistics

BENJAMIN L. WHORF

Every normal person in the world, past infancy in years, can and does talk. By virtue of that fact, every person—civilized or uncivilized—carries through life certain naïve but deeply rooted ideas about talking and its relation to thinking. Because of their firm connection with speech habits that have become unconscious and automatic, these notions tend to be rather intolerant of opposition. They are by no means entirely personal and haphazard; their basis is definitely systematic, so that we are justified in calling them a system of natural logic—a term that seems to me preferable to the term common sense, often used for the same thing.

According to natural logic, the fact that every person has talked fluently since infancy makes every man his own authority on the process by which he formulates and communicates. He has merely to consult a common substratum of logic or reason which he and everyone else are supposed to possess. Natural logic says that talking is merely an incidental process concerned strictly with communication, not with formulation of ideas. Talking, or the use of

Reprinted from *Language, Thought, and the School,* John B. Carroll (Ed.), by permission of The M.I.T. Press. Cambridge, Mass., 1956, pp. 207–219. Copyright 1956 by The Massachusetts Institute of Technology Press.

language, is supposed only to "express" what is essentially already formulated non-linguistically. Formulation is an independent process, called thought or thinking, and is supposed to be largely indifferent to the nature of particular languages. Languages have grammars, which are assumed to be merely norms of conventional and social correctness, but the use of language is supposed to be guided not so much by them as by correct, rational, or intelligent THINKING.

Thought, in this view, does not depend on grammar but on laws of logic or reason which are supposed to be the same for all observers of the universe—to represent a rationale in the universe that can be "found" independently by all intelligent observers, whether they speak Chinese or Choctaw. In our own culture, the formulations of mathematics and of formal logic have acquired the reputation of dealing with this order of things: i.e., with the realm and laws of pure thought. Natural logic holds that different languages are essentially parallel methods for expressing this one-and-the-same rationale of thought and, hence, differ really in but minor ways which may seem important only because they are seen at close range. It holds that mathematics, symbolic logic, philosophy, and so on are systems contrasted with language which deal directly with this realm of thought, not that they are themselves specialized extensions of language. The attitude of natural logic is well shown in an old quip about a German grammarian who devoted his whole life to the study of the dative case. From the point of view of natural logic, the dative case and grammar in general are an extremely minor issue. A different attitude is said to have been held by the ancient Arabians: Two princes, so the story goes, quarreled over the honor of putting on the shoes of the most learned grammarian of the realm; whereupon their father, the caliph, is said to have remarked that it was the glory of his kingdom that great grammarians were honored above kings.

The familiar saying that the exception proves the rule contains a good deal of wisdom, though from the standpoint of formal logic it became an absurdity as soon as "prove" no longer meant "put on trial." The old saw began to be profound psychology from the time it ceased to have standing in logic. What it might well suggest to us today is that, if a rule has absolutely no exceptions, it is not recognized as a rule or as anything else; it is then part of the background of experience of which we tend to remain unconscious. Never having experienced anything in contrast to it, we cannot isolate it and formulate it as a rule until we so enlarge our experience and expand our base of reference that we encounter an interruption of its regularity. The situation is somewhat analogous to that of not missing the water till the well runs dry, or not realizing that we need air till we are choking.

For instance, if a race of people had the physiological defect of being able to see only the color blue, they would hardly be able to formulate the rule that they saw only blue. The term blue would convey no meaning to them, their language would lack color terms, and their words denoting their various sensations of blue would answer to, and translate, our words "light, dark, white, black," and so on, not our word "blue." In order to formulate the rule or norm of seeing only blue, they would need exceptional moments in which they saw other colors. The phenomenon of gravitation forms a rule without exceptions; needless to say, the untutored person is utterly unaware of any law of gravitation, for it would never enter his head to conceive of a universe in which bodies behaved otherwise than they do at the earth's surface. Like the color blue with our hypothetical race, the law of gravitation is a part of the untutored individual's background, not something he isolates from that background. The law could not be formulated until bodies that always fell were seen in terms of a wider astronomical world in which bodies moved in orbits or went this way and that.

Similarly, whenever we turn our heads, the image of the scene passes across our retinas exactly as it would if the scene turned around us. But this effect is background, and we do not recognize it; we do not see a room turn around us but are conscious only of having turned our heads in a stationary room. If we observe critically while turning the head or eyes quickly, we shall see, no motion it is true, yet a blurring of the scene between two clear views. Normally we are quite unconscious of this continual blurring but seem to be looking about in an unblurred world. Whenever we walk past a tree or house, its image on the retina changes just as if the tree or house were turning on an axis; yet we do not see trees or houses turn as we travel about at ordinary speeds. Sometimes ill-fitting glasses will reveal queer movements in the scene as we look about, but normally we do not see the relative motion of the environment when we move; our psychic makeup is somehow adjusted to disregard whole realms of phenomena that are so all-pervasive as to be irrelevant to our daily lives and needs.

Natural logic contains two fallacies. First, it does not see that the phenomena of a language are to its own speakers largely of a background character and so are outside the critical consciousness and control of the speaker who is expounding natural logic. Hence, when anyone, as a natural logician, is talking about reason, logic, and laws of correct thinking, he is apt to be simply marching in step with purely grammatical facts that have somewhat of a background character in his own language or family of languages but are by no means universal in all languages and in no sense a common substratum of reason. Second, natural logic confuses agreement about subject matter, attained through use of language, with knowledge of the linguistic process by which agreement is attained: i.e., with the province of the despised (and to its notion superfluous) grammarian. Two fluent speakers, of English let us say, quickly reach a point of assent about the subject matter of their speech; they agree about what their language refers to. One of them, A, can give directions that will be carried out by the other, B, to A's complete satisfaction. Because they thus understand each other so perfectly, A and B, as natural logicians, suppose they must of course know how it is all done. They think, e.g., that it is simply a matter of choosing words to express thoughts. If you ask A to explain how he got B's agreement so readily, he will simply repeat to you, with more or less elaboration or abbreviation, what he said to B. He has no notion of the process involved. The amazingly complex system of linguistic patterns and classifications, which A and B must have in common before they can adjust to each other at all, is all background to A and B.

These background phenomena are the province of the grammarian—or of the linguist, to give him his more modern name as a scientist. The word linguist in common, and especially newspaper, parlance means something entirely different, namely, a person who can quickly attain agreement about subject matter with different people speaking a number of different languages. Such a person is better termed a polyglot or a multilingual. Scientific linguists have long understood that ability to speak a language fluently does not necessarily confer a linguistic knowledge of it, i.e., understanding of its background phenomena and its systematic processes and structure, any more than ability to play a good game of billiards confers or requires any knowledge of the laws of mechanics that operate upon the billiard table.

The situation here is not unlike that in any other field of science. All real scientists have their eyes primarily on background phenomena that cut very little ice, as such, in our daily lives; and yet their studies have a way of bringing out a close relation between these unsuspected realms of fact and such decidedly foreground activities as transporting goods, preparing food, treating the sick, or growing potatoes, which in time may become very much modified, simply because of pure scientific investigation in no way concerned with these brute matters themselves. Linguistics presents a quite similar case; the background phenomena with which it deals are involved in all our foreground activities of talking and of reaching agreement, in all reasoning and arguing of cases, in all law, arbitration, conciliation, contracts, treaties, public opinion, weighing of scientific theories, formulation of scientific results. Whenever agreement or assent is arrived at in human affairs, and whether or not mathematics or other specialized symbolisms are made part of the procedure, THIS AGREEMENT IS REACHED BY LINGUISTIC PROCESS, OR ELSE IT IS NOT REACHED.

As we have seen, an overt knowledge of the linguistic processes by which agreement is attained is not necessary to reaching some sort of agreement, but it is certainly no bar thereto; the more complicated and difficult the matter, the more such knowledge is a distinct aid, till the point may be reached—I suspect the modern world has about arrived at it—when the knowledge becomes not only an aid but a necessity. The situation may be likened to that of navigation. Every boat that sails is in the lap of planetary forces; yet a boy can pilot his small craft around a harbor without benefit of geography, astronomy, mathematics, or international politics. To the captain of an ocean liner, however, some knowledge of all these subjects is essential.

When linguists became able to examine critically and scientifically a large number of languages of widely different patterns, their base of reference was expanded; they experienced an interruption of phenomena hitherto held universal, and a whole new order of significances came into their ken. It was found that the background linguistic system (in other words, the grammar) of each language is not merely a reproducing instrument for voicing ideas but rather is itself the shaper of ideas, the program and guide for the individual's mental activity, for his analysis of impressions, for his syn-

thesis of his mental stock in trade. Formulation of ideas is not an independent process, strictly rational in the old sense, but is part of a particular grammar, and differs, from slightly to greatly, between different grammars. We dissect nature along lines laid down by our native languages. The categories and types that we isolate from the world of phenomena we do not find there because they stare every observer in the face; on the contrary, the world is presented in a kaleidoscopic flux of impressions which has to be organized by our minds—and this means largely by the linguistic systems in our minds. We cut nature up, organize it into concepts, and ascribe significances as we do, largely because we are parties to an agreement to organize it in this way—an agreement that holds throughout our speech community and is codified in the patterns of our language. The agreement is, of course, an implicit and unstated one, BUT ITS TERMS ARE ABSOLUTELY OBLIGATORY; we cannot talk at all except by subscribing to the organization and classification of data which the agreement decrees.

This fact is very significant for modern science, for it means that no individual is free to describe nature with absolute impartiality but is constrained to certain modes of interpretation even while he thinks himself most free. The person most nearly free in such respects would be a linguist familiar with very many widely different linguistic systems. As yet no linguist is in any such position. We are thus introduced to a new principle of relativity, which holds that all observers are not led by the same physical evidence to the same picture of the universe, unless their linguistic backgrounds are similar, or can in some way be calibrated.

This rather startling conclusion is not so apparent if we compare only our modern European languages, with perhaps Latin and Greek thrown in for good measure. Among these tongues there is a unanimity of major pattern which at first seems to bear out natural logic. But this unanimity exists only because these tongues are all Indo-European dialects cut to the same basic plan, being historically transmitted from what was long ago one speech community; because the modern dialects have long shared in building up a common culture; and because much of this culture, on the more intellectual side, is derived from the linguistic backgrounds of Latin and Greek. Thus this group of languages satisfies the special case of the clause beginning "unless" in the statement of the linguistic relativity principle at the end of the preceding paragraph. From this condition follows the unanimity of description of the world in the community of modern scientists. But it must be emphasized that "all modern Indo-European-speaking observers" is not the same thing as "all observers." That modern Chinese or Turkish scientists describe the world in the same terms as Western scientists means, of course, only that they have taken over bodily the entire Western system of rationalizations, not that they have corroborated that system from their native posts of observation.

When Semitic, Chinese, Tibetan, or African languages are contrasted with our own, the divergence in analysis of the world becomes more apparent; and, when we bring in the native languages of the Americas, where speech communities for many millenniums have gone their ways independently of each other and of the Old World, the fact that languages dissect nature in many different ways becomes patent. The relativity of all conceptual systems, ours included, and their dependence upon language stand revealed. That American Indians speaking only their native tongues are never called upon to act as scientific observers is in no wise to the point. To exclude the evidence which their languages offer as to what the human mind can do is like expecting botanists to study nothing but food plants and hothouse roses and then tell us what the plant world is like!

Let us consider a few examples. In English we divide most of our words into two classes, which have different grammatical and logical properties. Class 1 we call nouns, e.g., "house, man"; class 2, verbs, e.g., "hit, run." Many words of one class can act secondarily as of the other class, e.g., "a hit, a run," or "to man (the boat)," but, on the primary level, the division between the classes is absolute. Our language thus gives us a bipolar division of nature. But nature herself is not thus polarized. If it be said that "strike, turn, run," are verbs because they denote temporary or short-lasting events, i.e., actions, why then is "fist" a noun? It also is a temporary event. Why are "lightning, spark, wave, eddy, pulsation, flame, storm, phase, cycle, spasm, noise, emotion" nouns? They are temporary events. If "man" and "house" are nouns because they are longlasting and stable events, i.e., things, what then are "keep, adhere, extend, project, continue, persist, grow, dwell," and so on doing among the verbs? If it be objected that "possess, adhere" are verbs because they are stable relationships rather than stable percepts, why then should "equilibrium, pressure, current, peace, group, nation, society, tribe, sister," or any kinship term be among the nouns? It will be found that an "event" to us means "what our language classes as a verb" or something analogized therefrom. And it will be found that it is not possible to define "event, thing, object, relationship," and so on, from nature, but that to define them always involves a circuitous return to the grammatical categories of the definer's language.

In the Hopi language, "lightning, wave, flame, meteor, puff of smoke, pulsation" are verbs—events of necessarily brief duration cannot be anything but verbs. "Cloud" and "storm" are at about the lower limit of duration for nouns. Hopi, you see, actually has a classification of events (or linguistic isolates) by duration type, something strange to our modes of thought. On the other hand, in Nootka, a language of Vancouver Island, all words seem to us to be verbs, but really there are no classes 1 and

2; we have, as it were, a monistic view of nature that gives us only one class of word for all kinds of events. "A house occurs" or "it houses" is the way of saying "house," exactly like "a flame occurs" or "it burns." These terms seem to us like verbs because they are inflected for durational and temporal nuances, so that the suffixes of the word for house event make it mean long-lasting house, temporary house, future house, house that used to be, what started out to be a house, and so on.

Hopi has one noun that covers everything or being that flies, with the exception of birds, which class is denoted by another noun. The former noun may be said to denote the class (FC–B)—flying class minus bird. The Hopi actually call insect, airplane, and aviator all by the same word, and feel no difficulty about it. The situation, of course, decides any possible confusion among very disparate members of a broad linguistic class, such as this class (FC–B). This class seems to us too large and inclusive, but so would our class "snow" to an Eskimo. We have the same word for falling snow, snow on the ground, snow packed hard like ice, slushy snow, wind-driven flying snow—whatever the situation may be. To an Eskimo, this all-inclusive word would be almost unthinkable; he would say that falling snow, slushy snow, and so on, are sensuously and operationally different, different things to contend with; he uses different words for them and for other kinds of snow. The Aztecs go even farther than we in the opposite direction, with "cold," "ice," and "snow" all represented by the same basic word with different terminations; "ice" is the noun form; "cold," the adjectival form; and for "snow," "ice mist."

What surprises most is to find that various grand generalizations of the Western world, such as time, velocity, and matter, are not essential to the construction of a consistent picture of the universe. The psychic experiences that we class under these headings are, of course, not destroyed; rather, categories derived from other kinds of experiences take over the rulership of the cosmology and seem to function just as well. Hopi may be called a timeless language. It recognizes psychological time, which is much like Bergson's "duration," but this "time" is quite unlike the mathematical time, T, used by our physicists. Among the peculiar properties of Hopi time are that it varies with each observer, does not permit of simultaneity, and has zero dimensions; i.e., it cannot be given a number greater than one. The Hopi do not say "I stayed five days," but "I left on the fifth day." A word referring to this kind of time, like the word day, can have no plural. Actually, the only practical use of our tenses, in one-verb sentences, is to distinguish among five typical situations, which are symbolized in the picture. The timeless Hopi verb does not distinguish between the present, past, and future of the event itself but must always indicate what type of validity the SPEAKER intends the statement to have: (*a*) report of an event (situations 1, 2, 3 in the picture); (*b*) expectation of an event (situation 4); (*c*) generalization or law about events (situation 5). Situation 1, where the speaker and listener are in contact with the same objective field, is divided by our language into the two conditions, 1*a* and 1*b*, which it calls present and past, respectively. This division is unnecessary for a language which assures one that the statement is a report.

Hopi grammar, by means of its forms called aspects and modes, also makes it easy to distinguish among momentary, continued, and repeated occurrences, and to indicate the actual sequence of reported events. Thus the universe can be described without recourse to a concept of dimensional time. How would a physics constructed along these lines work, with no T (time) in its equations? Perfectly, as far as I can see, though of course it would require different ideology and perhaps different mathematics. Of course V (velocity) would have to go too. The Hopi language has no word really equivalent to our "speed" or "rapid." What translates these terms is usually a word meaning intense or very, accompanying any verb of motion. Here is a clue to the nature of our new physics. We may have to introduce a new term I, intensity. Every thing and event will have an I, whether we regard the thing or event as moving or as just enduring or being. Perhaps the I of an electric charge will turn out to be its voltage, or potential. We shall use clocks to measure some intensities, or, rather, some RELATIVE intensities, for the absolute intensity of anything will be meaningless. Our old friend acceleration will still be there but doubtless under a new name. We shall perhaps call it V, meaning not velocity but variation. Perhaps all growths and accumulations will be regarded as V's. We should not have the concept of rate in the temporal sense, since, like velocity, rate introduces a mathematical and linguistic time. Of course we know that all measurements are ratios, but the measurements of intensities made by comparison with the standard intensity of a clock or a planet we do not treat as ratios, any more than we so treat a distance made by comparison with a yardstick.

A scientist from another culture that used time and velocity would have great difficulty in getting us to understand these concepts. We should talk about the intensity of a chemical reaction; he would speak of its velocity or its rate, which words we should at first think were simply words for intensity in his language. Likewise, he at first would think that intensity was simply our own word for velocity. At first we should agree, later we should begin to disagree, and it might dawn upon both sides that different systems of rationalization were being used. He would find it very hard to make us understand what he really meant by velocity of chemical reaction. We should have no words that would fit. He would try to explain it by likening it to a running horse, to the difference between a good horse and lazy horse. We should try to show him, with a superior laugh, that his analogy also was a matter of different intensities, aside

from which there was little similarity between a horse and a chemical reaction in a beaker. We should point out that a running horse is moving relative to the ground, whereas the material in the beaker is at rest.

One significant contribution to science from the linguistic point of view may be the greater development of our sense of perspective. We shall no longer be able to see a few recent dialects of the Indo-European family, and the rationalizing techniques elaborated from their patterns, as the apex of the evolution of the human mind, nor their present wide spread as due to any survival from fitness or to anything but a few events of history—events that could be called fortunate only from the parochial point of view of the favored parties. They, and our own thought processes with them, can no longer be envisioned as spanning the gamut of reason and knowledge but only as one constellation in a galactic expanse. A fair realization of the incredible degree of diversity of linguistic system that ranges over the globe leaves one with an inescapable feeling that the human spirit is inconceivably old; that the few thousand years of history covered by our written records are no more than the thickness of a pencil mark on the scale that measures our past experience on this planet; that the events of these recent millenniums spell nothing in any evolutionary wise, that the race has taken no sudden spurt, achieved no commanding synthesis during recent millenniums, but has only played a little with a few of the linguistic formulations and views of nature bequeathed from an inexpressibly longer past. Yet neither this feeling nor the sense of precarious dependence of all we know upon linguistic tools which themselves are largely unknown need be discouraging to science but should, rather, foster that humility which accompanies the true scientific spirit, and thus forbid that arrogance of the mind which hinders real scientific curiosity and detachment.

Communication

EDWARD SAPIR

It is obvious that for the building up of society, its units and subdivisions, and the understandings which prevail between its members some processes of communication are needed. While we often speak of society as though it were a static structure defined by tradition, it is, in the more intimate sense, nothing of the kind, but a highly intricate network of partial or complete understandings between the members of organizational units of every degree of size and complexity, ranging from a pair of lovers or a family to a league of nations or that ever increasing portion of humanity which can be reached by the press through all its transnational ramifications. It is only apparently a static sum of social institutions; actually it is being reanimated or creatively reaffirmed from day to day by particular acts of a communicative nature which obtain among individuals participating in it. Thus the Republican party cannot be said to exist as such, but only to the extent that its tradition is being constantly added to and upheld by such simple acts of communication as that John Doe votes the Republican ticket, thereby communicating a certain kind of message, or that a half dozen individuals meet at a certain time and place, formally or informally, in order to communicate ideas to one another and eventually to decide what points of national interest, real or supposed, are to be allowed to come up many months later for discussion in a gathering of members of the party. The Republican party as a historic entity is merely abstracted from thousands upon thousands of such single acts of communication, which have in common certain persistent features of reference. It we extend this example into every conceivable field in which communication has a place we soon realize that every cultural pattern and every single act of social behavior involve communication in either an explicit or an implicit sense.

One may conveniently distinguish between certain fundamental techniques, or primary processes, which are communicative in character and certain secondary techniques which facilitate the process of communication. The distinction is perhaps of no great psychological importance but has a very real historical and sociological significance, inasmuch as the fundamental processes are common to all mankind, while the secondary techniques emerge only at relatively sophisticated levels of civilization. Among the primary communicative processes of society may be mentioned: language; gesture, in its widest sense; the imitation of overt behavior; and a large and ill defined group of implicit processes which grow out of overt behavior and which may be rather vaguely referred to as "social suggestion."

Language is the most explicit type of communicative behavior that we know of. It need not here be defined beyond pointing out that it consists in every case known to us of an absolutely complete referential apparatus of phonetic symbols which have the property of locating every known social referent, including all the recognized data of perception which the society that it serves carries in its tradition. Language is the communicative process par excellence in every known society, and it is exceedingly important to observe that whatever may be the shortcomings of a primitive society judged from the vantage point of civilization its language inevitably forms as sure, complete and potentially creative an apparatus of referential symbolism as the most sophisticated language that we know of. What this means for a theory of communication is that the mechanics of significant understanding between human beings are as sure and complex and rich in overtones in one society as in another, primitive or sophisticated.

Gesture includes much more than the manipulation of the hands and other visible and movable parts of the organism. Intonations of the voice may register attitudes and feelings quite as significantly as the clenched fist, the wave of the hand, the shrugging of the shoulders or the lifting of the eyebrows. The field of gesture interplays constantly with that of language proper, but there are many facts of a psychological and historical order which show that there are subtle yet firm lines of demarcation between them. Thus, to give but one example, the consistent message delivered by language symbolism in the narrow sense, whether by speech or by writing, may flatly contradict the message communicated by the synchronous system of gestures, consisting of movements of the hands and head, intonations of the voice and breathing symbolisms. The former system may be entirely conscious, the latter entirely unconscious. Linguistic, as opposed to gesture, communication tends to be the official and socially accredited one; hence one may intuitively interpret the relatively unconscious symbolisms of gesture as psychologically more significant in a given context than the words actually used. In such cases as these we have a conflict between explicit and implicit communications in the growth of the individual's social experience.

The primary condition for the consolida-tion of society is the imitation of overt behavior. Such imitation, while not communicative in intent, has always the retroactive value of a communication, for in the process of falling in with the ways of society one in effect acquiesces in the meanings that inhere in these ways. When one learns to go to church, for instance, because other members of the community set the pace for this kind of activity, it is as though a communication had been received and acted upon. It is the function of language to articulate and rationalize the full content of these informal communications in the growth of the individual's social experience.

Even less directly communicative in character than overt behavior and its imitation is "social suggestion" as the sum total of new acts and new meanings that are implicitly made possible by these types of social behavior. Thus, the particular method of revolting against the habit of church going in a given society, while contradictory, on the surface, of the conventional meanings of that society, may nevertheless receive all its social significance from hundreds of existing prior communications that belong to the culture of the group as a whole. The importance of the unformulated and unverbalized communications of society is so great that one who is not intuitively familiar with them is likely to be baffled by the significance of certain kinds of behavior, even if he is thoroughly aware of their external forms and of the verbal symbols that accompany them. It is largely the function of the artist to make articulate these more subtle intentions of society.

Communicative processes do not merely apply to society as such; they are indefinitely varied as to form and meaning for the various types of personal relationships into which society resolves itself. Thus, a fixed type of conduct or a linguistic symbol has not by any means necessarily the same communicative significance within the confines of the family, among the members of an economic group and in the nation at large. Generally speaking, the smaller the circle and the more complex the understandings already arrived at within it, the more economical can the act of communication afford to become. A single word passed between members of an intimate group, in spite of its apparent vagueness and ambiguity, may constitute a far more precise communication than volumes of carefully prepared correspondence interchanged between two governments.

There seem to be three main classes of techniques which have for their object the facilitation of the primary communicative processes of society. These may be referred to as: language transfers; symbolisms arising from special technical situations; and the creation of physical conditions favorable for the communicative act. Of language transfers the best known example is writing. The Morse telegraph code is another example. These and many other communicative techniques have this in common, that while they are overtly not at all like one another their organization is based on the primary symbolic organization which has arisen in the domain of speech. Psychologically, therefore, they extend the communicative character of speech to situations in which for one reason or another speech is not possible.

In the more special class of communicative symbolism one cannot make a word to word translation, as it were, back to speech but can only paraphrase in speech the intent of the communication. Here belong such symbolic systems as wigwagging, the use of railroad lights, bugle calls in the army and smoke signals. It is interesting to observe that while they are late in developing in the history of society they are very much less complex in structure than language itself. They are of value partly in helping out a situation where neither language nor any form of language transfer can be applied, partly where it is desired to encourage the automatic nature of the desired response. Thus, because language is extraordinarily rich in meaning it sometimes becomes a little annoying or even dangerous to rely upon it where only a simple this or that, or yes or no, is expected to be the response.

The importance of extending the physical conditions allowing for communication is obvious. The railroad, the telegraph, the telephone, the radio and the airplane are among the best examples. It is to be noted that such instruments as the railroad and the radio are not communicative in character as such; they become so only because they facilitate the presentation of types of stimuli which act as symbols of communication or which contain implications of communicative significance. Thus, a telephone is of no use unless the party at the other end understands the language of the person calling up. Again, the fact that a railroad runs me to a certain point is of no real communicative importance unless there are fixed bonds of interest which connect me with the inhabitants of the place. The failure to bear in mind these obvious points has tended to make some writers exaggerate the importance of the spread in modern times of such inventions as the railroad and the telephone.

The history of civilization has been marked by a progressive increase in the radius of communication. In a typically primitive society communication is reserved for the members of the tribe and at best a small number of surrounding tribes with whom relations are intermittent rather than continuous and who act as a kind of buffer between the significant psychological world —the world of one's own tribal culture— and the great unknown or unreal that lies beyond. Today, in our own civilization, the appearance of a new fashion in Paris is linked by a series of rapid and necessary events with the appearance of the same fashion in such distant places as Berlin, London, New York, San Francisco and Yokohama. The underlying reason for this remarkable change in the radius and rapidity of communication is the gradual diffusion of cultural traits or, in other words, of meaningful cultural reactions. Among the various types of cultural diffusion that of language itself is of paramount importance. Secondary technical devices making for ease of communication are also, of course, of great importance.

The multiplication of far-reaching techniques of communication has two important results. In the first place, it increases the sheer radius of communication, so that for certain purposes the whole civilized world is made the psychological equivalent of a primitive tribe. In the second place, it lessens the importance of mere geographical contiguity. Owing to the technical nature of these sophisticated communicative devices, parts of the world that are geographically remote may, in terms of behavior, be actually much closer to one another than adjoining regions, which, from the historical standpoint, are supposed to share a larger body of common understandings. This means, of course, a tendency to remap the world both sociologically and psychologically. Even now it is possible to say that the scattered "scientific world" is a social unity which has no clear cut geographical location. Further, the world of urban understanding in America contrasts rather sharply with the rural world. The weakening of the geographical factor in social organization must in the long run profoundly modify our attitude toward the meaning of personal relations and of social classes and even nationalities.

The increasing ease of communication is purchased at a price, for it is becoming increasingly difficult to keep an intended communication within the desired bounds. A humble example of this new problem is the inadvisability of making certain kinds of statement on the telephone. Another example is the insidious cheapening of literary and artistic values due to the foreseen and economically advantageous "widening of the appeal." All effects which demand a certain intimacy of understanding tend to become difficult and are therefore avoided. It is a question whether the obvious increase of overt communication is not constantly being corrected, as it were, by the creation of new obstacles to communication. The fear of being too easily understood may, in many cases, be more aptly defined as the fear of being understood by too many—so many, indeed, as to endanger the psychological reality of the image of the enlarged self confronting the not-self.

On the whole, however, it is rather the obstacles to communication that are felt as annoying or ominous. The most important of these obstacles in the modern world is undoubtedly the great diversity of languages. The enormous amount of energy put into the task of translation implies a passionate desire to make as light of the language difficulty as possible. In the long run it seems almost unavoidable that the civilized world will adopt some one language of intercommunication, say English or Esperanto, which can be set aside for denotive purposes pure and simple.

The Functions of Speech

DELL H. HYMES

Under this rubric, I want to raise questions about the functions of speech in a society, after a few words about the functions of speech in general. Whereas in the preceding section we considered language more as a "countersign of thought," here

"Linguistic aspects of cross-cultural personality study," by Dell H. Hymes from *Studying Personality Cross-culturally*, edited by B. Kaplan, pages 337–344. Reprinted with the permission of the author, editor, and the Harper & Row, Publishers.

we will consider it more as a "mode of action" (see Malinowski, 1923, page 326).

Many have classified language and speech into various aspects, one of the most popular classifications in American behavioral science being that of Morris (1939) into syntactics, semantics, and pragmatics. For relating the act of speech to personality and culture, Jakobson's classification is much more adequate. He has summarized it in remarks at conferences (1953, 1959). I can only adumbrate it here. As factors in the speech situation, Jakobson recognizes the sender, the receiver, the topic of reference, the code, and the message. All are involved in every communication, but focus on one or another may dominate. As tags for the associated functions, we may use the adjectives "expressive," "persuasive" or "rhetorical" (after Burke, 1951), "referential," "metalinguistic," and "poetic." According to Jakobson, one such function is dominant in each communication; the others are hierarchically arranged below it. In other words, focus on the several factors is hierarchically arranged, either from the viewpoint of the participants or of the analyst. To this classification, I believe that at least the factor of *context* or *scene* should be added (see Burke, 1945). There remain problems of interpretation and application which cannot be analyzed here, except to mention the point made earlier regarding the expressive function. One may either identify certain features as manifestations of a particular function or look at the whole message from the point of view of each function in turn. We may simply note, then, that Jakobson's classification of speech functions keeps a full set of relevant dimensions in mind, and can probably subsume many familiar but more limited concepts, such as Malinowski's "phatic communion" and Piaget's distinction between "egocentric" and "socialized" speech. It is worth pointing out that a sensitive analysis by Burke (1957) largely agrees with the Jakobson formulation.

In what follows, my general conception of the relevant dimensions of speech as a mode of social action is an application of recent theoretical work by Talcott Parsons. I would distinguish four broad aspects of speech activity: the cultural values and evaluations associated with speech activity; the social structure of the contexts of speech activity; the personalities who participate in speech activity (this and the preceding being connected by the speech aspects of roles); and the array of linguistic repertoires and routines available in the society for use in appropriate roles and situations. In Parsonian notation, these four aspects would be dubbed in order L I G A. Since I have but recently developed this conceptual scheme, what follows is not an analytic application of it, but a discursive essay on some of the questions which led to its formulation. I want to call attention to some of the neglected questions about the specific functions of speech. My premise is that speech is vital to personality, and that it varies significantly from society to society in its role as an oral activity and acquired skill. Differences in this regard seem as important as differences in the use of any other learned mode of behavior or of any other sensory modality. Because of space limitations, I shall be skimpy with illustrations, but there are many in the ethnographic literature.

First, cultural differences in the importance and evaluation of speech and language can be taken as something which reflects cultural personality and shapes the personality development of individuals. Speech communities differ in their insistence on skill and precision in speech, certainly as regards the use of their language by outsiders, probably as regards its use among themselves. People differ in their attitude towards speech material of foreign origin. Some refuse to borrow from other languages, some are extremely hospitable to foreign words. In multilingual situations there are differences in identification with the different languages, especially when one language is being replaced or threatened.

Swadesh comments: "Obviously we have here a rich area in which to observe the interplay of culture and personality" (Swadesh, 1948, page 234). Bruner (1956, pages 617–619) shows the crucial importance of this for the relation between primary group experience and acculturation. Peoples also differ in their conscious interest in the resources of their language and in their exploitation of them. I have mentioned sound symbolism in Korean. The coinage of words by sound symbolism has become a convention in American popular culture, especially in that part, such as comic books, directed ostensibly toward children. (For Russian attitudes see Mead and Metraux, 1953, pages 166 ff.) Newman has brilliantly contrasted the style of Yokuts, an Indian language of California, to that of English, as austere restraint vs. wild proliferation (Newman, 1940).

Peoples differ in their evaluation of talking, in the kinds of talk and talkers that are conventionally recognized, and in the way talking enters into the definition of statuses and roles. Differences in rewards and expectations will have a selective effect on the development of personalities. Peoples also differ in their criteria for verbal ability.

Second, personality is shaped and reflected by differences in the handling of speech situations. Barker and Wright (1954) have used the methods of psychological ecology to discover what they term the *behavior settings* of a community. By *speech situations* I mean the distribution of acts of speech in relation to behavior settings. Every society defines this relationship in a characteristic way. Most generally, there are some behavior settings in which speech is proscribed, some in which it is prescribed, and some in which it is optional. One must take into account a society's own theory as to who has the power of speech. Supernatural beings, animals, objects may variously be attributed this power. Wherever a society attributes speech, or the power of comprehension, it creates behavior settings in which speech can occur.

The first step in analyzing speech situations would be to discover which behavior settings fall into which general class. The second would be to analyze the contents of the classes. One major factor would be the relative number of settings in each class: societies differ markedly in their toleration of silence (or of talk, depending on the point of view). In what sort of settings is speech proscribed or prescribed? In relation to what persons and roles? Are there settings specifically defined as occasions for speech, such as confession, prayer, praise, oath-taking, therapy, verbal training of children? In our society family table-talk has been studied by Bossard (1948, Chapters VIII, IX). He finds it "a form of family interaction, important in the identification of personality roles and the development of personality traits" (page 175). In some societies the family is not together at meals; other behavior settings and different persons would be more important for the kind of subtle, indirect verbal conditioning of the child which Bossard describes.

In any society there is a congruence between speech and its setting, whether the setting be defined in terms of time, place, or personnel (e.g., Smith, 1957; Evans-Pritchard, 1948). Some settings not only require speech, but speech about certain topics or the use of certain expressions. From a psychoanalytic viewpoint, Devereux has highlighted cultural differences in the settings in which profanity can occur, the objects toward which it can be addressed, and what its use reveals about character structure (Devereux, 1951). What one cannot talk about, what one must talk about, when, where, and to whom—these differ in ways that involve differences in personality.

The content of speech plays a dual role regarding behavior settings. A situation may define what kind of speech is appropriate. Speech itself may serve to define a situation, and speech manipulation to define ambiguous situations may be an important skill. This dual role of speech involves usages shared by classes, regions, local communities, families, occupants of certain statuses and roles, and even pairs of individuals. On the broadest scale, levels of speech recognized throughout a society are involved (see Bloomfield, 1927). The way these differ from one society to another is itself significant. Thus, "the lack of congruence even between the conventional usage scales for English and French (slang-colloquial-standard vs. *vulgaire-populaire-familier*, etc.) reflects an important difference in the linguistic sociology of the two communities" (Weinreich, 1955, page 538).

Some differences in speech behavior seem constant across behavior settings, depending on the persons communicating. An Ainu husband uses his wife's personal name to her, but she may never address him by his. Sapir (1915) and Haas (1944) discuss phenomena of this sort, such as differences in the speech of men and women. Still, the persons involved communicate in certain behavior settings rather than others, so that particular usages become linked to particular situations. Occurrence of these usages elsewhere may refer to such situations, perhaps as a comment on personality, for instance, use of baby-talk to insult an adult.

An important point is made by Sapir:

Generally speaking, the smaller the circle, and the more complex the understanding already arrived at within it, the more economical can the act of communication afford to become. A single word passed between members of an intimate group, in spite of its apparent vagueness, and ambiguity, may constitute a far more precise communication than volumes of carefully prepared correspondence interchanged between two governments. (1931, page 79)

This seems to be the principle underlying effective use of speech surrogates, such as the Mazateco whistle speech or West African drum signals. It also underlies functionally specialized idioms, such as the argot of Ethiopian merchants, or the speech disguise of Tagalog young people (Conklin, 1956, 1959). Friedson (1956) suggests use of the principle as a measure of a speaker's

perception of his intimacy with his audience. In general, one would want to know what settings permit conventional or individual economizing in communication.

Behavior settings may differ in the very language or code used. The choice may be for concealment, prestige, or effective communication, and differences will reveal and shape personality. Weinreich (1953) analyzes many of the factors involved.

To function successfully as an adult personality, the child growing into a speech community must acquire a mastery of several sets of rules. He must of course learn the phonological rules, the grammatical rules, the semantic rules, which make an utterance a proper part of the language, and which make possible the vital cultural property of language, the production and understanding of novel utterances. There are the rules of the paralinguistic system, of speech as expressive and persuasive behavior. As Luria (1959a, 1959b) has shown, the child must also learn or grow to associate utterances with actions. Linked perhaps with this kind of "directive" or "adaptive" function of speech is another aspect of speech activity which is also separate from knowing the rules of the linguistic code proper. The successful adult must have mastered some part of the available linguistic routines and repertoires; he must judge not only of possible utterances, but also of their appropriate distribution among roles and behavior settings. He must learn not only how to say, but what to say. With all of this must go the internalization of certain attitudes toward speech activity and his language or languages.

Let us consider now the differences in the role that speech may play in the actual process of socialization, first regarding the onset and rate of language development, then regarding the context of development.

It is clear that children differ in the age at which speaking begins, and in the rate at which they master language. To some extent this is innate, but much depends upon cultural expectation and family situation. Number and relative age of siblings is one factor; only children have been found superior to children-with-siblings, and twins often develop special systems of communication, reducing the need for acquiring the language of adults, while singletons-with-siblings resemble twins more than only-children (Anastasi and Foley, 1949, pages 337 ff. summarize a number of studies). These results are from studies of North American children, but the cross-cultural implication is clear. Language development in children can be expected to vary with any social, cultural or ecological conditions affecting the makeup of the household.

Most studies of language development are linguistically inadequate, seizing upon external criteria such as number of words and length of utterances, whereas the essential thing is mastery of patterns, which must be studied in terms of a structural analysis of the language (Leopold, 1953–54). Only bare beginnings of such study have been made (Jakobson, 1941; Velten, 1943; Leopold, 1939–1949; Kahane, Kahane, and Saporta, 1958). Still the results discussed by Anastasi and Foley are significant. The importance of the age and rate at which language is achieved is succinctly stated by Bossard: "the acquisition of language is necessary to set into motion the two conditioning factors of social interaction and cultural background which mold the personality of the child" (1948, pages 177–178). Thus children who differ in the age at which language is acquired must differ in the age at which much of culture is acquired, particularly that whole range of culturally-defined reality which depends on language, such as the supernatural. They will also differ in the part of their first years that is accessible in later life (see Schachtel, 1947). A child who has successfully interacted with its environment without speech for a longer time may be more independent of language's shaping effect in later life.

Societies may differ not only in the age at which children typically acquire speech, but also in the context of its acquisition. For any society, one would want answers to such questions as: When is the child considered capable of understanding speech? Among the Tlingit, for instance, "when the infant is but a few months old the mother talks to him, tells him his moral tales, 'trains' him" (Olson, 1956, page 681). Is acquisition of speech accompanied by pressure, or treated as something that comes in due course? Are there special word games or speech patterns for teaching children? If there is pressure, at what stage of psychosexual development is the pressure applied? When are other socialization pressures applied, before or after the acquisition of speech? Various writings make clear that pressure, deprivation, and overprotection may variously induce speech defects or the preservation of infantile speech habits (Kluckhohn, 1954, page 944; Lemert, 1952; Henry and Henry, 1950; Klausner, 1955).

To what extent is a child rewarded by verbal praise, in contrast to material rewards such as candy, or physical affection? To what extent is the child punished by verbal reprimand, as opposed to deprivation, or physical pain? What is the conception of proper speech behavior on the part of the child, relative to particular persons and behavior settings? Are a child's questions about words and meanings welcomed or rebuffed? Overall, is a child allowed much or little oral gratification through speech? Is a child encouraged, discouraged, or ignored in efforts to find satisfaction in speech play? What is the proportion of speech activity to communication by other means, such as gestures, on the part of the child?

Are there special settings for verbal instruction of children? If there are, how frequent and with what personnel, and about what topics? Is the instruction conventionalized in content, as are proverbs and myths, or only in theme? Is the tone of instruction categorical, as among many American Indian groups, or not, as in West Africa? Is sex involved? There is no sex instruction of the young among the Nupe

(Nadel, 1951), but many American Indian children were forced to listen to a mythology rife with sexual incidents.

Does speech enter into the continuities and discontinuities in cultural conditioning (Benedict, 1938)? Every child learns a special version of its language first, usually its family's but that is a minor discontinuity; more significant may be "baby-talk." Is there a specialized "baby-talk"? How elaborated? What is its cultural content? Among American Indians, a Hidatsa mother stated: "We don't like baby talk . . . when they talk, we want them to talk just like us, right from the start" (Voegelin and Robinett, 1954, page 69, n. 6), whereas the Comanche had an unusually rich, formalized vocabulary of special words used to teach the child to speak between one year and three or four (Casagrande, 1948). Though thought of as simple, baby-talk may be as difficult as the adult language. Herzog (1948, page 97) says some features of Comanche baby-talk are as difficult to pronounce as corresponding features of the adult vocabulary, and Ferguson (1956) finds some of the most difficult sounds in the language to be among the most frequent in Arabic baby talk. The greatest discontinuity may come in the multilingual situation. Perhaps the most striking case is the Chontal of Zapotec, Mexico, where children are taught Spanish first, learning Chontal when as adolescents they enter the cultural life of the adult community (Waterhouse, 1949). Here an important factor seems parents' desire for children's success in the Spanish-using school. The children actually are forbidden the use of Chontal by their parents, for fear it will impede school progress.

One would expect differences in all these regards to correlate with differences in the functions of speech in the adult society and with the evaluation of speech activity in the adult culture. One could use the methods developed by Whiting and Ford to test hypotheses such as this: does the importance of verbal reward and punishment in socialization correlate with the importance of verbal interaction with the supernatural in adult life? Does late acquisition of speech correlate with an importance of glossolalia ("speaking in tongues") in adult religious life?

To conclude: language is a prerequisite of human society, but beyond this universal function, its significance varies from group to group. Speech is but one mode of communication, and its use involves the choice of one sensory modality as opposed to others. Societies and persons differ in the extent to which they choose this modality, the situations in which they choose it, and their evaluation of it. They differ in the ways speech enters into the definition of situations, conceptions of personality types, the socialization of the child. Its universality should not make us forget that speech activity, like sex and weaning, is a variable for the study of personality cross-culturally.

REFERENCES

Anastasi, Anne, and John P. Foley, Jr. *Differential psychology.* New York: Macmillan, 1949.

Barker, Roger G., and Herbert F. Wright. *Midwest and its children.* Evanston: Row, Peterson, 1954.

Benedict, Ruth. Continuities and discontinuities in cultural conditioning. *Psychiatry,* 1938, **1,** 161–67.

Bloomfield, Leonard. Literate and illiterate speech. *Amer. Speech,* 1927, **2,** 432–439.

Bossard, James H. S. *The sociology of child development.* New York: Harper, 1948.

———, E. S. Boll, and W. P. Sangor. Some neglected areas in family-life study. *Ann. Amer. Acad. Polit. Social Sci.,* 1950, **272,** 68–76.

Brunner, Edward M. Primary group experience and the processes of acculturation. *Amer. Anthropologist,* 1956, **58,** 605–623.

Burke, Kenneth. *A grammar of motives.* New York: Prentice-Hall, 1945.

———. *A rhetoric of motives.* New York: Prentice-Hall, 1951.

————. The poetic motive. *Hudson Rev.*, 1957, **11**, 54–63.

Casagrande, Joseph B. Comanche baby language. *Int. J. Amer. Linguistics*, 1948, **14**, 11–14.

Conklin, Harold C. Tagalog speech disguise. *Language*, 1956, **32**, 136–139.

————. Linguistic play in its cultural setting. *Language*, 1959, **35**, 631–636.

Devereux, George. Mohave Indian verbal and motor profanity. In Geza Roheim (Ed.), *Psychoanalysis and the social sciences.* New York: International Universities Press, 1951. Vol. 3, pp. 99–127.

Evans-Pritchard, E. E. Nuer modes of address. *Uganda J.*, 1948, **12**, 166–171.

Ferguson, Charles A. Arabic baby talk. In *For Roman Jakobson.* s'Gravenhague: Mouton, 1956. Pp. 121–128.

Friedson, Eliot. The varieties of individual speech. *Quart. J. Speech*, 1956, **42**, 355–362.

Haas, Mary H. Men's and women's speech in Koasati. *Language*, 1944, **29**, 142–149.

Henry, Jules, and Zenia Henry. Speech disturbances in pilaga children. *Amer. J. Orthopsychiat.*, 1950, **10**, 362–369.

Herzog, George. Linguistic approaches to personality. In S. Stansfeld Sargent, and Marian W. Smith (Eds.), *Culture and personality.* New York: Wenner-Gren Foundation for Anthropological Research, 1949. Pp. 93–102.

Jakobson, Roman. *Kindersprache, Aphasie und allgemeine Lautgesetze.* (Sprakvetenskaplija Sallskapets i Uppsala Forhandlinger, 1940–1942). Uppsala, 1941.

————. Chapter Two. In Claude Levi-Strauss et al. (Eds.), *Results of the Conference of Anthropologists and Linguists.* Baltimore: Waverly Press, 1953. Pp. 11–21.

————. Results of the Conference from the viewpoint of linguistics. In Thomas A. Sebeok (Ed.), *Aspects of style in language.* New York: Wiley, 1965.

Kahane, Henry, Rene Kahane, and Sol Saporta. *Development of verbal categories in child language.* (Publication Nine of the Indiana University Research Center in Anthropology, Folklore, and Linguistics) *Int. J. Amer. Linguistics*, 1958, **24**, No. 4, Part II.

Klausner, Samuel Z. Phonetics, personality, and status in Israel. *Word*, 1955, 11, 209–215.

Kluckhohn, Clyde. Culture and behavior. In Gardner Lindzey (Ed.), *Handbook of social psychology.* Reading, Mass., Addison-Wesley, 1954. Vol. II, pp. 921–976.

Leopold, Werner. *Speech development of a bilingual child.* Evanston, Ill.: Northwestern University Series, 1939–1949. 4 vols.

————. Patterning in children's language learning. *Language learning*, 1953–1954, **5**, 1–14.

Luria, A. R. The directive function of speech, I. *Word*, 1959a, **15**, 341–352.

————. The directive function of speech, II. *Word*, 1959b, **15**, 453–464.

Malinowski, Bronislaw. Meaning in primitive languages. Appendix A in G. K. Ogden and I. A. Richards, *The meaning of meaning.* London: Routledge, 1923.

Mead, Margaret, and Rhoda Metraux (Eds.). *The study of culture at a distance.* Chicago: University of Chicago Press, 1953.

Morris, Charles W. Foundations of the theory of signs. *Int. Enc. Unif. Sci.*, 1939, **1**, No. 2.

Nadel, S. F. *The foundations of social anthropology.* New York: Free Press, 1951.

Newman, Stanley S. Linguistic aspects of Yokuts style. In Ann Gayton, and Stanley S. Newman. *Yokuts and Western mono myths.* University of California Publications, Anthropological Records, No. 5, Berkeley: University of California, 1940. Pp. 4–8.

Olson, Ronald L. Channeling of character in Tlingit society. In Douglas G. Haring (Ed.), *Personal character and cultural milieu.* (3d ed.) Syracuse: Syracuse University Press, 1956. Pp. 675–687.

Sapir, Edward. *Abnormal types of speech in Nootka.* Canada, Geological Survey, Memoir 62, Anthropological Series No. 5. Ottawa: Government Printing Bureau, 1915.

Sapir, E. Communication. *Ency. Soc. Sci.*, 1931, **4**, 78–81.

Schachtel, E. G. On memory and childhood amnesia. *Psychiatry*, 1947, **10**, 1–26.

Smith, M. G. The empirical basis and theoretic structure of psychology. *Phil. Sci.*, 1957, **24**, 97–108.

Swadesh, Morris. Sociologic notes on obsolescent languages. *Int. J. Amer. Linguistics*, 1948, **14**, 226–235.

Velten, H. V. The growth of phonemic and lexical patterns in infant language. *Language*, 1943, **19**, 281–292.

Voegelin, C. F., and Florence M. Robinett. "Mother language" in Hidatsa. *Int. J. Amer. Linguistics*, 1954, **20**, 65–70.

Waterhouse, Viola. Learning a second language first. *Int. J. Amer. Linguistics*, 1949, **15**, 106–109.

Weinreich, Uriel. *Languages in contact.* Publications of the Linguistic Circle of New York, No. 2, New York, 1953.

————. Review of Ullmann, Precis de semantique française. *Language*, 1955, **31**, 537–543.

Language and Social Class:
Cognitive Disadvantage

_____ **3**

INTRODUCTION

With the problems of school integration and the education of the children of the poor in full prominence, educators are taking a new look at social class differences. As is true of most social and educational problems, we have considerably more pressure for immediate solutions than we have knowledge with which to provide them. We also have considerably more speculation than research, and considerably more proposals for action than theory and hypotheses for testing.

The study of social class differences is not new on the education and social-science scene (Bloom, Davis, Hess, 1965). As a product of the post-depression years, this study has concentrated on differences in such general phenomena as social class values, child-rearing practices, and developmental tasks. Occasionally these studies imply that the middle class has more to learn from the lower classes than it has to teach to them. They indeed seem to imply that the middle class may substitute high blood pressure, ulcers, and extravagantly high achievement needs for lower-class contentment with the immediate moment and sexual expression. In addition to confusing necessity with choice, this general point of view romanticizes the condition of the lower classes without suggesting ways of improving their lot.

There has been considerable recent interest in the study of social class differences in language and thought (Deutsch, 1963, 1964; Jensen, 1964; Fischer, 1958; Loban, 1964; Passow, 1963). Older studies simply compared IQ scores of middle-class Caucasian and minority children (Anastasi, 1958, Chapters 16, 17). The trend of these studies indicated the average intellectual superiority of the middle-class children, with of course considerable overlap of scores for the two classes and races. The studies left unanswered the questions about the causes of the observed differences (nature versus nurture), the character of the intellectual processes involved in answering the questions of the IQ test, and, finally, what changes in school organization and instruction would facilitate the intellectual development of children who performed poorly on IQ tests.

The discussions and research reported in this chapter generally assume that the linguistic and cognitive disabilities of underprivileged children are their most serious educational handicap. The deficiencies are often deep and extensive enough to condemn to futility much educational effort which is designed for middle-class children who often are able to supply for themselves what may be lacking in school instruction. Doubts about the quality of our teaching frequently arise only when we are asked to teach a subject matter, such as science and mathematics, and students, for example, the underprivileged, which are not at all amenable to conventional treatment. In our programs for the underprivileged child not only do we lack an appropriate teaching methodology, but we have not developed a conceptualization of linguistic and cognitive process that would enable us to diagnose their deficiencies.

Bernstein has been one of the original investigators of social class differences in the use of language (Bernstein, 1960, 1961, 1962, 1964). His investigations have been of English children, but his work is being successfully replicated with American children. In his most recent formulation of linguistic differences Bernstein refers to elaborated (formal) and restricted (public) codes. (The reader should recall that "public" in England refers to what we call "private" in the United States.) The restricted code describes language function in the lower class, the elaborated code in the middle class. Because Bernstein relates language and thought to modes of social interaction, his conceptualization is similar to that of the linguistic anthropologists [Chapter 2].

Like other investigators, Bernstein questions the basis of IQ differences reported for social classes. This skepticism is shared by Jensen in the article that follows. Bernstein's attention to the nonverbal aspects of communication, gesture, intonation, and so on, recall Sapir's definition of communication and the aural components of language emphasized by the linguists. The elaborated codes are similar to Chomsky's description of syntax, and the failure of lower-class children to learn the elaborated code may also be the failure to acquire mastery of the syntax of their native language. At this point in their development, Bernstein's codes have more implications for the diagnosis of language difficulties than for their treatment.

Employing a behavioristic frame of reference and utilizing the knowledge gained from the laboratory study of verbal learning, Jensen makes a most provocative analysis of the problem of social class differences in language and thought. In attempting to understand the educational handicaps of lower-class children, he regards emotional and motivational factors as secondary or derivative. He addresses himself instead to such factors as adequate repertories of prerequisite skills, provision of appropriate learning sets, and the effectiveness of reinforcing stimuli in particular instructional situations (Jensen, 1964). Jensen's central assumption is that "learning grows on learning." Our past experience to a large extent determines our future experience. This is essentially the behaviorist position, which seeks to relate antecedent conditions to consequent behavior or results. What an individual is able to learn at any given stage of his development is a function partly of what he has already learned in the past. Some forms of past learning have more transfer value for school learning than have other forms of past learning. Lower-class children have learned fewer things that transfer to school learning. Consequently, they become victims of a cumulative deficit. At each grade level they fail to acquire some of the essential prerequisites for learning the material of the later grades.

Jensen's analysis of verbal disability does not borrow heavily from linguistics or psycholinguistics. However, mediational processes and syntactical mediation fit into his associationist framework. Because Jensen's analysis leads to explicit description and manipulation of important variables, his approach may be more fruitful than the cognitive and linguistic approaches for research on linguistic differences and remedial instruction.

The studies by John, Semler, and Iscoe lean heavily on the description of verbal learning outlined by Jensen. John, however, also borrows from the study of the linguistic development of children [Chapter 7] and from Piaget's description of intellectual processes [Chapter 7]. In another sense (Jensen's), we can say that John is studying verbal mediation in Negro children—processes that she calls labeling, relating, and categorizing. John has three major hypotheses, one relating to each of these aspects of linguistic behavior. These hypotheses predicted that middle-class Negro children would show more labeling skill, more syntactical skill, and more skill in functional classification than would lower-class Negro children. As John suggests, similar research on the language development of preschool children of various subcultures may indicate improvements in educational methods for children of all social classes (see also John and Goldstein, 1964).

Semler and Iscoe used paired-associate learning in the study of learning abilities of Negro and white children. Previous studies have indicated a clear-cut correlation between mental age and the ability to learn paired-associate materials. In effect, these materials provide the opportunity to measure learning ability independently of previous learning, a task that Jensen and others believe IQ tests fail to perform. If IQ tests measure the present level of achievement rather than learning ability as such, we should expect to discover considerable variation in the learning ability of lower class children, all of whom may have equally low IQs. Semler and Iscoe also vary the learning tasks to shed further light on the relation of learning ability, IQ, and school achievement. Their findings seriously question the significance of the usual correlations of IQ and school achievement. Low IQ scores may not indicate that the child cannot learn, only that he *has* not learned. The "education of the masses" is possible after all. In our own time it may also be a moral obligation. Semler and Iscoe also believe that it is impossible to equate Negroes and whites for social class, a methodological difficulty that may support John's method of interclass comparison of Negro subjects. Although neither the John study nor the Semler and Iscoe study sufficiently weight the genetic factor or the irreversible effects of early deprivation, these studies do offer the public schools new challenge and hope in the education of the underprivileged child.

The study by Brown and Ford (1961) suggests how social class or social structure may be studied through the analysis of language. Their main source of data was modern American plays. What they studied was the form of American address, the use of the first name or the use of a title with the last name. Their evidence suggests two dimensions of social relation that may influence the choice of the form of address: (1) intimacy, which governs reciprocal address, and (2) status, defined in terms of age and occupational level, which governs nonreciprocal address.

REFERENCES

Anastasi, A. Race differences: Methodological problems. Race differences: Major results. In her *Differential psychology.* New York: Macmillan, 1958. Chaps. 16 and 17.

Bernstein, B. Language and social class. *Brit. J. Sociol.,* 1960, **11**, 271–276.

——. Social class and linguistic development: a theory of social learning. In A. H. Halsey, J. Floud, and C. A. Anderson (Eds.), *Education, economy and society.* New York: Free Press, 1961.

——. Linguistic codes, hesitation phenomena, and intelligence. *Lang. & Speech,* 1962, **5**, No. 1, 31–46.

——. Elaborated and restricted codes: their social origins and some consequences. London: University of London, 1964. (mimeo.)

Bloom, B. S., A. Davis, and R. Hess. *Compensatory education for cultural deprivation: Part 2. An annotated bibliography on education and cultural deprivation.* New York: Holt, Rinehart, and Winston, 1965.

Brown, R., and M. Ford. Address in American English. *J. abnorm. Psychol.,* 1961, **61**, 375–385.

Deutsch, M., The disadvantaged child and the learning process. In A. H. Passow (Ed.), *Education in depressed areas.* New York: Teachers College, 1963. Pp. 163–180.

——. *The role of social class in language development and cognition.* New York: Institute for Developmental Studies, 1964. (mimeo.)

——, A. R. Jensen, and T. Pettigrew (Eds.). *Social class, race, and psychological development.* Society for the Study of Psychological Issues, in press.

Fischer, J. L. Social influences on the choice of a linguistic variant. *Word,* 14, 47–56.

Jensen, A. R. Social class and verbal learning. Berkeley: University of California, 1964. (Mimeo.) This will also appear in the volume edited by Deutsch, Jensen, and Pettigrew (see above).

John, V., and L. S. Goldstein. The social context of language acquisition. *Merrill-Palmer Quart.,* 1964, **10**, No. 3, 265–275.

Loban, W., Language ability in the elementary school: Implications of findings pertaining to the culturally disadvantaged. In *Improving English skills of culturally different youth.* Washington, D.C.: U.S. Office of Education, 1964. Document No. OE-30012, Bulletin, 1964, No. 5.

Passow, A. H. (Ed.) *Education in depressed areas.* New York: Teachers College, 1963.

Social Structure, Language, and Learning

BASIL BERNSTEIN

No one in his right mind would plan an educational programme without taking into account the age of the pupils, their levels of maturity, intellectual and emotional, their interests and, of course, their social background. However, the extent to which we take account of these factors varies, and of equal importance is *how* we take account of them. It is the contention of this paper that we have failed to think through systematically the relationship between the pupil's background and the educational measures appropriate to successful learning. This is not to say that we have no information. Many researches have shown a relationship between a bit of the child and a bit of education. Often the teacher and the researcher is the same person at a later point in time but it seems that we are still engaged on psychological or sociological matching.

Although training colleges are aware of the importance of the pupil's social background and sociology is accepted as an important part of teacher training, there is little sign that an educational programme has been systematically thought through for the pupil whose origins are lower working class—approximately 29% of the population. This does not mean that we do not possess an armoury of visual aids, folk dancing, guitar playing, or text books for the slow but "normal" learner. The teacher does not lack advice on problems of discipline, from the suggestion that "louts should teach louts" to *From Innocence to Experience: without the aid of the cane*. Some think it is simply a matter of class-size but fail to see that it may be a question of which sized class for which particular group of normal children. A few pieces of contemporary research have indicated that it is equivocal to suggest that size of class matters; and yet we have no criterion by which to judge what constitutes a significant difference in size. Is it a drop in number from forty to thirty or a reduction to fifteen? Is it perhaps of greater importance whether the pupils come from the middle or lower working-class?

The general problems involved in teaching children from the lower working-class relative to those from the middle-class, are not necessarily problems of teaching children who differ in an innate capacity to learn as indicated by tests of intelligence. In fact, the evidence indicates that there must be a greater absolute number of children with very high intelligence in the lower than in the higher social groups.[1] What is of greater interest, is that there appears to be in different social groups a particular and different relationship between scores on group verbal and non-verbal tests (for example, the Mill Hill Vocabulary Test and Raven's Progressive Matrices). In lower

Reprinted with the permission of the author and the publisher from the article of the same title (with an addendum by the author), *Educational Research*, 1961, 3, 163–176.

[1] The statement refers to the *total* number of manual workers (the customary working-class group) *not* to the lower working-class considered as a sub-group.

working-class groups the verbal scores are grossly depressed in relation to the scores at the higher levels of the non-verbal test. The scores on the verbal test of the majority of children from this group tend to fall within the average range of the test whilst the scores on the non-verbal test tend to yield a normal curve of distribution skewed to the right, that is, in the direction of the highest scores.

Educational performance as judged by attainment in class is related to the scores on the group verbal test. A fairly consistent pattern emerges which reveals that as the boys' scores move towards the highest points possible on the non-verbal test the gap between the scores on the two types of test widens. As the present writer found, differences here are of the order of 20 + I.Q. points. In a sample of pupils attending a famous Public school this relationship, found in the working-class, was not present. The depressed scores on the verbal test for those working-class boys who have very high non-verbal scores, could be expected in terms of the linguistic deprivation experienced in their social background. This raises the question of the relationships between potential and developed intelligence and education.

In the light of what we know from much research, we can suggest a pattern of difficulties which the lower working-class pupil experiences in trying to cope with education as it is given in our schools. This will not hold in precise detail for every pupil, but we can say that the probability of finding such a pattern is greater if the pupil's origin is lower working-class.

Such children will experience difficulty in learning to read, in extending their vocabulary, and in learning to use a wide range of formal possibilities for the organisation of verbal meaning; their reading and writing will be slow and will tend to be associated with a concrete, activity-dominated, content; their powers of verbal comprehension will be limited; grammar and syntax will pass them by; the propositions they use

will suffer from a large measure of dislocation; their verbal planning function will be restricted; their thinking will tend to be rigid—the number of new relationships available to them will be very limited.

In arithmetic they may master the mechanical operations involved in addition, subtraction and multiplication, provided they have also mastered their tables, but they will have some difficulty in division. However, verbal problems based upon these operations may confuse them. They will have great difficulty in ordering the verbal argument before applying the operations. They will tend to learn a particular set of operations in relation to a discrete context and they will have difficulty in generalising the operations to a wide range of contexts. Their conception of number will be restricted. As the progression shifts from the mechanical application of fractions and simple percentages to relatively more sophisticated expressions, their lack of understanding of arithmetical *processes* will be revealed. Ratio may well be a point in the gradient of difficulty which they are unable to pass. As they develop, failure in their basic understanding will limit what they can do despite persistence and application.

Their time-span of attention will be brief and this will create the problem of holding and sustaining attention. They are not interested in following the detailed implications of a concept or object and the matrix of relationships which this involves; rather they are disposed towards a cursory examination of a series of different things. Their interest in *processes*, even those which are linked to their everyday experience, is limited. As soon as the formal dimension of the process is reached they begin to be uneasy. The interval between feeling and doing is short and this facilitates the acting out of impulse behaviour. Their curiosity is limited which removes an important dynamic from learning. They tend to require a very clear-cut educational experience with little ambiguity in direction and content. They are highly suspicious of anything which does not look like education as they traditionally conceive it. In the *short run* democratic appeals are less successful than dictatorial edicts.

Although the pupil may pass the primary stage without a great sense of unease, the discrepancy between what he is called upon to do and what he can do widens considerably at the secondary level. The character of the educational process changes at this level. It becomes increasingly analytic and relies on the progressive exploitation of what Piaget calls *formal* operations, whereas lower working-class pupils are more likely to be restricted to *concrete* operations. Finally, and with somewhat less confidence, we may say that there is a general flatness in their over-all educational achievements in the basic subjects. Although there may be one or two small peaks, in the main such pupils are confined to the average level. It is, I suggest, a peculiarly undifferentiated educational performance.

No mention has been made—deliberately —of the reduced motivation to learn, of the lack of involvement in the means and ends of education, of the standardised reactions, which are an unhappy defence against the despair and failure which school symbolises, and of the problems of discipline which are so generated. The central problem for the lower working-class child is, primarily, that of learning *how* to learn and secondly, that of learning *what* has to be learned. To make the educational experience happy and contented is not necessarily to solve the problems of learning, if this is achieved by by-passing the problem and playing directly into a concrete perceptual set as is done by much use of visual and concrete material. Sometimes class control is considered as a substitute, instead of as a condition, for learning. The problem however is *not* how to get the pupil interested but what to do *after* his interest has been elicited.

There is, of course, a wide range of individual differences and, it must be expected, such patterns will not be found with all children of the particular social background under discussion; nor are they confined to such pupils; it is suggested, however, that there is a higher expectation of finding this pattern of educational performance with the social group mentioned than with others.

How does this happen? What is the most important single factor in a boy's history, which generates this consistency of emotional and intellectual behaviour in the learning situation? It is not good enough to say that he thinks descriptively and is insensitive to abstract formulations, that he is concerned with substance rather than process, or, on a more sociological level, that there exists a clash in values between the school and the home, that the orientation of education is middle-class. These, and many others, are descriptive statements, which describe differences between some part of the boy and some part of the school. The question raised here is a dynamic one. How does the boy become like this and what is the main agency through which this becoming is facilitated and reinforced?

I suggest that forms of spoken language induce in their learning, orientations to particular orders of learning, and condition different dimensions of relevance. Teachers, research workers and educationalists have all commented on the limited linguistic skill and vocabulary of lower working-class pupils and the difficulty of sustaining and eliciting adequate communication.

It is therefore not new to focus upon the use of language as judged by educational criteria. Nisbet (1953) thought that part of the negative correlation between family size and I.Q. was the result of the type of speech model made available to the child. He considered that this linguistic limitation effected in some way a general cognitive impoverishment. Mitchell, 1956 (on the basis of an analysis of a battery of tests given to children of high and low social status), found that the verbal meaning and fluency scores for the low-status children could be used to predict their scores on a range of different factors. In this group there was a lack of differentiation among a number of functions whereas for the high-status group there was considerable differentiation. Studies reported by McCarthy (1954), of children in the special environments of residential institutions, indicate that they suffer a grave language deficiency and that their powers of abstraction are often impaired.

Luria and Yudovitch (1959) recently studied identical twins who were grossly retarded in speech for non-organic reasons. The twins were subjected to experimental changes in their environment and the speech changes subsequent to this were noted. It was found that the twin who had received special language training was able to perform more efficiently upon his environment, through the development of discursive operations which were not available to the twin who had received no training and who served as a control. These studies and others point to the critical role of spoken language in the process by which the developing child achieves self-regulation. Of particular interest, is the relationship between forms of spoken language and the mode of self-regulation. It is the nature of this inter-relation I want to consider and its educational implications.

There is little doubt that the social form of a relationship acts selectively on the mode and content of the communication. The language of the child in a group of other children (as shown by the Opies, 1959) is very different in structure and content from that he uses when speaking to an adult. Similarly the spoken language of combat units in the armed services is different from that normally used in civilian life. Vigotsky maintained that the more the subject of a dialogue was held in common, the more probable it is that the speech will be condensed and abbreviated, for example we may think of the communication pattern between a married couple of long standing or that between old friends. In these relationships, meaning does not have to be made fully explicit; a slight shift of pitch and stress, a small gesture can convey a complex meaning. Communication goes forward against a backcloth of closely shared identifications and affective empathy which removes the need for elaborate verbal expression.

This communion of the spirit which underlies and conditions the form of the communication may render what is actually said, gravely misleading to an observer who does not share the history of the relationship. The *how* of the communication is heavily burdened with implicit meanings. Some of the verbal meanings are restricted and not elaborated. The observer will be struck by the measure of his own exclusion and this will be reinforced by the expressive intimacy, vitality and warmth which accompanies what is said. The content is likely to be concrete and descriptive rather than analytical and abstract. The backcloth of closely shared identifications which create empathy gives to the speech sequences, from the point of view of the observer, a large measure of dislocation. The dialogue appears somewhat disjunctive because of the logical breaks which interrupt the flow of information.

What is the effect on behaviour if this form of spoken language is the *only* one which individuals have at their disposal? What are the implications if individuals are unused to signalling meaning unless it is against a background of common and closely held identification whose nature has rarely, if ever, been verbally elaborated and made explicit? What is the result of learning to operate with restricted speech structures where the burden of meaning may lie not so much in what is said, but how it is said, where language is used *not* to signal and symbolise, fairly explicitly, individual separateness and difference but to increase consensus? This does not mean that no disagreements will take place. What does it mean, in terms of verbal conceptual growth, if speech is only, or mainly, used in circumstances where the intent of the other person may be taken for granted and no pressure induces the need to create speech specially to fit the needs of those outside the group who do not share its experience? Where the number of situations which serve as stimuli for verbalisation is restricted by the conditions and form of the social relationship?

It is suggested that this is the situation in which many children of the lower working-class grow up. Their society is *limited* to a form of spoken language in which complex verbal procedures are made irrelevant by the system of non-verbal, closely shared, identifications which serve as a backcloth to the speech. The form of the social relationship acts selectively on language potential. Verbalisation is limited and organised by means of a narrow range of formal possibilities. These restricted formal strategies, for the sustained organisation of verbal meaning, are capable of solving a comparatively small number of linguistic problems, yet, for this social group they are the *only* means of solving all and every verbal problem requiring a sustained response. It is not a question of *vocabulary:* it is a matter of the *means* available for the organisation of meaning and these means are a function of a *special type of social relationship.* The size of the vocabulary is a function of other variables as will be shown: it is a symptom but not a cause of the speech form, although, in its own right it acts as a reinforcing agency.

The linguistic relationship between the lower working-class mother and her child is such that little pressure is placed upon the child to verbalise in a way which signals and symbolises his unique experience. The "I" of the mother, the way she organises and qualifies her experience, will be transmitted to the child *not* through evoking speech which is specially cut for this purpose. Spoken language is *not* perceived as a major vehicle for presenting to others inner states of the speaker. What can be said is limited by the rigid and limited possibilities for verbal organisation. It is a combination of non-verbal signals with a particular structure of verbal signals which originally elicits, and later reinforces, a preference in

the child for a special type of social relationship, which is limited in terms of verbal explicitness and relies heavily on a pattern of non-verbal signals. The "I" of the lower working-class mother is not, relatively, a verbally differentiated "I."

The shift of emphasis from non-verbal to verbal signals, in the middle-class mother-child relationship, occurs earlier and the pattern of the verbal signals is far more elaborate (Bernstein, 1961). Inherent in the middle-class linguistic relationship is a pressure to verbalise feeling in a relatively individual manner and this process is guided by a speech model which regularly and consistently makes available to the child the formal means whereby this process is facilitated.

It can be said that for the middle-class child there is a progressive development towards verbalising and making explicit, subjective intent, whilst this is *not* the case for the working-class child. This is not necessarily the result of a deficiency of intelligence but comes about as a *consequence* of the social relationship acting through the linguistic medium. It is through this developing medium that the child learns to internalise his social structure. His environment, and what is significant in his environment, is taken into himself, to become the sub-stratum of his consciousness by means of linguistic processing. And every time he speaks, his social structure is selectively reinforced. This does not deny the role of non-verbal learning but I suggest that even here, from an early age, the effects are fed through language and are stabilised by language. As speech marks out a pattern of stimuli to which the child adapts in the learning of this pattern, his perception is organised, structured and reinforced. The adequacy of his response is rewarded or punished by the adult model until the child is able to regulate his responses independently of the adult. In this way the outside gets into the inside from the very beginnings of speech. The appropriateness of the child's behaviour is thus conditioned to a wide variety of contexts by means of the vehicle of communication.

The lower working-class child learns a form of language which symbolises the normative arrangements of a local group rather than the individuated experience of each of its members. The form of the communication reinforces the pattern of social relationships but fails to induce in the child a need to create speech which uniquely fits his experience. Luria has suggested that speech may be considered as a complex of additional signals which leads to marked changes in the field of stimuli. It isolates, abstracts and generalises perceived signals and relates them to certain categories. Speech becomes a major means of selectively reinforcing perceptions. In the context of this discussion, forms of spoken language mark out what is relevant affectively, cognitively and socially and *experience is transformed by that which is made relevant.*

What is made relevant by the form of lower working-class speech is markedly different from that which is made relevant by the form of middle-class speech. The experience of children from these gross strata follows different paths from the very beginnings of speech. The type of learning, the conditions of learning and the dimensions of relevance initiated and sustained by the spoken language are completely different. In fact, it would not be too much to say that in strategic respects they are antithetical. The behaviour of the children is regulated according to separate and distinct principles. They have learned two different forms of spoken language; the only thing they have in common is that the words are English.

At this point a rather more rigorous definition is necessary of the two linguistic forms which, it is suggested, become the major instruments initiating and sustaining the socialisation process. The linguistic forms associated with the lower working-class I shall call a *public* language. Here it should be remembered that there will not be a one to one relationship between the lower

working-class and this form of spoken language but the probability of its use is certainly very high. With this in mind, we may dispense with social class concepts and refer to types of spoken language and the behaviour sustained by them. Operationally, it is more accurate to use the linguistic forms to distinguish the groups rather than a particular class affiliation.

A *public* language is a form of language use which can be marked off from other forms by the rigidity of its syntax and the restricted use of formal possibilities for verbal organisation. It is a form of relatively condensed speech in which certain *meanings* are restricted and the possibility of elaboration reduced. In this case speech[2] does not become the object of special perceptual activity, neither is a theoretical attitude adopted to sentence organisation. Whilst it may not be possible to predict any one content of this language, the formal organisation and syntax is predictable for any one individual. The class of the content is also predictable. The characteristics of a *public* language are as follows:

1. Short, grammatically simple, often unfinished sentences with a poor syntactical form stressing the active voice.
2. Simple and repetitive use of conjunctions (so, then, because).
3. Little use of subordinate clauses to break down the initial categories of the dominant subject.
4. Inability to hold a formal subject through a speech sequence; thus a dislocated informational content is facilitated.
5. Rigid and limited use of adjectives and adverbs.
6. Infrequent use of impersonal pronouns as subjects of conditional clauses.
7. Frequent use of statements where the reason and conclusion are confounded to produce a categoric statement.
8. A large number of statements/phrases which signal a requirement for the previ-

[2]This does not mean that the *quantity* of speech is necessarily reduced.

ous speech sequence to be reinforced: "Wouldn't it? You see? You know?" etc. This process is termed "sympathetic circularity."

9. Individual selection from a group of idiomatic phrases or sequences will frequently occur.

10. *The individual qualification is implicit in the sentence organisation: it is a language of implicit meaning.*

A *formal* language is one in which the formal possibilities and syntax are much less predictable for any one individual and the formal possibilities for sentence organisation are used to clarify meaning and make it explicit. The person, when he speaks a *public* language, operates within a mode of speech in which individual selection and permutation are grossly restricted. In the case of a *formal* language the speaker is able to make highly individual selection and permutation. Of course, a *formal* language speaker does not always do this, but the possibility always exists for him. The characteristics of a *formal* language are:

1. Accurate grammatical order and syntax regulate what is said.

2. Logical modifications and stress are mediated through a grammatically complex sentence construction, especially through the use of a range of conjunctions and subordinate clauses.

3. Frequent use of prepositions which indicate logical relationships as well as prepositions which indicate temporal and spatial contiguity.

4. Frequent use of the personal pronoun "I."

5. A discriminative selection from a range of adjectives and adverbs.

6. Individual qualification is verbally mediated through the structure and relationships within and between sentences.

7. Expressive symbolism discriminates between meanings within speech sequences rather than reinforcing dominant words or phrases, or accompanying the sequence in a diffuse, generalised manner.

8. It is a language use which points to the possibilities inherent in a complex conceptual hierarchy for the organising of experience.

These characteristics must be considered to give a *direction* to the organisation of thinking and feeling rather than to the *establishing* of complex modes of relationships. The characteristics are relative to those of a *public* language.

Each of these two sets of criteria refers to an ideal linguistic structure but what will be found empirically is an orientation to this or that form of language use. It is clear that some of these characteristics will occur in most forms of language use but a *public* language is a form of usage in which all the relevant characteristics will be found. It is possible to consider approximations to a *public* language to the extent that other characteristics are not found. Although any one example of a *public* language will be associated with a particular vocabulary and sequence frequency, it is worth while emphasising that the definition and characterisation are independent of content. Here we are concerned with the implications of a general mode, not with the isolated significance of particular words or speech sequences. This is not to suggest that middle-class children are the only ones oriented to a *formal* language but the probability is certainly much higher for this group. Neither do such children learn only a *formal* language. The mode of speech used can and does, in most cases, vary according to the type of social relationship involved. The speech behaviour of middle-class children, or for that matter children from any class, will in the peer group, approximate to a *public* language, and will tend to release behaviour regulated by the form of speech. Middle-class children will have access to both forms which will be used according to the social context. This will lead to an appropriateness of behaviour in a wide range of contexts. Other children, a goodly proportion of the total population in this and other countries, are likely to be restricted to one form, a *public* language. This will be the only form known: the only one that can be used.

Some of the implications of this restricted form of linguistic behaviour have a bearing on the educational picture described at the beginning of this discussion. Because of the simple, often broken, sentence structure and the rigid range of formal possibilities available, a *public* language will be one in which logical modification and stress can only be crudely rendered linguistically. This necessarily affects the length and type of the completed thought. Of equal importance, the verbal planning function is shortened. The shortening of this function often creates, in sustained speech sequences, a large measure of dislocation or disjunction. The thoughts are strung together somewhat like passing beads on a frame rather than following a planned sequence. The restricted verbal planning function also creates a high degree of redundancy, by which is meant a large measure of repetition of information or sequences which add little to what has previously been given. This is vividly illustrated by the two transcripts of tape-recorded discussion which follow:

"It's all according like these youths and that if they get into these gangs and that they most have a bit of a nark around and say it goes wrong and that and they probably knock someone off I mean think they just do it to be big getting publicity here and there."

Age 16.   I.Q. Verbal 104; Non-verbal 100

"Well it should do but it don't seem to nowadays, like there's still murders going on now, any minute now or something like that they get people don't care they might get away with it then they all try it and it might leak out one might tell his mates that he's killed someone it might leak out like it might get around he gets hung for it like that."

Age 17.   I.Q. Verbal 99; Non-verbal 126 +
(From a transcript of a tape-recorded discussion)

As there is a limited and rigid use of individual qualifiers, the adjectives and adverbs function as *social* counters through which the individual qualification will be made. This drastically reduces the verbal elaboration of the qualification which is given meaning by expressive signals. This does not ,mean that the gross number of adjectives and adverbs in speech samples taken from the two linguistic forms will differ very much but that the range will in one case be restricted. The qualifiers will be drawn from a lexicon *commonly* held, and (as it were) slotted into position, rather than being individually selected for a specific purpose. In this sense the qualification tends to be *impersonal*. Ongoing research tends to indicate that adjectives and adverbs used in *formal* language speech samples from subjects matched for age and very high nonverbal I.Q. with *public* language subjects, are only rarely not present in the active or passive vocabulary of the *public* language speakers. Feeling, then, is differentiated by referents which are the result of shared conditioning.

A *public* language is a vehicle for expressing and receiving concrete, global, descriptive relationships organised within a relatively low level of conceptualisation. The words and speech sequences refer to broad classes of contents rather than to progressive differentiation within a class. The reverse of this is also possible: a range of items within a class may be specified without knowledge of the concept which summarises the class. The categories referred to tend not to be broken down systematically and this has critical implications if the reference to be designated is a subjective state of the speaker. Despite the warmth and vitality, which is an expressive correlate of the language, it tends to be *impersonal* in the literal sense of that word. The original linguistic relationship between mother and child exerts no pressure on the child to make his experience explicit in a verbally differentiated way. It is perfectly possible, despite a restricted vocabulary, to create speech which fits individuated experience, but the orientation induced by this mode of communication does not make such characterisation appropriate.

The mode of speech, itself, will elicit and reinforce a special affective or emotional correlate. The speech delivery within a normal environment, outside the classroom, tends to be composed of fast, fluent, short, relatively unpaused utterances. Affect (expressive signals) is not used to discriminate finely among meanings carried within a speech sequence; rather it is used to reinforce dominant words or phrases, or accompanies the utterance in a diffuse manner. The feelings of the child would seem to be, relatively, undifferentiated for two reasons. Feeling is not differentiated, stabilised and made specific by linkage through language to a wide range of referents. Secondly, feeling which is regulated by the speech is conditioned by the form of the language. It is a vehicle for expressing concrete, direct, activity-dominated verbal sequences. It reinforces a relationship of immediacy with the environment. The gap between feeling and doing may well be brief. It should be unnecessary to add this, but nothing that has been said should be taken to mean that the natural feelings of sympathy, generosity, kindliness and warmth are not to be found, equally present, in all social groups.

A *public* language focuses upon the inhibiting function of speech by directing attention (the attention of the observer) towards potential referents which carry no stimulus value for the speaker. In as much as a *public* language induces in the user a sensitivity towards the concrete here and now—towards the direct, immediate, the descriptive, the global—then the dimensions of relevance will tend to preclude responses to other patterns of stimuli. Thus an orientation towards a particular type of learning under particular conditions is also involved. An example of this inhibiting function would also illustrate the significance of the seventh characteristic of the language. It was suggested that there would be frequent use of statements in which the reason and conclusion are confounded, to produce a categoric sentence.

Imagine the following two conversations on a bus. A mother has a child sitting on her lap.

MOTHER:	Hold on tight.
CHILD:	Why?
MOTHER:	Hold on tight.
CHILD:	Why?
MOTHER:	You'll fall.
CHILD:	Why?
MOTHER:	I told you to hold on tight, didn't I?

MOTHER:	Hold on tightly, darling.
CHILD:	Why?
MOTHER:	If you don't you will be thrown forward and you'll fall.
CHILD:	Why?
MOTHER:	Because if the bus suddenly stops you'll jerk forward on to the seat in front.
CHILD:	Why?
MOTHER:	Now darling, hold on tightly and don't make such a fuss.

In the first example a whole range of potential learning and connections have been cut out by the categoric statement. The natural curiosity of the child has been blunted. There is no causal chain between the mother's request and the child's expected response. The change in the behaviour has been brought about by a process akin to verbal conditioning rather than through instrumental learning. If the child challenges the statement then in a short period he is challenging the *right* of the mother to issue the request, that is, he is challenging the authority which inheres in the status of the mother. The potential social power in the form of the relation is revealed very quickly.

In the second example the child is exposed to an area of connection and sequence. If this is challenged then another set of reasons are elicited. Of course, after a time the categoric statement is applied but an order of learning has been made available in between. It should be noted that as the result of the linguistically elaborated relationship the initial challenges are of the reasons given to support the request. The challenge of the mother comes much *later* in the relationship and the latent social power is revealed later *and* under different conditions. If the categoric statement is used frequently in a *public* language then it limits learning and curiosity and induces a sensitivity towards a particular type of authority in which social power is quickly and nakedly revealed. The categoric statement becomes part of a language which narrows the range of stimuli to which the child responds. The length of this example also indicates how difficult it is to give concrete illustrations in a short paper.

An important psychological correlate of a *public* language is that it tends to discourage the experience of guilt. However, strong feelings of loyalty and responsibility to and for the local group will exist. Earlier it was suggested that the verbalising of subjective states, particularly of motivation, is not highly relevant. This implies that the referents of these states are not selectively reinforced by language. Koln (1959a, b) has drawn attention to the fact that middle-class parents are more likely to respond in terms of the child's *intent* in acting as he does, whilst working-class parents are more likely to respond in terms of the *immediate* consequence. Thus the working-class parent is responsive to ends directed to inhibiting disobedient or disreputable acts, while the middle-class parent is responsive to intent and acts with reference to individualised standards. Simply, there is little *talking through* of acts which require disciplinary measures in working-class homes, little verbal investigation of motive.

The rational control and manipulation of induced guilt is a major means available to the middle-class mother for disciplining the child. These means reinforce the individualising process in the child and transfer attention from consequence, or result, to *intent;* from the act to the *processes* underlying the act. This is not the case for a child whose mother speaks a *public* language. In this case behaviour is more likely to be made subordinate to shame. Shame indicates a diminution of *respect* accorded to conduct by a group. It is psychologically different from guilt. Of course, the middle-class child is sensitive to feelings of shame;

the point is that he is also sensitive to guilt.

A *public* language user will be aware that an act is wrong or that punishment is just, but feelings of guilt will tend to be divorced from the notion of wrongness. This would seem to make more likely the re-occurrence of the behaviour and to create a particular attitude to the punishment. It is not for one moment suggested that because motivational processes are verbally available to an individual, that these, in themselves, will always inhibit an action; only that the action would be accompanied by psychological states which might not be present if a child spoke a *public* language. There is a tendency for this to be recognised. Punishment of a *public* language user in a school will frequently tend to be corporal, threatened or actual, because it is difficult to elicit a sense of guilt or a sense of personal involvement in the act. Though caning, etc., does exist in Public schools where a *formal* language is spoken, other methods are *also* used to modify behaviour. With a *formal* language user, punishment can involve a temporary rejection, or a talking through of the misdemeanour aimed at increasing the experience of guilt, responsibility and so of personal involvement. Attempts to interchange the means of social control may lead at first to many difficulties. This is *not* to be taken to mean that corporal punishment is necessarily an effective means of social control. Where it is used as a substitute for the real difficulty of making a social relationship, it is rarely effective.

This rather difficult argument has tried to make clear how learning may be conditioned where the only language of the child is *public*. In the learning of this linguistic form, the child is progressively oriented to a relatively low level of conceptualisation. It induces a lack of interest in processes, a preference to be aroused by, and to respond to, that which is immediately given, rather than responding to the implications of a matrix of relationships. Such an orientation partly conditions the intensity and extent of curiosity, as well as the mode of establishing relationships. In turn, this will affect what is learned and how it is learned and so influence future learning. There will be a tendency to accept and respond to an authority which inheres in the form of the social relationship rather than in reasoned principles. It fosters a form of social relationship which maximises identifications with the aims and principles of a local group rather than with the complex differentiated aims of the wider society. Finally and of the greatest importance, it is a language of implicit meaning in which it becomes progressively more difficult to make explicit, and to elaborate verbally, subjective intent.

This behaviour is all of one piece and is maintained as a relatively "steady state" by protective devices built into the language system. Perhaps the most important of these protective devices is that a *formal* language (as used, for example, by the teachers) will be mediated through the *public* language. In the process of mediation, any alternative orientation which would sensitise the listener to a different dimension of significance is neutralised. Where a translation cannot be made there is no communication. It tends to inhibit the verbal expression—and hence the learning attendant on such expression—of those experiences of separateness and difference which would isolate the speaker from his group. It channels cognitive and affective states which, if expressed, might constitute a potential threat to the equilibrium. For example, curiosity is limited and focused by the relatively low level of conceptualisation. The restricted planning function and the concern with the immediate, tend to make difficult the development of a reflective experience. There is a tendency, too, to shift responsibility from self to the environment and his further reinforces the rigidity of the behaviour.

CONCLUSION

It can be seen that attempts to change the system of spoken language of children from certain environments will meet with great resistance, passive and active. It is an attempt to change a pattern of learning, a system of orientation, which language originally elicited and progressively reinforced. To ask the pupil to use language differently, to qualify verbally his individual experience, to expand his vocabulary, to increase the length of his verbal planning function, to generalise, to be sensitive to the implications of number, to order a verbally presented arithmetic problem, these requests when made to a *public* language user are very different from when they are made to a *formal* language user. For the latter it is a situation of linguistic development whilst for the former it is one of *linguistic change*. Two different psychological states underlie these situations. The *public* language speaker is called upon to make responses to which he is neither oriented nor sensitised. His natural responses are unacceptable. It is a bewildering, perplexing, isolated, and utterly defenceless position which ensures almost certain failure unless the teacher is very sensitive to the child's fundamental predicament.

This is by no means to say that a *public* language speaking pupil cannot learn. He can, but it tends to be mechanical learning and once the stimuli cease to be regularly reinforced there is a high probability of the pupil forgetting. In a sense, it is as if the learning never really gets inside to become integrated into pre-existing schemata. In fact, it looks as if this is so, for unlike the *formal* language oriented pupil, the *public* language pupil lacks these receptive schemata or if he possesses them they are weakly organised and are unstable.

The very conditions of the classroom situation often make effective education impossible. Large classes reduce the possibility of individual teaching, increase the probability of impersonal authoritarian methods of class control, which in turn increase the passivity of the pupil. If the teacher avoids this by small group techniques then, inevitably, he adds to his fatigue and in the long run may reduce his efficiency. There is a case for a general rule —the lower the status of the pupil, the smaller should be the number in the class. Expensive as this may seem at first sight, it might be economical in the long run. A small class is the basic condition for a close psychological relationship (inter-personal rather than inter-group) between teacher and pupil. The social organisation must enable the person, as well as the function, of the teacher to be felt and perceived. In an important sense, the teacher of a class of *public* language speakers is much more exposed, psychologically, if he is to teach efficiently. He cannot retreat into his formal role and impersonalise his communication. This does not mean that the appropriate teaching situation is one of all "pals" together. Nor does it require teachers who can "speak the language." In this respect there are only two types of teachers: those who can and those who cannot.

This is not the time to discuss techniques but perhaps it might be possible to seek agreement about the nature and ramifications of the educational problem. Although it appears very similar, the backwardness presented by the *public* language pupil is different in its dynamic form from that of the pupil whose backwardness is the result of psychological factors. It is a culturally induced backwardness transmitted and sustained through the effects of linguistic processing. The relationship, it is suggested, between potential and developed intelligence is mediated through a language system which encourages insensitivity to

the *means* whereby the pupil's dimensions of relevance may be expanded and enhanced. It follows also that the condition progressively worsens over the years. As the educational process becomes more analytic and relatively abstract at the secondary level the discrepancy between what the pupil can do and what he is called upon to do is painfully revealed.

A *public* language speaker has at his disposal a vast range of potential responses. His behaviour is by no means standardised. The general cognitive impoverishment is an impoverishment only from the point of view of the educator and, of course, it deprives society of potential talent. However, it is a form of language which symbolises a tradition where the individual is treated as an end in himself, not as a means to a further end. It psychologically unites the speaker to his kin and, on a sociological level, to his group. It should not be under-valued. Under the most hopeful circumstances the educational process increases the risk of the speaker's alienation from his origins. The task would seem to be to preserve for the speaker the aesthetic and dignity which inheres in the language, its powerful forthrightness and vitality but to make available the possibilities inherent in a *formal* language. We must be very sure that the new dimensions of relevance made available do not also include the measuring of human worth on a scale of purely occupational achievement.

REFERENCES

Bernstein, B. Some sociological determinants of perception. *Brit. J. Sociol.*, 1958, 9, 159–174.
———. Language and social class. *Brit. J. Sociol.*, 1960, 11, 271–276.
———. Social class and linguistic development: a theory of social learning. In J. Floud, A. H. Halsey, and A. Anderson (Eds.), *Society, economy and education*. New York: Free Press (in press).
Koln, M. L. Social class and parental authority. *Amer. Sociol. Rev.*, 1959a, 24, 352–366.

———. Social class and parental values. *Amer. J. Sociol.*, 1959b, 64, 337–351.
Luria, A. R. *Speech and the regulation of behaviour*. London: Pergamon Press, 1961.
———, and Ia. Yudovich. *Speech and the development of mental processes in the child*. London: Staples (in press).
McCarthy, D. Language development in children. In L. Carmichael (Ed.), *Manual of child psychology*. New York: Wiley, 1954, London: Chapman and Hall.
Mitchell, J. V. Jr. A comparison of the factorial structure of cognitive functions for a high and

low status group. *J. Educ. Res.*, 1956, **47**, 397–414.

Nisbet, J. D. Family environment. *Occasional Papers on Eugenics*, No. 8. London Eugenics Society, 1953.

Opie, I. and P. Opie, (1959). *The Lore and Language of School-children*. Oxford: Clarendon Press.

Vigotsky, L. S. Thought and speech. *Psychiatry*, 1939, **2**, 29-54.

POSTSCRIPT, SEPTEMBER 1961

Elaborated and Restricted Codes: A Note on Verbal Planning

I think it is possible to present the ideas developed in previous papers in a more economic and general manner. The concepts *public* and *formal* are not good analytic distinctions, they operate at too low a level of abstraction and they are probably semantically confusing. They will be replaced by the terms *elaborated* and *restricted* codes.

The two codes may be distinguished on the linguistic level in terms of the probabilities of predicting for any one speaker which structural elements will be used to organise meaning. In the case of an *elaborated* code, the speaker will select from a relatively extensive range of alternatives, therefore the probability of predicting the pattern of organising elements is considerably reduced. If the speaker is using a *restricted* code then the number of these alternatives is severely limited and the probability of predicting the pattern is greatly increased.

On a psychological level the codes may be distinguished in terms of the extent to which each facilitates or inhibits the orientation to symbolise intent in a verbally explicit form. Behaviour processed by these codes will develop different modes of self-regulation and thus different forms of orientation.

The codes themselves are functions of particular forms of social relationships, or more generally, qualities of social structures.

The *pure* form of a *restricted* code would be one where the lexicon is wholly predictable and, therefore, also the organising structure. Examples of this pure form would be ritualistic modes of communication. An actor, also, would be using a pure form of a *restricted* code, although from the point of view of the audience it would be an *elaborated* code. In fact his success in the role would depend on maintaining these two definitions. It is clear that in the *pure* form of the *restricted* code individual intent can only be signalled through the non-verbal components of the communication, i.e., intonation, stress, expressive features, etc.

In contemporary society what is found more often is a *restricted* code where prediction is only possible on the structural level. The simplification of structural alternatives is a function of the shared identifications which create the form of the social relationship. This reduces the tension to verbalise intent and make it explicit. Expressive features again will carry much of the burden of changes in meaning.

A limiting case of a *restricted* code is one where the user is linguistically wholly constrained by the code. This is the condition which corresponds to the analysis of a public language.

The following model and brief analysis may be helpful in drawing attention to the relationships between these codes and to verbal planning and modes of orientation.

In this model below the line represents the signal store in which inter-related verbal and non-verbal signals are contained. Above the line "E" and "D" represent the usual encoding and decoding processes controlled and integrated by the verbal planning function (V.P.). [See Fig. 3-1.]

When "A" signals to "B" I suggest that at least the following takes place:

Orientation: "B" scans the incoming message for a pattern of domi-

Association: nant signals. (This is the beginning of the verbal planning sequence.)

Associations to the pattern of dominant signals control selection from the signal store (V. + N.V.).

↑
Selection
↓

Organisation: Organisation and integration of signals (V. + N.V.) to produce a sequential reply.

The term code as I use it implies the principles which regulate these three processes. It follows that restricted and elaborate codes will establish different kinds of control which crystallise in the nature of verbal planning. The latter is a resultant of the conditions which establish the patterns of orientation, association and organisation. The originating determinants of this trio would be the form of the social relationship or more generally the quality of the social structure. This would allow the following postulate: The form of the social relationship acts selectively on the type of code which then becomes a symbolic expression of the relationship *and* proceeds to regulate the nature of the inter-action. Simply, the *consequences* of the form of the social relationship are transmitted and sustained by the code on a psychological level. Strategic learning would be elicited, sustained and generalised by the code which would mark out *what* has to be learned and would constrain the *conditions* of successful learning.

I should like to indicate very briefly four aspects of verbal planning control where the code is restricted.

1. The sequences will tend to be dislocated, disjunctive, relatively well-organised but with relatively poor syntactic control, stressing the active rather than the passive voice, and point to the concrete, the descriptive and the narrative. Non-verbal signals will be an important source of significant changes in meaning as the verbal sequences are relatively impersonal, i.e., not individuated and serve as social symbols reinforcing the form of the social relationship.

2. An example will best indicate the second aspect. When "A" meets "B" whom he does not know "A" will yet have some idea of "B". This idea will be translated in terms of the verbal planning of "A"s original signals to "B". If "B"s return signals indicate that "A"s original idea is inadequate, or, perhaps, inappropriate, "A" will modify his idea and through verbal planning control send different signals and note "B"s response. After an interval some type of equilibrium regulating the relationship will have become established with occasional fluctuations damped down by feedback achieved via verbal planning control, V.P.-transmission-return signals-check-verbal planning-transmission. By this process "A" will have internalised the "requirements" of "B" via speech. If the code is restricted, by definition, so is verbal planning consequently the range and type of others who can be so internalised is limited. By implication the social tie to those who

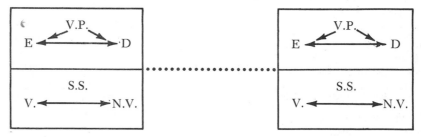

FIGURE 3-1.

can be so becomes a very powerful bond which is both positively and negatively strengthened by the code.

3. The third aspect relates to problem solving and the role of speech in orientating and thus changing the quality of the environment for the speaker.

As the problem to be solved moves in the direction of the relatively abstract it is likely that inner verbal sequences will be evolved (not necessarily throat movements, perhaps below the threshold of incipient articulation) which will proceed to orient the thinker and change the quality of the signals responded to in the environment. When the thinker is limited to a restricted code the verbal sequences evoked may direct perception to the more gross aspects of the environment and so his solution will become more and more inappropriate in direct relation to the degree of abstraction of the problem. This verbal feed-back in some problem solving activities will be continuously reinforced. The bond relating the thinker to the concrete and descriptive will become progressively tighter with the cumulative effect of the use of the restricted code.

4. The fourth aspect refers to the time dimension of verbal planning; that is to the delay between impulse and signalling.[3]

If the speaker can use, or is oriented to, an elaborate code he can tolerate the tension associated with delay in selection. Subsequent signalling is likely to be more appropriate and the tension will be reduced by the appropriateness of the signals. In this way (delay → tension → appropriate signalling → reduction in tension ↔ reinforcement of the total sequence), a channel for the reduction of tension through verbal control is facilitated with the continued use of an elaborate code.

In a *restricted* code the delay between impulse and signal will be shorter in a normal environment. Raising the level of coding difficulty, thus increasing the delay potential, may lead to a break-down in signalling or the signalling may not adjust to the new demands. The first solution results in a total drop in output; the second *avoids* increasing the delay between impulse and signal. Either way the code does not facilitate the toleration of tension and the reduction of tension by appropriate signalling. In a *restricted* code the channel for the release of tension will tend to be through changes in somato-motor and expressive sets.

Social Class and Verbal Learning

ARTHUR R. JENSEN

SOCIAL CLASS DETERMINANTS OF LANGUAGE DEVELOPMENT

So far we have only set the stage for introducing the chief agent of intellectual development—language. But it might be advisable in the following discussion to substitute the term *verbal behavior* in place of "language," a word which in some educational circles has taken on certain value connotations that are best avoided in the present context. Discussion of social class

Published with the permission of the author from a monograph of the same title. Berkeley: University of California, 1964. (mimeo.)

[3] The measures for this are the mean pause duration per word per utterance and the frequency of pauses. (greater than 0.25 seconds)

differences in "language" tends to arouse notions about the middle-class social advantages of "correct" pronunciation, "good" English, avoidance of slang, and so forth. Language differences along these dimensions, especially in the context in which they are usually discussed, are extremely superficial from a psychological viewpoint. If it were thought that social class influences on verbal behavior implied no more than factors such as these, the topic of verbal learning as it relates to social class would be of very little interest to us. As the term is used in the following discussion, however, verbal behavior—not just the *capacity* for verbal behavior, but verbal behavior itself—is what most distinguishes the human being from the rest of the animal world.

The psychological consequences of verbal behavior are extremely profound in ways and degrees scarcely appreciated by those who are unfamiliar with the recent research. To the extent that a person is prevented, by whatever reason, from falling heir to these consequences of his human potential for verbal learning, he will fall short of his potential as a human being. If some of the limiting influences on verbal development are intimately related to certain aspects of a lower-class style of life, certainly no other aspects of lower-class status can be viewed as sufficiently advantageous to off-set the waste of human potential that results from these adverse influences on verbal development. In speaking on this topic to middle-class groups, I am usually asked by one of the audience to say something about the "advantages" of living in the world of the lower-class. The question is probably prompted by a romanticized notion of poverty, which evokes in the middle-class outsiders imaginative visions of forbidden freedoms, spontaneity, instinctual gratifications, depths of feeling, hearty togetherness, and immunity to ulcers and other ills presumed to result from middle class striving and stress. But this is neither the view of lower-class individuals, nor of those who have studied the matter

and weighed the total human consequences of lower-class environment. So the answer as to its supposed advantages can be clear-cut: there are none! The disadvantages are great, however, and one of their major sources might be fruitfully sought in the area of verbal behavior.

The aims of the following discussion, therefore, are twofold: First, to indicate how social factors might in general affect verbal development; and second, to delineate specifically some of the psychological consequences of various stages and processes of verbal development.

Since the most important external factor affecting the rate of verbal development is the quality of a child's early linguistic environment (Carroll, 1960, page 749), we should first look at some of the contrasts between lower- and middle-class environments in this respect.

The child's vocalizations, which normally occur in the first year of life and are the forerunners of speech, must be reinforced or rewarded by certain kinds of responses from other persons if they are to persist and develop into speech. The more reinforcement, the better; and apparently the fewer the number of persons from whom reinforcement comes, the better. Brodbeck and Irwin (1946), for example, found that children reared by their parents or by foster parents vocalize more than children living in institutional settings, and this difference shows up as early as 6 months of age. Also, Rheingold and Bayley (1959) found that children who had a single mothering experience excelled children who had six to eight mother surrogates in the area of vocalization. Fewer lower-class children than middle-class children have a single mother-child relationship in their early years. Instead, the responsibility of caring for the child in the lower-class home tends to be assumed by a number of different persons, both adults and older children. In the typical lower-class home there is reportedly less verbal play, less verbal interaction, and less reinforcing behavior on the part of the older members of the household in response to the child's early vocalizations than is generally found in middle-class homes. The beginning of speech is therefore more apt to be delayed in a lower-class environment.

While the child can engage in other forms of learning such as the acquisition of motor skills largely through interaction with the inanimate environment, language acquisition depends entirely upon interaction with another person, and the emotional quality and intensity of this interpersonal relationship is believed to play a crucial role in the process. The "shaping" of the child's speech sounds through the differential reinforcing behavior of the parent is probably carried on more persistently by middle-class than by lower-class parents in their efforts to have the child's speech patterns match their own. This "shaping" of speech by the parent also constitutes training in auditory discrimination, which in turn facilitates further language acquisition.

Speech cannot develop without this spontaneous vocal interplay between child and adult, or between one child and another who is sufficiently mature to make the auditory discriminations which almost automatically give rise in the middle-class parent to differential reinforcing behavior (by gesture, facial expression, and vocal utterance). Children who are at the same stage of development, in playing together, can practice what they already "know" verbally, but this arrangement will not add further to their verbal knowledge for neither child is able to provide the other with standards for imitation or to "shape" the other's vocal behavior through differential reinforcement. Language learning takes place, as it were, by the child having to continually "reach" to a higher level set by the significant adults and older children with whom he interacts. And if the child is forced to spend a great deal of his time in the company of other children who are not his verbal superiors, his language development will be retarded. For this reason, twins and triplets are on the average some-

what slower in language development than singletons; and this shows up even later in childhood as a difference in IQ, twins being several points lower on the average than singletons. Koch (1954) has found that children with the greatest proficiency in verbal skills tend to be the first-born whose next sibling arrives 2 to 4 years later. To account for this, the relatively undivided attention of the mother during these first 2 to 4 years is thought to be the prime factor. Thus, if the mother's time is more divided in the lower-class family and if the children are more closely spaced and spend relatively more of their time in the company of their verbal peers than is the case in the middle-class family, the results are predictable along the lines already indicated.

When the child begins talking in his second year, his difficulties are increased if his vocal models must be perceived through a high "noise" background. The congested living conditions in many lower-class homes can be presumed to have a higher noise level plus a greater proportion of adult speech which does not constitute vocal interaction with the child. Again, the consequences are predictable.

Even after the child is already talking, the question-asking behavior which is so characteristic of young children, and which later becomes important for independent problem solving, will eventually be extinguished through lack of adequate reinforcement if the parents are too distracted to respond in a satisfying way to the child's questions.

The functions of language also seem to differ between the lower- and the middle-class family. Most of the research on social class differences in verbal behavior has been carried on in England by sociologist Basil Bernstein (1960), but many of his findings are probably valid among the lower- and middle-classes in America as well. Spoken language among the lower-class is, first of all, less like written language syntactically, grammatically, and in overall sequential organization and logical progression, than is true among the middle-class, which immediately suggests that there would be relatively less positive transfer from lower-class verbal experience to formal language—the language of books, newspapers, magazines, etc. Thus, for the lower-class person, reading and writing are very different from speech. Also, language in the lower-class is not as flexible a means of communication as in the middle-class. It is not as readily adapted to the subtleties of the particular situation, but consists more of a relatively small repertoire of stereotyped phrases and expressions which are used rather loosely without much effort to achieve a subtle correspondence between perception and verbal expression. Furthermore, much lower-class language consists of a kind of incidental "emotional" accompaniment to action here and now, whereas in contrast, middle-class language, rather than being a mere accompaniment to ongoing activity, serves more to represent things and events not immediately present. Thus middle-class language is more abstract and necessarily somewhat more flexible, detailed, and subtle in its descriptive aspects. In all social classes conversational language serves mainly as a social lubricant, but in the lower-class the expository function of language is relatively less prominent than in the middle-class. These differences are important for psychological development because of the intimate relationship between language and thought. It would be a mistake to think of language as merely a *vehicle* for thought; developmentally and functionally both are completely interdependent (Vigotsky, 1962).

One of the most thorough investigations of the relationship between reading readiness in first-grade children and patterns of parent-child interaction has been carried out by Esther Milner (1951). All of the children in her study were Negro, ranging on an index of social status from lower-lower to lower-upper class. A composite score from a number of reading readiness tests showed a correlation (Pearson *r*) of .86 with the social-class index. That is,

dividing the children into high and low groups on the basis of reading readiness resulted in about the same two groups as when they were divided on the basis of social class. Through interviews with the children and with their mothers a number of environmental differences between low and high scorers in reading readiness were discovered. Many of the differences seem to be directly related to verbal attainment. For example, it was found that the high-scoring children were surrounded by a richer verbal environment at home than the low-scoring children. More books were available to the high scorers, and they were read to by adults more than the low-scoring children. There also seemed to be more evidence of opportunities for emotionally positive interaction with the parents among the high scorers, and this often took place in a context favoring language development. For instance, mothers of low scorers indicated more frequently that as a rule they do not eat breakfast with their children or do not talk with the children during breakfast. The same was true for supper.

There appears to be a radically different atmosphere around the meal table from the child's point of view for the high scorers than for the low scorers. More frequently for the high scorers mealtime at home, particularly the first meal of the day, serves as a focus for total family interaction. Further, this interaction seems to be positive and permissive in emotional tone for these children and has a high verbal content—that is, the child is talked to by adults with mature speech patterns, and in turn he talks to them. The opposite situation apparently exists for the low scorers. There was, in fact, indication from the responses of some of these mothers that they actively discourage or prohibit their children's "chatter" and refuse to engage in conversation with them during meals; this prohibition is based on a belief that talking during meals is a "bad" practice. One low scorer's mother's response to "Did anyone talk to (child) while she was eating her meal?" was "I do not allow her to talk while she is eating; it is a bad habit." (Milner, 1951, page 109).

That much of the difference in reading readiness that Milner found between lower-

and middle-class children was due to the kinds of environmental factors she describes has been shown experimentally by introducing certain middle-class practices into lower-class homes and later comparing these children with those from other lower-class homes in a matched control group. Irwin (reported in McCandless, 1961, page 260), for example, had lower-class mothers read aloud to their children for at least 10 minutes a day from the age of one, a practice that is common in the middle-class but rare in the lower-class. A control group of similar mothers was given no such instructions. Measures of language development showed significant differences between the experimental and control groups in all phases of speech by 20 months of age.

Can a child's language level be changed by the age of entering nursery school or kindergarten? A study by Dawe (1942) suggests that it can be. Orphanage children ranging in age from 3 years 7 months to 6 years 10 months were given special speech and language training only on weekends for a total of 92 hours over a period of about $7\frac{1}{2}$ months. Compared with a well-matched control group, the experimental group showed a gain of 14 IQ points (their mean initial IQ was about 80). The language training, incidentally, did not consist of mere test coaching; the transfer of training was quite general and showed up in a variety of assessment procedures.

THE DEVELOPMENT OF VERBAL BEHAVIOR

The preceding discussion of verbal behavior in relation to social class has been conducted in quite gross and general terms. As long as we remain at this level of discussion, the significance of verbal behavior cannot be fully appreciated. A more thorough understanding of how verbal behavior develops and of how it affects other aspects of psychological development can be gained only through a more detailed and analytical approach.

This analysis can be facilitated by the use of a few simple S-R paradigms. First, it should be made clear that these paradigms do not represent psychological theories or models, and are not in any way intended as a description of what goes on in the brain when learning occurs. They are simply schemata for analyzing and classifying behavioral observations and types of experiments on learning.

The S-S paradigm has already been mentioned in connection with perceptual learning, which was conceived of as the formation of connections between various elements of sensory input and is thus represented as S-S.

Another basic form of learning, known as response integration, can be symbolized as R-R. Most forms of motor learning are good examples of this. Learning to walk, for instance, involves the integration of a large number of motor responses. To be sure, walking involves a good deal of sensory feedback, both from external cues and from proprioceptive and other internal sensations, but when the total act of walking has become perfected through practice, it depends largely upon the "playing-off" of a centrally integrated sequence of motor responses. It is this central integration that we symbolize as R-R. This integration of motor responses can be easily understood by anyone who has engaged extensively in any form of athletics involving complex motor skills or who plays a musical instrument, say the piano. The pianist who has memorized a piece of music later finds he cannot recall the notes unless he sits at the piano and begins to play. His "memory" of the composition seems to lie more in his motor behavior than in any symbolic representation of the music; he can play the piece at the piano even though at his desk he would be completely unable to write out a single bar of the score. And if he makes a mistake while playing, he cannot easily stop and start again at just any point. He usually has to go back to some "beginning" point in the music and continue from there. The sequence of integrated responses involved in playing seems to "unfold" without much conscious direction on the part of the player. Often, if he tries too hard to think of the notes in a difficult but well-practiced passage, he will be more apt to fumble. The same sort of thing is seen in athletic performance; once a complex motor action is underway, it becomes extremely difficult, or often impossible, to stop before the entire sequence has run off. This type of learning, like S-S learning, does not itself depend upon verbal or symbolic behavior. A good deal of verbal behavior, however, may involve such R-R connections. That is to say, vocal utterances tend to follow well-integrated sequences, which conform to the sequential aspects of our language. Thus, for example, it is utterly impossible for an adult to improvise totally nonsensical arrangements of words which do not markedly reflect the normal sequential properties of his own language.

Next, there is S-R learning, or the connection of stimuli with responses. A simple example would be Pavlov's dog salivating when the bell rings. The question of whether such learning takes place by sheer temporal contiguity of stimulus and response, or whether reinforcement is necessary for the formation of S-R connections, cannot be discussed here, and it is perhaps not a crucial issue for our present purpose. But we must introduce an elaboration of this S-R paradigm to represent those instances where a reinforcing stimulus (S_+) does, in fact, hasten and strengthen the formation of an S-R connection. This can be shown as follows: S-R (S_+), in the case of positive reinforcement or reward, and S-R (S_-), in the case of negative reinforcement or punishment. These forms of reward learning have been most thoroughly studied in animal psychology, which is not to say that such learning does not occur also in human subjects. Beyond an early age, however, simple S-R learning is rarely found in "pure" form; it is almost always accompanied by other response elements, usually

verbal. These are illustrated in some of the following paradigms.

Verbal learning begins with the child hearing words in connection with other stimuli in his environment. Words are at first just one of many kinds of auditory stimulation; through stimulus substitution the words come to evoke some of the same responses as do the objects with which they were associated; but since all of the stimulus elements in an object or situation that come to evoke a set of responses are not present when the word is heard alone, many of the response elements drop out or become very minimal in response to the word. Other response elements remain, however. These may consist of looking toward the object and of anticipatory movements involved in grasping or manipulating the object. There is also an affective side of this response; if the stimulus object is one which has been previously associated with affective arousal, such as the sight and sound of the parent, or touching a hot stove, or tasting a piece of candy, the words associated with these objects will also tend to arouse some of the same affective components.

In the first few months of life the child does not seem to distinguish vocal utterances from other auditory stimuli, and motor responses can be conditioned to both vocal and nonvocal sounds with about equal ease. By about one year of age, however, verbal stimuli (S_v) become much more potent than other forms of auditory stimulation. Responses can be conditioned some four times faster to words than to other, nonvocal sounds (Ervin and Miller, 1963, page 135). Therefore, at this age the acquisition of S_v-R connections begins to take place quite rapidly, and by two years of age the easiest kind of learning for the child is to learn to recognize the names of things. It would be interesting to speculate on the reasons for this prepotency of verbal stimuli. One explanation probably lies in the fact that verbal stimuli are more consistently associated with other affect-arousing stimuli, namely, the parents. The vocal sounds associated with parental attentions become singled out, so to speak, as the figure against a background of other sounds.

S_v-R learning is soon followed, usually during the child's second and third years, by S-V learning, in which the child makes his own verbal responses (V) to the stimuli (S) which had formerly been associated with their verbal labels as spoken by others (S_vR). The child's own verbal responses (V) gradually come to approximate the corresponding auditory model, that is, the parent's speech. Between two and three years of age the child constantly points to objects (S), hears their verbal labels (S_v) from the parents, and tries to imitate these sounds in his own vocal utterances (V). It is at this stage that a child begins to learn that certain discreet sounds or words are associated with specific objects and acts. Indeed, Piaget has suggested that words are an intrinsic part of objects to very young children. It is during this "labeling" period, as we shall call it, that some very important social class differences may exert their effects on verbal learning. Lower-class parents, it has been observed, engage in very little of this naming or "labeling" play with their children. Two main consequences of this have been noted: first of all, there results a retardation of S_v-R learning, due to the fact that the parents' verbal labels are less frequently associated with other stimuli in the environment; and thus S-V learning is also retarded, with the effect that the child will have less tendency to make verbal responses to the stimuli in its environment. Secondly, it has been noticed by first-grade teachers of lower-class children that such children seem to have greater difficulty than do middle-class children in discriminating and understanding isolated words; thus the lower-class child may reach school age before he begins to learn what the middle-class child has already acquired long before in his preschool years: learning how to associate single spoken words with objects, pictures of objects, or with printed words. These associations are made more

difficult for the lower-class child by the fact that many of these tasks require that the spoken words be identified out of the context of continuous speech. That words are discrete labels for things seems to be better known by the middle-class child entering first grade than by the lower-class child. Much of this knowledge is gained in the parent-child interaction, as, for example, when the parent looks at a picture book with the child, points to each picture while saying its name, and reinforces the child's behavior with some show of approval when he utters similar sounds. Apparently a great amount of this kind of learning takes place in middle-class homes, while it seems to take place hardly at all among lower-class families. We shall see shortly why this labeling behavior is so important for other kinds of learning.

The next developmental stage of learning is characterized by the emergence of voluntary behavior, that is, overt behavior which is under the child's own verbal control. It is thus represented as V-R, or the connection of verbal responses (whether overt or covert) with other motor behavior. Psychologically it is a rather large step from S-V to V-R learning. The infant's motor behavior is mostly involuntary reflex action. Later the child's motor behavior shows the effects of R-R, S-R, and S_v-R learning. It is not until much later, usually between 3 and 4 years of age, that we see clear evidence of the V-R control of behavior. Once V-R patterns are developed, they constitute, in conjunction with S-V learning, what we shall call the S-V-R- paradigm. It is when this stage is reached that we recognize fully human learning, and the ontogenetic psychological development from "animal" to "man" is, in all essentials, complete. Beyond the age of six or seven, in normal middle-class children, it is doubtful if we see many forms of learning in school that are not represented by the S-V-R paradigm. (The training of specific perceptual or motor skills such as might be involved in music, art, or athletic performance are possible exceptions.) By this stage, the child much of the time is no longer responding directly and solely to his physical environment; the environmental stimuli (S) give rise to verbal responses (V), either overtly or covertly, which in turn govern the overt motor response (R). Psychologically, one of the big differences between a young child and an adult, or between a lower animal and a human beyond the age of six or seven, can be represented as the difference between S-R and S-V-R.

An addition should be made to this paradigm, as follows: S-V-R-V_c; the V_c represents a verbal confirming response or "feedback." Overt behavior often results in certain environmental effects which, in terms of the person's needs or purposes, are desirable (S_+) and hence reinforcing, or they are undesirable (S_-) and hence negatively reinforcing or punishing. Adjusting the Hot and Cold faucets in the shower is a simple example of behavior with rather immediate environmental consequences. The person is able to respond verbally to these environmental consequences of his own behavior and this can be called a verbal confirmatory response (V_c). This verbal confirmation or "feedback" can have much the same effect on the speed of acquisition of S-R or S-V-R connections as the environmental consequent itself would have.

This capacity for self-reinforcement or symbolic reinforcement is extremely limited in lower animals, as it is in very young children. To establish S-R connections in an animal, it is usually necessary to follow the response to be learned by some form of primary reinforcement or reward, that is, reinforcement which has direct physiological consequences, such as biological need-reduction, pain-reduction, or some form of innately "pleasurable" stimulation. The V_c response is also more than merely a form of secondary reinforcement. A secondary reinforcer is a previously neutral stimulus which has gained reinforcing power through temporal contiguity with a primary or biologically relevant reinforcer. But secondary

reinforcers are known to extinguish very rapidly, at least in animals. This is not the case, however, with the verbal confirmatory response, V_c. It has the effect of strengthening behavior which has "desirable" environmental consequences even though the V_c itself does not have any primary reinforcing properties in the biological sense. The V_c response is most often covert, especially in adults, and it may even be quite "unconscious." It consists, in effect, of saying to oneself "Good!" or "That's right!" or "Wrong!"

The existence of the covert V_c response has been experimentally demonstrated in children by Russian psychologists (reported by Razran, 1959). In one experiment, for example, an autonomic conditioned response first was formed to the word "Right." Then the children were given a set of arithmetic problems, and it was found that when a child solved a problem correctly, the autonomic response previously conditioned to the word "Right" would occur. In other words, each time the child performed correctly, he confirmed or reinforced his own answer with some subvocal, or perhaps even unconscious, equivalent of the verbal response "Right." In another experiment a previously established conditioned response to the word "ten" occurred when the child was given arithmetic problems that resulted in the answer "ten." Thus, it appears that beyond a certain age the child himself—or rather his verbal behavior—may become his most important source of immediate reinforcement. Much more, however, remains to be learned about this form of self-confirmatory behavior and its developmental aspects; this is one of the important tasks of future research.

Then, words also become linked to words, and thus: V-V. The word association experiment in which the subject is presented with a stimulus word and is asked to respond as quickly as possible with the first word that comes to mind, is a good illustration of the existence of V-V connections. There is a great deal of communality among subjects from similar cultural backgrounds in their first two or three associations to a word; for example, *black-white, table-chair, man-woman*, etc. As a result of these connections between verbal responses, the S-V-R paradigm may be elaborated to S-V-V-R; there is ample experimental evidence that under certain conditions such chains of verbal mediators do, in fact, play an important role in learning.

Since two or more words which may not be directly associated with one another may be associated with a third word, one more type of paradigm must be described:

This diagram makes it apparent that verbal associations exist in hierarchical arrangement. In this illustration there are two words associated with each other, and both are associated with a higher-order, more general, word; and there is another word which is not associated with the first two, except indirectly through its association with the higher-order word. An example would be the words *table, chair,* and *bed. Table* and *chair* are strong associates of one another, but neither is strongly associated with *bed.* All three, however, are associated with the word *furniture.* Here, obviously, is a concept in its most rudimentary form.

Now the reader must imagine for himself extensive hierarchical networks elaborated along these lines. It is into such "verbal networks," which exist in older children and adults, that environmental stimuli, both verbal and non-verbal, enter and ramify. In terms of verbal learning theory, the adult psyche may be pictured as consisting, in part, of this extensive hierarchical network of verbal associations. A great deal of what we think of as intelligence, or as verbal ability, or learning ability, can be thought of in terms of the extensiveness and complexity of this verbal network and of the strength of the interconnections between its

elements. All of these connections between various verbal elements are by no means of equal strength. Word association tests and other related techniques can be used to roughly map out the structure of the network and the relative strengths of the connections between its elements. The relative strengths of the various associations determine the channels along which semantic generalization occurs when stimuli enter the network via any given element or set of elements. The strength and richness of the connections between elements at different levels of the hierarchy determine to a large degree the ease and speed of concept attainment and the person's level of ability for conceptual and abstract thinking. This vast verbal network, as it exists in the normal adult, is almost awesome to contemplate; thorough exploration of it is still far from an accomplishment, although in recent years psychologists have increasingly devoted their attentions to it. . . .

SYNTACTICAL MEDIATION

As a child matures, an increasingly prominent aspect of his verbal behavior is the degree to which it corresponds to the syntactical structure of his language. The structure of the language becomes incorporated as part of the underlying processes governing the individual's verbal behavior. The degree of subtlety, diversity, and complexity of syntactical structure of the verbal environment will determine the nature of the syntactical processes incorporated by the developing child. The extent to which these structures become incorporated is a function of the frequency with which they are experienced in the environment, the degree to which the social environment reinforces their overt manifestation, and the individual's basic capacity for learning. In view of the points made earlier concerning social class differences in spoken language, one would expect that somewhat different syntactical structures are incorporated by individuals according to their social class background.

The key question, however, is whether the tendency for syntactical verbal behavior is of any psychological importance to learning and intellectual ability. We now have considerable evidence that it is of great importance, but the specific mechanisms through which it exerts its facilitative effect on learning are still obscure. The problem is currently under investigation in our laboratory.

Syntactical mediation is one of the most powerful of all variables affecting the speed of paired-associate learning. That is, when pairs of items to be associated are imbedded in some syntactical structure, such as a sentence, the association is made almost at once, without the necessity of many repeated learning trials. Since subjects in paired-associate experiments are usually college students who have strong tendencies spontaneously to bring syntactical mediators to bear on the learning task, it is difficult to use them as experimental subjects when the variable we wish to control is syntactical mediation. Verbal mediational tendencies cannot be suppressed in bright college students.

Therefore, in our research on this problem we have used as subjects young children and mentally retarded adults, who show little or no spontaneous tendencies to verbally mediate their learning. A typical experiment (e.g., Jensen and Rohwer, 1963a, 1963b) consisted of having retarded subjects (IQs 50–60) learn a list of eight paired-associates composed of pictures of common objects, e.g., *shoe-clock, telephone-hammer, ball-house*, etc. The control group of subjects was asked only to name each picture on the first trial and on subsequent trials they learned by the usual anticipation method. When the pairs were presented for the first time to the mediation group, the experimenter stated a sentence containing each pair of items, e.g., "I threw the SHOE at the CLOCK," "I smashed the TELEPHONE with the HAMMER," etc. After this initial

trial, the mediation group was given subsequent trials the same as the control group, without any further verbalization from the experimenter. The result was that the mediation group learned, on the average twice as fast as the control group and made only one-fifth as many errors.

This experiment was repeated under conditions that required the retarded subjects to generate their own mediators, and again the great facilitative effect of such mediation was manifested. When retarded adults were compared on this task with fourth graders of the same mental age, it was found that the retardates were about 3 to 4 times slower than the normal children in learning, both under mediated and nonmediated conditions, which indicates that this task more nearly reflects IQ then mental age. The children also benefited markedly from the mediation instructions.

To investigate the effectiveness of this form of syntactical mediation as a function of age, Jensen and Rohwer (in press) have given a paired-associate task with and without mediation instructions to groups of children from kindergarten to the twelfth grade. The children were matched for IQ and social class over all grade levels. In the mediation condition subjects were always instructed to make up their own mediators. The control group learned by the usual method of anticipation, without any instructions from the experimenter to form verbal mediators. The items to be associated were again pairs of pictures of familiar objects.

Comparing the performance of the mediation group with that of the control group, it was found that the effectiveness of the mediation instructions was relatively slight at kindergarten age and increased steadily up to the sixth grade, after which it progressively decreased up to the twelfth grade. A reasonable interpretation of this finding is that the ability for syntactical mediation is not sufficiently developed at kindergarten age to be of much benefit, but rapidly increases thereafter with age. But at the same time there is an increase with age

In the subjects' spontaneous use of verbal mediation, so that in older subjects the mediation instructions add little if anything to what the subject would do on his own, and thus the difference between the mediation and control groups decreases.

Also, it was noted that the younger children made up syntactically less varied and complex mediators. Many kindergarteners, for example, could only make up noun phrases, such as "the HAT and the TABLE." Complete, but simple, sentences are common by the second grade, with a corresponding increase in facilitation of learning. And with increasing age the mediators seem to become syntactically more sophisticated.

In order to identify more precisely the nature of these syntactical variables involved in facilitation of paired-associate learning, Rohwer (1964) controlled syntactic structure experimentally by providing 244 sixth-grade children with various mediational contexts for the eight paired-associates they were required to learn. The total design of the experiment was quite complex, but essentially what Rohwer did was to imbed the pairs (e.g., HAT-COW) in a phrase or sentence on only the pretrial in all conditions (except the control group, which was given no verbal mediator). Three types of mediational context were used: (i) a noun phrase in which the two items of the pair were connected by a conjunction (e.g., "the HAT *and* the COW)"; (ii) a prepositional phrase in which the items were connected by a preposition and adjectives were added to enlarge the context (e.g., "the dirty HAT *on* the sleeping COW"). The control group on the pretrial had to read single random consonant letters in place of the words (e.g., "x HAT b j COW") which was intended to force the control subjects to take the same amount of time on the pretrial and also to inhibit to some extent their spontaneous formation of mediators.

Figure 3-2 shows the learning curve in the first six trails for the various conditions. The differences, which are highly significant, show clearly that different syntactical structures, representing different parts of speech and different degrees of complexity, have different degrees of power in facilitating learning. The largest difference in "connective power" is that between conjunctions and prepositions.

Another feature of Rohwer's experiment was a condition which included all the same words as the previously described mediators, but presented in a nonsyntactical arrangement; that is, they did not correspond to normal English word order. Thus, the phrase "the dirty HAT on the sleeping COW" was presented in the nonsyntactical condition as "on sleeping HAT the dirty the cow." It was found that when the words were not in normal syntactical order they had no facilitating effect on paired-associate learning. The learning curve for the nonsyntactical condition did not differ appreciably from that of the control condition shown in Figure 3-2.

Still another variation of the experiment was to substitute nonsense paralogs, which sound like words, for the words in the mediational phrases. Thus, "the dirty HAT rested quietly on the sleeping COW," was transformed in the nonsense condition to "sep fenty HAT fluted tofenly um sep shugling COW." As in the nonsyntactical condition, there was no facilitation of learning. The performance of the nonsense group was not significantly distinguishable from that of the control group.

A similar experiment was performed by Davidson (in press), with certain variations of additional interest. Davidson used 60 second-graders. The 20 paired-associates, consisting of pairs of pictures of common objects, were projected on a screen at a 6 sec. rate for the study trial. This was immediately followed by the test trial, which consisted of presenting only the stimulus member with each pair. The subjects were provided with a 20-page booklet; each page contained pictures of all 20 response items. The subjects responded by encircling what they thought was the correct associate of each stimulus item presented on the screen

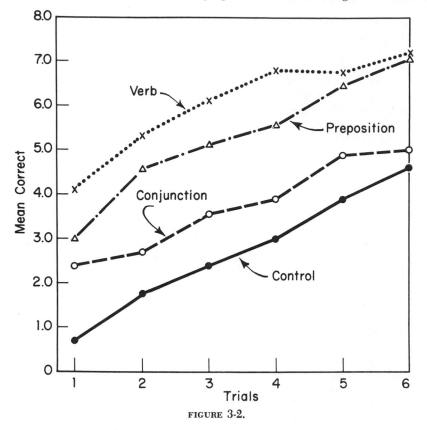

FIGURE 3-2.

during the test trial. This method eliminates the factor of response learning per se, and gets at only the associative aspect of paired-associate learning. The answer sheets were collected, new ones distributed, and a second study trial was given, followed by a second test trial.

All subjects were given a pretest, as described above, with the only instructions from the experimenter being that "these pictures always go together," along with directions for marking the answer sheets, etc. The distribution of learning scores (number of correct responses on the two test trials) was cut at the median to divide the subjects into High and Low scorers in paired-associate learning ability.

These subjects were then divided into five groups to receive different mediation instructions. Aside from the experimenter's

different verbalizations on the first study trial only, the procedure was essentially the same as for the pretest, although a different set of pictures was used. The five experimental conditions were as follows: A—same as pretest condition, B—experimenter named the pictures as they were presented (e.g., HAT-TABLE), C—named pictures jointed by meaningful preposition (e.g., HAT *on* TABLE), D—nàmed pictures put into complete sentence containing same preposition as in the condition C, E—same sentence as D, but the objects were shown together in the same picture, e.g., a picture of the HAT actually lying on the TABLE. The second study trial was the same for all subjects and corresponded to condition A, that is, no verbalization from the experimenter.

Figure 3-3 shows the mean correct responses in the two test trials for the High and Low pretest scorers on each of the five experimental conditions. Two effects are highly significant statistically: (i) The type of verbalization caused large differences in learning paired-associates. Practically all of this difference is between mere naming of the items and joining them by a preposition. Additional verbalization and the imagery stimulated by presenting the objects combined in one picture added a negligible increment to the subjects' performance.

One might wonder if the more complex verbalization would be relatively more facilitating for somewhat older children, who might show a greater difference between a prepositional mediator and a complete sentence. This possibility is suggested by Rohwer's data on sixth graders, although the conditions of his experiment were sufficiently different from Davidson's as to vitiate any such comparison.

(ii) The other highly significant effect is the overall difference between High and Low pretest scorers, which indicates that the paired-associate task has a good deal of reliability, even when based on only two trials in a group testing procedure.

While the interaction between groups and conditions is not significant, certain features of the curves of the two groups are in line with expectation. For example, naming results in slight improvement for Low scorers but results in a slight decrement for High scorers. The reason for this is probably that fewer Low scorers are naming spontaneously and are thus facilitated by being given the names. The High scorers, on the other hand, tend to name spontaneously, and if their own naming response is different from the experimenter's, they would suffer some interference. To check this notion, subjects were later asked to name the objects, and it was found on one item, for example, that many of the subjects said "gun" when the experimenter's verbal-

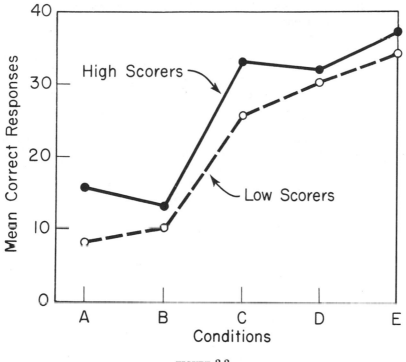

FIGURE 3-3.

ization was "rifle," a more precise label for the picture.

Also, it was originally hypothesized that the more complex verbal mediator would increasingly wipe out the differences between High and Low scorers, but as is apparent in Figure 3-3, there is no clear trend in this respect.

Both the Rohwer and Davidson experiments leave no doubt of the powerful effects of syntactical mediation in facilitating learning. What now needs to be found out is the degree to which subjects from different social classes differ in kinds of syntactical mediators they bring to a learning situation. It is known, for example, that actual objects elicit somewhat different mediators than do pictures of the objects, and pictures elicit different responses than do the mere names of the objects (Otto, 1962). And we have found that paired-associate learning of object pairs is easier than of picture pairs (e.g., Jensen and Rohwer, 1963a). In general, the greater the cue reduction in the stimulus terms, the fewer are the mediating associations elicited, and the more difficult is the paired-associate learning. In view of this, it is interesting that Semler and Iscoe (1963) found greater differences between lower-class Negro children and somewhat higher status white children in paired-associate learning when the pairs consisted of pictures than when they consisted of actual objects.

For the benefit of those who might complain that paired-associate learning does not warrant so much attention because it is a laboratory method with seemingly little relevance to the tasks of education, let it be pointed out that many forms of school learning are essentially paired-associate learning—graphemes-phonemes pictures-words, spoken words-written words, English words-foreign words, etc. Furthermore, performance on paired-associate learning is significantly related to such important forms of school learning as reading ability, independently of IQ (Otto, 1961). In combination with other laboratory procedures (many of which, like the paired-associate technique, can be adapted to group administration) the paired-associate paradigm can be a valuable analytical method in the study of individual and group differences in learning ability.

Other psycholinguistic methods are also available for studying individual differences in the degree to which syntactical structure has been incorporated by an individual. One method, known as the "cloze" procedure consists of deleting every *n*th word in a passage of normal English and having the subject fill in the blanks with what he thinks are the most appropriate words. Another method consists of comparing the rates of learning nonsense syllables which do or do not correspond to the syntactical structure of the language, such as learning "the maff vlems oothly um the glax nerfs," as compared with the less syntactical "maff vlems ooth um glax nerf." Though the latter phrase has fewer syllables, it is considerably more difficult to memorize because of its lack of syntactical resemblance to English. A person for whom the learning rates of these two types of materials did not differ appreciably probably has not incorporated the syntactical structure of the English language to any strong degree. We would predict that these measures would reflect social class differences, but tests of such hypotheses have not yet been made.

REFERENCES

Bernstein, B. Language and social class. *Brit. J. Sociol.*, 1960, 11, 271–276.

Brodbeck, A. J., and O. C. Irwin. The speech behavior of infants without families. *Child Develpm.*, 1946, 17, 145–156.

Carroll, J. B. Language development. In C. W. Harris (Ed.), *Encyclopedia educational research.* (3d ed.) New York: Macmillan, 1960. Pp. 744–752.

Davidson, R. E. Mnemonic mediation and ability in paired-associate learning. *J. educ. Psychol.* (in press).

Ervin, Susan M., and W. R. Miller. Language

development. In H. W. Stevenson (Ed.), *Child psychology*. Chicago: National Society for the Study of Education, 1963. Pp. 108–143.

Jensen, A. R., and W. D. Rohwer, Jr. The effect of verbal mediation on the learning and retention of paired-associates by retarded adults. *Amer. J. ment. Defic.*, 1963a, **68**, 80–84.

Jensen, A. R., and W. D. Rohwer, Jr. Verbal mediation in paired-associate and serial learning. *J. verb. Learn. verb. Behav.*, 1963b, **1**, 346–352.

Jensen, A. R., and W. D. Rohwer, Jr. Syntactical mediation of serial and paired-associate learning as a function of age. *Child Develpm.*, (in press, a).

Jensen, A. R., and W. D., Rohwer, Jr. What is learned in serial learning? *J. verb. learn. verb. Behav.* (in press, b).

Koch, Helen. The relation of primary mental abilities in five and six year olds to sex and characteristics of his siblings. *Child Develpm.*, 1954, **25**, 209–223.

McCandless, B. R. *Children and adolescents*. New York: Holt, Rinehart and Winston, 1961.

Milner, Esther. A study of the relationship between reading readiness in grade one school children and patterns of parent-child interaction. *Child Develpm.*, 1951, **22**, 95–112.

Otto, W. The acquisition and retention of paired associates by good, average, and poor readers. *J. educ. Psychol.*, 1961, **52**, 241–248.

Otto, W. No differential effects of verbal and pictorial representations of stimuli upon responses evolved. *J. verb. learn. verb. Behav.*, 1962, **1**, 192–196.

Razran, G. Soviet psychology and psychophysiology. *Behav. Sci.*, 1959, **4**, 35–48.

Rheingold, Harriet, and Nancy Bayley. The later effects of an experimental modification of mothering. *Child Develpm.*, 1959, **30**, 363–372.

Rohwer, W. D., Jr. The verbal facilitation of paired-associate learning. Unpublished doctoral dissertation, University of California, 1964.

Semler, I. J., and I. Iscoe. Comparative and developmental study of the learning abilities of Negro and white children under four conditions. *J. educ. Psychol.*, 1963, **54**, 38–44.

The Intellectual Development of Slum Children: Some Preliminary Findings

VERA P. JOHN

The traditional normative approach in the investigations of the cognitive life of children is being supplanted by new theory and new techniques. For example, the study by Kagan and Moss (1962) on styles of conceptualization has shown that some children, as well as adults, exhibit a stable approach to a great variety of cognitive tasks. A major value of their work lies in the stress they place on interrelationships among discrete behaviors characteristic of the growing organism. In a longitudinal study of infants, Thomas, Birch, and Chess (1961), working toward a similar goal, are seeking to discover stable primary patterns of reactivity through observation of the child up to and including his first years in school. These studies, though derived from theoretical frameworks differing from that of Piaget (1954), still resemble his work in deriving explanatory concepts from observed behavior.

However, these studies, as well as the majority of current research, employ readily available subjects, that is, newborn infants

Reprinted with permission of the author and publisher, *American Journal of Orthopsychiatry*, 1963, **33**, 813–822.

of professional colleagues or children who attend schools affiliated with universities. This is one reason why there is as yet little knowledge about the subject of this paper, developmental studies of the urban slum child. His methods of discovering his world, classifying information and manipulating objects or people have hardly been studied.

It is this child, however, who presents the most severe and abiding challenge to the nation's educators; a challenge not only in terms of human tragedy, as Conant (1961) reports in discussing the high percentage of boys out of school and out of work between the ages of 16 and 21, but in terms of the social and political health of the metropolis.

The Institute for Developmental Studies, whence this paper originates, is physically situated on the edge of a slum. The life of the children in this neighborhood differs from the life of the college-town subjects of typical developmental studies. Their play, their toys, the noises with which they live, the texture of their existence is not familiar to most research workers. An immediate problem facing an investigator is the selection of measures to use when assessing these children. How valid are traditional psychological tests for this purpose? Riessman (1962) views a test as deeply affected by the social context in which it is given. Similarly, the classroom behavior and achievement of slum children, the traditional criterion variables for studies of intelligence, may be evaluated inappropriately by psychologists and teachers.

In our current research, the impact of the early social environment on the patterning of intellectual skills in young children is being examined within a program that encompasses the study of elementary school children of varying social class and ethnic backgrounds. The aim of this program is to ascertain those patterns of linguistic and cognitive behavior that are characterized by internal consistency and are related to the socio-economic environment of the subjects. To focus primarily on the influence of the social environment on intellectual development, it was advantageous to compare groups of children from a single subculture. Therefore, the subjects of this study were Negro children of various social classes. Two aspects of the intellectual development of these children will be discussed: certain features of verbal behavior, such as the use of descriptive and integrative language, and the use of language as a conceptual tool, as in classificatory behavior.

VERBAL BEHAVIOR

Several studies show that children from lower-class backgrounds rely on shorter sentences in their speech than do their middle-class age-mates (John and Deutsch, 1960). They have a more limited vocabulary and poorer articulation. Investigators have hypothesized that these differences are partially due to the more restricted nature of the environment in which children from lower-class homes are raised. Though the findings are consistent from investigator to investigator, the aspects of language behavior chosen for study have usually not been derived from a theoretical approach to language or cognition.

In these studies we have delineated three major levels of language behavior: labeling, relating and categorizing. A multilevel system of language analysis is useful theoretically and methodologically. However, processes characteristic of one level of verbal behavior may also operate, though to a more limited extent, at another level of language. Language and nonlanguage approaches are continuously integrated in the child's attempts to deal with his environment. The social scientist must impose units of observation and analysis upon ongoing behavior and his methods of "cutting the pie" may occasionally seem forced. Hence, the distinction between verbal behavior and classificatory behavior may appear arbitrary.

Labeling is similar to morphological

analysis, in linguistic terms. When the child first learns to speak, he masters more or less precise relationships between perceived phenomena and their labels. This acquisition is both a receptive and expressive process. On the one hand the child is exposed to the word and its referent; subsequently, his own labeling actions become overt and these efforts receive social reinforcement.

Whereas motor exploration can be perfected by a child on his own, language as an effective internal process can only be learned from others. If the infant is to learn the skill of words, he needs the presence and active assistance of another speaker. Reliance upon language as a means of effective communication as well as cognitive exploration is particularly prevalent in the small, nuclear middle-class home. The lower-class child, on the other hand, is surrounded by many faces and cared for by many hands. He, too, experiences the hearing of a word and the seeing of an object, but his own first attempts at talking may go unrecognized.

Opportunities to hear simple labels repetitively are abundant in most normal environments. The names of foods, furniture and colors are repeated thousands of times in the hearing of the young child. Thus reinforcement for his own attempts at labeling may be of minimal importance for the child when faced with these "referents." The corrective feedback offered to the much-listened-to child gives him an opportunity to experiment with strategies of language behavior. He learns under what circumstances people listen to him, how he can attract attention, and hold it—what is easily understood. Thus, the child reared in a verbally rich environment, surrounded by adults who are responsive to his speech, can learn while rather young how to internalize the role of the speaker as well as the listener.

Measures of Labeling

The empirical findings to be reported in this paper have been drawn from a large ongoing study of the verbal skills, intellectual performance and motivational approaches of 250 school children from various neighborhoods in Metropolitan New York. Only some of the verbal and cognitive tasks drawn from the battery of the verbal survey will be discussed.

At this preliminary stage of the research, two questions seemed worth exploring: (a) Are relatively small differences in the socioeconomic environment of young Negro children reflected in their performance on certain selected tasks, and (b) is there a widening of socioeconomic differences as reflected in test performance when fifth-grade Negro children are compared with first-grade Negro children?

The Peabody Picture Vocabulary Test (PPVT) was used to measure receptive vocabulary and the WISC vocabulary scale to measure expressive vocabulary.

A third test of labeling behavior, designed by the author for this study, is aimed at testing two different processes in overt naming, using the same set of stimuli. In this "Verbal Identification Test," the children were first asked to *enumerate* what they saw on stimulus cards depicting simple events or groups of objects; then, the pictures were shown again and they were asked to give the most appropriate "title" for each picture, that is, to *integrate* the various parts of the picture. The first major hypothesis to be tested was that lower-class and middle-class children would differ little, if at all, in their enumerations, but they would manifest class differences in labeling tasks that require integrating.

Measures of Relating

Besides labeling and enumerating, the young child also masters intraverbal relationships in his attempts to approximate language as he hears it. The second level of this language model is comparable to syntactical analysis, in linguistic terms. At this level the child learns to chain responses, just as he had learned earlier to fit objects together into meaningful wholes, during the sensory-motor stage of intellectual development as described by Piaget (1954).

The Word Association Test, a method of eliciting behavior at the relating level, was utilized to study the patterns of associations children make to stimulus words. Susan Ervin (1957) has shown that responses to stimulus words in an association task can be analyzed by means of form-classes, that is, the similarity between the grammatical category of stimulus and response. In the process of word acquisition, children learn to group words into some kind of "filing system." Thus, even though two nouns seldom, if ever, follow each other in a spoken sentence, children gradually learn that they are functionally equivalent. Younger children are likely to give completion (or phrase) responses when participating in a word association experiment. The responses of older children are more adult-like, in that they associate noun with noun, verb with verb. In addition, children for whom the task of word association is difficult are expected to have longer latencies. Thus, the Word Association Test offers a highly sensitive, albeit indirect, measure of language socialization.

The second hypothesis tested in this study was that middle-class children would show a higher percentage of responses in the same form-class as the stimulus words and shorter latencies in this task than their lower-class age-mates. In this fashion, the middle-class child's behavior is more closely modeled after that of the adult, and may thus constitute a measure of the absorption of adult language patterns.

CLASSIFICATORY BEHAVIOR

The language-conceptual level specified in these studies relates to how the speaking organism uses language to categorize objects, people and events in his environment. Whereas labeling can be defined as the relationship between word and object

(or referent), relating deals with intraverbal relationships. However, classifying cannot be adequately defined by a single phrase. Classificatory behavior involves covert as well as internal language, a fact which greatly handicaps scientific inquiry into these processes.

Much of the behavior of the young child exploring his world is perceptual and motor. Words may be one of the primary and perhaps most essential methods by which the child pools his varied experiences in order to process incoming stimuli effectively. Luria (1959) has described in detail the types of cognitive deficit exhibited by speech-retarded children (twins). One of their difficulties is in relating the present to the future. Lower-class children, due to their relative poverty of language, may also experience difficulties when pooling and processing varied experiences.

Measures of Classification

Only a most limited account is presented here of the study of classificatory behavior in children, including the role of language in classification. The writer and co-workers designed a Concept Sorting task that consists of 16 cards. These pictorial stimuli can be grouped into functional pairs (sailor and boat, for instance) or in logically consistent piles or categories of four cards each (means of transportation, animals). After the child has finished sorting the cards into piles, the examiner elicits a verbal rationale about each sort from the child.

The third hypothesis in this study was that lower-class children would classify test stimuli according to functional criteria, and thus would sort into a greater number of piles of fewer cards each than middle-class children. Children high in verbal skills are more likely to group stimuli into categories distinguished by class names. The lower-class (and verbally less experienced) child was expected, even if he did sort cards according to concepts, to state the underlying concept indirectly, "they all have legs," instead of explicitly, "they are all animals."

Three dimensions of verbal and classificatory behavior have been emphasized as most likely to be affected by the social experience of the young child: (1) verbal behavior of the integrative type, as measured by part 2 of the Verbal Identification Test; (2) word associations, in which a higher percentage of form-class responses and shorter latencies were expected to be given by children from the more advantaged social groups; and (3) sorting behavior, in which middle-class children were likely to give concept-sorts accompanied by explicit verbalizations of the rationale for classifying.

COMPARISON OF THREE GROUPS OF NEGRO CHILDREN

For this preliminary report, a limited number of language and conceptual tasks likely to reflect differences in the socio-economic environment of young children have been chosen for a comparison of the performance of three groups of Negro children in verbal and classificatory tasks.

Subjects

For these comparisons, three groups of Negro children have been chosen from the larger verbal survey population. These children can be grossly labeled as lower-lower class (Class I, in this report), upper-lower class (Class II), and middle-class (Class III children). Sixty-nine of the subjects in this study are enrolled in the first grade, while 105 children are currently attending fifth grade.

The Index of Social Class developed at the Institute was used to categorize the subjects into these three social groupings. This Index is an appropriately weighted composite measure of the occupational status of the main breadwinner (akin to the Empey Scale of Occupational Prestige), education of the main breadwinner and the person-to-room ratio of the family. The weights assigned to the indicators are derived from a regression equation based on the degree of intercorrelation among these three variables. The information necessary to classify a child into one of the three social-class categories is elicited from the children being tested, and further verified by questionnaires mailed to the parents. Space does not permit us to describe in greater detail the very careful process by which these ratings have been calculated.

The parent of the Class I Negro child of this study is likely to be an unskilled worker with approximately nine years of schooling. Few of the mothers work, and many of the families have children of all ages. The main breadwinner in the Class II family is likely to be a semiskilled worker, such as a truck driver, who has attended but not always graduated from high school. Many of the mothers in this socioeconomic class work, and the families tend to be smaller. Perhaps the most striking difference between these two groups of children is in the condition of their housing. The Class I child lives in an apartment nearly twice as crowded as the Class II child. The occupation of mothers among the Class III children of this study is likely to be as high or higher than that of the fathers. Most of the parents attended college, though many of them did not graduate. The fathers tend to be civil servants and owners of small businesses, while the mothers are trained nurses and teachers. The father is absent in nearly one-third of the Class I and Class II Negro families in this study, but this is true of only 4 per cent of the Class III Negro families. Crowding, then, seems to be a psychologically significant difference between lower-lower and upper-lower class families; the intactness of the family and the higher level of education of the parents seems most to differentiate the middle-class Negro families from the lower-class families.

TABLE 3-1

Performance of Negro Children on Labeling Tasks: Analyses of Variance

	Grade 1: Socioeconomic status					Grade 5: Socioeconomic status				
	I (n = 27)	II (n = 23)	III (n = 19)	F (df = 2, 66)	P	I (n = 30)	II (n = 46)	III (n = 29)	F (df = 2, 102)	P
P.P.V.T.										
Mean	57.5	55.3	62.8	2.99	N.S.		P.P.V.T. not administered			
S.D.	7.9	13.9	10.9							
Verbal Ident.										
(a) Enumeration										
Mean	53.9	51.4	59.9	1.57	N.S.	64.3	69.5	71.2	1.63	N.S.
S.D.	15.6	14.6	15.8			16.7	14.6	17.5		
(b) Integration										
Mean	45.5	47.7	54.5	2.50	N.S.	63.6	67.4	69.2	4.16	<.05
S.D.	11.9	15.9	12.4			7.5	8.8	5.2		
Lorge-Thorndike (IQ scores)										
Mean	95.4	99.6	103.0	1.43	N.S.	88.6	97.5	100.0	6.14	<.01
S.D.	12.6	13.6	14.2			13.4	13.7	13.0		
	(n = 25)	(n = 25)	(n = 16)	(df = 2, 63)		(n = 31)	(n = 32)	(n = 15)	(df = 2, 75)	
WISC Vocabulary										
Mean	11.6	15.3	14.9	2.75	N.S.	26.1	30.2	33.7	4.82	<.025
S.D.	5.3	6.6	6.2			8.4	8.7	6.5		

RESULTS

The performances of the three classes of children were compared on measures of receptive and expressive labeling. Table 3-1 presents the findings at this first level of language behavior. We predicted that these children would differ more in verbal behavior, which requires integrative language, than in descriptive language. There are no statistically significant differences at this level of behavior among first-grade children, though the trends are in the predicted direction. The large intragroup variability and the smaller number of children at this age level may be responsible for this lack of statistical significance. The most interesting finding revealed by these data is this: The performance of the fifth-grade middle-class Negro children is significantly better on the integrative part of the Verbal Identification Test, whereas there are no statistically significant differences on the enumeration part. By requiring the child to perform two different types of labeling with the same set of pictures, the psychological processes involved in the relatively passive acquisition of overlearned responses elicited in the first part of the Verbal Identification Test are contrasted with the process of language production requiring summarizing and abstracting elicited in the second part.

One may argue that our findings merely substantiate trends revealed by the Lorge-Thorndike Intelligence Test, namely, that fifth-grade children, particularly Class I children, perform significantly worse on tasks requiring "intelligence." The results on the Verbal Identification Test may yield some insight into what is involved in performing well on an intelligence test. The middle-class children seem to have mastered the skill of choosing the most appropriate single response when presented with a complex task, while their behavior is similar to that of their poorer age-mates when they are required to enumerate and describe.

That differences among older children of differing socioeconomic backgrounds are wider than those among younger children has often been attributed to the increasing complexity of tasks designed for children in higher grades. It is interesting that, in these data, significant class differences are found with the younger children using the identical tests. It may be that the emergence of statistically significant differences among these groups is related less to the increase in the absolute differences in performance than to the decrease in intragroup variability. The highly uniform performance of the fifth-grade Negro children of Class III is particularly striking. This stabilization of responses within a group might reflect the action of cumulative, common social influences on these children. The widening of differences among these groups with time is further illustrated by the significant results of the WISC Vocabulary Test and the Lorge-Thorndike Intelligence Test. In the latter, the fifth-grade subjects were administered the Non-Verbal Battery, Level 3, while the first-grade children were given the Level 1 test. The Non-Verbal Battery requires a child to choose the most appropriate member of a number of alternatives. The superiority of the Class III children on the integrative section of the Verbal Identification Test, designed to measure this type of behavior, suggests that the apparent IQ superiority of the middle-class children largely arises from their mastery of the skill of choosing a best-fit response.

At the relating level, differences in performance reach a statistically significant difference on the latency scores of the first-grade children. (See Table 3-2 for results on the Word Association Test.) The remaining comparisons are in the predicted direction without reaching significance. The tendency to make more responses of the same form as the stimulus word increases sharply with age. This developmentally more advanced, or adultlike, behavior may be learned more indirectly by children than the integrative responses tapped by the Verbal Identifica-

TABLE 3-2

Performance of Negro Children on Word Association Test: Analyses of Variance

	Grade 1: Socioeconomic status					Grade 5: Socioeconomic status				
	I (n = 25)	II (n = 25)	III (n = 16)	F (df = 2, 63)	P	I (n = 31)	II (n = 32)	III (n = 16)	F (df = 2, 76)	P
Latency scores										
Mean	111.4	38.6	68.5	3.97	<.05	39.8	35.4	41.0	<1.00	N.S.
S.D.	126.6	20.8	94.3			19.0	21.3	28.9		
Form class										
Mean	2.4	3.9	3.9	2.81	N.S.	5.5	6.5	7.2	3.02	N.S.
S.D.	2.3	2.4	2.9			2.8	1.9	1.9		

tion Test, which reveals class differences. The second hypothesis, then, is not confirmed in this preliminary presentation of findings.

The Concept Sorting Test is aimed at eliciting classificatory behavior in children. Because this is a relatively time-consuming task, only half the children could be tested. The "perfect" performance in this task consists of grouping the 16 stimulus cards into four piles, each representing a concept. After the child has finished sorting, a rationale for each pile is elicited from him. The third hypothesis in this study was that lower-class children would classify test stimuli according to functional criteria, and thus would sort into more piles of fewer cards each than would middle-class children. This prediction was confirmed at the fifth-grade level. In addition, the lower-class child was expected to be able to give fewer explicit rationales for his concept-sorts than the other children. A chi-square test for two independent samples was performed to determine whether the relative number of explicit rationales differed among the three SES groups (Siegal, 1956). The results of these calculations are presented in Table 3-3.

Thus, fifth-grade lower-class children sort cards into more piles and give significantly fewer explicit verbalizations of their sorting behavior than do middle-class children. When evaluating these findings, as well as those presented above, it is important to remember that these preliminary results are based on relatively small numbers of subjects.

CONCLUSIONS

In brief, the following results were attained in this preliminary analysis of verbal and classificatory behavior in young Negro children. Middle-class children surpass their lower-class age-mates in possessing a larger vocabulary (WISC Vocabulary results) and a higher nonverbal IQ (Lorge-Thorndike), in their ability to produce a best-fit response (Verbal Identification,

Integrative section), and in their conceptual sorting and verbalization behavior. At the relational level of language, group differences are less striking (Word Association test).

The emergence of significant group differences on these various tasks at the fifth-grade level may reflect stable patterns of language-conceptual behaviors in the middle-class children. Although similar trends exist at the first-grade level, they may be attenuated by the fact that the younger children, independent of social class, are primarily occupied with the acquisition of the rudiments of language.

The middle-class child has an advantage over the lower-class child in tasks requiring precise and somewhat abstract language. The acquisition of more abstract and integrative language seems to be hampered by the living conditions in the homes of lower-class children. Opportunities for learning to categorize and integrate are rare in the lives of all young children; this type of learning requires specific feedback or careful tutoring. Such attention is far less available to the lower-class child.

Whatever their genesis, consistent class differences in language skills have here been shown to emerge between groups of children from the same subculture but of different socioeconomic class. By systematically examining features of the preschool lives of young children and clarifying their relationship to performance on language and conceptual tasks, it may be possible to facilitate the acquisition of these skills and thus improve educational methods for children of any class.

Throughout this report, the term "Class I children" has been used to characterize those children who live in our slums. The terms "socially disadvantaged" or "culturally deprived" enable us as social scientists to neutralize our feelings about life for children in the midst of abject poverty. The synthetic quality of these words perhaps reflects our anger and shame about the plight of these children and our ignorance and confusion about how best to help them.

TABLE 3-3

Performance of Negro Children on Concept Sorting Task: Analyses of Variance

	Grade 1: Socioeconomic status					Grade 5: Socioeconomic status				
	I (n = 11)	II (n = 13)	III (n = 13)	F (df = 2, 34)	P	I (n = 16)	II (n = 30)	III (n = 19)	F (df = 2, 62)	P
Concept sorting Number of piles°										
Mean	7.3	5.9	6.7	1.99	N.S.	6.4	5.6	5.0	3.75	<.05
S.D.	2.3	1.7	1.5			1.6	1.8	1.3		

Frequency of Explicit Concept Verbalization in Fifth-Grade Negro Children†

Socioeconomic status	Below median	Above median	Total
I	13	3	16
II	18	12	30
III	7	12	19
Total	38	27	65

°The number of piles ranges from a perfect score of 4 all the way to 12.

†$X^2 = 7.11$, df = 2, P <.05.

REFERENCES

Conant, J. B. *Slums and suburbs.* New York: McGraw-Hill, 1961.

Ervin, S. M. Grammar and classification. Presented at the meeting of the American Psychological Association, 1957.

Hunt, J. McV. *Intelligence and experience.* New York: Ronald, 1961.

John, V., and M. Deutsch. The role of language in the cognitive processes of middle-class and lower-class children. Presented at the annual meeting of the American Association for the Advancement of Science, New York, December 1960.

Kagan, J., and H. A. Moss. The psychological significance of styles of conceptualization. Unpublished manuscript, 1962.

Luria, A. R., and S. Y. Yudovitch. *Speech and the development of mental processes in children.* London: Staples, 1959.

Piaget, J. *The construction of reality in the child.* New York: Basic Books, 1954.

Riessman, F. *The culturally deprived child.* New York: Harper Inc., 1962.

Siegal, S. *Nonparametric statistics.* New York: McGraw-Hill, 1956.

Thomas, A., H. G. Birch, S. Chess, and L. C. Robbins. Individuality in responses of children to similar environmental situations. *Amer. J. Psychiat.*, 1961, **117**: 798–803.

Comparative and Developmental Study of the Learning Abilities of Negro and White Children under Four Conditions

IRA J. SEMLER

IRA ISCOE

Measured differences between Negroes and whites continues to be a controversial topic in the psychological and educational literature. Garrett (1945a, 1945b, 1947) and more recently Shuey (1958) have pointed out the generally inferior performance of Negroes on a wide assortment of intelligence tests, both group and individual. Dreger and Miller (1960), in an extensive review of psychological differences between Negroes and whites, while not disagreeing completely with the genetic explanations of Garrett and Shuey have stressed strongly the importance of the psychocultural environment and the need for further cross-cultural research. There is little mention in this review of studies involving the learning abilities of Negroes and whites. This is not due to the reviewers' laxity since the typical Negro-white study is limited characteristically to reports of existing intellectual differences without regard to the effect of such differences on specific task performance.

The concern of the present research was to compare the abilities of Negro and white children on paired-associate learning tasks where previous measurement had determined that the white children had significantly higher IQs. However, since the relationship between measured intellectual

Reprinted with the permission of the authors and the publisher from the article of the same title, *Journal of Educational Psychology*, 1963, **54**, 38–44.

status and learning ability is imperfectly understood (Sarason and Gladwin, 1958) and since paired-associate learning ability does not seem to be closely related to intelligence level (Berkson & Cantor, 1960; Eisman, 1958), it was hypothesized that no difference would be found between Negro and white children.

METHOD

Subjects

All subjects were enrolled in the public schools and private kindergartens in Austin, Texas. At the time of the study the schools were still segregated as a result of neighborhood housing situations rather than school policy. An attempt was made to select schools so as to minimize socioeconomic differences. Despite these efforts and not unexpectedly for this region of the country, a significant difference in favor of the white children was obtained.

The ages of the children ranged from 5 through 9 years. The mean age for the whites was 7-2 and for the Negroes 7-4. The subjects were randomly selected by ages from lists furnished by the schools. Each child was first administered a Wechsler Intelligence Scale for Children (WISC) using trained examiners. After approximately a week, each child was administered the paired-associate learning task having been randomly assigned previously to one of the four experimental conditions. In all some 275 children were tested for this portion of the study. Table 3-4 provides comparative WISC Full Scale IQ data for the 275 subjects by sex and age level. The superiority of the whites, especially at the lowest age level, is to be discussed in detail later.

Selection of Stimulus Pairs

Six pairs of stimuli were employed for the paired-associate learning task. Each stimulus pair was selected from a different conceptual classification involving items which were familiar to both groups and

TABLE 3-4

Mean WISC Full Scale IQs of White and Negro Children by Sex at Five Age Levels

| Subjects | Age in years | | | | | |
	5	6	7	8	9	Total
White (N = 141)						
Boys						
M	108.3	104.2	97.7	105.2	98.5	
N	19	22	12	15	12	80
Girls						
M	116.5	104.9	97.2	105.8	94.2	
N	7	15	15	12	12	61
Negro (N = 134)						
Boys						
M	83.4	92.6	90.6	98.3	89.5	
N	13	14	12	20	12	71
Girls						
M	82.5	103.0	90.8	96.5	85.0	
N	13	12	12	14	12	63

assumed to be informally learned early in the lives of all these subjects. Pretesting revealed that young children could sort the 12 stimulus objects into 6 pairs, based on functional utility or conceptual similarity, and could, in most cases, verbalize the basis for their pairings.

The six pairs employed were:

Stimulus	Response
Banana	Orange
Toothbrush	Comb
Pipe	Cigar
Doll	Toy Truck
Cup	Bowl
Glove	Shoe

The assumption was that the above pairs possess high associative value by virtue of conceptual or functional similarity. In order to provide item pairs which would require new learnings (associations) these Similar pairs were rearranged as follows:

Stimulus	Response
Banana	Shoe
Toothbrush	Orange
Pipe	Comb
Doll	Cigar
Cup	Toy Truck
Glove	Bowl

The assumption underlying the resulting Dissimilar condition was that the associative values in terms of categorical or functional similarity are much lower than in the case of the Similar condition. This assumption is supported by the findings of Underwood and Richardson (1956) with regard to verbal associations and concept formation.

In order to assess the effect of the availability of cue on the learning of the stimulus pairs employed, one set was composed of actual objects (Concrete) while the other consisted of high quality colored $3\frac{1}{4} \times 4\frac{1}{4}$ inch photographs (Abstract) of these same objects mounted on 5×7 inch neutral colored cardboard. Therefore, the labels Concrete and Abstract refer to operationally defined stimulus characteristics. Com-

binations of the two sets of stimulus pairs (Similar versus Dissimilar) and two degrees of cue presence (Concrete versus Abstract) were used to establish the four experimental conditions—i.e., Similar-Concrete, Similar-Abstract, Dissimilar-Concrete, and Dissimilar-Abstract.

Design and Procedure

Stimulus pairs were presented manually for all conditions. The stimulus object or picture was shown for approximately 5 seconds followed by the response object or picture for approximately 3 seconds regardless of the correctness of the subject's response. The intertrial interval was approximately 5 seconds. Each subject was run for 12 blocks of 6 pair presentations with a total of 72 pair presentations in all. Serial learning effects were avoided by randomizing order of pair presentations across trial blocks. An observer recorded the subject's response on each trial and the total number of correct anticipations in the 6 pair presentations for 12 blocks was used in the analysis of variance. The 275 subjects who had been administered the WISC previously were randomly assigned to one of the four experimental conditions and given the paired-associate learning task appropriate to their assignment. From this subject pool 31 Negro children and 31 white children were randomly selected from each of the four conditions providing 124 white and 124 Negro subjects for a race by condition analysis. Since analyzing data from such a design furnishes no age or race by age information a three-factor repeated measurement design was employed involving two races, four conditions, and five age levels. In order to equalize the number of subjects in each cell of this design, a proportional analysis using 120 (60 white subjects and 60 Negro subjects) was carried out. In addition, a race by age analysis of measured intelligence for these same 120 subjects was made in order to compare acquisition rate and intellectual level. A correlation analysis between intelligence and total learning score for each race was also computed for the original 275 subjects.

RESULTS

The analysis of variance for the 124 white and 124 Negro subjects under the four conditions yielded an F of 81.73 which, with 3 and 240 degrees of freedom, is significant at the .001 level. Nonsignificant Fs for race and the race by condition interaction were obtained. It is apparent that, while the conditions yielded significantly different rates of learning, the two races did not differ in this respect nor was any one condition significantly more difficult for either race.

The proportional analysis of variance for the 120 subjects which supports the previous analysis in greater detail is summarized in Table 3-5.

Again, the four experimental conditions yielded highly significant differences. The significant age effect ($p < .001$) and the race by age interaction ($p < .05$) are graphically illustrated by Figures 3-4 and 3-5.

In terms of age trends, the learning rate of white children was superior to Negro children under the Similar condition at the 5- and 6-year-old level (Figure 3-4) for both Concrete and Abstract paired-associate presentations. In addition, differences may be noted between whites and Negroes under the Dissimilar-Concrete and the Dissimilar-Abstract conditions. However, race differences in learning ability decreased steadily across the age levels stud-

TABLE 3-5

Summary of the Proportional Analysis of Variance of Paired-Associate Learning of White and Negro Children by Age under Four Conditions

Source	df	MS	F
Between subjects	149		
Race	1	6.137	.770
Condition	3	506.858	63.628°°°°
Age	4	44.445	5.579°°°°
Race × condition	3	5.815	.730
Race × age	4	20.768	2.607°
Condition × age	12	6.633	.833
Race × condition × age	12	7.760 ˙	.974
Error (b)	80	7.966	
Within subjects	1320		
Trials	11	166.916	200.139°°°°
Trials × race	11	.849	1.018
Trials × condition	33	7.001	8.394°°°°
Trials × age	44	.865	1.037
Trials × race × condition	33	.885	1.061
Trials × race × age	44	.836	1.002
Trials × condition × age	132	.525	.629
Trials × race × condition × age	132	1.031	1.236
Error (w)	880	.834	
Total	1439		

° $p < .05$.
°°°° $p < .001$.

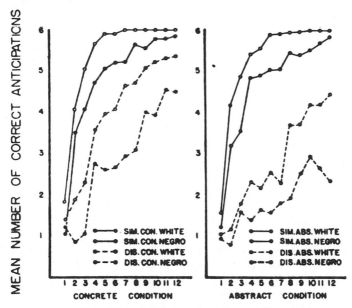

FIGURE 3-4. *Trials in blocks of six 5- and 6-year-olds.*

ied and were not significant in the summary analysis. This is illustrated by comparing the learning curves of Figure 3-4 for the combined 5- and 6-year-olds with the curves in Figure 3-5 for the combined 8- and 9-year-olds where learning ability differences have disappeared. A further analysis of race differences at the five age levels in terms of

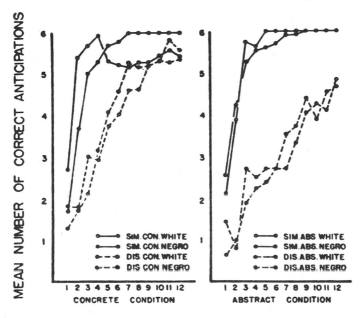

FIGURE 3-5. *Trials in blocks of six 8- and 9-year-olds.*

mean difference in total learning score is reported in Table 3-6 which shows in greater detail the developmental trend differences indicated by the significant race by age interaction reported in Table 3-5.

Figures 3-4 and 3-5 also show that learning was most rapid for both white and Negro 5- and 6-year-old children under the Similar-Concrete condition. This is the condition wherein the pairs to be associated were categorically similar and cue presence was maximized. The rate of acquisition under the Similar-Abstract condition was almost as rapid for both groups as under the Similar-Concrete condition. Cue reduction, regardless of race, does not exert a differential effect on the learning of conceptually similar pairs. However, the effect of pair dissimilarity was to lower learning rates. This was more pronounced under the Dissimilar-Abstract condition than under the Dissimilar-Concrete condition and was true for both races. It appears, then, that cue reduction has a significant effect on acquisi-

TABLE 3-7

Correlation of WISC IQs with Total Learning Score

Race	Verbal	Perform-ance	Full scale
White ($N = 141$)	.033	.127	.094
Negro ($N = 134$)	.117	.204°	.189°

° Reliably different from 0 at the .05 level of confidence.

tion rate when the pairs to be associated involved new learning as was the case under the Dissimilar condition.

In general, most of the between-subjects and within-subjects interactions were non-significant leaving "pure" main effects to be studied. The significant trials by condition interaction is clearly seen in a comparison of the learning curves in Figures 3-4 and 3-5 where acquisition rate differs depending upon the experimental treatment under consideration.

In order to determine the relationship between total learning score and intellectual level a comprehensive correlation analysis was carried out for both whites and Negroes. Part of these data is reported in Table 3-7 which indicates low but reliable correlations between WISC Performance and Full Scale IQs with total learning score for Negroes only. Since very low but reliable correlations were obtained, a further breakdown of Verbal, Performance, and Full Scale WISC IQs by race and age is reported in Table 3-8. It should be noted that the data in Table 3-8 were based on the 120 subjects used in the proportional analysis of variance of Table 3-5. Further, an analysis of variance of WISC Full Scale IQs for these same 120 subjects is reported in summary form in Table 3-9. This indicates a highly significant difference in WISC Full Scale IQ in favor of white subjects and significant differences across the age levels studied. However, the differences were more pronounced at the 5-year-old level which may partially account for the race by

TABLE 3-6

Mean of Total Learning Scores at Five Age Levels

Age level		White	Negro	t
5	M	48.92	38.25	10.67°°
	N	12	12	
6	M	56.17	50.08	3.73°°
	N	12	12	
7	M	52.67	56.42	−2.30°
	N	12	12	
8	M	54.16	56.42	−1.39
	N	12	12	
9	M	50.33	53.25	−1.79
	N	12	12	

NOTE.—Based on proportional analysis of variance.
° $p < .05$.
°° $p < .01$.

TABLE 3-8

Mean Verbal, Performance, and Full Scale WISC IQs of the 120
Subjects at Five Age Levels Used in the Proportional
Analysis of Variance

	Age in years				
WISC IQ	5	6	7	8	9
White (N = 60)					
Verbal	110.75	104.75	102.67	102.00	91.33
Performance	116.33	110.83	98.08	109.58	93.25
Full scale	114.67	108.33	100.58	106.08	91.42
N	12	12	12	12	12
Negro (N = 60)					
Verbal	87.75	105.50	92.50	99.42	90.17
Performance	86.92	97.25	89.83	100.00	85.50
Full scale	86.00	101.83	90.50	99.50	86.75
N	12	12	12	12	12

age interaction in view of the low (but reliable) correlation obtained between total learning and intelligence level. It is doubtful, however, if this is the main factor in the race by age interaction.

DISCUSSION

The lack of previous studies of a similar nature produces some difficulty in the eval-

TABLE 3-9

Summary Analysis of Variance of Full Scale WISC IQs for the 120 Subjects Used in the Proportional Analysis of Variance in Table 3-5

Source	df	MS	F
Race	1	3830.700	27.472°°°°
Age	4	975.138	6.993°°°°
Race × age	4	588.554	4.221°°°
Cells	9		
Within sub-groups (w)	110	139.436	
Total	119		

°°°$p < .005$.
°°°°$p < .001$.

uation of the findings of this study. It is not the purpose of this discussion to emphasize the race differences obtained in measured intelligence. The data indicate the limitation of measured intelligence in predicting performance under conditions where new learning is to take place. In the case of this study, the procedure and design suggest a variety of fruitful ways of studying factors which may have a significant effect on the acquisition of new learning. This is an important consideration in studies between races or between groups. The results provide developmental support, however, for a hypothesis of no difference in learning ability between the groups studied under the four experimental conditions.

Specifically, the results suggest that young Negro children have more difficulty than young white children in learning new associations, especially when cues are reduced by using photographs rather than actual objects. The greatest discrepancy in Full Scale IQ (about 28 points) existed at the 5-year-old level. However, in view of the decreasing difference between races in learning ability across age levels, and in spite of continuing significant differences in intelligence, and the low correlations between IQ and total learning score, it seems improbable that intellectual differences alone could explain the superior learning of the young white subjects. Some consideration is due, therefore, for environmental factors.

All of the 5-year-old and some of the 6-year-old subjects were obtained from nursery schools. Public school kindergartens per se did not exist and a child must be age 6 by September 1 of the school year to enter first grade. As far as nursery school attendance goes, the great majority of Negro children attend because the mother works. The Negro 5-year-old children were taken from a setting run by a church with over 120 children ranging in ages from 3 through 6. They were cared for all day in less than adequate circumstances. In contrast, the white children were not for the most part children of working mothers. Whatever their parents' reasons for sending them to nursery school, the facilities in terms of physical plant and staff were excellent. The children received some informal school training such as learning to write numbers and letters. The implication here is that the environment of the 5-year-old Negro children was not as stimulating towards new learning situations as that of the whites. There is also the added implication that, in terms of socioeconomic difference, the Negro children at the 5-year-old level were much lower than the whites. In terms of our overall sample of Negro and whites, the Negroes were also of lower socioeconomic status. This is, of course, a problem in comparing racial groups. It is virtually impossible to equate Negroes and whites on the basis of socioeconomic status. Standard of living, steadiness of employment, and number of persons in the family working all complicate the estimate of economic status.

Some comment is due also concerning the older Negro children and their public school facilities. They came from a school which had a very adequate physical plant, a good lunch program, and a dedicated, well-trained group of teachers. This school was certainly the equal of that of our older white children. Whether these factors really contributed to the gradual erasing of differences in learning ability with increasing age cannot be answered unequivocally, but they should at least be pointed out. A combination of environmental factors may well have contributed to the comparatively poor overall learning of the younger Negro children. At any rate, there is little to be gained by falling back on a genetic explanation inasmuch as these too cannot be separated from environmental conditions. What is important to note is the developmental support obtained in this study for no differences in overall learning with increasing age of our subjects.

There is a certain timeliness in the results of the present research. As new educational opportunities are opened for the Negro child in the United States, educators will be challenged to find methods whereby the optimum conditions for learning can be found and applied. The advent of integration has already produced a great many problems concerned with the learning and motivation of minority groups, especially Negroes. Our findings of no overall race differences in learning ability should not be minimized. They suggest that educators should exercise great caution in inferring learning ability from measured intellectual level alone. The developmental study of specific learning abilities of Negroes and whites could provide a more effective basis for the psychological and educational decisions that inevitably will have to be made by those who bear the responsibility of discovering and implementing the conditions for the maximum development of human potential. One study does not in itself prove anything definitive, especially in an area that has been replete with charges and counter-charges in the past. Further research, including possible replication of the present study, is indicated.

REFERENCES

Berkson, G., and G. N. Cantor. A study of mediation in mentally retarded and normal school children. *J. educ. Psychol.*, 1960, **51**, 82–86.

Dreger, R. M., and K. S. Miller. Comparative psychological studies of Negroes and whites in the United States. *Psychol. Bull.*, 1960, **57**, 361–402.

Eisman, Bernice S. Paired associate learning, generalization and retention as a function of intelligence. *Amer. J. ment. Defic.*, 1958, **63**, 481–489.

Garrett, H. E. A note on the intelligence scores of Negroes and whites in 1918. *J. abnorm. soc.*

Psychol., 1945a, **40**, 344–346.

———. Psychological differences as among races. *Science*, 1945b, **101**, 16–17.

———. Negro-white differences in mental ability in the United States. *Scient. Mon.*, 1947, **65**, 329–333.

Sarason, S., and T. Gladwin. Psychological and cultural problems in mental subnormality: A review of the research. *Genet. Psychol. Monogr.*, 1958, **57**, 7–269.

Shuey, Audrey M. *The testing of Negro intelligence.* Lynchburg, Va.: Randolph Macon Women's College, 1958.

Underwood, B. J., and J. Richardson. Some verbal materials for the study of concept formation. *Psychol. Bull.*, 1956, **53**, 84–95.

Language and Meaning:
The Union of Mind and Body

_____ *4*

INTRODUCTION

Chomsky states that no aspect of linguistic study is more subject to confusion than that which deals with the relation of syntax (or grammar) and meaning (or semantics). He believes that the question of how you construct a grammar without appealing to meaning is as inappropriate as the question of how you construct a grammar with no knowledge of the hair color of the speaker. (Chomsky, 1957, pages 92–105). Yet, as Katz and Fodor point out in their article in this chapter, we cannot identify grammatical structure with meaning, for the obvious reason that we can all recall sentences which are different in structure but have identical meaning, as well as sentences which are the same in structure but have quite different meaning. Chomsky's belief is that "meaning" tends to be a catchall term which includes all aspects of language about which we are almost totally ignorant. What is frequently called "meaning" or "cognitive structure" is only the fairly systematic use of available syntactic devices.

The major question of this chapter, therefore, is the meaning of meaning. The cognitive and behavioristic theorists take quite divergent positions. Unlike the behaviorists, the cognitive theorist is not primarily concerned with avoiding a mind-body dualism that postulates a physical world of stimuli and overt responses and a mental world of thought and meaning. Indeed, cognitive theorists do assert that there is only an indirect connection between the physical world and cognition. Words, for example, become meaningful when they recall images that are copies of the objects they name and when they are incorporated, with other words, in the cognitive structure of the individual. The acquisition of most new meaning is the "subsumption" of new material under more inclusive ideas already existing in the cognitive structure (Ausubel, 1965, page 68). It is a major characteristic of cognitive theory to describe intellectual processes and structure in terms of *hierarchical* organization. This characteristic of cognitive theory is more fully discussed later [Chapter 6].

The behaviorist position, as exemplified by Hull, Skinner, Underwood, and the authors of the articles in this chapter, utilizes very parsimonious definitions of meaning. For Skinner, to speak of meaning as some internal process isolated from the conditioning of verbal operants is to create a linguistic fiction [Chapter 8]. Although "meaning" as such is not discussed in the Hullian system, Hull conceived of a "pure stimulus act" to explain responses to the not-here and not-now and what we more generally refer to as knowledge and purpose (Hull, 1930). In Chapter 6 we discuss his habit family hierarchy and its relevance to the study of thinking and to meaning. Underwood, utilizing Noble's definition of meaning (in this chapter) describes meaningfulness as a product of the frequency with which words occur in the language (Underwood and Schulz, 1960). By reducing the definition of meaning and meaningfulness to fairly explicit operations and measurement, the behaviorists have reduced meaning to its simpler psychological components. They discuss meaning as a function of specific variables, such as word frequency. Word frequency is really an indirect measure of the frequency with which individuals are *exposed* to words (Underwood and Schulz, 1960).

The classic work on meaning is *The Meaning of Meaning,* by Ogden and Richards. An important selection from this book appears here. An important distinction in their discussion of meaning is between symbol (word) and referent (thing). The layman, when he bothers to think about words at all, believes that words are faithful copies of the physical objects to which they refer. He fails to grasp that the relation between the word and the object is "imputed." Meaning does not adhere in the direct word-object relation. This absence of a direct relation has allowed certain men, especially politicians, the opportunity for rather complex word games and ingenious deception (Chase, 1931).

Beginning with Korzybski (8th edition, 1948), the so-called "General Semanticists" have capitalized on this distinction between symbol and referent (Hayakawa, 1963). For them the ills of the international world as well as the mental illness of the individual are the results of confusing symbol with referent. The proper therapy for individuals and nations requires that everyone learn this important distinction and that he remain aware of it when he talks and listens to others. Confusion arises when individuals use the same words to refer to different things or different words to refer to the same things. We can restore harmony and peace to individuals and the world by understanding and utilizing this principle in our formal and informal communication. We cannot begrudge the General Semanticist the noble aspiration to bring peace and harmony to the world. We can, however, marvel over his failure to observe that it is often precisely at moments when individuals are imputing the *same* relations of referent and symbol that the most lively disagreements result. Harmony is often the result of tactfully declining to pursue clarification of meaning.

For the behaviorist, the separation of symbol and referent is a regression to mentalistic psychology, with the symbol belonging to one level of "existence," the mental, and the referent to another level of "existence," the physical. For this reason, as stated in the article here, Osgood rejects the position of Ogden and Richards. Osgood, however, is not satisfied with the position of the S-R behaviorist, which explains meaning as derived from simple conditioning—the direct pairing of word and object. According to this S-R view, the child acquires meaning when he properly associates the word and the object that the word signifies. Words become conditioned stimuli. The chief pitfall of the behaviorist position, according to Osgood, is that words frequently elicit responses that vary considerably from those elicited by the objects themselves. For example, our response to the name of an individual is not a duplication of our response to the physical presence of that individual. To account for this difference Osgood developed a "mediation hypothesis." He observes, first of all, that a word elicits only a part of the response which the associated object elicits. This word response he refers to as r_m (an abbreviation for mediating reaction). This mediating reaction (r_m) in turn produces a mediating stimulus (s_m) that, in turn, may result in a variety of overt responses. Although Osgood offers his theory in a behaviorist contest, r_m-s_m describes a process not accessible to observation and perhaps somewhat tenuously tied to observable stimuli and responses.

Noble's definition of meaning, as he discusses it in the article in this chapter, is considerably more parsimonious and behavioristic than that of Ogden and Richards and that of Osgood. For Noble, meaning is identified with associational strength rather than habit strength. It is *not* simply the result of the number of reinforced pairings of particular stimuli and response. In a strictly empirical definition of the term, Noble defines meaning as the mean number of continued, written responses given within a one-minute period to a particular word. A word increases in meaning when it is associated with a greater number of responses. Complex meaning is a product of certain responses producing stimuli that, in turn, give rise to a host of new responses. These stimuli, important in complex meaning, are internal or proprioceptive and have some similarity to the mediating stimulus (s_m) of Osgood. In the main, however, Noble's definition of meaning is strictly empirical, defined almost entirely in terms of word function. Because words are both stimuli and responses, they are treated as physical objects.

Is Noble talking about meaning or associative strength? We have referred to the confusion that the term meaning introduces into discussions of language and thought. Meaningful learning has introduced considerable confusion into discussions of teaching. There is a long tradition in psychology and education courses that treats meaningful learning as some process superior to and distantly related to rote learning. Meaningful learning results in "understanding," whereas rote learning results in the "empty" repetition of words. The very vagueness of this language should reveal to the reader how fruitless at this level the discussion of meaning, meaningfulness, and instruction is. Yet the specificity of Noble's definition seems to omit important components of "meaning" and "meaningfulness": for example, the syntactical relation words have to one another and to sentences, the ability of individuals to choose between alternative meanings, and the relation of the acquisition of meaning to previously acquired meaning and to the influences of one's society and culture. Associative strength is, no doubt, an important component of meaning and the acquisition of meaning, and its experimental usefulness has been demonstrated. If one places one's faith in this experimental parsimony and if one is patient enough not to demand answers to complex questions before he has found the answers to the simple one, it is not impossible to expect that this approach will result in understanding the more complex aspects of meaning.

The work of Bernard Riess, (e.g., 1946) more than that of Noble, identifies meaning with habit strength. Riess views meaning as a product of classical conditioning. Razran, together with Soviet psychologists, developed a conditioning technique that results in "mediated generalization" (Razran, 1939). The use of this technique has the effect of causing one conditioned stimulus (here a word) to spread to other words that are semantically related to the first word. Meaning is acquired (or, more technically, one is semantically conditioned) by the process of generalization and transfer. Mediated generalization describes both the technique and the learning that results. Words are treated as physical objects.

Riess attributes the observed results to semantic conditioning. Later studies by Berko, Ervin-Tripp, and Brown suggest that these developmental trends could be the result of the child's gradual acquisition of grammatical knowledge [Chapters 1, 7]. In these latter studies the tendency of adult subjects to associate words of the same parts of speech (for example, nouns with nouns, verbs with verbs) is analogous to their preference for synonyms in the Riess study.

The article by Katz and Fodor is of major importance in the study of language and meaning. These authors attempt to describe the characteristics required by a semantic theory. Semantic theory is a theory of the speaker's ability to interpret the sentences of his language. First, they distinguish between grammatical and semantic theory. Following Chomsky's conception of grammar, the authors assert that grammar enables the native speaker to use and understand any sentences of his language, including those he has never heard before. Grammar is able to do this by providing rules that generate the sentences of one's native language. The grammar of a language describes how a speaker distinguishes between well-formed and ungrammatical sentences, recognizes ambiguity in syntax, and understands the relation between sentences.

Grammar, however, does not complete the explanation of why the native speaker is able to use and understand new sentences. We can all recall sentences that are different in grammatical structure and yet identical in meaning. There are also sentences that have identical grammatical structure but different meaning. A semantic theory describes the ability of the speaker to *interpret* sentences. Katz and Fodor do not believe that a semantic theory must explain in what way social settings determine how an utterance is understood. No sentence can have meanings in social contexts that it lacks in isolation.

REFERENCES

Ausubel, D. P. *The psychology of meaningful verbal learning.* New York: Grune & Stratton, 1963.
Ausubel, D. P. A cognitive structure view of word and concept meaning. In R. C. Anderson and D. P. Ausubel (Eds.), *Readings in the psychology of cognition.* New York: Holt, Rinehart and Winston, 1965. Pp. 58–75.
Chase, S. *Tyranny of words.* New York: Harcourt, 1931.
Chomsky, N. *Syntactic structures.* 's-Gavenhage, Holland: Mouton, 1957.
Hayakawa, S. I. *Symbols, status, and personality.* New York: Harcourt, 1963.
Hull, C. L. Knowledge and purpose as habit mechanism. *Psychol. Rev.,* 1930, **37**, 511–525.
Korzybski, A. *Science and sanity: An introduction to non-Aristotelian systems and general semantics.* (8th ed.) Lakeville, Conn., 1948.
Razran, G. H. S. A quantitative study of meaning by a conditioned salivary technique (semantic conditioning). *Science,* 1939, **90**, 89–90.
Riess, B. Genetic changes in semantic conditioning. *J. exp. Psychol.,* 1946, **36**, 143–152.
Underwood, B. J., and R. W. Schulz. *Meaningfulness and verbal learning.* Philadelphia: Lippincott, 1960.

Thoughts, Words, and Things

CHARLES K. OGDEN

I. A. RICHARDS

In yet another respect all these specialists fail to realize the deficiencies of current linguistic theory. Preoccupied as they are— ethnologists with recording the details of fast vanishing languages; philologists with an elaborate technique of phonetic laws and principles of derivation; philosophers with "philosophy"—all have overlooked the pressing need for a better understanding of what actually occurs in discussion. The analysis of the process of communication is partly psychological, and psychology has now reached a stage at which this part may

Reprinted with the permission of the publishers, Harcourt, Brace, & World, Inc., and Routledge & Kegan Paul, Ltd., from the authors' *The Meaning of Meaning* (8th ed.), 1953, pp. 8–23.

be successfully undertaken. Until this had happened the science of Symbolism necessarily remained in abeyance, but there is no longer any excuse for vague talk about Meaning, and ignorance of the ways in which words deceive us.

Throughout the Western world it is agreed that people must meet frequently, and that it is not only agreeable to talk, but that it is a matter of common courtesy to say something even when there is hardly anything to say. "Every civilized man," continues the late Professor Mahaffy, to whose *Principles of the Art of Conversation* we owe this observation, "feels, or ought to feel, this duty; it is the universal accomplishment which all must practise"; those who fail are punished by the dislike or neglect of society.

There is no doubt an Art in saying something when there is nothing to be said, but it is equally certain that there is an Art no less important of saying clearly what one wishes to say when there is an abundance of material; and conversation will seldom attain even the level of an intellectual pastime if adequate methods of Interpretation are not also available.

Symbolism is the study of the part played in human affairs by language and symbols of all kinds, and especially of their influence on Thought. It singles out for special inquiry the ways in which symbols help us and hinder us in reflecting on things.

Symbols direct and organize, record and communicate. In stating what they direct and organize, record and communicate we have to distinguish as always between Thoughts and Things. It is Thought (or, as we shall usually say, *reference*) which is directed and organized, and it is also Thought which is recorded and communicated. But just as we say that the gardener mows the lawn when we know that it is the lawnmower which actually does the cutting, so, though we know that the direct relation of symbols is with thought, we also say that symbols record events and communicate facts.

By leaving out essential elements in the language situation we easily raise problems and difficulties which vanish when the whole transaction is considered in greater detail. Words, as every one now knows, "mean" nothing by themselves, although the belief that they did, as we shall see in the next chapter, was once equally universal. It is only when a thinker makes use of them that they stand for anything, or, in one sense, have "meaning." They are instruments. But besides this referential use which for all reflective, intellectual use of language should be paramount, words have other functions which may be grouped together as emotive. These can best be examined when the framework of the problem of strict statement and intellectual communication has been set up. The importance of the emotive aspects of language is not thereby minimized, and anyone chiefly concerned with popular or primitive speech might well be led to reverse this order of approach. Many difficulties, indeed, arising through the behaviour of words in discussion, even amongst scientists, force us at an early stage to take into account these "non-symbolic" influences. But for the analysis of the senses of "meaning" with which we are here chiefly concerned, it is desirable to begin with the relations of thoughts, words and things as they are found in cases of reflective speech uncomplicated by emotional, diplomatic, or other disturbances; and with regard to these, the indirectness of the relations between words and things is the feature which first deserves attention.

This may be simply illustrated by a diagram, in which the three factors involved whenever any statement is made, or understood, are placed at the corners of the triangle, the relations which hold between them being represented by the sides. The point just made can be restated by saying that in this respect the base of the triangle is quite different in composition from either of the other sides (Figure 4-1).

Between a thought and a symbol causal relations hold. When we speak, the symbolism we employ is caused partly by the

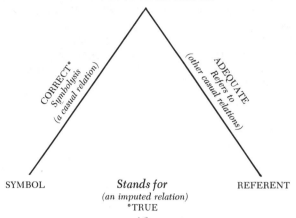

THOUGHT OR REFERENCE

CORRECT°
Symbolises
(a casual relation)

ADEQUATE
Refers to
(other casual relations)

SYMBOL   *Stands for*   REFERENT
(an imputed relation)
°TRUE

FIGURE 4-1.

reference we are making and partly by social and psychological factors—the purpose for which we are making the reference, the proposed effect of our symbols on other persons, and our own attitude. When we hear what is said, the symbols both cause us to perform an act of reference and to assume an attitude which will, according to circumstances, be more or less similar to the act and the attitude of the speaker.

Between the Thought and the Referent there is also a relation; more or less direct (as when we think about or attend to a coloured surface we see), or indirect (as when we "think of" or "refer to" Napoleon), in which case there may be a very long chain of sign-situations intervening between the act and its referent: word—historian—contemporary record—eye-witness—referent (Napoleon).

Between the symbol and the referent there is no relevant relation other than the indirect one, which consists in its being used by someone to stand for a referent. Symbol and Referent, that is to say, are not connected directly (and when, for grammatical reasons, we imply such a relation, it will merely be an imputed, as opposed to a real, relation) but only indirectly round the two sides of the triangle.

It may appear unnecessary to insist that there is no direct connection between say "dog," the word, and certain common objects in our streets, and that the only connection which holds is that which consists in our using the word when we refer to the animal. We shall find, however, that the kind of simplification typified by this once universal theory of direct meaning relations between words and things is the source of almost all the difficulties which thought encounters. As will appear at a later stage, the power to confuse and obstruct, which such simplifications possess, is largely due to the conditions of communication. Language if it is to be used must be a *ready* instrument. The handiness and ease of a phrase is always more important in deciding whether it will be extensively used than its accuracy. Thus such shorthand as the word "means" is constantly used so as to imply a direct simple relation between words and things, phrases and situations. If such relations could be admitted then there would of course be no problem as to the nature of Meaning, and the vast majority of those who have been concerned with it would have been right in their refusal to discuss it. But too many interesting developments have been occurring in the sciences, through the rejection of everyday symbolizations and the endeavour to replace them by more accurate accounts, for any naïve theory that "meaning" is just "meaning" to be popular at the moment. As a rule new facts in startling disagreement with accepted explanations of other facts are required before such critical analyses of what are generally regarded as simple satisfactory notions are undertaken. This has been the case with the recent revolutions in physics. But in addition great reluctance to postulate anything *sui generis* and of necessity undetectable was needed before the simple natural notion of simultaneity, for instance, as a two-termed relation came to be questioned. Yet to such questionings the theory of Relativity was due. The same two motives, new discrepant facts, and distaste for the use of obscure kinds *of* entities in eking out explanations, have led to disturbances in psychology, though here the required restatements have not yet been provided. No Copernican revolution has yet occurred, although several are due if psychology is to be brought into line with its fellow sciences.

It is noteworthy, however, that recent stirrings in psychology have been mainly if not altogether concerned with feeling and volition. The popular success of Psychoanalysis has tended to divert attention from the *older* problem of thinking. Yet in so far as progress here has consequences for all the other sciences and for the whole technique of investigation in psychology itself, this central problem of knowing or of "meaning" is perhaps better worth scrutiny and more likely to promote fresh orientations than any other that can be suggested. As the Behaviorists have also very properly pointed out, this question is closely connected with the use of words.

But the approach to Meaning, far more than the approach to such problems as those of physics, requires a thorough-going investigation of language. Every great advance in physics has been at the expense of some generally accepted piece of metaphysical explanation which had enshrined itself in a convenient, universally practised, symbolic shorthand. But the confusion and obstruction due to such shorthand expressions and to the naïve theories they protect and

keep alive, is greater in psychology, and especially in the theory of knowledge, than elsewhere; because no problem is so infected with so-called metaphysical difficulties—due here, as always, to an approach to a question through symbols without an initial investigation of their functions.

We have now to consider more closely what the causes and effects of symbols are. Whatever may be the services, other than conservative and retentive, of symbolization, all experience shows that there are also disservices. The grosser forms of verbal confusion have long been recognized; but less attention has been paid to those that are more subtle and more frequent. In the following chapters many examples of these will be given, chosen in great part from philosophical fields, for it is here that such confusions become, with the passage of time, most apparent. The root of the trouble will be traced to the superstition that words are in some way parts of things or always imply things corresponding to them, historical instances of this still potent instinctive belief being given from many sources. The fundamental and most prolific fallacy is, in other words, that the base of the triangle given above is filled in.

The completeness of any reference varies; it is more or less close and clear, it "grasps" its object in greater or less degree. Such symbolization as accompanies it—images of all sorts, words, sentences whole and in pieces—is in no very close observable connection with the variation in the perfection of the reference. Since, then, in any discussion we cannot immediately settle from the nature of a person's remarks what his opinion is, we need some technique to keep the parties to an argument in contact and to clear up misunderstandings—or, in other words, a Theory of Definition. Such a technique can only be provided by a theory of knowing, or of reference, which will avoid, as current theories do not, the attribution to the knower of powers which it may be pleasant for him to suppose himself to possess, but which are not open to the only kind of investigation hitherto profitably pursued, the kind generally known as scientific investigation.

Normally, whenever we hear anything said we spring spontaneously to an immediate conclusion, namely, that the speaker is referring to what we should be referring to were we speaking the words ourselves. In some cases this interpretation may be correct; this will prove to be what he has referred to. But in most discussions which attempt greater subtleties than could be handled in a gesture language this will not be so. To suppose otherwise is to neglect our subsidiary gesture languages, whose accuracy within their own limited provinces is far higher than that yet reached by any system of spoken or written symbols, with the exception of the quite special and peculiar case of mathematical, scientific and musical notations. Words, whenever they cannot directly ally themselves with and support themselves upon gestures, are at present a very imperfect means of communication. Even for private thinking thought is often ready to advance, and only held back by the treachery of its natural symbolism; and for conversational purposes the latitude acquired constantly shows itself to all those who make any serious attempts to compare opinions.

We have not here in view the more familiar ways in which words may be used to deceive. In a later chapter, when the function of language as an instrument for the *promotion of purposes* rather than as a means of *symbolizing references* is fully discussed, we shall see how the intention of the speaker may complicate the situation. But the *honnête homme* may be unprepared for the lengths to which verbal ingenuity can be carried. At all times these possibilities have been exploited to the full by interpreters of Holy Writ who desire to enjoy the best of both worlds. Here, for example, is a specimen of the exegetic of the late Dr Lyman Abbott, pastor, publicist, and editor, which, through the efforts of Mr Upton Sinclair, has now become classic.

Does Chrisitianity condemn the methods of twentieth-century finance? Doubtless there are some awkward words in the Gospels, but a little "interpretation" is all that is necessary.

"Jesus did not say 'Lay not up for yourselves treasures upon earth.' He said 'Lay not up for yourselves treasures upon earth *where moth and rust doth corrupt and where thieves break through and steal.*' And no sensible American does. Moth and rust do not get at Mr. Rockefeller's oil wells, and thieves do not often break through and steal a railway. What Jesus condemned was hoarding wealth."

Each investment, therefore, every worldly acquisition, according to one of the leading divines of the New World, may be judged on its merits. There is no hard and fast rule. When moth and rust have been eliminated by science the Christian investor will presumably have no problem, but in the meantime it would seem that Camphorated Oil fulfils most nearly the synoptic requirements. Burglars are not partial to it; it is anathema to moth; and the risk of rust is completely obviated.

Another variety of verbal ingenuity closely allied to this, is the deliberate use of symbols to misdirect the listener. Apologies for such a practice in the case of the madman from whom we desire to conceal the whereabouts of his razor are well known, but a wider justification has also been attempted. In the Christian era we hear of "falsifications of documents, inventions of legends, and forgeries of every description which made the Catholic Church a veritable seat of lying." A play upon words in which one sense is taken by the speaker and another sense intended by him for the hearer was permitted. Indeed, three sorts of equivocations were distinguished by Alfonso de Liguori, who was beatified in the nineteenth century, which might be used with good reason; a good reason being "any honest object, such as keeping our goods, spiritual or temporal." In the twentieth century the intensification of militant nationalism has added further "good reason"; for the military code includes all transactions with hostile nations or individuals as part of the process of keeping spiritual and temporal goods. In war-time words become a normal part of the mechanism of deceit, and the ethics of the situation have been aptly summed up by Lord Wolseley: "We will keep hammering along with the conviction that 'honesty is the best policy,' and that truth always wins in the long run. These pretty sentences do well for a child's copy-book, but the man who acts upon them in war had better sheathe his sword for ever."

The Greeks, as we shall see, were in many ways not far from the attitude of primitive man towards words. And it is not surprising to read that after the Peloponnesian war the verbal machinery of peace had got completely out of gear, and, says Thucydides, could not be brought back into use—"The meaning of words had no longer the same relation to things, but was changed by men as they thought proper." The Greeks were powerless to cope with such a situation. We in our wisdom seem to have created institutions which render us more powerless still.

On a less gigantic scale the technique of deliberate misdirection can profitably be studied with a view to corrective measures. In accounting for Newman's *Grammar of Assent* Dr E. A. Abbott had occasion to describe the process of "lubrication," the art of greasing the descent from the premises to the conclusion, which his namesake cited above so aptly employs. In order to lubricate well, various qualifications are necessary:

"First a nice discrimination of words, enabling you to form, easily and naturally, a great number of finely graduated propositions, shading away, as it were, from the assertion 'x is white' to the assertion 'x is black.' Secondly an inward and absolute contempt for logic and for words. . . . And what are words but toys and sweetmeats for grown-up babies who call themselves men?"

But even where the actual referents are not in doubt, it is perhaps hardly realized how widespread is the habit of using the power of words not only for *bona fide* communications, but also as a method of misdirection; and in the world as it is to-day the naïve interpreter is likely on many occasions to be seriously misled if the existence of this unpleasing trait—equally prevalent amongst the classes and the masses without distinction of race, creed, sex, or colour—is overlooked.

Throughout this work, however, we are treating of *bona fide* communication only, except in so far as we shall find it necessary in Chapter IX to discuss that derivate use of Meaning to which misdirection gives rise. For the rest, the verbal treachery with which we are concerned is only that involved by the use of symbols as such. As we proceed to examine the conditions of communication we shall see why any symbolic apparatus which is in general use is liable to incompleteness and defect.

But if our linguistic outfit is treacherous, it nevertheless is indispensable, nor would another complete outfit necessarily improve matters, even if it were ten times as complete. It is not always new words that are needed, but a means of controlling them as symbols, a means of readily discovering to what in the world on any occasion they are used to refer, and this is what an adequate theory of definition should provide.

But a theory of Definition must follow, not precede, a theory of Signs, and it is little realized how large a place is taken both in abstract thought and in practical affairs by sign-situations. But if an account of sign-situations is to be scientific it must take its observations from the most suitable instances, and must not derive its general principles from an exceptional case. The person actually interpreting a sign is not well placed for observing what is happening. We should develop our theory of signs from observations of other people, and only admit evidence drawn from introspection when we know how to appraise it. The adoption of the other method, on the ground that all our knowledge of others is inferred from knowledge of our own states, can only lead to the *impasse* of solipsism from which modern speculation has yet to recoil. Those who allow beyond question that there are people like themselves also interpreting signs and open to study should not find it difficult to admit that their observation of the behaviour of others may provide at least a framework within which their own introspection, that special and deceptive case, may be fitted. That this is the practice of all the sciences need hardly be pointed out. Any sensible doctor when stricken by disease distrusts his own introspective diagnosis and calls in a colleague.

There are, indeed, good reasons why what is happening in ourselves should be partially hidden from us, and we are generally better judges of what other people are doing than of what we are doing ourselves. Before we looked carefully into other people's heads it was commonly believed that an entity called the soul resided therein, just as children commonly believe that there is a little man inside the skull who looks out at the eyes, the windows of the soul, and listens at the ears. The child has the strongest introspective evidence for this belief, which, but for scalpels and microscopes, it would be difficult to disturb. The tacitly solipsistic presumption that this naïve approach is in some way a necessity of method disqualifies the majority of philosophical and psychological discussions of Interpretation. If we restrict the subject-matter of the inquiry to "ideas" and words, *i.e.,* to the left side of our triangle, and omit all frank recognition of the world outside us, we inevitably introduce confusion on such subjects as knowledge in perception, verification and Meaning itself.

If we stand in the neighbourhood of a cross road and observe a pedestrian confronted by a notice *To Grantchester* displayed on a post, we commonly distinguish three important factors in the situation. There is, we are sure, (1) a Sign which (2) refers to a Place and (3) is being interpreted by a person. All situations in which Signs are considered are similar to this. A doctor

noting that his patient has a temperature and so forth is said to diagnose his disease as influenza. If we talk like this we do not make it clear that signs are here also involved. Even when we speak of symptoms we often do not think of these as closely related to other groups of signs. But if we say that the doctor interprets the temperature, etc., as a Sign of influenza, we are at any rate on the way to an inquiry as to whether there is anything in common between the manner in which the pedestrian treated the object at the cross road and that in which the doctor treated his thermometer and the flushed countenance.

On close examination it will be found that very many situations which we do not ordinarily regard as Sign-situations are essentially of the same nature. The chemist dips litmus paper in his test-tube, and interprets the sign red or the sign blue as meaning acid or base. A Hebrew prophet notes a small black cloud, and remarks "We shall have rain." Lessing scrutinizes the Laocoön, and concludes that the features of Laocoön *père* are in repose. A New Zealand school-girl looks at certain letters on a page in her *Historical Manual for the use of Lower Grades* and knows that Queen Anne is dead.

The method which recognizes the common feature of sign-interpretation has its dangers, but opens the way to a fresh treatment of many widely different topics.

As an instance of an occasion in which the theory of signs is of special use, the subject dealt with in our fourth chapter may be cited. If we realize that in *all* perception, as distinguished from mere awareness, sign-situations are involved, we shall have a new method of approaching problems where a verbal deadlock seems to have arisen. Whenever we "perceive" what we name "a chair," we are interpreting a certain group of data (modifications of the sense-organs); and treating them as signs of a referent. Similarly, even before the interpretation of a word, there is the almost automatic interpretation of a group of successive noises or letters as a word. And in addition to the external world we can also explore with a new technique the sign-situations involved by mental events, the "goings on" or processes of interpretation themselves. We need neither confine ourselves to arbitrary generalizations from introspection after the manner of classical psychology, nor deny the existence of images and other "mental" occurrences to their signs with the extreme Behaviorists. The Double language hypothesis, which is suggested by the theory of signs and supported by linguistic analysis, would absolve Dr Watson and his followers from the logical necessity of affecting general anæsthesia. Images, etc., are often most useful signs of our present and future behaviour—notably in the modern interpretation of dreams. An improved Behaviorism will have much to say concerning the chaotic attempts at symbolic interpretation and construction by which Psycho-analysts discredit their valuable labours.

The problems which arise in connection with any "sign-situation" are of the same general form. The relations between the elements concerned are no doubt different, but they are of the same sort. A thorough classification of these problems in one field, such as the field of symbols, may be expected, therefore, to throw light upon analogous problems in fields at first sight of a very different order.

When we consider the various kinds of Sign-situations instanced above, we find that those signs which men use to communicate one with another and as instruments of thought, occupy a peculiar place. It is convenient to group these under a distinctive name; and for words, arrangements of words, images, gestures, and such representations as drawings or mimetic sounds we use the term *symbols*. The influence of Symbols upon human life and thought in numberless unexpected ways has never been fully recognized, and to this chapter of history we now proceed.

An Analysis of Meaning

CLYDE E. NOBLE

Intimately related to the production of research data and to the formulation of theory in psychology is the procedure of identifying and quantifying the relevant variables within its various domains. Concerning the field of verbal learning, such writers as Carr (1925), Robinson (1932), McGeoch (1936, 1942), Dashiell (1940), Melton (1936, 1950), and Underwood (1949) have emphasized the continuing need for this type of analytic research.

The analysis of the attributes of verbal material has, moreover, a more general application. The training of human perceptual and motor skills is often accompanied by verbal instructions intended to facilitate performance on such tasks. One factor which may determine the effectiveness of instructions is the nature of the verbal stimuli which are introduced. For example, particular words may vary in *meaningfulness*. Evidence reviewed in such sources as McGeoch (1942), Underwood (1949), and Woodworth (1938), indicates this to be a potential relevant variable in verbal learning. His-

Reprinted with the permission of the author and publisher from the article of same title, *Psychological Review*, 1952, 59, 421–430.

torically, however, there has been little agreement on the precise definition of meaning, with the result that few consistent scaling procedures have been developed with which its actual relevance may be evaluated.

The objective of the present study is a theoretical-experimental analysis of the attribute of meaning in verbal stimulus material. Defining operations will be designed in accordance with rational considerations about this concept. In addition, quantitative analysis will provide the scale values necessary to the discovery of accurate functional relationships among this and other better-known psychological variables.

AN ANALYSIS OF MEANING

The many problems of *meaning* have occupied the attention of philosophers and of psychologists for a long time. Some of these problems have been genuine, others spurious. Inasmuch as its necessary and sufficient operations are both logically possible and empirically feasible, it may be shown that at least one of these alleged issues constitutes a genuine problem. Such is the requirement of an analysis of meaning in verbal learning theory.

Within the framework of Hull's (1943) behavior theory this is a relatively straightforward task. Consider a stimulus element S_x, a class of conditioned responses R_1, R_2, R_3, . . . R_n, and a class of corresponding habit strengths H_1, H_2, H_3, . . . H_n, forming hypothetical bonds between them. Assume that these Rs have, by virtue of prior training, been connected at various times to S_x, and that, for simplicity, the Hs of these connections are severally equal. This hypothetical situation may be represented by the schema in Figure 4-2, where the broken-shafted arrows denote learned connections, and where the dotted line following D denotes a continuing need or motivational state. It will be seen that this model depicts an ordinary competing response situation, in which each R has an equal probability of occurrence (R_p) following the presentation of S_x, and in which, given a wider range of observations, such phenomena as alternation, blocking, and increased reaction latency (R_t) are predictable . . . . Should the Hs be altered considerably in value the principle of competition would still hold, except that to refer to the habit structure under such conditions one would use the term *hierarchy of habits*.

Since, by logical anaylsis, *meaning* is a relation between terms, let us define the meaningfulness of this *situation* as the number of Hs subsisting between S and the several Rs taken together. More specifically, the *particular* meanings of S_x are: H_1, H_2, H_3, . . . H_n, and different conceptual combinations of these Hs yield different *numbers* of meanings. In this definition the author presupposes, of course, that the system *S-H-R* is isomorphic with the system α-*means*-β.

Various possible *logical* "meanings" of meaning—e.g., signification, denotation, connotation, equality, equivalence, definitional equivalence, material implication, strict implication—are not at issue here. Throughout the present analysis one must clearly and persistently distinguish between logical and psychological notions about meaning; the former class of notions is conceptual (hypothetical), the latter empirical (categorical). Further, no confusion should result from referring to relations between S and R as *psychological* (empirical) meanings, since such relations are (a) purely empirical constructs, and (b) presently to be coordinated with an operational index, *m*.

The present analysis does not assert meaning and habit strength to be identical concepts, although they have some common properties. Meanings are postulated to increase in number not as an exponential growth function of the number of *particular S-particular R* reinforcements—as H in Hull's theory—but rather as a simple linear function of the number of *particular S-multiple R* connections established. Now in terms of excitatory strength (E), where

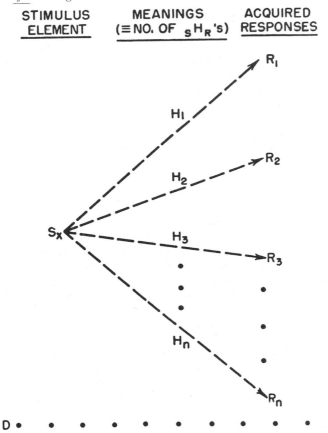

STIMULUS   MEANINGS   ACQUIRED
ELEMENT   ($\equiv$ NO. OF $_SH_R$'s)   RESPONSES

FIGURE 4-2. *Schema illustrating the development of stimulus meaning.*

$E \equiv H \cdot D$, a specific "energized" meaning may best be regarded as an unspecified supraliminal value of effective excitatory strength $(\bar{E})$, where $\bar{E} \equiv E - I$. To strengthen $\bar{E}$ beyond the value of the limen (L) required for reaction evocation (R) may alter R_p, R_a, R_n, or R_t, but the qualitative fact that S *sometimes evokes R* is unaltered. This is the psychological connotation of the assertion: *S means R.*

From an historical point of view it may be interesting to note that the present analysis is formally analogous to certain notions advanced by the British philosophers of the 18th and 19th centuries—especially by Berkeley and by James Mill. Later, from the standpoint of introspectional psychology, Titchener taught that meaning is the con-scious context which, under certain conditions, accrues to a "core" of sensory or imaginal content. This is his context "theory" of meaning, which Boring (1929, pages 185, 408) has implemented by suggesting the principle of 'accrual' to be that of association; i.e., learning. In terms of the Titchener-Boring viewpoint, then, *context* (or associated content) $=$ *meaning*. Boring has also attempted to describe Titchener's doctrine in S–R terminology by identifying S with "core" and R with "context" (Boring, 1929, page 588; 1942, page 18); hence with "meaning." However, since they can be shown to state infeasible demands (*cf.* Johnson, 1945), these and allied considerations—such as whether meaning is "palpable," "unconscious," or only "potential"—

are of no scientific concern to modern (behavioristic) psychology.

An interesting approach to a contextual theory of meaning at a more complex level of analysis is provided by the recent paper of Miller and Selfridge (1950). Defining meaningfulness in terms of dependent probabilities in successive free-association observations, these investigators have developed lists of varying orders of approximation to the structure of English.

So much for the formal definition of the concept of psychological meaning in terms of habit. Like habit, meaning is here a purely empirical construct. In order to impart significance to this notion—i.e., to relate it systematically to other constructs in behavior theory—it is first necessary to exhibit certain operations by means of which it may be given empirical verification. In other words, one must specify an empirical *index* with which the formal concept of meaning may be placed in correspondence. A few such indices are already available in the field of verbal learning. They are defined by the various operations used for calibrating the "association values" of stimulus items. The work of Cason (1926), Glaze (1928), Haagen (1949), Hull (1933), Kreuger (1934), and of Witmer (1935) represent important contributions to this problem. However, most of these indices are unsatisfactory either because they involved (a) very short response intervals, (b) free association techniques, (c) relative frequency measures, or (d) because their reliabilities were not reported. Since theoretically the number of *R*s is proportional to the number of supraliminal *Ē*s, frequency of response is proposed as a rational index of stimulus meaning (*m*). Therefore, the appropriate association value for the present analysis would be denoted by the central tendency of the frequency distribution of *continued* associations given by *S*s per unit time.[1]

[1]*Continued* associations are those which are successively elicited by the same stimulus, as distinguished from *free* or *controlled* associations.

Following these considerations an operational index of the attribute of stimulus meaning (*m*) was sought for each member of a list of 96 dissyllables, as indicated by the following definition:

$$m_s \equiv \frac{1}{N} \sum_{i=1}^{N} R_s,$$

where $S \equiv$ verbal stimulus; $R \equiv$ unit written response; $N \equiv$ number of subjects.

Procedure

A provisional list of 120 two-syllable nouns was taken from the Thorndike-Lorge tables (1944), the principal selection criterion being the *G* (general) frequency count. These items were drawn with the intention of representing (a) nearly all of the alphabet in the initial letters and (b) an extreme frequency-of-use range. It was hypothesized that frequency of occurrence in the written language would be highly correlated with *m* and therefore should provide a useful approximate ranking of the sample of stimuli to be calibrated.

The words from the Thorndike-Lorge list were supplemented by 18 artificial words which were also dissyllabic and in the form of nouns. They were selected from Dunlap's list (*cf.* Woodworth, 1938) or invented by the author. The purpose of including these paralogs was to insure a low-*m* extreme on the final scale, as well as to calibrate such items empirically on a scale continuous with that of actual words.

After a number of arbitrary and systematic rejections, the final list was reduced to 96 items. This list contained approximately

The present procedure is analogous to one reported by Cattell and Bryant (1889) and called, apparently by Woodworth (1938), the *method of continued association*. Krueger (1934) later used written responses in determining the association values of nonsense syllables, although the instructions to his *S*s would seem to define their responses as *free* associations.

20 per cent paralogs, 35 per cent infrequent items ($<$ 1 per 4 million), and 45 per cent frequent items ($>$ 1 per million). The last two frequency classes are defined by their Thorndike-Lorge relative frequency counts indicated in parentheses. The number 96 was selected because it was associated with a convenient maximum testing time for the prevailing military research schedules at the Human Resources Research Center. The time interval of 60 sec. was chosen because (a) preliminary tests showed that Ss reported 60 sec. to be an optimal interval, and (b) to insure a reliable time sample of the Ss' response hierarchy.

The stimulus items were administered in test booklet form with attached answer sheets. A uniform set was maintained by printing only one stimulus per page and by instructing S to return to the stimulus each time before responding anew. Furthermore, a given stimulus item was reproduced on each line in an effort to reduce S's inveterate tendency to free-associate. The sequence and order of presentation of the stimuli were varied by shuffling the answer sheets during the assembly of the test booklets. This device served to minimize constant errors due to fatigue, decreasing motivation, and inter-item interaction. After administering a pilot list to 15 Ss, in order to standardize the procedural variables, the final list of 96 items was given to a sample of 131 basic airmen from two flights undergoing routine classification testing at the Human Resources Research Center. These Ss were group-tested in four separate units of approximately half-flight size (about 33 men) in order to reduce inter-individual interaction. This source of variance was further reduced by varying the order and sequence of stimuli per S, as indicated. Two examiners tested two groups each, and the testing periods were held during the morning hours of two days one week apart. Response periods were of 60 sec. duration per stimulus, with an inter-item interval of 15 sec. Rest periods were given as follows: 5 min. at the end of the first 45 min. of

testing, 10 min. at the end of the second 45 min. period, and 5 min. at the end of the next 30 min. period.

Instructions to the Ss were as follows:

This is a test to see how many words you can think of and write down in a short time.

You will be given a *key* word and you are to write down as many *other* words which the key word brings to mind as you can. These other words which you write down may be things, places, ideas, events, or whatever you happen to think of when you see the key word.

For example, think of the word, KING. Some of the words or phrases which KING might bring to mind are written below:

queen	Kingdom
King Cole	England
ruler	imperial
Sky-King	kingfish

Ss were then given two practice sessions, using as stimuli the words HAM and KOREA. They were permitted to use two-word phrases, slang, long words or short words, provided they were associates of the stimulus words.

Instructions regarding motivation and set were as follows:

No one is expected to fill in all the spaces on a page, but write as many words as you can which each key word calls to mind. Be sure to think back to the *key* word after each word you write down because the test is to see how many other words the key word makes you think of. A good way to do this is to repeat each key word over and over to yourself as you write.

E also gave supplementary motivating instructions during the three rest periods.

The method of recording S's responses was sufficiently objective to require very little evaluation on E's part. However, in terms of the analysis of meaning proposed, it was decided to set up three objective criteria for unacceptable responses. These were:

1. *Illegible responses:* $S_x \rightarrow ?$

2. *Perseverative responses:*

$$S_x \rightarrow R_1(s_1) \rightarrow R_1(s_1) \cdots$$

TABLE 4-1

List of Dissyllable Words (Nouns) in Rank Order of Increasing Meaningfulness (m) as Defined by Mean Frequency of Continued Associations in 60 Sec. (N = 119)

Rank	Word number	m-Value	σ	Word	Rank	Word number	m-Value	σ	Word
1	24	0.99	2.05	GOJEY	49	58	2.69	3.43	OVUM
2	53	1.04	1.60	NEGLAN	50	72	2.73	3.24	ROSTRUM
3	49	1.05	1.85	MEARDON	51	84	2.76	2.92	VERTEX
4	8	1.13	1.89	BYSSUS	52	5	2.80	3.27	BODICE
5	4	1.22	1.95	BALAP	53	76	2.89	3.20	TANKARD
6	86	1.22	2.17	VOLVAP	54	60	3.06	3.04	PALLOR
7	77	1.24	2.03	TAROP	55	74	3.21	2.85	SEQUENCE
8	90	1.24	2.20	XYLEM	56	1	3.34	3.34	ARGON
9	41	1.26	2.16	LATUK	57	68	3.36	3.22	RAMPART
10	66	1.26	2.01	QUIPSON	58	35	3.51	3.50	JITNEY
11	25	1.27	2.20	GOKEM	59	17	3.55	3.19	ENTRANT
12	52	1.28	1.96	NARES	60	59	3.62	3.26	PALLET
13	96	1.28	2.19	ZUMAP	61	51	3.64	3.48	NAPHTHA
14	63	1.30	1.98	POLEF	62	62	3.77	3.45	PIGMENT
15	73	1.33	2.06	SAGROLE	63	57	3.91	3.42	ORDEAL
16	55	1.34	2.37	NOSTAW	64	94	4.44	3.19	ZENITH
17	6	1.39	2.12	BODKIN	65	91	4.60	3.82	YEOMAN
18	81	1.50	2.78	ULNA	66	67	4.68	3.13	QUOTA
19	88	1.53	2.05	WELKIN	67	64	5.10	3.45	QUARRY
20	29	1.54	2.84	ICON	68	15	5.13	3.19	EFFORT
21	40	1.55	2.45	KUPOD	69	83	5.32	3.24	UNIT
22	13	1.60	2.46	DELPIN	70	18	5.33	3.46	FATIGUE
23	3	1.71	2.55	ATTAR	71	37	5.47	3.11	KEEPER
24	48	1.73	2.69	MATRIX	72	38	5.52	3.70	KENNEL
25	12	1.74	2.69	DAVIT	73	47	5.61	3.32	MALLET
26	89	1.78	2.77	WIDGEON	74	42	5.94	3.17	LEADER
27	7	1.79	2.65	BRUGEN	75	65	5.98	3.16	QUARTER
28	36	1.82	2.95	KAYSEN	76	69	5.98	3.70	REGION
29	46	1.84	2.85	MAELSTROM	77	28	6.02	3.33	HUNGER
30	79	1.84	2.95	TUMBRIL	78	95	6.15	3.05	ZERO
31	70	1.86	2.85	RENNET	79	30	6.24	3.50	INCOME
32	71	1.90	2.35	ROMPIN	80	82	6.57	3.79	UNCLE
33	22	1.95	2.55	GAMIN	81	92	6.75	4.12	YOUNGSTER
34	19	2.09	3.11	FEMUR	82	80	6.83	3.29	TYPHOON
35	45	2.09	3.42	LOZENGE	83	10	6.88	3.11	CAPTAIN
36	20	2.13	2.77	FERRULE	84	93	7.12	3.75	ZEBRA
37	75	2.14	2.75	STOMA	85	23	7.17	4.48	GARMENT
38	26	2.15	3.09	GRAPNEL	86	85	7.28	4.05	VILLAGE
39	21	2.19	3.25	FLOTSAM	87	31	7.39	3.09	INSECT
40	11	2.26	3.35	CAROM	88	34	7.58	3.69	JEWEL
41	54	2.26	2.65	NIMBUS	89	32	7.70	3.53	JELLY
42	43	2.28	3.06	LEMUR	90	27	7.91	3.86	HEAVEN
43	9	2.41	3.13	CAPSTAN	91	56	7.95	3.66	OFFICE
44	61	2.43	2.88	PERCEPT	92	87	8.12	3.67	WAGON
45	44	2.48	2.96	LICHENS	93	14	8.33	4.21	DINNER
46	33	2.54	3.53	JETSAM	94	50	8.98	4.27	MONEY
47	16	2.59	3.08	ENDIVE	95	2	9.43	4.30	ARMY
48	78	2.63	3.04	TARTAN	96	39	9.61	4.30	KITCHEN

3. *Failures of set:* $S_x \nearrow \begin{array}{c} R_1 \\ \nearrow R_{2_1} \\ R_2(s_2) \to R_{2_2} \\ \searrow R_{2_3} \end{array}$

This last class of unacceptable responses was further classified into:

a. *Free or tangential associations:* e.g., LEMUR → Dorothy, Hope, faith, charity. . . .
b. *Clang or alliterative associations:* e.g., KAYSEN → caisson, Casey, casein, casement. . . .

Finally, a general rule of giving S the benefit of the doubt was adopted. This was occasionally necessary in the case of category 3 above, although free and clang associations were usually easily identified by the three scorers. Of the original 131 Ss tested, 12 protocols were rejected for persistent violations of the criteria cited. This brought the effective sample to 119 Ss.

Results

The index of meaning (m) of a particular stimulus was defined in equation [1] as the grand mean number of (acceptable) written responses given by all Ss within a 60 sec. period. Therefore, the scale values of the stimuli were determined directly by the average response frequencies of the 119 Ss. These m-values with the o's of their distributions are shown in Table 4-1, ranging in rank order from dissyllables of low response-evocation value (e.g., No. 1: GOJEY) to those of high response-evocation value (e.g., No. 96: KITCHEN). The empirical range is from 0.99 to 9.61. It will be noted that there is no discrete gap between the paralog items and the actual words. In fact, there are a few actual words low on the scale (e.g., No. 4: BYSSUS), while one paralog (No. 32: ROMPIN) appears at the third way point. It is also to be noted that response variability tends to increase with increasing m-value.

It was found that the m-values of partic-

TABLE 4-2

Intergroup Reliability Coefficients (r)
for m-Scale Based on Mean
m-Values for Four Groups of Ss

Group	I	II	III	IV	n
I	—	—	—	—	27
II	.98	—	—	—	30
III	.98	.98	—	—	30
IV	.96	.97	.98	—	32

N = 119.

ular items were quite stable from group to group. Intercorrelations of the four sets of mean m-values per word were carried out among all six combinations of groups. These Pearsonian r-values appear in Table 4-2. All are significantly different from zero ($P < 0.01$). Since the sampling distribution of r is skewed for large values, Fisher's Z-transformation was used to estimate the mean intergroup reliability coefficient of the m-scale: $\bar{r}_{mm} = 0.975$. It may be pointed out that a between-groups reliability coefficient[2] is the appropriate statistic to compute in this case since it was E's aim to determine the consistency of *different response samples* to the *same stimuli*. A more conventional reliability coefficient— such as one defined by the test-retest, split-half, or the alternate form procedure— would not have evaluated this particular relationship.

Of some interest in this investigation was the extent to which the assumptions of the product-moment correlational method were met. The family of response frequency distributions associated with the stimulus items exhibited skewness at the low-m extreme of the scale, but throughout the central and upper portions they were approximately symetrical. Hence, means were retained as measures of central tendency. When the six intercorrelations of the m-scale were plotted, it was found that the requirements

[2]Rather than a "reliability" coefficient, some might prefer to call this statistic a coefficient of "objectivity," "agreement," or of "consistency."

of linearity of regression and of homosce-
dasticity were reasonably satisfied.

DISCUSSION

MEANING. After reviewing the analysis of
meaning, one properly may ask whether
responses may acquire meanings also, or
whether only stimuli do so. As has been
indicated, meanings are considered relations
between Ss and Rs.[3] It is for convenience
that, instead of referring to m, one speaks
of "the meaning of a stimulus" or of "stimulus meaning," just as one speaks of "reinforcing a conditioned response," when
more precisely it is the S–R connection, or
H, which strictly is reinforced. To speak of
stimulus meaning is to imply an asymmetry
in the empirical meaning relation. Indeed,
common linguistic usage seems to concur
that meaning, like causation, be regarded
as a property of stimuli rather than of
responses.

Under certain conditions, however, it is
appropriate to refer loosely to the meaning

[3] Not all writers would agree to construe meaning thus (*cf.* 2, 3, 4, 17, 27).

of a *response*. One such condition would
arise if analysis should indicate that a certain class of responses results in proprioceptive stimulation (s) to an organism. This is
the well-known response-produced stimulus
situation, or feedback mechanism. Kines-
thesis is perhaps the best example. The
descriptive schema outlined in the section
on meaning applies equally well, as shown
in Figure 4-3. Here the situation becomes
more complex, but no different qualita-
tively. Hs develop between initial R ($\rightarrow s$)s
and subsequent Rs, thereby permitting
more complex degrees of development of
meaning.

The serial anticipation learning situation, for example, fits this schema well in
that each successive response functions as a
stimulus to the next response in the series,
while the verbal stimuli appearing serially
in the memory drum aperture serve as secondary reinforcing agents. This type of
analysis also suggests an explanatory approach for the relationships Miller and
Selfridge (1950) have found between reproductive recall and contextual dependencies.
The work of Thorndike (1931) on "belonging" may be similarly regarded.

The result of this analysis of meaning

FIGURE 4-3. *Schema illustrating the development of more complex degrees of
meaning.*

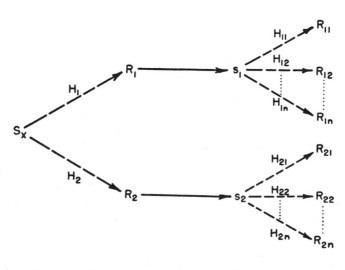

and its incorporation into learning theory is twofold: (a) it establishes a highly reliable, unequivocal new attribute of variation in learning, and (b) it provides an operational basis for explicating the common-sense notion of "meaning." Thus, if one were to ask a layman what he intended by saying that "home" to him *means:* "family, spouse, children, friends, love," etc., he would doubtless reply, "I think of these things when 'home' is mentioned." It is a simple matter to fit this statement to the model proposed in Figure 4-2. A learning theorist would explain that to the auditory (or visual) S *home,* these various verbal Rs have become conditioned during our imaginary layman's previous experience, and that under appropriate conditions (e.g., adequate D level, sufficient reinforcements to each L) these Rs are elicited. The meaning of S subsists in the Hs developed to it—nothing more[4]. A neutral S, by the present definitions, is meaning*less;* an S conditioned to twenty Rs is more meaning*ful* (i.e., has more meanings) than is one conditioned to ten, and so on. Speaking quite non-technically, meanings are habits. And as more habits accrue to a particular stimulus situation, so does its meaningfulness increase.

In the final analysis the index *m*, like *H*, emerges as a statistical concept. It is a function of the number of particular S-multiple R connections which are formed,

[4] In view of the fact that the class of responses defining the *m*-scale represents a set of individual-difference variables, one should properly denote the meaning relation in this case by the symbol *U* rather than by *H*. From a genetic standpoint, certain learning theorists preserve a distinction between innate *or* previously-acquired connections $(sUr's)$ and laboratory-established connections $(sHr's)$. However, in Hull's theory both *U* and *H* are considered habit or associational concepts, hence the proposed coordination with meaning is unimpaired. A similar argument holds for conditioned generalized connections $(s\bar{H}r's)$.

and it enjoys an existence independent of the cited operations no more than does any other empirical construct.

In view of its theoretical status and exceptional reliability, the *m*-scale is regarded with especial interest for research in verbal and in perceptual-motor learning. Using the *m*-scale, research may now be directed toward the solution of such current problems as the relationship between difficulty and meaningfulness, the effect of meaningfulness upon reminiscence, and the rôle of verbal instructions in the acquisition of motor skills.

SUMMARY AND CONCLUSIONS

This paper has presented a theoretical-experimental analysis of the attribute of meaning in verbal stimulus material. A word list of 96 dissyllables consisting of nouns and paralogs was presented to a sample of 119 USAF recruits in order to establish a quantitative scale for this attribute. The results of this analysis were as follows:

1. Meaning was formally defined as a relation between S and R. It was coordinated with Hull's theoretical construct *H* by postulating that meanings increase as a simple linear function of the number of S-multiple R connections acquired in a particular organism's history.

2. An index of stimulus meaning (*m*) was operationally defined in terms of the mean frequency of continued written associations made by subjects within a 60-sec. time interval.

3. A psychological performance scale of *m*-values was developed which exhibited a range extending from 0.99 to 9.61. The mean product-moment intergroup reliability coefficient was $\bar{r}_{mm} = 0.975$.

4. The significance of these findings for human learning theory was discussed.

REFERENCES

Bergmann, G., and K. W. Spence. The logic of psychophysical measurement. *Psychol. Rev.*, 1944, **51**, 1–24.

Boring, E. G. A *history of experimental psychology.* New York: Appleton, 1929.

———. *The physical dimensions of consciousness.* New York: Appleton, 1933.

———. *Sensation and perception in the history of*

experimental psychology. New York: Appleton, 1942.

Carr, H. A. *Psychology: A study of mental activity.* New York: Longmans, 1925.

Cason, H. Specific serial learning: A study of backward association. *J. exp. Psychol.*, 1926, **9**, 195–227.

Cattell, J. McK., and S. Bryant. Mental association investigated by experiment. *Mind*, 1889, **14**, 230–250.

Dashiell, J. F. A neglected fourth dimension to psychological research. *Psychol. Rev.*, 1940, **47**, 289–305.

Glaze, J. A. The association value of non-sense syllables. *J. genet. Psychol.*, 1928, **35**, 255–269.

Guilford, J. P. *Psychometric methods.* New York: McGraw-Hill, 1936.

Haagen, C. H. Synonymity, vividness, familiarity, and association value ratings of 400 pairs of common adjectives. *J. Psychol.*, 1949, **27**, 453–463.

Hebb, D. O. *The organization of behavior.* New York: Wiley, 1949.

Hull, C. L. The meaningfulness of 320 selected nonsense syllables. *Amer. J. Psychol.*, 1933, **45**, 730–734.

———. *Principles of behavior.* New York: Appleton, 1943.

Johnson, H. M. Are psychophysical problems genuine or spurious? *Amer. J. Psychol.*, 1945, **58**, 189–211.

Köhler, W. *The place of value in a world of facts.* New York: Liveright, 1938.

Krueger, W. C. F. The relative difficulty of nonsense syllables. *J. exp. Psychol.*, 1934, **17**, 145–153.

McGeoch, J. A. The vertical dimensions of mind. *Psychol. Rev.*, 1936, **43**, 107–129.

———. *The psychology of human learning.* New York: Longmans, 1942.

Melton, A. W. The methodology of experimental studies of human learning and retention: I. The functions of a methodology and the available criteria for evaluating different experimental methods. *Psychol. Bull.*, 1936, **33**, 305–394.

———. Learning. In W. S. Monroe (Ed.), *Encyclopedia of educational research.* New York: Macmillan, 1950. Pp. 668–690.

Miller, G. A., and J. A. Selfridge. Verbal context and the recall of meaningful material. *Amer. J. Psychol.*, 1950, **63**, 176–185.

Robinson, E. S. *Association theory today: An essay in systematic psychology.* New York: Appleton, 1932.

Thorndike, E. L. *Human learning.* New York: Appleton, 1931.

———, and I. Lorge. *The teacher's word book of 30,000 words.* New York: Columbia University Press, 1944.

Tolman, E. C. *Purposive behavior in animals and men.* New York: 1932.

Underwood, B. J. *Experimental psychology.* New York: Appleton, 1949.

Watson, J. B. *Behaviorism.* (2d, Ed.) New York: Norton, 1925.

Witmer, L. R. The association value of three-place consonant syllables. *J. genet. Psychol.*, 1935, **47**, 337–359.

Woodworth, R. S. *Experimental psychology.* New York: Holt, Rinehart and Winston, 1938.

The Nature of Meaning

CHARLES E. OSGOOD

The language process within an individual may be viewed as a more or less continuous interaction between two parallel systems of behavioral organization: sequences of central events ("ideas") and sequences of instrumental skills, vocalic, gestural, or orthographic, which constitute the communicative product. A communica-

Reprinted and abridged with the permission of the author and publisher from the article, "The nature and Measurement of meaning," *Psychological Bulletin*, 1952, **49**, 197–237.

tor vocalizes, "It looks like rain today; I'd better not wash the car." This output is a sequence of skilled movements, complicated to be sure, but not different in kind from tying one's shoes. Even the smallest units of the product, phonetic elements like the initial "l"-sound of "looks," result from precisely patterned muscle movements. The organization of these movements into word-units represents skill sequences of relatively high predictability; certain longer period sequences involving syntactical order are also relatively predictable for a given language system. But execution of such sequences brings the communicator repeatedly to what may be called "choice-points" —points where the next skill sequence is not highly predictable from the objective communicative product itself. The dependence of "I'd better not wash the car" upon "looks like rain today," the *content* of the message, reflects determinants within the semantic system which effectively "load" the transitional probabilities at these choice-points.

It is the communicative product, the spoken or written words which follow one another in varying orders, that we typically observe. Since we are unable to specify the stimuli which evoke these communicating reactions—since it is "emitted" rather than "elicited" behavior in Skinner's terminology (1938)—measurements in terms of rates of occurrence and transitional probabilities (dependence of one event in the stream upon others) are particularly appropriate (cf. Miller, 1951). Interest may be restricted to the lawfulness of sequences in the observable communicative product itself, without regard to the semantic parallel. This is traditionally the field of the linguist, but even here it has proved necessary to make some assumptions about meaning (cf. Bloomfield, 1933). On the other hand, one may be specifically interested in the semantic or ideational level. Since he is presently unable to observe this level of behavior directly, he must use observable characteristics of the communicative product as a basis for making inferences about what is going on at the semantic level. He may use sequential orderliness in the product to draw conclusions as to semantic orderliness in the speaker's or writer's mediation processes (i.e., which "ideas" tend to go together in his thinking with greater than chance probabilities). Or he may wish to study the ways in which central, semantic processes vary from concept to concept, from person to person, and so on. It is the problem of measuring meaning in this latter sense which will be discussed in the present paper.

Before inquiring into the measurement of the meaning of signs, for which there are no accepted, standardized techniques available, we may briefly mention certain fairly standard methods for measuring the comparative strength of verbal habits. Thorndike and his associates (1921, 1944) have made extensive *frequency-of-usage counts* of words in English; that this method gets at the comparative habit strengths of word skill sequences is shown by the fact that other measures of response strength, such as latency and probability within the individual (Thumb and Marbe, 1901; Cason and Cason, 1925), are correlated with frequency-of-usage. Zipf (1935, 1949, and elsewhere) has described innumerable instances of the lawfulness of such habit-strength measures. Whether samples be taken from Plautine Latin, newspaper English, or the English of James Joyce in his *Ulysses*, a fundamental regularity is found, such that frequency of occurrence of particular words bears a linear relation to their rank order in frequency, when plotted on double-log paper (Zipf's Law). Measurement of flexibility or diversity in communicative products is given by the *type-token ratio* (TTR): with each instance of any word counting as a token and each different word as a type, the greater the ratio of types to tokens the more varied is the content of a message. This measure can be applied comparatively to different forms of material, different kinds of individuals, and so forth (cf., Carroll, 1938, 1944; Johnson, 1944; Chotlos, 1944), provided the sizes of samples are constant. One may also count the ratios of adjectives to verbs (Boder, 1940), the frequencies of different pronouns, intensives, and so forth (cf., Johnson, 1944).

Although the above measures get at the comparative strengths of verbal skill sequences per se (i.e., without regard to meaning), this is not a necessary restriction. Frequency counts of this type can be applied to *semantic habit strengths* as well. Skinner (1937) has shown that a similar lawfulness applies to the frequencies of "free" associations in the Kent-Rosanoff tests. When frequencies of particular associates to given stimulus words for a group of subjects are plotted against their rank order in frequency, a straight-line function on double-log paper results (Zipf's Law). In other words, associations at the semantic level appear to be organized in such a way that few have very high probability of occurrence and many have low probabilities of occurrence. Bousfield and his collaborators (1944, 1950, 1937, 1944, 1950) have described a *sequential association method* for getting at comparative semantic habit strengths. When subjects associate successively from the same "pool," e.g., "names of four-legged animals," (*a*) the rate of successive associates shows a negatively accelerated curve, (*b*) varying in its constants with certain characteristics of materials and subjects, (*c*) the order of appearance of particular associates in individuals being predictable from the frequency of usage in the group, and (*d*) distortions in the function being related to particular transitional probabilities among associates, i.e., clustering. Useful though these measures are for many purposes, they do not get at meaning. The fact that "dog" has a higher probability of occurrence in sequential association than "otter" says nothing whatsoever about the differences in meaning of these two signs.

An extensive survey of the literature fails to uncover any generally accepted, standardized method for measuring meaning. Perhaps it is because of the philosophical haziness of this concept, perhaps because of the general belief that "meanings" are infinitely and uniquely variable, or perhaps because the word "meaning" as a construct in our language connotes mental stuff, more akin to "thought" and "soul" than to anything observable—for some combination of reasons there has been little attempt to devise methods here. Nevertheless, whether looked at from the viewpoints of philosophy or linguistics, from economic or sociological theory, or—interestingly enough—from within the core of psychological theories of individual behavior, the nature of meaning and change in meaning are found to be central issues. The proposals to be made in the latter portion of this paper are part of a program aimed at the development of objective methods of measuring meaning. Beyond obvious social implications, it is felt that this direction of research is a logical extension of scientific inquiry into an area generally considered immune to its attack.

THEORIES OF MEANING

Not all stimuli are signs. The shock which galvanizes a rat into vigorous escape movements usually does not stand for anything other than itself, nor does the pellet of food found at the end of a maze, nor a hammer in one's hand or a shoe on one's foot. The problem for any meaning theorist is to differentiate the conditions under which a pattern of stimulation is a sign of something else from those conditions where it is not. This certainly seems simple enough, yet it has troubled philosophers for centuries. By stating the problem somewhat formally, the chief differences between several conceptions of the sign-process can be made evident: let

$\dot{S}$ = object = any pattern of stimulation which evokes reactions on the part of an organism, and

$\boxed{s}$ = sign = any pattern of stimulation which is not this $\dot{S}$ but yet evokes reactions relevant to $\dot{S}$—conditions under which this holds being the problem for theory.

The definition of Ṡ is broad enough to include any pattern of stimulation which elicits any reaction from an organism. Although one usually thinks of "objects" as those things denoted by signs, actually any pattern of stimulation—a gust of northerly wind against the face, the sensations we call "belly-ache," the sensations of being rained upon—is an "object" at this level of discourse. One sign may be the "object" represented by another sign, as when the picture of an apple is called "DAX" in certain experiments. The definition of $\boxed{s}$ is purposely left incomplete at this point, since it depends upon one's conception of the nature of the sign-process.

We may start a logical analysis of the problem with a self-evident fact: *the pattern of stimulation which is the sign is never identical with the pattern of stimulation which is the object.* The word "hammer" is not the same stimulus as is the object hammer. The former is a pattern of sound waves having characteristic oscillations in frequency and intensity; the latter, depending upon its mode of contact, may be a visual form having characteristic color and shape, a pattern of tactual and proprioceptive sensations, and so on. Similarly, the buzzer in a typical rat experiment is not identical as a form of stimulation with the shock which it comes to signify. Yet these signs—the word "hammer" and the buzzer—do elicit behaviors which are in some manner relevant to the objects they signify, a characteristic *not* shared with an infinite number of other stimulus patterns that are *not* signs of these objects. In simplest terms, therefore, the question is: *under what conditions does something which is not an object becomes a sign of that object?* According to the way in which this question is answered we may distinguish several theories of meaning.

Mentalistic View

The classic interpretation derives directly from the natural philosophy of Western culture, in which the dualistic connotations of language dictate a correlation between two classes of events, material and nonmaterial. Since meanings are obviously "mental" events and the stimuli representing objects and signs are obviously "physical" events, any satisfying theory of meaning must specify interrelation between these levels of discourse. At the core of all mentalistic views, therefore, we find an "idea" as the essence of meaning; it is this mental event which links or relates the two different physical events, sign and object. The word "hammer" gives rise to the idea of that object in the mind; conversely, perception of the object hammer gives rise to the same idea, which can then be "expressed" in appropriate signs. In other words, *something which is not the object becomes a sign of that object when it gives rise to the idea associated with that object.* Probably the most sophisticated expression of this view is given by Ogden and Richards (1923) in their book, *The Meaning of Meaning.* Most readers will recall their triangular diagram of the sign-process: the relation between symbol and referent (the base of their triangle) is not direct but inferred, mediated through mental "thought" or "interpretation" (the third corner of their triangle).

Substitution View

Naive application of Pavlovian conditioning principles by early behaviorists like Watson led to the theory that signs achieve their meanings simply by being conditioned to the same reactions originally made to objects. This, in essence, is the view one encounters in many introductory texts in general psychology. An object evokes certain behavior in an organism; if another pattern of stimulation is consistently paired with the original object, it becomes conditioned to the same responses and thus gets its meaning. The object is the unconditioned stimulus and the sign is the conditioned stimulus, the latter merely being substituted for the former. The definition of the sign-process here is that *whenever some-thing which is not the object evokes in an organism the same reactions evoked by the object, it is a sign of that object.* The very simplicity of this theory highlights its in-adequacy. Signs almost never evoke the *same* overt responses as do the objects they represent. The word FIRE has meaning to the reader without sending him into head-long flight. Nevertheless, this represents a first step toward a behavioral interpretation of the sign-process.

Meaning as "Set" or "Disposition"

In a monograph entitled *Foundation of the Theory of Signs* (1938), Charles Morris, a semiotician working in the tradition estab-lished by Peirce and other American pragmatists, proposed a formula for the sign-process which avoids the pitfalls of sub-stitution theory but seems to step backward toward the mentalistic view. In essence he states that signs achieve their meanings by eliciting reactions which "take account of" the objects signified. The sign "hammer" may evoke quite different responses from those evoked by the object signified, but these responses must have the character of being relevant to the object. The response made to the sign is called "interpretant" which mediately takes account of the ob-ject signified. But it would seem that this process of "taking account of" is precisely what needs elucidation.

During the period intervening between this monograph and his recent book, *Signs, Language and Behavior* (1946), Morris stud-ied with two prominent behavior theorists, Tolman and Hull. The effects of this im-mersion in learning theory are evident in his book, which is a pioneer attempt to re-duce semiotic to an objective behavioral basis. He states that "if anything, A, is a preparatory stimulus which in the absence of stimulus-objects initiating response-sequences of a certain behavior-family causes a disposition in some organism to respond

under certain conditions by response-se-quences of this behavior-family, then A is a sign" (page 10). Reduced to its essentials and translated into our terms, this becomes: *any pattern of stimulation which is not the object becomes a sign of that object if it produces in an organism a "disposition" to make any of the responses previously elicited by that object.* There is no requirement that the *overt* reactions originally elicited by the object also be made to the sign; the sign merely creates a disposition or set to make such reactions, actual occurrence depending upon the concurrence of sup-porting conditions.

Beyond the danger that "dispositions" may serve as mere surrogates for "ideas" in this theory, there are certain other diffi-culties with the view as stated. For one thing, Morris seems to have revived the substitution notion. The sign is said to dis-pose the organism to make overt response-sequences of the *same* behavior-family origi-nally elicited by the object. But is this necessarily the case? Is my response to the word "apple" (e.g., free-associating the word "peach") any part of the behavior-family elicited by the object apple? For another thing, Morris formulation fails to differen-tiate sign-behavior from many instinctive reactions and from ordinary conditioning. To appreciate this difficulty will require a brief digression.

When a breach is made in a termite nest, the workers set up a distinctive pounding upon the floor of the tunnel and the warriors come charg-ing to the spot, where they take up defensive positions. Is this pounding sound a sign to the war-rior-termites that there is a breach in the nest? It happens that this behavior is purely instinc-tive, and most students of sign-behavior believe that signs must achieve their signification through *learning.* But is learning a sufficient criterion? Are all stimuli that elicit learned reactions auto-matically signs? In developing any skill, such as tying the shoes, the proprioceptive stimuli pro-duced by one response become conditioned to the succeeding reponse—but of what are these proprioceptive stimuli signs? With repeated ex-perience on an electrified grill a rat will often learn to rear up on its hind legs and alternately lift them, this act apparently reducing the total intensity of pain—the painful stimulation is thus conditioned to a new response, but of what is the pain a sign?

If only some of the stimuli which elicit learned responses are signs, we must seek a reasonable distinction *within* the class of learned behaviors. We cannot draw a line between human and subhuman learning: the buzzer is operationally as much a sign of shock to the rat in avoidance-training experiments as are dark clouds a sign of rain to the professor—both stimuli elicit reactions appropriate, not to themselves, but to something other than themselves. Is voluntariness of response a criterion? Meaningful reactions may be just as involuntary as perceptions—try to observe a familiar word and avoid its meaning! Is it variability of response to the stimulus? Meaningful reactions may be just as stable and habitual as motor skills.

The Mediation Hypothesis

I shall try to show that the distinguishing condition of sign behavior is the presence or absence of *a representational mediation process* in association with the stimulus. This conception of sign behavior is based upon a general theory of learning rather than being concocted specifically to account for meaning as seen in human communication. The essence of the viewpoint can be given as follows:

1. *Stimulus-objects* (Ṡ) *elicit a complex pattern of reactions from the organism, these reactions varying in their dependence upon presence of the stumulus-object for their occurrence.* Electric shock galvanizes the rat into vigorous jumping, squeaking, and running activities, as well as autonomic "anxiety" reactions. Food objects elicit sequences of salivating, chewing, lip-smacking, and so forth. Components like salivating and "anxiety" are relatively independent of the food or shock stimulation respectively and hence can occur when such objects are not present.

2. *When stimuli other than the stimulus-object, but previously associated with it, are later presented without its support, they tend to elicit some reduced portion of the total behavior elicited by the stimulus-object.* This reduction process follows certain laws: (a) mediating reactions which interfere with goal-achievement tend to extinguish; (b) the more energy expenditure involved in making a particular reaction, the less likely it is to survive the reduction process; (c) there is evidence that certain reactions (e.g., autonomic) condition more readily than others (e.g., gross skeletal) and hence are more likely to become part of the mediation process—this may merely reflect factor (b) above.

3. *The fraction of the total object-elicited behavior which finally constitutes the stable mediation process elicited by a sign* ($\boxed{s}$) *will tend toward a minimum set by the discriminatory capacity of the organism.* This is because the sole function of such mediating reactions in behavior is to provide a distinctive pattern of self-stimulation (cf., Hull's conception of the "pure stimulus act").

4. *The self-stimulation produced by sign-elicited mediation processes becomes conditioned in varying strengths to the initial responses in hierarchies of instrumental skill sequences.* This mediated self-stimulation is assumed to provide the "way of perceiving" signs or their "meaning," as well as mediating instrumental skill sequences —behaviors to signs which take account of the objects represented.

Whereas Morris linked sign and object through partial identity of object-produced and disposition-*produced* behaviors, we have linked sign and object through partial identity of the "disposition" *itself* with the behavior elicited by the object. Words represent things because they produce some replica of the actual behavior toward these things, as a mediation process. This is the crucial identification, the mechanism that ties particular signs to particular stimulus-objects and not to others. Stating the proposition formally: *a pattern of stimulation which is not the object is a sign of the object if it evokes in an organism a mediating reaction, this (a) being some fractional part of the total behavior elicited by the object and (b) producing distinctive self-stimu-*

lation that mediates responses which would not occur without the previous association of nonobject and object patterns of stimulation. This definition may be cumbersome, but all the limiting conditions seem necessary. The mediation process must include some part of the same behavior made to the object if the sign is to have its particularistic representing property. What we have done here, in a sense, is to make explicit what may be implicit in Morris' term "disposition." The second stipulation (*b*) adds the learning requirement—the response of warrior-termites to pounding on the tunnel floor is ruled out since it does not depend upon prior association of pounding with discovery of a breach in the nest.

Paradigm *A* in Figure 4-4 gives an abbreviated symbolic account of the development of a *sign*, according to the mediation hypothesis. Take for illustration the connotative meaning of the word SPIDER. The stimulus-object ($\dot{S}$), the visual pattern of hairy-legged insect body often encountered in a threat context provided by other humans, elicits a complex pattern of behavior

(R_T), which in this case includes a heavy loading of automatic "fear" activity. Portions of this total behavior to the spider-object become conditioned to the heard word, SPIDER. With repetitions of the sign sequence, the mediation process becomes reduced to some minimally effortful and minimally interfering replica—but still includes those autonomic reactions which confer a threatening significance upon this sign. This mediating reaction (r_m) produces a distinctive pattern of self-stimulation (S_m) which may elicit a variety of overt behaviors (R_x)—shivering and saying "ugh," running out of a room where a spider is said to be lurking, and even refusing a job in the South, which is said to abound in spiders.

The vast majority of signs used in ordinary communication are what we may term *assigns*—their meanings are literally "assigned" to them via association with other signs rather than via direct association with the objects represented. The word ZEBRA is understood by most six-year-olds, yet few of them have ever encountered

FIGURE 4-4. *Symbolic account of the development of sign processes:* A, *development of a sign;* B, *development of an assign.*

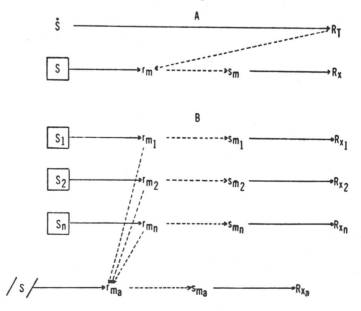

zebra-objects themselves. They have seen pictures of them, been told they have stripes, run like horses, and are usually found wild. As indicated in Figure 4-4, this new stimulus pattern, ZEBRA, "picks up" by the mechanisms already described portions of the mediating reactions already elicited by the primary signs. In learning to read, for example, the "little black bugs" on the printed page are definitely assigns; these visual patterns are seldom directly associated with the objects signified, but rather with auditory signs (created by the child and teacher as they verbalize). Obviously, the more quickly the child can learn to make the right noises to these visual stimuli (the modern phonetic approach to reading), the more quickly these new, visual assigns will acquire significance. The child already has meanings for HOUSE, DOG, and even TYPE-WRITER as *heard* stimulus patterns, but these mediation processes must be assigned to *seen* stimulus patterns.

It is apparent from the foregoing that the meanings which different individuals have for the same signs will vary with their behaviors toward the objects represented. This is because the composition of the mediation process, which *is* the meaning of a sign, is entirely dependent upon the composition of the total behavior occurring while the sign-process is being established. This indicates that to change the meaning of signs we must change behavior with respect to objects (keeping in mind that the "objects" for assigns are other signs). On the other hand, meanings are quite independent of the stimulus characteristics of the signs themselves, a point repeatedly stressed by linguists. According to the present theory, there is nothing sacred about the particular mouth-noises we use in communication any more than there is about the buzzer that becomes a sign of shock to the rat—a flash of light or a blast of air would serve as well. Of course, in human communication (in contrast to sign-behavior in the rat) it is necessary that the users of signs be able to produce as well as receive them.

REFERENCES

Bloomfield, L. *Language.* New York: Holt, 1933.

Boder, D. P. The adjective-verb-quotient: A contribution to the psychology of language. *Psychol. Rec.*, 1940, 3, 310–343.

Bousfield, W. A. An empirical study of the production of affectively toned items. *J. gen. Psychol.*, 1944, 30, 205–215.

———. The relationship between mood and the production of affectively toned associates. *J. gen. Psychol.*, 1950, 42, 67–85.

———, and W. D. Barclay. The relationship between order and frequency of occurrence of restricted associative responses. *J. exp. Psychol.*, 1950, 40, 643–647.

———, and H. Barry, Jr. Quantitative correlates of euphoria. *J. exp. Psychol.*, 1937, 21, 218–222.

———, and C. H. W. Sedgwick. An analysis of sequences of restricted associative responses. *J. gen. Psychol.*, 1944, 30, 149–165.

Carroll, J. B. Diversity of vocabulary and the harmonic series law of word-frequency distribution. *Psychol. Rec.*, 1938, 2, 379–386.

———. The analysis of verbal behavior. *Psychol. Rev.*, 1944, 51, 102–119.

Cason, H., and E. B. Cason. Association tendencies and learning ability. *J. exp. Psychol.*, 1925, 8, 167–189.

Chotlos, J. W. Studies in language behavior: IV. A statistical and comparative analysis of individual written language samples. *Psychol. Monogr.*, 1944, 56, No. 2 (Whole No. 255), 75–111.

Johnson, W. Studies in language behavior: 1. A program of research. *Psychol. Monogr.*, 1944, 56, No. 2 (Whole No. 255), 1–15.

Miller, G. A. *Language and communication.* New York: McGraw-Hill, 1951.

Morris, C. *Foundations of the theory of signs.* Internat. Encycl. Unif. Sci., Vol 1, No. 2, Chicago: University of Chicago Press, 1938.

———. *Signs, language and behavior.* New York: Prentice-Hall, 1946.

Ogden, C. K., and I. A. Richards. The meaning of meaning. London: Routledge, 1923.

Skinner, B. F. The distribution of associated words. *Psychol. Rec.*, 1937, 1, 69–76.

————. *The behavior of organisms.* New York: Appleton, 1938.

Thorndike, E. L. *The teacher's word book.* New York: Teachers College, 1921.

————, and I. Lorge. *The teacher's word book of 30,000 words.* New York: Teachers College, 1944.

Thumb, A., and K. Marbe. *Experimentelle Un-*

tersuchungen uber die psychologischen Grundlagen der sprachlichen Analogiebildung. Leipzig: Engleman, 1901.

Zipf, G. K. *The psychology of language.* New York: Houghton Mifflin, 1935.

————. *Human behavior and the principle of least effort.* Cambridge, Mass.: Addison-Welsey, 1949.

The Structure
of a Semantic Theory

JERROLD J. KATZ

JERRY A. FODOR

This paper does not attempt to present a semantic theory of a natural language, but rather to characterize the form of such a theory. A semantic theory of a natural language is part of a linguistic description of that language. Our problem, on the other hand, is part of the general theory of language, fully on a par with the problem of characterizing the structure of grammars of natural languages. A characterization of the abstract form of a semantic theory is given by the metatheory which answers such questions as these: What is the domain of a semantic theory? What are the descriptive and explanatory goals of a semantic theory? What mechanisms are employed in pursuit of these goals? What are the empirical and methodological constraints upon a semantic theory?

The present paper approaches the problem of characterizing the form of semantic theories by describing the structure of a semantic theory of English. There can be little doubt but that the results achieved will apply directly to semantic theories of languages closely related to English. The question of their applicability to semantic theories of more distant languages will be

left for subsequent investigations to explore. Nevertheless, the present investigation will provide results that can be applied to semantic theories of languages unrelated to English and suggestions about how to proceed with the construction of such theories.

We may put our problem this way: What form should a semantic theory of a natural language take to accommodate in the most revealing way the facts about the semantic structure of that language supplied by descriptive research? This question is of primary importance at the present stage of the development of semantics because semantics suffers not from a dearth of facts about meanings and meaning relations in natural languages, but rather from the lack of an adequate theory to organize, systematize, and generalize these facts. Facts about the semantics of natural languages have been contributed in abundance by many diverse fields, including philosophy, linguistics, philology, and psychology. Indeed, a compendium of such facts is readily

Reprinted and abridged with the permission of the authors and publisher from an article of the same title, *Language*, 1963, **39**, No. 2, 170–210.

available in any good dictionary. But at present the superabundance of facts obscures a clear view of their interrelations, while such theories as have been proposed to account for the facts have, in general, been either too loosely formulated or too weak in explanatory and descriptive power to succeed.

THE PROJECTION PROBLEM

A full synchronic description of a natural language is a grammatical and semantic characterization of that language (where the term "grammatical" is construed broadly to include phonology, phonemics, morphology, and syntax). Hence, a semantic theory must be constructed to have whatever properties are demanded by its role in linguistic description. Since, however, the goals of such description are reasonably well understood and since, in comparison to semantics, the nature of grammar has been clearly articulated, we may expect that by studying the contribution that semantics will be required to make to a synchronic description of a language we can clarify the subject, the form of generalizations, the goals, and the empirical and methodological constraints upon a semantic theory.

A fluent speaker's mastery of his language exhibits itself in his ability to produce and understand the sentences of his language, INCLUDING INDEFINITELY MANY THAT ARE WHOLLY NOVEL TO HIM (i.e. his ability to produce and understand ANY sentence of his language). The emphasis upon novel sentences is important. The most characteristic feature of language is its ability to make available an infinity of sentences from which the speaker can select appropriate and novel ones to use as the need arises. That is to say, what qualifies one as a fluent speaker is not the ability to imitate previously heard sentences but rather the ability to produce and understand sentences never before encountered. The striking fact about the use of language is the absence of repe-

tition: almost every sentence is uttered for the first time. This can be substantiated by checking texts for the number of times a sentence is repeated. It is exceedingly unlikely that even a single repetition of a sentence of reasonable length will be encountered.

A synchronic description of a natural language seeks to determine what a fluent speaker knows about the structure of his language that enables him to use and understand its sentences. Since a fluent speaker is able to use and understand any sentence drawn from the INFINITE set of sentences of his language, and since, at any time, he has only encountered a FINITE set of sentences, it follows that the speaker's knowledge of his language takes the form of rules which project the finite set of sentences he has fortuitously encountered to the infinite set of sentences of the language. A description of the language which adequately represents the speaker's linguistic knowledge must, accordingly, state these rules. The problem of formulating these rules we shall refer to as the projection problem.

This problem requires for its solution rules which project the infinite set of sentences in a way which mirrors the way that speakers understand novel sentences. In encountering a novel sentence the speaker is not encountering novel elements but only a novel combination of familiar elements. Since the set of sentences is infinite and each sentence is a different concatenation of morphemes, the fact that a speaker can understand any sentence must mean that the way he understands sentences which he has never previously encountered is compositional: on the basis of his knowledge of the grammatical properties and the meanings of the morphemes of the language, the rules which the speaker knows enable him to determine the meaning of a novel sentence in terms of the manner in which the parts of the sentence are composed to form the whole. Correspondingly, we can expect that a system of rules which solves the projection problem must reflect the compositional character of the speaker's linguistic knowledge.

SYNCHRONIC LINGUISTIC DESCRIPTION MINUS GRAMMAR EQUALS SEMANTICS

A description of a natural language is, inter alia, a solution to the projection problem for that language. If we are to discover the goals of semantics by subtracting from the goals of a description of a language whatever the grammar contributes to the solution of the projection problem, we must consider the respect in which a grammar is a solution for the grammatical aspect of the projection problem.

Grammars answer the question: What does the speaker know about the phonological and syntactic structure of his language that enables him to use and understand any of its sentences, including those he has not previously heard? They do so by providing rules which generate the sentences of the speaker's language. In particular, these rules generate infinitely many strings of morphemes which, though they are sentences of the language, have never been uttered by speakers. Moreover, a grammar generates the sentences which a speaker is, in principle, capable of understanding in such a way that their derivations provide their structural descriptions. Such descriptions specify the elements out of which a sentence is constructed, the grammatical relations between these elements and between the higher constituents of the sentence, the relations between the sentence and other sentences of the language, and the ways the sentence is syntactically ambiguous together with an explanation of why it is ambiguous in these ways. Since it is this information about a novel sentence which the speaker knows and which enables him to understand its syntactic structure if and when he encounters the sentence, an adequate transformational grammar of a language PARTIALLY

solves the projection problem for the language.

A semantic theory of a language completes the solution of the projection problem for the language. Thus, semantics takes over the explanation of the speaker's ability to produce and understand new sentences at the point where grammar leaves off. Since we wish to determine, when we have subtracted the problems in the description of a language properly belonging to grammar, what problems belong to semantics, we must begin by gaining some grasp of how much of the projection problem is left unsolved by an optimal grammar.

One way to appreciate how much of understanding sentences is left unexplained by grammar is to compare the grammatical characterizations of sentences to what we know about their semantic characterizations. If we do this, we notice that the grammar provides identical structural descriptions for sentences that are different in meaning and different structural descriptions for sentences that are identical in meaning. The former will be the case for all morphemically distinct substitution instances of a given sentential type; for example, *The dog bit the man* and *The cat bit the woman*. The latter will be the case for many instances of sentential synonymy; for example, *The dog bit the man* and *The man was bitten by the dog*.

In general, it is obvious that in no sense of meaning does the structural description which the grammar assigns to a sentence specify either the meaning of the sentence or the meaning of its parts. Such considerations must now be made precise in order that we may apply our formula 'linguistic description minus grammar equals semantics' to determine a lower bound on the domain of a semantic theory. Later in this section we will fix an upper bound by determining what problems lie outside the concerns of a complete linguistic description.

Grammars seek to describe the structure of a sentence IN ISOLATION FROM ITS POS-

SIBLE SETTINGS IN LINGUISTIC DISCOURSE (WRITTEN OR VERBAL) OR IN NONLINGUISTIC CONTEXTS (SOCIAL OR PHYSICAL). The justification which permits the grammarian to study sentences in abstraction from the settings in which they have occurred or might occur is simply that the fluent speaker is able to construct and recognize syntactically well-formed sentences without recourse to information about settings, and this ability is what a grammar undertakes to reconstruct. Every facet of the fluent speaker's linguistic ability which a grammar reconstructs can be exercised independently of information about settings: this is true not only of the ability to produce and recognize sentences but also of the ability to determine syntactic relations between sentence types, to implicitly analyze the syntactic structure of sentences, and to detect grammatical ambiguities. Since, then, the knowledge that a fluent speaker has of his language enables him to determine the grammatical structure of any sentence without reference to information about setting, grammar correspondingly forms an independent theory of this independent knowledge.

We may generalize to arrive at a sufficient condition for determining when an ability of speakers is the proper subject matter of a synchronic theory in linguistics. The generalization is this: IF SPEAKERS POSSESS AN ABILITY THAT ENABLES THEM TO APPREHEND THE STRUCTURE OF ANY SENTENCE IN THE INFINITE SET OF SENTENCES OF A LANGUAGE WITHOUT REFERENCE TO INFORMATION ABOUT SETTINGS AND WITHOUT SIGNIFICANT VARIATION FROM SPEAKER TO SPEAKER, THEN THAT ABILITY IS PROPERLY THE SUBJECT MATTER OF A SYNCHRONIC THEORY IN LINGUISTICS.

The first question in determining the subject matter of a semantic theory is: Can we find an ability which satisfies the antecedent of this generalization, which is beyond the range of grammatical description, and which is semantic in some reasonable sense? If we can, then that ability falls within the domain of a semantic theory.

In order to find such an ability, let us consider a communication situation so constructed that no information about setting can contribute to a speaker's understanding of a sentence encountered in that situation. Any extragrammatical ability that a speaker can employ to understand the meaning of a sentence in such a situation will ipso facto be considered to require semantic explanation.

The type of communication situation we shall consider is the following. A number of English-speakers receive an anonymous letter containing only the English sentence S. We are interested in the difference between this type of situation and one in which the same anonymous letter is received by persons who do not speak English but are equipped with a completely adequate grammar of English. To investigate what the first group can do by way of comprehending the meaning of S that the second group cannot is to factor out the contribution of grammar to the understanding of sentences. We will only investigate aspects of linguistic ability which are invariant from individual to individual within each group. We thus make sure that the abilities under investigation are a function not of idiosyncrasies of a speaker's personal history but only of his knowledge of his language.

Suppose S is the sentence *The bill is large*. Speakers of English will agree that this sentence is ambiguous, i.e. that it has at least two readings. According to one it means that some document demanding a sum of money to discharge a debt exceeds in size most such documents; according to the other it means that the beak of a certain bird exceeds in bulk those of most similar birds. However, the fact that this sentence is ambiguous between these readings cannot be attributed to its syntactic structure, since, syntactically, its structure on both readings is as shown in Figure 4-5. That is, the group who do not speak English but are equipped with a grammar can say no more about *The bill is large* than what is repre-

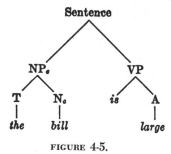

FIGURE 4-5.

sented in Figure 4-5. Thus, this sentence, which is marked as unambiguous by the grammar, will be understood as ambiguous by a fluent speaker. From this difference between the performances of the two groups, it follows that one facet of the speaker's ability that a semantic theory will have to reconstruct is that he can detect nonsyntactic ambiguities and characterize the content of each reading of a sentence.

Now suppose S is the sentence *The bill is large but need not be paid.* Speakers of English will understand this sentence only on readings in which *bill* means an order to pay a sum of money to discharge a debt. This shows that a speaker can disambiguate parts of a sentence in terms of other parts and thereby determine the number of readings of a sentence. Thus, another facet of the speaker's semantic ability is that of determining the number of readings that a sentence has by exploiting semantic relations in the sentence to eliminate potential ambiguities.

Now let S be the sentence *The paint is silent.* English speakers will at once recognize that this sentence is anomalous in some way. For example, they will distinguish it from such sentences as *The paint is wet* and *The paint is yellow* by applying to it such epithets as "odd," "peculiar," "paradoxical," and "bizarre." Though it is clear that the speaker does not have the explicit conceptual machinery to correctly characterize the difference between these sentences, his consistent use of such rough labels shows that he is aware of some sort of linguistic anomaly. But the group who do not speak

English and are equipped only with a grammar will regard all these sentences as fully regular, since there is no grammatical basis for distinguishing between them. Hence, another facet of the semantic ability of the speaker is that of detecting semantic anomalies. Correspondingly, a semantic theory will be needed to mark the distinction between semantically anomalous sentences and semantically regular sentences, so far as this distinction is not co-extensive with the distinction the grammar makes between ungrammatical and grammatical strings of morphemes.

Finally, whatever sentence the anonymous letter contains, as a rule, speakers of English can easily decide what sentences are paraphrases of it and what are not, in the sense that they can answer the questions What does the letter say? Does the letter say such-and-such? How can what the letter says be rephrased? This facet of the speaker's ability cannot be referred to his mastery of grammar either, for a person who is equipped with a grammar but who does not speak English will be unable to tell whether or not a sentence is a paraphrase of S. The reasons are simply that there need be no definite grammatical relation between a sentence and its paraphrases, e.g. between *Two chairs are in the room* and *There are at least two things in the room and each is a chair,* and that where a definite grammatical relation obtains between a pair of sentences, neither need be a paraphrase of the other, e.g. *The ball was hit by the man* and *The ball was hit, The man hit the ball* and *The man did not hit the ball.*[1] Thus, still another facet of the speaker's semantic ability which must fall within the domain of a semantic theory is his paraphrasing skill.

We can now tentatively characterize the lower bound on the domain of a semantic theory, since we have found an ability of speakers which cannot be accounted for by grammar, which is semantic in a reasonable sense, and which enables speakers to appre-

[1] Cf. *Syntactic structures,* Appendix II, for the transformations which relate these sentences.

hend the semantic structure of an infinite number of sentences without information about setting and independent of individual differences between speakers. We thus take the goals of a semantic theory to include at least the explication of each facet of this ability and of the interrelations between them.

The speaker's exercise of this ability, which henceforth we shall refer to as THE ABILITY TO INTERPRET SENTENCES, provides empirical data for the construction of a semantic theory, just as the construction of a grammar draws upon empirical data supplied by the exercise of the speaker's ability to distinguish well-formed sentences from ungrammatical strings, to recognize syntactic ambiguity, and to appreciate relations between sentence types. A semantic theory describes and explains the interpretative ability of speakers by accounting for their performance in determining the number and content of the readings of a sentence, by detecting semantic anomalies, by deciding on paraphrase relations between sentences, and by marking every other semantic property or relation that plays a role in this ability.

WHAT IS BEYOND THE DESCRIPTIVE SCOPE OF A SEMANTIC THEORY

Having fixed a lower bound on the domain of a semantic theory, our next step must be to fix an upper bound, thus uniquely determining the set of problems forming the domain of a semantic theory of a natural language.

Previous conceptions of semantics have usually defined the goals of a semantic description of a natural language in such a way that to achieve them a semantic theory would have to account for the manner in which settings determine how an utterance is understood. We shall now show that to set the goals of a semantic theory this high is to set them too high. Once we have

shown that a semantic theory cannot be expected to account for the way settings determine how an utterance is understood, we will have fixed an upper bound on the domain of semantic theories. That is, we will have shown that a semantic theory is a theory of the speaker's ability to interpret the sentences of his language.

The form of a theory of how settings control the understanding of utterances of sentences is as follows. Such a theory is a function F whose arguments are a sentence S; GS, a grammatical description of S; IS, a semantic interpretation of S (where IS is the set of possible readings of S); and C, an abstract characterization of a setting. $F(S, GS, IS, C)$ is

1. the particular reading in IS that speakers of the language give to S in settings of the type C, or
2. An n-tuple ($n \geq 2$) of the readings from IS that speakers of the language give to S if S is ambiguous n-ways in settings of type C, or
3. The null element if speakers of the language give to S none of the readings in IS when S occurs in settings of type C.

The value of $F(S, GS, IS, C)$ is (1) just in case C fully disambiguates S, i.e. C determines a unique reading from the one or more in IS; it is (2) just in case C fails to fully disambiguate S; it is (3) just in case an occurrence of S in C is token-odd.

An example of each of these cases will clarify this abstract formulation by showing how a theory of this form would explicate the speaker's ability to choose the reading(s) which a setting determines for a sentence occurring in it. As an example of case (1) consider the sentence *The shooting of the hunters was terrible*. This sentence is ambiguous between the reading r_1, on which it means that it was terrible that the hunters were shot, and the reading r_2, on which it means that the marksmanship of the hunters was very bad. This ambiguity will be represented in IS. The theory F must decide which of these readings the sentence bears in settings which disambiguate it, and it must decide in which settings the sentence remains ambiguous. If, then, an utterance of the sentence occurs as an answer to the question *How good was the marksmanship of the hunters?*, i.e. If C represents a situation in which the marksmanship of the hunters is clearly at issue, then, ceteris paribus, the value of F would have to be r_2. Now consider case (2). The ambiguous sentence *He follows Marx*, occurring in a setting in which it is clear that the speaker is discussing intellectual history, cannot bear the reading "He dogs the footsteps of Groucho." However, this setting leaves the sentence ambiguous between the readings "He is a disciple of Karl's" and "He post-dates Karl." Thus, F will have to have these latter two readings as its value for this sentence and this setting as arguments. Finally, as case (3), suppose the sentence *This is the happiest night of my life* is uttered in the middle of the day. Since the sentence is uttered in a setting that lacks conditions which utterances of this sentence presuppose, the occurrence is a case of token-oddity. Thus, for this sentence occurrence F must give the null element as its value, i.e. none of the readings of this sentence in IS are selected by C.

This, then, is the form of a theory about the effect of setting upon the way speakers understand sentences. Any particular theory is complete just to the extent that it solves the problems incorporated in this abstract formulation. A complete theory of this kind is more powerful in principle than a theory of the semantic interpretation of sentences in isolation. But a theory of settings must contain a theory of semantic interpretation as a proper part because the readings that a speaker attributes to a sentence in a setting are a selection from among those that the sentence has in isolation. It is clear that, in general, a sentence cannot have readings in a setting which it does not have in isolation. Of course, there are cases in which a sen-

tence may have a reading for some speakers in some settings which it does not have in isolation for all speakers. But these cases are essentially idiomatic in the sense that meaning is determined either by special stipulation (passwords, nonce senses, etc.) or special rules (codes, etc.) or else by special information about the intentions of the speaker. If a theory of the selective effect of setting were required to deal with such cases, no such theory would be possible, because any sentence may be made to mean anything you like simply by constructing the setting to include the appropriate stipulation. Since, then, the readings that a speaker gives a sentence in a setting are a selection from those which it has in isolation, a theory of semantic interpretation is logically prior to a theory of the selective effect of setting.

The abstract formulation given above may be realized in the form of a theory of either of two kinds, depending on how the notion of setting is construed. One kind of theory of setting selection construes the setting of an utterance to be the nonlinguistic context in which the utterance occurs, i.e. the full sociophysical environment of the utterance. The other kind takes the setting of an utterance to be the linguistic context in which the utterance occurs, i.e. the written or spoken discourse of which the utterance is a part. We shall consider, in turn, the possibility of constructing a theory of each of these types.

The first kind of theory of setting selection seeks to account for the way in which aspects of the sociophysical world control the understanding of sentences. Differing varieties of this kind of theory may be obtained by varying the aspects of the sociophysical environment of which the rules of the theory are permitted to take account, and by varying the spatiotemporal parameters of the environment. But clearly a necessary condition which any variety of this kind of theory must satisfy is that its construction of setting is so defined that it is able to represent all the nonlinguistic information required by speakers for understanding sentences. So far as a theory fails to satisfy this condition, it is incomplete, since there is then some information which determines the way speakers understand a sentence but which the theory fails to represent as part of the setting of that sentence.

But a complete theory of this kind is not possible in principle; for to satisfy the above necessary condition it would be required that the theory represent ALL the knowledge speakers have about the world. That this is so can be seen from even a few examples which show how nonlinguistic information of any kind may be involved in the understanding of a sentence. Consider (1) *Our store sells alligator shoes* and (2) *Our store sells horse shoes.* In normal settings (e.g. as signs in a store window or as newspaper advertisements), occurrences of (1) will be taken on the reading 'our store sells shoes made from alligator skins' while (2) will be taken on the reading 'our store sells shoes for horses'. Notice, however, that (1) is open to the reading 'our store sells shoes for alligators' and (2) is open to the reading 'our store sells shoes made from the skin of horses'. From this it follows that if a theory of setting selection is to choose the correct reading for (1), it must represent the fact that, to date, alligators do not wear shoes, although shoes for people are sometimes made from alligator skin. Conversely, if the theory is to choose the correct reading for (2), it must represent the fact that horses wear shoes, although shoes for people are not usually made from the skin of horses. Other examples illustrate the same point. Compare the three sentences: *Should we take junior back to the zoo? Should we take the lion back to the zoo? Should we take the bus back to the zoo?* Information which figures in the choice of the correct readings for these sentences includes the fact that lions, but not children and busses, are often kept in cages. Three further cases of the same sort are: *Can I put the wall-paper on?* and *Can I put the coat on?*; *Joe jumped higher than the Empire State Building* and *Joe jumped higher*

than you; Black cats are unlucky and *People who break mirrors are unlucky.*

The reader will find it an easy matter to construct an ambiguous sentence whose resolution requires the representation of practically any item of information about the world he chooses. Since a complete theory of setting selection must represent as part of the setting of an utterance any and every feature of the world which speakers need in order to determine the preferred reading of that utterance, and since, as we have just seen, practically any item of information about the world is essential to some disambiguations, two conclusions follow. First, such a theory cannot in principle distinguish between the speaker's knowledge of his language and his knowledge of the world, because, according to such a theory, part of the characterization of a LINGUISTIC ability is a representation of virtually all knowledge about the world that speakers share. Second, since there is no serious possibility of systematizing all the knowledge of the world that speakers share, and since a theory of the kind we have been discussing requires such a systematization, it is ipso facto not a serious model for semantics. However, none of these considerations is intended to rule out the possibility that, by placing relatively strong limitations on the information about the world that a theory can represent in the characterization of a setting, a LIMITED theory of selection by sociophysical setting can be constructed. What these considerations do show is that a COMPLETE theory of this kind is impossible.

The second kind of realization of the abstract formulation of a theory of setting selection is one in which the setting of an occurrence of a sentence is construed as the written or spoken discourse of which the occurrence is a part. Such a theory has a strong and a weak version. The strong version requires that the theory interpret a discourse in the same way that a fluent speaker would (i.e. mark the ambiguities that the speaker marks, resolve the ambiguities that the speaker resolves, detect the anomalous strings that the speaker detects, recognize paraphrase relations that the speaker recognizes, and do all this both within and across sentence boundaries). Since, however, in so interpreting a discourse a speaker may need to bring to bear virtually any information about the world that he and other speakers share, the argument given against a complete theory of selection by sociophysical setting applies equally against the strong version of a theory of selection by discourse. Hence we need only consider the weak version.

The weak version of such a theory requires only that the theory interpret discourses just so far as the interpretation is determined by grammatical and semantic relations which obtain within and among the sentences of the discourse. Thus, such a theory seeks to disambiguate sentences and sequences of sentences in terms of grammatical and semantic relations between these and the sentences which form their setting in a discourse, to determine when an occurrence of a sentence or of a sequence of sentences is rendered anomalous by the sentences which form its setting in a discourse, and to recognize paraphrase relations between pairs of sentences and pairs of sequences of sentences in a discourse.

But it is not at all clear that the weak version of a theory of discourse setting selection has greater explanatory power in these respects than a theory of semantic interpretation, since except for a few types of cases (see below), a discourse can be treated as a single sentence in isolation by regarding sentence boundaries as sentential connectives. As a matter of fact, this is the natural treatment. Consider the two-sentence discourse: *I shot the man with a gun. If the man had had a gun too, he would have shot me first.* The first sentence of this discourse is ambiguous in isolation, but not in this setting. But the problem of explaining this disambiguation is the same as the problem of explaining why the single sentence *I shot the man with a gun, but if the man had had a gun too, he would have shot me*

first does not have an ambiguous first clause. This technique of replacing discourses or stretches in discourse by single compound sentences, using sentence connectives in place of sentence boundaries, clearly has a very extensive application in reducing problems of setting selection to problems of semantic interpretation of sentences in isolation. Thus, given a theory of semantic interpretation, little is left for a theory of setting selection to explain.

The fact which underlies this technique is that, in the great majority of cases, the sentence break in a discourse is simply equivalent to the conjunction *and*. (In others it is equivalent to *but*, in others to *for*, in others to *or*, etc.) Sometimes, however, a discourse cannot be directly converted into a compound sentence in this way. For example, the discourse *How are you feeling today? I am fine, thanks.* does not convert to *How are you feeling today and I am fine, thanks.* because the compound sentence is ungrammatical. But the fact that sentences of different types cannot be run together in the obvious way may not pose a serious problem; for it is not at all clear that less obvious conversions will not lead to a satisfactory treatment of such cases within a theory of semantic interpretation. For example, we may convert the discourse just cited into the single sentence *X asked "How are you feeling today?" and Y replied "I am fine, thanks."* If such conversions can be carried out generally, then any problem about disambiguation, detection of anomaly, etc. that can be raised and/or solved in a theory of setting selection can be raised and/or solved by reference to an analogue in the theory of semantic interpretation. But even if such conversions cannot be carried out generally, the most interesting and central cases will still be within the range of a theory of semantic interpretation. Hence, for every discourse there is a single sentence which consists of the sequence of n sentences that comprise the discourse connected by the appropriate sentence connectives and which exhibits the same semantic relations exhibited in the discourse. But since the single sentence is, ex hypothesi, described by a theory of semantic interpretation, in every case in which a discourse can be treated as a single sentence, a theory of semantic interpretation is descriptively as powerful as a theory of setting selection.

We opened the discussion of theories of setting selection in order to fix an upper bound on the domain of a semantic theory of a natural language. The result of the discussion is that, where such a theory is not reducible to a theory of semantic interpretation, it cannot be completed without systematizing all the knowledge about the world that speakers share and keeping this systematization up to date as speakers come to share more knowledge. A limited theory of how sociophysical setting determines the understanding of an utterance is possible, but even such a theory blurs the distinction between the speaker's knowledge of his language (his linguistic ability) and his knowledge of the world (his beliefs about matters of fact). Therefore, since it is unlikely that anything stronger than a theory of semantic interpretation is possible and since such a theory is clearly an essential part of a linguistic description, it is reasonable to fix the upper bound of a semantic theory of a natural language at the point where the requirements upon a theory of semantic interpretation are satisfied.

THE COMPONENTS OF A SEMANTIC THEORY

We must now determine what mechanisms a semantic theory employs in reconstructing the speaker's ability to interpret sentences. We have seen that this ability is systematic in that it enables the speaker to understand sentences he has never heard before and to produce novel sentences that other speakers understand in the way that he understands them. To account for this ability a semantic theory must be so formulated that its output matches the interpretive performance of a fluent speaker. In this section, we describe the form of semantic theories.

It is widely acknowledged and certainly true that one component of a semantic theory of a natural language is a dictionary of that language. The reason for including a dictionary as a component of a semantic theory is based on two limitations of a grammatical description. First, a grammar cannot account for the fact that some sentences which differ ONLY morphemically are interpreted as different in meaning (e.g. *The tiger bit me* and *The mouse bit me*) while other sentences which differ only morphemically are interpreted as identical in meaning (e.g. *The oculist examined me* and *The eye doctor examined me*). Second, a grammar cannot account for the fact that some sentences of radically different syntactic structure are synonymous (e.g. *Two chairs are in the room* and *There are at least two things in the room and each is a chair*) while other syntactically different sentences are not. In each case, the interpretation of the sentences is determined in part by the meanings of their morphemes and by semantic relations among the morphemes. The reason for including a dictionary as a component of a semantic theory is precisely to provide a representation of the semantic characteristics of morphemes necessary to account for the facts about sentences and their interrelations that the grammar leaves unexplained.

What has always been unclear about a semantic theory is what component(s) it contains besides a dictionary, and how the components of a semantic theory relate to one another and to the grammar. We can find this out by asking in what respects a dictionary and grammar alone are NOT sufficient to match the fluent speaker's interpretations of sentences.

Let us imagine a fluent speaker of English presented with the infinite list of sentences and their structural descriptions generated by a grammar of English. Given an accurate dictionary of English WHICH HE APPLIES BY USING HIS LINGUISTIC ABILITY, the fluent speaker can semantically interpret any sentence on the list under any of its grammatical derivations. He can determine the number and content of the readings of a sentence, tell whether or not a sentence is semantically anomalous, and decide which sentences on the list are paraphrases of each other. Now contrast the fluent speaker's performance with the performance of a machine which MECHANICALLY applies an English dictionary to a sentence in the list by associating with each morpheme of the sentence its dictionary entry. It is clear that the dictionary usually supplies more senses for a lexical item than it bears in almost any of its occurrences in sentences. But the machine will not be able to select the sense(s) which the morpheme actually bears in a given sentence context, except so far as the selection is already determined by the grammatical markers assigned to the morpheme in the derivation of the sentence. (Thus the machine will be able to choose the correct sense of *seal* in *Seal the letter* so far as the choice is determined by the fact that in this sentence *seal* is marked as a verb, and the correct sense of *seal* in *The seal is on the letter* so far as the choice is determined by the fact that in this sentence *seal* is marked as a noun. But the machine will not be able to distinguish the correct sense of *seal* in *One of the oil seals in my car is leaking* from such incorrect senses as "a device bearing a design so made that it can impart an impression" or "an impression made by such a device" or "the material upon which the impression is made" or "ornamental or commemorative stamp" and so forth, since all of these senses can apply to nominal occurrences of *seal*.) What the machine is failing to do is to take account of or utilize the semantic relations between morphemes in a sentence. Hence it cannot determine the correct number and content of readings of a sentence. Nor can it distinguish semantically anomalous sentences from semantically regular ones. Since the machine will associate a dictionary entry with each morpheme in a sentence, it does not distinguish cases in which the sense of a morpheme or string of morphemes in a sentence precludes other morphemes in the sentence from bearing ANY of the senses that the dictionary supplies for them. (E.g. the machine cannot distinguish *The wall is covered with silent paint* from *The wall is covered with fresh paint*.) Finally, the machine cannot tell which sentences in the list are paraphrases of each other in any case except the one in which the sentences are of exactly the same syntactic structure and the corresponding words are either identical or synonymous.

The comparison between a fluent speaker and a machine reveals the respects in which a grammar and dictionary by themselves do not suffice to interpret sentences like a speaker of the language. What the fluent speaker has at his disposal that a machine has not are rules for applying the information in the dictionary—rules which take account of semantic relations between morphemes and of the interaction between meaning and syntactic structure in determining the correct semantic interpretation for any of the infinitely many sentences which the grammar generates. Thus, a semantic theory of a natural language must have such rules (which we shall call "projection rules") as one of its components if it is to match the speaker's interpretations of sentences.

The central problem for such a theory is that a dictionary usually supplies more senses for a lexical item than it bears in an occurrence in a given sentence, for a dictionary entry is a characterization of EVERY sense that a lexical item can bear in ANY sentence. Thus, the effect of the projection rules must be to select the appropriate sense of each lexical item in a sentence in order to provide the correct readings for each distinct grammatical structure of that sentence. The semantic interpretations assigned by the projection rules operating on grammatical and dictionary information must account in the following ways for the speaker's ability to understand sentences: they must mark each semantic ambiguity that a speaker can detect; they must explain the source of the speaker's intuitions of anomaly when a sentence evokes them; they must suitably relate sentences that speakers know to be paraphrases of each other.

Pictured in this way a semantic theory interprets the syntactic structure which the grammatical description of a language reveals. This conception gives content to the notion that a semantic theory of a natural language is analogous to a model which interprets a formal system. Further, it explicates the exact sense of the doctrine that the meaning of a sentence is a function of the meanings of its parts. The system of projection rules is just this function.

Instruction in Reading:
From Phoneme to Grapheme

5

INTRODUCTION

In this chapter we depart for the moment from consideration of basic theoretical issues and research on language and thought and turn our attention to the problem of instruction in reading. The reader should discover, however, how research and discussions on reading are connected with basic linguistic and psychological theory.

Many current debates on how reading should be taught have a stronger ideological than empirical flavor. No matter which instructional approach is defended or espoused (phonics, the look-and-say method, the basal-reader method, and so on), the appeal is based more on personal experience, tradition, intuition, love of children, or some faddish version of Gestalt psychology than on research (Brown, 1958). Undoubtedly, as occurs in the solution of so many complex practical pedagogical problems, each approach, exclusive of every other, has its assets and limitations. Furthermore, instruction in reading, like any teaching, must await the results of some highly involved research on instructional methodology so that we can combine knowledge with moral fervor in making our recommendations to teachers and students. What this chapter should indicate is that there are available in linguistics and psychology theoretical conceptions and research techniques which should be useful in the research on teaching.

The literature on instruction in reading is monumental (McCullough, 1957; Russell and Fea, 1963). Our selection of articles for this chapter has been guided by the psycholinguistic orientation of the anthology. In the first article, for example, Fries uses the concept of phoneme in making certain distinctions useful in the teaching of reading [Hamp, Chapter 1]. Fries distinguishes between phonemics, on one hand, and phonics and phonetics, on the other hand. The assertion of some teachers and laymen that the English language is not phonetic ignores the basic linguistic tenet about the primacy of speech. No natural language is unphonetic. Fries also recapitulates the history of writing from the primitive use of pictographs to the development of alphabets. He demonstrates the phonemic basis of alphabetic writing and urges respect for, and the teaching of, its phonemic basis.

The relation between the spoken and written language, often described as spelling-to-sound or grapheme-to-phoneme correspondence, is investigated by Gibson and her associates at Cornell University, as part of an extensive research program on reading. Grapheme-phoneme correspondence has been extensively studied by others (Hall, 1961; Higginbottom, 1962; and Venezky, 1962). The conceptual basis for this research is consistent with descriptive linguistics, which assumes the dependence of the written language on the spoken language. The Cornell investigators were attempting to discover rules of correspondence between spelling and sound that are not defined by speech alone, writing alone, or even by morphemes. What they are studying are letter-groups that have stable relations with phonemics patterns. These groups may be whole words or syllables. In effect, this research concerns the relation of written and spoken English.

We have made frequent reference to Chomsky's theory of language mastery. According to Chomsky, by mastering the syntax or rules of his native language, the child is able to generate and understand novel sentences, even though he is unable to state the rules he uses. Similarly, Gibson is assuming that the child who learns to read skillfully masters particular "superforms" (or rules) which define spelling-to-sound correspondence. The child is thus able to generate the reading of new words and sentences without single, explicit instruction. She also assumes that the child decodes the written materials into the phonemics of the spoken language that he has already mastered. The child's progress in reading is a function of his increasing mastery of these "superforms." The child discovers the grapheme-phoneme correspondences with and without explicit instruction. In one experimental test of this hypothesis (Experiment 1) the investigators observed whether pseudo words, constructed according to spelling-to-sound rules, were better perceived than were pseudo words that ignored these rules.

In referring to previous research, the authors discuss the relation of word frequency to auditory and visual perception and the technique for scaling meaningfulness [Noble, Chapter 5]. On the basis of their evidence they conclude that "meaningfulness," as defined by Underwood and Schulz, is not a variable in the recognition of words (Underwood and Schulz, 1960, pages 163–199).

Of considerable current popularity has been the use of the Initial Teaching Alphabet (i.t.a.), invented by Pittman, for the teaching of beginning reading. There has been no clear formulation of the theoretical basis for these particular spelling transformations or for their use in reading instruction. Both Pittman and Downing, however, refer to linguistics and research on grapheme-phoneme correspondence without clearly indicating how their system is derivative. Pittman and Downing assume that traditional orthography unnecessarily impedes the child's initial attempts to learn to read. Their alphabet uses special orthography that requires the learning of fewer characters, whole-word representations, and print signals. The Initial Teaching Alphabet shows the usual linguistic sophistication in its appreciation of the relation of the spoken to the written language, particularly in its use of the phoneme as the basis for the new print code. The new alphabet is an attempt to introduce a simplified regularity into the correspondence between written and spoken English. The underlying assumption seems to be that learning the simple correspondences earlier increases the rate at which the child learns the true correspondences later.

Following Gibson, if what the child must learn, in order to acquire reading skill, is the superordinate rules that define spelling-to-sound correspondence, then there is some question of whether the new alphabet facilitates the learning of these rules or simply burdens the child with the learning of additional rules, which later must be discarded. In an analogous situation, would the child acquire mastery of the grammatical rules of his language by first learning simplified but not entirely valid versions of rules that really comprise the syntax of his language?

The research that Downing reports does not answer this question. We have passed through a whole era of educational research on teaching methods that makes global comparisons of old and new instructional techniques, especially in connection with television, the film, lectures, discussions, and programed instruction. With little understanding of the basic variables and with little control over extraneous influences, such research has had few theoretical or practical results. At most it has a propagandistic and even commercial value. It seems, indeed, to be a broad jump from research on grapheme-phoneme correspondence to the complex and essentially unanalyzed problem of instruction in beginning reading.

Like Gibson and her associates, Silberman is interested in how the child learns to read letter-sound relations that he has never seen before. Theoretically, and methodologically, Silberman borrows from previous work on operant conditioning and from the technique used in the development of materials for programed instruction. The technique requires that the instructional materials be developed through a series of tryouts and revisions or, in the words of Skinner, developed by successive approximations. This position seems to be fastidiously empirical, and the final product is what actually works best. Silberman makes no reference to the child's mastery of "superforms" or complex rules of correspondence. The child, instead, is learning discrete discriminations. When the child transfers what he learns so that he is able to read new trigrams, the process is stimulus generalization. Rarely are educational materials developed with such detailed care and with such clear knowledge of their practical usefulness.

The fine-grain analysis of reading skill introduces precision into otherwise general and ambiguous discussions of instruction in reading. Yet Silberman's whole operation seems laborious and excruciatingly molecular. Would one ever complete the writing of the program? What is lacking in Silberman's approach is reference to constructs that describe complex reading skills or the acquisition of these skill patterns at the level at which we must teach and learn them.

REFERENCES

Brown, R. A dispute about reading. In his *Words and things.* New York: Free Press, 1958. Pp. 65–81.

Fries, C. C. *Linguistics and reading.* New York: Holt, Rinehart and Winston, 1963.

Hall, R. A., Jr. *Sound and spelling in English.* Philadelphia: Chilton, 1961.

Higginbottom, E. M. A study of the representation of English vowel phonemes in orthography. *Lang. & Speech,* 1962, **5,** 67–117.

McCullough, D. M. What does research reveal about practices in teaching reading? *English J.,* 1957, **46,** 475–490.

Russell, E. H., and H. R. Fea. Research on teaching reading. In N. L. Gage (Ed.), *Handbook of research on teaching.* Chicago: Rand McNally, 1963. Pp. 865–928.

Underwood, B. J., and R. W. Schulz. *Meaningfulness and verbal learning.* Philadelphia: Lippincott, 1960.

Venezky, R. I. A computer program for deriving spelling-to-sound correspondence correlations. Master's thesis, Cornell University, 1962.

Phonetics and Phonemics

CHARLES C. FRIES

A very few quotations, out of the abundance available, were given above to show something of the widespread assertion that "English is not a phonetic language." This or a somewhat equivalent statement appears in nearly every discussion of the problems of teaching phonics.

There is not a series of basic materials on the market today that does not include instruction in phonics, but it is functional phonics, not a superimposed system of reading. It is closely integrated with meaningful reading, and taught in close conjunction with other procedures such as context clues, structural clues, and word-form clues. The basis for this practice rests in the following assumptions:

> English is a language that follows no lawful pattern of pronunciation as German or Spanish. Consequently, no single method of word attack can be depended upon. This becomes increasingly obvious as the reader meets more involved polysyllabic words.
> Whereas one can sound out simple three- and

Reprinted with the permission of the author and publisher from *Linguistics and Reading.* New York; Holt, Rinehart, and Winston, Inc., 1963, pp. 146–156.

four-letter words with only a minimum loss of time, one's rate of perception is slowed down materially as he attempts to use a highly synthetic approach on more involved words.

English is an experimental rather than a phonetic language anyway.

In a purely phonetic language there are as many letters in the alphabet as there are elementary sounds. Having twenty-six letters in our alphabet we would expect to have twenty-six elementary sounds.

Actually there are forty-four elementary sounds in English and only twenty-three alphabet letters with which to indicate them because c, q, and x are superfluous. . . .

The authors' studies reveal, also, that our language is not purely phonetic. Thirteen percent of all English syllables are not phonetic. Eighty-seven percent of all syllables in our language are purely phonetic and the words in which unphonetic syllables occur are in part phonetic. Knowing the phonetic facts about our language, therefore, provides the tool with which pupils may recognize instantly nearly all of our English words.

Underlying statements such as these, and underlying also most of the practices of the phonics approach, is the assumption that *writing is the language* and that *the pronunciation is simply making sounds as directed by the spelling:* "Unfortunately, we have with us a large class of persons who speak without thinking how our words are spelled, and who, therefore, squeeze all the juice out of our speech by refusing to enunciate carefully all the niceties of sound that the words contain."

From this point of view it is insisted that the word *usually* must have four syllables and *every* must have three; that there must be no *p* in *warmth,* or in *something;* that the word *Arctic* has a *c* in the first syllable and must be pronounced [arktɪk]; that in the words *hundred* and *children* the *r* precedes the *e* in the final syllable and therefore these words must not be pronounced [həndərd] and [čɪldərn].

This assumption also underlies the usual instructions for pronunciation given in elementary textbooks of a foreign language.

These instructions, for the most part, deal with the pronunciation of the letters: "Since no letter of the Spanish alphabet is pronounced exactly like the corresponding English letter, it will be understood that the equivalents given in Lessons I–III are only approximate. . . . *qu* (*u* silent) pronounced like *k*. Occurs only with *e* and *i* (que, qui)."

With this assumption of the primacy of the written word, whenever the regular pronunciation of very common words does not follow the spelling, the "word" is said to be unphonetic: "The children [in the stories to be read] always 'run' but seldom 'walk,' because 'run' is phonetic and 'walk' is not."

A linguist, however, would insist that the vocal sounds are the primary material out of which a language code is made. These vocal sounds are *the phonetic features*, and their systematic analysis and description constitute the *phonetics* of the language. All the "syllables" and other sequences of "talk" consist of phonetic features—that is, of audible modifications of the breath stream that can be analyzed and described in terms of the muscular movements used to produce them. All sequences of vocal sounds whether the "words" of a philosopher or the "babbling" of an infant child are "phonetic." Graphic representations of the English language use, for the most part, the Roman alphabet. The "words" are "spelled" by writing sequences of the letters of this alphabet, or by naming orally the letters that constitute each sequence. This spelling of English words is not always consistent and regular.

When, then, in the quotations given above, "words" like *walk* or *laugh* are said to be "unphonetic" it is not that English "follows no lawful pattern of pronunciation" but simply that the *spelling* in these instances is at fault. . . .

English, then, like all other human languages, is and must be "phonetic." The pronunciation of English, like the pronunciation of all other languages has its own "lawful patterns." That pronunciation is one of its most stable features—so stable in fact that "phonetic laws" have furnished the basis for a soundly scientific approach to the study of its history and that of the language family to which it belongs.

Phonetics applied to English as to other languages has furnished an increasingly intricate and generally accepted set of techniques by which to identify, isolate, and describe the specific sound features. As a subject for study, "phonetics" has attempted to set up the criteria or the frames through which to grasp the complete range of sound differences producible by the human vocal apparatus. "Phonetics" also has provided the practical approach through which to learn to hear and to make whichever of these vocal differences occur in any particular language. Phonetic descriptions are in absolute terms—the same physical criteria apply to all languages. The phonetic approach has revealed something of the tremendous number of sound differences humans can and do make. A fully adequate *phonetic alphabet,* having a separate graphic sign for every different sound feature of all the various languages that exist, would need thousands of separate signs. For indicating the differences of English pronunciation in the northeastern section of the United States, the *Linguistic Atlas of New England* used a phonetic alphabet of 121 graphic units, 32 for vowels and 89 for consonants, plus sets of shift signs and double shift signs for each of the 32 vowel units and sets of diacritics for each of the 89 consonant units.

"Phonetics" has thus centered attention upon the physical differences that characterize each of the vocal sounds and has found the number of these differences far beyond our realization and belief. We are concerned here, however, not with items of vocal sound as items, but rather with those bundles of sound contrasts that function in identifying the word-patterns of a particular language. To know that two items of vocal sound are different is not enough; we want to know whether the differences between these two items constitute one of the func-

tioning contrasts that a particular language (English) uses to separate and identify word-patterns. The difference between the voiceless hiss [s] and the voiced buzz [z] is a phonetic difference, in whatever language it occurs. We can hear it in English and we can hear it in the Spanish of Mexico, as well as in the Portuguese of Brazil. In English this phonetic difference is used in contrast, to separate and identify many word-patterns: /raɪs/ (*rice*)—/raɪz/ (*rise*); /aɪs/ (*ice*)—/aɪz/ (*eyes*); /sil/ (*seal*)—/zil/ (*zeal*); /yus/ (*use* as in "a use")—/yuz/ (*use* as in "to use"). In the Spanish of Mexico this phonetic difference is *never used* in contrast to separate and identify any word-patterns. In the Portuguese of Brazil it *is used* in contrast to separate and identify word-patterns. In all three languages it is a *phonetic difference.* In the Spanish of Mexico it is *only a phonetic difference;* but in both English and Portuguese, because of its use in contrast to identify word-patterns, it is also a *phonemic* difference.

Phonetics is a set of techniques by which to identify and describe, in absolute terms, all the differences of sound features that occur in any language. *Phonemics* is a set of techniques by which to determine for a *particular language* which phonetic features form bundles of functioning contrasts to identify the word-patterns of that language. Phonetics can deal at the same time with the sound features of a single language or all or any number of languages. Phonemics can deal with only one language at a time. It is the *phonemes* of English that identify the various English word-patterns. The number of phonetic differences describable in any language runs into thousands; the number of phonemes identifiable in a language is by comparison very few—from twenty to sixty.

To repeat a statement made earlier: The habits of pronunciation that the child develops in learning his native language are not habits of producing and hearing the separate sounds as isolatable items in individual words but rather habits of patterns of functioning contrasts in the unique structured system of a particular language.

To bring all this to bear upon the problems of reading we must now consider the structural significance of the alphabet.

THE ENGLISH ALPHABET

During the preceding discussions we have used the terms "alphabet," "Roman alphabet," "Greek alphabet." In the preceding chapter it was the forms of the letters as used "in English writing," and now the heading of this section appears as "The English Alphabet." The matter may not be of very great importance, for we are concerned here primarily with "the alphabetic principle" in writing systems as opposed to other types of graphic representation. On the other hand because the various alphabets (Greek, Roman, Cyrillic, Runic, and so forth) do show a variety of differences in shapes, in number of letters, in order, and in use, I shall here use specific names in order to avoid possible confusions. By "English Alphabet" I mean simply the sets of letters usually used to represent graphically the English language in print and in writing.

Much has been added by discovery and research, to our knowledge and understanding of the writing systems of the world within the last fifty years and even within the last twenty-five years.

This knowledge has served not only to push farther back into the past the histories of the individual writing systems themselves but also to provide the evidence through which to work upon the problems of connection and relationships among the various systems.

Earlier in this book we made a point of stressing the antiquity of human language. There seems to be no evidence of any primitive human society without a language competent to grasp and to share the complete experience of its members. In comparison with this antiquity of language, writing systems must have developed much later. The history of writing systems, however, is

by no means short. With the evidence now available, competent scholars agree that a large number of the Sumerian cuneiform tablets go back to the fourth millennium before the Christian era—to 3100 B.C., to a period 5000 years ago: ". . . the Sumerians—that gifted and practical people who, as far as is known today, were the first to invent and develop a usable and effective system of writing."

These tablets, mostly from excavations at Nippur, an ancient Sumerian site about a hundred miles from Baghdad, have been copied, pieced together, studied, and only in part translated and interpreted within the last twenty-five years. They antedate the oldest Egyptian as well as the earliest Chinese writing systems.

The deciphering of Mycenean Linear B, now established as the oldest piece of Greek writing in existence, was achieved by Michael Ventris only ten years ago. It pushed back the history of Greek writing from about 800 B.C. to about 1400 B.C. The "alphabet" (syllabary) of Linear B equals in antiquity the Phoenician "alphabet" (syllabary) which also arose about the middle of the second millennium B.C.

But more important than any changes in the relative chronology or history of various individual writing systems—of Greece, or Egypt, or China, or Sumer—is the beginning of a new type of study directed to the connections and relationships between the structures of the various systems. I. J. Gelb's book of 1952 is such a study.

The aim of this study is to lay a foundation for a new science of writing which might be called grammatology. While the general histories of writing treat individual writings mainly from a descriptive-historical point of view, the new science attempts to establish general principles governing the use and evolution of writing on a comparative-typological basis. The importance of this study lies in its being the first systematic presentation of the history and evolution of writing as based on these principles.

This recently developing "structure" approach to the nature of the writing systems of the world has served to clarify and to emphasize a variety of matters that those who are concerned with the "reading" of any of these systems must consider. The basic "structure" of each particular writing system will necessarily determine what must be learned as the first steps to the reading of materials written in that system. Writing systems differ most significantly not in respect to the differences in the variety of graphic shapes used but in respect to what features of the language are represented by those shapes. From this point of view the history of the various writing systems is the history of man's earliest struggles to understand the elements that constitute his language. These struggles do not begin with the early nineteenth century—the date given above for the first steps in the modern "scientific" view of language. They reach back several thousands of years to the first efforts to invent a means of giving graphic expression to the meanings he could grasp and communicate through his language.

The first type of that graphic expression was through pictures—not pictures that represented his linguistic expression of these meanings, but pictures that represented directly the meanings themselves—pictures that showed the shapes of things, or the actions of the hunt or a battle, or of fighters swimming a river. There were series of pictures showing a sequence of events. Pictures of this kind often served as mnemonic devices to recall the occurrences of a legend. But although these pictures could and did record events and situations they were not the pictographs of *picture writing. Picture writing* requires the use, in the representation, of a "strict order of the signs following the order of the spoken words." On the other hand, pictures in which "the meaning is conveyed by the totality of little drawings without any convention as to the beginning of the message or the order in which it should be interpreted" are *not picture writing.*

On the whole, *pictographs* representing the meaning of the linguistic expression constitute the *forerunners* of writing, not *real* writing—that is, the graphic devices tied to the order of the linguistic signals as they come out in speech—*phonography.*

After the efforts to represent graphically the meaning of the linguistic whole, came the attention to the separate "words" as the first linguistic units to be symbolized in writing. This type of writing provided separate signs for each word. It was *logographic.* This is the kind of writing we use for our numerals. The graphic sign 7 stands in our English writing for the word pronounced /sɛvən/ (spelled *seven*). The single sign 7 stands for the whole sound-pattern which constitutes this word in English, not for the separate parts of this sound-pattern. Thus as a representation for the total *sound-pattern* which constitutes the word it is phonographic; and as a graphic representation of a total word-pattern, it is logographic. The sign 7 is thus a phonographic *logogram.* It is *not* an *ideogram,* a representation of an "idea" or a "meaning"—of "seven-ness." It is strictly a word sign, as is 75 for /sɛvəntɪ faɪv/ (*seventy-five*), or 57 for /fɪftɪ-sɛvən/ (*fifty-seven*), or 777 for /sɛvən həndrəd ənd sɛvəntɪ sɛvən/ (*seven hundred and seventy seven*). Other languages use this graphic shape (often slightly modified as 𝒯) as a representation of their own words: *sieben* (German), *sept* (French), *shichi* (Japanese), *siete* (Spanish), *sette* (Italian). Most of Chinese writing consists of logograms and thus requires an immense number of separate graphic signs. Large Chinese dictionaries have forty to fifty thousand logographic "characters." A typewriter may have 5500.

The next linguistic unit that was symbolized in writing was the syllable. Many of the languages of the world have used and still do use syllabaries for their system. In a syllabary the separate signs do not represent the words as wholes except, of course, when the whole word consists of a single syllable, as do many of the words in Chinese. Nor do the signs of a syllabary represent the separate phonetic units which constitute the syllable. Japanese writing uses a large number of word-signs (Chinese characters, called by the Japanese *kanji*) and two types of syllabary, the *katakana* with only 47 basic signs, and *hiragana* with more variant forms of its basic syllabary shapes. The syllabary of Linear B used at least 69 signs. According to I. J. Gelb there were only 22 to 30 signs in the Semitic syllabaries, 56 in the Cypriotic syllabary, 100 to 130 in the Sumerian cuneiform syllabaries. As with the Japanese writing, some of these syllabaries were used together with a rather large number of word-signs (logograms). Sumerian writing, for example, in addition to its syllabic signs used some 600 other signs.

The next linguistic features to be symbolized by writing were the separate phonetic units of syllables—the writing that constitutes an *alphabet.* A syllabary as well as an alphabet symbolizes the sounds of a language, but in a different way. We are familiar with the way the letters of our alphabet represent the sound units of a word-pattern. It may help to stress the difference between an alphabet and a syllabary if, for illustration, here, we use some of these same letters as syllabary signs.

Each of our letters has a name which consists of a separate syllable. Examples are the following.

Letter	*Name*
D	dee /di/
T	tee /ti/
J	jay /ǰ e/
K	kay /k e/
L	ell /ɛ l/
M	em /ɛ m/
N	en /ɛ n/
U	yu /y u/
S	es /ɛ s/

If then we use each of our letters to represent its full name as it sounds, each letter will stand for a *syllable* rather than the single phonetic units it usually represents when used as a letter in our alphabet. As syllabary signs then the following letters I C U symbolize the single syllable words *I see you.* The following, as syllable signs, represent a few more words in context.

O A B C D 2 B S
L M N O B S
O S A R, 1 S

The chief difficulty of using our letters as syllabary signs arises out of the great limitation of signs for syllables with other vowels than /i/ and /e/ in open syllables, as B, D, C, with /i/, and J, K, with /e/, and only /ɛ/ in closed syllables, as F, L, M, N, S with /ɛ/.

Alphabetic writing is not phonetic writing—with each letter representing one *phone* in the pronunciation of a word. As indicated in Chapters Two and Three and earlier in this chapter, the bundles of sound contrasts that constitute the functioning units to identify our word-patterns are the *phonemes. Alphabetic writing is basically phonemic.* Just as the habits of pronunciation that a child develops in learning his native language are not habits of producing and hearing the separate sounds as isolatable items, so the habits of reading alphabetic writing are not habits of responding to the individual letters as representative of isolatable phones. Just as he responds to the phonemic patterns that identify the word-patterns in speech he must learn to respond to the graphic representations of these phonemic patterns in reading.

But practically none of the writing systems in actual use are "pure" systems using only one of the types of linguistic units for graphic representation—words, syllables, phonemes. Logographic systems often contain syllable and alphabet representations. Our own alphabetic system contains also a variety of examples of word-writings. All the systems have some advantages. For our own language with its fairly large number of vowel phonemes our alphabetic representation has special advantages.

The great advantage of the Greco-Russian-Greco-Roman type of alphabet is not that it specifies phonemic features incapable of specification by all other alphabet types, but rather that it is the only type which has alphabetic resources which permit a writer to distinguish between *consonant clusters* and *vowel clusters* and *consonant-vowel* sequences without extra work.

SUMMARY

At this point it may be useful to bring together in brief statements the particular features that differentiate the four terms we have discussed.

Phonics has been and continues to be a way of teaching beginning reading. It consists primarily in attempting to match the individual letters by which a word is spelled with the specific "sounds" which these letters "say." *Phonics* is used by some teachers as one of the methods of helping pupils, who have acquired a "sight-vocabulary" of approximately 200 words, to solve the problems presented by "new" words by "sounding" the letters.

Phonetics is *not* the same set of materials and activities as *phonics*. *Phonetics* is a set of techniques by which to identify and de-

scribe, in absolute terms, all the differences of sound features that occur in any language. *Phonetics* is not concerned with the ways in which words are spelled in English by the traditional alphabet. "Phonetic" alphabets have been constructed to serve as tools to represent graphically the actual pronunciations of linguistic forms, and these alphabets have been tried from time to time in the efforts to achieve a more effective way of teaching beginning reading.

Phonemics is a set of techniques by which to identify and to describe, especially in terms of distribution, the bundles of sound contrasts that constitute the structural units that mark the word-patterns. It is the *phonemes* of the language that alphabetic writing represents.

An *alphabet* is a set of graphic shapes that can represent the separate vowel and consonant phonemes of the language. All *alphabets* are phonemically based, and the procedures of teaching the process of reading alphabetic writing must take into account this essential fact of the structural base of alphabetic writing.

The Role of Grapheme-Phoneme Correspondence in the Perception of Words

ELEANOR J. GIBSON

ANNE PICK

HARRY OSSER

MARCIA HAMMOND

What is the critical unit of language for the reading process—the perception of written words? Recommendations for the teaching of reading have usually depended on the choice and definition of a unit. It was once assumed that the letters of the

alphabet were the units, so children began reading instruction by learning their ABCs.

Reprinted with the permission of the senior author and the publisher from the article of the same title, *American Journal of Psychology*, 1962, **75**, 554–570.

The advent of Gestalt psychology (applied in a very simple-minded way) changed all this. Several generations of children, as a result, were taught by the "whole word" method. As Bloomfield points out, such a method loses all the advantages of an alphabetical language.[1] One might as well learn picture-writing. Yet the letters of our alphabet in many cases do not have a one-to-one correlation with phonemic units. Is there, then, a proper unit?

It is the purpose of this paper to investigate the hypothesis that a unit is constituted by spelling-to-sound correlations. This is a higher-order unit formed by grapheme-phoneme correspondences. It is not defined by speech alone, or writing alone, nor is it a morpheme. It is the letter-group which has an invariant relationship with a phonemic pattern. Whole words usually have such a relationship; but often they can be broken into smaller clusters of letters which still have the kind of relationship referred to when they are in a stated position relative to other such clusters. The clusters may be of different sizes and the rules for the grapheme-phoneme correspondence are conditional on what precedes or what follows. The correspondence is not a matter of "sequential probability" but it is to be found in the structure of written English *as it is related to spoken English.*

The existence of such correspondence has been demonstrated in a study by Charles F. Hockett and a group of co-workers in the Department of Linguistics at Cornell University. This group has classified English graphic monosyllables (1) according to the arrangements of letters in them, and (2) in terms of their pronunciation. The aim of the classification is to discover the rules by which pronunciation can be predicted from spelling. A graphic monosyllable includes a vowel-spelling, an initial-consonant spelling, and a final-consonant spelling. An initial-

consonant spelling might be *CL;* a vowel-spelling, *EA;* a final consonant spelling, *TS.* The monosyllable is *CLEATS.* Rules for pronunciation are formulated conditionally on what precedes and follows as well as in terms of the letter-group as such. Regularities in spelling-to-sound predictability may be termed spelling-to-sound correlations, or grapheme-phoneme correspondences.

A child who learns to read (well) is forming useful spelling-to-sound habits based on these rules, whether he could tell you so or not. Even if he is taught by some method which makes it difficult, he must eventually discover the important spelling-to-sound correlations, if he is to be able to generate for himself the way to read new words.

From this starting position, we can proceed to the statement of a psychological hypothesis which has some testable consequences. Reading consists of decoding graphic material to the phonemic patterns of spoken language which have already been mastered when reading is begun. The units to be decoded are not single letters, for these have no invariant acoustic match in our language. The whole word is possible, but is uneconomical as a training unit for it provides no basis for independent decoding of new graphic combinations. The hypothesis advanced is that the reading task is essentially that of discovering higher-order invariants, the spelling-to-sound correlations. These are constants which are presumably discovered by exposure to both the graphic and the phonemic stimuli at the same time and in different contexts, so that the invariant combinations can be recognized in many different words. There are not a fixed number of units, such as all the words in the dictionary. There are, rather, all the potential ones which the rules of correspondence generate.

It is assumed that the individual discovers these grapheme-phoneme correspondences as he learns to read, even if he is not specifically taught them. He may not be able to draw up a set of rules but he "has"

[1] Leonard Bloomfield, Linguistics and reading, *Elementary Engl. Rev.,* 19, 1942, 125–130, 183–186.

them, if he is a good reader, just as a young child "has" grammar long before he can formulate rules for it. Once he has them, any letter-combinations which follow the rules are functional units.

From this hypothesis we predict that a skilled reader should discriminate better visually, letter-groups (pseudo-words) which are constructed according to the rules of spelling-to-sound correlation (found in the structure of written and spoken English) than ones which are not, or are only partially so. This hypothesis is tested in the experiments described below. Recognition of letter-groups presented tachistoscopically was the criterion chosen for discrimination. Ability to perceive a letter-group presented tachistoscopically was found by Crausman to correlate with reading ability.[2] There is reason to think, therefore, that it is a valid measure of word-discriminability in the reading process.

Historical Background

There is a certain amount of relevant material in the literature of experimental psychology which it may repay us to examine in the light of this hypothesis. Particularly, a number of experiments on word- and letter-recognition have been conducted in recent years with the method of tachistoscopic viewing. Howes and Solomon said, in reporting one of these, "any general property of words . . . should be operative in the word-threshold experiment, and the dependent variable (duration threshold) some function of it."[3] What is the logic of this statement, and what are the properties of words (or letter groups) which have been treated as parameters in a "word-threshold" experiment?

The logic is discussed by Solomon and Howes. Perception, they say, is defined by both stimulus properties and response-properties. When linguistic responses are elicited in a perceptual experiment, "any variable that is a general property of

linguistic responses must also be a property of any perceptual concept that is based upon these responses."[4] *Word-frequency* was the property investigated by Solomon and Howes. They defined it simply in terms of frequency in the Thorndike-Lorge tables, but pointed out that frequency could refer to "frequency of visual exposure of a linguistic *stimulus*" or "the frequency of occurrence of a linguistic *response*." The two are different, they thought, but probably correlated. The assumption has been expressed by Postman and Conger that *emitted* frequency of a word, as such, affects the visual recognitive threshold.[5] Osgood, on the other hand, questions this assumption: "frequency-of-conversational-usage would not affect recognizability of words as *visual* stimuli."[6]

Postman and Rosenzweig found, in line with Osgood's position, that auditory training (hearing and speaking) did not significantly decrease visual recognitive thresholds for printed syllables, although it did decrease auditory thresholds, and visual training decreased visual thresholds.[7] Sprague also found that oral practice alone had no effect on tachistoscopic recognitive thresholds.[8] On the other hand, Forrest found that visual thresholds (determined by increasing sharpness of focus) varied with relative familiarity of paralogs, although the method of familiarizing was by auditory presentation.[9] (It should be noted that the paralogs were all "pronounceable" and that they were exhibited twice in written form so that S would be familiar with the spelling of the words.)

The hypothesis proposed in this paper attempts to cut across the dichotomy of

[2] Burt Crausman, Temporal perception of good and poor readers, *Canad. Psychol.*, 1, 1960, 113 (abstract).

[3] D. H. Howes and R. L. Solomon, Visual duration threshold as a function of word probability, *J. exp. Psychol.*, 41, 1951, 401.

[4] R. L. Solomon and D. H. Howes, Word frequency, personal values, and visual duration thresholds, *Psychol. Rev.*, 58, 1951, 257.

[5] Leo Postman and Beverly Conger, Verbal habits and the visual recognition of words, *Science*, 19, 1954, 671–673.

[6] C. E. Osgood, *Method and Theory in Experimental Psychology*, 1053, 203.

[7] Leo Postman and M. R. Rosenzweig, Practice and transfer in the visual and auditory recognition of verbal stimuli, this JOURNAL, 69, 1956, 209–226.

[8] R. L. Sprague, Effects of differential training on tachistoscopic recognition thresholds, *J. exp. Psychol.*, 58, 1959, 227–231.

[9] D. W. Forrest, Auditory familiarity as a determinant of visual threshold, this JOURNAL, 70, 1957, 634–636.

stimulus- and response-frequency by proposing that the critical unit to be considered in word-recognition involves both—that it is, in fact, a stimulus-response *correspondence* which the individual becomes skilled in detecting as it recurs in an invariant relationship in different words. Neither frequency of visual exposure alone or emitting the oral response alone is of significance. Rather, it is frequency of experiencing a grapheme-phoneme coincidence which leads to skilled recognition.

No experiments have been performed heretofore with this concept in mind, but the experiments which have attempted to relate some property of words or letter-groups to visual discriminability will be briefly summarized.

WORD-FREQUENCY. The hypothesis that greater frequency of words in the language should be correlated with speed and accuracy of recognition has been verified in a number of experiments. Cattell's early experiments with groups of letters and words exposed on a revolving drum laid the foundation for this research,[10] followed by Erdmann and Dodge.[11] Vernon,[12] Howes and Solomon,[13] Solomon and Postman,[14] McGinnies, Comer and Lacey,[15] Postman and Conger,[16] King-Ellison and Jenkins,[17] Baker and Feldman,[18]

[10] J. McK. Cattell, Ueber der Zeit der Erkennung und Benennung von Schriftzeichen, Bildern, und Farben, *Philos. Stud.*, 2, 1885, 635–650.
[11] Benno Erdmann and Raymond Dodge, *Psychologische Untersuchungen über das Lesen auf experimenteller Grundlage*, 1898, 360 pp.
[12] M. D. Vernon, *Studies in the Psychology of Reading: A. The Errors Made in Reading*, Med. Res. Council, Spec. Rep. Ser., No. 130, 1–40.
[13] Howes and Solomon, 1951, *op. cit.*, 401–410.
[14] R. L. Solomon and Leo Postman, Frequency of usage as a determinant of recognition thresholds for words, *J. exp. Psychol.*, 13, 1952, 195–201.
[15] E. M. McGinnies, P. B. Comer, and O. L. Lacey, Visual recognition thresholds as a function of word length and word frequency, *ibid.*, 44, 1952, 65–69.
[16] Postman and Conger, *op. cit.*, 671–673.
[17] Patricia King-Ellison and J. J. Jenkins, The durational threshold of visual recognition as a function of word frequency, this JOURNAL, 67, 1954, 700–703.
[18] K. E. Baker and Herman Feldman, Threshold-luminance for recognition in relation to frequency of prior exposure, this JOURNAL, 69, 1956, 278–280.

and Moscovici and Humbert[19] have all confirmed the role of word-frequency (in some cases built in experimentally) in lowering visual recognitive thresholds.

Experimental findings for "familiarity" of words are comparable. Using Noble's technique of scaling words for familiarity by means of a rating scale,[20] Kristofferson obtained recognition-thresholds for 20 items, some real and some pseudo-words, and found a significant correlation between rated familiarity and recognition-threshold.[21]

A developmental study by Hoffmann compared children in grades 1 through 8 and adults on tachistoscopic viewing of (1) groups of consonants, (2) nonsense-syllables (pronounceable), (3) unfamiliar words, and (4) familiar words.[22] The number of letters read correctly increased from condition (1) through (4). The developmental curves differ, as well. The slope is least steep for consonants and increases with the conditions. In other words, groups of consonants are not recognized much better by adults than by first-graders, but the advantage increases as approximation to familiar linguistic units increases.

Miller, Bruner, and Postman compared accuracy of visual recognition for groups of letters having four orders of "approximation to English."[23] Accuracy of recognition was greater as approximation to English increased. That frequency as such of either single letters, bigrams, etc., is the critical principle here is unlikely. When the four lists are examined, it is obvious that pronunciability increases with order of approximation to English, and with each stage, more and more "real" syllables appear. Pronounceable and familiar subgroups may have played a very important role in increasing accuracy.

TRIGRAM-FREQUENCY. Postman and Conger investigated the effect of trigram-frequency (sequences

[19] S. Moscovici and T. C. Humbert, Usage et disponibilité comme facteurs déterminant la durée de stimuli verbaux, *Bull. de Psychol.*, 13, 1960, 406–412.
[20] C. E. Noble, The meaning-familiarity relationship, *Psychol. Rev.*, 60, 1953, 89–98.
[21] A. B. Kristofferson, Word recognition, meaningfulness, and familiarity, *Percep. mot. Skills.* 7, 1957, 219–220.
[22] Jakob Hoffmann, Experimentell-psychologische Untersuchungen über Leseleistungen von Schulkindern, *Arch. gesam. Psychol.*, 58, 1927, 325–388.
[23] G. A. Miller, J. S. Bruner, and Leo Postman, Familiarity of letter sequences and tachistoscopic identification, *J. gen. Psychol.*, 50, 1954, 129–139.

of three letters which appear as parts of words with different frequencies) on recognition-threshold.[24] Two experiments failed to show any relationship between recognition-thresholds and trigram-frequency.

An experiment by Taylor investigated the effect of experimentally produced frequency on trigrams.[25] The trigrams were chosen so as to be approximately equal for summed (individual-letter) frequency. They were selected also for easy pronunciability. An experimental list was presented to the Ss 15 times. S looked at each letter-group for 2 sec. and pronounced it aloud. Afterward, duration-thresholds were obtained for these and for a matched control-list. Frequency of practice of this type did lead to a lowered recognition-threshold. Thus, when a letter-group is viewed and pronounced as a unit, frequency is effective.[26] But mere frequency of sequences embedded in words is not.

Trigrams which form sub-units (that is, pronounceable syllables) of words are another matter. Postman and Rosenzweig compared recognitive thresholds for sets of trigrams which were high and low, respectively, for frequency of occurrence both as actual syllables in English words and as trigrams.[27] The more "familiar" syllables had lower mean recognitive thresholds. In fact, English words yielded no lower thresholds than familiar syllables.

MEANINGFULNESS. Whether "meaningfulness" has any role in word-recognition has been the subject of a few experiments. The earliest of these by Peixotto did not use a short-exposure technique, but the results are relevant.[28] She used syllables scaled for association-value from the lists of Glaze,[29] Hull,[30] and Krueger.[31] The Ss simply read a list of 30 syllables printed in columns on pages of a booklet. After reading through three pages (the same list repeated in random order) they found syllables they had read mixed with 90 others on the fourth page. They marked the ones they recognized as having seen before. She found little or no relationship between associative value and recognitive score.

A different criterion of meaning was used by Taylor, who had Ss study syllables accompanied by a picture of a familiar object which was designed as their "meaning."[32] Recognitive thresholds were not lowered for this group as compared with one which had equal frequency of practice with the syllable without the picture (see above). Neither did the degree of associative value of the syllable (as determined by Glaze) have any effect upon performance. She concluded that the variable of meaningfulness, as defined by these procedures, did not influence visual thresholds of duration.

Kristofferson[33] found a significant correlation between meaning (as scaled by Noble[34]) and threshold for word-recognition. In this case, however, meaning covaried with "familiarity." It is probable that the latter variable was the effective one, in view of the usual positive results with word-frequency and the negative ones for meaningfulness.

The finding of Postman and Rosenzweig that three-letter English words were not recognized any sooner than familiar syllables (sub-units) of words is consistent with the rejection of "meaning" as a variable in word recognition.[35] Their words all had a referent (*e.g. bun, pen*, etc.), whereas the syllables did not (*e.g. ing, est*, etc.). They commented that "the failure of the English words to yield lower thresholds than the nonsense-syllables suggests that S is no less ready to use syllables as response-units than he is English words of comparable linguistic frequency."

SUMMARY. These experimental results taken together seem to us consistent with our hypothesis that letter-groups which have an invariant spelling-to-sound relationship form functional units for reading. Frequency in one sense would be a necessary condition for the formation of such units, for invariance cannot be discovered without repetition. It would be expected, therefore, that whole words of high frequency and syllables (sub-units of

[24] Postman and Conger, *op. cit.*, 671–673.

[25] J. A. Taylor, Meaning, frequency, and visual duration threshold, *J. exp. Psychol.*, 55, 1958, 329–334.

[26] See also Solomon and Postman, *op. cit.*, 105, 201.

[27] Postman and Rosenzweig, *op. cit.*, 209–226.

[28] H. E. Peixotto, The recognitive value of three hundred nonsense syllables, this JOURNAL, 61, 1948, 352–360.

[29] J. A. Glaze, The associative value of nonsense syllables, *J. genet. Psychol.*, 35, 1928, 255–267.

[30] C. L. Hull, The meaningfulness of 320 selected nonsense syllables, this JOURNAL, 45, 1933, 730–734.

[31] W. C. F. Krueger, The relative difficulty of nonsense syllables, *J. exp. Psychol.*, 17, 1934, 145–153.

[32] Taylor, *op. cit.*, 329–334.

[33] Kristofferson, *op. cit.*, 219–220.

[34] Noble, An analysis of meaning, *Psychol. Rev.*, 59, 1952, 421–430.

[35] Postman and Rosenzweig, *op. cit.*, 216.

words having a consistent pronunciation) would have high recognitive value, whereas mere sequential frequency would not unless it had a consistent acoustic match. The evidence to be drawn from these experiments is, however, merely supportive; a real test of the hypothesis remains to be made.

Preliminary Experiment

The purpose of the experiment was to test the hypothesis that skilled readers would discriminate visually pseudo-words constructed according to the rules of spelling-to-sound correlation better than words which are not, or are only partially, so constructed. Three lists of pseudo-words were constructed, one with an invariant relation between spelling and sound (*e.g.* NOOSH), one in which all the words were pronounceable, but there were two alternative pronunciations (*e.g.* DRIEND), and one in which the words had low spelling-to-sound correlation (were relatively unpronounceable by rules of English pronunciation, *e.g.* SCRIGW). Word-length varied, but was equated for the three lists. There were 15 words in each list.

The words were presented tachistoscopically, one at a time for 100 m.sec. each. The three lists were mixed in a random order. Items were projected on a screen so that Ss could be run in groups. (A second projector and tachistoscope, synchronized with the first, provided a pre- and post-exposure field of a brightness equal to that of the background of the projected word.) The pre-ëxposure field contained two horizontal lines so arranged as to frame the projected word if they were superposed on it. These lines took the place of a fixation-point. The slides containing the words were prepared by typing in bold-face type with a sign-typewriter (typed letters were $\frac{3}{8}$ in. high).

The Ss were given a "ready" signal, fixated the lines, and after the word was flashed, tried to write what they saw. They were told to guess when they could. Each word was exposed only once. There were 21 Ss, members of a class in the Psychology of Language.

Results were scored right or wrong for the whole word (scoring of parts was tried but discarded as being difficult and no more informative). The mean number correct was about twice as great for the two pronounceable sets of words as for the unpronounceable. A Tukey-test for multiple comparison of means showed that the means for the two pronounceable series were both different from the unpronounceable, but not from each other. If these two had differed, it might have

been hypothesized that two alternate pronunciations interfere with one another and reduce discriminability in comparison with a single "good" pronunciation. This was not the case.

EXPERIMENT I

The hypothesis tested in Experiment I was the same as in the preliminary experiment, but only two sets of words were constructed: one with high spelling-to-sound correlation (referred to as the *P* or pronounceable list) and one with low spelling-to-sound correlation (the *U* or unpronounceable list). Summed letter-frequency, which has not been controlled in the preliminary experiment, was equated for the two lists.

CONSTRUCTION OF LISTS. The 25 words in the pronounceable list consisted of (1) an initial consonant-spelling having a single regular pronunciation, (2) a final consonant-spelling having a single, regular pronunciation, and (3) a vowel-spelling placed between the two consonant-spellings, and having a single regular pronunciation when it follows and is followed by the given initial and final consonant-spellings, respectively. An example would be B/1, E/3, SKS/2. Some of the consonant- and vowel-spellings were single letters, some were "clusters." A cluster-type of vowel-spelling may actually contain a consonant-letter as in "aw."[36]

The words in the second list—those with low spelling-to-sound correlation—were constructed from the words in the first list. The initial consonant-spelling of the pronounceable words became the final consonant-spelling of the unpronounceable words. Similarly, the final consonant-spelling of the pronounceable words became the initial consonant-spelling of the unpronounceable words. The position of the vowel spellings remained the same.[37] For example: Pronounceable, B E SKS;

[36] Spelling must often be "mapped" into phonemes by clusters or groups of letters, rather than by single letters. Rules for invariance are thus phrased in terms of "consonant-spelling" and "vowel-spelling."

[37] To obtain a pronounceable and an unpronounceable list using the same letters, it was necessary to choose initial consonant-spellings that are not also final ones, and vice versa; or at least one of the consonant-spellings in each pair had to be of this type.

TABLE 5-1

Correct Responses and Pronunciability Ratings for Pronounceable (*P*) and Unpronounceable (*U*) Words

P words	Total correct	Pronunciability-rating	*U* words	Total correct	Pronunciability-rating
(1) DINK	118	1.06	NKID	105	5.85
(2) VUNS	110	1.53	NSUV	90	6.34
(3) GLOX	117	1.59	XOGL	108	6.12
(4) SULB	95	1.95	LBUS	115	5.64
(5) LODS	107	1.28	DSOL	118	4.99
(6) BESKS	79	2.30	SKSEB	50	6.77
(7) CLATS	91	1.47	TSACL	102	6.05
(8) BRELP	91	3.01	LPEBR	35	7.72
(9) FRAMB	112	2.40	MBAFR	36	7.31
(10) GRISP	113	1.62	SPIGR	77	5.24
(11) FUNTS	119	1.62	NTSUF	77	6.10
(12) TILMS	97	2.18	LMSIT	70	6.44
(13) SLAND	120	1.71	NDASL	69	6.73
(14) BLASPS	67	2.88	SPSABL	35	7.28
(15) SPRILK	38	3.21	LKISPR	14	7.40
(16) SMAWMP	3	6.20	MPAWSM	20	7.23
(17) BLORDS	54	2.29	DSORBL	49	6.00
(18) PREENT	56	2.86	NTEEPR	7	7.47
(19) DRIGHK	36	6.34	KIGHDR	0	6.72
(20) KLERFT	37	4.18	FTERKL	33	6.77
(21) GLURCK	51	2.94	CKURGL	37	6.59
(22) QUEESK	45	3.05	SKEEQU	35	4.63
(23) TIRPTH	42	4.50	PTHIRT	31	6.12
(24) PRILTHS	28	4.63	LTHSIPR	0	8.36
(25) TRILFTHS	13	5.29	LFTHSITR	0	8.50

Unpronounceable, SKS E B. The complete list of words appears in Table 5-1.

The reader may ask, at this point, whether one list is, in fact, pronounceable while the other is not. Actually, the term pronounciability is used here as a convenient means of referring to a correlation of spelling-with-sound, according to the rules of English spelling and pronunciation. One can make an attempt to pronounce "TSACL" some way or other, but there is no invariant correlation between this spelling and a standard way of pronouncing it in the English language.

PROCEDURE. The task required of S was to identify a word as it was projected on a screen, and to write it down. The procedure was similar to the preliminary experiment in the method of projection and apparatus employed; but it differed in that five presentations of the lists were given, with an increasing exposure-time for each presentation.[38] The 50 words were projected in a random order for 30 m.sec. each. They were then reordered and projected for 50, 100, 150, and 250 m.sec. The words were reordered after each series. The Ss were seated about 4 ft. from the screen and were told to write down what they saw and to guess when they could. They were run in small groups to permit good viewing angles for all Ss. The height of the letters projected on the screen was $3\frac{3}{4}$ in., the width about $2\frac{1}{2}$ in. The entire field of projection was 82 in. wide. There were 25 Ss (adult, summer-school students); their native language was English.

[38] This technique was copied from Miller, Bruner, and Postman, *op. cit.*, 129–139.

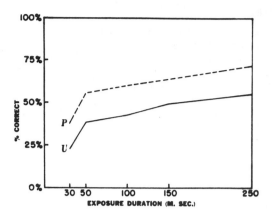

FIGURE 5-1. *Mean percentage of* P *and* U *words correct at 5 exposure-durations.*

Results

The words recorded by the Ss were scored right or wrong, and separate means for *P* and *U* words were obtained for each time-interval. The mean percentage of *P* words correct and *U* words correct is plotted for each of the five successive exposure-durations in Figure 5-1. The curve for *P* words is consistently higher than the curve for *U* words. The percentage correct rises sharply from the first exposure to the second, and thereafter increases very little. The two curves are parallel throughout.

The Wilcoxon Matched Pairs Signed Ranks Test[39] was used to compare the total *P* and *U* scores (see Table 5-1). The pairs in each case were composed of the two pseudo-words constructed from the same group of letters, one pronounceable, one not. The difference between the total *P* score and the total *U* score is significant at better than the 1 per cent level (two-tail).

It was also possible to test the consistency of the trend for Ss, with Wilcoxon's test. When the scores (number correct) of the *P* and *U* words were compared for the Ss, the difference between them was significant beyond the 1 per cent level. The difference between them at every time-interval was also significant beyond the 1 per cent level (two-tail test in all cases).

[39] F. Wilcoxon, *Some Rapid Approximate Statistical Procedures,* 1949.

Because of a long established habit of reading from left to right, it might be expected that more errors would occur for the final consonant-spelling than for the initial one. The Ss' reproductions were scored for initial and final consonant-clusters separately, and this expectation was borne out. But the difference between words of the *P* and *U* lists was still present ($p < 0.01$ by a chi-square test for both initial and final clusters).

Errors can also be expected to increase with length of word. Such was the case. Errors were fewest in the case of four-letter words and increased with length. The difference between *P* and *U* words occurred for all lengths of word but was smallest for four-letter words and greatest for five-letter words. The interaction could not be measured, since the number of cases for the different lengths of word was not equal, but the difference is quite obvious. A short word of four letters is so seldom missed that the difference between *P* and *U* can have only a small effect. On the other hand, a word of eight letters is so difficult that not even pronunciability will permit perfect discrimination to occur with great frequency.

The errors were studied and classified also for the kinds of changes made. "Real" word-errors occurred infrequently, probably because the Ss were told in the instructions that they would be shown "nonsense" words. More real words were given for *P* combinations than for *U* combinations (27 in all, as against 15).

Errors which changed the projected letter-group in the direction of a more pronounceable one were frequent. This was accomplished in some cases by adding a vowel (*e.g.* NIKID for NKID), by omitting a consonant (*e.g.* SKEB for SKSEB), or by changing a consonant-cluster (*e.g.* BLUS for LBUS). An error of this type was often repeated on later trials.

Errors of omission (writing nothing) were more frequent for the unpronounceable words, but such errors did not occur often. They occurred most often for the longer words.

Discussion

The results of this experiment demonstrate that a letter-group with a high spelling-to-sound correlation is reproduced more accurately than an equivalent letter-group with a low spelling-to-sound correlation. This result cannot be caused by a difference in the familiarity of the letters taken alone, or even the vowel- and consonant-clusters taken alone, for the same clusters were used in the two lists. It must be due to the existence of higher-order graphic units: the letter-combinations of English writing that function as relatively stable units in grapheme-phoneme correspondences.

Practically, this result suggests strongly that the proper unit for analyzing the process of reading (and writing) is not the alphabetical letter but the spelling pattern which has an invariant relationship with a phonemic pattern. This may be of great importance for children's learning to read and write.

Among the theoretical implications for psychology, perhaps the most general is this, that while reading is based on the discrimination and identification of visual forms such as letters, it becomes, in the skilled reader, a process of perceiving "super-forms," and that these tend to be constituted (organized) by their relation to auditory-vocal temporal patterns. Insofar as frequency has a role in the constitution of these units, it is the frequency of grapheme-phoneme coincidence which is crucial, not frequency of exposure to the seen or uttered units alone. The reading of words is thus inseparable from the hearing of words. Since the hearing of words is also inseparable from the speaking of words, reading must be conceived, however, as part of a circular response-process, not simply as a stimulus-response process. The stimuli are complex, and the eventually effective stimuli are response-produced, in the sense that the visual stimuli which come to function as units are structured partly by feedback from response. Verbal perception, unlike certain other kinds of perception, will have to be explained in terms of a still emerging theory of self-stimulation or feedback.

EXPERIMENT II

The above interpretation of the results in Experiment I assumes that the pseudo-words having high spelling-to-sound correspondences are actually perceived (read) more quickly and accurately than those with low correspondence. Proponents of theories emphasizing *emitted* frequency or "response-bias" will be tempted to object that the difference between the two sets of words was not due to a difference in perceptibility, but instead due to the *S*'s tendency to emit, whatever the stimulus presented, the responses which were in the past made most frequently.[40]

The "spew hypothesis" of Underwood and Schultz[41] states the operation of re-

[40] See, for example, Israel Goldiamond and W. F. Hawkins, Vexierversuch: The log relationship between word-frequency and recognition obtained in the absence of stimulus words, *J. exp. Psychol.,* 56, 1958, 457–463; C. R. Brown and Herbert Rubenstein, Test of response bias explanation of word-frequency effect, *Science,* 133, 1961, 280–281.

[41] B. J. Underwood and R. W. Schulz, *Meaningfulness and Verbal Learning,* 1960, 36.

sponse-bias as follows, "the order of emission of verbal units is directly related to frequency of experience with those units." Are the pronounceable words recorded correctly more often by the Ss only because they are nearer the threshold of availability as responses, or are they actually perceived better?

If emitted frequency, in the past, is responsible for the words recorded, one might expect that *errors* in the previous experiments would include many which changed spelling without changing pronunciation. An example would be writing KLERPHT for KLERFT or GLURK for GLURCK. Some errors of this type were made, but fewer than seem consistent with a serious consideration of the hypothesis. Only 16 errors (out of a total of 7250 opportunities to respond) could be classified as identical in pronunciation with the pseudo-word exposed on the screen. But there are so many possible causes of error that one has no expected frequency with which to compare this number. A more direct test therefore seemed advisable.

If the S is not required to *emit* a word-response at all, but is instead asked to recognize or match one word with another, we can be fairly sure we are testing what he has perceived, not merely the response which is most available and easy to emit. He does not have to produce the response at all, in this case. One could use a judgment of same or different, or a match from a list including the word shown and some incorrect versions.

Our second experiment was designed to test the hypothesis that an S would *recognize* the word shown, from a multiple-choice list including this word, more accurately when the word shown had a high spelling-to-sound correlation.

CONSTRUCTION OF LISTS. The pseudo-words exposed for recognition were 20 from the two lists (pronounceable and unpronounceable) used in Experiment I. The "misleads" for the multiple-choice series for each one posed a problem. Artificial construction of these by made-up rules would yield unknown and probably unequal difficulty for different words. Also, the S might discover some of the rules before finishing and thereafter choose on a problem-solving basis, rather than perceptual matching. The series was obtained empirically, therefore, by including for each word the three most frequent errors recorded in the previous experiment, whatever they were. For example: for GLURCK the following words were used: GLURK, GLUCK, GLURGK, and GLURCK; for CKURGL the following were used: CKUGL, CKURL, CKUGEL, and CKURGL. Since one position in the choice-list might be more favorable than another, four lists were so constructed for each word that each choice appeared once in each of the four positions.

Practice-effects were equated by making two random orders of the words to be presented tachistoscopically, the second one so constructed that the unpronounceable version of a pronounceable combination now appeared in the position the pronounceable one had occupied in the first order (and vice versa). There were therefore 8 sub-groups constituted by the two orders, each with four versions of the multiple-choice series.

PROCEDURE. S was seated 5 to 7 ft. from a screen on which the words were projected, as before. The width of the total field projected was 31 in. The width of the word on this field varied from 12 to 24 in., depending on number of letters. The letters, as projected, were $3\frac{1}{2}$ in. high. Ss were run individually. The instructions read to S were as follows:

On the screen before you, between the two black lines, a nonsense-word will appear for only a fraction of a second. Immediately afterward, a list of four nonsense words will appear, *one* of which will be the word just exposed.

Choose the one you think is the same as the word you have just seen and place a number in the blank corresponding to its order on the screen. Number 1 is at the top and Number 4 at the bottom. A "ready" signal will be given before the first exposure. When the "ready" signal is given, please be sure to fixate between the two lines so as not to miss the word.

Do not try to make inferences about the alternatives provided in the choice-list, because they were obtained experimentally. Just look at the word flashed, and pick the one in the list which looks most like it.

Ten practice-words were given first to accustom S to the timing of the exposure. A pseudo-word was exposed tachistoscopically for 30 m.sec. and was followed after $\frac{1}{2}$ sec. by projection of the appropriate choice-list. This list was projected for a duration of 8 sec. The duration was long enough to permit S to read the words and record one, but not to study the alternatives in detail.

The 40 experimental words followed, in the order assigned to the sub-group. The entire experiment lasted about 18 min. There were 60 Ss, all university students. Each sub-group contained at least 6 Ss. An S took part in only one sub-group.

Results

The results were first scored separately for each sub-group, to see whether trends changed depending on order in the whole series of position in the choice-list. Table 5-2 contains the results by sub-groups. The mean number correct with a given order can be read across the table. The mean number correct for a given order in the choice-list can be read downward. For every sub-group (Order A combined, Order B combined, and Choice-Lists 1, 2, 3, and 4) the pronounceable words were matched correctly more often than the unpronounceable words. It seemed justifiable, therefore, to combine all the results. The over-all means were 14.62 correct for pronounceable words and 11.48 correct for unpronounceable words.

Since a quarter of the choices would be expected to be correct by chance, the number perceived correctly beyond chance was 9.62 for P words and 6.48 for U words. This is a gain of 48 per cent for P words over U words.

When the words (pronounceable and unpronounceable) were matched by pairs, 15 of the 20 pronounceable words were perceived correctly more often than their unpronounceable mates. In four cases, the unpronounceable version was perceived correctly more often, and in one case there was no difference. By the Wilcoxon Matched-Pairs Signed-Rank Test (two-tailed) the difference between the lists was significant at $p < 0.002$. The differences were also significant ($P < 0.01$) when tested by Ss.

The results of this experiment, then, corroborate those of the previous one and provide further positive evidence that pseudo-words constructed according to rules of invariant spelling-to-sound correlation of the English language are perceived more accurately under conditions of tachistoscopic viewing than their matches with no invariant spelling-to-sound prediction. It seems reasonable to conclude that the *perception* of the stimulus-word is affected by this correspondence; that we are not observing simply a "response-bias" to emit pronounceable combinations.

When responses must be emitted, however (as in Experiment I), there might conceivably be a combined effect of the perceptual bias toward grasping the higher-order invariant and a response-bias toward pronunciability. In that case, the difference between the two word-lists in Experiment I should be considerably greater than that in Experiment II. It is impossible to make a

TABLE 5-2

Number of Correct Choices of P and U Words Separated for Order and Multiple Choice Matching List

Order	Words	List 1	List 2	List 3	List 4	Mean
A	P	121°	171†	105°	106‡	14.37
	U	92°	130†	83°	91‡	11.31
B	P	96§	91§	84§	103‡	14.96
	U	63§	74§	68§	88‡	11.72
Mean	P	15.50	14.56	13.50	14.93	14.62
Mean	U	11.07	11.33	10.79	12.79	11.48

°$N = 8$;   †$N = 12$;   ‡$N = 7$;   §§$N = 6$.

direct comparison here, since a longer list (25 pairs) was used in Experiment I, as well as a different method (reproduction vs. recognition). The advantage of the pronounceable words over the unpronounceable words at the first exposure (30 m. sec.) was 65 per cent in Experiment I, as against 48 per cent in Experiment II. It is possible, therefore, that both effects are operative in Experiment I, resulting in greater difference in the results.

The question now to be answered is how the rules of invariance for grapheme-phoneme correspondence are learned. To answer this question it may be feasible to "build in" such units experimentally. If this can be done, the learning process presumably could be studied. Meanwhile, a simple associational model does not seem the best to entertain, for the rules of correspondence are conditional (whether a cluster is at the beginning or the end or the middle, etc.). A trigram such as "ign" functions as a predictable cluster for pronunciation at the end of a word (*e.g.* sign, malign) but the prediction will be different in another context (*e.g.* significant). A model more like a paradigm for concept-formation, with conditional isolation from context, seems more promising. Hopefully, a workable model can be formulated. Developmental experiments which may reveal the presence or absence of functional units of the kind posited at different age-levels are now in progress, and should provide some clues.

Control Experiments on Pronunciability

RATING OF PRONUNCIABILITY. Are letter-combinations which have, according to the rules, an invariant grapheme-phoneme correspondence, actually more "pronounceable"? The term "pronunciability" has been used in this paper as if such a statement could be made. But the matter is not merely one of convenience of reference, since Underwood and Schulz found that pronunciability, as defined by their scaling procedure, was a very important variable in verbal learning.[42] Ratings were therefore obtained of the pronunciability of the words in the *P* and *U* lists.

The rating method devised by Underwood and Schulz was copied verbatim except for references

[42] Underwood and Schulz, *op. cit.*, 163–199.

to word-length and "common" words (some of theirs were common words, while all of ours were pseudo-words). The two sets of words were mixed and presented to a group of 165 Ss (students in an introductory class in psychology) for rating on a 9-point scale. A score of 1 equals high and 9 equals low. Order was reversed for half the Ss in case scale changes would occur with practice.

The results showed a clear difference in pronunciability between the two lists. Mean ratings were computed for each of the 50 pseudo-words (see Table 5-1). The over-all mean rating of the pronounceable words was 2.88 (SD = 1.48); that of the unpronounceable words was 6.57 (SD = 0.94). For every one of the matched pairs the pronounceable combination received a lower mean rating (*i.e.* more pronounceable) than the unpronounceable combination. In all cases the mean for a pronounceable combination was lower than the over-all mean for the unpronounceable ones; similarly, the rating of each unpronounceable combination was higher than the over-all mean of the pronounceable combinations. There was considerable inter-individual variability in rating, probably related to differences in background of language, but the results fully justify the characterization of one list as more pronounceable than the other.

INVARIANCE OF PRONUNCIATION. A second question may be asked regarding the actual pronunciation of the pseudo-words. The rules of grapheme-phoneme correspondence imply that there should be a relatively invariant pronunciation of the *P* words, but a variety of pronunciations for the *U* words, which do not follow the rules. Is this indeed a fact? To answer the question, 16 Ss were asked to read the 50 words aloud. They first read quickly aloud through the two lists, one and then the other. The total time was noted for each list. Then they read the words, mixed in a random order, with a 5-sec. pause between words. The words were exposed, one at a time, on cards. A tape recording was made for each S. Order was balanced among the Ss.

The first reading served both as practice and as a time-check. If readability under conditions of tachistoscopic exposure is related to reading skill under normal conditions, the total reading time should differ for the two lists. The mean reading time was 38.8 sec. for the *P* list and 57.5 sec. for the *U* list, thus confirming this expectation. The trend was consistent for individual Ss.

The tape recordings (all 50 words for each of the 16 Ss) were given to two linguists for analysis of the pronunciations. They worked individually. The method used on their first transcriptions was

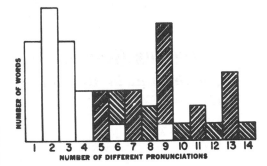

FIGURE 5-2. *Distribution of frequencies of* different *pronunciations for* P *and* U *words.* (Cross-hatching indicates U words.)

partly phonetic and partly phonemic. The sequences of letters in the *U* list, and perhaps occasionally in the *P* list, were such that the *Ss* sometimes brought in phonemes from other languages to make them easier to pronounce. In general, however, the *Ss* included extra sounds, so as to push the sequence toward a possible English one. On their second analysis, the linguists tried to put all the phonetic transcriptions in terms of the phonemic system of English (that is, in terms of significant contrasts). When the two linguists had disagreed on a transcription, the word was played several times and usually an agreement resulted. There was finally 98 per cent agreement between them.

Figure 5-2 shows the distributions of different pronunciations for the *P* list and the *U* list. There is very little overlapping, though two *P* words (DRIGHK and SMAWMP) were quite inconsistently pronounced and fell within the *U* distribution. The mean of different pronunciations was 2.68 for the *P* words and 9.12 for the *U* words. When *P* words were compared with their *U* counterparts, all *P* words had fewer different pronunciations except one (DRIGHK) which had a number equal to its counterpart.

The words in the *U* list were invariably pronounced as bisyllabic words, whereas the words in the *P* list were almost always pronounced as monosyllables.

It can be concluded that pseudo-words constructed according to rules of grapheme-phoneme correspondence are pronounced more consistently when read aloud when those which are not.

RELATION BETWEEN SCALED PRONUNCIABILITY AND INVARIANCE OF PRONUNCIATION. Whether pronunciability, as measured by a rating scale, is related to invariance of pronunciation (relative to rules of grapheme-phoneme correspondence) can be determined by comparing the results of the two experiments above. The results are independent, since none of the *Ss* took part in both experiments.

Both sets of scores (ratings and variability of pronunciation) for the 50 words were transformed into standard-scores and correlated by means of a Pearson *r*. A positive correlation of 0.85 was found (not corrected for attenuation). The magnitude of this correlation is very interesting, for it suggests that the rules of grapheme-phoneme correspondence, which exist objectively in the language, are reflected psychologically in individual ratings of pronunciability of words and also in group conformity of pronunciation.

These two experiments seem to us to provide quite impressive empirical validation of the rules used in constructing the lists.

SUMMARY AND CONCLUSIONS

The hypothesis has been proposed that the proper unit of the reading process is neither the single letter nor the whole word but a higher-order invariant derived from grapheme-phoneme correspondences. Rules can be drawn up for predicting spelling from sound if temporal patterning of "clusters" is taken into account. It was proposed that the skilled reader has learned to perceive as units the letter-patterns conforming to these rules and that such patterns have, therefore, an advantage in reading.

Several experiments were performed to test this hypothesis. Pseudo-words conforming to rules of spelling-to-sound correlation were compared with ones of low correlation under conditions of tachistoscopic viewing.

In the first experiment, it was found that the *Ss* reproduce pseudo-words of high correlation more accurately than ones matched for summed letter-frequency, but of low correlation.

Teaching Reading with i.t.a. in Britain

JOHN DOWNING

In Britain more than eight thousand children are learning or have learned to read with an augmented and modified writing system for English, originally known as "Augmented Roman" but later renamed the "Initial Teaching Alphabet" (i.t.a.) by its inventor, Sir James Pitman. The new name emphasizes its purpose as an aid to beginning reading. The Initial Teaching Alphabet is left behind as soon as fluency has been achieved, and reading skills are transferred to traditional orthography (t.o.). This new writing system and its aims have been described previously by Pitman,[1] and I have related the characteristics of i.t.a. to teaching methods[2] and to young children's needs in the learning situation.[3] The history of previous attempts to develop special orthographies for beginning reading also has been discussed and related to our current research.[4] This article is limited to an account of the empirical research into i.t.a.'s application in beginning reading classes in Britain.

AIMS OF THE RESEARCH

Our current experiments with i.t.a. are designed to obtain reliable and valid objective data to answer three questions:

1. Is the traditional orthography of English an important source of difficulty in beginning reading?
2. If children learn to read more rapidly and with greater success in the simplified and regularized i.t.a. reading system, can they transfer their superior reading skill from i.t.a. over to t.o.?
3. Is this two-stage process worthwhile in the final outcome? Are reading attainments in t.o. superior, after transfer, to what they would have been without the intervention of the special i.t.a. writing system for beginners?

THE RESEARCH PLAN

Reliability and validity have been sought through the design of a program of rigorous

[1] I. J. Pitman, "Learning To Read: An Experiment," *Journal of Royal Society of Arts*, 109, 1961, pp. 149–180; I. J. Pitman, "Learning To Read: A Suggested Experiment," *Times Educational Supplement*, 29, May, 1959; and I. J. Pitman, *The Ehrhardt Augmented (40 Sound-42 Character) Lower Case Roman Alphabet*. London: Pitman, 1959.

[2] J. A. Downing, "Experiments with an Augmented Alphabet for Beginning Readers in British Schools," *Frontiers of Education*, Ed., A. E. Traxler. Washington, D.C.: American Council on Education, 1963; J. A. Downing, *The Initial Teaching Alphabet*. London: Cassell, 1963.

[3] J. A. Downing, "Experiments with Pitman's Initial Teaching Alphabet in British Schools," *Proceedings of the 8th Annual Convention of the International Reading Association*, Miami, Florida, May 1–4, 1963.

[4] J. A. Downing, "The Relationship Between Reading Attainment and the Inconsistency of English Spelling at the Infants' School Stage," *British Journal of Educational Psychology*, 32, 1962, pp. 166–177. See also footnote 2.

Reprinted with the permission of the author and publisher from the article of the same title, *Phi Delta Kappan*, 1964, 45, No. 7, 322–329.

scientific experimentation and testing conducted in normal and representative classroom environments.

An experimental group of classes consisting of over 2,000 four- and five-year-old children from seventy-five primary schools are using i.t.a. for their first instruction in reading and writing, and a control group has been established in which pupils are beginning with t.o. From each group classes and pupils are selected for best match on important school and pupil variables. We are attempting to insure that the only major difference between the two groups is the orthography in which reading and writing instruction is given. Practically all of the books used by experimental group classes are printed in i.t.a., while the control group books are in t.o. For example, both groups use the same basal reader series (the most popular in Britain), but the series used by experimental classes is printed in i.t.a.

All other factors have been controlled as far as possible within an experiment being conducted under representative real-life school conditions. For example, in both the experimental and control classes the teachers have been asked not to change their normal methods of teaching but to continue to operate their usual timetables and instructional procedures. Special precautions have been taken to control the "Hawthorne effect." For instance, the workshops, research meetings, and school visits necessary for the experimental classes are matched by similar activities for the control classes designed to help them obtain the best possible results with t.o., and also to demonstrate that their important role in this research is recognized by the research team.

The i.t.a. teachers' workshops occupy two full days at some point before the class experiment begins. Teachers learn the new i.t.a. characters and how to arrive at i.t.a. spellings used. Discussions are also held to show how methods of teaching reading, writing, and spelling need little modification in the experimental i.t.a. classes. These two-day workshops appear to have been quite adequate for the teachers' training needs for i.t.a. experimentation.

The pupils' parents are informed about the experiments and are encouraged to maintain normal attitudes towards their children's reading and writing activities. Parents of i.t.a. pupils can buy books printed in i.t.a. or borrow them through the free public library service.

In the i.t.a. classes teachers have started reading instruction in accordance with their normal approach to judging reading readiness. As is usual in British infants' schools, each pupil is encouraged to progress at his own rate. When a child reaches the fifth primer (Grade 2-ii) and the teacher is satisfied that he is ready for transfer (e.g., able to read from minimal cues and to use contextual clues), she encourages him to use only books printed in t.o. and begins to teach him the use of t.o. in writing.

RESULTS OF THE FIRST TWO YEARS

We can report at this time on only that part of the sample which was recruited during the school year September, 1961, to July, 1962. We did not complete the recruitment of the total sample until April, 1963. This imposes two limitations on our findings: (1) It is smaller than we consider necessary. (2) Since final matching of experimental and control classes could not be completed until the whole sample was available, some comparisons have to be made between classes which are not matched as precisely as we consider necessary. However, we have investigated the composition of the experimental and control groups in respect to age, sex, social class, and intelligence and found no significant differences between them, and therefore it seems reasonable to publish these preliminary findings on the three major questions listed above.

QUESTION 1: *Is t.o. an important source of difficulty in beginning reading?*

Pitman and others who have devised special writing systems for beginners assume that complexities and inconsistencies in t.o. are an important cause of failure in beginning reading. They propose their more simple and more reliable orthographies to make it easier for children to learn to read. In i.t.a., Pitman appears to have simplified the initial learning task in three ways:

1. *Fewer characters need to be learned.* Lower case characters only are used. Capitalization is achieved in i.t.a. by making a larger lower case shape in place of a quite different shape, as is often the case in t.o.

2. *Fewer whole word representations*

Conventional print	*i.t.a.*
1. dog	dog
2. dog	
3. Dog	
4. Dog	
5. DOG	

FIGURE 5-3

need to be learned. Because only one form of letter is used, each whole word printed in i.t.a. has only one single printed form. (E.g., Figure 5-3.)

3. *Less phonemic print-signals need to be learned.* The number of alternative spell-

Conventional print		*i.t.a.*	
1. u	ruby	ꙍ	rꙍby
2. u.e	rule		rꙍl
3. o	do		dꙍ
4. o.e	move		mꙍv
5. ui	fruit		frꙍt
6. ui.e	bruise		brꙍꟗ
7. ou	group		grꙍp
8. ough	through		þhrꙍ
9. oo	moon		mꙍn
10. ooe	wooed		wꙍd
11. oo.e	loose		lꙍs
12. heu	rheumatism		rꙍmatiꟗm
13. ue	flue		flꙍ
14. eu	maneuver		manꙍver
15. ew	grew		grꙍ
16. oe	canoe		canꙍ
17. wo	two		tꙍ
18. U.E	RULE		rꙍl
19. O.E	MOVE		mꙍv
20. UI.E	BRUISE		brꙍꟗ
21. OUGH	THROUGH		þhrꙍ
22. OOE	WOOED		wꙍd
23. OO.E	LOOSE		lꙍs
24. HEU	RHEUMATISM		rꙍmatiꟗm
25. UE	FLUE		flꙍ
26. EU	MANEUVER		manꙍver
27. EW	GREW		grꙍ
28. OE	CANOE		canꙍ

FIGURE 5-4

TABLE 5-3

Reading Primer Reached at End of Second School Year (July, 1963)
in Control t.o. and Experimental i.t.a. Groups

Reading primer	Control t.o. group (N = 610)		Experimental i.t.a. group (N = 306)	
	Frequency	Frequency, percentage	Frequency	Frequency, percentage
0	5	0.8	2	0.65
Intro.	21	3.45	1	0.3
I	120	19.7	11	3.6
II	109	17.85	30	9.8
III	137	22.45	30	9.8
IV	93	15.25	44	14.4
V	30	4.9	24	7.85
Beyond	95	15.6	164	53.6

Group differences on Kolmogorov Smirnov Test significant at 0.1%
level (D = 13.66). All pupils commenced school in September, 1961.
Control Median: Book III.
Experimental Median: Beyond Book V.

ings for English phonemes is greatly reduced in i.t.a. For example, the eighteen lower case, plus twelve upper case t.o. print-signals for the phoneme *oo* in zoo, too, woo, shoe, flew, do, through, etc. is cut to one only in i.t.a. (See Figure 5-4.)

In these three ways, Pitman has attempted to reduce the amount that the pupil needs to learn before starting off to read books. Therefore our first hypothesis for testing is that *this reduction will lead to significantly more rapid progress through a series of basal readers.*

Careful records are kept of the dates when pupils successfully complete each of the basal readers. Table 5-3 shows the results of an analysis of these records from the experimental and control classes which began instruction in September, 1961. It was made at the end of the second year (July, 1963) when the pupils were between 6 and 7¼ years old.

These results show clearly that experimental i.t.a. pupils are very significantly in advance of children using the t.o. readers. If these results are confirmed by analyses of the records of the remainder of the sample,

our first hypothesis will have been strongly supported by the evidence. Since children progress much more rapidly through the series printed in the simplified writing system of i.t.a., we may then conclude that t.o. is such an important source of difficulty that it seriously retards children's progress through the basal readers.

Pitman also seems to have made i.t.a. a more systematic print code for English phonemes than t.o. Recent research by Durrell[5] in the United States and Elkonin[6] in Russia indicates that prereading training in the development of the abstract concept of the phoneme produces very significant improvements in beginning reading, and that we should not lose sight of the fact that both English and Russian are written in alphabetic codes.

Pitman's i.t.a. appears to be more con-

[5] D. D. Durrell and H. A. Murphy, "The Auditory Discrimination Factor in Reading Readiness and Reading Disability," *Education*, 73, 1953, pp. 556–561.

[6] D. B. Elkonin, "The Psychology of Mastering the Elements of Reading," *Educational Psychology in the U.S.S.R.* Eds., B. Simon and J. Simon. London: Routledge and Kegan Paul, 1963.

sistent or, at least, less complex than t.o. in three respects:

1. *Less ambiguity of spelling is permitted.* Pitman's i.t.a. provides a more[7] consistent set of clues for decoding English words than does t.o. For example, in i.t.a. children are not faced with the ambiguity produced by the erratic use of the letter *o* in words such as those shown in Figure 5-5. The different phonemes in these words are indicated by different print-signals. (It is important to note that Pitman does not claim that i.t.a. is a phonetic alphabet. His invention is an *initial teaching* alphabet for *reading.* He claims only that it is *less* ambiguous than t.o. in the way that it signals English in the reading situation.)

Conventional print	*i.t.a.*
do	dꙍ
go	gœ
women	wimen
gone	gon
one	wun

FIGURE 5-5

2. *Ambiguity of direction of reading is removed.* In i.t.a. the directional rule, i.e., left to right, is maintained consistently. For example, in each of the words shown in Figure 5-6 the three phonemes are signaled in consecutive order from left to right in i.t.a. so that the ambiguity of direction in the t.o. code produced by spelling patterns in which the second phoneme in the word

[7]This summary of Pitman's views may be somewhat oversimplified. Sir James comments in a personal communication that his claim is that i.t.a. "furnishes sufficiently indicative signals for English in the reading situation. It leaves it to the reader to supply from his knowledge of the spoken language and its meaning the many variations in the pronunciations of colloquial speech. As for instance that of the word *to* in the sentence '*to* make sure, he asked the boy *to* close the door *to*,' that of the syllable *ar* in *polarity* and *polar*, and that of the two pronunciations of the word *either.*"

is indicated by the second and fourth letters is removed.

Conventional print	*i.t.a.*
cape	cæp
dive	diev
home	hœm
tune	tuen

FIGURE 5-6

3. *The complexity of the print-code for phonemes is reduced.* In i.t.a. beginners do not have to learn that the *c* in *cat* and the *h* in *hat* represent quite a different phoneme at the beginning of *chat*. In i.t.a. that different phoneme is provided with its own different letter. Other phonemes which have no individual print-signal of their own in t.o. are generally represented by their own individual letters in i.t.a. They may be learned as individual print-signals in their own right representing their own particular phonemes. (For further examples, see Figure 5-7.)

Conventional print	*i.t.a.*
cat	cat
hat	hat
chat	¢hat
which	whi¢h
thigh	þhie
thy	ðhie

FIGURE 5-7

In these three ways, i.t.a. seems to be a more systematic code for English than t.o. and therefore a second hypothesis which we are testing is that *pupils learning to read with i.t.a. will achieve significantly higher scores on those types of reading tests in which the lower-order decoding skills have a prominent role in solution* (e.g., where contextual clues are not available).

The Schonell[8] Graded Word Reading

[8]F. Schonell, *Psychology and Teaching of Reading.* Edinburgh: Oliver and Boyd, 1949.

TABLE 5-4

Results of Schonell Graded Word Reading Test in Control t.o. and
Experimental i.t.a. Groups Halfway Through Second School Year
(February, 1963)

Score on Schonell Graded Word Reading Test	Control t.o. group (N = 623)		Experimental i.t.a. group (N = 345)	
	Frequency	Frequency, percentage	Frequency	Frequency, percentage
0–9	351	56.35	74	21.75
10–19	169	27.15	36	10.4
20–29	67	10.75	43	12.45
30–39	21	3.35	43	12.45
40–49	9	1.45	35	10.15
50–59	3	0.45	28	8.1
60–69	2	0.3	38	11.00
70–79	1	0.15	23	6.65
80–89			10	2.65
90–100			15	4.35

Group differences on Kolmogorov Smirnov Test significant at 0.1% level (D = 13.09). All pupils commenced school in September, 1961.
Control t.o. group mean, 10.9; standard deviation, 10.6.
Experimental i.t.a. group mean, 37.1; standard deviation, 27.

Test appears to be fairly well suited for a test of this hypothesis. The child is credited with one point in score for each word read and pronounced correctly. The norm for age 5 is a score of 0. Beyond that the norms increase by 10 for each year of age. Schonell did not design the test specifically to measure what we have termed decoding ability, but since there are no contextual clues in such a word list it appears to place a premium on decoding ability in *very young* children who are unlikely to have learned many difficult whole-word print configurations.

To test this hypothesis children in i.t.a. classes have been tested on an i.t.a. version of the Schonell test and their attainments compared with those of pupils in the t.o. classes tested in t.o. All conditions besides the orthography have been held constant (e.g., words, size of print, testing environment, etc.).

The results of administering the Schonell test to the September, 1961, entrants after they had been in school less than 1½ years are shown in Table 5-4. These children were then between 5½ and 6¾ years of age.

The superiority of the scores of the i.t.a. pupils is very significant. If the results of subsequent tests and retests of the remainder of the sample confirm these then our second hypothesis will be strongly supported. We may then conclude that the greater consistency of i.t.a. appears to produce superior attainments in decoding print into speech, and that therefore t.o. seriously frustrates children's attempts to translate print-signals into their own English language.

QUESTION 2: *Can pupils transfer their training in reading i.t.a. to reading t.o.?*

If pupils who have learned to read in a simplified system cannot transfer readily to the traditional system, then most of the value of the transitional system is lost, for it is impractical to advocate reforming traditional orthography now.

Pitman lays special stress on the care he has taken to design i.t.a. for easy transfer to t.o. The degree of compatability between i.t.a. and t.o. may be judged from Figure 5-8. Pitman claimed that transfer from i.t.a. to t.o. would be easy, because he had designed his new characters and devised rules of spelling in i.t.a. which preserve in most words the main cues for fluent reading in t.o. In the minority of cases where the i.t.a. print-configuration is quite different from its t.o. counterpart, he believes that children will guess the word correctly from contextual clues.

Another hypothesis to be tested, therefore, is that *in i.t.a. classes reading achievements in t.o. will not be significantly inferior to achievements in i.t.a. once an appropriate level of skill has been attained by pupils learning to read with i.t.a.*

To test this hypothesis a sub-sample of seven carefully matched schools was selected from those which joined the experiment in September, 1961. Their September,

1961, entrants were tested twice with the Neale[9] Analysis of Reading Ability, a comprehensive test consisting of six passages of English narrative prose which the child reads aloud in an individual testing situation.

Tables 5-5, 5-6, and 5-7 also contain the data relevant to this hypothesis. With regard to speed of reading, the hypothesis is not supported, for although the i.t.a. group appears to read t.o. more rapidly than the t.o. group, the difference is not significant at the 5 per cent level of confidence. But the superiority of the i.t.a. group in accuracy and comprehension in reading t.o. is highly significant. If these results are confirmed when the sample is extended, then our hypothesis will be strongly supported with respect to accuracy and comprehension and we may conclude that children who use i.t.a. for beginning reading not only can transfer their training to t.o., but, $1\frac{1}{2}$ years after commencing instruction in i.t.a., they can read t.o. with much greater accuracy and comprehension than children who have been attempting to learn t.o. from the very beginning.

paul and sally at the see

heer wee ar at the see,"
sed paul's muther.
sally and paul ran
doun tω the see.
paul ran very fast
intω the see
and sally ran in after him.
"dω not gœ sœ fast,"
ʃhee sed.
"ie cannot gœ
as fast as yω."

FIGURE 5-8. *Page 40 from "get up zip," one of the Downing readers. (The original is in four colors.)*

CONCLUSIONS AND DISCUSSIONS

Only very tentative conclusions can be drawn at this stage in our research because, as we have already pointed out, the experiments have still to be completed and the data available for this interim report are, therefore, inevitably limited in some respects.

The evidence even with these limitations does appear to indicate rather strongly that t.o. is an important source of difficulty in beginning reading. Transfer from the simplified writing system of i.t.a. to t.o. seems possible and it appears likely that ultimate standards of reading in t.o. may be improved by this two-stage process. However, the

[9] M. D. Neale, *Neale Analysis of Reading Ability.* London: Macmillan, 1963.

TABLE 5-5
Transfer of Training: Reading Speed as Measured by Neale Analysis of Reading Ability
(September, 1961, Entrants in Seven Matched Pairs of Schools)

FORM C

Reading speed	Control t.o. group tested February, 1963 In t.o. $(N = 190)$		Experimental i.t.a. group tested February, 1963 In i.t.a. $(N = 146)$	
	Frequency	Frequency, percentage	Frequency	Frequency, percentage
0	67	35.25	10	6.85
1–10	8	4.2	12	8.2
11–20	61	32.1	39	26.7
21–30	36	18.95	35	24.0
31–40	10	5.25	22	15.1
41–50	3	1.6	15	10.3
51–60	2	1.05	6	4.1
61–70	1	0.55	1	0.7
71–80			2	1.35
81–90	2	1.05	2	1.35
91–100			2	1.35

FORM A

Reading speed	Control t.o. group tested March, 1963 In t.o. $(N = 190)$		Experimental i.t.a. group tested March, 1963 In t.o. $(N = 146)$	
	Frequency	Frequency, percentage	Frequency	Frequency, percentage
0	67	35.2	17	11.65
1–10	3	1.6	9	6.15
11–20	43	22.65	24	16.45
21–30	35	18.4	20	13.7
31–40	18	9.45	25	17.1
41–50	11	5.8	14	9.6
51–60	6	3.15	14	9.6
61–70	3	1.6	10	6.85
71–80	3	1.6	7	4.8
81–90	1	0.55	4	2.75
91–100			2	1.35

FORM C: Group differences on Kolmogorov Smirnov Test significant at 1% level (D = 20.28).

FORM A: Group differences on Kolmogorov Smirnov Test not significant at 5% level (D = 17.14).

EXPERIMENTAL i.t.a GROUP: Comparison between i.t.a. test (Form C) and t.o. test (Form A), t-test significant at 0.1% (t = 4.9).

	Control t.o. group		Experimental i.t.a. group	
	Mean	Standard deviation	Mean	Standard deviation
Form C	14.5	15.0	27.0	18.9
Form A	18.7	18.9	33.9	24.2

TABLE 5-6

Transfer of Training: Reading Accuracy as Measured by Neale Analysis of Reading Ability
(September, 1961, Entrants in Seven Matched Pairs of Schools)

FORM C

Reading accuracy	Control t.o. group tested February, 1963 In t.o. (N = 190)		Experimental i.t.a. group tested February, 1963 In i.t.a. (N = 146)	
	Frequency	Frequency, percentage	Frequency	Frequency, percentage
0	81	42.65	10	6.85
1–10	71	37.35	24	16.45
11–20	20	10.5	21	14.4
21–30	8	4.2	33	22.6
31–40	4	2.1	24	16.45
41–50	3	1.6	17	11.65
51–60	2	1.05	8	5.45
61–70	1	0.55	6	4.1
71–80			2	1.35
81–90			1	0.7

FORM A

Reading accuracy	Control t.o. group tested March, 1963 In t.o. (N = 190)		Experimental i.t.a. group tested March, 1963 In t.o. (N = 146)	
	Frequency	Frequency, percentage	Frequency	Frequency, percentage
0	74	38.95	21	14.4
1–10	54	28.4	26	17.8
11–20	32	16.85	17	11.65
21–30	18	9.45	39	26.7
31–40	7	3.7	19	13.0
41–50	2	1.05	12	8.2
51–60	3	1.6	9	6.15
61–70			3	2.05

FORM C: Group differences on Kolmogorov Smirnov Test significant
at 0.1% level (D = 21.46).
FORM A: Group differences on Kolmogorov Smirnov Test significant
at 0.1% level (D = 21.46).
EXPERIMENTAL i.t.a. GROUP: Comparison between i.t.a. test (FORM
C) and t.o. test (Form A), sign test significant at 0.1%
level (Z = 5.97).

	Control t.o. group		Experimental i.t.a. group	
	Mean	Standard deviation	Mean	Standard deviation
Form C	7.2	11.3	27.4	18.9
Form A	9.3	11.9	22.7	17.4

TABLE 5-7

Transfer of Training: Reading Comprehension as Measured by Neale Analysis of Reading Ability
(September, 1961, Entrants in Seven Matched Pairs of Schools)

FORM C

Reading compre-hension	Control t.o. group tested February, 1963 In t.o. (N = 190)		Experimental i.t.a. group tested February, 1963 In i.t.a. (N = 146)	
	Frequency	Frequency, percentage	Frequency	Frequency, percentage
0	79	41.55	13	8.9
1– 5	81	42.65	49	33.55
6–10	19	10.0	44	30.15
11–15	7	3.7	27	18.5
16–20	2	1.05	9	6.15
21–25	2	1.05	4	2.75

FORM A

Reading compre-hension	Control t.o. group tested March, 1963 In t.o. (N = 190)		Experimental i.t.a. group tested March, 1963 In t.o. (N = 146)	
	Frequency	Frequency, percentage	Frequency	Frequency, percentage
0	71	37.3	20	13.7
1– 5	80	42.1	37	25.35
6–10	23	12.1	45	30.8
11–15	11	5.8	29	19.85
16–20	3	1.6	9	6.15
21–25	2	1.05	5	3.45
26–30			1	0.7

FORM C: Group differences on Kolmogorov Smirnov Test significant
at 0.1% level (D = 21.46).
FORM A: Group differences on Kolmogorov Smirnov Test significant
at 0.1% level (D = 21.46).
EXPERIMENTAL i t a GROUPS: Comparison between i.t.a. test
(Form C) and t.o. test (Form A), t-test not significant at
5% level (t = 1.08).

	Control t.o. group		Experimental i.t.a. group	
	Mean	Standard deviation	Mean	Standard deviation
Form C	3.0	4.1	7.6	5.6
Form A	3.5	4.4	7.9	6.1

i.t.a. research conducted so far throws up many other questions which require answering, and a great deal more research on these problems needs to be done.

For instance, it is clearly possible to obtain objective evidence as to the effects of i.t.a. on creative writing and spelling, both before and after the transfer to t.o. The teachers' subjective reports indicate that creative writing is improved both in quantity and in quality by i.t.a. Spelling after the transfer is alleged to be, at least, no worse than usual and some claim that it is better. Obviously, it will be important to evaluate these aspects more objectively and this is part of our plan. We are also actively engaged in measuring the more general educational effects of the use of i.t.a. by comparing the development of problem-solving ability in the i.t.a. and t.o. classes. The influence of i.t.a. on children's attitudes towards reading, writing, and learning in general is also clearly of importance and can be investigated easily if more adequate research funds are provided. Subjective reports from teachers suggest that children using i.t.a. are more independent and less anxious, but again more objective evidence should be obtained.

A whole program of research is needed to investigate what teaching materials and methods can be developed to maximize the advantages of i.t.a. during each stage of learning to read and write, and still another program is needed to inquire into the effects of using i.t.a. on other subjects of the school curriculum. Some of our i.t.a. schools in Britain have reported that children have passed through the early stages "too quickly" as far as present curricula are concerned, and that there is now free time to be filled.

These are but a few examples of the outstanding problems to be investigated in the research into the use of i.t.a. for beginning reading. No doubt i.t.a. has other potential uses which should be investigated more extensively. For example, we have conducted pilot experiments which show that i.t.a. may have an important use in recovering children who have failed previously to learn to read with t.o. One of these experiments has been reported in the *Reading Teacher*.[10] Also we are conducting pilot studies of i.t.a.'s use in teaching English as a second language. Quite apart from practical school needs, the i.t.a. research has served to focus attention on theoretical issues on the borderline of linguistics and psychology (e.g., the significance of grapheme-phoneme correspondence in the process of learning to read), and a growth in research in this whole area seems likely in the immediate future. (See, for example, Bloomfield and Barnhart[11] and Fries.[12])

There are three parallel forms (A, B, C) of the test. When Form C was administered to all pupils in the seven matched pairs of classes in February, 1963, the i.t.a. pupils were tested on an i.t.a. version of Form C while the control group had the same test in t.o. In the following month, March, 1963, Form A was used in the test but this time both the experimental i.t.a. group and the t.o. control group were tested in t.o. (The complete results of these two tests on the two groups for the three measures—reading speed, accuracy, and comprehension—are shown in Tables 5–5, 5–6, and 5–7, respectively.)

It should be noted that at the time of the second test (Neale, Form A) in March, 1963, just under one-half of the pupils in the i.t.a. group had been completely taken off i.t.a. books by their teachers. Therefore, some of the i.t.a. pupils could not have achieved "an appropriate level of skill" for transfer in the terms of our third hypothesis.

Nevertheless, the overall comparison between the i.t.a. group's performance in i.t.a. and its performance in t.o., even without a further breakdown of the i.t.a. group in

[10] J. A. Downing, "The Augmented Roman Alphabet for Learning to Read," *The Reading Teacher,* March, 1963, pp. 325–336.

[11] L. Bloomfield and C. L. Barnhart, *Let's Read.* Detroit: Wayne State University Press, 1961.

[12] C. C. Fries, *Linguistics and Reading.* New York: Holt, Rinehart and Winston, 1962.

terms of readiness for transfer, supports this hypothesis. The pupils in the i.t.a. experimental classes read t.o. faster than they had read i.t.a. a month previously. They were less accurate at reading t.o. than they had been in i.t.a., but they were just about as good at comprehending t.o. prose as they had been in comprehending i.t.a. prose a month earlier. (The improvement in speed is probably due to practice in this testing situation.)

If the results of similar tests of later entrants into the experimental group and control group samples confirm the above then we may conclude that even at this early stage pupils can effectively transfer their training in i.t.a. reading to reading in t.o., at least as far as comprehension is concerned.

QUESTION 3: *After the whole process of learning with i.t.a. and transferring to t.o., are reading attainments in t.o. superior to what they would have been without the intervention of a special orthography for beginners?*

Most educators would probably agree that the expense of changing beginning reading materials, training teachers, etc., can only be justified if the end result after transfer from the simplified orthography to t.o. is significantly superior attainments in reading t.o. Our final hypothesis for testing is, therefore, that *pupils who have first learned with i.t.a. will at the stage of transfer to t.o. read t.o. with significantly greater speed, accuracy, and comprehension than pupils who have not used i.t.a. in the initial stages.*

Experimental Analysis of a Beginning Reading Skill

HARRY F. SILBERMAN

This report is an historical account of the development of a first-grade phonics program as part of a two-year research project supported by the Office of Education, U.S. Department of Health, Education and Welfare.

An initial version of the program was constructed on the assumption that if the child received frequent exposure to words in a variety of contexts, he would induce letter-sound relationships that would enable him to read novel words which he had not seen before. Minimally contrasting pairs of three letter consonant-vowel-consonant trigrams (rat, fat) were presented in this version of the program.

A tutorial procedure, using one child at a time, was tried to determine what changes

should be made in the program. If in the judgment of the experimenter the child was making a sufficient number of errors to warrant assistance, his progress through the program was halted to ascertain the cause of his difficulty. Then the experimenter attempted to remedy the difficulty by a variety of tutorial techniques. When the child resolved his difficulty the experimenter recorded the program variation that seemed effective. This process of tutorial modification was continued until a sufficient number of tutorial changes were recorded to warrant a major revision of the program. The

Reprinted with the permission of the author and the publisher from the article of the same title, *Programed Instruction*, 1964, 3, No. 7, 4–8.

revised version of the program was then given to other children, and a second revision was made. Subsequent revisions were made in the same manner.

Formal experimental comparisons were made periodically between the latest revision and the original version of the program. If no significant difference was obtained, the revision process was continued. Empirical iterations were continued until differences were not only statistically significant but also judged to be practically significant in favor of the revised program. When comparisons of the original and revised program yielded clear superiority for the revised version, empirical iterations were halted. The data which had been collected during the tutoring sessions and the student responses to the different versions of the program were then analyzed for consistencies and patterns. The analysis resulted in hypotheses concerning modifications which accounted for the improvement in the program.

The objective of the program was to teach the child to sound out and read trigram combinations of the initial consonants *f, r, s, m* and word endings *an, it, at,* and *in* as shown in Table 5–8.

Four words were reserved as a test of the child's ability to transfer the skill acquired in the program to novel trigram combinations. These trigrams were not included within the program. They are indicated by x's along the diagonal of the matrix in Table 5–8.

Early revisions were primarily concerned with sequencing problems. At first, words were grouped with a common ending, e.g., *man, ran.* With this procedure, it was found that children were responding only to the variable initial consonant. When later confronted with an item such as *rin* they would say *ran.* The solution to this problem appeared to be a matter of holding the initial consonants and varying the word endings. The program was accordingly changed so that words were grouped by common initial consonants. This procedure resulted in greatly increased error rates, accompanied by an annoying tendency of the children to avoid looking at the words.

A series of discrimination exercises was then inserted. Trigram pairs were presented which contrasted in order of increasing difficulty: in all three letters (rat, fin), in the first letter (rat, fat), in the last two letters (man, mit), in the last letter (man, mat), and finally in the middle letter (san, sin). This procedure reduced the number of errors in the program somewhat but did not alter criterion performance at all.

The next model featured a cumulative sequencing procedure in which each new word was contrasted with all preceding words before the next word was presented.

TABLE 5-8

Program Objectives

		Trigram endings			
		an	it	at	in
	f	x			
Initial consonants	r		x		
	s			x	
	m				x

In addition, an assortment of other techniques was used further to improve the program prior to a formal experimental comparison with the initial version. Item formats were simplified; pictures and mnemonics were used to evoke vowel sounds, e.g., Indian for *i*, apple for *a*; stories were designed around the trigrams, e.g., "Mr. Ban is a man with a fan"; verbal reminders were issued such as "Remember the letter *a* goes with the /ae/ sound" and so on.

The comparison of the newly revised version and the original version yielded no significant differences on program or transfer words. The assumption that children would quickly induce the phonic generalizations without explicit development of these subskills within the program was abandoned.

The program was redesigned using a synthetic approach which began with a single letter as the unit and proceeded to the whole trigram in a fashion similar to a chaining procedure described by James Evans at Teaching Machines Incorporated; i.e., grapheme ⟨ran⟩ → phoneticization (/r/ /an/) → saying the word (/ran/). Part of the new program taught children to phoneticize trigrams.

Another part was designed to teach children to blend or amalgamate the sound elements. The sound elements produced by the child when "sounding out" the trigrams were supposed to provide the occasion for his saying the whole trigram. Instead, the phoneticizing response and the whole trigram response appeared to be separately and independently associated with the grapheme; the phoneticization did not evoke the whole trigram pronunciation;

i.e., ran ⟨ /r/ /an/ ⟩ rather than ran → /ran/

/r/ /an/ → /ran/. Consequently, children had no success on the transfer words even though they could read the program words.

Various solutions to this problem were tried. Breaking the trigram into three elements rather than two merely intensified the problem. Making the partition between the vowel and final consonant rather than between the initial consonant and the vowel was also ineffective.

Other techniques which were tried included preliminary practice on amalgamating syllables and gradually increasing the time interval between audio segments of phoneticized trigram stimuli. Another technique which had a short run was the use of 5 × 8 cards whose ends were folded over the inscribed grapheme. [   ] → [r   ] → [ran]. Children were to sound out the elements as they unfolded left and right flaps respectively. The rate of this manipulation was increased until the whole word was exposed at once.

After several other methods were tried, a simple combination of an echoic and fading procedure was found most effective in teaching children to amalgamate the sound elements. For example, at first /m/ /an/ /man/ was echoed rhythmically by the child. Later he responded to /m/ /am/ with /m/ /an/ /man/. It was found particularly important here not to allow the child to continue with the program until this segment had been completely mastered. When children faltered on this segment, they were branched back and given extended practice until their pronunciation was brought under control of their own phoneticization.

At this point, children taking the program were still unable to cope with the transfer words. Special practice in making the transfer to novel trigram combinations within the program had to be given before they were able to decode the novel combinations on the criterion test. This practice was accomplished by omitting the feedback stimulus following four selected words within the program. If the child was unable to sound out and read these words, he was branched to familiar review words that contained the elements of the word giving him trouble. If he still did not read the novel word, he was branched to other familiar words that rhymed with that word. Then he was led through the sounding out procedure step-by-step once again for another chance at it before he was given the correct pronunciation. This procedure was repeated for each of the four words.

Other changes were made to improve the program further before making another formal comparison with the original version. These consisted primarily of removing those segments of the program that required irrelevant responses which were more of a distraction than a help to the child. It was interesting to observe how an absolutely essential ingredient in a previous version became irrelevant in the current one.

In the course of developing the final program, it was observed that taped versions did not do as well as the identical versions presented orally by an experimenter. One hypothesis for explaining this phenomenon is that the experimenter modifies the pacing and the prosodic features of his language in response to subtle cues provided by the learner. In other words, the experimenter presenting the program is simultaneously making frequent diagnostic assessments of the student's behavior. For example, if the student is smiling and giving quick loud responses, the pace is increased; if he is frowning and hesitant, even though answering correctly, the pace is reduced and discriminative cues are provided to the learner by the experimenter's changing the inflection of his words and giving small unintentional gestural responses. Thus, even if the experimenter uses the same words as have been recorded on tape, a certain responsiveness is lost in the instrumentation of the program with a consequent reduction in performance. An alternative hypothesis attributes this effect primarily to a history of social conditioning that endows a human teacher with certain reinforcing properties not shared

by the equipment. Further research is needed to test such hypotheses.

The final version of the program contains eight segments. The first segment requires the learner to make an auditory discrimination between initial-consonant sounds. In the second and third segments, common words are presented, and children must press a key on which is inscribed the initial consonant or the vowel-consonant ending contained in the word. The fourth and fifth segments contain a series of discrimination items which require students to match a visual element to an auditory sample. The sixth and seventh segments teach pupils to amalgamate the sound elements and have them use skills acquired in earlier parts of the program. The final segment gives them practice in transferring the reading skill to novel words.

The latest version of the program was adopted for use in CLASS for the final comparison with the initial version. A group of thirty pupils from three B-1 class-rooms were assigned to two treatment groups. Groups were equated on reading readiness pretest scores. The initial version of the program was given to one group, the final version to the other. The initial version required eight forty-minute sessions; the final version required an average of eleven forty-minute sessions. The final version used branching and included more items than the initial linear program.

The results of the comparison showed that the final group read significantly more words than the initial group on the criterion test. The greatest difference was found on the transfer words. On the average, the final group read three of the four transfer words while none of the initial group read any transfer words.

The Study of Thought:
From Associations
to Strategies

_____ 6

INTRODUCTION

The central purpose of this anthology is to collect under one cover important theoretical discussions and experimental studies of the relation of language and thought. We do not intend to duplicate the fine collections of readings on the psychology of cognition that have recently appeared (Harper, Anderson, Christensen, and Hunka, 1964; Anderson and Ausubel, 1965). In order to give our subject matter somewhat more rounded treatment it is necessary to devote one chapter to current research and discussions on cognition.

In a recent discussion of theoretical issues surrounding the psychology of cognition two approaches have been distinguished: that of the cognitive theorists and that of the behaviorists (Anderson and Ausubel, 1965). Later we shall consider whether the issues are basic or chiefly the result of personal preferences for models and terminology. In general, the cognitive theorists assert that (in their language) thought is the product of inner organization and restructuring. Their attention focuses on the present inner mental states of the individual. These states are variously described as cognitive structures (Ausubel, 1965), images [Miller, Pribam, and Galanter, Chapter 6], and strategies of thinking [Bruner, Chapter 6], and cognitive styles (Kagan et al., 1964). For the cognitive theorists, thought is linked more closely to perception than to learning, although they acknowledge the necessity of learning in the development of thought. Terms like "subsumption" (Ausubel, 1965), "schemata" (Bartlett, 1950), "strategy" [Bruner, Chapter 6], and "Plans" [Miller, Galanter, and Pribam, Chapter 6] all suggest an important characteristic of cognitive theory: thought is described in terms of internal *hierarchies*. There is a superordinate and subordinate organization of knowledge and behavior. This hierarchical conception of thought has enabled the cognitive theorists to accept Chomsky's theory of transformational grammar and the complex organization of thought that his theory implies.

The exploration of the implications of cognitive theory for teaching (Bruner, 1961a, 1961b), the advent of computers capable of simulating and even surpassing the operations and products of human intelligence, and the development of information theory as a means of explaining the processing and storage of information have given the cognitive theorists many new research problems and techniques and considerable popularity. Soviet psychology has remained loyal to the Pavlovian tradition and continues to view thought as a "second signal system" (conditioned reflexes are the first signal system) (Berlyne, 1965, page 3). Most cognitive theorists are found in the English-speaking and French-speaking countries. In the French-speaking countries the theory and methodology of Piaget have largely determined the research problems. Piaget has been embarked on a study of perceptual and cognitive development from infancy to adulthood in the hope of discovering the processes of knowledge gathering—what Piaget calls "genetic epistomology" (Flavell, 1963). [See Berlyne, Chapter 7; Piaget, Chapter 7.]

The behaviorist and the neo-behaviorist have been unwilling to sacrifice either theory or methodology, which they use to correlate antecedent stimulus events and subsequent response events for what may be the fruitless pursuit of such fictional notions as, "images," "strategies," "styles," and "structures." In the view of the behaviorist, thought is largely the product of learning. The study of thought is most profitably pursued by systematically manipulating the environmental conditions that control learning. Whereas the cognitive theorist studies mainly the individual's present, inner states, the behaviorist studies his past conditions of learning.

The research of modern behaviorists is no longer tied to the single stimulus-response association, as we have seen in the work of Jensen [Chapter 3] and Osgood [Chapter 4], and as we will see in the work of Maltzman [Chapter 6], Staats [Chapter 9], and Kendler [Chapter 9]. The neo-behaviorist postulates internal stimuli and internal responses. He does not believe that there is a one-to-one relation between stimulus and response corporealized in the reflex arc, or bond. Basically the notion of an S-R association is statistical (Berlyne, 1965, page 10). As such it merely predicts that a certain type of behavior is more likely to occur in the presence of a certain type of stimulus situation than in the presence of some randomly selected stimulus situation. Current critiques of stimulus-response theory ignore these later reformulations.

With the passing of the reflex arc there has appeared the mediating process. We have already referred to Osgood's mediating stimuli and responses. The behaviorists defend on two grounds the introduction of mediating processes into their theoretical speculation and experimentation. 1. These processes refer essentially to overt behavior. Their postulation enables experimentors to preserve the gains of stimulus-response psychology and at the same time undertake the study of complex human function. 2. The postulation of these processes is in the best tradition of the physical sciences, which utilize similar constructs in seeking explanations for physical events. Hypothetical constructs must rise or fall with the evidence. Their theoretical, methodological, and empirical fruitfulness must determine their future.

Research in linguistics and psycholinguistics has favored a cognitive over a behaviorist language. Even Osgood's recent reformulation of his position indicates a shift in this direction (Osgood, 1963). The current status of the study of the relation of language and thought may only reflect the trend of the last ten years in American psychology, which favors the study of complex intellectual functions over the study of simple functions. Berlyne asserts that "there has been almost exclusive concentration on difficult and creative intellectual exploits to the neglect of more humdrum and prosaic forms of thinking" (Berlyne, 1965, page 4). He suggests that we must understand the kind of thinking a waitress employs in adding up the check or the lawyer uses in deciding which statute to apply in a common law case (examples of reproductive thinking) before we can understand the mental processes of the scientist producing a new invention, a mathematician a new discovery, or the artist a new work of art, (examples of productive thinking). Because the human nervous system is tied through evolution to that of primitive animals, we should expect the existence of continuity, which links the knee jerk to sophisticated intellectual development.

The editor is inclined to agree with Kendler that many of the issues between cognitive and behavioral theorists, especially the mediational behaviorists, reflect "personal preference for models and language systems adopted to represent behavior instead of fundamental theoretical assumptions" (Kendler, 1964, page 229). Kendler suggests that terms like "principles," "plans," and "strategies" can be expressed by means of cues that arise from chains of stimulus-response associations. The knowledge of hierarchies of Gagné may well illustrate how stimulus-response language can describe the range of human learning from simple response learning to problem solving (Gagné, 1962, 1964, 1965). Gagné's description of types of human learning includes both horizontal sequences or response chains and vertical hierarchies of concepts, principles, and rules.

After reviewing our present state of knowledge about thinking, Kendler makes this statement:

It is easy to get depressed about the current status of our knowledge of conceptual behavior. We know so little. We have so much to learn. Yet depression, or even disappointment, is not justified. Different empirical techniques have been developed, knowledge is being gathered, and some integrating ideas, even if they are limited in scope, are being offered. (Kendler, 1964)

The first article, by Carroll, describes the nature of concepts as "classes of mental experience learned by organisms in the course of their life histories." The formation of particular concepts depends on experiences with positive and negative examples of these concepts. These are the *necessary* conditions. The sufficient conditions include set, reinforcement of responses, and sequencing of the positive and negative examples. Concept formation may be preverbal, and it has affective components. [See Ervin-Tripp and Foster, Chapter 7.] A most interesting part of Carroll's discussion is his consideration of the relation between words, meanings, and concepts. He conceives of these as forming three relatively independent series with complex interrelations.

The remaining articles in this chapter, of course, reflect the different theoretical positions we have discussed. In the tradition of Clark Hull and the neo-behaviorists, Maltzman describes thinking as an intervening variable. His basic construct is the habit family hierarchy, which operates as a convergent or divergent mechanism. We are reminded of Kendler's assertion that in the psychology of learning there has been a shift of interest from the development of single S-R associations to the competition between associations (Kendler, 1964, page 232). With the intersection of the convergent and divergent mechanisms there is the compound habit family hierarchy, which may explain human problem solving. To account for the changes that occur in the compound habit family hierarchies, Maltzman utilizes our knowledge of conditioning and mediated generalization. Maltzman's broad conceptualization of thinking is, perhaps, the best behavioristic model we have. The model more fully explains reproductive rather than productive thinking. The behaviorist always has some difficulty in explaining what the individual does when he meets a truly unprecedented situation calling for unique responses. We are left wondering whether there really is anything new under the sun and whether we are ever as naive as we often seem to be.

In the last decade Bruner has achieved considerable prominence among the cognitive theorists. Also his publications on education and teaching have attracted the attention of lay and professional audiences (Bruner, 1961a, 1961b). He has discussed the importance of structure in teaching subject matter, intuitive and analytical thinking strategies, and the necessity of learning through "discovery." Bruner's concern is for productive thinking. In discussing productive thinking and learning by discovery he uses such concepts as "hypothetical modes" and "cumulative constructionism" to describe typical patterns of student thought. He emphasizes the learner's need to be actively involved in what he learns and to organize information into cognitive structures that are meaningful to him. Intellectual capacities are developed and intellectual competence achieved when the student is allowed the freedom of search and discovery (Bruner, 1961a). The selection strategies that he and his associates discuss in their article in this chapter are the intellectual processes through which we acquire concepts or ideas. They are ways of handling and processing information.

Much of the research on thinking, especially as it relates to concept formation, has been tied to information theory and processes (Hovland, 1952; Hunt, 1962). Unfortunately, the definition of information easily shifts in the research literature (Shannon and Weaver, 1949; Miller, 1953; Attneave, 1959; Luce, 1960). Utilizing information theory, there has been growing interest in the study of complex human behavior through simulation by high-speed, digital computers. The computer, we know, has capabilities of information processing that far surpass those of man. Computer research on thinking is illustrated in the study by (1958). Newell, Shaw, and Simon. The attractiveness of this research is the explicitness with which these investigators can describe the processes they study. The question is whether they are studying the operation of the computer rather than human thought and problem solving. Everyone will concede that computers have capabilities lacking in human beings and vice versa. Verbal reports made while the subjects are solving problems may not mirror the subjects' thinking processes (Kendler, 1964). The basic postulates of Newell and his associates seem clear and parsimonious. They assume a number of storage centers ("memories"), primitive processes that use the stored information, and a set of rules for combining these processes into programs of information processing. They believe that their theory of problem solving has more in common with cognitive than with associationist theory. They reject the behaviorist conception of the nervous system as a passive photographic plate or switchboard because this conception overlooks the importance of the system's responding in complex and highly selective ways to simple stimulation. The neurophysiology of the modern behaviorist is more sophisticated than these authors report, especially with Hebb and his theory of reverberating circuits. Stimulus-response psychologists have not given enough attention to selectivity and direction in thinking. This statement does not mean, however, as Berlyne has demonstrated, that a behaviorist approach cannot encompass these variables and a considerable amount of information theory (Berlyne, 1965).

Miller, Galanter, and Pribam assume that behavior is organized in hierarchies. These hierarchies are not the habit family hierarchies of Maltzman and Hull, which refer to the ordering of responses in terms of response strength. Instead, they describe their hierarchies as levels of representations. Moreover, they are concerned not only with the organization of knowledge but with how knowledge becomes action. Tolman was criticized for leaving his rats thinking in the maze. Their bridge between knowledge and action is the "Plan." A Plan is any hierarchical process in the organism that can control the order in which a sequence of operations can be performed. The computer programs of Newell, Shaw, and Simon illustrate such Plans. Image is the name given to organized knowledge or cognitive structure. In foregoing the language of stimulus-response psychology, the authors borrow from a number of sources. They refer to the similarity between William James' concept of "will" and their definition of Plan. They refer to Bartlett's "schemata" (Bartlett, 1950) as ways of organizing our past experiences for recall and use. Finally, they discuss the similarity between Lewin's concept of intention and their own description of thought and action.

REFERENCES

Anderson, R. C., and D. P. Ausubel (Eds.), *Readings in the psychology of cognition.* New York: Holt, Rinehart and Winston, 1965.

Attneave, F. *Applications of information theory to psychology.* New York: Holt, Rinehart and Winston, 1959.

Ausubel, D. P. Introduction. In R. C. Anderson and D. P. Ausubel (Eds.), *Readings in the psychology of cognition.* New York: Holt, Rinehart and Winston, 1965. Pp. 3–11.

Bartlett, F. S. *Remembering: A study in experimental and social psychology.* New York: Cambridge, 1950. Pp. 197–214.

Berlyne, D. E. *Structure and direction in thinking.* New York: Wiley, 1965.

Bruner, J. S. The act of discovery. *Harvard Educ. Rev.,* 1961a, **31,** 21–32.

———. *The process of education.* Cambridge, Mass.: Harvard University Press, 1961b.

———, J. J. Goodnow, and G. A. Austin. *A study of thinking.* New York: Wiley, 1956.

Flavell, J. H. *Developmental psychology of Jean Piaget.* Princeton, N.J.: Van Nostrand, 1963.

Gagné, R. M. The acquisition of knowledge. *Psychol. Rev.,* 1962, **69,** 355–365.

———. Problem solving. In A. W. Melton (Ed.), *Categories of human learning.* New York: Academic Press, 1964. Pp. 294–317.

———. *The conditions of learning.* New York: Holt, Rinehart and Winston, 1965.

Harper, J. C., C. C. Anderson, C. M. Christensen, and S. M. Hunka (Eds.). *The cognitive processes: Readings.* Englewood Cliffs, N.J.: Prentice-Hall, 1964.

Hovland, C. I. A communication analysis of concept learning. *Psychol. Revi.,* 1952, **59,** 461–472.

Hunt, E. B. *Concept learning: An information processing problem.* New York: Wiley, 1962.

Kagan, J., B. Rosman, D. Day, J. Albert, and W. Phillips. Information processing in the child. Significance of analytic and reflective attitudes. *Psychol. Monogr.,* 1964, **78,** 1–37.

Kendler, H. H., The concept of a concept. In A. W. Melton (Ed.), *Categories of human learning.* New York: Academic Press, 1964.

Luce, R. D. *Developments in mathematical psychology.* Glencoe, Ill.: Free Press, 1960.

Miller, G. A., What is information measurement? *Amer. Psychologist,* 1953, **8,** 3–11.

Newell, A., J. C. Shaw, and H. A. Simm. Elements of a theory of human problem solving. *Psychol. Rev.,* 1958, **65,** 151–166.

Osgood, C. E. On understanding and creating sentences. *Amer. Psychol.,* 1963, **18,** 735–751.

Shannon, C. D., and W. Weaver. *Mathematical theory of communication.* Urbana: University of Illinois Press, 1949.

Words, Meanings, and Concepts:
Part I. Their Nature[1]

JOHN B. CARROLL

The teaching of words, and of the meanings and concepts they designate or convey, is one of the principal tasks of teachers at all levels of education. It is a concern of textbook writers and programmers of self-instructional materials as well. Students must be taught the meanings of unfamiliar words and idioms; they must be helped in recognizing unfamiliar ways in which familiar words may be used; and they must be made generally aware of the possibility of ambiguity in meaning and the role of context in resolving it. Often the task that presents itself to the teacher is not merely to explain a new word in familiar terms, but to shape an entirely new concept in the mind of the student.

Whether the teaching of words, meanings, and concepts is done by the teacher, the textbook writer, or the programmer, it is generally done in an intuitive, unanalytic way. The purpose of this article is to sketch, at least in a first approximation, a more analytical approach to this task. One would have thought that volumes would have been written on the subject, but apart from such brief treatments as those of Brownell and Hendrickson[2], Serra[3], and Levit[4], and Vinacke[5], for example, one searches the literature in vain for any comprehensive treatment of concept teaching. One is reassured that there are gaps to be filled.

There is, in the first place, an unfortunate hiatus between the word "meaning" and the very word "concept" itself. *Meaning* and *concept* have usually been treated as quite separate things by different disciplines. *Meaning*, for example, has been considered the province of a somewhat nebulous and insecure branch of linguistics called *semantics*.[6] *Concept* is almost any-

---

[1] Part II appears in Chapter 10.

[2] William A. Brownell and Gordon Hendrickson, "How Children Learn Information, Concepts, and Generalizations" *Forty-Ninth Yearbook, National Society for the Study of Education, Part I*, ed. N. B. Henry (Chicago: University of Chicago Press, 1950), 92–128.

[3] Mary C. Serra, "How to Develop Concepts and Their Verbal Representations," *Elem. Sch. J.*, LIII (1953), 275–285.

[4] Martin Levit, "On the Psychology and Philosophy of Concept Formation," *Educ. Theory*, III (1953), 193–207.

[5] W. Edgar Vinacke, "Concept Formation in Children of School Ages," *Education*, LXXIV (1954), 527–534.

[6] Even if a technical science of "semantics" is a comparatively modern invention,—dating, say, from Bréal's article on the subject published in a classical journal in 1883,—the field might be said to have been thoroughly discussed. The classic work of Ogden and Richards (C. K. Ogden and I. A. Richards, *The Meaning of Meaning* (3rd ed.; New York: Harcourt, Brace, 1930).), the somewhat faddish writings stemming from Korzybski's doctrines of "general semantics" (A. Korzybski, *Science and Sanity; an Introduction to Non-Aristotelian Systems and General Semantics* (8th ed.; Lakeville, Conn.: 1948).), and the recent work in psychology of Osgood *et al.* (Charles E. Osgood, George J. Suci, and Percy Tannenbaum, *The Measurement of Meaning* (Urbana, Illinois: Univ.

Reprinted with the permission of the author and publisher from the article of the same title, *Harvard Educational Review*, 1964, **34**, 178–190.

body's oyster: it has continually been the concern of the philosopher, but has received generous attention from psychology. While the meanings of these two terms can be usefully distinguished in many contexts, it is also the case that a framework can be made for considering their intimate interconnections.

Second, there is a gap between the findings of psychologists on the conditions under which very simple "concepts" are learned in the psychological laboratory and the experiences of teachers in teaching the "for real" concepts that are contained in the curricula of the schools. It is not self-evident that there is any continuity at all between learning "DAX" as the name of a certain geometrical shape of a certain color and learning the meaning of the word "longitude." Even if such a continuity exists, it is not clear how the relative difficulty or complexity of concepts can be assessed.

Third, a problem related to the second arises when we ask whether there is any continuity, with respect to psychological "processes," between the inductive, nonverbal type of learning studied in the psychological laboratory under the guise of "concept learning" and the usually more deductive, verbal-explanatory type of teaching used in the classroom and in typical text materials. Take, for example, the kind of concept learning that has been explored so fruitfully by Bruner and his associates.[7] The experimental setting they employed is essentially a game between the experimenter and the subject: the experimenter says he is thinking of a concept— and perhaps he shows an example of his "concept," whereupon the subject's task is to make guesses about other possible instances of the concept in such a way that he will eventually be able to recognize the concept as defined by the experimenter. But in every case, one feels that the experimenter could have "taught" the subject the con-

---

of Illinois Press, 1957).), Brown (Roger Brown, *Words and Things* (Glencoe, Illinois: The Free Press, 1958).), and Skinner (B. F. Skinner, *Verbal Behavior* (New York: Appleton-Century-Crofts, 1957).) might be said to have disposed of most of the general problems of a science of meaning. On the other hand, Stephen Ullmann's recent book (Stephen Ullmann, *Semantics, an Introduction to the Science of Meaning* (Oxford: Basil Blackwell, 1962).) claims only to be in the nature of a "progress report," pointing to the "revolution" that has taken place in modern linguistics and the "advances in philosophy, psychology, anthropology, communication engineering and other spheres" that have had "important repercussions in the study of meaning."

There has been a rash of papers on the implications of linguistics for the teaching of English, the teaching of reading, the teaching of foreign languages, and so on. In fact, the idea that linguistics has much to contribute to educational problems in the "language arts" has become almost embarrassingly fashionable. One's embarrassment comes from the fact that despite certain very definite and positive contributions that linguistics can make to these endeavors, these contributions are of relatively small extent. Once we accept such fundamental tenets of linguistics as the primacy of speech over writing, the structure of the language code as a patterning of distinctive communicative elements, and the arbitrariness of standards of usage, and work out their implications in detail, we find we are still faced with enormous problems of methodology in the teaching of such subjects as English, reading, and foreign languages. The position is particularly difficult in connection with the study of meaning, because most branches of linguistics have paid little attention to this study; some linguists have seemed to go out of their way to exclude the study of meaning from their concerns as linguists. Although there are recent attempts (Paul Ziff, *Semantic Analysis* ([Ithaca, N.Y.: Cornell Univ. Press, 1960]) and Jerrold J. Katz and Jerry A. Fodor, "The Structure of a Semantic Theory," *Language*, XXXIX [1963], 170–210.) to systematize semantic studies, these efforts may be less than completely successful if they fail to take account of the fundamentally psychological problem of how individuals attain concepts and how these individually-attained concepts are related to word meanings. The treatment of this problem offered in the present paper is exceedingly sketchy and must be regarded as only a first approximation.

[7] Jerome S. Bruner, Jacqueline J. Goodnow, and George A. Austin, *A Study of Thinking* (New York: Wiley, 1956).

cept by a very simple verbal communication like "three circles" (for a "conjunctive" concept in which two attributes must occur together) or "any card that has either redness or two borders" (for a "disjunctive" concept) or "any card with more figures than borders" (for a "relational" concept). Teaching a concept in school is usually not all that simple.

In an effort to fill these gaps, we will sketch out a framework for conceptualizing problems of Meaning and Concept. For reasons that will eventually become clear, we must start with the notion of Concept.

THE NATURE OF CONCEPTS

In a totally inorganic world there could be no concepts, but with the existence of organisms capable of complex perceptual responses, concepts become possible. In brief, concepts are properties of organismic experience—more particularly, they are the abstracted and often cognitively structured classes of "mental" experience learned by organisms in the course of their life histories. There is evidence that animals other than human beings behave with regard to concepts in this sense, but we shall confine our attention to human organisms. Because of the continuity of the physical, biological, and social environment in which human beings live, their concepts will show a high degree of similarity; and through language learning, many concepts (classes of experience) will acquire names, that is, words or phrases in a particular language, partly because some classes of experience are so salient and obvious that nearly every person acquires them for himself, and partly because language makes possible the diffusion and sharing of concepts as classes of experience. We use the term "experience" in an extremely broad sense defining it as any internal or perceptual response to stimulation. We can "have experience of" some aspect of the physical, biological, or social environment by either direct or indirect

means; we can experience heat, or light, or odor directly, while our experiences of giraffes or atoms, say, may be characterized as being indirect, coming only through verbal descriptions or other patterns of stimuli (pointer readings, etc.) that evoke these concepts.

One necessary condition for the formation of a concept is that the individual must have a series of experiences that are in one or more respects similar; the constellation of "respects" in which they are similar constitutes the "concept" that underlies them. Experiences that embody this concept are "positive instances" of it; experiences that do not embody it may be called "negative instances." A further necessary condition for the formation of a concept is that the series of experiences embodying the concept must be preceded, interspersed, or followed by other experiences that constitute negative instances of the concept. As the complexity of the concepts increases (i.e., as there is an increase in the number of interrelations of the respects in which experiences must be similar in order to be positive instances), there is a greater necessity for an appropriate sequencing of positive and negative instances in order to insure adequate learning of the concept.[8] At least this is true when the concept has to be formed from *non-verbal* experiences only, i.e., from actual exemplars or referents of the concept as contrasted with non-exemplars. But concept learning from verbal explanation, as will be noted below, must, as it were, put the learner through a series of vicarious experiences of positive and negative instances. For example, in telling a child what a lion is, one must indicate the range of positive and negative instances—the range of variations that could be found in real lions and the critical respects in which other animals—tigers, leopards, etc. —differ from lions.

We have been describing what is often called the process of abstraction. We have

[8] Earl B. Hunt, *Concept Learning: An Information Processing Problem* (New York: Wiley, 1962).

given a number of *necessary* conditions for the formation of a concept; exactly what conditions are *sufficient* cannot yet be stated, but in all likelihood this will turn out to be a matter of (a) the number, sequencing, or timing of the instances presented to the individual, (b) the reinforcements given to the individual's responses, and (c) the individual's orientation to the task. The evidence suggests that the learner must be oriented to, and attending to, the relevant stimuli in order to form a concept. The public test of the formation of a concept is the ability to respond correctly and reliably to new positive and negative instances of it; we do not wish to imply, however, that a concept has not been formed until it is put to such a test.

The infant acquires "concepts" of many kinds even before he attains anything like language. One kind of concept that is acquired by an infant quite early is the concept embodied in the experience of a particular object—a favorite toy, for example. As the toy is introduced to the infant, it is experienced in different ways—it is seen at different angles, at different distances, and in different illuminations. It is felt in different positions and with different parts of the body, and experienced with still other sense-modalities—taste, smell. But underlying all these experiences are common elements sufficient for the infant to make an identifying response to the particular toy in question—perhaps to the point that he will accept only the particular specimen that he is familiar with and reject another specimen that is in the least bit different. The acceptance or rejection of a specimen is the outward sign of the attainment of a concept— as constituted by the class of experiences associated with that particular specimen. The experiences themselves are sufficiently similar to be their own evidence that they constitute a class—a perceptual invariant, therefore, together with whatever affective elements that may be present to help reinforce the attainment of the concept (pleasure in the sight, taste, smell, and feel of the toy, for example).

Even the concept contained in a particular object represents a certain degree of generality—generality over the separate presentations of the object. But pre-verbal infants also attain concepts which from the standpoint of adult logic have even higher degrees of generality. A further stage of generality is reached when the infant comes to recognize successive samples of something—e.g., a particular kind of food—as equivalent, even though varying slightly in taste, color, temperature, etc. Because the different samples of food are about equally reinforcing, the infant gradually learns to overcome the initial tendency to reject a sample that is experienced as not quite the same as one previously experienced. That is, what seems to be initially a negative instance turns out to be a positive instance because it provides the same reinforcement as the earlier instance—the reinforcement being in this case a "sign" that the new experience is to be taken in the same class as former ones. An even higher stage of generality is achieved when the child will accept and make a common response to any one of a number of rather different stimuli —for example, any one of a number of different foods. In adult terms, he has attained the concept of "food" in some elementary sense. The explanation of this phenomenon may indeed draw upon the usual primary reinforcement theory (the equivalence of different foods in satisfying a hunger drive) but it also depends upon various secondary reinforcements, as when the parent punishes the child for eating something not considered "food," like ants or mud. This is an elementary case in which culture, as represented by parents, provides signs as to what the positive and negative instances of a concept are.

Direct experience, i.e., the recognition of experiences as identical or similar, allows the infant to attain concepts that in adult language have names such as redness, warmth, softness, heaviness, swiftness, sweetness, loudness, pain, etc. In some cases, the infant's concepts of sensory qualities may be rather undifferentiated. For example, because big things are generally experienced as heavy and strong, and small things are generally experienced as lightweight and weak, the infant's concept of size may not be adequately differentiated from his concepts of weight and strength. Without any social reinforcement to guide him, his concept of "redness" may range over a rather wide range of the color spectrum, and if he happens to have been born into a culture which pays little attention to the difference, say, between what we would call "red" and "orange," his concept of "redness" may remain relatively undifferentiated even after he has learned a language —just as it has been demonstrated that different varieties of blue are not well coded in everyday English.[9]

Furthermore, we can infer from various investigations of Piaget[10] that the child's concepts of size, weight, and other physical attributes of objects do not contain the notion of "conservation" that his later experiences will teach him. For all the infant or young child knows of the physical universe, objects can change in size, weight, etc., in quite arbitrary ways. It is only at a later stage, when the child has had an opportunity to form certain concepts about the nature of the physical universe that his concepts of size, weight, and number can incorporate the notion of constancy or conservation that mature thinking requires. Experience with objects that can expand or contract through stretching or shrinking gives the child a concept of size that can properly explain the fact that a balloon can be blown up to various sizes. Indeed, this explanation may involve the concepts of "expansion" and "contraction." At a still later stage, the child may learn enough about the relation of heat to expansion to explain why it is necessary to have seams in concrete roads, or why one allows for

expansion in the building of large bridges. And it will be relatively unlikely that even as an adult he will learn enough about the concept of size to understand the concept of relativity—that the size of a body is relative to the speed at which it is traveling and the system in which it is measured.

Thus, concepts can in the course of a person's life become more complex, more loaded with significant aspects. Concepts are, after all, essentially idiosyncratic in the sense that they reside in particular individuals with particular histories of experiences that lead them to classify those experiences in particular ways. My concept of "stone" may not be precisely your concept of "stone" because my experiences with stones may have included work with pieces of a peculiar kind of vitreous rock that you have seldom seen. To a large extent, how I sort out my experiences is my own business and may not lead to the same sortings as yours.

Nevertheless, I can specify the way I sort out my experiences by noting the *critical attributes* that differentiate them. I can specify what sensory qualities and attributes are necessary before I will classify an experience as being an experience of what I call a stone. But it is not even necessary for a person to be able to specify such attributes. A child who has learned a certain concept—who has learned to recognize certain experiences as being similar—may not necessarily be able to verbalize what attributes make them similar; he may not even be aware of the fact that he has attained a certain concept, since it may be the case that only his behavior—the fact that he consistently makes a certain response to a certain class of stimuli—indicates that he has formed a concept. Such would be the case, for example, for the classic instance where the child is afraid of the barber because he wields instruments (scissors) that look like those of the doctor whom he has already learned to fear, and because he wears a similar white smock.

Indeed, this last instance exemplifies the fact that concepts may include affective components. Because concepts are embod-

[9] Roger W. Brown and Eric H. Lenneberg, "A Study in Language and Cognition," *J. Abnorm. Soc. Psychol.*, XLIX (1954), 454–462.

[10] John H. Flavell, *The Developmental Psychology of Jean Piaget* (Princeton: Van Nostrand, 1963).

ied in classes of experiences they include all the elements of experiences that may occur in common—perceptual and cognitive elements as well as motivational and emotional elements. My concept of "stone" may reflect, let us say, my positive delight in collecting new varieties of minerals, whereas your concept may reflect the fact that you had unpleasant experiences with stones—having them thrown at you in a riot, or finding lots of them in your garden. Osgood's "semantic differential,"[11] in which one is asked to rate one's concepts on scales such as good-bad, strong-weak, fast-slow, active-passive, light-heavy, pungent-bland, etc., is a way of indexing certain relatively universal cognitive and affective components of individual experiences as classed in concepts; it would perhaps more properly be called an "experiential differential" than a "semantic differential." The fact that fairly consistent results are obtained when concept ratings from different people are compared or averaged implies that people tend to have generally similar kinds of experiences, at least within a given culture.

It has already been suggested earlier that since man lives in an essentially homogeneous physical and biological environment and a partially homogeneous social environment, it is inevitable that a large number of concepts arrived at by individual people should be the same or at least so nearly identical in their essential attributes as to be called the same; these concepts we may call *conceptual invariants*. We can be sure that throughout the world people have much the same concepts of *sun, man, day, animal, flower, walking, falling, softness,* etc. by whatever names they may be called. The fact that they have names is incidental; there are even certain concepts that for one reason or another (a taboo, for example) may remain nameless.

It is probably when we enter into the

realms of science and technology and of social phenomena that the concepts attained by different people will differ most. In science and technology concepts vary chiefly because of differences, over the world, in the levels of scientific and technological knowledge reached; and in the social sphere they will differ chiefly because of the truly qualitative differences in the ways cultures are organized. Nevertheless, within a given community there will be a high degree of commonality in the concepts recognized and attained, in the sense that there will be relatively high agreement among people as to the attributes that are criterial for a given concept. For example, even though types of families vary widely over the world, the concept of *family* within a given culture is reasonably homogeneous. At the same time, differences in intellectual and educational levels will account for differences in the sheer number of concepts attained by individuals within a given culture.

WORDS AND THEIR MEANINGS

In the learning of language, words (and other elements in a linguistic system, including phonemes, morphemes, and syntactical patterns) come to be perceived as distinct entities, and in this sense they form one class of perceptual invariants along with the perceptual invariants that represent common objects, feelings, and events. The child must learn to perceive the various instances of a given sound or word as similar, and eventually to differentiate the several contexts in which a given sound or sound pattern is used. (We know of an instance of a very young child who somehow learned to react violently to the word "no," but she would react just as violently to the word "know," even when it was embedded in a sentence. The process of differentiation took a considerable time.)

Many words or higher units of the linguistic system come to stand for, or name,

[11] Charles E. Osgood, George J. Suci, and Percy H. Tannenbaum, *The Measurement of Meaning* (Urbana, Illinois: Univ. of Illinois Press, 1957).

the concepts that have been learned pre-verbally. Certainly this is true for a long list of words that stand for particular things or classes of things, qualities, and events. For the English language, these categories correspond roughly to proper and common nouns; adjectives; and verbs of action, perception, and feeling. It is perhaps less clear that "function words" like prepositions and conjunctions, or grammatical markers like the past tense sign can represent concepts, but a case can be made for this. For example, prepositions like *in, to, above, below, beside, near* correspond to concepts of relative spatial position in a surprisingly complex and subtle way; and conjunctions like *and, but, however, or* correspond to concepts of logical inclusion and exclusion, similarity and difference of propositions, etc.

The processes by which words come to "stand for" or correspond to concepts can best be described in psychological terms. Without going into the details here, we can only say that in every case there is some sort of reinforcing condition that brands a word as being associated with a given concept. This is true whether the word is learned as what Skinner[12] calls a *mand* (as when a child learns the meaning of *water* as a consequence of having water brought whenever he says "water") or as a *tact* (as where the child is praised or otherwise reinforced for saying "water" when he sees or experiences water), because in either case the word is paired contiguously with the concept *as an experience*. The connection between a word and the concept or experience with which it stands in relation must work in either direction: the word must evoke the concept and the concept must evoke the word.

As a physical symbol, a word is a cultural artifact that takes the same, or nearly the same, form throughout a speech community. It is a standardized product on which the

[12] B. F. Skinner, *Verbal Behavior* (New York: Appleton-Century-Crofts, 1957).

speech community exercises a considerable degree of quality control. Not so with concepts, which as we have seen may vary to some extent with the individual, depending on his experiences of the referents of the words. Society does, however, maintain a degree of "quality control" on the referential meaning of words. The conditions under which the use of words is rewarded or not rewarded—either by successful or unsuccessful communication or by direct social approval or disapproval—can be looked upon as constituting the "rules of usage" of a word, and these rules of usage define the *denotative meaning* of a term. Thus, there is a rule of usage such that the noun *mother* can be used only for a certain kind of kinship relation. One thinks of denotative meaning as something that is socially prescribed. Connotative meaning, however, banks heavily on those aspects of concepts that are widely shared yet non-criterial and perhaps affective (emotional) in content. "Mother" as a noun might evoke various emotional feelings depending upon one's experience with mothers.

Perhaps it is useful to think of words, meanings, and concepts as forming *three* somewhat independent series. The words in a language can be thought of as a series of physical entities—either spoken or written. Next, there exists a set of "meanings" which stand in complex relationships to the set of words. These relationships may be described by the rules of usage that have developed by the processes of socialization and communication. A "meaning" can be thought of as a standard of communicative behavior that is shared by those who speak a language. Finally, there exist "concepts"; the classes of experience formed in individuals either independently of language processes or in close dependence on language processes.

The interrelations found among these three series are complex: almost anyone can give instances where a word may have many "meanings," or in which a given "meaning" corresponds to several different words. The relationships between societally-standardized "meanings" and individually-formed "concepts" are likewise complex, but of a somewhat different nature. It is a question of how well each individual has learned these relationships, and at least in the sphere of language and concepts, education is largely a process whereby the individual learns either to attach societally-standardized words and meanings to the concepts he has already formed, or to form new concepts that properly correspond to societally-standardized words and meanings. A "meaning" of a word is, therefore, a societally-standardized concept, and when we say that a word stands for or names a concept it is understood that we are speaking of concepts that are shared among the members of a speech community.

To the extent that individual concepts differ even though they possess shared elements, misunderstandings can arise. My concept of "several" may correspond to the range "approximately three to five," where yours may correspond to "approximately five to fifteen." Speech communities may differ, too, in the exact ranges in which they standardize meanings. The word *infant* seems to include a higher age range in Great Britain (in the phrase "infants' schools") than it does in the United States, and in legal contexts the word may even refer to anyone who has not attained some legal age like twenty-one years.

The fact that words vary in meaning according to context has given rise to one form of a "context theory of meaning" which seems to allege that the meaning of a word is to be found in its context; this is only true, however, in the sense that the context may provide a *clue* as to the particular meaning (or standardized concept) with which a word is intended to be associated. In fact, the clue usually takes the form of an indication of one or more elements of a concept. For example, in the phrase *A light load* the context suggests (though it does not determine absolutely) that *light* is to be taken as the opposite of heavy because

loads vary more importantly in weight than in their color, whereas the context in *A light complexion* suggests the element of color because complexions can vary in color but only very improbably in weight. It is not surprising that normal language texts have been found to have redundancy, for the elements of concepts suggested by the words in a sentence are often overlapping.

Frequently context is the key to the fact that a word is being used in an archaic or unusual sense. A student who cannot square the usual meaning of *smug* with its use in the following lines from Shakespeare's *Henry IV (Part I)*:

> And here the smug and silver Trent shall run
> In a new channel, fair and evenly

had better resort to a dictionary, where he will find that an earlier meaning of *smug* is *trim, neat.* We cannot dwell here on the interesting ways in which words change in meaning historically, often in response to changes in emphasis given to the various criterial attributes embodied in the concepts corresponding to words. Just as one example, though, consider the historical change of meaning of "meat" from (originally) "any kind of food" to "edible part of animal body, flesh," where the criterial attribute "part of animal body" gradually came to be reinforced alongside the attribute "edible thing."

DEFINITIONS

What, by the way, is the function of a dictionary definition in the light of the system of ideas being presented here? Aside from the few instances where dictionary definitions present pictures or drawings of the items being defined, two main techniques are used in dictionary entries: (1) the use of verbal equivalents, and (2) the use of formal definition by stating *genus et differentia.* The use of verbal equivalents, as where we are told that *smug* can mean "trim, smooth, sleek," has the function of evoking either a (hopefully) previously known concept to which both the defined word and the defining word stand in the same relation, or a series of (hopefully) previously known concepts from whose common elements the reader can derive the concept to which the defined word properly stands in relation. The use of a formal definition, on the other hand, literally "marks off the boundaries of" the concept by first indicating what it has in common with other experiences (*genus*) and then indicating in what respects or attributes (*differentia*) it differs from other experiences. For example, if we are told that *tarn* is a small mountain lake or pool, we know that in many respects it is similar to other lakes or pools—that it is an enclosed, contained body of water, but that it is a special kind of lake of a given size and location. One could, therefore, presumably acquire the concept named *tarn* by learning to make this response only in connection with the criterial attributes defining it. What could be simpler, particularly if one is verbally told what the criterial attributes are? The only kind of intellectual mishap would occur, one would think, when one of the attributes is misunderstood or overlooked. Calling Lake George (in the Adirondacks) a *tarn* would be grossly to neglect or misunderstand the element of small size.

CONCEPT FORMATION RESEARCH

We are now in a position to inquire into the possible relevance of concept formation research to the learning of the meanings and concepts associated with words in a language.

Practically all concept formation research since the days of Hull[13] has been concerned with essentially the following task: the subject is presented with a series of instances which are differentiated in some way; either the task is finding out in what way the several instances match up with one of a small number of names, or (in the simpler case) it is one of discovering why some instances are "positive" (i.e., instances of the "concept" the experimenter has in mind) or "negative" (not instances of the "concept"). Typically the stimulus material consists of simple visual material characterized by a number of clearly salient dimensions—e.g., the color of the figures, the geometrical shape of the figures, the number of figures, the number of borders, the color of the background, etc. Occasionally the critical characteristics of the concept are not clearly in view—as in Hull's experiment where the critical stroke elements of Chinese characters tended to be masked by the rest of the figures, or as in Bouthilet's[14] experiment where the critical feature was the inclusion of letters found in the stimulus word. Sometimes the critical elements are semantic elements of words, as in Freedman and Mednick's experiment[15] in which the task was to find the common semantic element in a series of words such as *gnat, needle, stone,* and *canary.*

Thus, there are two elements to be studied in any concept-formation task: (1) the attributes which are criterial to the concept —their nature and number, the number of values each attribute has and the discriminability of these values, and the salience of the attributes themselves—that is, whether the attributes command attention and are readily perceivable, and (2) the information-handling task required of the subject in view of the order in which positive and negative instances are presented and the amount of information concerning the concept that is furnished by each presentation. Most of what we know about this kind of

[13] C. L. Hull, "Quantitative Aspects of the Evolution of Concepts," *Psychol. Monogr.,* No. 123, (1920).

[14] L. Bouthilet, "The Measurement of Intuitive Thinking" (unpublished Ph.D. Thesis Univ. of Chicago, 1948).

[15] J. L. Freedman and S. A. Mednick, "Ease of Attainment of Concepts as a Function of Response Dominance Variance," *J. Exp. Psychol.,* LV (1958), 463–466.

concept attainment task can be summarized in the following statements:

1. Concept attainment becomes more difficult as the number of relevant attributes increases, the number of values of attributes increases, and the salience of the attributes decreases.

2. Concept attainment become more difficult as the information load that must be handled by the subject in order to solve the concept increases, and as the information is increasingly carried by negative rather than positive instances.

3. Various strategies for handling the information load are possible, and some are in the long run more successful than others.

Thinking: from a Behavioristic Point of View

IRVING MALTZMAN

Hull (1934) has demonstrated that the habit family hierarchy and related principles may generate many hypotheses concerning behavior in relation to objects in space such as might occur in the *Umweg* problem or simple kinds of novel behavior. He has thus shown that the elementary laws of behavior may be applicable to behavior of nonspeaking organisms in so-called reasoning situations.

The purpose of this paper is to demonstrate that the principles formulated by Hull and by Spence may also be applicable to the problem solving of articulate humans. In this respect the present analysis has much in common with the important formulations concerning mediated generalization and problem solving by Cofer and his associates (1942, 1951), Dollard and Miller (1950), Doob (1947), and Osgood (1953). The behavior theory involved may be outlined as follows. Behavior is a function of effective reaction potential $(_S\bar{E}_R)$, which in turn is a multiplicative function of habit strength $(_SH_R)$ and the effective drive state (D) minus the total inhibitory potential (I_E). The latter represents the summation of reactive (I_r) and conditioned $(_SI_R)$ inhibition. It is assumed here that the effective

drive state represents the summation of the anticipatory goal response (*rg-sg*) as well as the primary and secondary drives (Spence, 1951). Furthermore, the multiplicative effect of the anticipatory goal response is restricted to its associated class of instrumental responses.

The principal theoretical conception necessary for our account of problem solving is an extension of Hull's spatial habit family hierarchy (1934). The great complexity of human thinking requires the formulation of what might be called compound temporal habit family hierarchies. In the spatial habit family hierarchy, alternative locomotor responses are elicited as a function, in part, of spatial and temporal distance from a goal. But in adult human problem solving, responses in changing spatial relations to a goal are not usually elicited, although there are problems involving motor skills in which this may be the case. A typical performance change in problem solving is in terms of verbal responses, and the change is solely a temporal one (Cohen, 1953). Nevertheless, it is assumed that the

Reprinted with the permission of the author and the publisher from the article of the same title, *Psychological Review*, 1955, **62**, 275–286.

principles operating in the spatial habit family hierarchy will to a large extent operate in the temporal hierarchy. Recent evidence in support of this assumption has been obtained by Rigby (1954).

The conception of a compound temporal habit family hierarchy is based upon the prior assumption that the elementary laws of behavior derived from conditioning and applicable to trial-and-error and discrimination learning are also applicable, at least in part, to primary problem solving or reasoning, and thinking in general. That different kinds of behavior are observed in conditioning, trial-and-error, discrimination, and problem-solving situations is not to be denied. But these different behaviors need not necessarily involve fundamentally different laws. Different behavior is observed in these situations because the initial conditions are different, and the situations represent varying degrees of complexity in the sense of the number of different variables and principles operating in them. Nevertheless, it is reasonable to assume that at least some of the elementary laws derived from conditioning will lead to the development of the composition laws operating in human problem solving.

As Hull (1952) has demonstrated, these elementary laws can account for many of the phenomena of simple trial-and-error learning. A hierarchy of responses elicitable

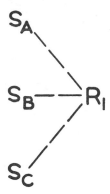

FIGURE **6-2.** *A convergent mechanism. The alternative stimuli have varying tendencies to elicit a given response.*

by a given stimulus, in which the correct response is relatively low in the hierarchy, characterizes this form of behavior, as shown in Figure 6-1. Learning is said to be complete when the order of the response hierarchy has so changed that the correct response is now dominant in the hierarchy. Hull has called this hierarchy of responses, elicitable by a given class of stimuli, the divergent mechanism (1934).

As Spence (1936) and Hull (1952) have demonstrated, the elementary laws of behavior derivable from conditioning situations can also account for many of the phenomena of simple discrimination learning. A hierarchy of stimuli eliciting a given response in which the correct cue is relatively low in the hierarchy characterizes this form of behavior, as shown in Figure 6-2. Such learning is said to be complete when the order of the stimulus hierarchy has so changed that the correct cue is dominant. Hull has called this hierarchy of stimuli eliciting a given response the convergent mechanism (Hull, 1934).

A synthesis of the divergent and convergent mechanisms gives rise to the habit family hierarchy involved in behavior sequences in relation to objects in space (Hull, 1934, 1952). A hierarchy of this sort is shown in Figure 6-3.[1]

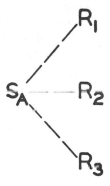

FIGURE **6-1.** *A divergent mechanism. The stimulus has varying tendencies to elicit the alternative responses.*

[1] There have been a few minor deviations from Hull in the manner of diagramming the stimulus-

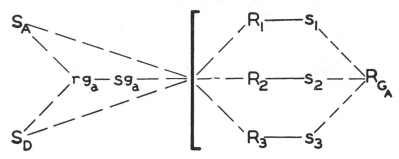

FIGURE 6-3. *A habit family hierarchy produced by a divergent and a convergent mechanism.*

As seen in this figure, S_A (the external stimulus) and S_D (an internal drive stimulus) are capable of eliciting a given habit family hierarchy and equivalent responses leading to a given goal. Common to all responses in the hierarchy is a fractional anticipatory goal response (rg_a-sg_a) which is associated with both the external and internal sources of stimulation. Responses in the hierarchy may be elicited directly by either the external or internal stimuli, or by both. The effects of reinforcement or extinction of individual members of the hierarchy generalize to other members through the mediating mechanism of the anticipatory goal response and its stimulus. It therefore follows that the principles of conditioning and trial-and-error learning should also apply, at least in a general way, to the habit family hierarchy.

For example, if the reaction potential of the correct response leading to a goal is low in the hierarchy, then the generalized conditioned inhibition from the repeated failures of the dominant incorrect responses

may reduce its effective reaction potential below the response threshold. Attainment of the goal would never occur under the conditions present. Or, if the subject has a high degree of an irrelevant need such as anxiety, aside from the possible interfering effects coming from the competing responses aroused by this drive, failure to attain the goal under the above conditions would be even more pronounced. The increased effective drive state multiplying the habit strengths for the dominant incorrect responses and the weak correct responses would increase the absolute difference in reaction potential between the two.[2] Such a condition would produce a greater amount of conditioned inhibition generated through the repeated extinction of incorrect responses. This in turn would increase the probability of failure.

Another way in which changes in the habit family may occur is through the arousal of the fractional anticipatory goal response (rg_a-sg_a). Its arousal may produce an immediate increase in effective reaction

response relationships in order to simplify their presentation. Instead of having a dashed line between the stimulus and each response member of the divergent mechanism, a single dashed line leading to a bracket is used. All bracketed responses are associated with the stimulus. The number and length of the response sequences have also been reduced. A dashed line between a stimulus and a response signifies a learned association, while a solid line between a response and the cue it produces indicates an unlearned association.

[2] For illustrative purposes we may substitute numerical values in the formula for reaction potential ($_sE_R = {_sH} \times D$). The $_sH_R$ value for the dominant incorrect response is 5; the $_sH_R$ value for the weaker correct response is 2; drive has a value of 1. The absolute difference in reaction potential between the correct and incorrect responses is therefore 3. If the drive state is increased to a value of 2, then the absolute difference between responses becomes 6. A greater difference in reaction potential must now be overcome before the correct response can become dominant in the response hierarchy.

potential for the related responses. This effect occurs because it presumably enters into a multiplicative relationship with habit strength in the determination of reaction potential.

A synthesis of habit family hierarchies gives rise to the compound habit family hierarchy involved in human problem solving. A hierarchy of this sort is shown in Figure 6-4. It is formed when the stimulus of a divergent mechanism becomes a mem-

ber of a convergent mechanism as well. By the same learning process, responses of the divergent mechanism in question become responses in convergent mechanisms. In the compound habit family hierarchy not only does S_A have the disposition for arousing its habit family hierarchy, but to varying degree the habit family hierarchies of S_B and S_C as well. There is a hierarchy of habit families elicitable by S_A. An analogous condition holds for the other stimulus com-

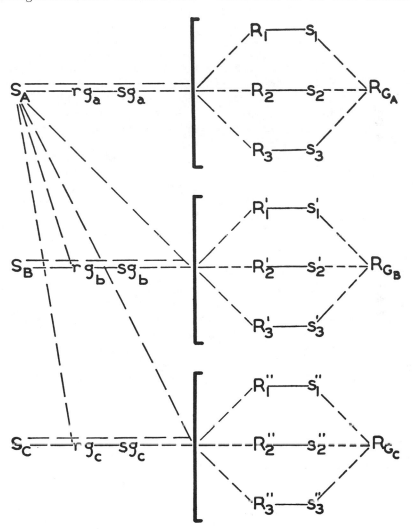

FIGURE 6-4. *A compound habit family hierarchy produced by a combination of habit family hierarchies.*

plexes, S_B and S_C. They have varying amounts of reaction potential for the elicitation of the other habit family hierarchies. These relations as well as the drive stimuli have been omitted in Figure 6-4, in order to avoid confusing details.

When the compound hierarchy is formed, R_1, for example, originally only a member of the divergent mechanism elicitable by S_A, becomes a member of a convergent mechanism. There is now a hierarchy of stimuli, S_A, S_B, S_C with differing amounts of effective reaction potential for its elicitation. A similar state of affairs exists for the other response members of a hierarchy, as well as for the anticipatory goal responses. The stimulus complex S_A has varying amounts of reaction potential for the elicitation of the anticipatory goal response rg_b-sg_b and rg_c-sg_c as well as its original anticipatory response. We now have a hierarchy of habit family hierarchies or a class of classes of stimulus-response relationships.[3] Thinking in general, and problem solving in particular, thus may involve the selection of habit family hierarchies as well as the selection of specific response sequences within a hierarchy.

If the selection of response classes or habit family hierarchies obeys the same principles as the selection of individual responses, then the task of discovering the principles of problem solving may be greatly facilitated. The laws derived from conditioning could then be used to account for changes in the compound hierarchy, without, of course, necessarily excluding other principles. Maltzman and his associ-

[3] This presentation of the compound habit family hierarchy is an oversimplification. For one thing, it does not indicate that individual response members of a habit family may potentially serve as the anticipatory goal response for other habit families. Also, the stimulus aspects of the compound hierarchy, and how they are related to concept formation and perception, are not developed here.

Theories of problem solving by Duncker (7), Duncker and Krechevsky (8) and by Wolters (25), although stemming from different points of view, have a number of characteristics in common with the compound habit family hierarchy.

ates have obtained some experimental evidence in support of this assumption (Maltzman, Fox, and Morrisett, 1953; Maltzman and Morrisett, 1952, 1953).

An additional basis for such an assumption is that the difference between instrumental conditioning and problem solving in this respect may not be as great as it seems. In problem solving the members of a response class are qualitatively different—for example, different verbal responses. Effects upon one member may influence other members through mediated generalization, as previously indicated. In instrumental conditioning, changes in a response class, however, are also involved, because precisely the same response may not occur on successive trials (Hull, 1952). There are differences in intensity and, perhaps, in quality in the successive bar-pressing responses in the Skinner box. Nevertheless the rate of bar pressing increases with successive reinforcements. Learning occurs even though a given response is not precisely repeated, because a class of similar responses is reinforced as a result of simple stimulus and simple response generalization. The limits and the precise manner in which generalization occurs in the two situations are probably different. But because of its important theoretical implications for a theory of problem solving, the similarity between the two situations in this respect should not be discounted.

Changes in the order of dominance in the compound hierarchy may occur as a result of either or both of two effects. First, the effective reaction potential of the incorrect dominant habit families and their individual members may be decreased as the result of extinction. The initial response elicited in a given problem situation would tend to be the dominant response in a dominant habit hierarchy. If this response does not lead to a solution, as by definition it would not, it would receive an increment in inhibitory potential, and responses next in the order of dominance would tend to occur. There would be temporary extinction and spontaneous recovery of these incorrect responses. Eventually the inhibitory potential of these responses would reduce their effective reaction potential below that of the responses contained in the hierarchy next in the order of dominance, and so on. Each response in the hierarchy need not be elicited and extinguished, however, since mediated conditioned inhibition may generalize from one member of a hierarchy to another. The anticipatory goal response of this hierarchy presumably would also acquire inhibitory potential, thereby further reducing the effective reaction potential of the related class of responses.

A second general way in which changes in the order of dominance in a compound hierarchy may occur is by increasing the effective reaction potential of the habit family or families initially low in the hierarchy which contain the correct responses. One way in which this may come about is as a result of previous reinforcement of individual members of the hierarchy in that situation. Through mediated generalization all members of the hierarchy would receive an increment in reaction potential.

Another way in which a habit family may be raised in the compound hierarchy is through the arousal of the anticipatory response of the habit family. Elicitation of the anticipatory goal response produces an immediate increase in effective reaction potential for the related class of responses, for the reason previously mentioned (Maltzman and Eisman, 1954). The antecedent condition for the anticipatory goal response is assumed to be commerce with a goal or a substitute, often symbolic, for the goal. In adult human problem solving the latter is the typical condition. Recent research indicates that verbal instructions given by the experimenter provide an important condition determining the arousal of the anticipatory response (Coffer, 1951; Maltzman and Eisman, 1954). The consequent condition of its arousal is an increased probability of occurrence of responses instrumental in attaining the goal in question.

These different ways in which changes in the compound habit family hierarchy may occur are related to the different kinds of problem solving distinguished by certain

writers. As Hull (1952) has pointed out, any learning situation other than classical conditioning involves problem solving of some sort. The essential characteristics of a problem-solving situation are that an organism is motivated, and that attainment of some goal object satisfying that drive is dependent upon the organism's performing in a given manner. It is characteristic of problem solving that the appropriate response leading to goal attainment does not immediately occur. This is true to some extent in instrumental conditioning, and to a greater extent in trial-and-error learning and in what has traditionally been called problem solving.

Further distinctions between different kinds of problem solving have also been made. Maier (1940, 1945) has repeatedly distinguished between different functions responsible for problem solving, and has classified problem solving as either productive or reproductive. The latter kind of thinking according to Maier involves the application of previously acquired experiences which lead to a correct solution in a new situation. It is problem solving based on the transfer of training, or equivalent stimuli. Productive thinking on the other hand is the consequence of the integration of previously unrelated experiences. The integration is produced by a direction which is an "outside" force not itself a habit.

The present treatment of problem solving, as previously indicated, makes use of the concept of the fractional anticipatory goal response. Certain functional characteristics of the anticipatory goal response appear to make it an analogue of Maier's concept of a new direction. However, among other things, we do not accept Maier's restriction that only productive thinking involves the combination of previously isolated habit segments, to use Hull's terminology. To some extent this is the distinguishing characteristic of all thinking. It is the feature that sets it off from simple retention, and trial-and-error learning. All forms of thinking involve mediated generalization, and hence compounding of previously isolated habit segments.

Nevertheless, there are differences between reproductive and productive thinking. Situations eliciting reproductive thinking often involve the presentation of a succession of problems. The solution of each of these requires the elicitation of different response members of the same habit family hierarchy. This habit family will then become dominant in the compound hierarchy, as the result of reinforcement of its response members and the extinction of responses belonging to different habit families. As previously indicated, the increase in reaction potential of the entire class of responses as the result of reinforcement of individual members would occur as a consequence of mediated generalization. For example, subjects given a series of anagrams whose solutions all belong to the same word category will have a greater frequency of success on subsequent anagrams of the same category than subjects without such prior experience (Rees and Isreal, 1935). However, failure on individual problems may occur because a solution is still dependent upon selection of particular responses within this one habit family.

The occurrence of reproductive thinking in situations where only a single problem is presented is also the consequence of the factors outlined. As a result of past training the dominant habit family in the compound hierarchy contains the correct response. Solution of the given problem depends upon extinction of the initially dominant incorrect responses within this one hierarchy.

In productive thinking, on the other hand, a habit family initially low in the compound hierarchy must become dominant before a correct solution can be attained. This occurs as the result of the extinction of the dominant incorrect response hierarchies. Once the appropriate habit family is dominant a solution will occur, provided that the correct responses within that hierarchy in turn become dominant. The protocols of subjects in Duncker's radiation problem exemplify this mode of thinking (1945).

If a subject incorrectly anticipates the goal or solution to the problem—e.g., "destroy the tumor by means of rays sent over a path as free as possible from healthy tissue"—the proposed solutions are alternative responses within the same dominant habit family, and are all attempts to achieve this end. Repeated failure of these proposals will produce extinction of the anticipatory goal response and its related instrumental responses. As a consequence, another habit family may become dominant. The subject will now anticipate a different kind of solution, such as "reduce the intensity of radiation." As a result, all potential response sequences in the subject's habit family leading to this goal are facilitated. If the correct solution (converging rays from different angles) is not the dominant response in this hierarchy, extinction of incorrect responses must occur before the solution will be attained.

In an actual protocol this orderly progression from one habit family to another is probably an infrequent occurrence. The more typical case would be one in which the reaction potentials of two or more habit families overlap. This would probably be the case after the first few responses from the dominant hierarchy have been extinguished. Thus reproductive and productive thinking differ with respect to the kinds of changes which must occur in the compound hierarchy before a correct solution can be attained. In reproductive thinking the habit families containing the correct responses are dominant at the outset of the problem, as the result of training and generalization from other situations. Or they rapidly become dominant in the compound hierarchy through the reinforcement of individual response members of the habit family. In productive thinking the habit families containing the correct responses are initially low in the compound hierarchy. They become dominant following the extinction of the dominant habit families which lead to incorrect solutions.

Experiments on the effects of direction

in the pendulum problem by Maier (1930) and by Weaver and Madden (1949) are a special case of productive thinking, in that instructions and demonstrations are employed to increase the reaction potential of the anticipatory goal response and individual response members of the habit families leading to a correct solution. The problem is to construct two pendulums which would make chalk marks on two different places on the floor. In Maier's experiment (1930) one group of subjects was given only the statement of the problem. Other groups received the statement of the problem plus various additional instructions or demonstrations. One of these groups was given three different demonstrations of operations on the material which were necessary for solution of the problem. They were shown how to make a plumb line, how to combine poles by using a clamp, and how to wedge poles against a surface. A third group was given these demonstrations and told that they must combine them for a solution of the problem. A fourth group was told that it would be advantageous if the pendulum could hang from the ceiling. They were given a "direction." The fifth group received the demonstrations and the direction. All of the problem solutions except one occurred in this last group.

According to the present formulation the experimenter's statement that it would be advantageous to hang the pendulum from the ceiling tended to elicit an anticipatory response for this goal. A wide variety of equivalent responses instrumental in leading to this goal therefore received an immediate increment in reaction potential. However, for a correct solution to occur, certain specific responses must be elicited. The three demonstrations given the last group increased the tendency of these responses to occur within their respective habit family hierarchies. The increased frequency of solutions under these conditions would follow from the differential increase in reaction potential of the relevant responses and the lawful nature of trial and error

learning. However, since a large number of responses belong to a given hierarchy, and the correct responses may still not be dominant, extensive extinction of incorrect responses must occur. If the correct responses are very low in the dominant hierarchy, a solution may not occur at all because of the extensive generalization of the effects of extinction of the incorrect responses. Another basis for failure in this group is that despite the instructions tending to arouse the appropriate anticipatory goal response, some subjects, presumably as the result of self-instructions, induce different anticipatory goal responses. These are the subjects that adopt an inappropriate approach to the problem, according to Maier.

Groups 2 and 3, which are not given the directional instructions but receive the demonstrations, also have an increase in reaction potential for the three response sequences necessary for a solution. However, the anticipatory goal response and the related class of responses necessary to suspend the pendulum from the ceiling are not increased in strength, which is presumably why these subjects failed to solve the problem. However, contrary to Maier, Weaver and Madden (1949) found no difference between the performance of groups 3 and 5.

Their experiment implies that the appropriate habit family for suspending the pendulums from the ceiling may be elicited by self-instructions, or that the increase in habit strength of the three necessary response sequences by itself may be sufficient for the solution of the problem in some individuals. Why there was this discrepancy between the two studies, however, is not at all apparent.

Throughout the previous discussion the systematic and theoretical status of the concept of thinking has only been implied. We shall now try to make it more explicit. According to the present systematic position, thinking is a defined concept or hypothetical variable. The specific definition that is given to it is the problem of theory, and will be discussed presently. Now we must explore further the consequences of the assumed systematic status of the concept. For one thing, thinking is not a response, verbal or otherwise, just as learning is not a response, and just as electricity is not the temperature of a conductor. All of these are dispositional concepts that are given empirical meaning by statements referring to their antecedent as well as their consequent conditions (Carnap). They are not equivalent to their manifestations or consequent conditions. The insistence that thinking *is* a verbal response, a contraction of certain muscles, or activity in the central nervous system, is thus based on an inappropriate use of language. The verbal response, for example, is just one of several different kinds of responses that may be taken as a criterion or manifestation of thinking. Other response criteria might be gestures, mimicry, motor skills, etc. Questions as to which ones may be taken as criteria, and under which conditions, as well as how they are related to thinking, are to be answered by experiments and theory.

The present systematic position with respect to the relationship between thinking and verbal responses (the most frequently used criterion of thinking) may be made clearer by using the analogy of bar pressing in the Skinner box. The assumptions here are analogous to the assumption that bar pressing is a function of other variables besides learning. If a bar depression does not occur, it need not necessarily imply the absence of learning. The rat's motivation may have been reduced to a minimum; there may be temporary extinction of the response, or inhibition due to the arousal of competing responses by extraneous stimuli, etc. Similarly, the absence of a verbal or some other kind of response does not necessarily mean the absence of thinking. It may be due to the absence of effective reaction potential for that particular response; perhaps the relevant motivation is absent; or other response tendencies inhibit its appearance, etc. On the other hand, the presence of bar pressing does not necessarily imply that learning has occurred. It may be

an operant level, some unconditioned response strength—in Hull's terminology, $_s U_R$. Likewise, verbal responses may occur in the absence of thinking. One aspect of this condition will be discussed shortly.

In the foregoing we have tried to explicate the systematic status of the concept of thinking. We shall now turn to the more specific problem of how it may be treated within the framework of Hull's theory of behavior.

Since it is assumed that thinking as well as learning is a disposition or hypothetical variable, the problem now is to distinguish between the two concepts. If the two are defined in terms of the same operations and consequences, they have the same empirical meaning and the distinction is purely a verbal one. As commonly employed, the term learning refers to the acquistion of a hypothetical state, $_s H_R$, as a result of antecedent conditions such as the number of reinforcements. The consequent conditions are changes in some response criteria such as decreased latency, increased rate of responding, etc.

The term thinking as it is employed here refers to the utilization of new combinations of habit strength by articulate organisms. In other words, we assume that thinking is equivalent to a complex form of effective habit strength which is produced by mediated generalization. The reason for arbitrarily restricting the usage of "thinking" to humans is the belief that extensive mediated generalization is necessary for the recombination of habit strengths to occur, and complex mediated generalization of this sort is made possible primarily by linguistic responses.

We have stated that thinking involves the utilization of learning in new combinations, as distinguished from the acquisition of learning. A further problem is to distinguish between thinking and retention, since the latter also involves the utilization of habit strength.

The distinction is not always easy to make, and at times may be arbitrary. But so is the commonly accepted distinction between learning and retention (McGeoch, 1952). As previously noted, learning refers to the acquisition of a hypothetical state as a function of the number of reinforcements. Retention is a term referring to the persistence and subsequent manifestation of that hypothetical state. In a learning experiment, performance on trials after the first is a function of the persistence of previous learning, or retention, from earlier trials. Only on the first trial is nothing more than the acquisition of habit strength involved. This entire process, however, is called learning even though much of it is actually retention. After the subject has reached some predetermined criterion, he is required to utilize in some manner the habit strengths previously acquired. He is asked to recall the material previously learned, recognize, or relearn it, etc. In every case the responses originally acquired are elicited again to some extent. This implies that the habit strengths utilized in the test of retention are substantially the same as that originally acquired. Retention has as its consequent condition the elicitation of some previously acquired response, presumably as a result of the persistence of previously acquired habit strength. The term thinking has as its consequent condition the elicitation of a response other than the previously acquired response as a result of past learning. Habit strength previously acquired has entered into new compounds, has changed as the result of mediated generalization.

A fundamental problem for a behavioristic psychology of thinking is to determine the laws governing these combinations and recombinations of habit strengths. Hull's equations (1952) for combining habit strengths in generalization and compound stimulus situations are approximations of such composition laws. But they are only first approximations, because the generalization and compounding of habit strengths occurring in thinking are undoubtedly a good deal more complex than those that Hull has treated. A basic problem in this

respect would be the development of the laws of mediated generalization which, theoretically, produce the new compounds of habit strength, and empirically, produce the formation of new stimulus-response classes. It is likely that the close connection between language and thinking (or even their equating) in certain theories results from the fact that language permits the greatest degree of mediated generalization and therefore thinking.

Admittedly the theory of thinking and problem solving outlined here is loosely formulated and incomplete. Nevertheless, it at least has the merit that it relates human problem solving to behavior in simpler situations. It is an attempt to integrate the two, as distinguished from the usual gestalt approach which treats problem solving as divorced from the relatively large number of principles derived from conditioning and trial-and-error learning. Although many of the principles derived from conditioning may not entirely apply to human problem solving, this is certainly an empirical question worth investigating. At the very least, these principles should yield significant hypotheses as to the factors determining problem solving.

SUMMARY

A theory of human problem solving has been outlined, based upon the concept of a compound temporal habit family hierarchy, which is assumed to function, at least in part, according to the principles of conditioning and trial-and-error learning. Some of the characteristics of the compound hierarchy were noted, and its role in different kinds of problem-solving situations was indicated.

The systematic status of thinking from a behavioristic point of view was described as a disposition or hypothetical state of the organism. Within the present theory it is equivalent to a new combination of habit strengths produced, primarily, by mediated generalization.

REFERENCES

Carnap, R. Logical foundations of the unity of science. *Int. Enc. unif. Sci.,* 1938, 1, 42–62.

Cofer, C. N. Verbal behavior in relation to reasoning and values. In H. Guetzkow (Ed.), *Groups, leadership and men.* Pittsburgh: Carnegie, 1951. Pp. 206–217.

——, and J. P. Foley, Jr. Mediated generalization and the interpretation of verbal behavior: I. Prolegomena. *Psychol. Rev.,* 1942, 49, 513–540.

Cohen, J. The concept of goal gradients: A review of its present status. *J. gen. Psychol.,* 1953, 49, 303–308.

Dollard, J., and N. E. Miller. *Personality and psychotherapy.* New York: McGraw-Hill, 1950.

Doob, L. W. The behavior of attitudes. *Psychol. Rev.,* 1947, 54, 135–156.

Duncker, K. On problem solving. *Psychol. Monogr.,* 1945, 58, No. 5 (Whole No. 270).

——, and I. Krechevsky. On solution-achievement. *Psychol. Rev.,* 1939, 46, 176–185.

Hull, C. L. The concept of the habit-family hierarchy and maze learning. *Psychol. Rev.,* 1934, 41, 33–54, 134–152.

——. *A behavior system.* New Haven, Conn.: Yale University Press, 1952.

McGeoch, J. A., and A. L. Irion. *The psychology of human learning.* New York: Longmans, 1952.

Maier, N. R. F. Reasoning in humans: I. On direction. *J. comp. Psychol.,* 1930, 10, 115–143.

——. The behavior mechanisms concerned with problem solving. *Psychol. Rev.,* 1940, 47, 43–58.

——. Reasoning in humans: III. The mecha-nism of equivalent stimuli and of reasoning. *J. exp. Psychol.,* 1945, 35, 349–360.

Maltzman, I., and E. Eisman. Two kinds of set in problem solving. Paper read at American Psychological Association, New York, September, 1954.

——, J. Fox, and L. Morrisett, Jr. Some effects of manifest anxiety on mental set. *J. exp. Psychol.,* 1953, 46, 50–54.

——, and L. Morrisett, Jr. Different strengths of set in the solution of anagrams. *J. exp. Psychol.,* 1952, 44, 242–246.

——, and L. Morrisett, Jr. The effects of single and compound classes of anagrams on set solutions. *J. exp. Psychol.,* 1953, 45, 345–350.

Osgood, C. E. *Method and theory in experimental psychology.* New York: Oxford University Press, 1953.

Rees, H., and H. Isreal. An investigation of the establishment and operation of mental sets. *Psychol. Monogr.,* 1935, 46, No. 6 (Whole No. 210).

Rigby, W. K. Approach and avoidance gradients and conflict behavior in a predominantly temporal situation. *J. comp. physiol. Psychol.,* 1954, 47, 83–89.

Spence, K. W. The nature of discrimination learning in animals. *Psychol. Rev.,* 1936, 43, 427–449.

——. Theoretical interpretations of learning. In C. P. Stone (Ed.), *Comparative psychology.* New York: Prentice-Hall, 1951. Pp. 239–291.

Weaver, H. E., and E. H. Madden. "Direction" in problem solving. *J. Psychol.,* 1949, 27, 331–345.

Wolters, A. W. On conceptual thinking. *Brit. J. Psychol.,* 1933, 24, 133–143.

Selection Strategies in Concept Attainment

JEROME S. BRUNER

JACQUELINE J. GOODNOW

GEORGE A. AUSTIN

Whenever one seeks to "find out something," one is immediately faced with deciding upon the order in which to make one's inquiries. It is commonplace to remark that some orders of inquiry are better than others. We say of a scientist's research that it is a beautiful series of experiments, or of a lawyer that he has mastered the art of asking

Reprinted with the permission of the senior author and the publisher, John Wiley & Sons, Inc., from the authors' *A Study in Thinking;* 1956, pp. 81–90.

questions. It is with the ordering of inquiry, the steps in research or testing, that the present chapter is concerned.

We begin with an example. A neurologist is interested in the localization of pattern vision in monkeys. More specifically, he is interested in six cortical areas and their bearing on pattern vision. He knows that, with all six areas intact, pattern vision is unimpaired. With all six areas destroyed, pattern vision is absent. His technique of research is extirpation. In planning his research, how shall he proceed? Destroy one area at a time? All but one at a time? In what order shall he do his successive experiments?

The prime question is "What is to be gained by choosing one order as compared to another order of testing instances?"

The first thing to be gained is, of course, an opportunity to *obtain information appropriate to the objectives of one's inquiry.* One may wish to choose an instance at any given point in concept attainment that can tell one the most about what the concept might be. One may seek to avoid redundant instances, or may want such an instance for reassurance. It also happens that at different points in the choice sequence negative and positive instances have different informative value. By choosing instances in a certain order, it is possible for a person to increase the chances of encountering a negative or a positive instance when he needs them. This may seem at first to be absurd, for how can a person choose a positive or a negative instance before he knows what the concept really is? Later, we will see that certain strategies guarantee that *within a set of choices* a person can assure such an encounter. To sum up, controlling the sequence of instances allows the person to ensure that the instances before him *contain appropriate information.*

A second benefit inherent in controlling the order of instances tested is to *increase or decrease the cognitive strain involved in assimilating information.* Ideally, instances should be chosen for test in such an order that whatever their potential informational

value and whatever their status, whether positive or negative, their information can be assimilated without undue strain on memory or inference. There are several ways, as we shall see, in which the assimilability of information may be controlled by choosing instances in a certain order. A well-contrived order of choice—a good "selection strategy"—makes it easier to *keep track* of what hypotheses have been found tenable or untenable on the basis of information encountered. We shall have a great deal to say in later sections about this feature of selection strategies.

A third advantage is not at first obvious. By following a certain order of selecting instances for testing one *controls the degree of risk involved.* There are conservative orders and highly speculative ones. One may test instances in such an order as to guarantee that the concept will definitely be attained after a certain number of choices. But one may also choose instances in an order such that there is either the chance of very rapid attainment with good luck, or very slow attainment with bad. "Taking a flier" is within the power of the person who controls the order in which he will select instances. And by the same token, a safe course may be chosen.

In sum, selection strategies bestow three potential benefits upon their users:

a. They increase the likelihood that instances encountered will contain appropriate information.
b. They render less strainful the task of assimilating and keeping track of information.
c. They regulate the amount of risk one will undergo in attaining a correct solution within a limited number of choices.

Before turning to an examination of the conditions that affect the adoption of various selection strategies, we must first examine four ideal selection strategies with respect to their usefulness in achieving the benefits just described.

IDEAL SELECTION STRATEGIES
AND THEIR BENEFITS

We concentrate in this chapter on conjunctive concepts. Let us set before a subject all of the instances representing the various combinations of four attributes, each with three values—specifically, all the instances illustrated in Figure 1°—an array of 81 cards, each varying in shape of figure, number of figures, color of figure, and number of borders. We explain to the subject what is meant by a conjunctive concept—a set of the cards that share a certain set of attribute values, such as "all red cards," or "all cards containing red squares and two borders"—and for practice ask the subjects to show us all the exemplars of one sample concept. The subject is then told that we have a concept in mind and that certain cards before him illustrate it, others do not, and that it is his task to determine what this concept is. We will always begin by showing him a card or instance that is illustrative of the concept, a positive instance. His task is to choose cards for testing, one at a time, and after each choice we will tell him whether the card is positive or negative. He may hazard an hypothesis after any choice of a card, but he may not offer more than one hypothesis after any particular choice. If he does not wish to offer an hypothesis, he need not do so. He is asked to arrive at the concept as efficiently as possible. He may select the cards in any order he chooses. That, in essence, is the experimental procedure.

There are four discernible strategies by which a person may proceed in this task. These we label the *simultaneous-scanning strategy,* the *successive-scanning strategy,* the *conservative-focusing strategy,* and the *focus-gambling strategy.* Let us describe each of these briefly and consider the manner in which each bestows upon its users the three benefits mentioned previously.

° This figure has been omitted—J. P. De C.

Simultaneous Scanning

In the present array . . . composed of instances that may exhibit any of three values of four different attributes, there are 255 possible ways of grouping instances into conjunctive concepts. A first positive card *logically* eliminates 240 of these, and the informational value of any other positive or negative card thereafter presented can similarly be described in terms of the remaining hypotheses that it logically eliminates. Now, simultaneous scanning consists in essence of the person using each instance encountered as an occasion for deducing which hypotheses are tenable and which have been eliminated. This is a highly exacting strategy, for the subject must deal with many independent hypotheses and carry these in memory. Moreover, the deductive process is exacting.

If the subject is able to follow the strategy successfully, his choice of next instances to test will be determined by the objective of eliminating as many hypothetical concepts as possible per instance chosen. Suppose, for example, that a subject in our experiment has narrowed the possible concepts down to three: the concept must either be all *red* cards, all cards with *circles,* or all cards with *red circles.* Prior choices have eliminated all other hypotheses. Since we are dealing with an ideal strategy here, let us also assume an ideal subject: a subject with perfect rationality and perfect discriminative capacities. Such a subject would certainly know how to avoid choosing redundant instances that eliminated no hypotheses. By choosing a card for testing that contained at least one of the two features, circles or red color, he would guarantee that the next instance encountered contained appropriate information. He would have to decide whether to choose an instance containing *one* of the relevant features or *both* of them: the next instance will contain a circle and no other relevant feature, contain red and no other relevant

TABLE 6-1

Properties of instance chosen for testing	If correct concept is		
	Red only	Circle only	Red circle
Red only	Instance positive Eliminates: circle red circle	Instance negative Eliminates: red	Instance negative Eliminates: red
Circle only	Instance negative Eliminates: circle	Instance positive Eliminates: red red circle	Instance negative Eliminates: circle
Red and circle	Instance positive Eliminates: nothing	Instance positive Eliminates: nothing	Instance positive Eliminates: nothing

feature, or it will contain red circles. Consider now the consequences of each of these decisions for each of the three possible concepts [see Table 6-1]. Such an analysis of the nine possible outcomes should suggest to the subject that his next choice should contain only one of the relevant attributes; at the least, such a choice will eliminate one hypothetical concept, at best two of them. To choose a card containing both relevant attribute values means that no information will be obtained regardless of what the correct concept is.

Now, if the subject can figure out the nine possible outcomes (and has enough time to do so), he will be able to make a wise decision about how next to proceed. The decision is important, for it will determine whether he will be able to solve the problem with one more choice; if these were expensive experiments rather than simple tests of the status of instances, the difference might be critical. But it is quite obvious that most human beings cannot or will not go through such an elaborate analysis of the situation in order to determine their best next step. Indeed, if there had been ten hypotheses still remaining in our example, the paper and pencil work involved in assessing next moves would have been prohibitive. So we can sum up by remarking

that while it is possible in principle for the person using simultaneous scanning to plan the best next step, the task of guaranteeing *maximum* informativeness of a next choice is in practice too difficult to accomplish.

With respect to rendering easier the assimilation and retention of information contained in instances encountered, simultaneous scanning has little to recommend it. After each choice the subject must go through the difficult process of deducing which hypothetical concepts have been eliminated and carrying the result of these deductions in memory. There appears to be no means whereby simultaneous scanning can reduce this heavy load on inference and memory.

Nor does simultaneous scanning provide a way of regulating the riskiness of one's next choices—no practical way, at least. We shall leave the matter at that, hoping that it will become much clearer in a later section. The best one can do is to compute the riskiness of a choice by the method just outlined.

Successive Scanning

This strategy consists in testing a single hypothesis at a time. The subject has the hypothesis that *red* is the feature common to all correct cards, and chooses instances containing red in order to test whether they are positive instances. He goes on testing hypotheses until he hits the correct concept. The typical successive scanner then *limits his choices to those instances that provide a direct test of his hypothesis.*

Now it is quite apparent that such a technique for choosing instances cannot assure that the person will encounter instances containing the maximum information possible. That is to say, since instances are chosen only to test one hypothesis at a time, one is likely to choose logically redundant cards some feature of which has been used before to test some previous hypothesis. On this point more will be said later, for it is evident that this is much like discontinuity in learning.

It also follows that the strategy has little worth from the point of view of regulating risk. There is little the user can do either to take bigger gambles or lesser gambles in his choice of instances. His only possible maneuver here is a rather far-fetched one, but one that subjects nonetheless indulge in. This consists really of playing a guessing game with the experimenter in choosing an order of hypotheses to test. For example, subjects will often operate on the assumption that the experimenter is out to "trick" them and that, therefore, the correct concept cannot be a "simple" one, namely, that it will not be a single-attribute concept like "red" or "circles." In consequence, users of successive scanning begin, more frequently than would be expected by chance, by "guessing" that the hypothesis is defined by more than one attribute and choose cards to test such multiattribute hypotheses.

What then is served by the use of successive scanning? The gain is nearly all in the relief of cognitive strain. Limited inference is required and the principal strain on memory is to keep track of what hypotheses have already been tested and found wanting.

A closer examination of the manner in which strain on inference is reduced brings

us directly to a most characteristic feature of cognitive activity which we shall encounter on subsequent occasions in analyzing the behavior of subjects in probability situations. It is this. Human subjects—and the same may be true of other species as well— prefer a direct test of any hypothesis they may be working on. To recall the meaning of direct test, a subject is faced with deciding whether a white door or a black door is the correct entrance to a reward chamber and adopts the hypothesis that the white door is correct. There are two ways of testing this hypothesis. The *direct way* is to try the white door. The *indirect way* is to try the black door. In a direct test, as we have noted, the knowledge obtained needs no further transformation for testing the hypothesis. White is either correct or incorrect. The indirect test requires a transformation: if the black door is correct, then the white door was not correct and therefore the hypothesis is wrong; if the black door is wrong then the white door must have been correct and the hypothesis is right. It may be that the reason for the preference for direct test is in the interest of cognitive economy: saving the person from having to transform his knowledge. Another possible explanation, one which does not preclude the first, is that we do not fully accept the possibilities of correctness and incorrectness being mutually exclusive. We have a backlog of experience in which it has not always followed that if white is correct black is wrong or vice versa. We have also experienced situations where more than two alternatives were possible, and only a direct test would be effective.[1]

In any case, when a subject behaves in the typical manner of the successive scanner and limits himself to testing instances directly related to his hypothesis, his behavior appears to follow the principle of direct

---

[1] It is of interest that the first experiment which drew attention to a preference for direct test— in the form of participant behavior—used a situation where more than two alternatives were possible (Heidbreder, 1924).

test. In sum, then, successive scanning has little utility either in guaranteeing maximum informativeness of one's choices or in regulating risk. Its chief benefit is in the reduction of cognitive strain by limiting its user to direct test of hypotheses. As such, its principal utility may be as a procedure that is useful when the cognitive going gets rough or when one has good reason to believe that a particular hypothesis will turn out to be correct.

Conservative Focussing

In brief, this strategy may be described as finding a positive instance to use as a focus, then making a sequence of choices each of which alters but one attribute value of the first focus card and testing to see whether the change yields a positive or a negative instance. Those attribute values of the focus card which, when changed, still yield positive instances are *not* part of the concept. Those attribute values of the focus card that yield negative instances when changed *are* features of the concept. Thus, if the first positive card encountered contains three red circles with two borders (3RO2b), and if the concept is "red circles," the sequence of choices made would be as follows, each choice changing a *single* attribute value of the focus card:

3RO2b (+) focus card[2]

2RO2b (+) first choice: eliminate "three figures" as a relevant attribute value

3GO2b (−) second choice: retain "red" as a relevant attribute value

3R+2b (−) third choice: retain "circle" as a relevant attribute value

3RO1b (+) fourth choice: eliminate "two borders" as a relevant attribute value

Ergo, concept is "red circles."

Note one thing. When a subject has changed an attribute value of the focus card and the

[2]The symbol (+) denotes a positive instance; (−) a negative instance.

new card chosen turns out to be positive, this result logically eliminates the attribute in question from consideration. *No* value of such an attribute can be relevant to the concept. The subject need not sample any further values of it.

Several other features of this strategy are especially noteworthy. From the point of view of guaranteeing that each instance encountered be informative, the strategy does just that. By following it, redundancy can be completely avoided. The strategy guarantees, moreover, that each instance encountered will contain a "safe maximum" of information, as we will see when the risk-regulating property of the strategy is examined below.

The benefits in cognitive economy to be gained by using this strategy are striking. The first of these is that by its use the subject is enabled to disregard completely the bewildering business of eliminating possible hypotheses from the domain of 255 possible concepts in terms of which he may group instances. For in fact, the technique is designed to *test the relevance of attributes.* Given an initial positive card, his choices are designed to consider the four attribute values of the focus card one at a time to see which of these may be eliminated. In the present example there are four single attribute values to be considered, much less than the 15 rather complex hypotheses that would have to be considered in simultaneous scanning. A second contribution of this strategy to cognitive economy is that it guarantees that the relevance of all attribute values in the focus card will be *tested relatively directly.* If a change in an attribute value of the focus instance makes a difference, then that attribute value of the focus is relevant; if not, it is irrelevant. A third benefit is more subtle. By choosing a particular positive instance as a focus, the person *decreases the complexity and abstractness of the task* of keeping track of information he has encountered. All subsequent choices and their outcomes can be referred back to this focus instance much as if it were a score card. The attributes of the focus card are ticked off on the basis of subsequent tests.

There is one notable disadvantage to the strategy from the point of view of cognitive economy. Unless the universe of instances to be tested is arrayed in an orderly fashion so that a particular instance may be easily located on demand, the task of search imposed on the user of conservative focussing may become rather severe. We shall see examples of this disadvantage later.

Now for risk regulation. The expression "conservative focussing" has been chosen with good reason. Every choice is safe, safe in the sense that it logically guarantees the presence of information in the instance chosen for testing. This guaranteed information is not the maximum possible. On the other hand, the choice never carries the risk of yielding *no* information. We have already noted that by following the strategy, the subject will never choose a redundant instance, one that carries no new information. To understand fully why it is that a chosen instance almost never contains the maximum amount of information possible, we must turn to a consideration of focus gambling.

Focus Gambling

The principal feature of this strategy is that the subject uses a positive instance as a focus and then changes *more than one* attribute value at a time. In the present array . . . from which our examples are drawn, the subject might change two or three attribute values at once. This may not seem very different from conservative focussing, but a closer examination will make clear that it is. In particular, several features of focus gambling are of interest from the point of view of the risk-regulating nature of a strategy, and these we shall consider first.

In most tasks involving concept attainment, whether in the laboratory or in every-day life, one objective is to get the job done in as few choices or tests as possible, particularly if choices or tests are costly. It is always possible, given the use of conservative focussing, to complete the job with only as many tests as there are attributes to be tested. Focus gambling provides a way of attaining the concept in *fewer* trials than this limit. But in doing so it also imposes a risk. The risk is this. By using the strategy, one *may* succeed in attaining the concept in fewer test choices than required by conservative focussing. But the strategy also *may* require many more test choices than this. If one is in a position to take such a risk—the risk that solution may be very fast, very slow, or in between—then focus gambling is an admirable procedure. Such a position would be one where, presumably, quick solution paid off very handsomely compared to the losses to be suffered by slow solution.

It can readily be seen how the gambling feature is built into this interesting strategy. Again consider an example. Our subject as before takes as his focus the first positive card given him as an example: three red circles with two borders (3R$\bigcirc$2b). Rather than change only *one* attribute value of this focus, he will take a flier and change *three* of them. Let us say then that his next choice is 3G+1b. Now, if the change should "make no difference," i.e., if the instance chosen is still positive, then the concept must be that attribute value shared by the positive focus card and the next card chosen (also positive): namely, "three figures." In one fell swoop, the user of this strategy has eliminated three attributes and attained the concept. Similarly, if two attributes of the focus are changed and a positive instance still results, then the two changed attributes are eliminated. So far, the strategy seems risk-less enough.

The difficulty arises when a change in more than one attribute of the focus yields a *negative* instance. For when this happens, the only way in which a person can assimilate the information contained in the instance is to revert to the method of simultaneous scanning: to use the instance as an aid to eliminating possible hypotheses. This has the effect, of course, of diminishing drastically the economical nicety of a focus-gambling strategy. It is now no longer possible to proceed by testing *attributes* for their relevance. Instead, one must deal with *hypothesis elimination* by the method described in connection with simultaneous scanning or throw away the potential information contained in negative instances.

From the point of view of guaranteeing that instances chosen contain new information, focus gambling does not have the feature that makes conservative focussing notable. It does not guarantee that redundant instances will be avoided. For in so far as the person using this procedure does not use the information contained in negative instances, he is likely to, and frequently does, choose instances in the course of solution that contain the same information that might have been assimilated from such prior negative instances.

Finally, with respect to making the cognitive task of information assimilation easier, the strategy has most of the features of conservative focussing. One does not have to consider the full array of possible hypothetical concepts (unless one wishes to utilize the information of negative instances). It is geared to the testing of attributes in the focus card rather than to hypothesis elimination in the pure sense. It also provides for direct testing of hypotheses about the relevant attributes. As before, it reduces complexity by the use of a focus instance as a "score card." But it is lacking in economical benefits whenever negative instances occur. The user can do nothing with these unless he shifts strategy. And there is a temptation to do just this. Finally, the strategy also has the fault of requiring a considerable amount of search-behavior if one is to find appropriate instances to test.

Images and Plans

GEORGE A. MILLER

EUGENE GALANTER

KARL L. PRIBRAM

Consider how an ordinary day is put together. You awaken, and as you lie in bed, or perhaps as you move slowly about in a protective shell of morning habits, you think about what the day will be like—it will be hot, it will be cold; there is too much to do, there is nothing to fill the time; you promised to see him, she may be there again today. If you are compulsive, you may worry about fitting it all in, you may make a list of all the things you have to do. Or you may launch yourself into the day with no clear notion of what you are going to do or how

long it will take. But, whether it is crowded or empty, novel or routine, uniform or varied, your day has a structure of its own —it fits into the texture of your life. And as you think what your day will hold, you construct a plan to meet it. What you expect to happen foreshadows what you expect to do.

Reprinted with the permission of the senior author and the publisher from *Plans and the Structure of Behavior*. New York: Holt, Rinehart and Winston, Inc., 1960, pp. 5–20.

The authors of this book believe that the plans you make are interesting and that they probably have some relation to how you actually spend your time during the day. We call them "plans" without malice —we recognize that you do not draw out long and elaborate blueprints for every moment of the day. You do not need to. Rough, sketchy, flexible anticipations are usually sufficient. As you brush your teeth you decide that you will answer that pile of letters you have been neglecting. That is enough. You do not need to list the names of the people or to draft an outline of the contents of the letters. You think simply that today there will be time for it after lunch. After lunch, if you remember, you turn to the letters. You take one and read it. You plan your answer. You may need to check on some information, you dictate or type or scribble a reply, you address an envelope, seal the folded letter, find a stamp, drop it in a mailbox. Each of these subactivities runs off as the situation arises —you did not need to enumerate them while you were planning the day. All you need is the name of the activity that you plan for that segment of the day, and from that name you then proceed to elaborate the detailed actions involved in carrying out the plan.

You *imagine* what your day is going to be and you make *plans* to cope with it. Images and plans. What does modern psychology have to say about images and plans?

Presumably, the task of modern psychology is to make sense out of what people and animals do, to find some system for understanding their behavior. If we, as psychologists, come to this task with proper scientific caution, we must begin with what we can see and we must postulate as little as possible beyond that. What we can see are movements and environmental events. The ancient subject matter of psychology— the mind and its various manifestations—is distressingly invisible, and a science with invisible content is likely to become an invisible science. We are therefore led to underline the fundamental importance of

behavior and, in particular, to try to discover recurrent patterns of stimulation and response.

What an organism does depends on what happens around it. As to the way in which this dependency should be described, however, there are, as in most matters of modern psychology, two schools of thought. On the one hand are the optimists, who claim to find the dependency simple and straightforward. They model the stimulus-response relation after the classical, physiological pattern of the reflex arc and use Pavlov's discoveries to explain how new reflexes can be formed through experience. This approach is too simple for all but the most extreme optimists. Most psychologists quickly realize that behavior in general, and human behavior in particular, is not a chain of conditioned reflexes. So the model is complicated slightly by incorporating some of the stimuli that occur after the response in addition to the stimuli that occur before the response. Once these "reinforcing" stimuli are included in the description, it becomes possible to understand a much greater variety of behaviors and to acknowledge the apparently purposive nature of behavior. That is one school of thought.

Arrayed against the reflex theorists are the pessimists, who think that living organisms are complicated, devious, poorly designed for research purposes, and so on. They maintain that the effect an event will have upon behavior depends on how the event is represented in the organism's picture of itself and its universe. They are quite sure that any correlations between stimulation and response must be mediated by an organized representation of the environment, a system of concepts and relations within which the organism is located. A human being—and probably other animals as well—builds up an internal representation, a model of the universe, a schema, a simulacrum, a cognitive map, an Image. Sir Frederic C. Bartlett, who uses the term "schema" for this internal representation, describes it in this way:

"Schema" refers to an active organisation of past reactions, or of past experiences, which must always be supposed to be operating in any well-adapted organic response. That is, whenever there is any order or regularity of behavior, a particular response is possible only because it is related to other similar responses which have been serially organised, yet which operate, not simply as individual members coming one after another, but as a unitary mass. Determination by schemata is the most fundamental of all the ways in which we can be influenced by reactions and experiences which occurred some time in the past. All incoming impulses of a certain kind, or mode, go together to build up an active, organised setting: visual, auditory, various types of cutaneous impulses and the like, at a relatively low level; all the experiences connected by a common interest: in sport, in literature, history, art, science, philosophy, and so on, on a higher level.[1]

The crux of the argument, as every psychologist knows, is whether anything so mysterious and inaccessible as "the organism's picture of itself and its universe," or "an active organisation of past reactions," etc., is really necessary. Necessary, that is to say, as an explanation for the behavior that can be observed to occur.

The view that some mediating organization of experience is necessary has a surprisingly large number of critics among hard-headed, experimentally trained psychologists. The mediating organization is, of course, a theoretical concept and, out of respect for Occam's Razor, one should not burden the science with unnecessary theoretical luggage. An unconditional proof that a completely consistent account of behavior cannot be formulated more economically does not exist, and until we are certain that simpler ideas have failed we should not rush to embrace more complicated ones. Indeed, there are many psychologists who think the simple stimulus-response-reinforcement models provide an adequate description of everything a psychologist should concern himself with.

For reasons that are not entirely clear,

the battle between these two schools of thought has generally been waged at the level of animal behavior. Edward Tolman, for example, has based his defense of cognitive organization almost entirely on his studies of the behavior of rats—surely one of the least promising areas in which to investigate intellectual accomplishments. Perhaps he felt that if he could win the argument with the simpler animal, he would win it by default for the more complicated ones. If the description of a rodent's cognitive structure is necessary in order to understand its behavior, then it is just that much more important for understanding the behavior of a dog, or an ape, or a man. Tolman's position was put most simply and directly in the following paragraph:

[The brain] is far more like a map control room than it is like an old-fashioned telephone exchange. The stimuli, which are allowed in, are not connected by just simple one-to-one switches to the outgoing responses. Rather, the incoming impulses are usually worked over and elaborated in the central control room into a tentative, cognitivelike map of the environment. And it is this tentative map, indicating routes and paths and environmental relationships, which finally determines what responses, if any, the animal will finally release.[2]

We ourselves are quite sympathetic to this kind of theorizing, since it seems obvious to us that a great deal more goes on between the stimulus and the response than can be accounted for by a simple statement about associative strengths. The pros and cons cannot be reviewed here—the argument is long and other texts[3] exist in which an interested reader can pursue it—so we shall simply announce that our theoretical preferences are all on the side of the cognitive theorists. Life is complicated.

[1] Frederic C. Bartlett, *Remembering, A Study in Experimental and Social Psychology* (Cambridge: Cambridge University Press, 1932), p. 201.

[2] Edward C. Tolman, Cognitive maps in rats and men, *Psychological Review*, 1948, 55, 189–208.

[3] See, for example, either E. R. Hilgard, *Theories of Learning* (New York: Appleton-Century-Crofts, ed. 2, 1956), or W. K. Estes *et al.*, *Modern Learning Theory* (New York: Appleton-Century-Crofts, 1954), or D. O. Hebb, *The Organization of Behavior* (New York: Wiley, 1949).

Nevertheless, there is a criticism of the cognitive position that seems quite important and that has never, so far as we know, received an adequate answer. The criticism is that the cognitive processes Tolman and others have postulated are not, in fact, sufficient to do the job they were supposed to do. Even if you admit these ghostly inner somethings, say the critics, you will not have explained anything about the animal's behavior. Guthrie has made the point about as sharply as anyone:

> Signs, in Tolman's theory, occasion in the rat *realization,* or *cognition,* or *judgment,* or *hypotheses,* or *abstraction,* but *they do not occasion action.* In his concern with what goes on in the rat's mind, Tolman has neglected to predict what the rat will do. So far as the theory is concerned the rat is left buried in thought; if he gets to the food-box at the end that is his concern, not the concern of the theory.[4]

Perhaps the cognitive theorists have not understood the force of this criticism. It is so transparently clear to them that if a hungry rat knows where to find food—if he has a cognitive map with food-box located on it —he will go there and eat. What more is there to explain? The answer, of course, is that a great deal is left to be explained. The gap from knowledge to action looks smaller than the gap from stimulus to action—yet the gap is still there, still indefinitely large. Tolman, the omniscient theorist, leaps over that gap when he infers the rat's cognitive organization from its behavior. But that leaves still outstanding the question of the rat's ability to leap it. Apparently, cognitive theorists have assumed that their best course was to show that the reflex theories are inadequate; they seem to have been quite unprepared when the same argument —that things are even more complicated than they dared to imagine—was used against them. Yet, if Guthrie is right, more cognitive theory is needed than the cognitive theorists normally supply. That is to say, far from respecting Occam's Razor, the

cognitive theorist must ask for even *more* theoretical luggage to carry around. Something is needed to bridge the gap from knowledge to action.

It is unfair to single out Tolman and criticize him for leaving the cognitive representation paralytic. Other cognitive theorists could equally well be cited. Wolfgang Köhler, for example, has been subjected to the same kind of heckling. In reporting his extremely perceptive study of the chimpanzees on Tenerife Island during the first World War, Köhler wrote:

> We can . . . distinguish sharply between the kind of behavior which from the very beginning arises out of a consideration of the structure of a situation, and one that does not. Only in the former case do we speak of insight, and only that behavior of animals definitely appears to us intelligent which takes account from the beginning of the lay of the land, and proceeds to deal with it in a single, continuous, and definite course. Hence follows this criterion of insight: *the appearance of a complete solution with reference to the whole lay-out of the field.*[5]

Other psychologists have been less confident that they could tell the difference between behavior based on an understanding of the whole layout and behavior based on less cognitive processes, so there has been a long and rather fruitless controversy over the relative merits of trial-and-error and of insight as methods of learning. The point we wish to raise here, however, is that Köhler makes the standard cognitive assumption: once the animal has grasped the whole layout he will behave appropriately. Again, the fact that grasping the whole layout may be necessary, but is certainly not sufficient as an explanation of intelligent behavior, seems to have been ignored by Köhler. Many years later, for example, we heard Karl Lashley say this to him:

> I attended the dedication, three weeks ago, of a bridge at Dyea, Alaska. The road to the

[4] E. R. Guthrie, *The Psychology of Learning* (New York: Harper, 1935), p. 172.

[5] Wolfgang Köhler, *The Mentality of Apes* (translated from the second edition by Ella Winter; London: Routledge and Kegan Paul, 1927), pp. 169–170.

bridge for nine miles was blasted along a series of cliffs. It led to a magnificent steel bridge, permanent and apparently indestructible. After the dedication ceremonies I walked across the bridge and was confronted with an impenetrable forest of shrubs and underbrush, through which only a couple of trails of bears led to indeterminate places. In a way, I feel that Professor Köhler's position is somewhat that of the bridge. . . . The neurological problem is in large part, if not entirely, the translation of the afferent pattern of impulses into the efferent pattern. The field theory in its present form includes no hint of the way in which the field forces induce and control the pattern of efferent activity. It applies to perceptual experience but seems to end there.[6]

Many other voices could be added to this dialogue. Much detailed analysis of different psychological theories could be displayed to show why the cognitive theorists feel they have answered the criticism and why their critics still maintain that they have not. But we will not pursue it. Our point is that many psychologists, including the present authors, have been disturbed by a theoretical vacuum between cognition and action. The present book is largely the record of prolonged—and frequently violent—conversations about how that vacuum might be filled.

No doubt it is perfectly obvious to the reader that we have here a modern version of an ancient puzzle. At an earlier date we might have introduced the topic directly by announcing that we intended to discuss the will. But today the will seems to have disappeared from psychological theory, assimilated anonymously into the broader topic of motivation. The last serious attempt to make sense out of the will was the early work of Kurt Lewin and his students. Lewin's contributions are so important that we will treat them in detail in Chapter 4; we cannot dismiss them summarily by a paragraph in this introduction. In order to show what a psychology of will might be like, therefore, it is necessary to return to an earlier and more philosophical generation of psychologists. William James provides the sort of discussion that was once an indispensable part of every psychology text, so let us consider briefly how he handled the topic.

The second volume of *The Principles* contains a long chapter (106 pages) entitled "Will." The first third of it is James's struggle against theories based on "sensations of innervation"—the notion that the innervation required to perform the appropriate action is itself a part of the cognitive representation. James maintains instead that it is the anticipation of the kinesthetic effects of the movement that is represented in consciousness. He then turns to the topic of "ideo-motor action," which provides the foundation for his explanation of all phenomena of will. If a person forms a clear image of a particular action, that action tends to occur. The occurrence may be inhibited, limited to covert tensions in the muscles, but in many cases having an idea of an action is sufficient for action. If there is anything between the cognitive representation and the overt action, it is not represented in consciousness. Introspectively, therefore, there seems to be no vacuum to be filled, and James, had he heard them, would have felt that criticisms of the sort made by Guthrie and Lashley were not justified.

But what of the more complicated cases of willing? What occurs when we force ourselves through some unpleasant task by "the slow dead heave of the will?" According to James, the feeling of effort arises from our attempt to keep our attention focused on the unpleasant idea. "The essential achievement of the will," he tells us, "is to *attend* to a difficult object and hold it fast before the mind."[7] If an idea can be maintained in attention, then the action that is envisioned in the idea occurs automatically —a direct example of ideo-motor action. All of which helps us not in the least. The bridge

---

[6] Lloyd A. Jeffress, ed., *Cerebral Mechanisms in Behavior* (New York: Wiley, 1951), p. 230.

[7] William James, *The Principles of Psychology*, Vol. II (New York: Holt, 1890), p. 561.

James gives us between the *ideo* and the *motor* is nothing but a hyphen. There seems to be no alternative but to strike out into the vacuum on our own.

The problem is to describe how actions are controlled by an organism's internal representation of its universe. If we consider what these actions are in the normal, freely ranging animal, we must be struck by the extent to which they are organized into patterns. Most psychologists maintain that these action patterns are punctuated by goals and subgoals, but that does not concern us for the moment. We wish to call attention to the fact that the organization does exist—configuration is just as important a property of behavior as it is of perception. The configurations of behavior, however, tend to be predominantly temporal—it is the *sequence* of motions that flows onward so smoothly as the creature runs, swims, flies, talks, or whatever. What we must provide, therefore, is some way to map the cognitive representation into the appropriate *pattern* of activity. But how are we to analyze this flowing pattern of action into manageable parts?

The difficulty in analyzing the actions of an animal does not arise from any lack of ways to do it but from an embarrassment of riches. We can describe an action as a sequence of muscle twitches, or as a sequence of movements of limbs and other parts, or as a sequence of goal-directed actions, or in even larger units. Following Tolman, most psychologists distinguish the little units from the big units by calling the little ones "molecular," the big ones, "molar." Anyone who asks which unit is the correct size to use in describing behavior is told that behavioral laws seem more obvious when molar units are used, but that just how molar he should be in any particular analysis is something he will have to learn from experience and observation in research.

The implication is relatively clear, however, that the molar units must be composed of molecular units, which we take to mean

that a proper description of behavior must be made on *all levels simultaneously.* That is to say, we are trying to describe a process that is organized on several different levels, and the pattern of units at one level can be indicated only by giving the units at the next higher, or more molar, level of description. For example, the molar pattern of behavior X consists of two parts, A and B, in that order. Thus, $X = AB$. But A, in turn, consists of two parts, a and b; and B consists of three, c, d, and e. Thus, $X = AB = abcde$, and we can describe the same segment of behavior at any one of the three levels. The point, however, is that we do not want to pick one level and argue that it is somehow better than the others; the complete description must include all levels. Otherwise, the configurational properties of the behavior will be lost—if we state only $abcde$, for example, then $(ab)(cde)$ may become confused with $(abc)(de)$, which may be a very different thing.

This kind of organization of behavior is most obvious, no doubt, in human verbal behavior. The individual phonemes are organized into morphemes, morphemes are strung together to form phrases, phrases in the proper sequence form a sentence, and a string of sentences makes up the utterance. The complete description of the utterance involves all these levels. The kind of ambiguity that results when all levels are not known is suggested by the sentence, "They are flying planes." The sequence of phonemes may remain unchanged, but the two analyses $(They)(are\ flying)(planes)$ and $(They)$ $(are)(flying\ planes)$ are very different utterances.[8]

---

[8] The traditional method of parsing a sentence is the prototype of the kind of behavioral description we demand. Noam Chomsky, in Chapter 4 of his monograph, *Syntactic Structures* (The Hague: Mouton, 1957), provides a formal representation of this kind of description, which linguists refer to as "constituent analysis." We shall discuss Chomsky's method of representing verbal behavior in more detail in Chapter 11. The suggestion that linguistic analysis provides a model for the

Psychologists have seldom demonstrated any reluctance to infer the existence of such molar units as "words" or even "meanings" when they have dealt with verbal behavior, even though the actual responses available to perception are merely the strings of phones, the acoustic representations of the intended phonemes. Exactly the same recognition of more molar units in nonverbal behavior deserves the same kind of multi-level description. Unfortunately, however, the psychologist usually describes behavior —or some aspect of behavior—at a single level and leaves his colleagues to use their own common sense to infer what happened at other levels. The meticulous recording of every muscle twitch, even if anyone were brave enough to try it, would still not suffice, for it would not contain the structural features that characterize the molar units— and those structural features must be *inferred* on the basis of a *theory* about behavior. Our theories of behavior, in this sense of the term, have always remained implicit and intuitive. (It is rather surprising to realize that after half a century of behaviorism this aspect of the problem of describing behavior has almost never been recognized, much less solved.)

In those fortunate instances that do give us adequate descriptions of behavior—instances provided almost entirely by linguists and ethologists—it is quite obvious that the behavior is organized simultaneously at several levels of complexity. We shall speak of this fact as the "hierarchical organization

of behavior."[9] The hierarchy can be represented in various ways. The diagram of a hierarchy usually takes the form of a tree, the arborizations indicating progressively more molecular representations. Or it can be cast as an outline:

> X.
> 　A.
> 　　a.
> 　　b.
> 　B.
> 　　c.
> 　　d.
> 　　e.

This outline shows the structure of the hypothetical example introduced on page 250. Or it can be considered as a collection of lists: X is a list containing the two items, A and B; A is a list containing two items, a and b; B is a list containing three items, c, d, and e. Or it can be considered as a set of rules governing permissible substitutions: Where X occurs, we can substitute for it AB; where A occurs we can substitute ab; etc.[10] Each of these methods of presentation of a hierarchy has its special advantages in special situations.

---

description of all kinds of behavior is, of course, no novelty; it has been made frequently by both linguists and psychologists. For example, in *The Study of Language* (Cambridge: Harvard University Press, 1953), John B. Carroll, a psychologist, observed that, "From linguistic theory we get the notion of a hierarchy of units—from elemental units like the distinctive feature of a phoneme to large units like a sentence-type. It may be suggested that stretches of any kind of behavior may be organized in somewhat the same fashion" (p. 106).

[9] Many psychologists are familiar with the notion that behavior is hierarchically organized because they remember Clark Hull's use of the phrase "habit-family hierarchy." We must hasten to say, therefore, that Hull's use of the term "hierarchy" and our present use of that term have almost nothing in common. We are talking about a hierarchy of levels of representation. Hull was talking about an ordering of alternative (interchangeable, substitutable) responses according to their strengths. See, for example, C. L. Hull, The concept of the habit-family hierarchy and maze learning, *Psychological Review*, 1934, 41, 33–54; 134–152. Closer to the spirit of the present discussion is the system of behavioral episodes used by Roger G. Barker and Herbert F. Wright, in *Midwest and Its Children* (Evanston: Row, Peterson, 1954), to describe the molar behavior of children in their natural habitats. The work of Barker and Wright is a noteworthy exception to our assertion that psychologists have not tried to describe the structural features of behavior.

[10] Chomsky, *op. cit.*, p. 26.

Now, if the hierarchical nature of the organization of behavior can be taken as axiomatic, the time has come to set aside a few terms for the special purposes of the present discussions. Because definitions make heavy reading, we shall keep the list as short as possible.

PLAN. Any complete description of behavior should be adequate to serve as a set of instructions, that is, it should have the characteristics of a plan that could guide the action described. When we speak of a Plan in these pages, however, the term will refer to a *hierarchy of* instructions, and the capitalization will indicate that this special interpretation is intended. *A Plan is any hierarchical process in the organism that can control the order in which a sequence of operations is to be performed.*

A Plan is, for an organism, essentially the same as a program for a computer, especially if the program has the sort of hierarchical character described above. Newell, Shaw, and Simon have explicitly and systematically used the hierarchical structure of lists in their development of "information-processing languages" that are used to program high-speed digital computers to simulate human thought processes. Their success in this direction—which the present authors find most impressive and encouraging —argues strongly for the hypothesis that a hierarchical structure is the basic form of organization in human problem-solving. Thus, we are reasonably confident that "program" could be substituted everywhere for "Plan" in the following pages. However, the reduction of Plans to nothing but programs is still a scientific hypothesis and is still in need of further validation. For the present, therefore, it should be less confusing if we regard a computer program that simulates certain features of an organism's behavior as a theory about the organismic Plan that generated the behavior.[11]

Moreover, we shall also use the term "Plan" to designate a rough sketch of some course of action, just the major topic headings in the outline, as well as the completely detailed specification of every detailed operation.[12]

STRATEGY AND TACTICS. The concept of the hierarchical organization of behavior was introduced earlier with the distinction between molar and molecular units of analysis. Now, however, we wish to augment our terminology. The molar units in the organization of behavior will be said to comprise the behavioral *strategy,* and the molecular units, the *tactics.*

EXECUTION. We shall say that a creature is executing a particular Plan when in fact that Plan is controlling the sequence of operations he is carrying out. When an organism executes a Plan he proceeds through it step by step, completing one part and then moving to the next. The execution of a Plan need not result in overt action— especially in man, it seems to be true that

---

[11] It should be clearly recognized that, as Newell, Shaw, and Simon point out, comparing the sequence of operations executed by an organism and by a properly programed computer is quite different from comparing computers with brains, or electrical relays with synapses, etc. See Allen Newell, J. C. Shaw, and Herbert A. Simon, Elements of a theory of human problem solving. *Psychological Review*, 1958, 65, 151–166. Also, Herbert A. Simon and Allen Newell, Models, their uses and limitations, in L. D. White, ed., *The State of the Social Sciences* (Chicago: University of Chicago Press, 1956), pp. 66–83.

[12] Newell, Shaw, and Simon have also used "plan" to describe a general strategy before the details have been worked out, but they distinguish between such a plan and the program that enables a computer to use planning as one of its problem-solving techniques. See Allen Newell, J. C. Shaw, and Herbert A. Simon, A report on a general problem solving program. *Proceedings of the International Conference on Information Processing,* Paris, 1959 (in press).

Other workers have used the term "machine" rather loosely to include both the Plan and the instrument that executes it. For example, see M. L. Minsky, *Heuristic Aspects of the Artificial Intelligence Problem,* Group Report 34–55, Lincoln Laboratory, Massachusetts Institute of Technology, 17 December 1956, especially Section III.3.

there are Plans for collecting or transforming information, as well as Plans for guiding actions. Although it is not actually necessary, we assume on intuitive grounds that only one Plan is executed at a time, although relatively rapid alternation between Plans may be possible. An organism may—probably does—store many Plans other than the ones it happens to be executing at the moment.

IMAGE. The Image is all the accumulated, organized knowledge that the organism has about itself and its world. The Image consists of a great deal more than imagery, of course. What we have in mind when we use this term is essentially the same kind of private representation that other cognitive theorists have demanded. It includes everything the organism has learned—his values as well as his facts—organized by whatever concepts, images, or relations he has been able to master.

In the course of prolonged debates the present authors heard themselves using many other terms to modify "Plan" in rather special ways, but they will not be listed here. New terms will be defined and developed as they are needed in the course of the argument that follows. For the moment, however, we have defined enough to be able to say that the central problem of this book is *to explore the relation between the Image and the Plan.*

Stated so, it may seem to imply some sharp dichotomy between the two, so that it would be meaningful to ask, "Is such-and-such a process exclusively in the Plan or exclusively in the Image?" That the two points of view cannot be used in that way to classify processes into mutually exclusive categories should become apparent from such considerations as these:

——A Plan can be learned and so would be a part of the Image.

——The names that Plans have must comprise a part of the Image for human beings, since it must be part of a person's Image of himself that he is able to execute such-and-such Plans.

——Knowledge must be incorporated into the Plan, since otherwise it could not provide a basis for guiding behavior. Thus, Images can form part of a Plan.

——Changes in the Images can be effected only by executing Plans for gathering, storing, or transforming information.

——Changes in the Plans can be effected only by information drawn from the Images.

——The transformation of descriptions into instructions is, for human beings, a simple verbal trick.

Psychologists who are accustomed to think of their problem as the investigation of relations between Stimulus and Response are apt to view the present undertaking in a parallel way—as an investigation of relations between a subjective stimulus and a subjective response. If that were all we had to say, however, we would scarcely have written a book to say it. Stimulus and response are physiological concepts borrowed from the discussion of reflexes. But we have rejected the classical concept of the reflex arc as the fundamental pattern for the organization of all behavior, and consequently we do not feel a need to extend the classic disjunction between stimulus and response variables into the realm of Images and Plans. To assume that a Plan is a covert response to some inner Image of a stimulus does nothing but parallel objective concepts with subjective equivalents and leaves the reflex arc still master—albeit a rather ghostly master—of the machinery of the mind. We are not likely to overthrow an old master without the help of a new one, so it is to the task of finding a successor that we must turn next.

The Development
of Language and Thought:
Ages and Stages

7

INTRODUCTION

In the study of linguistic and cognitive development the basic issue, according to Sigel (1964, pages 211–212) is this: Does development always follow the same pattern so that there is a fixed order of ages and stages, or is development a product of learning experiences which differentiate ability, knowledge, and skill for each child? The first position is called the age-dependent theory. The second position is the experiential approach. As in the controversy between cognitive and behaviorist theorists on the nature of thought, the issue here may be more a product of the tradition of research within which one works and the models and language one uses rather than the product of contrary assumptions. The gap that has long separated research in developmental and learning psychology has been detrimental to both areas. In Europe and America the two isolated areas of research have made most difficult a synthesis of the work of Piaget and his followers and experimental American psychologists. There are indications, however, in the new experimental rigor of Piaget and in the developmental interests of American learning psychologists, that this gap will be bridged.

In this introduction we shall first discuss the theory and research on the development of thought. The reader will later observe, however, that much of the study of language development employs the same techniques and normative designs. Stage-dependent theory has been the basis of most research on the development of thought. This theory is based on inferences drawn from cross-sectional studies that compare the performances of different children at various ages. The best test of the theory, however, requires longitudinal studies of the same children over extended periods.

There are few if any published longitudinal studies of this type (Sigel, 1964, page 213). Further testing of the stage-dependent theory requires experimental manipulation of the environment to discover how development can be altered by external influences.

The stage-dependent theory is criticized on several grounds (Sigel, 1964, page 212): (1) there is decided overlap among chronological age groups in all areas of performance; (2) the apparent continuity of development conceals from observation gaps existing between stages; (3) the tremendous instability of response in children makes it difficult to determine which stages they have reached; and (4) the theory does not explain the individual differences in intelligence that appear.

Despite these drawbacks the stage-dependent theory enjoys considerable attention among English-speaking and French-speaking psychologists. Piaget and his collaborators for more than thirty years, at the Rousseau Institute in Geneva, Switzerland, have observed the development of intellectual functions and logic in children. Until recently the experimental rigor that American psychologists require has often been absent in Piaget's research, but he has shown exceptional ingenuity in building theoretical models based on naturalistic observation. In his early study of the development of logic in children (before 1937), Piaget emphasized the relation of language and thought and developed his well-known distinction between egocentric and social language and between animistic and symbolic thought (Hunt, 1961, page 110). Later, partly as a result of the severe criticism of his early work, he began to observe carefully how children manipulated objects. From these later studies he developed the conception of logic as "operations" or "structure."

Piaget has studied the development of intellectual processes of children —how children learn to think. This development of thought is the result of a continuous interaction of the child and his environment. In embryology this interaction results in the growth and increased complexity of the bodily organs and functions. For Piaget, intellectual development is analogous to embryological development. As the child continues to cope with his environment his mental processes become more and more complex.

Piaget divides the interaction between the child and his environment into two phases. There is *assimilation,* which, like the eating of food, involves taking something from the environment. In this process, the environment acts as the stimulus. The child responds with the responses he has already acquired. But assimilation, or simple response, is not enough. The child needs to cope with a changing and expanding environment as he grows toward adulthood. The coping, according to Piaget, requires more than making simple, habitual responses. Instead, the child must reorganize his thinking. This reorganization develops new *patterns* of responses, which Piaget calls *schemata.* In effect, the child must change old into new schemata. *Accommodation* defines the process of reorganizing schemata in ways that allow the child to cope more fully with his environment. The process of reorganization is probably continuous, but it is frequently described as occurring in stages and substages. In the article that follows Berlyne defines the stages and substages.

Berlyne also discusses the correspondence of Piaget's study of operations and schemata to the strategies for information processing discussed in Chapter 6. Although Berlyne is inclined to classify Piaget with the neobehaviorists, especially those who use operant conditioning models, Piaget does not employ stimulus-response models or terminology in describing his system. As demonstrated in the article by Piaget that appears in this chapter, the thought processes he describes seem to be of a much higher level than are the mediational processes of the modern behaviorist, and they seem to be more representational in nature than implicit and explicit responses. His description of the dynamic aspects of thought is closer to the cognitive Plans of Miller, Galanter, and Pribam [Chapter 6] than to the antecedent-subsequent correlations of the behaviorists. The fruitful translation of one position into the language of the other may reveal merely terminological differences.

A study by Ervin-Tripp (1960) illustrates how Piaget's ideas of age-correspondence can be experimentally tested. In effect, this investigator attempts to discover how experimental intervention or training can modify the course of logical development. We recall that Piaget's methodology is usually based on observation rather than controlled intervention. His research also provides for no control of previous learning. Ervin-Tripp uses a transfer-of-training design, which equalizes the effects of previous training and allows a test of Piaget's maturational factor through the use of children of different ages. In finding that success on the transfer task was related to spatial and verbal ability, which in turn correlate with age, she provides evidence that supports Piaget's position.

This chapter also concerns the study of the development of language. There are several useful reviews of the literature on language development that are too lengthy to reprint in this anthology (McCarthy, 1954; Carroll, 1960; Ervin-Tripp and Miller, 1963). In the comments here we have followed closely the review and summary of Ervin-Tripp and Miller, which emphasizes the research on language development that has been guided by modern linguistics.

When acquiring a language the child must learn its sound system or phonology and its grammar or syntax. In the prelinguistic stage the child first develops control over volume, pitch, and articulation. By the end of the first year the child is able to vocalize almost all conceivable sounds, including those that are not part of the parental tongue. Later, in a period of passive control, he is able to hear differences in intonation, stress, and voice quality even though he is unable to produce these differences. A third stage is marked by the child's use of meaningful words. It is preceded by a transition period in which there is decreased babbling or complete silence. In this third stage it is possible to study the child's system of sound contrasts to discover how he distinguishes meaningful words. According to Ervin-Tripp and Miller, by the time the child reaches the fourth year his phonological system corresponds closely to that of the adult.

The acquisition of grammar is a complex process and not as easily described. At the age of ten months, when children first use words, they show no knowledge of grammar. By the age of four, however, they seem to have mastered the complex syntactical structure of their native language. The first stage is one of "passive grammatical control" during which we can assume that the child is learning the transformational rules of grammar well enough to understand adult communication but not well enough to utter anything more than one-word sentences. The second stage may be one of "unmarked grammatical system" in which certain regularities of grammatical sequences may occur. As Ervin-Tripp and Miller state, it is difficult to determine whether these are memorized sequences or the generation of novel sentences. Nevertheless, at about two years of age, two-word sentences appear. Between the ages of twenty-seven to thirty months a third stage, "the marked grammatical system," may appear. Examples of *markers* are the appearance of *the* before nouns and the appearance of verbs after *can* and before *-ing*. The child's grammatical system appears to be a simplified model of the adult's. Finally, by the age of four the child has acquired knowledge of the basic structure of his language. Then follows a period of consolidation and overlearning which finally result in skilled adult speech (Ervin-Tripp and Miller, 1963, page 125). While acknowledging the controversial position of transformational grammar in the field of linguistics, Ervin-Tripp and Miller are enthusiastic about its usefulness for the study of language acquisition. The great advantage of transformational theory is that "a small number of rules compared with a large number of possible sentences results in an economy of description and a potential economy of learning as well" (page 125).

The last four articles in this chapter investigate language development beyond four years of age. All of these studies are psycholinguistically oriented. Ervin-Tripp and Foster use Osgood's semantic differential scale to study the acquisition of denotative and connotative meaning. In an attempt to find the origin of connotative meaning, they studied the ability of first- and second-grade children to make proper discrimination of weight, strength, and size, as measures of evaluation. The differences in the performances of younger and older children indicate that what survives as metaphor and connotation in adults may begin as denotative confusion in children. For example, "big-strong-heavy" acquire distinctive meaning (or denotation) as children learn the discriminations between them. However, their initial overlap of meaning survives as connotation.

Werner and Kaplan investigate the acquisition and generalization of meaning. Their major concern is how children between the ages of eight and fourteen use verbal context to derive meaning. In discussing the "context theory of meaning" Carroll states that meaning is not found in the context but that the context provides a clue to the particular meaning with which a word should be associated [Chapter 6]. The present study shows how children of various ages may use contextual clues to learn and generalize the meaning of nonsense words. Werner and Kaplan distinguish two ways: (1) the sentence-contextual method, in which the nonsense word carries the whole or part of the sentence context; and (2) the nonsentence contextual method, in which the nonsense word is clearly differentiated from the sentence context but retains a broad contextual meaning. The differences in sentence manipulation that these investigators discovered between older and younger children suggest the greater mastery of syntax in the older children.

The study of syntactical function of particular words may well shed light on perception and cognition. Asch and Nerlove use words such as "cold," "soft," and "bright," which have double syntactical functions. These words refer to both psychological and physical properties. As in the study of Werner and Kaplan, they compare the linguistic behavior of children of different ages. The experimental design permits the observation of the order in which the two functions are mastered or the simultaneity with which they are mastered. The results suggest that the development of concepts is not the product of discrete discrimination and associations. In learning that words have multiple rather than single syntactical relations or meanings, the child may be demonstrating a hierarchical organization of thought.

The article by Brown and Berko deals with syntactic categories as somewhat distinct from syntactical functions. This study gives us some knowledge of how children gradually develop grammatical sophistication. Since this acquisition of grammatical knowledge appears to be the result of intuitive comprehension of the rules of grammar, the evidence here lends support to the linguistic and psychological processes postulated by Chomsky and Miller [Chapter 1].

REFERENCES

Berko, J. The child's learning of English morphology. *Word*, 1958, **14**, 150–177.

Brown, R. Linguistic determinism and the part of speech. *J. abnorm. soc. Psychol.*, 1957, **55**, 1–5.

————, and U. Bellugi. The child's acquisition of syntax. *Harvard Educ. Rev.*, 1964, **34**, No. 2, 133–151.

Carroll, J. B. Language development in children. *Encyclopedia of Educational Research*. New York: Macmillan, 1960.

Ervin-Tripp, Susan M. Training and logical operation of children. *Child Develpm.*, 1960, **31**, 555–563.

————, and W. Miller. Language development. Child's psychology. In the *Sixty-second Yearbook, National Society for the Study of Education*. Chicago: University of Chicago Press, 1963. Pp. 108–143.

Flavell, J. H. *The developmental psychology of Jean Piaget*. Princeton, N.J.: Van Nostrand, 1963.

Hunt, J. McV. *Intelligence and experience.* New York: Ronald, 1961.

Keppel, G. Verbal learning in children. Psychol. Bull. 1964, 61, No. 1, 63–80.

Kessen, W., and C. Kuhlman (Eds.). Thought in the young child. *Monogr. Soc. Res. Child Develpm.*, 1962, 27, No. 2.

Luria, A. R. The directive function of speech: I. Its development in early childhood. *Word*, 1959, 15, No. 2, 341–352.

McCarthy, D. Language development in children. In L. Carmichael (Ed.), A *manual of child development.* (2d ed.), New York: Wiley, 1954, Pp. 492–630.

Piaget, J. *The psychology of intelligence.* London: Routledge, 1950.

Sigel, I. W. Developmental trends in the abstraction ability of children. *Child Develpm.*, 1953, 24, 132–144.

————. The attainment of concepts. In M. S. Hoffman and L. W. Hoffman (Eds.), *Review of child development research.* New York: Russell Sage Foundation, 1964. Pp. 209–248.

Weir, R. *Language in the crib.* 's-Gravenhage: Mouton, 1962.

Recent Developments in Piaget's Work

D. E. BERLYNE

Piaget is known to English-speaking psychologists mainly for his early writings, with their thought-provoking but, according to some critics, disputable accounts of the quaint notions of young children. Doubts have been expressed about the validity of the method of interrogation used for these studies and about the generality of the findings. Repetitions with other populations have not always produced the results that Piaget's works would lead one to expect. At least one writer was moved to dismiss his "subjective approaches to the analysis of child behaviour" as "little removed from ordinary literary speculation."[1]

Since the 1930s, however, Piaget's researches have been undergoing some gradual but profound changes. He has been turning to more exact and behaviouristic methods of collecting data: close observation of infants, setting older children practical tasks or putting precise questions to them about events enacted in front of them, and psychophysical experiments with both child and adult subjects. His theory has become more detailed and more ambitious in scope, drawing on his knowledge of biology, logic and history of science, all of them fields to which he has contributed. These developments can be summed up by saying that he has changed from one of the most celebrated *developmental* psychologists into one of the most important of contemporary *general* psychologists. But this does not mean that his work has lost any of its importance for those faced with the practical problems of childhood in their everyday work.

Like most contemporary psychologists, Piaget starts from the biological concept of "adaptation." He sees adaptation as an

[1] Pratt, K. C. The neonate. In C. Murchison (Ed.), *A Handbook of Child Psychology.* Worcester, Mass.: Clark University Press, 1933.

Reprinted with the permission of the author and the publisher, Methuen & Co., Ltd., article of the same title, *British Journal of Educational Psychology*, 1957, 27, 1–12.

interplay of two complementary processes, which he calls *"assimilation"* and *"accommodation."* Assimilation occurs when an organism uses something in its environment for some activity which is already part of its repertoire. At the physiological level, it is exemplified by the ingestion of food, and, at the psychological level, it embraces a variety of phenomena. Piaget sees assimilation at work, for example, whenever a situation evokes a particular pattern of behaviour because it resembles situations that have evoked it in the past, whenever something new is perceived or conceived in terms of something familiar, whenever anything is invested with value or emotional importance. Accommodation, on the other hand, means the addition of new activities to an organism's repertoire or the modification of old activities in response to the impact of environmental events.

Psychologists accustomed to other conceptual schemes may wonder whether it really helps to group together such multifarious processes under the same rubrics. Is the role played by a cow which a child confuses with a horse really analogous to that played by a cow appearing as roast beef on the child's dinner plate? Although Piaget discusses assimilation and accommodation at great length, some readers may feel that the concepts need to be analyzed more minutely before they can yield unequivocal predictions rather than describing facts already discovered. At all events, assimilation seems to include what learning theorists call "generalization" and "discrimination," processes determining which response a particular stimulus will elicit, while accommodation covers "differentiation of responses" and the learning of new responses.

As the child's development proceeds, a more and more complete balance and synthesis between assimilation and accommodation is achieved. The child is able to take account of stimuli more and more remote from him in space and time, and to resort to more and more composite and indirect methods of solving problems.

Piaget agrees with many other theorists in distinguishing "affective" and "cognitive" factors. The former release energy, while the latter determine how the energy will be applied. Piaget's writings have concentrated on the "cognitive" aspect of behaviour rather than on motivation and emotion, but he insists that neither aspect must be overlooked. The child does not undergo separate intellectual and emotional developments. The most dispassionate pursuit of knowledge must be driven by some motive, and the directions in which drives and emotions impel behaviour must depend on the structures made available by the growth of intelligence.

THE PERIOD OF SENSORI-MOTOR INTELLIGENCE (BIRTH TO TWO YEARS)[2]

During his first two years, the child gradually advances towards the highest degree of intelligence that is possible without language and other symbolic functions. He begins life with innate reflexes, but these are, from the start, modified and made more effective by learning. New responses are soon acquired, and then complex solutions to problems are achieved by piecing together familiar responses in novel combinations. By the end of the second year, the first signs of the human capacity for symbolization appear: he invents new patterns of behaviour which show him to be representing the results of his actions to himself before they occur. In short, the sensorimotor period sees attainments comparable to the highest found in sub-human animals.

This growing ingenuity in the face of practical problems goes hand in hand with the formation of a less "egocentric" and more "objective" conception of the world. For some weeks after birth, the world must consist of a succession of visual patterns, sounds and other sensations. The infant comes naturally to pay attention to those

[2] See References (Piaget, 1950b, chap. IV; 1953b; 1955a).

external events which are associated with satisfactions or which are brought about by his own actions. Gradually, he builds up a view of the world as a collection of objects continuing to exist even when they are out of his sight and generally preserving the same sizes and shapes, despite the changes in their appearance that come with changes in position. Whereas no distinction between himself and what is outside him can have any meaning for him at first, he comes to conceive of himself as one object among the many that people the world, most of them unaffected by his activities.

The concept of an *object* is bound up with objective notions of *space, time* and *causality*, which the child does not possess as part of his native endowment but has to build up gradually through interaction with the world. After learning to select appropriate spatial directions and temporal successions for his actions, he comes to respond to the positions and times of occurrence of events outside himself, using his own body and his own actions as reference-points. Finally, he conceives of a space and a time in which both he himself and external objects are located. He learns, for example, to distinguish occasions when objects are moving independently of him from occasions when they merely appear to be changing positions because he is moving among them. Similarly, he progresses from an understanding of the relationship between his responses and their consequences to an understanding of the causal influence inanimate objects can exert on one another and even on him.

THE ORIGIN OF
SYMBOLIC PROCESSES[3]

Anything the child has achieved during the sensori-motor period is dwarfed by the prospects introduced by signs and symbols, particularly words and images. They expose him to a world of real and imaginary enti-

[3]See References (Piaget, 1949a; 1950b, chap. V; 1951).

ties extending far beyond his momentary range of vision or even his life-span. It is a stable and consistent world, whereas the objects he perceives come and go.

Piaget deprecates the long-established belief that images are mere reactivations of traces of past experiences, passively registered by the nervous system. He insists that imagery is an extremely complex and active process, as can be seen from the time it takes to appear after birth. It grows out of the child's imitative capacities and is, in fact, *"internalized imitation."* The gradual extension of imitation during the sensori-motor period proceeds from a tendency to reproduce sounds and visual effects which have just been produced by the infant himself or by somebody else to an ability to copy an increasing range of new responses from an increasing range of models. It reaches its climax and the point at which it can perform symbolic functions with "deferred imitation," the imitation of the behaviour of an absent person of whom the child is "reminded."

Inanimate objects also can evoke imitation, as, for example, when a child opens his mouth on finding it difficult to open a match-box. Imagery consists of just such symbolic imitation "internalized" i.e., so reduced in scale that only the subject himself is aware of it. It consists, in other words, of what behaviourists call *"implicit"* or *"fractional"* responses. When the first indications of imagery emerge about the middle of the second year, the child is beginning, significantly enough, to turn from "practice" games, in which pleasure is derived from exercising simple activities, to "symbolic games," which involve make believe or role-playing. The child understands, however, the nature of the relation between a symbol and what it signifies; he knows that the doll is not really a baby or that he is not really a cowboy.

Having learned to use *actions and images as symbols* and having by now acquired a sufficient vocabulary, he finds himself using words in a similar way. But words, more than images, are responsible for the progressive socialization of thought. Words and the concepts corresponding to them are taken over from the social group. They are, therefore, bound to edge the child's thoughts into line with those of other persons. He can influence and be influenced by, benefit from or suffer from, the beliefs and values of other members of his group and so arrive at an equilibrium and harmony with his social as well as his physical environment.

RELATIONS BETWEEN PERCEPTION AND THOUGHT[4]

In recent years, Piaget has been spending a great deal of time, together with Lambercier and other collaborators, on the painstaking investigation of visual illusions and related phenomena. This area of research, a time-honoured preserve of the more prosaic type of experimental psychology, may seem remote from the work for which he is best known. It has, nevertheless, given rise to some of his most original and comprehensive ideas, forming the kernel of his whole theory of intellectual functions. Whereas writers influenced by Gestalt psychology or by certain trends in American social psychology have tended to lump all "cognitive" processes together, Piaget finds the differences between perceptual and conceptual processes illuminating.

There are two obvious ways in which perception contrasts with thought. One arises from the fact, emphasized by the Gestalt school, that the perceived properties of a stimulus vary according to the pattern of which it is a component. The concepts participating in thought do not share this instability. The essential nature of a number does not change, no matter what the structure into which a mathematician fits it. A journey between two towns may seem longer or shorter in different circumstances, but the distance separating the towns

[4] See References (Piaget, 1950b, chap. III; 1954–1955).

according to our knowledge or our calculations does not fluctuate.

Secondly, perceptions are notoriously variable from person to person and from moment to moment. If we take 1,000 subjects, show them a line three inches long and another two inches long, and ask them to select a third line equal in length to the two combined, we shall expect a distribution of results with a high variance. We shall even expect each subject's response to vary from trial to trial, especially if the two lines are shown in different arrangements. On the other hand, if we take the same 1,000 subjects, show them the figure 2 and the figure 3, and ask them to select a third figure, equal to the sum of the two, the uniformity of the responses will be remarkable.

These differences can be traced back to two related factors which inevitably distort all perception. First, perception is always "centred" (*centré*). Sense-organs have to be oriented in one direction at once, and the optical apparatus in particular is so constructed that the centre of the visual field is seen more clearly and in more detail than other parts. As some of Piaget's psychophysical experiments show, the size of a fixated object is over-estimated in comparison with the sizes of peripheral objects. The various parts of the visual field expand and shrink in turn as the gaze wanders from one point to another. The second source of error is the fact that larger portions of a figure are likely to catch the eye more often than others, with the result that the distortions that arise when they are the centre of attention play a disproportionately large part in the net impression of the figure. What we have is, in fact, a biased sample of all possible fixations. From these assumptions, Piaget has derived a formula predicting the direction and extent of "primary" visual illusions, i.e., those which are found in infants and lower animals as much as, if not more than, in adult human beings and which can be ascribed to the inherently "probabilistic" nature of perception.

Perception is analogous to certain processes in physics, notably in statistical mechanics, which are likewise governed by probability. These processes are irreversible, since they always lead from a less probable to a more probable state. For example, when a hot body is brought into contact with a cool body, heat is transmitted from the former to the latter and not *vice versa.* A spoonful of sugar diffuses evenly through a cupful of tea, but particles of sugar in a mixture do not forgather at one spot. Similarly, the distortions to which perceived figures are subject work predominantly in one direction. They cannot be relied on to balance out.

Thinking can escape from these limitations, because it is comparable with physical systems of a different type, namely those possessing *reversibility.* An example is a balance with equal weights in the two pans. The depression of one pan is followed by an upward swing which restores the original situation. Such systems are in stable equilibrium precisely because a change can be cancelled by an equal change in the opposite direction. A balance, however, is inflexible in the sense that there is one state to which it invariably reverts. Thought processes require structures which permit of more mobility without threatening disequilibrium. They must be free to flit rapidly from one idea to another and to arrange ideas in new combinations. But systems of concepts must preserve their organization, despite this mobility, if thoughts are to be consistent and if they are to produce a stable conception of the world. The "dynamic equilibrium" which Piaget attributes to thought can perhaps best be compared with that of a lift and its counterweight. The lift can move freely up and down, and the system remains intact and in equilibrium, no matter what floor is reached. This is because of its reversibility: any movement of the lift is compensated by an equal and opposite movement of the counterweight, and it can also be nullified by an equal and opposite movement of the lift.

The reversibility of logical thought is acclaimed by Piaget as the acme in which the growth of intelligence culminates. The spoken word and the performed action can never be recalled. The influence of something which has been perceived and then disappears from view lingers to infect subsequent perceptions. But a thought can be entertained and then unthought, and everything is as if it had never occurred. We are consequently able to conceive possible solutions for problems which it would be costly, dangerous or impossible to test by action. And no matter how extravagant an idea is considered and then rejected, the coherence of conceptual systems is not threatened. The world represented by thought, unlike that presented by perception, is relatively free from "centring" (*centration*). It does not change with the location of the thinker or the direction of his attention.

These contrary characteristics are found in a pure form only in the naïve perception of the infant on the one hand and in the rigorous thought of the scientist, mathematician or logician on the other. The principal merit of this part of Piaget's work, as far as child psychology is concerned, is the light it sheds on certain processes forming compromises between perception and thought. As we shall see when we return to the chronological sequence, the first attempts at thinking are still contaminated with the short-comings of perception. And perception, after the first months of life, is usually accompanied by "perceptual activities," which mitigate its imperfections. There is no way of removing distortion completely from perception, but one distortion can be set against another. The focus of attention can be systematically varied, so that information from a succession of fixations is compared and collated to yield something approaching an objective impression. What appears from one point of view can be related to the perseveration or anticipation of what has been or will be seen from a different angle. "Perceptual activities" thus contribute to the "decentring" (*decentration*) of perception and the achievement of "semireversibility," so called because errors are not corrected exactly but merely tend to cancel out in the long run. Although these activities generally enhance accuracy of perception, they can on occasion lead to "secondary illusions," which are less pronounced in younger than in older children. An example is the "size-weight illusion," which makes a small object seem heavier than a larger one of equal weight.

THE PERIOD OF PRE-CONCEPTUAL THOUGHT (TWO TO FOUR YEARS)[5]

Before his use of symbolic processes can reach fruition, the child has to re-learn on a conceptual level some of the lessons he has already mastered on the sensori-motor level. For instance, he may have learned to recognize transient stimulus-patterns as shifting appearances assumed by enduring objects. But this does not immediately make him at home with the *concept* of an object. Adults are familiar with the concept of a particular *object* (*"this table," "Socrates"*), with the concept of a *class* (*"all four-legged tables," "all men"*) and with the relation of *class-membership* which joins them (*"This is a four-legged table," "Socrates is a man."*). These underlie our deductive reasoning, since having, for example, placed Socrates in the class of men, we can infer that Socrates has all the properties characteristic of this class.

The three-year-old child still lacks this equipment and has to use something midway between the concept of an object and that of a class, which Piaget calls the "pre-concept." On a walk through the woods, for example, he does not know whether he sees a succession of different snails or whether the same snail keeps on re-appearing. The distinction, in fact, means nothing to him; to him they are all "snail." Similar phenomena are, in some hazy way, identified, so that a

shadow under a lamp in a room has something to do with the shadows under the trees in the garden. Contrariwise, a person in new clothes may be thought to require a new name.

Unlike adults, who reason either *deductively* from the general to the particular or *inductively* from the particular to the general, the child at the pre-conceptual stage reasons *trans*ductively from the particular to the particular. It is a form of argument by analogy: "A is like B in one respect, therefore A must be like B in other "respects." Transduction may often lead to valid conclusions, e.g., that if Daddy is getting hot water he must be going to shave, since he shaved after getting hot water yesterday. But it will at other times lead the child into errors of a sort said to be common in psychotics but certainly not unknown in intellectual circles.

THE PERIOD OF INTUITIVE THOUGHT (FOUR TO SEVEN YEARS)[6]

When the child's reasoning has overcome these deficiencies, other limitations remain, mainly because thought has not yet freed itself from perception and become "decentred." Intuitive thought can best be understood from an experiment Piaget is fond of quoting. The child sees some beads being poured out of one glass into a taller and thinner glass. It is made clear to him that all the beads that were in the first glass are now in the second; none has been added or removed. He is asked whether there are now more or fewer beads in the second glass than there were in the first. The usual answer at this stage is either that there are more (because the level has risen) or that there are fewer (because the second glass is narrower).

To explain such errors, it may be worth asking why we, as adults, are able to avoid

[5] See References (Piaget, 1950b, chap. V; 1951).

[6] *Ibid.*

them. The first reason is that we are told by our thought processes that the number of objects in a set, if nothing is added or subtracted, must necessarily remain the same. We usually regard our thought processes as more trustworthy than our perceptions whenever the two conflict. At a conjurer's performance, for example, we do not really believe that the rabbit has been created *ex nihilo* or the lady has been sawn in half. The child at the intuitive stage is, on the other hand, still dominated by his perceptions. His conclusions are still at the mercy of the changes resulting from successive "centrings." The second reason is that we take into account several aspects of the situation at once or in turn. We can see that the height of the column of beads has increased and that the width has decreased just enough to compensate for the increase in height. But the child focusses on one aspect and overlooks others. In his reasoning as in his perception, "centring" causes one element to be overemphasized and others to be relatively ignored. The instructiveness of such examples for adults, who might smile at the child's mistakes in the bead experiment but be liable to precisely the same sort of misjudgment in relation to, say, political or social problems, needs hardly be laboured.

THE PERIOD OF CONCRETE OPERATIONS (SEVEN TO ELEVEN YEARS)[7]

We come at last to the first reasoning processes that would satisfy logicians. Logical (or, as Piaget calls it, "operational") thought emerges when a certain basic stock of concepts has been acquired and when these concepts have been organized into coherent systems. The *concepts* which figure in operational thought are called "operations" because they *are internalized re-*

[7]See References (Piaget, 1949a and b; 1950b, chaps. II, V; 1953a.

sponses. They grow out of certain overt actions in exactly the same way as images grow out of imitation. Three sorts in particular are of importance:

1. *Classes.* The concept of a "class" or the operation of "classification" is an internalized version of the action of grouping together objects recognized as similar. Having learned to pick out all the yellow counters in a heap and *place* them together in one spot, the child acquired the ability to *think of* all yellow objects together and thus form the concept of the "class of all yellow objects." This means that some part of what happens in the nervous system and musculature when yellow objects are manually gathered together occurs whenever yellow objects are grouped together in thought. Once formed, classes can be joined to form more inclusive classes, so that elaborate systems of classification are built up, the one used by biologists being the clearest illustration.

2. *Relations.* Asymmetrical relations, such as "a is longer than b" or "x is the father of y," derive by internalization from *ordering* activities, e.g., from placing objects in a row in order of increasing size. The best example of the complex systems which ordering relations can form is the family tree.

3. *Numbers.* The number system is the joint product of classification and ordering. The number 17, for instance, depends on the operation of grouping 17 objects together to form a class and that of placing 17 between 16 and 18 in the sequence of natural numbers.

Systems of operations are called "groupings" (*groupements*), and their stability depends on their having five properties. Unless these properties are present, the relations between the elements of a grouping will change as attention is directed to different parts of them, as happens with perceptual patterns, and thought will not be immune from inconsistency. The five properties are as follows:

1. *Closure.* Any two operations can be combined to form a third operation (e.g., $2 + 3 = 5$; *all men and all women = all human adults; A is 2 miles north of B and B is 1 mile north of C = A is 3 miles north of C.*
2. *Reversibility.* For any operation there is an opposite operation which cancels it (e.g., $2 + 3 = 5$ but $5 - 3 = 2$; *all men and all women = all human adults,* but *all human adults except women = all men; A is 2 miles north of B and B is 1 mile north of C = A is 3 miles north of C, but A is 3 miles north of C and C is 1 mile south of B = A is 2 miles north of B*).
3. *Associativity.* When three operations are to be combined, it does not matter which two are combined first. This is equivalent to the possibility of arriving at the same point by different routes (e.g., $(2 + 3) + 4 = 2 + (3 + 4)$; *all vertebrates and all invertebrates = all human beings and all sub-human animals; a is the uncle of b and b is the father of c = a is the brother of d and d is the grandfather of c*).
4. *Identity.* There is a "null operation" formed when any operation is combined with its opposite (e.g., $2 - 2 = 0$; *all men except those who are men = nobody; I travel 100 miles to the north and I travel 100 miles to the south = I find myself back where I started*).
5. The fifth property has two versions, one for classes and relations and the other for numbers:
a. *Tautology.* A classification or relation which is repeated is not changed. This represents the fact, recognized by logicians but not always by con-

versationalists, that saying something over and over again does not convey any more information than saying it once (e.g., *all men and all men = all men; a is longer than b and a is longer than b = a is longer than b*).
b. *Iteration.* A number combined with itself produces a new number (e.g., $3 + 3 = 6$; $3 \times 3 = 9$).[8]

THE PERIOD OF FORMAL OPERATIONS (ELEVEN TO FIFTEEN YEARS)[9]

The eleven-year-old can apply "operational" thinking to practical problems and concrete situations. The adolescent takes the final steps towards complete "decentring" and "reversibility" by acquiring a capacity for abstract thought. He can be guided by the *form* of an argument or a situation and ignore its *content*. He need no longer confine his attention to what is real. He can consider hypotheses which may or may not be true and work out what would follow if they were true. Not only are the hypothetico-deductive procedures of science, mathematics and logic open to him in consequence but also the role of would-be social reformer. The adolescent's taste for theorizing and criticizing arises from his ability to see the way the world is run as only one out of many possible ways it could be run and to conceive of alternative ways that might be better.

Quite a variety of new intellectual techniques become available at the same time. The most important new equipment of all is the *calculus of propositions*. At the concrete-operations stage, he was able to use the branches of logic known as the *algebra*

[8]Readers with mathematical interests will notice that, in so far as these properties refer to numbers, they are equivalent to the defining characteristics of a *group.* Groupings of classes and relations, on the other hand, are almost, but not quite, *groups* and almost, but not quite, *lattices.*

[9]See References (Inhelder, 1954, 1955; Piaget, 1949b; 1953a and c; 1954b).

of classes and the *algebra of relations*. Now he can supplement these with forms of reasoning bearing on the relations between propositions or sentences. Propositional calculus uses "second-order operations" or operations on operations. An example would be *"either sentence p is true or sentence q is true."* Another would be *"if sentence r is true, then sentence s must be true"* or, in the parlance favoured by logicians, *"r implies s."*

A large part of Piaget's information on this period comes from Inhelder's ingenious experiments, in which children were invited to discover elementary laws of physics for themselves with the help of simple apparatus. Children at the intuitive-thought stage vary conditions haphazardly and observe what happens in particular cases without deriving any *general principles*. At the concrete-operations stage, one factor at a time is varied, and its effects are duly noted. Not before the formal-operations stage does the child plan truly scientific investigations, varying the factors in all possible combinations and in a systematic order. The pedagogical implications of Inhelder's work are unmistakeable. Children with no previous instruction appear to be capable of learning scientific laws in this way, with, presumably, more motivation and more understanding than are produced by traditional teaching methods. But, according to Piaget and Inhelder, they are not capable of the sort of thinking that makes use of such laws before the advances of the formal-operations stage have been completed.

Piaget asks why so many new ways of thinking become available about the same time, despite their superficial dissimilarity. It is, he concludes, because they all require systems of *operations with similar structures*, and the child is not able to organize his thinking in accordance with such structures before adolescence. He has recently been much impressed with the possibilities of modern symbolic logic and certain non-numerical branches of mathematics as means of describing the structures common

to apparently different intellectual processes. This is not one of the ways in which logic has usually been used by psychologists in the past; Piaget is interested in using "logical models" for much the same purpose as other psychologists have begun to use "mathematical models."

One new acquisition is the ability to use systems of operations in which each operation has two distinct opposites. A class (e.g., *"all vertebrate animals"*) has the sort of opposite called an *inverse* (*"all invertebrate animals"*). A relation (e.g., *"a is twice as heavy as b"*) has a *reciprocal* (*"b is twice as heavy as a"*). But *"p implies q"* has both an inverse (*"q does not imply p"*) and a reciprocal (*"q implies p"*). Likewise, when the adolescent experiments with a balance, he discovers that the effects of one operation (e.g., increasing the weight in the right-hand pan) can be cancelled either by the inverse operation (reducing the weight in the right-hand pan to its original value) or by the reciprocal operation (increasing the weight in the left-hand pan by the same amount.) Such systems with two opposites have a structure known to mathematicians as the "four group."

The four group can be shown to provide the operations necessary for dealing with *proportionality*. It is no accident that the laws governing equilibrium between weights in the pans of a balance are understood at about the same age as the laws governing the sizes of shadows. In one of Inhelder's experiments, the subject is given two vertical rings of different diameters and has to place the rings between a candle and a screen in such a way that their shadows will coincide. Adolescents discover that the problem is solved when the ratio between the distances of the two rings from the candle is the same as the ratio between their diameters. Understanding proportionality opens the way to understanding *probability*, since, when we speak of the probability of a six in a game of dice, we mean the proportion of throws that will produce sixes in the long run.

Combinatorial analysis, depending on the structures mathematicians call *"lattices,"* is another equally fruitful new attainment. Suppose that we have two ways of dividing up animals—into "vertebrates (V)" and "invertebrates (v)" and into "flying (F)" and "non-flying (f)." A child at the concrete-operations stage is capable of allotting a particular animal to one of the four possible classes, $(V.F.)$, $(V.f.)$, $(v.F.)$ and $(v.f.)$. An adolescent at the formal-operations stage is capable of going further and considering all the sorts of animals that there are in the world or the sorts there conceivably could be. There are now *sixteen* possibilities: there might be no animals at all, there might be animals of all four classes, there might be $(v.F.)$ only, there might be $(V.F.)$, $(V.f.)$ and $(v.f.)$ animals but no $(v.F.)$, etc. Now each of these sixteen combinations corresponds to one of the sixteen relations between two propositions recognized by modern logic. For example, *"if an animal can fly, it must be a vertebrate"* would correspond to $(V.F.)$ or $(V.f.)$ or $(v.f.)$, i.e., the $(v.F.)$ possibility is excluded. We can understand, therefore, why permutations and combinations and complex logical relations are mastered more or less simultaneously.

The mastery of logical relations between propositions is well illustrated in Inhelder's experiments. All attempts to study the relations between the phenomena of nature, whether in the laboratory or in practical life, must use them: *"If I put the kettle on the stove and light the gas, the water will boil"; "It will rain or snow tomorrow unless the forecast was wrong or unless I read a description of today's weather and thought it was the forecast for tomorrow,"* etc. The ability to think in terms of all possible combinations, which appears together with the ability to use complex statements like these, is clearly revealed when adolescents are set one of Inhelder's most instructive problems. Five vessels, all containing colourless liquids, are provided; A, B and C, when mixed, will turn pink, D will remove the colour, and E will have no

effect. The properties of the liquids can be discovered only by systematically examining mixtures of every possible pair, every possible trio, etc., in turn.

AFFECTIVE DEVELOPMENT[10]

The child's physiological constitution makes him liable, right from birth, to emotional and drive states. These pleasant and unpleasant states come to be aroused, through some sort of conditioning, by the external stimulus patterns which regularly accompany them, and, when he had learned to perceive in terms of objects, he comes to like or dislike these. Human beings are naturally more important sources of satisfaction and distress than other objects, and so their actions and they themselves will have especially strong positive and negative values attached to them.

The social influences to which the appearance of language and other symbols makes the child amenable are manifested particularly clearly in the formation of "inter-individual feelings." The ability to picture how the world looks from another person's point of view includes the power to represent to oneself the feelings aroused in him by one's own actions. The child takes over other people's evaluations of his own behaviour and builds up an attitude to himself derived from his estimates of their attitudes to him. The stage is then set, during the pre-conceptual and intuitive periods, for the first moral feelings. These take the form of a belief in absolute prohibitions and prescriptions, derived from parental orders but somehow enjoying an existence and validity in their own right. Acts are felt to deserve punishment according to how far they depart from what is permitted, without reference to intentions or other mitigating circumstances.

When he reaches the period of concrete

[10] See References (Piaget 1950b, chap. VI; 1953-1954).

operations, the child can form groupings of values, as of other classifications and orderings. He can systematize his values according to their relative priorities and their mutual affinities, so that his evaluations and his motives may be consistent with one another. He can subordinate his actions to future needs, thereby achieving that "decentring" from the present which we call *will*. His addiction to "games with rules," which replace "symbolic games" about this time, shows him to have arrived at a less primitive conception of moral rules. He now sees them as conventions, accepted by a social group for the benefit of all, capable of being changed by common consent, and arising out of mutual respect between equals.

By the end of the formal-operations stage, feelings become "decentred" still further, as they are released from the domination of what is known to be actually true. Motivation and evaluation now depend on *ideals*, and everything tends to be judged by how far it approximates to or falls short of the theoretical states of affairs that would fulfil these ideals. The adolescent views his own activities and plans as part of the total activity of the social group. He begins to think of himself as a fully fledged member of society, free to imitate or criticise adults. With the "decentring" which implants the individual in the community and subordinates his activities to collective goals, the formation of the personality is complete.

CONCLUSIONS

It is evident that Piaget's latest work will not silence his critics altogether. He still does not pay much attention to questions of sampling. Some projects, e.g., Inhelder's on adolescents, seem to have used a large part of the school population of Geneva. The data on the sensori-motor period, on the other hand, come mainly from observation of Piaget's own three children, hardly the children of the Average

Man! But Piaget might well retort, like Kinsey, that such bodies of data, however imperfect, are all we have of comparable density.

Except for some means and mean deviations in his reports of perceptual experiments, he provides few statistics. There are generally no measures of variance, which one suspects must be considerable, no tests of significance, just a categorical statement that at such and such an age children do such and such, with a few specific illustrations. He is not much affected by the growing vogue for rigorous theories, with precise statement of assumptions, derivation of predictions and operational definition of concepts.

Be that as it may, Piaget is, without any doubt, one of the outstanding figures in contemporary psychology, and his contributions will eventually have to be reckoned with much more than they are both in the management of children and in many areas which may not seem directly connected with child psychology. His ideas are closely tied to observation of behaviour, and this makes them the sort of psychology which moves science forward because it is testable by reference to the facts of behaviour. At the same time, it goes beyond the facts just sufficiently to open up new lines of research and to attempt the sort of synthesis which is one of the chief aims of science.

Not the least reason for paying attention to Piaget's work is the relation it bears to trends followed by English-speaking psychologists. At times, his conclusions parallel those reached independently by other investigators; at other times, they serve to correct or supplement what psychologists with other approaches have to say. Like those influenced by Gestalt psychology, Piaget affirms that perceptions and thoughts cannot be understood without reference to the wholes in which they are organized. He disagrees with them in denying that wholes are unanalyzable into component relations and in insisting that the wholes figuring in thought are radically different from those figuring in perception. There are, throughout his writings, many reminders of psychoanalytic concepts—the "omnipotence" and "oceanic feeling" of infancy, "functional pleasure," the formation of the ego and the super-ego, the advance from the pleasure principle to the reality principle. But he makes many detailed criticisms of psychoanalytic theories, and the child as described by him certainly seems tranquil and studious by comparison with the passion-torn "polymorphous pervert" that emerges from Freudian writings.

But Piaget's closest affinities are undoubtedly with the neo-behaviourists. He does not hold with early attempts to explain everything by "conditioned reflexes" or "association." But many of his observations and many aspects of his theory harmonize extremely well with conceptions of learning based on studies of what has come to be called "instrumental" or "operant conditioning." The sequence of more and more complex behaviour patterns which he depicts as outgrowths of simple reflexes and habits parallels Hull's list of progressively more intricate "adaptive behaviour mechanisms," found in animals.[11] And Piaget's view of images and thought operations as "internalized" overt responses approximates very closely to the view prevalent among stimulus-response learning theorists.

One body of work which has grown up in Great Britain and the U.S.A. and which Piaget is eagerly endeavouring to bring into relation with his own findings is that centering on cybernetics, information theory and game theory.[12] But it is to be hoped that other common ground between his psychology and others with different starting-points will be explored. It is certainly high time that the national self-sufficiences which disfigure psychology in contradistinction to other branches of science were left behind.

[11] Hull, C. L.: *A behavior system.* New Haven: Yale University Press, 1952, pp. 347–50.
[12] See Piaget (1953).

REFERENCES

Inhelder, B. Les attitudes expérimentales de l'enfant et de l'adolescent. *Bull. de Psychol.,* 1954, **7,** 272–282.

———, and J. Piaget. *De la logique de l'enfant à la logique de l'adolescent.* Paris: Presses Universitaires, 1955.

Mays, W. Professor Piaget's épistémologie génétique. *Proc. II. Int. Cong. Phil. Sci.,* 1954, **5,** 94–99.

———. How we form concepts. *Sci. News,* 1955, **35,** 11–23.

Piaget, J. Le problème neurologique de l'intériorisation des actions en opérations réversibles. *Arch. Psychol., Genève,* 1949a, **32,** 241–258.

———. *Traité de logique.* Paris: Colin, 1949b.

———. *Introduction à l'épistémologie génétique:* Tome I. *La pensée mathématique.* Tome II. *La pensée physique.* Tome III. *La pensée biologique, La pensée psychologique, La pensée sociologique.* Paris: Presses Universitaires, 1950a.

———. *The psychology of intelligence.* London: Routledge, 1950b.

———. *Play, dreams and imitation in childhood.* London: Heinemann, 1951.

———. Genetic psychology and epistemology. *Diogenes,* 1952, **1,** 49–63.

———. *Logic and psychology.* Manchester: Presses Universitaires, 1953a.

———. *The origin of intelligence in the child.* London: Routledge, 1953b.

———. Structures opérationelles et cybernétique. *Année Psychol.,* 1953c, **53,** 379–388.

———. Les relations entre l'intelligence et l'affectivité dans le développement de l'enfant. *Bull. Psychol., Paris,* 1953–1954, **7,** *passim.*

———. Les lignes générales de l'épistémologie genetique. *Proc. II. Int. Cong. Phil. Sci.,* 1954a, **1,** 26–45.

———. La période des opérations formelles et le passage de la logique de l'enfant à celle de l'adolescent. *Bull. Psychol., Paris,* 1954b, **7,** 247–253.

———. Le développement de la perception de l'enfant à l'adulte. *Bull. Psychol., Paris,* 1954–1955, **8,** *passim.*

———. *The child's construction of reality.* London: Routledge, 1955a.

The Genetic Approach
to the Psychology of Thought

JEAN PIAGET

From a developmental point of view, the essential in the act of thinking is not contemplation—that is to say, that which the Greeks called "theorema"—but the action of the dynamics.

Taking into consideration all that is known, one can distinguish two principal aspects:

1. The formal viewpoint which deals with the configuration of the state of things to know—for instance, most perceptions, mental images, imageries.

2. The *dynamic* aspect, which deals with transformations—for instance, to disconnect a motor in order to understand its functioning, to disassociate and vary the components of a physical phenomenon, to understand its causalities, to isolate the elements of a geometrical figure in order to investigate its properties, etc.

The study of the development of thought shows that the dynamic aspect is at the same time more difficult to attain and more important, because only transformations make us understand the state of things. For instance: when a child of 4 to 6 years transfers a liquid from a large and low glass into a narrow and higher glass, he believes in general that the quantity of the liquid has increased, because he is limited to comparing the initial state (low level) to the final state (high level) without concerning himself with the transformation. Toward 7 or 8 years of age, on the other hand, a child discovers the preservation of the liquid, because he will think in terms of transformation. He will say that nothing has been taken away and nothing added, and, if the

level of the liquid rises, this is due to a loss of width, etc.

The formal aspect of thought makes way, therefore, more and more in the course of the development to its dynamic aspect, until such time when only transformation gives an understanding of things. To think means, above all, to understand; and to understand means to arrive at the transformations, which furnish the reason for the state of things. All development of thought is resumed in the following manner: a construction of operations which stem from actions and a gradual subordination of formal aspects into dynamic aspects.

The operation, properly speaking, which constitutes the terminal point of this evolution is, therefore, to be conceived as an internalized action reversible (example: addition and subtraction, etc.) bound to other operations, which form with it a structured whole and which is characterized by well defined laws of totality (example: the groups, the lattice, etc.). Dynamic totalities are clearly different from the "gestalt" because those are characterized by their nonadditive composition, consequently irreversible.

So defined, the dynamics intervene in the construction of all thought processes; in the structure of forms and classifications, of relations and serialization of correspondences, of numbers, of space and time, of the causality, etc. One could think at first glance that space and geometry add to the formal aspect of thought. In this way one con-

Reprinted with the permission of the publisher from the article of the same title, *Journal of Educational Psychology*, 1961, **52**, 275–281.

ceived of the geometric science in the past, considering it impure mathematics, but applicable to perception and intuition. Modern geometry, since *Le Programme d'Erlangen* by F. Klein, has tended, like all other precise disciplines, to subordinate the formal to the dynamic. The geometries are, indeed, understood today as relying all on groups of transformation, so that one can go from one to the other by characterizing one less general "subgroup" as part of a more inclusive group. Thus geometry too rests on a system of dynamics.

Any action of thought consists of combining thought operations and integrating the objects to be understood into systems of dynamic transformation. The psychological criteria of this is the appearance of the notion of conservation or "invariants of groups." Before speech, at the purely sensory-motor stage of a child from 0 to 18 months, it is possible to observe actions which show evidence of such tendencies. For instance: From 4–5 to 18 months, the baby constructs his first invariant, which is the schema of the permanent object (to recover an object which escaped from the field of perception). He succeeds in this by coordinating the positions and the displacements according to a structure, which can be compared to what the geometricians call "group displacements."

When, with the beginning of the symbolic function (language, symbolic play, imagerie, etc.), the representation through thought becomes possible, it is at first a question of reconstructing in thought what the action is already able to realize. The actions actually do not become transformed immediately into operations, and one has to wait until about 7 to 8 years for the child to reach a functioning level. During this preoperative period the child, therefore, only arrives at incomplete structures characterized by a lack in the notion of combinations and, consequently, by a lack of logic (in transitivity, etc.).

In the realm of causality one can especially observe these diverse forms of pre-causality, which we have previously described in detail. It is true that a certain number of authors—Anglo-Saxon above all—have severely criticized these conclusions, while others have recognized the same facts as we have (animism, etc.). Yet, in an important recent book (which will appear soon) two Canadian authors, M. Laurendeau and A. Pinard, have taken the whole problem up once again by means of thorough statistics. In the main points they have come to a remarkable verification of our views, explaining, moreover, the methodological reasons for the divergencies among the preceding authors.

At about 7 to 8 years the child arrives at his first complete dynamic structures (classes, relations, and numbers), which, however, still remain concrete—in other words, only at the time of a handling of objects (material manipulation or, when possible, directly imagined). It is not before the age of 11 to 12 years or more that operations can be applied to pure hypotheses. At this latter level, a logic of propositions helps complete the concrete structures. This enlarges the structures considerably until their disposition.

The fundamental genetic problem of the psychology of thought is hence to explain the formation of these dynamic structures.

Practically, one would have to rely on three principal factors in order to explain the facts of development: maturation, physical experience, and social interaction. But in this particular case none of these three suffice to furnish us with the desired explanations—not even the three together.

MATURATION. First of all, none of these dynamic structures are innate, but they form very gradually. (For example: The transitivity of equalities is acquired at approximately $6\frac{1}{2}$ to 7 years, and the ability of linear measure comes about only at 9 years, as does the full understanding of weights, etc.) But progressive construction does not seem to depend on maturation, because the achievements hardly correspond to a particular age. Only the order of succession is constant. However, one witnesses innumerable accelerations or retardations for reasons of education (cultural) or acquired experience. Certainly one cannot deny the inevitable role which maturation plays, but is determined above all by existing possibility (or limitation). They still remain to be actualized, which brings about other factors. In addition, in the domain of thought, the factors of innateness seem above all limitative. We do not have, for example, an intuition of space in the fourth dimension; nevertheless we can deduce it.

PHYSICAL EXPERIENCE. Experiencing of objects plays, naturally, a very important role in the establishment of dynamic structures, because the operations originate from actions and the actions bear upon the object. This role manifests itself right from the beginning of sensory-motor explorations, preceding language, and it affirms itself continually in the course of manipulations and activities which are appropriate to the antecedent stages. Necessary as the role of experience may be, it does not sufficiently describe the construction of the dynamic structures—and this for the following three reasons.

First, there exist ideas which cannot possibly be derived from the child's experience —for instance, when one changes the shape of a small ball of clay. The child will declare, at 7 to 8 years, that the quantity of the matter is conserved. It does so before discovering the conservation of weight (9 to 10 years) and that of volume (10 to 11 years). What is the quantity of a matter independently of its weight and its volume? This is an abstract notion corresponding to the "substance" of the pre-Socratic physicists. This notion is neither possible to be perceived nor measurable. It is, therefore, the product of a dynamic deduction and not part of an experience. (The problem would not be solved either by presenting the quantity in the form of a bar of chocolate to be eaten.)

Secondly, the various investigations into the learning of logical structure, which we were able to make at our International Center of Genetic Epistemology, lead to a very unanimous result:[1] one does not "learn" a logical structure as one learns to discover any physical law. For instance, it is easy to bring about the learning of the conservation of weight because of its physical character, but it is difficult to obtain the one of the transitivity of the relationship of the weight:

$$A = C \text{ if } A = B \text{ and } B = C$$

or the one of the relationship of inclusion, etc. The reason for this is that in order to arrive at the learning of a logical structure, one has to build on another more elementary logical (or prelogical) structure. And such structures consequently never stem from experience alone, but suppose always a coordinating activity of the subject.

Thirdly, there exist two types of experiences:

1. The physical experiences show the objects as they are, and the knowledge of them leads to the abstraction directly from the object (example: to discover that a more voluminous matter is more or less heavy than a less voluminous matter).

2. The logicomathematical experience supposes to interrelate by action individual facts into the world of objects, but this refers to the result of these actions rather than to the objects themselves. These interrelations are arrived at by process of abstractions from the actions and their coordinates. For instance, to discover that 10 stones in a line always add up to 10, whether they are counted from left to right or from right to left. Because then the order and the total sum have been presented. The new knowledge consists simply in the discovery that the action of adding a sum is independent of the action of putting them in order. Thus the logicomathematical experience does not stem from the same

[1]See *Etudes d'epistomologie genetique*, Vols. 7 and 10.

type of learning as that of the physical experience, but rather from an equilibration of the scheme of actions, as we will see.

SOCIAL INTERACTION. The educative and social transmission (linguistic, etc.) plays, naturally, an evident role in the formation of dynamic structures, but this factor does not suffice either to entirely explain its development, and this for two reasons:

First, a certain number of structures do not lend themselves to teaching and are prior to all teaching. One can cite, as an example, most concepts of conservation, of which, in general, the pedagogs agree that they are not problematic to the child.

The second, more fundamental, reason is that in order to understand the adult and his language, the child needs means of assimilation which are formed through structures preliminary to the social transmission itself—for instance, an ancient experience has shown us that French-speaking children understand very early the expression *"quelques unes de mes fleurs"* [some of my flowers] in contrast to *"toutes mes fleurs"* [all my flowers], and this occurs when they have not yet constructed the relation of inclusion:

Some A are part of all B;
therefore A < B

In conclusion, it is not exaggerated to maintain that the basic factors invoked before in order to explain mental development do not suffice to explain the formation of the dynamic structures. Though all three of them certainly play a necessary role, they do not constitute in themselves sufficient reason and one has to add to them a fourth factor, which we shall try to describe now.

This fourth factor seems to us to consist of a general progression of equilibration. This factor intervenes, as is to be expected, in the interaction of the preceding factors. Indeed, if the development depends, on one hand, on internal factors (maturation), and on the other hand on external factors (physical or social), it is self-evident that these internal and external factors equilibrate

each other. The question is then to know if we are dealing here only with momentary compromises (unstable equilibrium) or if, on the contrary, this equilibrium becomes more and more stable. This shows that all exchange (mental as well as biological) between the organisms and the milieu (physical and social) as composed of two poles: (*a*) of the *assimilation* of the given external to the previous internal structures, and (*b*) of the *accommodation* of these structures to the given ones. The equilibrium between the assimilation and the accommodation is proportionately more stable than the assimilative structures which are better differentiated and coordinated.

It is this equilibrium between the assimilation and accommodation that seems to explain to us the functioning of the reversible operations. This occurs, for instance, in the realm of notions of conservation where the invariants of groups do not account for the maturation and the physical experience, nor for the sociolingual transmission. In fact, dynamic reversibility is a compensatory system of which the idea of conservation constitutes precisely the result. The equilibrium (between the assimilation and the accommodation) is to be defined as a compensation of exterior disturbances through activities of the subject orientated in the contrary direction of these disturbances. This leads us directly to the reversibility.

Notice that we do not conceive of the idea of equilibrium in the same manner as the "gestalt theory" does, which makes great use of this idea too, but in the sense of an automatical physical equilibrium. We believe, on the contrary, that the mental equilibrium and even the biological one presumes an activity of the subject, or of the organism. It consists in a sort of matching, orientated towards compensation—with even some overcompensation—resulting from strategies of precaution. One knows, for instance, that the homeostasis does not always lead to an exact balance. But it often leads to overcompensation, in response to exterior disturbances. Such is the case in nearly all occurrences except precisely in the case of occurrences of a superior order, which are the operations of reversible intelligence, the reversible logic of which is characterized by a complete and exact compensation (inverted operation).

The idea of equilibrium is so close to the one of reversibility that G. Brunner, in a friendly criticism of one of our latest books appearing in the *British Journal of Psychology,* proposes to renounce the idea of equilibrium because the notion of the reversibility seems sufficient to him. We hesitate to accept this suggestion for the following three reasons:

First, reversibility is a logical idea, while the equilibrium is a causal idea which permits the explanation of reforms by a means of a probabilistic schema. For instance, in order to explain the formation of the idea of conservation, one can distinguish a certain number of successive stages, of which each is characterized by the "strategy" of a progress of compensation. Now it is possible to show[2] that the first of these strategies (only bearing upon one dimension, to the neglect of others) is the most probable at the point of departure, and further, that the second of these strategies (with the emphasis on a second dimension) *becomes* the most likely—as a function of the result of the first. And, finally, that the third of these strategies (oscillation between the observed modifications upon the different dimensions and the discovery of their solidarity) *becomes* the most likely in the functioning of the results of the preceding, etc. From such a point of view the process of equilibration is, therefore, characterized by a sequential control with increasing probabilities. It furnishes a beginning for causal explanations of the reversibility and does not duplicate the former idea.

Secondly, the tendency of equilibrium is much broader for the operation than the

reversibility as such, which leads us to explain the reversibility through the equilibrium and not the reverse. In effect, it is at this level of the obvious regulations and sensory-motor feedbacks that the process of equilibration starts. This in its higher form becomes intelligence. Logical reversibility is therefore conceivable as an end result and not as a beginning and the entire reversibility follows the laws of a semireversibility of various levels.

Thirdly, the tendency to equilibrate does not only explain this final reversibility, but also certain new synthesis between originally distinct operations. One can cite in this regard an example of great importance: the serial of whole numbers. Russell and Whitehead have tried to explain the basic set of numbers through the idea of equivalent classes, without recourse to the serial order. This means that two classes are believed to be equivalent, if one can put their respective elements into a reciprocal arrangement. Only when this relationship relies on the quality of the objects (an A put into relation with an A, a B with a B, etc.) one does not get the quantity. If this relationship is made exclusive of the qualities (an Individual A or B put into relationship with an Individual B or A) then there exists only one way to distinguish the elements from each other. In order not to forget one, or not to count the same twice, one must deal with them in succession and introduce the serial factor as well as the structure of classes. We may then say, psychologically speaking, that the sequence of whole numbers is synthesis between two groupings qualitatively distinct, the fitting of the classes and serialization, and that this synthesis takes place as soon as one excludes the qualities of the elements in question. But how does this synthesis occur? Precisely by a gradual process of equilibration.

On the one hand the child who develops his ideas from numbers is in possession of structures enabling him to fit them into classes (classifications). But if he wants to be exclusive of qualities in order to answer

[2]*Logique et equilibre* (Vol. 2 of *Etudes d'epistomologie genetique*).

to the question "how many," he becomes unable to distinguish the elements. The disequilibrium which appears, therefore, obliges the child to resort to the idea of order and take recourse to arranging these elements into a lineal row. On the other hand, if the child arranges the elements as 1, 1, 1, etc., how would he know, for instance, how to distinguish the second from the third? This new disequilibrium brings him back to the idea of classification: The "second" is the element which has but one predecessor, and the "third" is one that has two of them. In short, every new problem provokes a disequilibrium (recognizable through types of dominant errors) the solution of which consists in a re-equilibration, which brings about a new original synthe-sis of two systems, up to the point of independence.

During the discussion of my theories, Brunner has said that I have called dis-equilibrium what others describe as motiva-tion. This is perfectly true, but the advan-tage of this language is to clarify that a cognitive or dynamic structure is never independent of motivational factors. The motivation in return is always solidary to structural (therefore cognitive) determined level. The language of the equilibrium pre-sents that activity, that permits us to reunite into one and the same totality those two aspects of behavior which always have a functional solidarity because there exists no structure (cognition) without an ener-gizer (motivation) and vice versa.

The Development of Meaning in Children's Descriptive Terms

SUSAN M. ERVIN-TRIPP

GARRETT FOSTER

Children frequently confuse the names for physical dimensions. If two objects differ in size, they may say one is STRONGER than the other. If they differ in weight, one may be called BIGGER than the other. This is, of course, just what one would expect in the early stages of learning if size, weight, and strength are empirically correlated.

Osgood, Suci, and Tannenbaum (1957) have found correlations of a similar sort in examining the structure of meanings meas-ured by semantic differential scales. Three factors have been found repeatedly—Eval-uation, Potency, and Activity. Little atten-tion has been given to the development or origin of these factors. Inspection of the scales defining each factor suggests that two conditions would create correlations. One is verbal conjunction; if whatever is said to be GOOD is also said to be FAIR the scales will be correlated through verbal associations. Secondly, "ecological covariation" (Bruns-wik, 1947) exists for certain sensory dimen-sions. We would thus expect BIG, HEAVY, and STRONG to be correlated for all cultural groups.

It is clear that adults can discriminate the sensory dimensions that children con-fuse verbally. On the semantic differential, however, they are normally asked to extend terms metaphorically, as in judging the size and weight of FREE PRESS or EDUCATION.

Reprinted with the permission of the authors and the publisher from the article of the same title, *Journal of Abnormal and Social Psychol-ogy*, 1960, **61**, 271–275.

Even on the semantic differential, the correlation of size and weight scales can be destroyed by inclusion of items like DIAMOND and MIST where a check with sense experience is possible and the usual trait correlation is reversed. To the extent that the semantic differential reflects covariation in experience of traits that are logically independent, we would expect that there would be an increase with age in denotative discrimination of the terms that are correlated on the differential. In the following study, age changes in children's verbal confusions are examined.

The more highly correlated two attributes are, the less probable are encounters with discrepant instances. It is useful to note three different variants on this situation. One category may constitute a subclass of a larger category. Thus, if 98 per cent of a child's encounters with men, in which there is direct address or verbal reference to a man, involve his father, we would expect that the child might at first call all adult males DADDY. Discrepant instances would at first be too few for a differentiation to take place. If there were two adult males in the family such an extension would be unlikely. Thus Leopold (1939) noted that while his daughter called all men PAPA, women had individual names and there was no word for FRAU.

The subclass of a hierarchy of classes is actually an extreme instance of the second variant of correlation, a partial overlap of two classes. The degree of correlation or overlap should predict the probability of two terms being confused. Thus, communism and atheism might be confused by those unaware of discrepancies such as religious communist settlements. From a matrix showing the probability of being right in applying the term COMMUNIST to an atheist, we can see that the higher the correlation of the two terms, the greater the probability of being right, and the greater the likelihood that the two ideologies are called by one term. There are other features that enter into the failure to differentiate terms. One is the relative size of the

two categories. If there are more atheists than communists, one is more likely to be wrong in calling an atheist a COMMUNIST than calling a communist an ATHEIST. The extreme case would be that in which the whole size of the class of communists is equal to the overlapping class. That is, for example, all communists are atheists but the reverse is not true. This case is identical with the one cited earlier of hierarchical classes. Other relevant factors are the perceptibility of an attribute or class, the consequences of correct and incorrect class discrimination (which may not be the same for the classes involved), the frequency of the terms in usage, and degree of logical independence.

If the dimensions of reference are continuous attributes rather than classes, then the relation may be described by a scatterplot rather than a matrix of frequencies. The same observations apply; the probability of being correct in saying that a bigger object is HEAVIER is a function of the attribute correlations.

In adult speakers of English, the differentiation of the attributes weight, size, and strength is such that if speakers can make appropriate tests, they are unlikely to say that the heavier of two like-sized objects is BIGGER. There are, however, situations in which the attribute extension in this simple physical case is appropriate. One is in the situation of prediction, where a value on one attribute only is known. Then it becomes useful to be able to predict the probable value on the other attribute. The second situation is one in which metaphor is exploited in verbal or pictorial communication, and one attribute may be used to suggest another.

Thus, we would expect that correlated attributes would appear in experienced speakers' usage, in situations of prediction and metaphorical extension, but not in denotation where the evidence for attribute discrimination is available.

In new learners, however, one term may apply to both attributes, which are not in fact discriminated, or both terms may appear as interchangeable synonyms for the two undiscriminated attributes.

In the following study two semantic differential factors, Evaluation and Potency, are presented as far as possible in conditions requiring denotative discrimination of three attribute expressions of each. A reduction with age is predicted with respect to the use of the wrong terms when a difference in only one attribute of the correlated set is present.

METHOD

SUBJECTS. There were two groups of Ss, a group of 16 male and 17 female first grade children, and a group of 18 male and 18 female sixth graders. Both groups were from the same school in a lower socioeconomic Negro district. To reduce variability, the extremely bright and extremely dull children were excluded, the criterion being the teacher's rating in the first grade, and deviations of 20 points from the norm on available IQ tests in the sixth grade.

MATERIALS. In Part I of the experiment, materials were selected to vary successively three of the dimensions on Osgood's potency factor. These three dimensions—weight, strength, and size—had been found to have loadings of .62 with the rotated factor analysis, involving concepts rated against scales, and coordinates of 1.68, 1.81, and 1.76, respectively, on another analysis of scales judged against scales. These were the largest components of the factor in each case.

The objects used were: (*a*) opaque salt shakers identical but for weight, (*b*) opaque jars identical but for weight, (*c*) cork balls differing in size, (*d*) sterofoam balls differing in size, (*e*) a pair of insulated wires with the wire removed from the middle third of one, leaving it flexible, and (*f*) a dry sponge and a damp one matched in size.

In Part II drawings of a girl's face were used to represent three of four dimensions representing Osgood's evaluative factor. The pictured dimensions were CLEAN-DIRTY, HAPPY-SAD, and PRETTY-UGLY. A fourth was included in the questioning: GOOD-BAD. These had loadings, respectively, of .82, .76, .86 (BEAUTIFUL-UGLY), and .88, and coordinates of 2.38, 2.09, 2.40, 2.29 on the first factor.

PROCEDURE. All of the Ss were individually tested with the following questions:

I would like to ask you some questions and you can give me the correct answers. . . OK? [For first graders:] It's kind of a game and lots of fun. First I'm going to ask about these objects. [2 objects contrasting in weight put in subject's hands.] Is one of these heavier and one lighter or are they both the same weight? [If says different] Which is heavier? Is one black and one white or are they both the same color? Is one bigger and one smaller or are they both the same size? [If says different] Which is bigger? Is one stronger and one weaker or are they both the same strength? [If says different] Which is stronger?

If the child failed to indicate the item that was heavier on the first question, he was eliminated from the rest of Part I. The second question, to which the answer was "the same" was to control set. A similar series of questions was asked about all the items, starting with the actual contrast as a screening question. One of the six possible key questions was omitted, concerning perception of weight in objects differing in size. If weight in the objects were controlled, the smaller object might be called heavier on the grounds of its scale weight. Because of the ambiguity of the term HEAVY applied to objects differing in size, the question was omitted.

In the analysis the percentages were computed over the whole set of responses, which included two for each question for each child because of the double set of materials. The Ns used in the significance tests were for the actual number of children tested.

In Part II a similar procedure was followed, with the control question "Does one picture have red hair and one black hair or are they both the same?" The questions and pictures were rotated, with every fourth question a control question.

RESULTS

In Table 7-1 it can be seen that between 39 and 66 per cent of the first-grade children offered contaminated responses for the various dimensions of the physical materials. In the sixth grade the proportion was reduced to a range between 21 and 44 per cent. While none of the individual changes in percentage was significant, there was a reduction for every comparison, including

TABLE 7-1

Proportion Ascribing Correlated Attribute Differences to Objects

Stimulus differences	Response	First grade			Sixth grade			
		Boys	Girls	Total	Boys	Girls	Total	Differences
Heavy	BIG	40.6	36.0 [a]	38.6 [a]	16.7	25.0	20.8	17.8
Strong	BIG	31.2	52.0	39.7	30.6	25.0	27.8	11.9
Strong	HEAVY	37.5	46.2	41.4	33.3	33.3	33.3	8.0
Big	STRONG	50.0	53.8	51.7	36.1	38.9	37.5	14.2
Heavy	STRONG	56.2	76.9	65.5	41.7	47.2	44.4	21.1
	N [b]	16	13	28	18	18	36	

[a] The number of cases in this cell is reduced by one due to loss of data.

[b] The Ss reported were those who correctly differentiated the stimulus attribute for all three attributes on all materials.

the subgroups by sex. A sign test is significant at the .01 level. The dimension that changes the least is the response that the heavier object is STRONGER; this is also the statement of highest frequency at both ages for both sexes. Since strength is less evident than weight, it is possible that this particular inference would continue in adult Ss. The inference that a bigger object is STRONGER is next in probability, supporting the notion that it is the inferred character of strength that is involved. Size is least often presented as a contaminated response, and it is also the most obvious.

It might be thought that the reduction in the sixth grade is due to a tendency to be more careful about differentiating at all, and thus to an increase in *same* responses. This was not the case. While the percentage of reversals was relatively low, it increased in the sixth grade. This increase occurred in stating that the heavier was SMALLER, that the stronger was SMALLER and LIGHTER. In the latter case these frequencies probably arise because a wet sponge is usually larger, and contains water. Only boys gave the last reversal, 22 per cent of the boys in the sixth grade saying the stronger was LIGHTER, and no girls. Nine percent of the boys and 28 per cent of the girls said the stronger was SMALLER. In the last case this was a larger proportion than those saying it was larger. It might be argued, then, that the reduction in the last two cases was due to sophistication with respect to one of the objects used.

On the study of the evaluative dimension using faces, almost no reversals occurred at either age. The age differences on Table 7-2 are striking. It may be noted that they do not occur markedly on three cases. Two of these refer to CLEAN. The frequency of children saying one child was CLEANER than the other for the other attributes was small at both ages. Clean may be said to be the most visible of the attributes. In fact it could be argued that it is the only one with a clear-cut physical criterion.

The third instance of lack of marked change was one in which the proportions were very high at both ages. The smiling face was said to be PRETTIER.

With the CLEANER dimension excluded, the range in the first grade is between 42 and 97 per cent offering a contaminated response. The highest are those offering the smiling face as more GOOD and the cleaner face as PRETTIER. All of the first grade boys gave these responses. In the sixth grade the range is between 14 and 75 per cent with the highest now being the smiling face which is seen as PRETTIER about as often as it was in the first grade. Thus, there is a shift in responses as with the physical attributes, but it is markedly different for the different attributes.

DISCUSSION

The slight rate of change with respect to discrimination of physical dimensions suggests the kind of learning to be expected where the criteria are most obvious.

With the personal attributes the findings are both more extreme and more uneven. It is clear that the only term of those used which designates a simple visible trait—CLEAN—is the one seldom offered to describe any other attribute. This finding agrees with the fact that BIG, the most obvious physical attribute, was less often used with the physical materials to describe other differences.

The other evaluative dimensions refer to more complex traits that are not entirely logically independent. PRETTY may also be said to designate a physical characteristic, but one that adults use both as a constant and a temporary trait, so that a clean smiling face might be deemed prettier than a dirty or frowning one. Thus, while the traits are discriminable they are not independent in the sense that the physical traits are.

HAPPY was used to designate a smiling face, but as children learn the use of the term they may find that it refers to a state of feeling only partially correlated with

TABLE 7-2

Proportion Ascribing Correlated Attribute Differences to Faces

Stimulus differences	Response	First grade			Sixth grade			Differences
		Boys	Girls	Total	Boys	Girls	Total	
Happy	CLEAN	12.5	5.9	9.1	0.0	11.1	5.6	3.5
Pretty	CLEAN	28.6	7.7	18.5	5.6	5.6	5.6	12.9
Clean	HAPPY	37.5	47.0	42.4	5.6	22.2	13.9	28.5°
Pretty	HAPPY	85.7	91.7	88.5	67.1	38.9	50.0	38.5°
Clean	PRETTY	100.0	82.4	90.9	50.0	50.0	50.0	40.9°
Happy	PRETTY	81.2	82.4	81.8	83.3	66.7	75.0	6.8°
Clean	GOOD	50.0	70.6	60.6	27.8	33.3	30.6	30.0°
Happy	GOOD	100.0	94.1	97.0	77.8	55.6	66.7	30.3°
Pretty	GOOD	78.6	50.0	65.4	44.4	22.2	33.3	32.0°
N[a]		16	17	33	18	18	36	

[a] Changes in N due to failure to name stimulus difference correctly: first-grade boys for PRETTY stimulus 14, girls 12; sixth-grade boys, 17, and girls, 16.
° Significant at the .01 level.

external evidence. Thus even the smiling–nonsmiling distinction might bear only an imperfect relation to the term HAPPY. One of the largest changes was in the use of HAPPY in describing the prettier girl, and the drop was most extreme in girls—a drop of 53 per cent. The children were from the start, especially the boys, only moderately likely to describe the cleaner girl as HAPPIER.

One possible reason for a drop in the ascription of terms to a correlated difference is a change in metaphorical treatment of pictures. Occasionally children would refuse to say that both children were the same in hair color, but said that one had red and one black hair. The hair in the drawing was white, that is, not filled in in the black-and-white outline picture. Younger children, used to story-book imagination, may be less literal about what is on the page. While this might account for the increase in *same* responses with age, it does not predict the direction of the ascription, by the first graders, which was in no case in the opposite direction from that predicted.

Does the failure to differentiate on this test imply that the children use the terms as virtual synonyms for an undifferentiated referent? With respect to the physical dimensions, only one child was so extreme as to use the same terms interchangeably for all three attributes on all the materials. But if we examine the faces test and omit CLEAN which seems to fall out of the pattern, it appears that 62 per cent of the children used HAPPY-GOOD-PRETTY synonymously, in the first grade.

We would like to argue that the factors that appear as clusters of correlated terms in the semantic differential studies of adults derive from empirical correlations of attributes. They could, of course, be linked purely by verbal associations, as in "He's a good clean player." If this were the case, differentiation of reference might still be accompanied by semantic differential correlations, since many of the terms on the semantic differential can be applied to the

"concept" only metaphorically. DEMOCRACY is clean, fragrant, and sweet only in the poetic sense.

While verbal associations may be one source of such dimensions, we are proposing that the history of concept development in the child provides another source. What remains as a connotative, metaphorical relationship in adults may in many cases start as denotative nondifferentiation. In a sense, the child might be said to acquire first a concept, for instance, of "big-strong-heavy . . ." in other words, a potency referent. The terms he applies to this referent may variously be BIG, STRONG, HEAVY. He may prefer one of these terms for people, another for boats, another for baseballs. Presumably he will only come to differentiate the terms and apply them appropriately to different stimulus dimensions when uncorrelated instances occur and he is corrected, or hears others differentiate the terms. By chance, the sample he selects may have a 100 per cent correlation and he may not encounter errors immediately.

SUMMARY

The physical dimensions of size, weight, and strength are empirically correlated. If the correlation delays discrimination of these attributes as referents for descriptive terms, then younger children should more often use incorrect terms to describe differences between objects. The terms GOOD, PRETTY, CLEAN, and HAPPY should also be used as synonyms prior to differentiation.

A set of materials was prepared in which size, weight, and strength were independently varied in pairs of objects. First-grade children more often than sixth graders said that the pairs of objects differed on other dimensions in addition to the attribute actually contrasted. In a set of pictures of faces, over half of the youngest children treated GOOD, PRETTY, and HAPPY as interchangeable synonyms. The proportion dropped markedly with age.

The more easily identified traits, such as the referents of BIG and CLEAN, were least often confused with other attributes.

The results are interpreted as showing that attributes which have metaphorical and connotative links in adult usage, may be denotatively confused at first. The factors found by Osgood on the semantic differential studies of verbal meaning may actually be the referents for several terms used as synonyms, prior to differentiation of finer distinctions between attributes.

REFERENCES

Brunswik, E. *Systematic and representative design of psychological experiments.* Berkeley: University of California Press, 1947.

Leopold, W. F. *The speech development of a bilingual child.* Evanston, Ill.: Northwestern University Press, 1939–1950.

Osgood, C. E., G. J. Suci, and P. H. Tannenbaum. *The measurement of meaning.* Urbana: University of Illinois Press, 1957.

The Development of Double Function Terms in Children: An Exploratory Investigation

SOLOMON E. ASCH

HARRIET NERLOVE

Most, probably all, of the terms that describe psychological activities or the properties of persons also describe the properties and activities of things. Words such as *hard, deep, bright* are obvious examples; we will call them "double-function" terms since they refer jointly to physical and psychological data. Their presence in speech is far from coincidental or occasional; a previous study (Asch, 1955, 1958) has demonstrated that languages belonging to different families possess such terms, and that the languages agree significantly in the meanings assigned to them.

Such double-function terms are important for several reasons. They promise to clarify the cognition of psychological events, and its relation to the cognition of physical events. They are also an elementary instance of metaphorical thinking, which is essential to the understanding of language.

The purpose of this investigation was to trace the development of the use and understanding of double function terms in children, as they improve in the mastery of their native tongue. The children were

Reprinted with the permission of the senior author and the publisher from the article of the same title in B. Kaplan and S. Wapner (Eds.), *Perspectives in Psychological Theory: Essays in Honor of Heinz Werner.* New York: International Universities Press, 1960, pp. 47–60.

English-speaking. Our aim was exploratory rather than definitive; we will formulate the relevant problems, the developmental trends we were able to observe, and some questions that await further study.

The historical evidence often fails to show how the double reference accrued to a given term—whether the physical or psychological reference came first, or whether both were present jointly from the start. But to judge by the available evidence, the extension of terms is a frequent occurrence; and probably many terms, particularly those that designate ubiquitous properties in the environment, referred first to the physical domain. Of this, however, we can be relatively certain: when a term that has exclusively referred to one region, say, the physical, is first "extended" to the other, this is the consequence of a directly experienced similarity between the respective data. Whoever first called a person *brittle* was at the time sensing a resemblance between a property of certain objects and of a certain way of acting. This is another way of saying that double-function terms are distinct from homonyms or homophones.

One can, however, establish more directly the course of this development in the individual. This was the aim of the present study: to observe whether children mastered double-function terms first in their physical or psychological sense, or simultaneously in both. Accordingly, we attempted to observe the earliest usages of these terms and the changes they undergo subsequently. We were particularly concerned to establish how children understood the nexus between the physical and psychological meanings, and whether the awareness of duality coincided with dual usage.

(It was not our intention in this genetic study to throw light on the historical problem mentioned earlier. The questions are indeed different; one has only to consider that the child is engaged in mastering a relatively completed product, of whose past he has no inkling.)

THE EXPERIMENT

To trace this development it is necessary to establish the meanings of the terms in question at different ages. This we undertook to do with five groups of children, ranging in age from three to twelve years. The most direct procedure would have been to observe and record the natural flow of speech; we followed a more controlled design, questioning the children directly about a limited set of terms. There were ten children in each of the age groups studied. It was not our intention in this first study to establish norms or a scale but rather to seek a trend; for this purpose the small number of children was adequate. Since the particulars of observation and recording varied according to age, they will be described separately in connection with the findings for each group.

The Three- to Four-Year Group

The youngest group, consisting of six boys and four girls, ranged between 3:1 and 4:11. The children, who were from predominantly upper middle-class homes, attended a nursery school in Swarthmore. Specific information concerning mental level was not available, but they were at least of normal intelligence.

The observations were made in a nursery school room set aside for the purpose. The experimenter (who was somewhat known, having previously visited the playground) met each child individually and invited him to play a game of words. In the course of the game the experimenter displayed a number of familiar objects, each of which illustrated a particular physical property. (Among these objects were a cube of sugar, iced water, hot water, a wooden block, a gold-colored metal disk, a branch, a powder puff and a cylinder.) The properties on which we centered were: *sweet, hard, cold, soft, bright, deep, warm,* and *crooked.* The child was shown each object in turn; after some discussion the experimenter mentioned one of the words, asking the child to pick an object that the word named. He was then asked to name a few other objects that the term described, to ascertain whether he had a firm grasp of the physical meaning. If he had (not every child knew the physical meaning of each term), he was asked whether the term could describe persons. This involved a series of questions phrased as follows: "Are people, too, *sweet?*" Do you know any *sweet* people? How do you know they are *sweet?* What do they do or say when they are *sweet?*" Since the discussion could become lengthy and trying, each child was questioned on one half of the list, but each was asked about the term *sweet.*

The results can be summarized as follows:

1. Most of the double-function terms were known only in relation to physical objects. The children readily called blocks and boxes *hard,* milk *cold,* water *deep,* and trees *crooked.*

2. In the few instances in which the terms were used to describe persons, the reference was most often to *physical* properties of persons. In explaining how they knew that a person had a given quality, the children gave such replies as: "Poor people are *cold* because they have no clothes"; "Daddy and Mommy are *deep* because they look big"; "Santa Claus is *warm* because he has a long beard"; "If there were gold people, they would be *bright.*"

3. *Sweet* was the only word applied to persons in a sense other than physical. Seven of the ten children applied it to persons, and all of them did so to mean generally "good," "nice," "likable."

4. Several of the children were surprised and indignant at the suggestion that some of the terms could be used to describe

persons: "No people are *cold!*" "I never heard of *deep* people anyway!" This strong denial of applicability disappeared in the older groups.

The Five- to Six-Year Group

The children, six girls and four boys, ranging in age from 5:10 to 6:1, attended the kindergarten of the Swarthmore public school.

Since we could rely at this age on a knowledge of the terms, the objects employed with the younger group were discarded. The experimenter mentioned one of the terms, asking the child to name an object to which it applied; all were able to do this. Thereupon they were asked whether the term could also apply to persons (e.g., "Are people *soft?* Do you know any *soft* people? How can you tell if someone is *soft?* What does a *soft* person do?"). If a child used the term in the psychological sense, we proceeded to question him further about its relation to the physical meaning (e.g., "Why do we call sugar *sweet,* and kind, nice people *sweet?*"). Each child was questioned about all eight terms.

1. As with the three-to-four-year-olds, these children understood and used the terms mainly in their object reference.

2. When they applied the terms to persons they did so predominantly in their physical sense, as did the younger children.

3. There were only ten instances (out of a possible eighty) in which a term was used to describe a psychological property. Five of these occurred for *sweet,* which continued to stand for what is generally good ("Debby is a *sweet* girl because she is nice." "*Sweet* people are nice; they play with you and give you candy."). The psychological sense of a few other terms began to appear at this stage: *hard* and *soft* each occurred twice, and *bright* once. The terms

tended to have a strongly affective charge; *hard* was described as "bad," *soft* as "kind."

4. In only a small proportion of the few cases in which the terms appeared with a psychological reference, could the children suggest a basis for the double function. When they did so, the explanations were also in global, affective terms ("Nice people and sugar are both *sweet* because we like both of them.").

5. At this age we introduced a further step, questioning the children about the homonym, *ring*. They were asked to suggest why the same word named jewelry worn on the finger and the sound of the telephone. This question, which was also put to all later groups, was included in order to check whether the children would distinguish between homonyms and double-function terms. Eight children disclaimed any similarity; one invented a similarity, suggesting that both might be black. One child proposed that the similarity resided in the name.

From this point on, the step referring to the object sense of the terms was omitted. The children were asked to give examples of the application of each term to persons; when they did so, they were to describe the meaning. They were then questioned about the relation between the object and person meanings. If they gave evidence of understanding the double function, we inquired whether they knew or had thought of this relation earlier.

The Seven- to Eight-Year Group

The children were five boys and five girls, ranging in age from 7:6 to 8:0, all pupils in the second grade of the Swarthmore public school.

1. This group showed evidence of a great increase in the use and understanding of the psychological sense of the terms. They showed an adequate understanding

in forty-seven (out of a possible eighty) cases. ("*Hard* people are tough and soldier-like"; "*Soft* people are gentle and nice"; "*Soft* people are weak and don't fight"; "*Bright* people are cheerful and friendly"; "*Crooked* people do bad things.")

2. Although they frequently understood the application of the terms to persons, the children had great difficulty in formulating a connection with the physical meanings. A very few came up with more or less adequate formulations: rocks and *hard* people are alike in that "they don't move easily," or "you can't get into the main thing in them"; or, pillows and *soft* people both "give to the touch," "both are comfortable." Most of the children could think of no reason why the same word had two meanings, and several suggested that there was no similarity: "They are two different kinds of *deep*"; "Ice cubes and people are a lot different" (referring to *cold*). These children have moved from a rejection of the psychological applicability of the terms to not acknowledging a relation between the several meanings.

3. The children rarely reported having thought about the double function. They could not explain the homonym *ring*, although a few tried to force a similarity.

The Nine- to Ten-Year Group

These were four girls and six boys, age 9:3 to 10:0, in the fourth grade of the Swarthmore public school.

They showed a further marked increase in comprehension of the psychological meanings. Five children adequately understood each of the eight terms. There was an equally strong increase in ability to state the dual function. "The sun and *bright* (gay) people are both beaming, both look happy"; "*Soft* things and *soft* people are both easy to reach, are not remote"; "Neither *crooked* people nor *crooked* things are upright, straight"; "*Hard* things and *hard* people are alike in that neither of them break." There was no evidence that they had been aware in the past of the double function.

The Eleven- to Twelve-Year Group

These were sixth-grade children, five boys and five girls, ranging in age from 10:11 to 12:1.

Their understanding of the psychological meanings was not much more advanced than that of the preceding group. But this age group showed a noticeable advance in the comprehension of the dual function. This is evident in the cogency of their comments: "*Hard* things and *hard* people are both unmanageable." "*Bright* things and *bright* people are alike in that they are both outstanding, you notice them first." "*Crooked* things and *crooked* people are roundabout and may be dangerous." The ability to state the relation does not keep pace with the understanding of the terms, but the progress in this direction is striking. We also noted a change when the children responded inadequately. Rather than employ the terms to denote physical properties of persons, they erred by assigning faulty psychological meanings to them: "A *deep* person is gruff and abrupt"; "A *cold* person is independent."

There were few reports of having earlier thought about the dual meanings, surely no more than in the younger groups. But the distinguishing feature of these children was their interest in the questions and in the general subject of the investigation. Many were completely fascinated by the problem and often turned from the consideration of one term to another with great reluctance.

The results for the several age groups are summarized in Tables 7-3 and 7-4. Table 7-3 contains the frequencies with which the terms were correctly employed to name psychological qualities of persons;

TABLE 7-3

Frequencies of Psychological Meanings

Age	Number of words									Total	Percentage
	0	1	2	3	4	5	6	7	8		
3–4	3	7								7	—
5–6	4	3	2	1						10	13
7–8			2	1	2		3	2		47	59
9				1		2	2	1	5	72	90
11							1	1	8	77	96

TABLE 7-4

Frequencies of Comprehension of the Dual Relation

Age	Number of words									Total	Percentage
	0	1	2	3	4	5	6	7	8		
3–4										—	—
5–6	7	2	1							4	40
7–8	2	3	2	2	1					17	36
9	2	1	1	2	1	1	1		1	32	44
11		1		2	2	2	3		1	62	81

the last column gives the mean frequencies in percentages. Excepting the three- to four-year group, for which the observations were more limited than for the others, there is a marked increase at each age up to nine. (The lack of substantial increase between the ages of nine and eleven need have no general significance; it may only reflect the ease of the particular terms that were studied.) Table 7-4 gives the frequencies with which each age group adequately explained the relation between the physical and psychological meanings. The percentage values of the last column were obtained by dividing the totals at each age by the corresponding totals of Table 7-3; they thus give us the proportion between the comprehension of the double meaning and the comprehension of their relation. (a) There was a continuous increase at each age level, which corresponds in general to the increases of Table 7-3. (b) As was to be expected, understanding of the dual relation lagged behind knowledge of the dual meanings. (c) Most noteworthy, though, is the lack of detailed parallelism between the age changes recorded in Tables 7-3 and 7-4 (see last columns). Up to and including the age of nine, the relative frequency with which the double function was understood remained appreciably constant; a marked change is observable only at the age of eleven, in clear contrast to the rate of growth of the psychological meanings.

DISCUSSION

We found the following trends in the course of the preceding observations: (1) Children first master the object reference of double-function terms. (2) They acquire the psychological sense of these terms later, and then apparently as a separate meaning, as if in independence of the object reference the term already possesses. (3) The dual property of the terms is realized last, and then not spontaneously as a rule.

How are we to account for the first finding, namely, the prior mastery of the object reference of such terms? One might propose that this is a direct effect of teaching, since adults are far more likely to call the child's attention to these properties in things; for example, children are more often warned to avoid *sharp* or *cold* things than persons. Although the effect of such teaching should not be ignored, it is not convincing as a complete explanation. One should also consider the possibility that the physical properties in question are less complex than the corresponding psychological properties. A term such as *deep* organizes a more inclusive and intricate set of events in persons than in things. It is not as easily isolable from the flux of accompanying events, and may on this account be more difficult to name. Here we must guard against a misunderstanding. The failure to use or understand a term is not evidence of failure to have the corresponding experience. It would indeed be strange to hold that children are insensitive to a person's properties such as *warm* or *cold* on the ground that they have not yet included them in their speech. This comment suggests that the present finding is part of a larger problem, which concerns the conditions that determine the naming of experiences, and particularly those pertaining to persons.

The striking finding is not that psychological meanings appear later in development, but that they are initially divorced from the corresponding object reference. The acquisition of psychological meanings does not, it appears, make contact with the physical meaning that the terms already possess. Taken at face value, this result signifies that, for the child, double-function terms are initially homonyms, and that only later he reaches a stage when he can discern the relation between them.

Instances of failure to experience the identity of a term occurring in systematically different contexts are by no means rare. A proper name, say *Robert*, is imbued with the character of its bearer to such a degree that it seems not to be the same name when it identifies a different person. Homonyms generally are excellent examples of this effect. They illustrate the role of context as a segregating condition, or the strength of part-whole determination. Stated differently, the perceived identity of a term is a function of its phonetic and contextual properties; apparently the constancy of the former does not suffice to preserve identity against variations of the latter. But the double-function terms are, unlike the preceding examples, not only phonetically identical but also similar in meaning when they occur in different contexts. To be sure, adults too are most often not aware of these relations, but once their attention is called to it, they are quite capable, as were the older children in this study, of realizing and explaining them. The younger children, however, most often failed and at times firmly rejected the relation. The segregation of the dual meanings is much stronger at earlier stages of development, as if the name were less a conventional symbol and more an indelible part of the thing itself.

It is surprising to find so little evidence for the role of similarity in the process of acquisition. When the child first hears or uses a term such as *hard* to refer to a person, he already possesses its physical meaning, yet apparently he does not recall it at this point. Does this weakness or absence of the similarity function imply that the child would continue to make equally good progress in mastering the language if he had to learn that *hard* meant gentleness in persons, or that it does not matter whether the dual meanings are compatible or incompatible?

The evidence compels us to say that the similarity relation responsible for the emergence of double-function terms in the growth of a language is not active in children's acquisition of these terms. In this respect individual mastery follows a course fundamentally different from the history of the language. In one sense this is not surprising, since the child masters the language of his community, as he does other cultural

products, without knowledge of their past. Therefore he does not necessarily "recapitulate" the history of the language, and the genetic study does not directly clarify the historical question mentioned earlier.

The question may be raised whether the children were perhaps aware of the relations between the dual meanings, but were unable to formulate them for the experimenter. We did not find this a problem, and believe that it did not significantly affect the trend of the observations. At no point did we have the sense that the children were struggling unsuccessfully to express what they knew. A related question concerns the adequacy with which the utterances of the children were categorized or interpreted. For the most part the decisions to be made were straightforward. When a ten-year-old says that a *hard* person is "stubborn, rough, doesn't give in" we know that he has the psychological sense of the term; when the same child says that rocks and persons are *hard* because neither "can be broken into, you can't get into the main thing in them," it seems fairly certain that he has grasped the similarity. Other statements were more difficult to decide. Let us take a nine-year-old who says that *warm* persons are "kind and nice." This formulation was considered adequate; it is overgeneral but well in line with the term's meaning. This child also stated, when attempting to explain the dual meaning, that *warm* things and people keep one warm, adding that the latter do so by hugging and talking. We were not certain whether the child spoke of the same thermal property in persons as in things; this answer was rejected as inadequate. Such uncertainties as arose would have to be resolved if one were concerned with establishing a scale, but they did not appreciably influence the trends that were observed.

The data give evidence of a clear trend, but they do not tell of the detailed steps responsible for the changes. We need to understand the conditions responsible for the transition from the exclusively physical usage, and for the time lag between the presence of dual meanings and the comprehension of their relations. Some observations we made are pertinent to the first question. We saw that at the five- to six-year level children apply the terms to persons in their physical reference. For example, a child explains that her mother is *warm* "because mommy kissed me right here [pointing to her cheek] and made it real warm," or that *warm* people are "warm inside," or that they make you feel warm." Statements of this kind raise the question whether this step serves as a bridge to the later, distinctively psychological usage, or whether the physical usage has to be superseded if the progress we have described is to occur. Assertions such as that *warm* people are kind because "people usually feel warm if they are kind," provide a bare hint that the bridging procedure may be operative.

Other utterances of the younger children point to a process that has not yet been mentioned. Three- and four-year-olds sometimes said of particular persons that they are *sweet* because they like sweet things, or *soft* because they like soft things. One five-year-old stated that "mommy is *sweet* because she cooks sweet things." These observations, if confirmed, would be evidence of an important effect of contact. It might appear that we have an instance of association by contiguity, but more is involved. Contiguity is a necessary condition for this effect, but most noteworthy is the apparent migration of a quality from thing to person.

SUMMARY

Children's mastery of double-function terms, or terms that name properties of persons and things, shows a regular development with age. Children first use the terms in their reference to objects. When they begin to apply the terms to the psychological properties of persons, they do not realize the relation to the physical reference. Recognition of the double function is last to appear and, as far as we were able to observe, does not occur spontaneously within the age groups studied. In this respect the course of individual development departs from the historical development of the language.

The processes responsible for the trends here observed await further investigation. Such investigation would throw light on the development of cognition of persons.

REFERENCES

Asch, S. On the use of metaphor in the description of persons. In H. Werner (Ed.), *On expressive language*. Worcester, Mass.: Clark University Press, 1955. Pp. 29–38.

————. The metaphor: A psychological inquiry. In R. Tagiuri and L. Petrullo (Eds.), *Person perception and interpersonal behavior*. Stanford, Calif.: Stanford University Press, 1958. Pp. 86–94.

Development of Word Meaning through Verbal Context: An Experimental Study

HEINZ WERNER

EDITH KAPLAN

A. THE TEST

In the main, a child learns the meaning of a word in two ways. One way is direct and explicit, i.e., the adult names a thing or defines a word for the child. The other way is indirect and implicit, through experience with concrete and/or verbal contexts.

This study is concerned with the acquisition of word meanings through verbal contexts. The children participating in this investigation ranged from $8\frac{1}{2}$ to $13\frac{1}{2}$ years of age and were divided into five age groups with 25 children at each age level. The interquartile *IQ* range was from 101 to 111.

The test was as follows: The child's task was to find the meaning of an artificial word, which appeared in six different verbal contexts. In all, there were 12 sets of six sentences each. The 12 artificial words denoted either an object or an action. For example, the artificial word in the first set of six sentences was CORPLUM, for which the correct translation was "stick" or "piece of wood." The contexts for CORPLUM were as follows:

1. A CORPLUM may be used for support.
2. CORPLUMS may be used to close off an open place.
3. A CORPLUM may be long or short, thick or thin, strong or weak.
4. A wet CORPLUM does not burn.
5. You can make a CORPLUM smooth with sandpaper.
6. The painter used a CORPLUM to mix his paints.

B. PROCEDURE

The experimental procedure was as follows: After the child was made thoroughly familiar with the task, he was presented with a card on which Sentence 1 of Series I was printed. After the child responded to the first sentence, he was asked how and why the meaning he gave for the word fit into the sentence. He then was presented with the second sentence while the first context was still in view. After having given his interpretation of the word as it appeared in the second sentence (which may or may not have differed from his first response) the child was again asked how and why it fit and also whether it could be applied to the preceding sentence. This procedure was carried out until all six contexts had been presented to the child. The child's responses were carefully recorded.

C. ANALYSIS AND RESULTS

Although correctness was not the major aspect of the study, it may be briefly mentioned that correctness of responses increased significantly from age level to age level.

Our main concern was with the ways

Reprinted with the permission of the author and the publisher, the Journal Press, from the article of the same title, *Journal of Psychology*, 1950, **29**, 251–257.

children gave signification to the artificial words; we were especially interested in the development of the signification process. For the purpose of analysis, three judges derived 60 criteria from a preliminary inspection of the protocols. These criteria, pertaining to linguistic as well as semantic characteristics, were then employed by the three judges in the final analysis.

Studying the protocols one is impressed with the great variety of processes by which children acquired and generalized word meanings from verbal contexts. Many responses of the younger children indicate a *lack in the differentiation between the meaning of the word and the given verbal context.* Instead of conceiving the word as referring to a circumscribed meaning, many of the younger children regarded the artificial word as carrying the meaning of the whole or part of the context in which it appeared. We may call this type of conception a *sentence-core concept.* For instance, one sentence, containing the artificial word, BORDICK, (faults) was the following: PEOPLE TALK ABOUT THE BORDICKS OF OTHERS AND DON'T LIKE TO TALK ABOUT THEIR OWN. One child, dealing with this sentence, remarked: "Well, BORDICK means 'people talk about others and don't talk about themselves,' that's what BORDICK means." That this child seriously thought that BORDICK meant the whole sentence became clear when he tried to fit this meaning into the context: PEOPLE WITH BORDICKS ARE OFTEN UNHAPPY. The child fitted his sentence-core concept into this context as follows: "People talk about others and don't talk about themselves —they are often unhappy." To the question: "How does this meaning fit?", the child had this answer: "Say this lady hears that another lady is talking about her, so she'll get mad at her and that lady will be very unhappy."

A frequent method of fitting a sentence-core concept, formed for one sentence, into another context was by a process we have termed *assimilation.* The child interprets the context of a new sentence as the same or similar to the context of the previous sentence. Through such assimilation, the concept for the previous sentence now fits into the new sentence. To illustrate, in one series the artificial word is HUDRAY (for which such concepts as "increase," "enlarge" or "grow" are adequate). Sentence 6 of this series read: YOU MUST HAVE ENOUGH SPACE IN THE BOOKCASE TO HUDRAY YOUR LIBRARY. One child said: "Hudray means 'to have enough space.'" He took a part of the context as the referent for HUDRAY. Returning to the previous sentences, he said that the concept, "to have enough space," fit all six sentences. For example, it fit Sentence 1 (IF YOU EAT WELL AND SLEEP WELL YOU WILL HUDRAY): "If you eat well, that is, if you do not overeat, you will have enough room in your stomach and won't get too chubby; if you sleep well, but not too much, you don't get overlazy; so you leave some room for more sleep—so you leave space—like."

Not infrequently, the child derived two independent sentence-core concepts pertaining to two successive sentences. In attempting to apply the second solution to the first sentence, he often combined the two solutions. For instance, for the two sentences:

JANE HAD TO HUDRAY THE CLOTH
SO THE DRESS WOULD FIT MARY.

YOU HUDRAY WHAT YOU KNOW BY
READING AND STUDYING.

one child gave as respective solutions: "Jane had to 'let out the hem' of the cloth" and "You 'learn by books' what you know." Coming back from the second to the first sentence the child said, "'Learn by books' fits here. Jane had to 'learn by books' how to 'let out the hem' in the cloth. Jane used an encyclopedia of sewing." For this girl, the first solution "let out the hem" was so completely embedded in the sentence context that it became a part of the sentence and no longer a substitute for HUDRAY. The child could now introduce the subsequent solution ("learn by books") above and beyond the first, original solution. At times, we obtained as many as three independent solutions combined in one sentence.

Another indication that word and sentence were not clearly differentiated at the earlier levels was the frequent manifestation of what we have called *holophrastic gradient*. Here, the concept was not limited to the unknown word, but spread to neighboring parts, thus carrying pieces of the sentence with it; e.g., for the word, LIDBER (collect, gather), one child stated for the sentence: JIMMY LIDBERED STAMPS FROM ALL COUNTRIES, "Jimmy 'collected' stamps from all countries." The concept was extended from "collect" to "collect stamps." Thus the concept, "collect stamps" was applied to another sentence: THE POLICE DID NOT ALLOW THE PEOPLE TO LIDBER ON THE STREET, in the following manner: "Police did not permit people to 'collect stamps' on the street."

Thus far, we have considered only those forms of signification of a word which are based on an intimate fusion of word and sentence (or sentence-parts). In our analysis, we found other forms of signification, in which the concepts, though they did not display sentence-word fusion, were still lacking the circumscribed, stable character of the more mature concepts. We called such products *simple contextual or simple holophrastic concepts*. Here the word meaning was definitely set apart from the context of the sentence; nevertheless, it differed from conventional word meanings in that it bore a wide situational connotation rather than a circumscribed, stable one. The artificial word did not refer, for the child, to a single object or action, but to a more inclusive context. Sometimes the broad situational connotation of the word was explicitly stated by the child, i.e., he employed a whole phrase to express the meaning of the word. In other cases, the child used a single word, seemingly delimited in its meaning, which on probing was found to be far more inclusive than it appeared on the surface. The following may serve as examples of explicitly stated holophrastic concepts.

The artificial word, ASHDER (obstacle), appears in the sentence, THE WAY IS CLEAR IF THERE ARE NO ASHDERS. One child responded: "The way is clear if there are no 'parts of a radio that don't fit in right' (together)." In the mind of this child, the word, ASHDER, referred to a radio-repair situation.

In the case of the sentence: THE POLICE DID NOT ALLOW THE PEOPLE TO LIDBER ON THE STREET, one child's translation of LIDBER was "throw paper around" (i.e., cluttering up the street by throwing paper around).

An illustration of implicit holophrastic concepts is the following, involving the word ONTRAVE (hope): ONTRAVE SOMETIMES KEEPS US FROM BEING UNHAPPY. A child substituted for ONTRAVE the seemingly circumscribed word "want." However, on probing, it became apparent that "want" referred to a broad contextual situation: "If you 'want a bow and arrow set and you get it,' that keeps you from being unhappy."

For this same sentence, another child came to the solution, "mother." " 'Mother' keeps you from being unhappy." However, "mother" actually meant "mother when she gives you things you want."

One may note an important characteristic attached to such situational word meanings; the word has not only a broad situational content, but this content is fluid and lacks closure: i.e., the concept may change in range from sentence to sentence, elements being added or subtracted etc. This can be seen from the way children quite typically expanded a concept in order to fit it into another sentence. This process of expansion, denoting fluidity of conceptualization, we have termed *contextual* or *holophrastic expansion*. An example of this holophrastic expansion is the following: One child had developed the concept "books to study" for HUDRAY. "Books" became expanded to "throwing books" when the child attempted to fit the concept into the sentence: MRS. SMITH WANTED TO HUDRAY HER FAMILY. The child stated: "Mrs. Smith wanted to 'throw books,' at her family."

Another child, who had arrived at the

concept "long" for one sentence, expanded it to "get long hair" in another: THE OLDER YOU GET THE SOONER YOU WILL BEGIN TO SOLDEVE, ". . . the sooner you will begin to 'get long hair.' ".

On occasion the contextual expansion was more systematically employed. The child formed a conceptual nucleus, which remained constant throughout the six contexts; and added to this nucleus elements varying with each sentence. We have termed this procedure *pluralization.* For example, one child formed a nucleus for all the sentences of one series containing the artificial word, LIDBER. This nucleus was "collect." In one sentence LIDBER meant "collect ribbons" (ALL THE CHILDREN WILL "collect ribbons" AT MARY'S PARTY); in another sentence, it was "collect autographs" (THE PEOPLE "collected autographs" from THE SPEAKER WHEN HE FINISHED HIS TALK); in a third sentence, it meant "collect information" (PEOPLE "collect information" QUICKLY WHEN THERE IS AN ACCIDENT), and so on.

We should like to mention two other forms of signification of a word, that were essentially based on contextual or holophrastic conceptualization. One we have termed *generalization by juxtaposition;* the other *generalization by chain.*

In the case of juxtaposition, a concept of an object *A* obtained in one sentence is applicable to a second sentence through the mediation of a concept of an object *B* that is spatially contiguous to the object *A.* For instance, a child gave the solution "plaster" for CONTAVISH in the sentence: BEFORE THE HOUSE IS FINISHED, THE WALLS MUST HAVE CONTAVISHES. "Plaster" also fit into the sentence, A BOTTLE HAS ONLY ONE

CONTAVISH. Here the child used "label" for CONTAVISH, saying, "A bottle has only one 'label.' " Nevertheless "plaster" was retained as the solution because "plaster," as the child explained, "is used to put on the 'label.' " In other words, the concept of an object such as "plaster" could be used as an overall solution because the juxtaposed object ("label") fit into the sentence. Most likely, the concept was contextual: not just "plaster" but "plaster +."

A similar mechanism seemed to be operative in generalization by chain. This type of generalization probably differs from juxtaposition only insofar as the two objects in question are conceived of as temporally rather than spatially connected (e.g., cause and effect). As an example, "honor" was substituted for SACKOY in one sentence: WE ALL ADMIRE PEOPLE WHO HAVE MUCH SACKOY. In the next sentence, "guts" was the meaning attributed to SACKOY. "You need 'guts' to fight with a boy bigger than you." But "honor" still fit because, as the child explained, "If you have 'guts,' you are 'honored' aren't you?"

Finally, the two main groups of immature signification discussed in this paper may be briefly compared statistically. As will be recalled, in the first group, the word carries with it the whole or parts of the sentence context; in the second group, the word is clearly differentiated from the sentence context, though it still possesses a broad contextual meaning. Table 7-5 summarizes the occurrence of these two types of contextual word meanings at the various age levels.

The figures represent the mean occurrence per child at each age group. Both forms of word meanings decreased as age

TABLE 7-5

Age	$8\frac{1}{2}$–$9\frac{1}{2}$	$9\frac{1}{2}$–$10\frac{1}{2}$	$10\frac{1}{2}$–$11\frac{1}{2}$	$11\frac{1}{2}$–$12\frac{1}{2}$	$12\frac{1}{2}$–$13\frac{1}{2}$
I Sentence-contextual	11.9	9.2	1.8	0.2	0.5
II Non-sentence-contextual	11.7	10.8	7.9	4.6	3.3

increased; however, there is a clearcut difference between the two developmental curves. Signification based on sentence-word fusion (Type I) decreased most sharply between the second and third age levels (around 10–11 years), with practically no occurrence after the third age level. The other type of contextual signification (in which there is no fusion of word meaning and sentence) showed an entirely different developmental trend: it gradually decreased, and even at the 13-year level there were as many as 3.3 such solutions per child.

The abrupt decrease of Type I, the most immature form of signification, around the 10- to 11-year level suggests a rather fundamental shift in language attitude, toward a task, which, as in our test, is on a relatively abstract verbal plane. This points to important implications which will be treated at greater length in a future paper.

In closing, we should like to mention briefly that there are aspects of language development other than semantic, discussed in this paper, which showed similar abrupt changes at the same age levels. This is particularly true with respect to grammatical structure. The data indicate that there is a growing comprehension of the test sentence as a stable, grammatical structure. Younger children manipulated the sentence as a fluid medium, lacking closure; that is, in the case of giving meaning to the artificial word they frequently altered the grammatical structure of the test sentence. The frequency of such manipulation showed an abrupt drop at the end of the second age level with practically no occurrence at the fourth and fifth levels.

One of the most significant and little explored problems of language development concerns the relationship between the semantic and grammatical aspects of language. The close correspondence of the developmental curves, indicated by our data, between two seemingly independent aspects of language lends support to those theories that assume a genetic interdependence of meaning and structure.

Word Association and the Acquisition of Grammar

ROGER BROWN

JEAN BERKO

Every natural language is a system. From knowledge of one part it is possible to anticipate correctly many other parts. The linguistic scientist studies some finite set of utterances (his linguistic "corpus") in search of the recurrent elementary units and patterns of combination that will generate the infinite set of utterances belonging to the language. Every child, in learning his first language, does much the same thing with the difference that he does not explicitly formulate most of the rules that govern his language behavior. A child is not, in his first few years, exposed to all possible utterances belonging to the community language but only to that small sample brought to him by his family, his friends, and television.

Reprinted with the permission of the authors and the publisher from *Child Development*, 1960, **31**, 1–14.

Exposure to this sample, however, teaches him to understand and to produce utterances not actually experienced but implied by what has been experienced. The child may begin as a parrot imitating what others say, but he will end as a poet able to say things that have not been said before but which will be grammatical and meaningful in his community. This is the terminal achievement which a theory of language acquisition must explain.

The linguistic scientist describes language systems at several levels: the *phonological* level of distinctive sound elements and their permissible combinations; the *morphological* level of elementary meaningful forms (*morphemes*) and their combination to make words; the *syntactic* level of sentence creation from words. We have described elsewhere (Berko and Brown, 1960) these three levels and have reported two studies (Berko, 1958; Brown, 1957) concerning the acquisition by children of morphology and syntax. The present study is concerned with syntax and, more particularly, with the child's utilization of the English parts-of-speech.

The linguistic scientist defines the parts-of-speech in purely syntactic or formal terms. He has shown that the English teacher's semantic definitions (e.g., "a noun is the name of a person, place, or thing") are imprecise approximations to the underlying but less obvious syntactic facts. The noun, in descriptive linguistics, is a class of words having similar "privileges of occurrence." Nouns are words that can follow articles and can occur in subject and object positions and, in this respect, are distinct from such other classes of words as the verb, adjective, and adverb. The fact that the words of any language fall into classes of approximate syntactic equivalents is of great interest to the student of language acquisition because it suggests one of the ways in which the lawful flexibility of speech is developed. A new word is ordinarily introduced to a child in a sentence, and this sentence will often serve to identify the part-of-speech to which the new word belongs. If the parts-of-speech have been internalized, this would mean that one vast array of sentence positions is available for the new word and other arrays are not. From the fact that X is a noun one can anticipate all of the grammatically acceptable uses of X and set aside all of the unacceptable uses. Is there evidence that children learn to operate with the parts-of-speech? We suspect that such evidence is to be found in certain well-established facts concerning word association.

Since the experiment of Woodrow and Lowell (1916), it has been known that the word associations of children show consistent differences from the associations of adults. Woodworth (1938) offers as examples of these differences the words appearing in Table 7-6. Woodrow and Lowell and others after them have conceptualized these differences in terms that are primarily semantic. Children are said to give more "contiguity" responses and more "whole-part" responses while adults are said to give more "coordinate," "contrast," and "similarity" re-

TABLE 7-6

Word Associations from Adults and Children

Stimulus	Response	1000 Children	1000 Men and Women
Table	Eat	358	63
	Chair	24	274
Dark	Night	421	221
	Light	38	427
Man	Work	168	17
	Woman	8	394
Deep	Hole	257	32
	Shallow	6	180
Soft	Pillow	138	53
	Hard	27	365
Mountain	High	390	246
	Hill	91	184

sponses. In several cases Woodrow and Lowell desert their semantic concepts and speak of "adjective-noun" associations and "verb-object" associations (both of which are more common in children's than in adult's responses). These classifications by parts-of-speech suggest a very general formal principle which contrasts the word associations of children and adults, a principle which so far as we know was first suggested by Ervin (1957). The associative responses of adults belong to the same part-of-speech as the stimulus word more often than do the associative responses of children. We shall speak of the adult type of association as homogeneous-by-part-of-speech (abbreviated Hmg.) and the child's type as heterogeneous-by-part-of-speech (Htg.).

Looking again at the examples of Table 7-6, we see that the response favored by adults is almost invariably Hmg. while that favored by children is Htg. Many of the largest differences found in the Woodrow and Lowell study conform to this syntactic principle though they were not so classified by the authors. In addition to these data from the past there are recent findings of Ervin (1957) who used a list of common words belonging to various parts-of-speech with groups of children in kindergarten and the first, third, and sixth grades. She found large increases with age in Hmg. responses to nouns, verbs, prepositions, adjectives, and adverbs. What is the significance of this apparently reliable developmental trend in word association?

There are, of course, many kinds of association that can link one word with another; similarity or contrast of referents, spatio-temporal contiguity of referents, and high transition probabilities between words are obvious possibilities. Similarity and contrast and contiguity between referents would sometimes lead to Hmg. responses (e.g., *table-chair*) and sometimes to Htg. responses (e.g., *table-eat*). Immediate transitions of high probability will very seldom exist between two words of the same part-of-speech, and so such pairs as *dark-night, deep-hole,* and *soft-pillow* are Htg. Elaborating a suggestion of Ervin's (Berko and Brown, 1960), we propose that the word associations of very young children are governed by such principles as we have cited but that, with increasing age, another principle of association begins to operate which has the effect of increasing the number of Hmg. responses.

From the time that a child begins to use phrases his speech repertoire will manifest the morphological structure that is a universal characteristic of adult speech in any language. The same meaningful forms (morphemes and words) occur in a variety of contexts; not all forms can occur in all contexts but some forms can occur in some of the same contexts. From these morphological universals it follows that words resemble one another in the degree to which they have similar privileges of occurrence. This syntactic similarity is always objectively present in speech involving phrases but probably it takes considerable time and maturity to analyze out syntactic similarity. The appreciation of syntactic similarity is, however, prerequisite to the ability to form meaningful and grammatical sentences that are not imitated from someone else. Suppose a child has learned that such words as *house, barn, table,* and *fence* can all occur in such positions as: "See the ——"; "I own a ——"; "The —— is new"; and "This —— is mine." If now he hears for the first time such a sentence as "See the *car*" in which *car* is a new word, he can be prepared to say "I own a *car*"; "The *car* is new"; and "This *car* is mine." Of course, the particular sentence uttered on a given occasion depends on semantic and motivational factors but the universe of sentences from which the particular can be drawn is established by the syntactic kinship linking *car* with *house, barn, table,* and *fence.*

Modern methods of teaching second or foreign languages begin, as does first language learning, with the repetition of phrases which recombine a limited set of meaningful elements. In second language learning, as in first, there comes a time when the student "creates" a phrase by realizing the syntactic implications of the material practiced. This is often accomplished nowadays by implicit induction without any explicit tuition in syntactic rules, and that is exactly the way it is accomplished by all children who become full participants in a first language.

Syntactic similarity is a matter of degree. The parts-of-speech are simply very large and very useful classes of approximate combinational equivalents. Animate nouns are more closely equivalent than nouns in general, and transitive verbs are more closely equivalent than verbs in general. Such popular adult word associations as *bright-dark* are not only semantic antonyms; they are also adjectives having highly similar privileges of occurrence. *Bright* has more sentence contexts in common with *dark* than with such another adjective as *virtuous*. It is our general hypothesis that, as utilization of syntax develops in children, syntactic similarity in words becomes an increasingly important determinant of word association and that the developmental trend from Htg. responses toward Hmg. responses is a manifestation of this great step forward into syntactic operations. We have undertaken to test this hypothesis by relating the child's tendency to give Hmg. word associations to his ability to make correct grammatical use of new words after hearing them in a couple of sentences.

METHOD

We worked with four groups of 20 subjects each. In each group there were equal numbers of male and female subjects. Groups I, II, and III were students from, respectively, the first, second, and third grades of the Michael Driscoll School in Brookline, Massachusetts. The Driscoll School is a public school in a middle-income residence area. Children in a given group

were all taken from the same classroom and simply drawn in the order of the seating arrangement until 20 had served. The fourth group (Group Ad.) consisted of 20 adults, students or staff at M.I.T., who responded to an advertisement asking for subjects.

Word Association Test

This test consisted of 36 stimulus words such that there were six words representing each of six parts-of-speech. The words were selected because all have high frequency in the speech of American elementary-school children (Rinsland, 1945) and because in earlier studies they yielded large differences between the associations of children and adults. The words were presented in a constant order to all subjects.

Verbs in English may be subdivided into transitive and intransitives. Intransitive verbs can appear without an object (e.g., "We *laugh*") while transitives almost always occur with some sort of object (e.g., "We *sent* something"). For the present experiment the transitives and intransitives were treated as two parts-of-speech, and there were six words representing each of them.

Nouns in English can be separated into "count nouns" and "mass nouns." The names are suggested from a distinction of reference; count nouns usually name bounded objects (e.g., *table, house*) while mass nouns name extended substances (e.g., *milk, sand*). However, there is also a clear syntactic distinction; count nouns in the singular can be preceded by *a* while mass nouns cannot (e.g., *a table* but not *a sand*) and, in addition, count nouns, when preceded by *some,* appear in the plural whereas mass nouns appear in the singular (e.g., *some tables* but *some milk*). On the present list of stimulus words there were six mass nouns and six count nouns.

In addition to the two varieties of noun and two varieties of verb, there were six adjectives and six adverbs on the list. The complete list is as follows:

Count Nouns (C.N.): table, house, foot, needle, apple, doctor.

Mass Nouns (M.N.): milk, water, sand, sugar, air, cheese.

Adjectives (Adj.): dark, soft, cold, white, sweet, hard.

Transitive Verbs (T.V.): to send, to bring, to find, to take, to hit, to invite.

Intransitive Verbs (I.V.): to skate, to come, to live, to laugh, to stand, to walk.

Adverbs (Adv.): quickly, slowly, sadly, now, softly, gently.

Many English words belong to more than one part-of-speech. It is possible in English to *table* a motion and to *foot* a bill but *table* and *foot,* in the vast majority of their occurrences, function as nouns and, when presented in isolation as stimulus words, are apprehended as nouns by most English-speaking adults. The words on the present list belong primarily to one part-of-speech though they may have secondary membership in others. The verbs were presented as infinitives with preceding *to* so that their verbal character would be clear.

Usage Test

The general plan of this test was to introduce to S a new word (actually a pronounceable nonsense syllable) by using it in two sentences. The two sentences were adequate to place the word in one of six parts-of-speech: the count noun, mass noun, transitive verb, intransitive verb, adjective, or adverb. After this introduction to the word, S was asked to use it in sentences of his own creation, and these were scored as correct if the new word was used as it ought to be in view of the part-of-speech implied by the introductory sentences.

As "new words" 12 nonsense syllables were used: *wug, boff, latt, roog, stog, huft, nass, sib, bik, rik, nare,* and *pilk.* There were 12 problems in all with two syllables assigned to each of the six parts-of-speech. The syllables were rotated through all 12 problems so that there was no regular association between any syllable and any particular problem. The syllable *wug* will be used here to indicate the general character of the presentations.

For each problem, S was shown a colorful picture of either a girl, a boy, a man, a woman, a cat, or a dog, and E read text of the following kind: "Do you know what a *wug* is? This is a picture of a little girl thinking about a *wug*. Can you make up what that might mean?" This was the presentation identifying *wug* as a count noun. Where *wug* was to be identified as an intransitive verb, E would say: "Do you know what it means to *wug*? This is a picture of a little boy who wants to *wug*." With *wug* as mass noun there would be such sentences as: "This is a cat thinking about some *wug*." With wug as transitive verb such a sentence as this was used: "This is a woman who wants to *wug* something." Where *wug* was to be identified as an adverb, E spoke of a dog thinking of doing something *wuggily*.

There were two problems for each part-of-speech and a different syllable for each problem. There were two identifying sentences for each problem and, in the case of the adjectives and adverbs, the appended suffixes -*y* and -*ly*. The pictures gave no clue to the meaning of the new word and were only included to interest the child and keep his attention. The figures in the pictures were always simply thinking about the new word, not demonstrating its meaning.

Procedure

E was introduced to the children in a class by the teacher, and the class was told that each member would have a chance to look at some pictures and play some games. The children were interviewed individually either in the corridor outside the classroom or in an unused classroom. The Word Association Test was presented first with the remarks: "This is a game called "say a word." Have you ever played "say a word"? Well, this is the way it works. I'm going to say a word and I want you to listen to my word and then say another word, not my word but a different word. Any word is all right so long as it's the first word that comes into your head when you hear my word. Are you ready?"

When the word associations had been recorded, E brought out the picture cards and said: "Now we're going to play a making-up game. How are you at making things up? Pretty good? Well, let's see." The problems were presented so as to go through all parts-of-speech once before repeating any of them.

The procedure with adults was the same except that S knew he was participating in an experiment on language and E did not call either part a game. In explanation of the brightly colored pictures and rather childish text, the adults were told that the tests had been designed for use with children as well as with adults.

Scoring

Scoring on the Word Association Test involves assigning response words to a part-of-speech; scoring on the Usage Test involves determining from S's use of a new word the part-of-speech to which S has implicitly assigned the new word. Because English words can belong to more than one part-of-speech and because single sentences employing a new word do not always unequivocally indicate the part-of-speech membership of the new word, there were sometimes problems in scoring.

On the Free Association Test those response words that were marked with characteristic suffixes (adjectives and adverbs) or with the *to* of the verbal infinitive could be confidently classified. With most potentially doubtful responses membership in one part-of-speech is so much more common than membership in another that it was safe to assign the word this primary membership. Where there was some doubt, however, E asked S to use the response word in a sentence and, in doing so, S revealed the part-of-speech he had in mind. It was necessary for E mentally to score the responses as they were elicited so that he could resolve scoring problems where necessary.

On the Usage Test S sometimes translated the new word into a conventional English word. When told that a man was thinking about some *wug* and asked to "tell what that might mean," S sometimes provided a familiar word as a translation, saying for instance, "He is thinking about some *milk*." In such a case the part-of-speech membership of the familiar equivalent was scored and would be correct, in the present instance, as *milk* is a mass noun and that is the part-of-speech implied for *wug*. Where the translation word was not clearly of one part-of-speech, E encouraged S to "say some more about it."

In other cases S interpreted the Usage Test as calling for use of the new word in a sentence and so might provide: "The man has some *wugs* for breakfast every day." In such a case the part-of-speech was inferred from the sentence and, in the present instance, would be scored incorrect as *wug* has been used as a count noun. Not every sentence is unequivocal in this regard, and so it was sometimes necessary to urge S to say a little more.

RESULTS

There were 36 stimulus words on the Free Association Test, six words for each of six parts-of-speech. Each of the 36 response words (or phrases) was scored as Hmg. or Htg. with reference to its stimulus word, and so for every subject there was a possible maximal score of six Hmg. responses for each of six parts-of-speech. There were 12 new words on the Usage Test, two words for each of six parts-of-speech. Each of the new words was scored Hmg. or Htg. according to the agreement between the part-of-speech implied by the introductory sentences and the part-of-speech implied by S's use or translation of the new word. For each S, therefore, there was a possible maximal score of two Hmg. responses on each of six parts-of-speech. After the rules of scoring had been developed by one judge, another judge independently scored 10 complete protocols (360 response words on word association and 120 new words on usage) from the rules. The two scorings agreed perfectly except for three instances where more information should have been elicited, and so it appears that this is essentially an objective scoring problem with no difficulties in the reliability sphere. The mean Hmg. scores for each part-of-speech and each age group appear in Table 7-7.

A two-way analysis of variance with 20 cases in each cell was carried out for the Free Association means and another for the Usage means. The results are summarized in Tables 7-8 and 7-9. Both age and part-of-speech account for large amounts of variance. In addition, there is a significant interaction between the two variables, and it can be seen in both the Free Association and Usage means that the increase with age of Hmg. responses is far less for count nouns than for the other parts-of-speech.

We are not primarily interested in the effects of age and of part-of-speech and so will not compare the 24 individual means for each test. It is, however, worth noting the extraordinary uniformities in Table 7-7. The individual means have been arranged in the order of the grand means of the rows (age groups) and columns (parts-of-speech). When this is done for Free Association, there are only three reversals of one position each in the age order, only four reversals of one position, and a single reversal of two positions in the part-of-speech data. The same sort of ordering of the Usage means results in only three reversals of one position each in the age order, only one reversal of three positions, and one reversal

TABLE 7 7

Mean HMG. Scores on Free Association and Usage
for Each Part-of-speech and Each Age Group

			FREE ASSOCIATION				
Group	C.N.	Adj.	I.V.	T.V.	Adv.	M.N.	Total
Ad.	5.10	5.00	4.80	4.45	4.95	2.35	4.44
3rd	4.65	3.65	3.40	2.95	1.95	2.40	3.17
2nd	4.55	3.90	2.75	2.40	2.25	1.90	2.96
1st	3.95	1.25	1.60	1.40	.80	1.20	1.70
Total	4.56	3.45	3.14	2.80	2.49	1.96	3.07

			USAGE				
Group	C.N.	Adj.	I.V.	T.V.	M.N.	Adv.	Total
Ad.	1.85	1.75	1.70	1.60	.95	1.20	1.51
3rd	1.45	1.65	1.65	1.75	.55	.55	1.27
2nd	1.55	1.50	1.20	1.10	.70	.45	1.08
1st	1.20	.75	.90	.90	.45	.10	.72
Total	1.51	1.41	1.36	1.34	.66	.58	1.15

TABLE 7-8

Analysis of Variance for Free Association Means

Source	Sum of squares	df	Variance estimate
Age (rows)	453.6167	3	151.2056
Parts-of-Speech (columns)	321.2167	5	64.2433
Interaction	84.6833	15	5.6456
Individual differences (within cells)	1345.3500	456	2.9503
Total	2204.8667	479	

Interaction $F = 1.91; p < .05.$
Age $F = 26.78; p < .001.$
Parts-of-speech $F = 11.38; p < .001.$

of two positions in the part-of-speech order. There is clear confirmation in this table of the increase with age of Hmg. responses found by Ervin (1957) and also clear evidence that the count noun and adjective function in child speech in advance of other parts-of-speech. Finally, ordering the Free Association and Usage cell means in the order of their grand means results in identical age and part-of-speech orders (except for a reversal of the Adv. and M.N. columns) in the two sets of data. This is a good first indication of the covariation in free association and usage which is the effect predicted by our hypothesis. We proceed to a more detailed presentation of the evidence for this effect.

It would have been possible to compute correlations between the individual scores on usage and the individual scores on free association for each part-of-speech and each age group. We examined these scores and saw that the correlations would be very small, probably because the usage scores can only range from zero to two and because this small sample of usage from each S is not a very reliable measure of S's grammatical skills. We decided to work instead with the means of Table 7-7 which yield a greater range of scores and a more reliable estimate of grammatical skill in a kind of S. The rank-order correlation between the 24 means from the Free Association Test and the 24 means from the Usage Test is .84, and this is a relationship significant at far better than the .001 level.

TABLE 7-9

Analysis of Variance for Usage Means

Source	Sum of squares	df	Variance estimate
Age (rows)	40.0896	3	13.3632
Parts-of-Speech (columns)	67.2688	5	13.4538
Interaction	11.1673	15	.7445
Individual differences (within cells)	208.5556	456	.4574
Total	327.0813	479	

Interaction $F = 1.63; p$ about .05.
Age $F = 17.95; p < .001.$
Parts-of-Speech $F = 18.07; p < .001.$

Contributing to the rank-order correlation of all 24 means is the tendency for usage and free association scores to increase with age as well as the tendency for scores on the six parts-of-speech to covary for usage and free association. Insofar as the correlation is generated by the former factor it is possible that we have nothing more here than a tendency for all sorts of language performance scores to move together with increasing age towards adult values. We are interested in something more particular than this. We want to know whether the increasing tendency to give Hmg. responses in free association can be interpreted as evidence of the developing organization of vocabulary into parts-of-speech which define correct grammatical usage for new words. We shall have better ground for this interpretation if correlations exist with the age variation taken out. One way of accomplishing this effect is to correlate the grand means (across all age groups) for the six part-of-speech columns for free association and usage. This rank order *rho* is .94 and even with only six cases that value is significant at about .01. Another way of testing for this relationship is to correlate the six paired means for each of the four age groups. The results appear in Table 7-10 (together with the previously mentioned *rhos*); three are significant and one is not. The *p* values for these four samples can be combined to yield a single *p* value for the relationship of free association to usage.

Mosteller and Bush (1954) suggest transforming the individual *p* values into normal deviates, summing them, and dividing the sum by the square root of the number of observations. The resultant value is itself a normal deviate with a *p* of about .0002. It seems very certain, therefore, that Hmg. scores for free association are related to Hmg. scores for usage.

DISCUSSION

The change with age in both free association and usage is very striking when one examines individual protocols. For free association, consider the stimulus words *to send.* One first grade child responds *away,* another *letter,* another *a card,* another *mail,* etc. In response to this same word adults give: *to receive, to get, to deliver, to bring, to mail, to fetch.* Both the child responses and the adult responses are semantically related to the stimulus word, and the one set does not seem to be any more so than the other. The difference lies with the fact that the child responses are phrase completions (words that commonly follow the stimulus) while the adult words would almost never follow *to send* in an English sentence but are very closely matched with it in that they are transitive verbs. More specifically, the adult responses are transitive verbs naming human actions which ordinarily have some small inanimate thing

TABLE 7-10

Rank Order Correlations Between Free Association and
Usage Hmg. Scores

Rho for all paired means, N = 24	.84	*p* < .00
Rho for grand means of the parts-of-speech, N = 6	.94	*p* = .01
Rho for Adults, N = 6	.83	*p* = .05
Rho for 3rd grade, N = 6	.46	*p* = .40
Rho for 2nd grade, N = 6	.94	*p* = .01
Rho for 1st grade, N = 6	.83	*p* = .05
Combined *p* value for adults, 3rd grade, 2nd grade, 1st grade		*p* = .00

as object. This further similarity is semantic but, in addition, involves a closer syntactic match than would be true for transitive verbs in general.

Consider now the sort of thing that happens on the Usage Test with a nonsense syllable intended to be a transitive verb. One first grade child was told: "This is a cat who wants to *niss* something. Can you make up what that might mean?" The child replied: "The cat wants a fish. A *niss* is a fish." To this same problem an adult responded: "The cat wants to catch something. To *niss* is to catch." The child seems to have put together knowledge about cats and the sound of *niss* to come up with a count noun—*fish*. He was not troubled by the fact that this translation violates the part-of-speech membership of *niss*. When *E* says "to *niss* something," that should exclude the possibility of saying "A *niss* is a fish," but, for this child, it does not. Apparently the first grade children paid little attention to the formal marks of the syntactic potentialities of *niss*. The adult, on the other hand, principally attended to these marks. In many cases the translations provided by adults seem to have been suggested by the sound of the new word even as *niss* suggested *fish* to the first grader. However, when this happened with adults, it was almost always within the limits of the class of words suggested by the syntactic cues. In general, then, both the free association results and the usage results seem to be manifestations of the developing organization of vocabulary into syntactic classes.

As the analyses of variance have demonstrated, both age and part-of-speech are highly significant determinants of the number of Hmg. responses on both the Free Association and Usage tests. These two variables may perhaps be conceptualized as a single determinant—the amount of experience with words belonging to a part-of-speech. Experience of words in all six parts-of-speech is bound to increase with age, and Hmg. responses on all parts-of-speech

clearly do increase with age. In addition, however, we note in Table 7-7 that the count noun and the adjective produce more Hmg. responses across all age levels than do the other parts-of-speech. While we do not know of any exact tests of the frequency of occurrence in English of words belonging to the various parts-of-speech, it seems to us that no test is needed to persuade the native speaker that count nouns and adjectives are more common than intransitive verbs or transitive verbs or adverbs or mass nouns. This is to say that at any given age a speaker of English is likely to have had more experience of count nouns and adjectives than of the other parts-of-speech we have studied.

The count noun has always the highest number of Hmg. responses and, indeed, does not change greatly in this respect from the first grade to adulthood because it is already at a near peak level in first graders. The count noun is, of course, the kind of word adults regularly undertake to teach children, for these are the names of denotable things: a *man*, a *dog*, a *car*, a *bike*. Surely speakers of English have greater experience of words in this class than of words in any other class.

The low number of Hmg. responses generally obtained for mass nouns requires a special comment. The Htg. responses given to mass nouns were usually count nouns, i.e., members of the same major part-of-speech. There is a good reason why these two varieties of noun were not usually distinguished even by adults. Mass nouns in English can always be used as count nouns. Ordinarily one says *some sand, some water, some marble* but one can say *some sands, some marbles,* and even *some waters*. The difference is that in the former cases a quantity of a uniform substance is suggested while in the latter case varieties or subspecies of some category of substances are suggested. This syntactic overlap seems to result in an overlap on the word association and usage tasks.

We have suggested that degree of experience of words in a part-of-speech is the basic determinant of the degree to which that part-of-speech functions in free association and usage. The significant sort of experience might be the number of words belonging to the part-of-speech or the variety of sentences for each word or the number of occurrences for each sentence. Probably all of these kinds of experience are close correlates in the natural situation. There are many different count nouns in English; there are many different sentences for most count nouns; and there are many sentences involving count nouns that occur very frequently. Without deliberate experimental manipulation of experience it probably will not be possible to determine the relative importance of these factors.

SUMMARY

It is a reliable finding that the response words provided by adults in a word association test usually belong to the same parts-of-speech as the respective stimulus words. There are fewer of these homogeneous-by-part-of-speech responses with young children; the tendency to associate words within a part-of-speech increases with age. The present paper suggests that this change in word associations is a consequence of the child's gradual organization of his vocabulary into the syntactic classes called parts-of-speech. To test the degree to which S has accomplished this latter grammatical task, a Usage Test was designed. In this test a new word was used in a couple of sentences which sufficed to indicate the part-of-speech to which the new word belonged. After hearing these sentences, S was asked to create some sentences of his own using the new word, and his performance was scored correct if it employed the word in ways permitted by its part-of-speech membership. Four groups of Ss (adults and first, second, and third grade children) were given a Word Association Test (consisting of stimulus words belonging to six different parts-of-speech) and also a Usage Test (consisting of new words assigned to the same six parts-of-speech). The Word Association Test was scored for homogeneous responses within each part-of-speech and the Usage Test for correct usage in accordance with each part-of-speech. It was found that scores on both tests regularly increased with age and that scores on the two tests were closely related to one another. It was concluded that the formal change in word association and the ability to make correct grammatical use of new words are two manifestations of the child's developing appreciation of English syntax.

REFERENCES

Berko, Jean. The child's learning of English morphology. *Word*, 1958, 14, 150–177.

———, and R. Brown. Psycholinguistic research methods. In P. Mussen (Ed.), *Handbook of research methods in child development*. New York: Wiley, 1960.

Brown, R. Linguistic determinism and the part of speech. *J. abnorm. soc. Psychol.*, 1957, 55, 1–5.

Ervin-Tripp, Susan M. Grammar and classification. Paper read at the American Psychological Association, New York, September, 1957.

Mosteller, F., and R. R. Bush. Selected quantitative techniques. In G. Lindzey (Ed.), *Handbook of social psychology*. Cambridge, Mass.: Addison-Wesley, 1954. Vol. I, pp. 289–334.

Rinsland, H. D. *A basic vocabulary of elementary school children*. New York: Macmillan, 1945.

Woodrow, H., and F. Lowell. Children's association frequency tables. *Psychol. Monogr.*, 1916, 22, No. 97.

Woodworth, R. S. *Experimental psychology*. New York: Holt, Rinehart and Winston, 1938.

Language and Learning:
How Do We Acquire Language?

8

INTRODUCTION

Psychologists have long been interested in how human beings learn their native language. The study of human verbal behavior has frequently used nonsense syllables or single words as the linguistic unit. The assumption of this program of research is that syllables and words are the smallest linguistic unit and that the acquisition of these units probably preceded the learning of more complex units such as phrases and sentences. This research largely ignores the phoneme and morpheme as linguistic units, although the influence of syllable pronounciability has been studied (Underwood and Schulz, 1960, pages 23–25). In general, the study of human verbal behavior has preceded and ignored both the structural linguistic and transformational description of language. There is, therefore, considerable debate concerning what verbal responses are learned. Is it specific letters, syllables, phonemes, morphemes, words, markers, phrases, sentences, or even unverbalized rules?

The most impressive part of the corpus of psychological knowledge is the psychology of learning. Stimulus-response language has made accessible to careful experimental research a wide range of human behavior. In the tradition of the natural sciences the psychology of learning has emphasized the importance of public observation and public evidence. Even when mediating variables are hypothesized, they must be tied down to explicit stimulus-response events, even if these events operate only as cues that trigger internal processes. The use of performance learning models has made great strides in the understanding of simple animal and human learning. There has also been the underlying assumption that there is evolutionary continuity between animal and human learning even if this learning extends to the sophisticated level of human language and thought.

There has always been a large number of educators, laymen, and psychologists who for several reasons have been impatient with this program of research; it has seemed irrelevant to human behavior, an oversimplification of that behavior, and perhaps, in both methodology and conceptualization, quite inadequate to tackle such important problems as language and thought. Many learning psychologists have been around long enough or they have read enough to conclude that direct research attacks on complex human behavior which ignore what we have discovered about simple behavior have frequently generated more heat than light. In this way the cognitive theorists are at least (and they are undoubtedly much more) a mote in the eye of the behaviorists. They may frequently spark the behaviorists to new conceptual and empirical feats. The study of human verbal and conceptual behavior is a lively and productive area of research. In studying more complex behavior the behavioral learning psychologist has been willing to use hypothetical constructs or intervening variables to explain observable S-R relations. It is these mediational hypotheses of psychologists such as Osgood [Chapter 6] and Kendler [Chapter 9] that offer considerable hope in bridging the gap between cognitive and behavioral theory.

Not only empirical fruitfulness but also subjective preference determine the theoretical models or technical language system a research psychologist employs. Currently the models and the language of the cognitive theorists enjoy considerable popularity and status. Their language has a familiar ring to laymen and educators, who often assume, therefore, that the models hold great promise for solutions of educational problems. It remains to be seen whether the relevance of cognitive theory to problems of school learning is more apparent than substantial. Fortunately, the behaviorists invented programed instruction, and this provided their platform for discussing practical problems of teaching and learning. Even though S-R correlational and mediational psychology has been the product of rigorous theory and experimentation, paradoxically enough, we find some behavioral psychologists with more enthusiasm than knowledge, extrapolating from findings on fairly prosaic human and animal behavior to the solution of complex problems of teaching and learning in the school. At this level of discussion one sometimes concludes that the object of the debate between cognitive and behavioral theorists is ideological control of the school rather than increased knowledge of human behavior.

Three of the articles in this chapter rise to the battle with considerable eloquence and conviction. The first article, however, is Jenkins' relatively dispassionate description of the associationist learning theory of Guthrie, Hull, and Skinner, and the somewhat cognitive learning theory of Tolman. Jenkins includes in his discussion an interesting distinction between three levels of psychological theory and the affirmation of the need for all theory to be testable, reliable, and coherent.

The publication of Skinner's *Verbal Behavior* (1957) marked the first attempt of the behaviorists to state the whole problem of human language. Skinner calls his behavioral analysis "functional." A functional analysis explains behavior by telling us what conditions are relevant to the occurrence of the behavior. In Skinner's model of operant conditioning these conditions are external to the organism. His system does not account for the contributions of the organism to verbal behavior. Skinner's analysis avoids the use of terms such as "ideas," "images," "meaning," and so on. Such concepts he considers traditional and prescientific. These terms usually refer to interior states of the organism that are inaccessible to scientific investigation. Although Skinner insists on empirical explanations of verbal behavior, his own analysis of linguistic behavior rests entirely on a speculative extension of his experimental analysis of animal behavior [Jenkins, Chapter 8]. For Skinner, verbal behavior is that behavior we observe in everyday life. All the facts are known, but they require ordering. The current, widespread interest in the operant conditioning of verbal behavior and the evidence this research has yielded may be convincing support for Skinner's position (Wolpe, 1958; Verplanck, 1962; Krasner and Ullman, 1965).

Chomsky's chief objection to Skinner's analysis of verbal behavior is the attempt to explain its causes without considering the neurological makeup of the speaker and what the speaker contributes to learning and performance. For Skinner the organism is hollow, and his explanations of all behavior are always in terms of external stimuli. According to Chomsky, Skinner dismisses the contribution of the speaker as trivial and elementary by appealing more to aphorism than to evidence. The crucial test of Skinner's analysis is its potential and actual fruitfulness in advancing our knowledge of verbal behavior. Chomsky believes that Skinner's rendering of the problem is no more scientific than is the traditional description of language behavior. By "metaphoric extension" Skinner applies the technical language of the laboratory to complex human behavior in a way that renders meaningless the laboratory terms of "stimulus," "response," and "reinforcement." Chomsky even believes that the laboratory guise of these terms may conceal their "mentalistic" use. For example, to say the "X is reinforced by Y" is to say nothing more than "X wants Y" or "X wishes Y were the case." Skinner may have accomplished little more than a terminological revision that may even obscure useful distinctions made in traditional descriptions of verbal behavior. The use of terms such as "reinforcement" and "generalization" may cover up everything that is important in language acquisition. In Chomsky's view what may be of central importance is our ability to generalize, hypothesize, and process information—a view that identifies him with the cognitive theorists. . . . What learning theory must explain, according to Chomsky, is the fact that "all normal children acquire essentially comparable grammars of great complexity with remarkable rapidity." This suggests that human beings are specially designed to carry out complex data-handling and hypothesis-formulating functions.

If Chomsky and Skinner could accept the *cue function* of words as external stimuli that mediate internal processes, and if they could accept the possibility of behavior chains capable of both horizontal and vertical arrangements, their positions would not be as opposed as they now seem to be. Gagné's "knowledge hierarchy" is one attempt to combine both arrangements. At this time the editor sees no insuperable obstacles, in either technique or theory, to the closer union of cognitive and behavioral theory.

Miller, on the other hand, finds that the behaviorist model which generalizes across species and from verbal to nonverbal behavior is hazardous and unproductive. In his view the major shortcomings of the behaviorist approach are the identification of speech with its possible physical features, the confusion of reference with meaning, and the use of words as the unit of analysis. The behaviorist approach ignores the syntax of sentences, the distinction between language and the language user, and the biological substructure necessary for speech. Miller has used Chomsky's transformational grammar as the basis for psycholinguistic research [Chapter 1]. The language system of the cognitive theorists accommodates transformational theory more easily than the language system of the behaviorists does. Miller's present position, as described in the articles in this anthology [Chapters 1, 6, and 8] represents a considerable departure from his previous behaviorist position (Miller, 1951). Whether the use of sentences and phrase markers will reveal more about the nature of human language and thought than present research on single words and syllables reveals remains to be seen.

REFERENCES

Hebb, D. O. *Organization of behavior.* New York: Wiley, 1949.

Hilgard, E. R. *Theories of behavior.* (2d ed.) New York: Appleton, 1956.

Krasner, L., and L. P. Ullman. *Research in behavior modification.* New York: Holt, Rinehart and Winston, 1965.

Miller, G. A. *Language and communication.* New York: McGraw-Hill, 1951.

Skinner, B. F. *Verbal behavior.* New York: Appleton, 1957.

Underwood, B. J., and R. W. Schulz. *Meaningfulness and verbal learning.* Philadelphia: Lippincott, 1960.

Verplanck, W. S. Unaware of where's awareness: Some verbal operants—notates, moments, and notants. In C. W. Erikson, (Ed.), *Behavior and awareness.* Durham, S.C.: Duke University Press, 1962.

Wolpe, J. *Psychotherapy by reciprocal inhibition.* Stanford, Calif.: Stanford University Press, 1958.

Learning Theories

JAMES J. JENKINS

Since "theory" is a somewhat ambiguous word, it seems advisable to outline briefly the conceptual framework which the seminar utilized in its discussion of learning theory.

General nature of psychological theories

A fully developed scientific theory contains three distinguishable levels. *Level I* contains the relatively raw "immediately apprehended" sense data (e.g., the speech sounds, the observations of a dial reading, the perceived movements of a rat). All sciences contain this level, but they differ in their selection of events. *Level II* contains the concepts which are the special concerns of the science (e.g., the stimulus, the phoneme, energy) and laws which are summaries of their observed relations or hypotheses predicting relations not yet observed. Such concepts are meaningful only if they are unambiguously related directly or indirectly to Level I events. Such a relation is equivalent to an *operational definition*. Concepts which are not operationally defined, and systems containing many such concepts, are called *meaningless*. The criterion of meaningfulness is related to that of testability since only meaningful concepts can be used in stating testable hypotheses and laws. *Level III* contains a formal mathematical or logical system. All concepts on this hypothetical level are purely formal or logical in contrast to those of Level II, which are "descriptive" of Level I events. Level III ordinarily consists of statements defining the elements in the hypothetical system, statements defin-

ing operations and relations in terms of the elements, and statements of rules of inference to be used in deriving the theorems of the system. The theorems may be regarded as the logical results of the assumed relations in the postulate set. The *interpretation* of this formal system consists of placing its entities and relations into correspondence with the concepts of Level II. Thus, a theorem on Level III leads directly to an hypothesis on Level II by means of translation of terms indicated by the interpretation. In turn, the laws or hypotheses of Level II are summaries of observed or predicted Level I events. Because of these relations between the levels of a theory, the formal system of Level III is said to explain the laws of Level II which, in turn, explain the events of Level I.

A scientist is free to select or develop any mathematical or logical system which he desires to use. The utility of his choice is then determined by examining the correspondence between his model or system and the concepts or empirical data which he observes. Ordinarily, it is desired that the experimental model be *testable* (that it generate meaningful predictions), *reliable* (that it generate consistent predictions), *coherent* (not in conflict with itself), *comprehensive* (that it explain a wide variety of phenomena) and *simple*. Obviously, both comprehensiveness and simplicity are subjective and debatable, but the other requirements are relatively clear.

Reprinted and abridged with the permission of the author and the publisher from Psycholinguistics: A Survey of Theory and Research Problems, *Journal of Abnormal and Social Psychology*, 1954, **49**, No. 4, Pt. 2, 25–34.

Theory-building in psychology has not, of course, proceeded self-consciously to develop level by level as our description above might imply. Psychology developed as a branch of philosophy, as did the other sciences, but the weaning was longer than for most. As late as 1900 most psychology departments were subdivisions within philosophy departments; some still are. Along with the mentalistic tradition of the 19th century, psychologists and pseudo-psychologists were prone to "theorize" by sticking into the organism whatever faculties, aptitudes, instincts, etc., seemed to serve their immediate purpose. There were practically as many intervening "explanatory" constructs as there were things to be explained. This has been aptly entitled "junk shop" psychology.

In the early part of the present century there was a general revulsion against this kind of theorizing, typified by the writings of such men as Watson, Kantor, Weiss, and more recently, Skinner. This stress on objectivity paralleled a similar revolution taking place in linguistics through the same period. These men went to the other extreme, the "empty organism" position. This view held that the psychologist should concentrate on exploring the many functional relations between objectively verifiable S (stimulus) events and objectively verifiable R (response) events, avoiding intervening variables which involve "going into" the organism. Thus, Skinner is content to study the behavior of the rat in the lever box under various stimulus conditions where the only observations are tracings on a recording drum—the actual movements of the animal itself not even being observed. If all variations in R were in fact predictable from knowledge of the current stimulus field, then this model would be sufficient. It is quite apparent, however, that with S conditions constant, the characteristics of R will still vary as functions of factors like past history (previous learning), individual differences in

aptitudes, motivation, personality, and so forth. Facts of this order led Woodworth in the middle 30's, for example, to insert an O in the formula, i.e., S—O—R, where the O refers rather vaguely to gross classes of intervening "organismic" variables.

Most contemporary learning theorists utilize models which introduce certain terms between the S and R. These terms may be thought of as falling roughly into two classes: *first,* terms which imply nothing about the internal mechanics of the organism but act as convenient summary terms, for example, "drive" defined only in terms of hours since last feeding, "habit" defined in terms of response probabilities or histories, etc.; and *second,* terms which are intended to describe internal states or activities, such as "drive" defined in terms of blood chemistry, neural and muscular activity, "habit" defined in terms of neural connections and strengths, etc. Most systems use both types of concepts and attempt to avoid the "junk shop" kind of psychology by introducing such terms only when they are unavoidable and by anchoring these variables firmly to antecedent (S) and subsequent (R) observable conditions.

At present, the models of learning theory are sets of Level II concepts and laws—some of which are little better than plausible hypotheses. There have been no acceptable attempts to develop or apply formal Level III systems except on a very limited basis.

Four Current Theories of Learning

While it is obviously impossible to develop in detail even one theory of learning in the space available here, an attempt will be made to outline, and present the contrasts between, four current theories which have great influence at the present time. These are the theories of Guthrie, Tolman, Skinner, and Hull. The interested reader is referred to the more adequate accounts of these and other systems given in the list of references following this section.

GUTHRIE'S ASSOCIATION THEORY

Of the theories to be considered here, perhaps the system which is simplest in appearance is that of E. R. Guthrie. This system, which is one of the early offshoots of Watsonian Behaviorism, reduces all learning to a simple associative rule: *any combination or totality of stimuli which has accompanied a movement will be followed by that movement when the combination occurs again.* Complete learning thus occurs on the first occasion on which a stimulus is paired with a response.

At first glance this simple association rule may seem to be in direct disagreement with the phenomena discussed previously, but this is not at all the case. Guthrie is concerned with stimuli and responses at a "molecular" level. Viewed in minute detail, no total stimulus pattern is ever exactly like another. Even if all external stimuli were rigidly controlled, changes are taking place within the organism (it is getting hungrier, thirstier, older, weaker, etc.; it is tense, relaxed, asleep, etc.; ad infinitum). Similarly, no two movements are ever exactly alike. They differ in the precise musculature involved, the state of the musculature, etc. The consequences of this infinite shading and change in both stimuli and responses is that learning appears to increase gradually through practice and time as more and more of the total possible stimuli and patterns of stimuli become associated with more and more of the relevant responses or muscle actions.

Generalization is taken care of by thinking of similar gross stimuli as actually consisting of overlapping pools of minute stimuli. As the stimuli become more dissimilar, the pools of stimuli overlap less and less until finally there are too few common elements to mediate the appropriate response. In order to handle *temporal delays and sequences,* Guthrie makes extensive use of movement-produced-stimulation as the actual stimulus field to which the responses are associated. *Motivation and reward* have no primary status in Guthrie's system. They operate only as they affect the central principle. Motivation is important in that it determines and intensifies sets of movements which then are available for associative connections. It supplies members to both the stimulus and response pools. Reward is important in that it terminates a class of movements and changes the stimulus situation—removing the organism, so-to-speak, from the situation before other movements can be associated with the stimuli. Thus, reward acts to prevent associations being formed with incompatible responses; it has no "positive" function. *Extinction* occurs, according to Guthrie, when the "correct" response no longer terminates the situation. Other movements follow and in turn are associated with the stimuli. In this manner on successive trials more and more stimuli are related to other movements and responses until finally the "correct" response disappears. With ever changing stimulus pools, *competing responses* which are close to the same strength will occur in various alternations, depending on the exact number of stimulus-movement associations present, until one of them gains a clear superiority.

It may be seen even in this brief presentation that Guthrie's theory deals with inferred elements of external and internal stimuli and inferred elements of responses. If everything is exactly the same, the organism will do exactly as it did the previous time. If it does not, then it may be argued that things really were not all the same. This amounts to saying that critical tests of the theory are difficult, if not impossible, to devise. The theory is facile in explanation but weak in prediction; it can be used to explain almost any (even directly opposite) outcomes. Its generality and simplicity are advantages, but it leaves much to be desired in the way of precision, reliability, and testability.

TOLMAN'S SIGN-GESTALT THEORY

A sharp contrast to Guthrie's theory both as to sources and complexity is the sign-gestalt theory of E. C. Tolman. Drawing from virtually all psychology from Watson's behaviorism on one side to Lewin's gestalt psychology on the other, Tolman builds a purposive, behavioristic theory of learning. The theory breaks sharply with the association of elemental stimuli and elemental movements and attempts to deal with goal-directed, whole acts of the organism. The level of description employed is molar, showing the relation of the organism to the goal. Most significantly perhaps, Tolman insists that what is learned is not movements or responses but "sign-significate expectations," The organism learns meanings and "what-leads-to-what" relationships. The relationship between a sign and its significate (an early stimulus and a later stimulus) is established in accord with the usual contiguity rule of association, and this relation is the "expectation." Thus, to Tolman, classical conditioning may be interpreted by saying that the buzzer comes to mean food-in-the-mouth and the salivation is a consequence of this meaning or expectancy.

This system stresses contiguity of stimuli in building up expectations. The closer in time two stimuli occur the greater the likelihood that an expectation will be set up. Practice plays a role in confirming and strengthening expectations. The more often S_2 follows S_1 the higher is the expectancy. It may be seen that expectancy can be viewed as a cognition of the probability that a given event will follow another. What increases, then, is not response potentials or habits but cognitions, which may be acted on in a variety of ways depending on the cumulative past experiences of the organism with objects and situations in its environment. This gives Tolman's system flexibility and allows him to predict the striking changes which are sometimes observed in the behavior of organisms when the learning situation is radically changed (such as providing alternative routes to a goal, changing the goal object, etc.).

Generalization is regarded as the result of stimulus sign-equivalence. Alterations in stimuli only affect performance by changing the expectancies of the organism. *Reward and motivation* have no direct effect upon *learning* in this system but affect *performance*, which is regarded as clearly different from learning. Thus, a rat may "know" how to run a maze (i.e., he may know the sign-significate relationships of all of the pathways) but not demonstrate this in performance until he is rewarded for it, at which time his "knowledge" should suddenly become evident. Reward does, of course, enter in as a stimulus significate whose presence or absence confirms or weakens an expectation. Motivation enters in as a sensitizer or emphasizer of certain significates or sign-significate relations which have been associated with it. *Extinction* is treated as a progressive disconfirmation of expectancies which cumulatively couples with the pattern of preceding situations to eliminate the learned performance. *Spontaneous recovery* takes place because the pattern of preceding situations is changed and the expectancy is still at some strength. When alternative responses are available, the pattern of behavior will ensue which is in accord with the strongest expectancy, and when that expectancy is disconfirmed the next strongest will control behavior and so on.

Tolman also points out that individual differences in organisms (heredity, age, training, special physical conditions) act to define particular behaviors on any occasion. He is thus one of the few learning theorists to comment on capacity laws, but even he has done little with them. In general, Tolman's position is a very broad one. He recognizes levels of learning and lately has come to suggest that there may be several kinds of learning. His system has stimulated much research, especially in the area of cognition. He has been criticized for vagueness and nonquantitativeness, but in part this is true of all of these theories.

SKINNER'S DESCRIPTIVE ACCOUNT

B. F. Skinner himself would deny that his approach is a theory or that psychology needs theories. He prefers, as indicated above, to collect and classify phenomena on Level II, using the most rigorous and simple descriptive categories he can develop, toward the end of systematizing knowledge about the basic phenomena of learning. The first major difference between Skinner and the other theorists discussed here is that he regards the two paradigms, conditioning and instrumental learning, as representing different kinds of learning.

Pavlovian conditioning is regarded as a highly specialized form of learning which plays little part in most human behavior. Skinner terms it *respondent* conditioning, emphasizing that it utilizes a response which can be *elicited* by a specific stimulus. The laws of respondent conditioning state (1) that contiguity of stimulation is the condition for increasing the strength of the CS-R relation and (2) that the exercise of the CS-R without the US results in decreased strength. These laws are summary descriptive statements with little elaboration, and in general Skinner has little concern with this kind of learning.

In instrumental conditioning stimulus conditions sufficient to elicit the behavior cannot be specified and are in fact irrelevant to the understanding of this behavior. The important aspect in this model is that responses are *emitted* and that they generate consequences. Skinner calls this *operant* behavior, stressing the role of the response. He is most concerned with the laws of this model and is convinced that most human behavior (including specifically language behavior) is dependent on this kind of learning. The basic laws of operant conditioning state that (1) if an operant is followed by the presentation of a reinforcing stimulus, its strength is increased and (2) if an operant is not followed by a reinforcing stimulus, its strength is decreased. In most situations an operant does become related to the stimulus field. It may come to occur, for example, only in the presence or absence of given stimuli. It is then termed a *discriminated operant*, but it is still not elicited. The stimulus conditions merely furnish the occasion for the appearance of the operant.

Skinner's system is somewhat like Tolman's in that it tends to deal with acts (not specific muscle movements) but unlike it in that it stresses the role of reinforcement. The all-important contiguity is that of the response and the reward, and one of the major determinants of the strength of an operant is the number of times the response-reward pairing occurs. These pairings summate in a non-linear but increasing fashion to increase the probability of occurrence or rate of occurrence of the operant.

Skinner introduces the concept of a reflex reserve[1] which may be defined loosely as the amount of "available activity" of a given sort which the organism is capable of emitting. Rewarding an operant increases the size of the reserve and non-reward decreases it. The rate of responding at any given moment is the function of the size of the reserve. Responses are emitted as some proportion of the total reserve remaining.

The size of the reserve is not a simple function of the number of reinforcements, however. Skinner has found that periodic reinforcement (one rewarded response every few minutes), aperiodic reinforcement (rewards on a random time schedule), fixed ratio reinforcement (reward every n^{th} response), etc., generate very great reserves. His theory lays considerable stress on the important role played by secondary reinforcement (the discriminatory stimuli), and he finds this quite useful in discussing language behavior.

The proportionality which exists between the reserve and the rate of responding may be altered by differing "states" of the organism. "States" are carefully defined intervening variables such as drive, emotion, etc. The hypothetical term "state" is introduced when it can be shown that several operations affect several reflexes in a similar fashion. States are defined by the operations and their effects and imply no physiological correlates. (It is this aspect of the system which has led to its being labeled as an "empty organism" approach.) Certain states increase the proportionality; others decrease it, but none of them are said to change the size of the reserve. As an example, in a state of high drive a rapid rate of responding would be established and, if the operant were not rewarded, rapid extinction would take place; in a state of low drive the rate of response would be low and extinction slow. Presumably, the same number of responses would be made in either case.

Skinner has studied stimulus discrimination and response differentiation exten-

---

[1] This concept was used in *Behavior of Organisms* but has been dropped in later work.

sively. When reward is made experimentally dependent on stimulus conditions, discrimination takes place. When it is dependent on response characteristics, differentiation of response takes place. Skinner's view is roughly one of mass behavior in a context of generalized stimuli, both becoming progressively more defined as the situation demands it. The problem, as he sees it, is not explaining generalization but rather the lack of it and, similarly, not response variability but lack of it. This aspect of his approach has some great advantages in dealing with progressively changing behaviors. In situations in which alternative responses are available, the response of highest strength has the greatest probability of occurrence. Alternative responses become available as earlier responses are weakened.

Skinner's system has been criticized on the grounds of its narrowness, its concern with only the lever box situation as an experimental base, and its use of the reflex reserve concept. It is, however, basically an empirical, descriptive approach and in the main there can be little argument with its basic laws. It has been valuable and stimulating in its somewhat different analysis of the learning process and in the attention it has directed towards special facets of learning phenomena.

HULL'S DEDUCTIVE SYSTEM

The most ambitious attempt to develop a rigorous, formal learning theory is unquestionably that of C. L. Hull. This system consists of a basic set of postulates from which, it is hoped, the laws of learning may be deduced in clear and quantitative form. The system stems most directly from Watsonian behaviorism and Thorndike's connectionism.

At the center of the Hullian system are two notions: habit strength and drive reduction. *Habit* is a tendency for a given stimulus discharge in the nervous system to evoke a given response. It is what is learned. *Drive*

reduction is the diminution of the neural state accompanying a need. It is the condition which effects learning; it is reinforcement. It is apparent that Hull does not hesitate, as some other theorists discussed here, to "get inside" the organism and to make positive claims about the nature of physiological events. It should be kept in mind, however, that he anchors these variables (in their role as constructs) to observable events.

Step by step Hull's postulates describe the process of learning as follows:

Stimuli impinge on the organism and generate neural activity which persists for some time before disappearing (P-1).[2] Complex stimuli interact in the nervous system to produce modified stimulus patterns (P-2). Organisms have innate general responses which are set in action by needs. These are not random responses but are selectively sensitized responses which have relatively high probabilities of terminating the specific need (e.g., withdrawal from pain, general movement and locomotion when hungry, etc.) (P-3). When a stimulus trace and a response occur in close contiguity and, at the same time, need is reduced, an increment is added to the habit strength of the particular stimulus-response pair (P-4). This constitutes learning.

Stimuli which are similar evoke the same responses, and the amount of generalization is a function of the difference between the stimuli in terms of "just noticeable differences" (a commonly used form of measurement in psychology of sensation) (P-5). Drives have stimulus properties and the intensity of a drive stimulus increases with intensity of the drive (P-6). Reaction potential is a product of habit strength and drive (P-7), but does not in itself lead directly to responding. Reaction potential to be effective must be greater than the resistances to response, reactive inhibition (similar to fatigue), conditioned inhibition (learned nonresponding) and the oscillating inhibitory potential associated with the reaction potential (P-8, 9, 10). If the momentary effective reaction potential is above the reaction threshold and stronger than competing responses, the

[2]This is the postulate number, here Postulate 1. The postulates themselves are quite lengthy and detailed. The sentences here are crude approximations.

response will occur (P-11). The remaining postulates discuss response measurement and incompatible responses.

Since Hull's system embraces both of the paradigms given above and is at the same time a reinforcement theory, his concern with contiguity is two-fold. He is concerned with the contiguity of the stimulus and the response and the response and reward. Learning is a function of the time lapse between the stimulus and the response according to a rather steep gradient and also a function of the time lapse between the response and the reward according to a gradient of reinforcement. This gradient of reinforcement is believed to be quite short. The gradient of reinforcement, however, can in effect be lengthened into a goal gradient. Stimuli within the range of the gradient of reinforcement acquire secondary reinforcing power and develop reinforcement gradients of their own. These small overlapping gradients summate to produce a major gradient extending considerable distances in space and time from the primary reinforcement itself. This complex treatment of contiguity proves to be a very useful tool in discussing many learning situations.

Habits are formed and increase in strength as a function of the number of reinforcements and the amount of need reduction. Since Hull specifies his position on generalization, it is easy to see how the summation can take place even though exact conditions are not reproduced. One interesting facet of Hull's theory is that habits are never "unlearned." Habit strength can only increase or remain the same since it is a function only of rewarded trials. Unrewarded trials do decrease responses, however, because they lead to increased reactive and conditioned inhibition. A response which had been "completely learned" and "completely extinguished" would be represented here by maximum habit strength and maximum conditioned inhibition with the net result that it would not appear. Drive and drive reduction are also obviously important in this system. Drive has an activational role through its multiplicative relation with habit strength and in addition exercises a stimulus role. Emphasis of this stimulus role permits Hull

to explain experiments which otherwise would be classed as cognitions and has led to interesting work on generalization gradients and discriminative characteristics of drives.

At every step Hull attempts to state at least tentatively the nature of the mathematical functions relating his constructs to each other and to the observable antecedent and subsequent conditions. He also derives corollaries or secondary principles which amplify the basic principles. Hull's position is that all behavior should be deducible from the system. He urges that such attempts be made and, when confirmation is not obtained, the postulate set be appropriately revised. He (as indeed all other theorists) regards the system as a self-correcting one, continuously predicting, verifying, and altering until it is complete.

Hull's system has been criticized for a variety of reasons—its excursions into the nervous system, its insistence upon reinforcement as a necessary condition for all learning, its lack of adequate definition of response, its peculiar mixture of levels in postulates, etc. In the main, however, it has proved to be quite durable. The system has been tremendously successful in stimulating research and providing a frame of reference for new material. It has been, and is being, widely extended to applications in social psychology, personality, and language behavior.

All of the theories outlined above are part of the behavioristic and functionalist tradition. As such they are primarily concerned with the phenomena of learning as manifested in overt behavior and, with the partial exception of Tolman, they all use "mechanistic" terms in describing their concepts. Some critics believe that these theorists have not sufficiently considered physiological knowledge in developing their concepts. A seemingly larger group of critics object to the apparently "mechanistic" and "atomistic" nature of these concepts and feel that such concepts cannot do justice to the full range of human and animal behavior. While such criticism has been expressed in many diverse ways, much of the basis for such objections may be found in the work of the gestalt psychologists, whose name comes from the emphasis they have placed on "wholes" and "organizing principles." Because the primary concern of this group has been the study of perception and problem solving rather than learning, a summary of their theorizing has not been included in this section. (A brief discussion of some of the gestalt phenomena in perception may be found in section 3.1. of this report.)

REFERENCES

Guthrie, E. R. *The psychology of learning.* New York: Harper, 1935.
A presentation of Guthrie's theory with applications to many everyday behavioral situations. Highly readable.

Hilgard, E. R. *Theories of learning.* New York: Appleton, 1948.
A fairly recent and comprehensive survey and evaluation of various contemporary conceptions of learning, including gestalt and behavioristic theories.

———, and D. G. Marquis. *Conditioning and learning.* New York: Appleton, 1948.
A more advanced and tightly argued analysis of the fundamental concepts and phenomena of learning. One of the most important critical books in the field.

Hull, C. L. *Principles of behavior.* New York: Appleton, 1943.
A systematic presentation of Hull's learning postulates and their application to phenomena. Although more recent revisions have appeared, this is probably the best comprehensive statement.

Koffka, K. *Principles of gestalt psychology.* New York: Harcourt, 1935.
Probably the most detailed and extensive presentation of the gestalt point of view, including materials on perception and learning.

Lewin, K. *Principles of topological psychology.* New York: McGraw–Hill, 1936.
Behavior of organisms treated in terms of field theory.

McGeoch, J. A., and A. L. Irion. *The psychology of human learning.* New York: Longmans, 1952.
An extensive coverage of the facts and theories of learning as applied particularly to human behavior.

Miller, N. E. Learnable drives and rewards. In Stevens (Ed.), *Handbook of experimental psychology.* New York: Wiley, 1951.
A penetrating analysis of the nature and development of secondary motivation and reward mechanisms, with presentation of experimental findings.

———, and J. Dollard. *Social learning and imitation.* New Haven: Yale University Press, 1941.
An application of Hull-type learning theory to a variety of social problems. Provides a very readable introduction.

Mowrer, O. H. *Learning theory and personality dynamics.* New York: Ronald, 1950.
A collection of Mowrer's best papers relating learning theory to personality dynamics. Also presents Mowrer's two-factor theory of learning.

National Society for the Study of Education. *The psychology of learning.* 41st Yearbook, Part II. Bloomington, Indiana: Public School, 1942.
Presents in careful, systematic form several important summaries of contemporary theories as written by their sponsors.

Osgood, C. E. *Method and theory in experimental psychology.* New York: Oxford, 1953.
A graduate text in experimental psychology, including sections on sensory processes, perception, learning, and symbolic processes. Includes critical analyses of contemporary learning theories and a presentation of the author's mediation hypothesis.

Skinner, B. F. *The behavior of organisms.* New York: Appleton, 1938.
The most complete presentation of Skinner's conception of learning and data derived from his type of instrumental situation. Important for its methodological contributions as well as for its viewpoint.

Spence, K. W. Theoretical interpretations of learning. In Stevens (Ed.), *Handbook of experimental psychology.* New York: Wiley, 1951.

A critical comparative evaluation of contemporary theories of learning by one of the most active theorists and investigators on the scene today.

Tolman, E. C. *Purposive behavior in animals and men.* New York: Appleton, 1932.

A systematic presentation of Tolman's early views with results of numerous experiments. A classic in the field, and a book which has had great influence upon contemporary psychology.

Wertheimer, M. *Productive thinking.* New York: Harper, 1945.

A Functional Analysis of Verbal Behavior

B. F. SKINNER

Men act upon the world, and change it, and are changed in turn by the consequences of their action. Certain processes, which the human organism shares with other species, alter behavior so that it achieves a safer and more useful interchange with a particular environment. When appropriate behavior has been established, its consequences work through similar processes to keep it in force. If by chance the environment changes, old forms of behavior disappear, while new consequences build new forms.

Behavior alters the environment through mechanical action, and its properties or dimensions are often related in a simple way to the effects produced. When a man walks toward an object, he usually finds himself closer to it; if he reaches for it, physical contact is likely to follow; and if he grasps and lifts it, or pushes or pulls it, the object frequently changes position in appropriate directions. All this follows from simple geometrical and mechanical principles.

Much of the time, however, a man acts only indirectly upon the environment from which the ultimate consequences of his behavior emerge. His first effect is upon other men. Instead of going to a drinking fountain, a thirsty man may simply "ask for a glass of water"—that is, may engage in behavior which produces a certain pattern of sounds which in turn induces someone to bring him a glass of water. The sounds themselves are easy to describe in physical terms; but the glass of water reaches the speaker only as the result of a complex series of events including the behavior of a listener. The ultimate consequence, the receipt of water, bears no useful geometrical or mechanical relation to the form of the behavior of "asking for water." Indeed, it is characteristic of such behavior that it is impotent against the physical world. Rarely do we shout down the walls of a Jericho or successfully command the sun to stop or the waves to be still. Names do not break bones. The consequences of such behavior are mediated by a train of events no less physical or inevitable than direct mechanical action, but clearly more difficult to describe.

Behavior which is effective only through the mediation of other persons has so many distinguishing dynamic and topographical properties that a special treatment is justified and, indeed, demanded. Problems raised by this special mode of action are usually assigned to the field of speech or language. Unfortunately, the term "speech" emphasizes vocal behavior and is only awkwardly applied to instances in which the mediating person is affected visually, as in writing a note. "Language" is now satisfactorily remote from its original commitment to vocal behavior, but it has come to refer to the practices of a linguistic community rather than the behavior of any one member. The adjective "linguistic" suffers from the same disadvantage. The term "verbal behavior" has much to recommend it. Its etymological sanction is not too powerful, but it emphasizes the individual speaker and, whether recognized by the user or not, specifies behavior shaped and maintained by mediated consequences. It also has the advantage of being relatively unfamiliar in traditional modes of explanation.

A definition of verbal behavior as behavior reinforced through the mediation of other persons needs, as we shall see, certain refinements. Moreover, it does not say much about the behavior of the listener, even though there would be little verbal behavior to consider if someone had not already acquired special responses to the patterns of energy generated by the speaker. This omission can be justified, for the behavior of the listener in mediating the consequences of the behavior of the speaker is not necessarily verbal in any special sense. It cannot, in fact, be distinguished from behavior in general, and an adequate account of verbal behavior need cover only as much of the behavior of the listener as is needed to explain the behavior of the speaker. The behaviors of speaker and listener taken together compose what may be called a total speech episode. There is nothing in such an episode which is more than the combined behavior of two or more individuals. Nothing "emerges" in the social unit. The speaker can be studied while assuming a listener, and the listener while assuming a speaker. The separate accounts which result exhaust the episode in which both participate.

It would be foolish to underestimate the difficulty of this subject matter, but recent advances in the analysis of behavior permit us to approach it with a certain optimism. New experimental techniques and fresh formulations have revealed a new level of order and precision. The basic processes and relations which give verbal behavior its special characteristics are now fairly well understood. Much of the experimental work responsible for this advance has been carried out on other species, but the results have proved to be surprisingly free of species restrictions. Recent work has shown that the methods can be extended to human behavior without serious modification. Quite apart from the possibility of extrapolating specific experimental findings, the formulation provides a fruitful new approach to human behavior in general, and enables us to deal more effectively with that subdivision called verbal.

The "understanding" of verbal behavior is something more than the use of a consistent vocabulary with which specific instances may be described. It is not to be confused with the confirmation of any set of theoretical principles. The criteria are more demanding than that. The extent to which we understand verbal behavior in a "causal" analysis is to be assessed from the extent to which we can predict the occurrence of specific instances and, eventually, from the extent to which we can produce or control such behavior by altering the conditions under which it occurs. In representing such a goal it is helpful to keep certain specific engineering tasks in mind. How can the teacher establish the specific verbal repertoires which are the principal end-products of education? How can the therapist uncover latent verbal behavior in a therapeutic interview? How can the writer evoke his own verbal behavior in the act of composition? How can the scientist, mathematician, or logician manipulate his verbal behavior in productive thinking? Practical problems of this sort are, of course, endless. To solve them is not the immediate goal of a scientific analysis, but they underline the kinds of processes and relationships which such an analysis must consider.

TRADITIONAL FORMULATIONS

A science of behavior does not arrive at this special field to find it unoccupied. Elaborate systems of terms describing verbal behavior have been developed. The lay vocabulary abounds with them. Classical rhetoric, grammar, logic, scientific methodology, linguistics, literary criticism, speech pathology, semantics, and many other disciplines have contributed technical terms and principles. In general, however, the subject here at issue has not been clearly identified, nor have appropriate methods for studying it been devised. Linguistics, for example, has recorded and analyzed speech sounds and semantic and syntactical practices, but comparisons of different languages and the tracing of historical changes have taken precedence over the study of the individual speaker. Logic, mathematics, and scientific methodology have recognized the limitations which linguistic practices impose on human thought, but have usually remained content with a formal analysis; in any case, they have not developed the techniques necessary for a causal analysis of the behavior of man thinking. Classical rhetoric was responsible for an elaborate system of terms describing the characteristics of literary works of art, applicable as well to everyday speech. It also gave some attention to effects upon the listener. But the early promise of a science of verbal behavior was never fulfilled. Modern literary criticism, except for some use of the technical vocabulary of psychoanalysis, seldom goes beyond the terms of the intelligent layman. An effective frontal attack, a formulation appropriate to all special fields, has never emerged under the auspices of any one of these disciplines.

Perhaps this fact is responsible for the rise of semantics as a general account of verbal behavior. The technical study of meaning was already under way as a peripheral field of linguistics when, in 1923, Ogden and Richards demonstrated the need for a broader science of symbolism. This was to be a general analysis of linguistic processes applicable to any field and under the domination of no special interest. Attempts have been made to carry out the recommendation, but an adequate science of verbal behavior has not been achieved. There are several current brands of semantics, and they represent the same special interests and employ the same special techniques as heretofore. The original method of Ogden and Richards was philosophical, with psychological leanings. Some of the more rigorous systems are frankly logical. In linguistics, semantics continues to be a question of how meanings are expressed and how they change. Some semanticists deal mainly with the verbal machinery of society, particularly propaganda. Others are essentially therapists who hold that many of the troubles of the world are linguistic error. The currency of the term "semantics" shows the need for a science of verbal behavior which will be divorced from special interests and helpful wherever language is used, but the science itself has not emerged under this aegis.

The final responsibility must rest with the behavioral sciences, and particularly with psychology. What happens when a man speaks or responds to speech is clearly a question about human behavior and hence a question to be answered with the concepts and techniques of psychology as an experimental science of behavior. At first blush, it may not seem to be a particularly difficult question. Except on the score of simplicity, verbal behavior has many favorable characteristics as an object of study. It is usually easily observed (if it were not, it would be ineffective as verbal behavior); there has never been any shortage of material (men talk and listen a great deal); the facts are substantial (careful observers will generally agree as to what is said in any given instance); and the development of the practical art of writing has provided a ready-made system of notation for reporting verbal behavior which is more convenient and precise than any available in the nonverbal field. What is lacking is a satisfactory causal or functional treatment. Together with other disciplines concerned with verbal behavior, psychology has collected facts and sometimes put them in convenient order, but in this welter of material it has failed to demonstrate the significant relations which are the heart of a scientific account. For reasons which, in retrospect, are not too difficult to discover, it has been led to neglect some of the events needed in a functional or causal analysis. It has done this because the place of such events has been occupied by certain fictional causes which psychology has been slow in disavowing. In examining some of these causes more closely, we may find an explanation of why a science of verbal behavior has been so long delayed.

It has generally been assumed that to explain behavior, or any aspect of it, one must attribute it to events taking place inside the organism. In the field of verbal behavior this practice was once represented by the doctrine of the expression of ideas. An utterance was felt to be explained by setting forth the ideas which it expressed. If the speaker had had a different idea, he would have uttered different words or words in a different arrangement. If his utterance was unusual, it was because of the novelty or originality of his ideas. If it seemed empty, he must have lacked ideas or have been unable to put them into words. If he could not keep silent, it was because of the force of his ideas. If he spoke haltingly, it was because his ideas came slowly or were badly organized. And so on. All properties of verbal behavior seem to be thus accounted for.

Such a practice obviously has the same goal as a causal analysis, but it has by no means the same results. The difficulty is that the ideas for which sounds are said to stand as signs cannot be independently observed. If we ask for evidence of their existence, we are likely to be given a restatement in other words; but a restatement is no closer to the idea than the original utterance. Restatement merely shows that the idea is not identified with a single expres-

sion. It is, in fact, often defined as something common to two or more expressions. But we shall not arrive at this "something" even though we express an idea in every conceivable way.

Another common answer is to appeal to images. The idea is said to be what passes through the speaker's mind, what the speaker sees and hears and feels when he is "having" the idea. Explorations of the thought processes underlying verbal behavior have been attempted by asking thinkers to describe experiences of this nature. But although selected examples are sometimes convincing, only a small part of the ideas said to be expressed in words can be identified with the kind of sensory event upon which the notion of image rests. A book on physics is much more than a description of the images in the mind of physicists.

There is obviously something suspicious in the ease with which we discover in a set of ideas precisely those properties needed to account for the behavior which expresses them. We evidently construct the ideas at will from the behavior to be explained. There is, of course, no real explanation. When we say that a remark is confusing because the idea is unclear, we seem to be talking about two levels of observation although there is, in fact, only one. It is the *remark* which is unclear. The practice may have been defensible when inquiries into verbal processes were philosophical rather than scientific, and when a science of ideas could be imagined which would some day put the matter in better order; but it stands in a different light today. It is the function of an explanatory fiction to allay curiosity and to bring inquiry to an end. The doctrine of ideas has had this effect by appearing to assign important problems of verbal behavior to a psychology of ideas. The problems have then seemed to pass beyond the range of the techniques of the student of language, or to have become too obscure to make further study profitable.

Perhaps no one today is deceived by an "idea" as an explanatory fiction. Idioms and expressions which seem to explain verbal behavior in term of ideas are so common in our language that it is impossible to avoid them, but they may be little more than moribund figures of speech. The basic formulation, however, has been preserved. The immediate successor to "idea" was "meaning," and the place of the latter is in danger of being usurped by a newcomer, "information." These terms all have the same effect of discouraging a functional analysis and of supporting, instead, some of the practices first associated with the doctrine of ideas.

One unfortunate consequence is the belief that speech has an independent existence apart from the behavior of the speaker. Words are regarded as tools or instruments, analogous to the tokens, counters, or signal flags sometimes employed for verbal purposes. It is true that verbal behavior usually produces objective entities. The sound-stream of vocal speech, the words on a page, the signals transmitted on a telephone or telegraph wire—these are records left by verbal behavior. As objective facts, they may all be studied, as they have been from time to time in linguistics, communication engineering, literary criticism, and so on. But although the formal properties of the records of utterances are interesting, we must preserve the distinction between an activity and its traces. In particular we must avoid the unnatural formulation of verbal behavior as the "use of words." We have no more reason to say that a man "uses the word *water*" in asking for a drink than to say that he "uses a reach" in taking the offered glass. In the arts, crafts, and sports, especially where instruction is verbal, acts are sometimes named. We say that a tennis player uses a drop stroke, or a swimmer a crawl. No one is likely to be misled when drop strokes or crawls are referred to as things, but words are a different matter. Misunderstanding has been common, and often disastrous.

A complementary practice has been to assign an independent existence to meanings. "Meaning," like "idea," is said to be something expressed or communicated by an utterance. A meaning explains the occurrence of a particular set of words in the sense that if there had been a different meaning to be expressed, a different set of words would have been used. An utterance will be affected according to whether a meaning is clear or vague, and so on. The concept has certain advantages. Where "ideas" (like "feelings" and "desires," which are also said to be expressed by words) must be inside the organism, there is a promising possibility that meanings may be kept outside the skin. In this sense, they are as observable as any part of physics.

But can we identify the meaning of an utterance in an objective way? A fair argument may be made in the case of proper nouns, and some common nouns, verbs, adjectives, and adverbs—roughly the words with respect to which the doctrine of ideas could be supported by the appeal to images. But what about words like *atom* or *gene* or *minus one* or *the spirit of the times* where corresponding nonverbal entities are not easily discovered? And for words like *nevertheless, although,* and *ouch!* it has seemed necessary to look inside the organism for the speaker's intention, attitude, sentiment, or some other psychological condition.

Even the words which seem to fit an externalized semantic framework are not without their problems. It may be true that proper nouns stand in a one-to-one correspondence with things, provided everything has its own proper name, but what about common nouns? What is the meaning of *cat?* Is it some one cat, or the physical totality of all cats, or the class of all cats? Or must we fall back upon the idea of cat? Even in the case of the proper noun, a difficulty remains. Assuming that there is only one man named Doe, is Doe himself the meaning of *Doe?* Certainly *he* is not conveyed or communicated when the word is used.

The existence of meanings becomes even more doubtful when we advance from single words to those collocations which "say something." What is said by a sentence is something more than what the words in it mean. Sentences do not merely refer to trees and skies and rain, they say something about them. This something is sometimes called a "proposition"—a somewhat more respectable precursor of speech but very similar to the "idea" which would have been said to be expressed by the same sentence under the older doctrine. To define a proposition as "something which may be said in any language" does not tell us where propositions are, or of what stuff they are made. Nor is the problem solved by defining a proposition as all the sentences which have the same meaning as some one sentence, since we cannot identify a sentence as a member of this class without knowing its meaning—at which point we find ourselves facing our original problem.

It has been tempting to try to establish the separate existence of words and meanings because a fairly elegant solution of certain problems then becomes available. Theories of meaning usually deal with corresponding arrays of words and things. How do the linguistic entities on one side correspond with the things or events which are their meanings on the other side, and what is the nature of the relation between them called "reference"? Dictionaries seem, at first blush, to support the notion of such arrays. But dictionaries do not give meanings; at best they give words having the same meanings. The semantic scheme, as usually conceived, has interesting properties. Mathematicians, logicians, and information theorists have explored possible modes of correspondence at length. For example, to what extent can the dimensions of the thing communicated be represented in the dimensions of the communicating medium? But it remains to be shown that such constructions bear any close resemblances to the products of genuine linguistic activities.

In any case the practice neglects many important properties of the original behavior, and raises other problems. We cannot successfully supplement a framework of semantic reference by appealing to the "intention of the speaker" until a satisfactory psychological account of intention can be given. If "connotative meaning" is to supplement a deficient denotation, study of the associative process is required. When some meanings are classed as "emotive," another difficult and relatively undeveloped psychological field is invaded. These are all efforts to preserve the logical representation by setting up additional categories for exceptional words. They are a sort of patchwork which succeeds mainly in showing how threadbare the basic notion is. When we attempt to supply the additional material needed in this representation of verbal behavior, we find that our task has been set in awkward if not impossible terms. The observable data have been preempted, and the student of behavior is left with vaguely identified "thought processes."

The impulse to explicate a meaning is easily understood. We ask, "What do you mean?" because the answer is frequently helpful. Clarifications of meaning in this sense have an important place in every sort of intellectual endeavor. For the purposes of effective discourse the method of paraphrase usually suffices; we may not need extraverbal referents. But the explication of verbal behavior should not be allowed to generate a sense of scientific achievement. One has not *accounted for* a remark by paraphrasing "what it means."

We could no doubt define ideas, meanings, and so on, so that they would be scientifically acceptable and even useful in describing verbal behavior. But such an effort to retain traditional terms would be costly. It is the general formulation which is wrong. We seek "causes" of behavior which have an acceptable scientific status and which, with luck, will be susceptible to measurement and manipulation. To say that these are "all that is meant by" ideas or meanings is to misrepresent the traditional *practice*. We must find the functional relations which govern the verbal behavior to be explained; to call such relations "expression" or "communication" is to run the danger of introducing extraneous and misleading properties and events. The only solution is to reject the traditional formulation of verbal behavior in terms of meaning.

A NEW FORMULATION

The direction to be taken in an alternative approach is dictated by the task itself. Our first responsibility is simple *description:* what is the topography of this subdivision of human behavior? Once that question has been answered in at least a preliminary fashion we may advance to the stage called explanation: what conditions are relevant to the occurrence of the behavior—what are the variables of which it is a function? Once these have been identified, we can account for the dynamic characteristics of verbal behavior within a framework appropriate to human behavior as a whole. At the same time, of course, we must consider the behavior of the listener. In relating this to the behavior of the speaker, we complete our account of the verbal episode.

But this is only the beginning. Once a repertoire of verbal behavior has been set up, a host of new problems arise from the interaction of its parts. Verbal behavior is usually the effect of *multiple causes*. Separate variables combine to extend their functional control, and new forms of behavior emerge from the recombination of old fragments. All of this has appropriate effects upon the listener, whose behavior then calls for analysis.

Still another set of problems arises from the fact, often pointed out, that a speaker is normally also a listener. He reacts to his own behavior in several important ways. Part of what he says is under the control of other parts of his verbal behavior. We refer to this interaction when we say that the speaker qualifies, orders, or elaborates his behavior at the moment it is produced. The

mere emission of responses is an incomplete characterization when behavior is *composed*. As another consequence of the fact that the speaker is also a listener, some of the behavior of listening resembles the behavior of speaking, particularly when the listener "understands" what is said.

The speaker and listener within the same skin engage in activities which are traditionally described as "thinking." The speaker manipulates his behavior; he reviews it, and may reject it or emit it in modified form. The extent to which he does so varies over a wide range, determined in part by the extent to which he serves as his own listener. The skillful speaker learns to tease out weak behavior and to manipulate variables which will generate and strengthen new responses in his repertoire. Such behavior is commonly observed in the verbal practices of literature as well as of science and logic. An analysis of these activities, together with their effects upon the listener, leads us in the end to the role of verbal behavior in the problem of knowledge.

The present book sets forth the principal features of an analysis from this point of view. Part II sketches the topography of verbal behavior in relation to its controlling variables and Part III some of the consequences of the interaction of variables. Part IV describes the manipulation of verbal behavior in the act of composition, while Part V considers the activities involved in editing and in the creative production of behavior which are usually called verbal thinking. No assumption is made of any uniquely verbal characteristic, and the principles and methods employed are adapted to the study of human behavior as a whole. An extensive treatment of human behavior in general from the same point of view may be found elsewhere. The present account is self-contained.

One important feature of the analysis is that it is directed to the behavior of the individual speaker and listener; no appeal is made to statistical concepts based upon data derived from groups. Even with respect to the individual speaker or listener, little use is made of specific experimental results. The basic facts to be analyzed are well known to every educated person and do not need to be substantiated statistically or experimentally at the level of rigor here attempted. No effort has been made to survey the relevant "literature." The emphasis is upon an orderly arrangement of well-known facts, in accordance with a formulation of behavior derived from an experimental analysis of a more rigorous sort. The present extension to verbal behavior is thus an exercise in interpretation rather than a quantitative extrapolation of rigorous experimental results.

The lack of quantitative rigor is to some extent offset by an insistence that the conditions appealed to in the analysis be, so far as possible, accessible and manipulable. The formulation is inherently practical and suggests immediate technological applications at almost every step. Although the emphasis is not upon experimental or statistical facts, the book is not theoretical in the usual sense. It makes no appeal to hypothetical explanatory entities. The ultimate aim is the prediction and control of verbal behavior.

Review of Skinner's Verbal Behavior

NOAM CHOMSKY

1. A great many linguists and philosophers concerned with language have expressed the hope that their studies might ultimately be embedded in a framework provided by behaviorist psychology, and that refractory areas of investigation, particularly those in which meaning is involved, will in this way be opened up to fruitful exploration. Since this volume is the first large-scale attempt to incorporate the major aspects of linguistic behavior within a behaviorist framework, it merits and will undoubtedly receive careful attention. Skinner is noted for his contributions to the study of animal behavior. The book under review is the product of study of linguistic behavior extending over more than twenty years. Earlier versions of it have been fairly widely circulated, and there are quite a few references in the psychological literature to its major ideas.

The problem to which this book is addressed is that of giving a "functional analysis" of verbal behavior. By functional analysis, Skinner means identification of the variables that control this behavior and specification of how they interact to determine a particular verbal response. Furthermore, the controlling variables are to be described completely in terms of such notions as stimulus, reinforcement, deprivation, which have been given a reasonably clear meaning in animal experimentation. In other words, the goal of the book is to provide a way to predict and control verbal behavior by observing and manipulating the physical environment of the speaker.

Skinner feels that recent advances in the laboratory study of animal behavior permit us to approach this problem with a certain optimism, since "the basic processes and relations which give verbal behavior its special characteristics are now fairly well understood . . . the results [of this experi-

Reprinted and abridged with the permission of the author and the publisher from the review in *Language*, 1959, **35**, 26–58.

mental work] have been surprisingly free of species restrictions. Recent work has shown that the methods can be extended to human behavior without serious modification" (3).°

It is important to see clearly just what it is in Skinner's program and claims that makes them appear so bold and remarkable. It is not primarily the fact that he has set functional analysis as his problem, or that he limits himself to study of 'observables', i.e. input-output relations. What is so surprising is the particular limitations he has imposed on the way in which the observables of behavior are to be studied, and, above all, the particularly simple nature of the 'function' which, he claims, describes the causation of behavior. One would naturally expect that prediction of the behavior of a complex organism (or machine) would require, in addition to information about external stimulation, knowledge of the internal structure of the organism, the ways in which it processes input information and organizes its own behavior. These characteristics of the organism are in general a complicated product of inborn structure, the genetically determined course of maturation, and past experience. Insofar as independent neurophysiological evidence is not available, it is obvious that inferences concerning the structure of the organism are based on observation of behavior and outside events. Nevertheless, one's estimate of the relative importance of external factors and internal structure in the determination of behavior will have an important effect on the direction of research on linguistic (or any other) behavior, and on the kinds of analogies from animal behavior studies that will be considered relevant or suggestive.

Putting it differently, anyone who sets himself the problem of analyzing the causation of behavior will (in the absence of independent neurophysiological evidence) concern himself with the only data available, namely the record of inputs to the

° Numbers in parentheses refer to the page numbers in B. F. Skinner, *Verbal Behavior*, Appleton-Century-Crofts, Inc., 1957.

organism and the organism's present response, and will try to describe the function specifying the response in terms of the history of inputs. This is nothing more than the definition of his problem. There are no possible grounds for argument here, if one accepts the problem as legitimate, though Skinner has often advanced and defended this definition of a problem as if it were a thesis which other investigators reject. The differences that arise between those who affirm and those who deny the importance of the specific 'contribution of the organism' to learning and performance concern the particular character and complexity of this function, and the kinds of observations and research necessary for arriving at a precise specification of it. If the contribution of the organism is complex, the only hope of predicting behavior even in a gross way will be through a very indirect program of research that begins by studying the detailed character of the behavior itself and the particular capacities of the organism involved.

Skinner's thesis is that external factors consisting of present stimulation and the history of reinforcement (in particular the frequency, arrangement, and withholding of reinforcing stimuli) are of overwhelming importance, and that the general principles revealed in laboratory studies of these phenomena provide the basis for understanding the complexities of verbal behavior. He confidently and repeatedly voices his claim to have demonstrated that the contribution of the speaker is quite trivial and elementary, and that precise prediction of verbal behavior involves only specification of the few external factors that he has isolated experimentally with lower organisms.

Careful study of this book (and of the research on which it draws) reveals, however, that these astonishing claims are far from justified. It indicates, furthermore, that the insights that have been achieved in the laboratories of the reinforcement theorist, though quite genuine, can be applied to complex human behavior only in the most gross and superficial way, and that speculative attempts to discuss linguistic behavior in these terms alone omit from consideration factors of fundamental importance that are, no doubt, amenable to scientific study, although their specific character cannot at present be precisely formulated. Since Skinner's work is the most extensive attempt to accommodate human behavior involving higher mental faculties within a strict behaviorist schema of the type that has attracted many linguists and philosophers, as well as psychologists, a detailed documentation is of independent interest. The magnitude of the failure of this attempt to account for verbal behavior serves as a kind of measure of the importance of the factors omitted from consideration, and an indication of how little is really known about this remarkably complex phenomenon.

The force of Skinner's argument lies in the enormous wealth and range of examples for which he proposes a functional analysis. The only way to evaluate the success of his program and the correctness of his basic assumptions about verbal behavior is to review these examples in detail and to determine the precise character of the concepts in terms of which the functional analysis is presented.

The notions "stimulus," "response," "reinforcement" are relatively well defined with respect to the bar-pressing experiments and others similarly restricted. Before we can extend them to real-life behavior, however, certain difficulties must be faced. We must decide, first of all, whether any physical event to which the organism is capable of reacting is to be called a stimulus on a given occasion, or only one to which the organism in fact reacts; and correspondingly, we must decide whether any part of behavior is to be called a response, or only one connected with stimuli in lawful ways. Questions of this sort pose something of a dilemma for the experimental psychologist. If he accepts the broad definitions, characterizing any physical event impinging on the organism as a stimulus and any part of

the organism's behavior as a response, he must conclude that behavior has not been demonstrated to be lawful. In the present state of our knowledge, we must attribute an overwhelming influence on actual behavior to ill-defined factors of attention, set, volition, and caprice. If we accept the narrower definitions, then behavior is lawful by definition (if it consists of responses); but this fact is of limited significance, since most of what the animal does will simply not be considered behavior. Hence the psychologist either must admit that behavior is not lawful (or that he cannot at present show that it is—not at all a damaging admission for a developing science), or must restrict his attention to those highly limited areas in which it is lawful (e.g. with adequate controls, bar-pressing in rats; lawfulness of the observed behavior provides, for Skinner, an implicit definition of a good experiment).

Skinner does not consistently adopt either course. He utilizes the experimental results as evidence for the scientific character of his system of behavior, and analogic guesses (formulated in terms of a metaphoric extension of the technical vocabulary of the laboratory) as evidence for its scope. This creates the illusion of a rigorous scientific theory with a very broad scope, although in fact the terms used in the description of real-life and of laboratory behavior may be mere homonyms, with at most a vague similarity of meaning. To substantiate this evaluation, a critical account of his book must show that with a literal reading (where the terms of the descriptive system have something like the technical meanings given in Skinner's definitions) the book covers almost no aspect of linguistic behavior, and that with a metaphoric reading, it is no more scientific than the traditional approaches to this subject matter, and rarely as clear and careful.

3. Consider first Skinner's use of the notions "stimulus" and "response." In *Behavior of organisms* (9) he commits himself to the narrow definitions for these terms. A part of the environment and a part

of behavior are called stimulus (eliciting, discriminated, or reinforcing) and response, respectively, only if they are lawfully related; that is, if the "dynamic laws" relating them show smooth and reproducible curves. Evidently stimuli and responses, so defined, have not been shown to figure very widely in ordinary human behavior. We can, in the face of presently available evidence, continue to maintain the lawfulness of the relation between stimulus and response only by depriving them of their objective character. A typical example of "stimulus control" for Skinner would be the response to a piece of music with the utterance *Mozart* or to a painting with the response *Dutch*. These responses are asserted to be "under the control of extremely subtle properties" of the physical object or event (108). Suppose instead of saying *Dutch* we had said *Clashes with the wallpaper, I thought you liked abstract work, Never saw it before, Tilted, Hanging too low, Beautiful, Hideous, Remember our camping trip last summer?* or whatever else might come into our minds when looking at a picture (in Skinnerian translation, whatever other responses exist in sufficient strength). Skinner could only say that each of these responses is under the control of some other stimulus property of the physical object. If we look at a red chair and say *red,* the response is under the control of the stimulus "redness"; if we say *chair,* it is under the control of the collection of properties (for Skinner, the object) "chairness" (110), and similarly for any other response. This device is as simple as it is empty. Since properties are free for the asking (we have as many of them as we have nonsynonymous descriptive expressions in our language, whatever this means exactly), we can account for a wide class of responses in terms of Skinnerian functional analysis by identifying the "controlling stimuli." But the word "stimulus" has lost all objectivity in this usage. Stimuli are no longer part of the outside physical world; they are driven back into the organism. We identify the stimulus when we hear the

response. It is clear from such examples, which abound, that the talk of "stimulus control" simply disguises a complete retreat to mentalistic psychology. We cannot predict verbal behavior in terms of the stimuli in the speaker's environment, since we do not know what the current stimuli are until he responds. Furthermore, since we cannot control the property of a physical object to which an individual will respond, except in highly artificial cases, Skinner's claim that his system, as opposed to the traditional one, permits the practical control of verbal behavior is quite false.

Other examples of "stimulus control" merely add to the general mystification. Thus a proper noun is held to be a response "under the control of a specific person or thing" (as controlling stimulus, 113). I have often used the words *Eisenhower* and *Moscow,* which I presume are proper nouns if anything is, but have never been "stimulated" by the corresponding objects. How can this fact be made compatible with this definition? Suppose that I use the name of a friend who is not present. Is this an instance of a proper noun under the control of the friend as stimulus? Elsewhere it is asserted that a stimulus controls a response in the sense that presence of the stimulus increases the probability of the response. But it is obviously untrue that the probability that a speaker will produce a full name is increased when its bearer faces the speaker. Furthermore, how can one's own name be a proper noun in this sense? A multitude of similar questions arise immediately. It appears that the word "control" here is merely a misleading paraphrase for the traditional "denote" or "refer." The assertion (115) that so far as the speaker is concerned, the relation of reference is "simply the probability that the speaker will emit a response of a given form in the presence of a stimulus having specified properties" is surely incorrect if we take the words "presence," "stimulus," and "probability" in their literal sense. That they are not intended to be taken literally is indicated by many examples, as when a response is said to be "controlled" by a situation or state of affairs as "stimulus." Thus, the expression *a needle in a haystack* "may be controlled as a unit by a particular type of situation" (116); the words in a single part of speech, e.g. all adjectives, are under the control of a single set of subtle properties of stimuli (121); "the sentence *The boy runs a store* is under the control of an extremely complex stimulus situation" (335); *"He is not at all well* may function as a standard response under the control of a state of affairs which might also control *He is ailing"* (325); when an envoy observes events in a foreign country and reports upon his return, his report is under "remote stimulus control" (416); the statement *This is war* may be a response to a "confusing international situation" (441); the suffix *-ed* is controlled by that "subtle property of stimuli which we speak of as action-in-the-past" (121) just as the *-s* in *The boy runs* is under the control of such specific features of the situation as its "currency" (332). No characterization of the notion "stimulus control" that is remotely related to the bar-pressing experiment (or that preserves the faintest objectivity) can be made to cover a set of examples like these, in which, for example, the "controlling stimulus" need not even impinge on the responding organism.

Consider now Skinner's use of the notion "response." The problem of identifying units in verbal behavior has of course been a primary concern of linguists, and it seems very likely that experimental psychologists should be able to provide much-needed assistance in clearing up the many remaining difficulties in systematic identification. Skinner recognizes (20) the fundamental character of the problem of identification of a unit of verbal behavior, but is satisfied with an answer so vague and subjective that it does not really contribute to its solution. The unit of verbal behavior—the verbal operant—is defined as a class of responses of identifiable form functionally related to one or more controlling varia-

bles. No method is suggested for determining in a particular instance what are the controlling variables, how many such units have occurred, or where their boundaries are in the total response. Nor is any attempt made to specify how much or what kind of similarity in form or "control" is required for two physical events to be considered instances of the same operant. In short, no answers are suggested for the most elementary questions that must be asked of anyone proposing a method for description of behavior. Skinner is content with what he calls an "extrapolation" of the concept of operant developed in the laboratory to the verbal field. In the typical Skinnerian experiment, the problem of identifying the unit of behavior is not too crucial. It is defined, by fiat, as a recorded peck or bar-press, and systematic variations in the rate of this operant and its resistance to extinction are studied as a function of deprivation and scheduling of reinforcement (pellets). The operant is thus defined with respect to a particular experimental procedure. This is perfectly reasonable, and has led to many interesting results. It is, however, completely meaningless to speak of extrapolating this concept of operant to ordinary verbal behavior. Such "extrapolation" leaves us with no way of justifying one or another decision about the units in the "verbal repertoire."

Skinner specifies "response strength" as the basic datum, the basic dependent variable in his functional analysis. In the bar-pressing experimental response strength is defined in terms of rate of emission during extinction. Skinner has argued that this is "the only datum that varies significantly and in the expected direction under conditions which are relevant to the 'learning process.' In the book under review, response strength is defined as 'probability of emission'" (22). This definition provides a comforting impression of objectivity, which, however, is quickly dispelled when we look into the matter more closely. The term "probability" has some rather obscure meaning for Skinner in this book. We are told, on the one hand, that "our evidence for the contribution of each variable [to response strength] is based on observation of frequencies alone" (28). At the same time, it appears that frequency is a very misleading measure of strength, since, for example, the frequency of a response may be "primarily attributable to the frequency of occurrence of controlling variables" (27). It is not clear how the frequency of a response can be attributable to anything BUT the frequency of occurrence of its controlling variables if we accept Skinner's view that the behavior occurring in a given situation is "fully determined" by the relevant controlling variables (175, 228). Furthermore, although the evidence for the contribution of each variable to response strength is based on observation of frequencies alone, it turns out that "we base the notion of strength upon several kinds of evidence" (22), in particular (22–28): emission of the response (particularly in unusual circumstances), energy level (stress), pitch level, speed and delay of emission, size of letters etc. in writing, immediate repetition, and— a final factor, relevant but misleading— over-all frequency.

Of course, Skinner recognizes that these measures do not co-vary, because (among other reasons) pitch, stress, quantity, and reduplication may have internal linguistic functions. However, he does not hold these conflicts to be very important, since the proposed factors indicative of strength are "fully understood by everyone" in the culture (27). For example, "if we are shown a prized work of art and exclaim *Beautiful!*, the speed and energy of the response will not be lost on the owner." It does not appear totally obvious that in this case the way to impress the owner is to shriek *Beautiful* in a loud, high-pitched voice, repeatedly, and with no delay (high response strength). It may be equally effective to look at the picture silently (long delay), and then to murmur *Beautiful* in a soft, low-pitched voice (by definition, very low response strength).

It is not unfair, I believe, to conclude from Skinner's discussion of response strength, the "basic datum" in functional analysis, that his "extrapolation" of the notion of probability can best be interpreted as, in effect, nothing more than a decision to use the word "probability," with its favorable connotations of objectivity, as a cover term to paraphrase such low-status words as "interest," "intention," "belief," and the like. This interpretation is fully justified by the way in which Skinner uses the terms "probability" and "strength." To cite just one example, Skinner defines the process of confirming an assertion in science as one of "generating additional variables to increase its probability" (425), and more generally, its strength (425–429). If we take this suggestion quite literally, the degree of confirmation of a scientific assertion can be measured as a simple function of the loudness, pitch, and frequency with which it is proclaimed, and a general procedure for increasing its degree of confirmation would be, for instance, to train machine guns on large crowds of people who have been instructed to shout it. A better indication of what Skinner probably has in mind here is given by his description of how the theory of evolution, as an example, is confirmed. This "single set of verbal responses . . . is made more plausible—is strengthened—by several types of construction based upon verbal responses in geology, paleontology, genetics, and so on" (427). We are no doubt to interpret the terms "strength" and "probability" in this context as paraphrases of more familiar locutions such as "justified belief" or "warranted assertability," or something of the sort. Similar latitude of interpretation is presumably expected when we read that "frequency of effective action accounts in turn for what we may call the listener's 'belief'" (88) or that "our belief in what someone tells us is similarly a function of, or identical with, our tendency to act upon the verbal stimuli which he provides" (160).

I think it is evident, then, that Skinner's use of the terms "stimulus," "control," "response," and "strength" justify the general conclusion stated in the last paragraph of §2 above. The way in which these terms are brought to bear on the actual data indicates that we must interpret them as mere paraphrases for the popular vocabulary commonly used to describe behavior, and as having no particular connection with the homonymous expressions used in the description of laboratory experiments. Naturally, this terminological revision adds no objectivity to the familiar "mentalistic" mode of description.

4. The other fundamental notion borrowed from the description of bar-pressing experiments is "reinforcement." It raises problems which are similar, and even more serious. In *Behavior of Organisms,* "the operation of reinforcement is defined as the presentation of a certain kind of stimulus in a temporal relation with either a stimulus or response. A reinforcing stimulus is defined as such by its power to produce the resulting change [in strength]. There is no circularity about this: some stimuli are found to produce the change, others not, and they are classified as reinforcing and non-reinforcing accordingly" (62). This is a perfectly appropriate definition for the study of schedules of reinforcement. It is perfectly useless, however, in the discussion of real-life behavior, unless we can somehow characterize the stimuli which are reinforcing (and the situations and conditions under which they are reinforcing). Consider first of all the status of the basic principle that Skinner calls the "law of conditioning" (law of effect). It reads: "If the occurrence of an operant is followed by presence of a reinforcing stimulus, the strength is increased" (*Behavior of Organisms* 21). As "reinforcement" was defined, this law becomes a tautology. For Skinner, learning is just change in response strength. Although the statement that presence of reinforcement is a sufficient condition for learning and maintenance of behavior is vacuous, the claim that it is a necessary condition may have some content, depending on how the class of reinforcers (and

appropriate situations) is characterized. Skinner does make it very clear that in his view reinforcement is a necessary condition for language learning and for the continued availability of linguistic responses in the adult. However, the looseness of the term "reinforcement" as Skinner uses it in the book under review makes it entirely pointless to inquire into the truth or falsity of this claim. Examining the instances of what Skinner calls "reinforcement," we find that not even the requirement that a reinforcer be an identifiable stimulus is taken seriously. In fact, the term is used in such a way that the assertion that reinforcement is necessary for learning and continued availability of behavior is likewise empty.

To show this, we consider some example of "reinforcement." First of all, we find a heavy appeal to automatic self-reinforcement. Thus, "a man talks to himself because of the reinforcement he receives" (163); "the child is reinforced automatically when he duplicates the sounds of airplanes, streetcars . . ." (164); "the young child alone in the nursery may automatically reinforce his own exploratory verbal behavior when he produces sounds which he has heard in the speech of others" (58); "the speaker who is also an accomplished listener 'knows when he has correctly echoed a response' and is reinforced thereby" (68); thinking is "behaving which automatically affects the behaver and is reinforcing because it does so" (438; cutting one's finger should thus be reinforcing, and an example of thinking); "the verbal fantasy, whether overt or covert, is automatically reinforcing to the speaker as listener. Just as the musician plays or composes what he is reinforced by hearing, or as the artist paints what reinforces him visually, so the speaker engaged in verbal fantasy says what he is reinforced by hearing or writes what he is reinforced by reading" (439); similarly, care in problem solving, and rationalization, are automatically self-reinforcing (442–443). We can also reinforce someone by emitting verbal behavior as such (since this rules out a class of aversive stimulations, 167), by not emitting verbal behavior (keeping silent and paying attention, 199), or by acting appropriately on some future occasion (152: "the strength of [the speaker's] behavior is determined mainly by the behavior which the listener will exhibit with respect to a given state of affairs'; this Skinner considers the general case of "communication" or "letting the listener know"). In most such cases, of course, the speaker is not present at the time when the reinforcement takes place, as when "the artist . . . is reinforced by the effects his works have upon . . . others" (224), or when the writer is reinforced by the fact that his "verbal behavior may reach over centuries or to thousands of listeners or readers at the same time. The writer may not be reinforced often or immediately, but his net reinforcement may be great" (206; this accounts for the great "strength" of his behavior). An individual may also find it reinforcing to injure someone by criticism or by bringing bad news, or to publish an experimental result which upsets the theory of a rival (154), to describe circumstances which would be reinforcing if they were to occur (165), to avoid repetition (222), to "hear" his own name though in fact it was not mentioned or to hear nonexistent words in his child's babbling (259), to clarify or otherwise intensify the effect of a stimulus which serves an important discriminative function (416), etc.

From this sample, it can be seen that the notion of reinforcement has totally lost whatever objective meaning it may ever have had. Running through these examples, we see that a person can be reinforced though he emits no response at all, and that the reinforcing "stimulus" need not impinge on the "reinforced person" or need not even exist (it is sufficient that it be imagined or hoped for). When we read that a person plays what music he likes (165), says what he likes (165), thinks what he likes (438–439), reads what books he likes (153), etc. BECAUSE he finds it reinforcing to do so, or that we write books or inform others of facts BECAUSE we are reinforced by what we

hope will be the ultimate behavior of reader or listener, we can only conclude that the term "reinforcement" has a purely ritual function. The phrase "X is reinforced by Y stimulus state of affairs, event, etc.)" is being used as a cover term for X wants Y," "X likes Y," "X wishes that Y were the case," etc. Invoking the term "reinforcement" has no explanatory force, and any idea that this paraphrase introduces any new clarity or objectivity into the description of wishing, liking, etc., is a serious delusion. The only effect is to obscure the important differences among the notions being paraphrased. Once we recognize the latitude with which the term "reinforcement" is being used, many rather startling comments lose their initial effect—for instance, that the behavior of the creative artist is "controlled entirely by the contingencies of reinforcement" (150). What has been hoped for from the psychologist is some indication how the casual and informal description of everyday behavior in the popular vocabulary can be explained or clarified in terms of the notions developed in careful experiment and observation, or perhaps replaced in terms of a better scheme. A mere terminological revision, in which a term borrowed from the laboratory is used with the full vagueness of the ordinary vocabulary, is of no conceivable interest.

It seems that Skinner's claim that all verbal behavior is acquired and maintained in "strength" through reinforcement is quite empty, because his notion of reinforcement has no clear content, functioning only as a cover term for any factor, detectable or not, related to acquisition or maintenance of verbal behavior. Skinner's use of the term "conditioning" suffers from a similar difficulty. Pavlovian and operant conditioning are processes about which psychologists have developed real understanding. Instruction of human beings is not. The claim that instruction and imparting of information are simply matters of conditioning (357–366) is pointless. The claim is true, if we extend the term "conditioning" to cover these processes, but we know no more about them after having revised this term in such a way as to deprive it of its relatively clear and objective character. It is, as far as we know, quite false, if we use "conditioning" in its literal sense. Similarly, when we say that "it is the function of predication to facilitate the transfer of response from one term to another or from one object to another" (361), we have said nothing of any significance. In what sense is this true of the predication *Whales are mammals?* Or, to take Skinner's example, what point is there in saying that the effect of *The telephone is out of order* on the listener is to bring behavior formerly controlled by the stimulus *out of order* under control of the stimulus *telephone* (or the telephone itself) by a process of simple conditioning (362)? What laws of conditioning hold in this case? Furthermore, what behavior is "controlled" by the stimulus *out of order,* in the abstract? Depending on the object of which this is predicated, the present state of motivation of the listener, etc., the behavior may vary from rage to pleasure, from fixing the object to throwing it out, from simply not using it to trying to use it in the normal way (e.g. to see if it is really out of order), and so on. To speak of "conditioning" or "bringing previously available behavior under control of a new stimulus" in such a case is just a kind of play-acting at science.

5. The claim that careful arrangement of contingencies of reinforcement by the verbal community is a necessary condition for language learning has appeared, in one form or another, in many places.[1] Since it is based not on actual observation, but on

[1] See, for example, Miller and Dollard, *Social learning and imitation* 82–83 (New York, 1941), for a discussion of the 'meticulous training' that they seem to consider necessary for a child to learn the meanings of words and syntactic patterns. The same notion is implicit in Mowrer's speculative account of how language might be acquired, in *Learning theory and personality dynamics*, Chapter 23 (New York, 1950). Actually, the view appears to be quite general.

analogies to laboratory study of lower organisms, it is important to determine the status of the underlying assertion within experimental psychology proper. The most common characterization of reinforcement (one which Skinner explicitly rejects, incidentally) is in terms of drive reduction. This characterization can be given substance by defining drives in some way independently of what in fact is learned. If a drive is postulated on the basis of the fact that learning takes place, the claim that reinforcement is necessary for learning will again become as empty as it is in the Skinnerian framework. There is an extensive literature on the question of whether there can be learning without drive-reduction (latent learning). The "classical" experiment of Blodgett indicated that rats who had explored a maze without reward showed a marked drop in number of errors (as compared to a control group which had not explored the maze) upon introduction of a food reward, indicating that the rat had learned the structure of the maze without reduction of the hunger drive. Drive-reduction theorists countered with an exploratory drive which was reduced during the prereward learning, and claimed that a slight decrement in errors could be noted before food reward. A wide variety of experiments, with somewhat conflicting results, have been carried out with a similar design.[2] Few investigators still doubt the existence of the phenomenon. Hilgard, in his general review of learning theory,[3] con-

[2] For a general review and analysis of this literature, see Thistlethwaite, A critical review of latent learning and related experiments, *Psych. bull.* 48.97–129 (1951). MacCorquodale and Meehl, in their contribution to *Modern learning theory*, carry out a serious and considered attempt to handle the latent learning material from the standpoint of drive-reduction theory, with (as they point out) not entirely satisfactory results. Thorpe reviews the literature from the standpoint of the ethologist, adding also material on homing and topographical orientation (*Learning and instinct in animals* [Cambridge, 1956]).

[3] *Theories of learning* 214 (1956).

cludes that "there is no longer any doubt but that, under appropriate circumstances, latent learning is demonstrable."

More recent work has shown that novelty and variety of stimulus are sufficient to arouse curiosity in the rat and to motivate it to explore (visually), and in fact, to learn (since on a presentation of two stimuli, one novel, one repeated, the rat will attend to the novel one); that rats will learn to choose the arm of a single-choice maze that leads to a complex maze running through this being their only "reward," that monkeys can learn object discriminations and maintain their performance at a high level of efficiency with visual exploration (looking out of a window for 30 seconds) as the only reward, and, perhaps most strikingly of all, that monkeys and apes will solve rather complex manipulation problems that are simply placed in their cages, and will solve discrimination problems with only exploration and manipulation as incentives. In these cases, solving the problem is apparently its own "reward". Results of this kind can be handled by reinforcement theorists only if they are willing to set up curiosity, exploration, and manipulation drives, or to speculate somehow about acquired drives for which there is no evidence outside of the fact that learning takes place in these cases.

There is a variety of other kinds of evidence that has been offered to challenge the view that drive-reduction is necessary for learning. Results on sensory-sensory conditioning have been interpreted as demonstrating learning without drive-reduction.[4] Olds has reported reinforcement by direct stimulation of the brain, from which he concludes that reward need not satisfy a physiological need or withdraw a drive stimulus.[5] The phenomenon of imprinting, long observed by zoologists, is of particular

interest in this connection. Some of the most complex patterns of behavior of birds, in particular, are directed towards objects and animals of the type to which they have been exposed at certain critical early periods of life.[6] Imprinting is the most striking evidence for the innate disposition of the animal to learn in a certain direction, and to react appropriately to patterns and objects of certain restricted types, often only long after the original learning has taken place. It is, consequently, unrewarded learning, though the resulting patterns of behavior may be refined through reinforcement. Acquisition of the typical songs of song birds is, in some cases, a type of imprinting. Thorpe reports studies that show "that some characteristics of the normal song have been learnt in the earliest youth, before the bird itself is able to produce any kind of full song."[7] The phenomenon of imprinting has recently been investigated under laboratory conditions and controls with positive results.[8]

Phenomena of this general type are certainly familiar from everyday experience. We recognize people and places to which we have given no particular attention. We can look up something in a book and learn it perfectly well with no other motive than to confute reinforcement theory, or out of boredom, or idle curiosity. Everyone engaged in research must have had the experience of working with feverish and prolonged intensity to write a paper which no

---

[4] Cf. Birch and Bitterman, Reinforcement and learning: The process of sensory integration, *Psych. rev.* 56.292–308 (1949).

[5] See, for example, his paper A physiological study of reward in McClelland (ed.), *Studies in motivation* 134–143 (New York, 1955).

[6] See Thorpe, op. cit., particularly 115–118 and 337–376, for an excellent discussion of this phenomenon, which has been brought to prominence particularly by the work of K. Lorenz (cf. Der Kumpan in der Umwelt des Vogels, parts of which are reprinted in English translation in Schiller (ed.), *Instinctive behavior* 83–128 (New York, 1957).

[7] Op.cit. 372.

[8] See e.g. Jaynes, Imprinting: Interaction of learned and innate behavior, *Jour. of comp. physiol. psych.* 49.201–206 (1956), where the conclusion is reached that "the experiments prove that without any observable reward young birds of this species follow a moving stimulus object and very rapidly come to prefer that object to others."

one else will read or to solve a problem which no one else thinks important and which will bring no conceivable reward—which may only confirm a general opinion that the researcher is wasting his time on irrelevancies. The fact that rats and monkeys do likewise is interesting, and important to show in careful experiment. In fact, studies of behavior of the type mentioned above have an independent and positive significance that far outweighs their incidental importance in bringing into question the claim that learning is impossible without drive-reduction. It is not at all unlikely that insights arising from animal behavior studies with this broadened scope may have the kind of relevance to such complex activities as verbal behavior that reinforcement theory has, so far, failed to exhibit. In any event, in the light of presently available evidence, it is difficult to see how anyone can be willing to claim that reinforcement is necessary for learning, if reinforcement is taken seriously as something identifiable independently of the resulting change in behavior.

Similarly, it seems quite beyond question that children acquire a good deal of their verbal and nonverbal behavior by casual observation and imitation of adults and other children. It is simply not true that children can learn language only through "meticulous care" on the part of adults who shape their verbal repertoire through careful differential reinforcement, though it may be that such care is often the custom in academic families. It is a common observation that a young child of immigrant parents may learn a second language in the streets, from other children, with amazing rapidity, and that his speech may be completely fluent and correct to the last allophone, while the subtleties that become second nature to the child may elude his parents despite high motivation and continued practice. A child may pick up a large part of his vocabulary and "feel" for sentence structure from television, from reading, from listening to adults, etc. Even a very young child who has not yet acquired a minimal repertoire from which to form new utterances may imitate a word quite well on an early try, with no attempt on the part of his parents to teach it to him. It is also perfectly obvious that, at a later stage, a child will be able to construct and understand utterances which are quite new, and are, at the same time, acceptable sentences in his language. Every time an adult reads a newspaper, he undoubtedly comes upon countless new sentences which are not at all similar, in a simple, physical sense, to any that he has heard before, and which he will recognize as sentences and understand; he will also be able to detect slight distortions or misprints. Talk of "stimulus generalization" in such a case simply perpetuates the mystery under a new title. These abilities indicate that there must be fundamental processes at work quite independently of "feedback" from the environment. I have been able to find no support whatsoever for the doctrine of Skinner and others that slow and careful shaping of verbal behavior through differential reinforcement is an absolute necessity. If reinforcement theory really requires the assumption that there be such meticulous care, it seems best to regard this simply as a reductio ad absurdum argument against this approach. It is also not easy to find any basis (or, for that matter, to attach very much content) to the claim that reinforcing contingencies set up by the verbal community are the single factor responsible for maintaining the strength of verbal behavior. The sources of the "strength" of this behavior are almost a total mystery at present. Reinforcement undoubtedly plays a significant role, but so do a variety of motivational factors about which nothing serious is known in the case of human beings.

As far as acquisition of language is concerned, it seems clear that reinforcement, casual observation, and natural inquisitiveness (coupled with a strong tendency to imitate) are important factors, as is the remarkable capacity of the child to generalize, hypothesize, and "process information" in a variety of very special and apparently highly complex ways which we cannot yet describe or begin to understand, and which may be largely innate, or may develop through some sort of learning or through maturation of the nervous system. The manner in which such factors operate and interact in language acquisition is completely unknown. It is clear that what is necessary in such a case is research, not dogmatic and perfectly arbitrary claims, based on analogies to that small part of the experimental literature in which one happens to be interested.

The pointlessness of these claims becomes clear when we consider the well-known difficulties in determining to what extent inborn structure, maturation, and learning are responsible for the particular form of a skilled or complex performance. To take just one example, the gaping response of a nestling thrush is at first released by jarring of the nest, and, at a later stage, by a moving object of specific size, shape, and position relative to the nestling. At this later stage the response is directed towards the part of the stimulus object corresponding to the parent's head, and characterized by a complex configuration of stimuli that can be precisely described. Knowing just this, it would be possible to construct a speculative, learning-theoretic account of how this sequence of behavior patterns might have developed through a process of differential reinforcement, and it would no doubt be possible to train rats to do something similar. However, there appears to be good evidence that these responses to fairly complex "sign stimuli" are genetically determined and mature without learning. Clearly, the possibility cannot be discounted. Consider now the comparable case of a child imitating new words. At an early stage we may find rather gross correspondences. At a later stage, we find that repetition is of course far from exact (i.e. it is not mimicry, a fact which itself is interesting), but that it repro-

duces the highly complex configuration of sound features that constitute the phonological structure of the language in question. Again, we can propose a speculative account of how this result might have been obtained through elaborate arrangement of reinforcing contingencies. Here too, however, it is possible that ability to select out of the complex auditory input those features that are phonologically relevant may develop largely independently of reinforcement, through genetically determined maturation. To the extent that this is true, an account of the development and causation of behavior that fails to consider the structure of the organism will provide no understanding of the real processes involved.

It is often argued that experience, rather than innate capacity to handle information in certain specific ways, must be the factor of overwhelming dominance in determining the specific character of language acquisition, since a child speaks the language of the group in which he lives. But this is a superficial argument. As long as we are speculating, we may consider the possibility that the brain has evolved to the point where, given an input of observed Chinese sentences, it produces (by an "induction" of apparently fantastic complexity and suddenness) the "rules" of Chinese grammar, and given an input of observed English sentences, it produces (by, perhaps, exactly the same process of induction) the rules of English grammar; or that given an observed application of a term to certain instances it automatically predicts the extension to a class of complexly related instances. If clearly recognized as such, this speculation is neither unreasonable nor fantastic; nor, for that matter, is it beyond the bounds of possible study. There is of course no known neural structure capable of performing this task in the specific ways that observation of the resulting behavior might lead us to postulate; but for that matter, the structures capable of accounting for even the simplest kinds of learning have similarly defied detection.

Summarizing this brief discussion, it seems that there is neither empirical evidence nor any known argument to support any SPECIFIC claim about the relative importance of "feedback" from the environment and the "independent contribution of the organism" in the process of language acquisition. . . .

11. The preceding discussion covers all the major notions that Skinner introduces in his descriptive system. My purpose in discussing the concepts one by one was to show that in each case, if we take his terms in their literal meaning, the description covers almost no aspect of verbal behavior, and if we take them metaphorically, the description offers no improvement over various traditional formulations. The terms borrowed from experimental psychology simply lose their objective meaning with this extension, and take over the full vagueness of ordinary language. Since Skinner limits himself to such a small set of terms for paraphrase, many important distinctions are obscured. I think that this analysis supports the view expressed in §1 above, that elimination of the independent contribution of the speaker and learner (a result which Skinner considers of great importance, cf. 311–312) can be achieved only at the cost of eliminating all significance from the descriptive system, which then operates at a level so gross and crude that no answers are suggested to the most elementary questions. The questions to which Skinner has addressed his speculations are hopelessly premature. It is futile to inquire into the causation of verbal behavior until much more is known about the specific character of this behavior; and there is little point in speculating about the process of acquisition without much better understanding of what is acquired.

Anyone who seriously approaches the study of linguistic behavior, whether linguist, psychologist, or philosopher, must quickly become aware of the enormous difficulty of stating a problem which will define the area of his investigations, and which will not be either completely trivial or hopelessly beyond the range of present-day understanding and technique. In selecting functional analysis as his problem, Skinner has set himself a task of the latter type. In an extremely interesting and insightful paper, K. S. Lashley has implicitly delimited a class of problems which can be approached in a fruitful way by the linguist and psychologist, and which are clearly preliminary to those with which Skinner is concerned. Lashley recognizes, as anyone must who seriously considers the data, that the composition and production of an utterance is not simply a matter of stringing together a sequence of responses under the control of outside stimulation and intraverbal association, and that the syntactic organization of an utterance is not something directly represented in any simple way in the physical structure of the utterance itself. A variety of observations lead him to conclude that syntactic structure is "a generalized pattern imposed on the specific acts as they occur," and that "a consideration of the structure of the sentence and other motor sequences will show . . . that there are, behind the overtly expressed sequences, a multiplicity of integrative processes which can only be inferred from the final results of their activity." He also comments on the great difficulty of determining the "selective mechanisms" used in the actual construction of a particular utterance.

Although present-day linguistics cannot provide a precise account of these integrative processes, imposed patterns, and selective mechanisms, it can at least set itself the problem of characterizing these completely. It is reasonable to regard the grammar of a language L ideally as a mechanism that provides an enumeration of the sentences of L in something like the way in which a deductive theory gives an enumeration of a set of theorems. ("Grammar," in this sense of the word, includes phonology.) Furthermore, the theory of language can be regarded as a study of the formal properties of such grammars, and, with a precise enough formulation, this general theory can provide a uniform method for determining, from the process of generation of a given sentence, a structural description which can give a good deal of insight into how this sentence is used and understood. In short, it should be possible to derive from a properly formulated grammar a statement of the integrative processes and generalized patterns imposed on the specific acts that constitute an utterance. The rules of a grammar of the appropriate form can be subdivided into the two types, optional and obligatory; only the latter must be applied in generating an utterance. The optional rules of the grammar can be viewed, then, as the selective mechanisms involved in the production of a particular utterance. The problem of specifying these integrative processes and selective mechanisms is nontrivial and not beyond the range of possible investigation. The results of such a study might, as Lashley suggests, be of independent interest for psychology and neurology (and conversely). Although such a study, even if successful, would by no means answer the major problems involved in the investigation of meaning and the causation of behavior, it surely will not be unrelated to these. It is at least possible, furthermore, that such notions as "semantic generalization," to which such heavy appeal is made in all approaches to language in use, conceal complexities and specific structure of inference not far different from those that can be studied and exhibited in the case of syntax, and that consequently the general character of the results of syntactic investigations may be a corrective to oversimplified approaches to the theory of meaning.

The behavior of the speaker, listener, and learner of language constitutes, of course, the actual data for any study of language. The construction of a grammar which enumerates sentences in such a way that a meaningful structural description can be determined for each sentence does not in itself provide an account of this actual behavior. It merely characterizes abstractly the ability of one who has mastered the language to distinguish sentences from nonsentences, to understand new sentences (in part), to note certain ambiguities, etc. These are very remarkable abilities. We constantly read and hear new sequences of words, recognize them as sentences, and understand them. It is easy to show that the new events that we accept and understand as sentences are not related to those with which we are familiar by any simple notion of formal (or semantic or statistical) similarity or identity of grammatical frame. Talk of generalization in this case is entirely pointless and empty. It appears that we recognize a new item as a sentence not because it matches some familiar item in any simple way, but because it is generated by the grammar that each individual has somehow and in some form internalized. And we understand a new sentence, in part, because we are somehow capable of determining the process by which this sentence is derived in this grammar.

Suppose that we manage to construct grammars having the properties outlined above. We can then attempt to describe and study the achievement of the speaker, listener, and learner. The speaker and the listener, we must assume, have already acquired the capacities characterized abstractly by the grammar. The speaker's task is to select a particular compatible set of optional rules. If we know, from grammatical study, what choices are available to him and what conditions of compatibility the choices must meet, we can proceed meaningfully to investigate the factors that lead him to make one or another choice. The listener (or reader) must determine, from an exhibited utterance, what optional rules were chosen in the construction of the utterance. It must be admitted that the ability of a human being to do this far surpasses our present understanding. The child who learns a language has in some sense constructed the grammar for himself on the basis of his observation of sentences and nonsentences (i.e. corrections by the verbal community). Study of the actual observed ability of a speaker to distinguish sentences from nonsentences, detect ambiguities, etc., apparently forces us to the conclusion that this grammar is of an extremely complex and abstract character, and that the young child has succeeded in carrying out what from the formal point of view, at least, seems to be a remarkable type of theory construction. Furthermore, this task is accomplished in an astonishingly short time, to a large extent independently of intelligence, and in a comparable way by all children. Any theory of learning must cope with these facts.

It is not easy to accept the view that a child is capable of constructing an extremely complex mechanism for generating a set of sentences, some of which he has heard, or that an adult can instantaneously determine whether (and if so, how) a particular item is generated by this mechanism, which has many of the properties of an abstract deductive theory. Yet this appears to be a fair description of the performance of the speaker, listener, and learner. If this is correct, we can predict that a direct attempt to account for the actual behavior of speaker, listener, and learner, not based on a prior understanding of the structure of grammars, will achieve very limited success. The grammar must be regarded as a component in the behavior of the speaker and listener which can only be inferred, as Lashley has put it, from the resulting physical acts. The fact that all normal children acquire essentially comparable grammars of great complexity with remarkable rapidity suggests that human beings are somehow specially designed to do this, with data-handling or "hypothesis-formulating" ability of unknown character and complexity. The study of linguistic structure may ultimately lead to some significant insights into this matter. At the moment the question cannot be seriously posed, but in principle it may be possible to study the problem of determining what the built-in structure of an information-processing (hypothesis-forming) system must be to enable it to arrive at the grammar of a language from the available data in the available time. At any rate, just as the attempt to eliminate the contribution of the speaker leads to a "mentalistic" descriptive system that succeeds only in blurring important traditional distinctions, a refusal to study the contribution of the child to language learning permits only a superficial account of language acquisition, with a vast and unanalyzed contribution attributed to a step called "generalization" which in fact includes just about everything of interest in this process. If the study of language is limited in these ways, it seems inevitable that major aspects of verbal behavior will remain a mystery.

Some Preliminaries to Psycholinguistics

GEORGE A. MILLER

The success of behavior theory in describing certain relatively simple correlations between stimulation and response has encouraged experimental psychologists to extend and test their theories in more complicated situations. The most challenging and potentially the most important of these extensions, of course, is into the realm of linguistic behavior. Consequently, in recent years we have seen several attempts to

Reprinted with the permission of the author and publisher from the article of the same title, *American Psychologist*, 1965, **20**, 15–20.

characterize human language in terms derived from behavioristic investigations of conditioning and learning in animals. These proposals are well known, so I will make no attempt to summarize them here. I will merely say that, in my opinion, their results thus far have been disappointing.

If one begins the study of a new realm of behavior armed with nothing but hypotheses and generalizations based on experience in some quite different area, one's theoretical preconceptions can be badly misleading. Trivial features may be unduly emphasized, while crucially important aspects may be postponed, neglected, or even overlooked entirely. These hazards are particularly dangerous when we generalize across species, or from nonverbal to verbal behavior.

The impulse to broaden the range of phenomena to which our concepts can be applied is commendable. But when this enthusiasm is not guided by a valid conception of the new phenomena to be explained, much intelligent enterprise can end in frustration and discouragement. Human language is a subtle and complex thing; there are many aspects that, if not actually unique, are at least highly distinctive of our species, and whose nature could scarcely be suspected, much less extrapolated from the analysis of nonverbal behavior.

It was with such thoughts in mind that I decided to take this opportunity to summarize briefly seven aspects of human language that should be clearly understood by any psychologist who plans to embark on explanatory ventures in psycholinguistics. The ideas are familiar to most people working in the field, who could no doubt easily double or treble their number. Nevertheless, the seven I have in mind are, in my opinion, important enough to bear repeating and as yet their importance does not seem to have been generally recognized by other psychologists.

Without further apologies, therefore, let me begin my catalogue of preliminary admonitions to anyone contemplating language as a potential subject for his psychological ratiocinations.

A POINT OF VIEW

It is probably safe to say that no two utterances are identical in their physical (acoustic and physiological) characteristics. Nevertheless, we regularly treat them as if they were. For example, we ask a subject to repeat something we say, and we count his response as correct even though it would be a simple matter to demonstrate that there were many physical differences between his vocal response and the vocal stimulus we presented to him. Obviously, not all physical aspects of speech are significant for vocal communication.

The situation is more complicated than that, however. There are also many examples—homophones being the most obvious—where stimuli that are physically identical can have different significance. Not only are physically different utterances treated identically, but physically identical utterances can be treated differently. It may often happen that the difference in significance between two utterances cannot be found in any difference of a physical nature, but can only be appreciated on the basis of psychological factors underlying the physical signal.

The problem of identifying significant features of speech is complicated further by the fact that some physical features are highly predictable in nearly all speakers, yet have no communicative significance. For example, when a plosive consonant occurs initially, as in the word *pen*, American speakers pronounce it with aspiration; a puff of air accompanies the *p* (which you can feel if you will pronounce *pen* holding the back of your hand close to your lips). When *p* occurs as a noninitial member of a consonant cluster, however, as in *spend*, this puff of air is reduced or absent. The same phoneme is aspirated in one position and unaspirated in the other. This physical feature, which is quite reliable in American speech, has no communicative significance, by which I mean that the rare person who does not conform is perfectly intelligible and suffers no handicap in communicating with his friends. Facts such as these, which are well known to linguists, pose interesting problems for psychologists who approach the acquisition of language in terms of laboratory experiments on discrimination learning.

In order to discuss even the simplest problems in speech production and speech perception, it is necessary to be able to distinguish significant from nonsignificant aspects of speech. And there is no simple way to draw this distinction in terms of the physical parameters of the speech signal itself. Almost immediately, therefore, we are forced to consider aspects of language that extend beyond the acoustic or physiological properties of speech, that is to say, beyond the objective properties of "the stimulus."

Since the concept of significance is central and unavoidable, it is important to notice that it has two very different senses, which for convenience, I shall call "reference" and "meaning."

For example, in most contexts we can substitute the phrase, "the first President of the United States" for "George Washington," since both of these utterances refer to the same historical figure. At least since Frege's time, however, it has been customary to assume that such phrases differ in meaning even though their referent is the same. Otherwise, there would be no point to such assertions of identity as "George Washington was the first President of the United States." If meaning and reference were identical, such an assertion would be as empty as "George Washington was George Washington." Since "George Washington was the first President of the United States" is not a pointless assertion, there must be some difference between the significance of the same "George Washington" and of the phrase "the first President of the United States," and, since this difference in significance is not a difference of referent, it must be a difference in something else—something else that, for want of a better name, we call its meaning.

This distinction between reference and meaning becomes particularly clear when we consider whole utterances. An utterance can be significant even though it might be extremely difficult to find anything it referred to in the sense that "table" refers to four-legged, flat-topped piece of furniture, etc. Sentences are meaningful, but their meaning cannot be given by their referent, for they may have none.

Of course, one might argue that psycholinguists should confine their attention to the significance of isolated words and avoid the complexities of sentences altogether. Such an approach would be marvelously convenient if it would work, but it would work only if words were autonomous units that combined in a particularly simple way. If the meaning of a sentence could in some sense be regarded as the weighted sum of the meanings of the words that comprise it, then once we knew how to characterize the meanings of individual words, it would be a simple matter to determine the meaning of any combination of words. Unfortunately, however, language is not so simple; a Venetian blind is not the same as a blind Venetian.

Perhaps the most obvious thing we can say about the significance of a sentence is that it is not given as the linear sum of the significance of the words that comprise it. The pen in "fountain pen" and the pen in "play pen" are very different pens, even though they are phonologically and orthographically identical. The words in a sentence interact.

In isolation most words can have many different meanings; which meaning they take in a particular sentence will depend on the context in which they occur. That is to say, their meaning will depend both on the other words and on their grammatical role in the sentence. The meanings to be assigned to word combinations can be characterized in an orderly way, of course, but not by some simple rule for linear addition. What is required is an elaborate description of the various ways in which words can interact in combination.

As soon as we begin to look carefully at the relations among words in sentences, it becomes obvious that their interactions depend on the way they are grouped. For example, in sentences like, "They are hunting dogs," one meaning results if we group "are hunting" together as the verb, but another meaning results if we group "hunting dogs" together as a noun phrase. We cannot assign meanings to words in a sentence without knowing how the words are grouped, which implies that we must take into account the syntactic structure of the sentence.

Moreover, when we consider the psychology of the sentence, the problem of productivity becomes unavoidable. There is no limit to the number of different sentences that can be produced in English by combining words in various grammatical fashions, which means that it is impossible to describe English by simply listing all its grammatical sentences. This fairly obvious fact has several important implications. It means that the sentences of English must be described in terms of *rules* that can generate them.

For psychologists, the implication of this generative approach to language is that we must consider hypothetical constructs capable of combining verbal elements into grammatical sentences, and in order to account for our ability to deal with an unlimited variety of possible sentences, these hypothetical constructs must have the character of linguistic rules.

Language is the prime example of rule-governed behavior, and there are several types of rules to consider. Not only must we consider syntactic rules for generating and grouping words in sentences; we must also consider semantic rules for interpreting word combinations. Perhaps we may even need pragmatic rules to characterize our unlimited variety of belief systems. Only on the assumption that a language user knows a generative system of rules for producing and interpreting sentences can we hope to account for the unlimited combinatorial productivity of natural languages.

Rules are not laws, however. They can be broken, and in ordinary conversation they frequently are. Still, even when we break them, we usually are capable of recognizing (under appropriate conditions) that we have made a mistake; from this fact we infer that the rules are known implicitly, even though they cannot be stated explicitly.

A description of the rules we know when we know a language is different from a description of the psychological mechanisms involved in our use of those rules. It is important, therefore, to distinguish here, as elsewhere, between knowledge and performance; the psycholinguist's task is to propose and test performance models for a language user, but he must rely on the linguist to give him a precise specification of what it is a language user is trying to use.

Finally, it is important to remember that there is a large innate component to our language-using ability. Not just any self-consistent set of rules that we might be able to invent for communicative purposes could serve as a natural language. All human societies possess language, and all of these languages have features in common—features that are called "language universals," but are in fact prelinguistic in character. It is difficult to imagine how children could acquire language so rapidly from parents who understand it so poorly unless they were already tuned by evolution to select just those aspects that are universally significant. There is, in short, a large biological component that shapes our human languages.

These are the seven ideas I wished to call to your attention. Let me recapitulate them in order, this time attempting to say what I believe their implications to be for psycholinguistic research.

SOME IMPLICATIONS
FOR RESEARCH

1. Not all physical features of speech are significant for vocal communication, and not all significant features of speech have a physical representation. I take this to imply that the perception of speech involves grouping and interpreting its elements and so cannot be simply predicted from studies of our ability to discriminate among arbitrary acoustic stimuli. Such studies can be useful only in conjunction with linguistic information as to which distinctions are significant. Linguists seem generally agreed that the absolute physical characteristics of a particular phone are less important than the binary contrasts into which it enters in a given language. It is noteworthy that after many decades of acoustic phonetics, we are still uncertain as to how to specify all the physical dimensions of the significant features of speech, particularly those that depend on syntactic or semantic aspects of the utterance.

2. *The meaning of an utterance should not be confused with its reference.* I take this to imply that the acquisition of meaning cannot be identified with the simple acquisition of a conditioned vocalization in the presence of a particular environmental stimulus. It may be possible to talk about reference in terms of conditioning, but meaning is a much more complicated phenomenon that depends on the relations of a symbol to other symbols in the language.

3. *The meaning of an utterance is not a linear sum of the meanings of the words that comprise it.* I take this to imply that studies of the meanings of isolated words are of limited value, and that attempts to predict the meaning of word compounds by weighted averages of the meanings of their components—an analogy with the laws of color mixture—cannot be successful in general. In Gestalt terminology, the whole is greater than (or at least, different from) the sum of its parts.

4. *The syntactic structure of a sentence imposes groupings that govern the interactions between the meanings of the words in that sentence.* I take this to imply that sentences are hierarchically organized, and that simple theories phrased in terms of chaining successive responses cannot provide an adequate account of linguistic behavior. Exactly how concepts are combined to produce organized groupings of linguistic elements that can be uttered

and understood is a central problem for psycholinguistics.

5. *There is no limit to the number of sentences or the number of meanings that can be expressed.* I take this to imply that our knowledge of a language must be described in terms of a system of semantic and syntactic rules adequate to generate the infinite number of admissible utterances. Since the variety of admissible word combinations is so great, no child could learn them all. Instead of learning specific combinations of words, he learns the *rules* for generating admissible combinations. If knowledge of these rules is to be described in our performance models as the language user's "habits," it is necessary to keep in mind that they are generative habits of a more hypothetical and less abstract nature than have generally been studied in animal learning experiments.

6. *A description of a language and a description of a language user must be kept distinct.* I take this to imply that psycholinguists should try to formulate performance models that will incorporate, in addition to a generative knowledge of the rules, hypothetical information-storage and information-processing components that can simulate the actual behavior of language users. In general, limitations of short-term memory seem to impose the most severe constraints on our capacity to follow our own rules.

7. *There is a large biological component to the human capacity for articulate speech.* I take this to imply that attempts to teach other animals to speak a human language are doomed to failure. As Lenneberg has emphasized, the ability to acquire and use a human language does not depend on being intelligent or having a large brain. It depends on being human.

In science, at least half the battle is won when we start to ask the right questions. It is my belief that an understanding of these seven general propositions and their implications can help to guide us toward the right questions and might even forestall ill-considered forays into psycholinguistics by psychologists armed only with theories and techniques developed for the study of non-verbal behavior.

A CRITIQUE

I have now stated twice my seven preliminary admonitions. In order to make sure that I am being clear, I want to repeat it all once more, this time in the form of a critical analysis of the way many experimental psychologists write about language in the context of current learning theory.

For the purposes of exposition, I have chosen a sentence that is part of the introduction to the topic of language in a well-known and widely used textbook on the psychology of learning. After remarking that, "language seems to develop in the same way as other instrumental acts," the author says:

Certain combinations of words and intonations of voice are strengthened through reward and are gradually made to occur in appropriate situations by the process of discrimination learning.

This, I believe is fairly representative of what can be found in many other texts. I have chosen it, not because I bear any malice toward the author, but simply because I think that all seven of my admonitions are ignored in only 27 words. Let me spell them out one by one.

First, since infants are not born with a preconception of what words are, they could hardly be expected to begin acquiring language by uttering combinations of words. Perhaps the author was not thinking of infants when he wrote this sentence. If he had been, he would probably have written instead that, "Certain combinations of *sounds* and intonations of voice are strengthened through reward and made to occur by the process of discrimination learning." In either case, however, he ignores my first admonition that not all physical features of speech are significant and not all significant features are physical.

A child does not begin with sounds or words and learn to combine them. Rather, he begins by learning which features are significant, and progressively differentiates his utterances as he learns. It is conceivable, though not necessary, that he might acquire those significant distinctions that have some physical basis "by the process of discrimination learning," but it would require an extensive revision of what we ordinarily mean by discrimination learning in order to explain how he acquires significant distinctions that are not represented in the physical signal, or why he acquires those features (such as aspiration only on initial plosives) that are not significant and are not systematically rewarded or extinguished.

Second, as I have already admitted (too generously, perhaps), it is possible to argue that a referential relation might be established between a visual input and a vocalization "by the process of discrimination learning." I deny, however, that it is reasonable to speak of acquiring meaning in this way.

Exactly what should be included in the meaning of a word is open to debate, but any interpretation will have to say something about the relation of this word's meaning to the meanings of other words and to the contexts in which it occurs—and these are complicated, systemic interrelations requiring a great deal more cognitive machinery than is necessary for simple discrimination. Since the author says specifically that *words* are acquired by discrimination learning, and since words have meaning as well as reference, I can only assume that he has ignored my admonition not to confuse reference and meaning. Perhaps a more accurate interpretation, suggested by the phrase "occur in appropriate situations," would be that he has not really confused reference and meaning, but has simply ignored meaning entirely. In either case, however, it will not do as a basis for psycholinguistics.

There is unfortunate ambiguity in the

phrase, "Certain combinations of words and intonations of voice." I am not sure whether the author meant that each word was learned with several intonations, or that we learn several intonations for word combinations, or that we learn both to combine words and to modulate the pitch of our voice. Consequently, I have been forced to cheat on you by examining the context. What I found was no help, however, because all the formal propositions referred simply to "words," whereas all the examples that were cited involved combinations of words.

Perhaps I am being unfair, but I think that this author, at least when he is writing on learning theory, is not deeply concerned about the difference between words and sentences. If this distinction, which seems crucial to me, is really of no importance to him, then he must be ignoring my third admonition that the meaning of words are affected by the sentences in which they occur.

My fourth admonition—that the syntactic structure of a sentence imposes groupings that govern the interactions between the meanings of its words—is also ignored. No matter how I interpret the ambiguous phrase about, "Certain combinations of words and intonations of voice," it must be wrong. If I read it one way, he has ignored the problem of syntax entirely and is concerned only with the conditioning of isolated word responses.

Or, if I put a more generous interpretation on it and assume he meant that combinations of words are strengthened and made to occur by discrimination learning, then he seems to be saying that every word and every acceptable combination of words is learned separately.

By a rough, but conservative calculation, there are at least 10^{20} sentences 20 words long, and if a child were to learn only these it would take him something on the order of 1,000 times the estimated age of the earth just to listen to them. Perhaps this is what the word "gradually" means? In this interpretation he has clearly violated my fifth admonition, that there is no limit to the number of sentences to be learned, and so has wandered perilously close to absurdity. Any attempt to account for language acquisition that does not have a generative character will encounter this difficulty.

Sixth, from the reference to responses being "strengthened" I infer that each word-object connection is to be characterized by an intervening variable, along the lines of habit strength in Hull's system. This is a rather simple model, too simple to serve as a performance model for a language user, but it is all our author has to offer. As for keeping his performance model distinct from his competence model, as I advise in my sixth admonition, he will have none of it. He says—and here I resort to the context once more—that language "is a complex set of responses [*and*] also a set of stimuli." It may be defensible to talk about speech as a set of responses and stimuli, but what a language user knows about his language cannot be described in these performance terms.

A language includes all the denumerable infinitude of grammatical sentences, only a tiny sample of which ever have or ever will occur as actual responses or stimuli. The author would blush crimson if we caught him confusing the notions of sample and population in his statistical work, yet an analogous distinction between speech and language is completely overlooked.

Finally, we need to make the point that the kind of reinforcement schedule a child is on when he learns language is very different from what we have used in experiments on discrimination learning. No one needs to monitor a child's vocal output continually and to administer "good" and "bad" as rewards and punishments. When a child says something intelligible, his reward is both improbable and indirect. In short, a child learns language by using it, not by a precise schedule of rewards for grammatical vocalizations "in appropriate situations." An experimenter who used such casual and unreliable procedures in a discrimination experiment would teach an animal nothing at all.

The child's exposure to language should not be called "teaching." He learns the language, but no one, least of all an average mother, knows how to teach it to him. He learns the language because he is shaped by nature to pay attention to it, to notice and remember and use significant aspects of it. In suggesting that language can be taught "by the process of discrimination learning," therefore, our author has ignored my final admonition to remember the large innate capacity humans have for acquiring articulate speech.

In summary, if this sentence is taken to be a description of the fundamental processes involved in language acquisition, it is both incomplete and misleading. At best, we might regard it as a hypothesis about the acquisition of certain clichés or expressive embellishments. But as a hypothesis from which to derive an account of the most obvious and most characteristic properties of human language, it is totally inadequate.

This completes the third and final run through my list of preliminaries to psycholinguistics. If I sounded a bit too contentious, I am sorry, but I did not want to leave any doubt as to why I am saying these things or what their practical implications for psycholinguistic research might be.

My real interest, however, is not in deploring this waste of our intellectual resources, but in the positive program that is possible if we are willing to accept a more realistic conception of what language is.

If we accept a realistic statement of the problem, I believe we will also be forced to accept a more cognitive approach to it: to talk about hypothesis testing instead of discrimination learning, about the evaluation of hypotheses instead of the reinforcement of responses, about rules instead of habits, about productivity instead of generalization, about innate and universal human capacities instead of special methods of teaching vocal responses, about symbols instead of conditioned stimuli, about sentences instead of words or vocal noises, about linguistic structure instead of chains of responses—in short, about language instead of learning theory.

The task of devising a cognitive production model for language users is difficult enough without wearing blinders that prevent us from seeing what the task really is. If the hypothetical constructs that are needed seem too complex and arbitrary, too improbable and mentalistic, then you had better forgo the study of language. For language is just that—complex, arbitrary, improbable, mentalistic—and no amount of wishful theorizing will make it anything else.

In a word, what I am trying to say, what all my preliminary admonitions boil down to, is simply this: Language is exceedingly complicated. Forgive me for taking so long to say such a simple and obvious thing.

Language and Problem
Solving: From Word to Deed

_____ 9

INTRODUCTION

There are both behaviorist and cognitive (or Gestalt) theories of problem solving. Maltzman's theory of thinking [Chapter 6] is one of the most serious attempts to develop and test a behavioral theory of problem solving (Duncan, 1959). Basic to Maltzman's theory is Hull's notion of habit family hierarchies with divergent and convergent mechanisms [Maltzman, Chapter 6]. More recently, Gagné has discussed problem solving as a form of learning that combines two or more previously learned rules into a higher order rule (Gagné, 1964). According to Gagné, problem solving must be preceded by simpler forms of learning that are more directly tied to the stimulus situation, such as response learning, chaining, and the learning of paired associates. These forms are succeeded by concept learning, principle learning, and, finally, problem solving. In both Maltzman's and Gagné's formulation there is an attempt to embrace within one behavioral model simple and complex mental processes. Very little has been done to expand Gestalt theory, and most Gestalt theory of problem solving is prelinguistic (Duncan, 1959). Van de Geer (1957) has formulated a phenomenological theory of problem solving in which he depicts thinking as the reduction of nontransparent situations to transparency.

The articles in this chapter emphasize the relation of linguistic responses to problem solving. According to Maltzman, linguistic responses are the primary mediators [Maltzman, Chapter 6]. In S-R mediational theory most forms of mediation are verbal or have an important verbal component. The research in this chapter is psycholinguistic in that it concerns the relation of language and thought.

The articles in this chapter emphasize behavioral theory because in recent years this theory has been most productive. In behavioral theory the chief ingredient of success is the individual's previous learning. This learning can either facilitate or inhibit adaptive responses. Problems elicit a number of responses, but only some of the responses will result in a solution to the problem. The response must already exist in the response repertory. It must be of sufficient strength to compete successfully with maladaptive responses, which in turn must extinguish as they meet with failure. The word "hierarchy" refers to the differences in strength of the responses in the individual's response repertory. The more nearly dominant the desirable response is, the more easily will the problem be solved (Staats and Staats, 1963, pages 202–203).

One of the most popular problems in experimental study is the Maier two-string problem (Maier, 1931). The solution of this problem requires the subject to tie together two strings that are too far apart to be reached by hand. Usually the subject is required to tie a weight to one string and to swing the weight and string as a pendulum. The objects provided as weights are frequently objects that have other, more common functions (for example, screwdriver, clamp, electrical relay). As the object swings closer at one end of its arc, the subject is able to grasp the object while holding the other string. Two of the following articles use this problem.

In the first article, Staats uses Maltzman's model of thinking to discover whether learning relevant verbal responses helps in the actual motor solution of the two-string problem. He is investigating the relation between verbal and instrumental hierarchies or, more popularly, the relation between saying and doing, preaching and practice. The procedure requires the subject to list uses of the screwdriver both before and after he is presented with the two-string problem. Staats treats verbal and motor (or instrumental) responses in the same way—as discrete behavioral units each with its hierarchical domain. The word, in the Staats experiment, is a physical stimulus. Consistent with the laws of simple learning, unless an association is established between the actual use of the screwdriver as a weight and the verbal response to the screwdriver as an instrument of weight, most subjects would not discover the relation. The experiment does not provide evidence of whether the verbal association of the screwdriver with the idea of weight facilitates the later use of the screwdriver for this function.

This latter question is answered in a series of studies by Cofer, Judson, and their associates. Although the authors phrase their research in terms of "set" and "direction," their studies furnish evidence for the relation of language and problem solving. Before subjects attempt to solve the experimental problem, they are required to learn various word lists, one of which, by the contextual arrangement of the words, implies the solution to the two-string problem. This procedure is altered in the special verbal problem by the provision of reinforcement of a verbal mediator in order to influence a chain of verbal association. The results show how the association of particular verbal responses can mediate the instrumental solution of a problem. As in the Staats experiment, their use of language is nonsyntactical and nonstructural (in the linguistic sense). What these authors describe as the evocation of solution-related verbal responses may have less to do with language and more to do with the concepts and conceptual relation that these words evoke. Chains of physical objects, analogous to the verbal chains, may well result in successful problem solutions.

Mediational processes in thinking and problem solving have received extended attention in the work of the Kendlers and their associates (Kendler and Kendler, 1959; Kendler, Kendler, and Wells, 1960; Kendler and Kendler, 1962). These investigators have been particularly ingenious in the study of intellectual processes within the framework of contemporary learning theory and developmental psychology. In the article that follows, Kendler defines "mediating response" and describes its role as a link between simple and complex behavior. She also describes the development of mediating responses, in an interesting conjoining of learning and developmental psychology. The Kendlers have studied a particular type of conceptual thinking—reversal and nonreversal shifts. Using brightness and size as stimuli, the article distinguishes between a reversal shift, which, for example, may reinforce the subject for responding to white instead of black on the brightness dimension, and the nonreversal shift, which, for example, may reinforce the subject for responding to an aspect of size— large or small—rather than to brightness. Predictions of successful shifts can be made on the basis of associational or mediational S-R theory. The observed differences between younger and older children in the performance of the two types of shifts strongly support the mediational hypothesis. Kendler suggests a three-stage hierarchy of development, ranging from (bottom to top) inconsistent, nonreversal, to reversal behavior. This development is related to language, although the relation is not easy to describe. The mere possession of the appropriate verbal responses in children does not guarantee their use. Kendler provides evidence that verbalization relevant to the shifts does produce faster shifts for children who possess the words but who use them only with experimental prompting.

Anderson observes that there has been no direct test of the mediational hypothesis (Anderson, 1965, page 402). He also suggests that Piaget's description of the development of intellectual processes in children between the ages of 5 and 7, as class inclusions operations, may be a better account for what may be happening in this transition period. The Kendlers describe the evolving mental processes in terms of stimulus characteristics rather than in terms of the mediational process itself.

Gagné and Smith question the implication of Gestalt psychological and educational theory that learning is essentially nonverbal and perhaps not even conceptual and that the learner intuitively discovers solutions to problems. For these theorists, verbalization is identified with rote learning, and rote learning is the antithesis of problem solving. In designing their study, Gagné and Smith were able to isolate the effects of verbalization. Also, departing from earlier experimental procedure, the verbalization of relevant principles is done by the subjects rather than the experimentor. They also compared solution and nonsolution sets for verbalization. Their study seems to have important implications for instruction. Their findings seem consistent with research on discovery learning, which requires students to induce principles [Kersh and Wittrock, Chapter 10]. Gagné and Smith also discovered that the subjects who verbalized took more time to make successive moves. Verbalization may develop a set or disposition for analytical thinking and may result in more successful problem solutions. Gagné and Smith suggest that verbalization may simply force subjects to think. Whether it is the verbalization process or the set it creates or some complex interaction of the two must await further investigation.

REFERENCES

Anderson, R. C. Introduction. In R. C. Anderson and D. Ausuble (Eds.), *Readings in the psychology of cognition.* New York: Holt, Rinehart and Winston, 1965.

Duncan, C. P. Recent research on human problem solving. *Psychol. Bull.,* 1959, **56,** 397–427.

Gagné, R. M. Problem solving. In A. Melton (Ed.), *Categories of human behavior.* New York: Academic Press, 1964. Pp. 294–317.

Kendler, T. S., and H. H. Kendler. Reversal and nonreversal shifts in kindergarten children. *J. exp. Psychol.,* 1959, **58,** 56–60.

——— and ———. Mediated responses to size and brightness as a function of age. *Amer. J. Psychol.,* 1962, **75,** 571–586.

———, ———, and D. Wells. Reversal and nonreversal shifts in nursery school children. *J. comp. physiol. Psychol.,* 1960, **53,** 83–87.

Maier, N. R. Reasoning in humans: II. The solution of a problem and its appearance in consciousness. *J. comp. Psychol.,* 1931, **12,** 181–194.

Staats, A. W., and C. K. Staats. *Complex human behavior.* New York: Holt, Rinehart and Winston, 1963. Pp. 199–219.

Van de Geer, J. P. *A psychological study of problem solving.* Haarlem: Uitgeverij de Toorts, 1957.

Verbal and Instrumental Response-Hierarchies and Their Relationship to Problem Solving

ARTHUR W. STAATS

There have been a number of recent attempts to account for human problem-solving in S-R terms.[1] Osgood, for example, has suggested that S learns hierarchies of perceptual responses to objects which mediate hierarchies of instrumental responses,

[1] C. N. Cofer, The role of language in human problem solving, Conference on Human Problem Solving Behavior, New York University, 1954 (unpublished); Irving Maltzman, Thinking: From a behavioristic point of view, *Psychol. Rev.,* 62, 1955, 275–286; C. E. Osgood, *Method and Theory in Experimental Psychology,* 1953, 603–637.

Reprinted with the permission of the author and the publisher from the article of the same title, *American Journal of Psychology,* 1957, **70,** 442–446. This study is based on a doctoral dissertation submitted to the University of California at Los Angeles in 1955. The writer is grateful to Professor Irving Maltzman and Carolyn K. Staats for assistance on this work.

with the result that problem-solving behavior can be predicted from verbal responses.[2] Thus, the latency with which S states how an object might be used would indicate the latency of the actual use of the object in a problem situation. Osgood did not discuss the possibility that there might be a difference between the verbal and the instrumental hierarchies, although it seems quite possible that the two classes of responses might be acquired independently. A study by Saugstad has indicated that there is at least a gross relationship between verbal and instrumental responses to objects in a problem-solving situation, but he was not interested in relative verbal response-strengths, *e.g.* latency.[3]

In the present study, possible verbal uses of a screwdriver were given by S before and after attempts to solve a problem which required the use of that implement as a weight. The verbal response measures were related to the latency of the response to the screwdriver as a weight in the problem-situation. Other relationships were also studied: (a) between two different indices of verbal response-strength;[4] (b) between verbal fluency and problem-solving ability;[5] (c) between verbal fluency and anxiety;[6] (d) between sex and problem-solving ability;[7] and (e) between performance on the

[2] Osgood, 631–632.

[3] Per Saugstad, Problem solving as dependent upon availability of functions, Unpublished Doctoral dissertation, University of Chicago, 1952, 28–35.

[4] A. A. Campbell (The interrelations of two measures of conditioning in man, *J. exp. Psychol.,* 22, 1938, 225–243) has found correlations between non-verbal measures.

[5] Harold Guetzkow (An analysis of the operation of set in problem solving behavior, *J. gen. Psychol.,* 45, 1951, 219–244) has also found such a relation.

[6] J. A. Taylor (Drive theory and manifest anxiety, *Psychol. Bull.,* 53, 1956, 303–320) has summarized evidence which suggests that the relationship should be positive.

[7] Guetzkow (*op. cit.,* 219 f.) and N. R. F. Maier (An aspect of human reasoning, *Brit. J. Psychol.,* 24, 1933, 144–155) have reported masculine superiority. If verbal and instrumental functions are related, the same superiority should be found at the verbal level.

Abstract Reasoning Test of the Differential Aptitude Tests and both problem solving and verbal fluency.

PROCEDURE

Subjects

Sixty-one Ss were used, 40 women and 21 men. The Ss were undergraduate students in general psychology at the University of California at Los Angeles.

Apparatus

Two strings were so hung from the ceiling in diagonal corners of a room that S could not reach one string while holding the other. The problem-solving objects, arranged close together on a table, were, from left to right: a 1 × 4-in. sheet of balsa wood, a 1-in. screw, a 7½-in. screwdriver, a 2 × 3-in. piece of paper, and a 3-in. pencil.

Method

S was first given the Abstract Reasoning Test, then verbal hierarchies of functional responses to a pencil, a screw, and a piece of paper were obtained—S simply being asked to list all of the different ways that each object might be used (with 5 min. given for each object). S was then given the Manifest Anxiety Scale and dismissed. During the following week S participated in the problem-solving phase of the study. Before the problem was given, S listed uses for the other problem-solving objects—screwdriver, balsa wood, and piece of string. Each S was allowed 10 min. in which to solve the problem, *i.e.* to get one string in each hand. To accomplish this, the screwdriver had to be tied to one string and swung in pendular fashion. Then S was again shown the screwdriver and given 5 min. to list its uses, following which he was asked to clarify any uses given which were ambiguous. S was cautioned not to discuss the experiment with other members of his classes.

Measures

The measure of problem-solving ability employed was time to solution of the problem. Six of the 61 Ss did not solve the problem in the allotted time, *i.e.* 10 min. The distribution of times was skewed, but that for log time appeared essentially normal.

A "weight" response to the screwdriver was defined as a verbal response which depended only upon the weight-property of the screwdriver, not its length, rigidity, sharpness, and so forth, *e.g.* fishing sinker, ballast, paperweight. When the response-measures were obtained subsequent to problem-participation, a response was not counted as a weight-response if it referred specifically to the use of the screwdriver to bring two strings together.

The rank of the first weight-response in the verbal response-hierarchies was considered the latency of the response. If S did not give a weight-response, his rank was the number of responses *plus* 1. The distribution of this measure, to be called Latency Weight-Response, was skewed. Frequency of the weight-type of response was the other measure of response-strength (Frequency-Weight-Responses). Its distribution also was skewed.

Another category of response, "hammer"-response, was defined to include responses which specified that the screwdriver was held by the shaft and so swung that the handle struck and applied force to some other object. Again two indices of the strength of the response-tendencies, latency and frequency of the hammer-responses, were tabulated. Both distributions were somewhat skewed.

The total number of pre-problem verbal responses made to each of the problem-solving objects was tabulated. There was a measure for each of the objects as follows: Total Screwdriver-Responses (pre- and post-problem), Total String-Responses, Total Screw-Responses, Total Wood-Responses, Total Paper-Responses, and Total Pencil-Responses. The last four were summed to yield another measure, Total Responses

Other-Objects. These measures were distributed in a somewhat skewed manner, as were the raw scores of the anxiety- and reasoning-tests which were used.

RESULTS

Weight-Response and Problem Solving

Only 7 of the 61 Ss gave a verbal weight-response to their pre-problem hierarchies, yet all but 6 Ss solved the problem. Thus, contrary to Osgood's expectation and Saugstad's results, in this situation it did not appear feasible to predict problem-solving performance from verbal responses to the problem-object. This lack of relationship may indicate that the verbal responses do not closely parallel the instrumental responses which are learned.

Time required for the solution of the problem was correlated with the two weight-response measures obtained subsequent to problem-participation. Since all three of these measures were correlated with Total Screwdriver Responses, the influence of this variable was controlled by partial correlation. The correlation between log time and latency of the Weight-Response was 0.25 (p = 0.053, two-tailed). The correlation of log time and frequency of the Weight-Responses was -0.27 (p = 0.05, two-tailed). Although the distribution of Frequency Weight-Responses was skewed, the assumption necessary for the use of the product-moment r appeared to be met, *i.e.* when the mean times of Ss with 1, 2, 3, ... n weight-responses were calculated, the relationship appeared to be linear. The assumption of linearity appeared to have been met also in all other uses of the statistic.

Thus, although verbal weight-responses were not frequently given prior to problem-participation, the Ss did frequently respond to the screwdriver as a weight subsequent to the problem. This result did demonstrate a relationship between the instrumental response-hierarchy and the subsequent verbal response-hierarchy, *i.e.* between a rein-

TABLE 9-1

Correlations of Fluency-Measures with Log Time and Manifest Anxiety

Total responses	Anxiety	p	Log time	p
Screwdriver (pre-problem)	0.17	—	−0.53	0.001
Screwdriver (post-problem)	—	—	−0.52	0.001
String	0.30	0.01	−0.47	0.001
Screw	0.21	0.105	—	—
Wood	0.05	—	—	—
Paper	0.26	0.05	—	—
Pencil	0.14	—	—	—
Other objects (screw, wood, paper, pencil)	—	—	−0.28	0.05

forced instrumental use of the screwdriver as a weight and subsequently verbalized weight-responses. This result has significance for recent studies of verbal behavior which have demonstrated that reinforcement can affect classes of verbal responses.[8] Furthermore, these verbal responses were emitted in strength proportional to the time it took the Ss to solve the problem, a relationship not explained by the effect of problem-participation upon the subsequent verbal weight-response, since only one reinforcement was involved whether the problem was solved quickly or slowly. The difference in the strength of verbal weight-responses which the Ss later demonstrated might have been learned prior to the problem. Problem-participation, with the reinforcement of the instrumental use of the screwdriver, might have brought the class of verbal weight-responses into a more dominant position for all the Ss who solved the problem. This interpretation suggests that, if the verbal weight-responses could have been elicited prior to problem-participation, the strength of the responses would have been positively related to time. Notwithstanding the interpretation, however, the results show only a relationship between

[8] B. D. Cohen, H. I. Kalish, J. R. Thurston, and E. Cohen, Experimental manipulation of verbal behavior, *J. exp. Psychol.*, 47, 1954, 106–110; W. S. Verplanck, The control of the content of conversation: Reinforcement of statements of opinion, *J. abnorm. soc. Psychol.*, 51, 1955, 668–676.

problem-solving participation and subsequent verbal responses.

Latency and Frequency

Latency and frequency of the Weight-Responses were correlated −0.67 (p = 0.001, two-tailed). Again the influence of Total Screwdriver-Responses was controlled by partial correlation. The partial correlation of latency and frequency of the Hammer-Responses was −0.76 (p = 0.001). The results corroborate the expectation that the different indices of verbal response-strength would be correlated.

Fluency and Problem Solving

The correlations of the fluency-measures and log time are shown in Table 9-1. A greater number of responses was associated with more rapid problem-solution.

Fluency and Anxiety

The Manifest Anxiety scores were correlated with the total number of responses given to each of the objects involved in the problem-situation, as shown in Table 9-1. In each case the correlation was positive, but in only two cases were they statistically reliable.

Sex-Differences

As expected, men solved the problem more quickly than women. The Mann-Whitney *U*-test of this difference yielded a Z of 2.95 (p = 0.003). Men also gave more responses to the screwdriver.[9] On the Mann-Whitney *U*-test, the Z was 2.79 (p = 0.005). Men gave their first hammer-response lower in their verbal response-hierarchies (pre-problem). The Z was 4.70 (p < 0.0001). Women gave more hammer-responses. To analyze the results, men and women were classified into two categories, those who gave no hammer-responses, and those who gave one or more hammer-responses. Twelve men were in the first category, 8 in the second. For women the tabulation was 9 and 32. The X^2 was 8.52 (p < 0.005). Thus, both indices indicated that women had learned a stronger hammer-response to the screwdriver. The corresponding comparisons on the strength of the weight-response yielded (a) a Z of 0.76 (p = 0.45) and (b) a X^2 of 0.08 (p = 0.80). No sex-difference was shown.

These results demonstrate that the responses learned to the screwdriver differ for the sexes in quantity and quality. Women appeared to have learned a stronger hammer-response to the screwdriver,[10] even while giving fewer total responses. Thus, it may be inferred that men and women Ss have different experience with respect to the screwdriver, and that this difference in experience may be reflected in their differential ability to solve the "two-string" problem.

---

[9] To save space, the sex-differences in the number of responses made to the other problem-solving objects are not presented here. None of the differences was significant, although in each case men gave more responses.

[10] To save space, the inconclusive and cumbersome analyses of the relationships between strength of hammer-response and problem-solving are not presented. Some evidence, however, suggested a negative relationship.

Other Results

(a) Men and women did not differ significantly on the Abstract Reasoning Test; the Mann-Whitney *U*-test yielded a Z of 0.52 (p = 0.60). (b) Scores on the Abstract Reasoning Test and log time correlated −0.33 (p < 0.01). (c) Latency and frequency of Weight-Response correlated −0.02 (p = 0.88) and −0.05 (p = 0.70) with abstract reasoning, respectively. Thus, more intelligent Ss did not give stronger post-problem weight-responses to the screwdriver than did less intelligent ones. (d) The correlation of abstract reasoning with Total Screwdriver-Responses was 0.05 (p = 0.70). Thus, fluency, an asset in problem-solving, was not accounted for by individual differences in intelligence. (e) Manifest Anxiety was not significantly correlated (−0.11, p = 0.41) with log time.

SUMMARY

Verbal responses to objects used in problem-solving were obtained before and after problem-participation. (a) The results indicated no relationship between pre-problem verbal responses and problem-solution, but (b) there was a relationship between rapidity of problem-solution and the strength of verbal responses subsequently given. (c) The two indices of strength of verbal response which were used were significantly correlated. (d) Fluency of verbal responding was positively related to problem-solving. (e) Positive relationships among anxiety-level and fluency-measures appeared, but four of the six correlations were not significant. (f) High scores in Abstract Reasoning went with rapid problem-solution, but not with fluency. (g) Men exhibited superior ability in problem solving but evidence indicated that the difference may have been due to differential experience with the objects used in the problems. (h) The sexes did not differ in abstract reasoning.

Reasoning as an Associative Process: II. "Direction" in Problem Solving as a Function of Prior Reinforcement of Relevant Responses

ABE J. JUDSON

CHARLES N. COFER

SIDNEY GELFAND

In the first paper of this series (Judson, 1956), it was shown that "direction" in the solution of a verbal classification or concept problem could be accounted for in terms of priority of activation of problem-related response systems and in terms of the activation of highly available and pervasive response systems (attitudes) already existing in Ss. The studies reported in the present paper were designed to explore the effects of reinforcement of a response system on the solution of problems to which the system is relevant. Both sets of studies were performed in an effort to learn something of the nature of set and direction in problem solving situations, with the expectation that set and direction could be reinterpreted as response systems or habit families, capable of influence by characteristics of the problem and by reinforcement. Three problems were used in these studies: the two string problem and the hat rack problem devised by Maier (1931, 1945) and another verbal problem set up in the light of free associations obtained from the Ss.

METHOD

The Two String Problem and the Hat Rack Problem

The designs used in work with these problems were similar. First, several lines of words were learned by Ss, in the setting of a retroactive inhibition experiment. In one of the word lists a series of words relevant to problem solving occurred together for one group. Following this learning, the problem was worked on, and then a recall for the word lists was obtained.

The Guetzkow (1931, 1945) group form of the two string problem and a group form of the hat rack problem developed for this investigation were used.

In the first study with the two string problem, 5 successive class hours were

Reprinted with the permission of the senior author and the publisher from the article of the same title, *Psychological Reports*, 1956, **2**, 501–507.

required. The first 4 hours were devoted to learning 8 5-word lists. On a given day, each list was read by E and then S attempted to recall it. Each list was given one practice trial a class hour for 4 days. On the fifth day a recall for the 8 lists was obtained. Work on the two string problem followed immediately, and then a further recall of the word lists was made.

Four classes were used in this first study. Group D took only the two string problem. The other 3 groups learned word lists: the sixth of the 8 lists for Group A was *rope swing pendulum clock time;* of these words, only *rope* occurred in any list for Group B, and *rope* was associated in Group B with *hemp twine tie package;* in Group C, *rope* was associated with *hemp twine tie package, pendulum* occurred as the last word in the list, *dream sleep bed clock,* and *swing* was inserted in another list between the words *band* and *time.*

In Group A words relevant to the pendulum solution of the two string problem were associated in 1 of the 8 lists; only one of these words occurred at all in any list for Group B; all of these words occurred in the lists for Group C but in associative contexts presumably irrelevant to the pendulum solution.

In performance of the two string problem, the illustrated group form was first passed out, and the problem was explained with reference to two strings actually suspended from the classroom ceiling. 6 min. were allotted for working on the problem, and Ss were urged to produce as many solutions as possible.

Two partial replications of this experiment with the two string problem were carried out, with new groups of Ss. Two differences in procedure were introduced. First, there was no Group D in the repetitions. Second, all of the learning was carried out in one class hour, and during the following class hour the word lists were recalled and the two string problem was completed. Work with the hat rack problem followed essentially the same design. Group D was not used, and the entire procedure was

run through during one class hour. The key words, learned in associative relationship by Group A in one list and not by the other groups, were *plank prop reach ceiling floor. Plank* occurred in one list for Group B, and all of the words occurred in lists for Group C but in different associative contexts. The words associated together in Group A were expected to lead to the solution of the problem in which two boards are wedged between the ceiling and the floor.

The Special Verbal Problem and Free Associations

20 Ss were asked, individually, to give 10 single word free associations to each of 10 stimulus words. At a second session, 6 weeks later, S was presented a problem consisting of 4 words, each typed on a separate card. His task was to select the "correct" word. The "correct" word was actually the first response he had made in free association to one of the original stimulus words; the other 3 words had not appeared before in the experiment. After S made his choice, he was told whether it was right or wrong, and then the same 4 words were presented again, in different positions, and S again was asked to choose the "correct" word. This procedure was continued, information being given about the correctness of the choice, until S made correct choices on 5 consecutive trials.

Following achievement of this criterion, S was shown a second set of 4 words. 1 of the 4 was the second word from the associative chain, and the other 3 were new words. One trial was given with this set, and S chose the "correct" word but was not told whether he was right or wrong. Additional non-informative single trials were run in which the successive members of the original 10-word associative chain were presented, each with 3 words not previously used in the experiment. Each S served as his own control (see below).

This procedure may be clarified by an example. Let us suppose that S has responded to the stimulus words, *rose, sorrow, melody,* with the following associations: *Rose:* flower, thorn, bush, stem, apple, tree, orange, lemon, grapefruit, watermelon; *Sorrow:* tears, cry, weep, relax, sleep, snore, eyelid, eyebrow, ear, hear; *Melody:* tune, music, note, staff, sharp, flat, clef, range, gun, elevation. 6 weeks later, S is first given *flower,* together with 3 new words. After he has learned that *flower* is the "correct" word, *tnorn* is then presented once with 3 new words, *bush* once with 3 new words, and so on through *watermelon.* Each time S chooses the "correct" word, but following the trials with *flower* he is never told whether his choice is right or wrong. The hypothesis here is that the reinforcement of *flower* in the learning situation should raise the availability of the other words associatively linked with it; hence in the additional 9 trials S should more often select the associated words than any of the new words.

As a control, *tears* would be learned as the "correct" word in another learning series; the words used in the 9 test trials, however, would be from another associative chain, e.g., *music, note,* etc. The reinforcement of *tears* should not affect the choices in this control test series. It may be seen that the specific words used would vary from S to S.

Subjects

The Ss used in all of these experiments were students enrolled in undergraduate psychology classes at the University of Maryland and the George Washington University. The experiments were carried out during regular class meetings with each total class.

RESULTS

The Two String Problem

The major results for the three runs of this experiment, for *men,* are presented in Table 9-2, which gives the percentage of pendulum solutions obtained. It may be seen that, as anticipated, a greater proportion of Ss in the 3 Groups A produced pendulum solutions than in the other 3 groups. Critical ratios for the differences between Groups A and C, Groups A and D, and between Group A and the other three groups combined for the first run were significant at beyond the .05 level. The difference between Groups A and B in this run does not reach significance. In the second run, the differences between Groups A and B and between A and C are significant at the .06 and .11 levels, respectively. The difference in the third run of the two string problem did not reach significance.

As an additional check on these results, comparisons were made on the frequency of solutions obtained for the groups by methods other than the pendulum method. There are three such methods: lengthening one string, anchoring one string, extension of reach with a pole. In none of the three runs

TABLE 9-2

Percentage of Pendulum Solutions Given by Men to the Two String Problem in the Various Groups of the Three Experimental Runs

	First run		Second run		Third run	
	N	%	N	%	N	%
Group A	62	68	54	74	54	54
Group B	53	58	45	56	49	49
Group C	38	47	70	61	49	49
Group D	119	52	—	—	—	—

was there a significant difference in the frequencies with which the male Ss of the various groups used these other methods.

It is noteworthy that the male Ss of the third run used the anchoring and extension of reach methods significantly less frequently than did the male Ss of the first two runs. This finding suggests either that the experimental procedure in the third run was defective or that the groups were not comparable. The significance of this finding is not clear, however.

Female Ss gave relatively few pendulum solutions, and the several groups did not differ systematically or significantly. This finding is consistent with that reported by Guetzkow (1947, 1951). Women used as frequently as did men the lengthening and anchoring methods, but they used the method involving extension of reach significantly less frequently (p = .01) than did men.

The Hat Rack Problem

Analysis of the solutions to this problem provided by the Ss revealed 5 methods by which solution was accomplished: (a) Ceiling to floor solutions. This includes all solutions in which the boards are arranged to contact both ceiling and floor. It includes Solution b and is the one specifically "suggested" by the words associatively linked by the learning carried out in Group A. (b) Clamp solutions. Ceiling to floor solutions in which the boards are held together by means of the C clamp. (c) Support solutions. Any solution in which the walls or corners of the room are used as supports. (d) Base solutions. Solutions in which one board is placed flat on the floor to serve as a base for the other one. (e) Balance solutions. The boards are arranged in a "T" or an "X" structure, for example, and precariously balanced.

Table 9-3 presents percentages of solutions by all groups and all methods. It may be seen that female Ss produce very few solutions by either Method (a) or Method (b), and discussion of results will again be confined to those for males.

39 per cent of the males of Group A produced ceiling to floor solutions, as against 19 per cent and 15 per cent of the males of Groups B and C, respectively. The difference between Groups A and B is significant at the .10 level, between Groups A and C at the .05 level, and between Group A and Groups B and C combined, at the .05 level. None of the other differences for other methods approaches significance for

TABLE 9-3

Percentages of Ss Solving Hat Rack Problem by Various Methods

	Group											
	A				B				C			
	Men		Women		Men		Women		Men		Women	
Method	N	%	N	%	N	%	N	%	N	%	N	%
Ceiling to floor	36	39	10	10	36	19	30	00	39	15	16	13
Clamp	36	8	10	00	36	17	30	00	39	13	16	6
Support	36	53	10	20	36	42	30	20	39	64	16	75
Base	36	58	10	50	36	58	30	57	39	38	16	44
Balance	36	41	10	80	36	56	30	50	39	44	16	50

males. It is clear that Group A produced more ceiling to floor solutions than the other groups, in accordance with the verbal associations acquired.

The Special Verbal Problem

Over the 9 experimental test trials, the 20 Ss chose 116 previously associated words and 64 words not previously associated. In the 9 control trials the values were 96 and 84 respectively. A chi square value of 4.13, significant at the .05 level, is given by these results. This suggests that effects of reinforcement of the "correct" word in the learning series transferred to the associated words which followed in the test series.

DISCUSSION

These results suggest that there are operations of reinforcement by which the availability or the strength of a class of words in some way relevant to problem solution may be increased and that problem solution is affected by such differential reinforcement.

In the adaptations of the Maier problems we may argue that in the Groups A a solution-relevant pattern of verbal associations was acquired. If the stimulus of the string is perceived as a rope or if through mediated generalization (Cofer and Foley, 1942; Osgood, 1952) the responses learned to *rope* transfer to the strings of the problem, then the solution-related verbal responses may occur to the Ss of Groups A and lead to the formulation of the pendulum solution. One could argue that this pattern of verbal associations provides the direction or set necessary for this solution to occur. A similar analysis applies to the hat rack problem. In this case the relevant verbal associative pattern would occur to the Ss of Group A if they perceive the boards of the problem as planks or if the

associative pattern transfers through generalization from the word *plank* to the word *board*. The results from the special verbal problem suggest that differential reinforcement effects, occurring in one phase of the problem, can transfer along pre-experimentally established lines and affect problem solution in other phases of the problem.

In these experiments, we were concerned to prevent the Ss from "catching on" to what was being done to them. To achieve this objective, the Maier problem experiments were disguised as studies of retroactive inhibition, and the solution-relevant verbal associative pattern was contained in 1 list embedded among 7 others. 6 weeks were allowed to pass between the collection of free associations and the presentation of the special verbal problem, and free associations were collected to many more stimulus words than necessary in order to make difficult recognition and recall of those actually used in the verbal problem. Such evidence as we have suggests that these measures were effective in hiding from Ss the purposes of these studies. The use of group methods probably also made the deception easier. No S interviewed after the Maier problem experiments recognized the relationship between the words learned and the two string or the hat rack problem. In the control series of the special verbal problem, the critical words were as familiar to the Ss as were the critical words of the experimental series, because both sets were free association responses obtained at the same time.

In view of these controls it is perhaps not surprising that the amount of transfer obtained in these various experiments was not greater than that found. It is possible that the experiments were "over-controlled."

However, we now feel reasonably confident that it is fruitful to conceive such processes in problem solving as set and direction as being names for complex response systems or habit families, which, once activated or strengthened in the problem situation, guide the course of problem solving. Whether solution attempts will be successful or not, of course, will depend upon the relevance of the response system to the requirements of the particular problem.

SUMMARY

Several studies are described in which relevant patterns of verbal associations, set up by learning in the first stage of the experiment, are shown to be associated with the frequences of certain types of solution in the Maier two string and hat rack problems. It is also shown, in the case of a simple verbal problem, that problem solution requiring choice of members of a chain of free associations is affected by prior reinforcement of one member of the chain. These investigations are interpreted as giving support to and indicating the fruitfulness of a conception of set or direction in problem solving as consisting of complex response systems or habit families.

REFERENCES

Cofer, C. N., and J. P. Foley, Jr. Mediated generalization and the interpretation of verbal behavior: I. Prolegomena. *Psychol. Rev.,* 1942, 49, 513–540.

Guetzkow, H. An analysis of the operation of set in problem solving behavior. Unpublished doctor's dissertation, University of Michigan, 1947.

———. An analysis of the operation of set in problem solving behavior. *J. gen. Psychol.,* 1951, 45, 219–244.

Judson, A. J., and C. N. Cofer. Reasoning as an associative process: I. "Direction" in a simple verbal problem. *Psychol. Rep.,* 1956, 2, 469–476.

Maier, N. R. F. Reasoning in humans: II. The solution of a problem and its appearance in consciousness. *J. comp. Psychol.,* 1931, 12, 181–194.

———. Reasoning in humans: III. The mechanisms of equivalent stimuli and of reasoning. *J. exp. Psychol.,* 1945, 35, 349–360.

Osgood, C. F. The nature and measurement of meaning. *Psychol. Bull.,* 1952, 49, 197–237.

Development of Mediating Responses in Children

TRACY S. KENDLER

Learning theory and general behavior theory have, for the most part, shown little concern with developmental research. This is not to be taken as reflecting a lack of interest in children. There is an honorable, but spotty, tradition of experimental studies that used children as subjects dating back to Watson and his famous Albert. But the use of children does not automatically make the research developmental, especially if the emphasis is on the generality of behavior principles across species or across age levels within any one species.

Reprinted with the permission of the author and the publisher from the article of the same title in J. C. Wright and J. Kagan (Eds.), *Basic cognitive processes in children.* Monograph of the Society for Research on Child Development, Inc., Purdue University, 1963, pp. 33–48.

Perhaps this indifference arises because developmental research appears to be more concerned with finding *differences* between age groups than in finding general laws of behavior applicable to all age groups. Learning theory, on the other hand, commits the investigator to studying general processes that relate the organism to its environment through its past history. "The organism," which may range from amoeba to homo sapiens, is often either a white rat or a pigeon. The use of these animals is not due to any particular interest in the species but rather to some very important advantages they provide to the researcher. For example, their past histories and motivational states can be manipulated or controlled at will and there are few ethical limitations imposed on the tasks they may be required to perform. Though he may restrict his research to some convenient laboratory organism, the behavior theorist implicitly assumes that at least some aspect of his findings are common to a wide range of organisms, usually including mankind. Within this tradition investigators who use human beings as subjects, and are explicit about the species, are often more interested in demonstrating the universality of the behavioral laws derived from animal experiments than in obtaining differences that might appear to reduce their generality.

If a discipline like comparative or developmental psychology is as much interested in differences as in similarities, then its findings may supply the ammunition for an attack on the vital assumption of the generality of behavioral laws. This is possible, but it is not necessarily so. If the principles generated by research with laboratory animals are applicable to higher level human behavior, then research directed at understanding the changes that take place with increasing maturity can extend the range and the vitality of behavior theory. If some of the knowledge derived from learning experiments can give direction to developmental research and can help to explain and organize its findings, behavior theorists

may yet convert a potential enemy into a valuable ally.

It will come as no surprise to the reader that the developmental research to be described, which was conducted jointly with Howard H. Kendler and our colleagues, derives from an S-R learning theory pretheoretical framework. Among the reasons for this choice (besides the fact that we were trained in this discipline) are the substantial body of relevant knowledge and the well developed experimental techniques that can be adapted to the study of higher mental processes. Moreover, learning theory possesses a rigor that may help to tighten a field where the temptation to be vague is great.

The mediated response is one of the mechanisms most often used to find a common theme between simple and complex behavior within this theoretical framework. The mediator is a response, or series of responses, which intercede between the external stimulus and the overt response to provide stimulation that influences the eventual course of behavior. These responses may be overt, but they are usually presumed to be covert. The mediated response is not an original idea. All theories of thinking, motor or central, behaviorist or phenomenological, dealing in the second-signal system or using computer models, postulate internal processes that intervene between the presentation of the problem and its solution, between the input and output, or between the stimulus and the response. The differences arise in the model used to generate hypotheses about the nature of this internal process and in the methods used to validate these hypotheses. Watson, who coordinated thinking with sub-vocal talking, used conditioning as his model and sought verification by direct measurement of the muscles of speech. The contemporary behaviorist approach allows for a wider range of mediating responses and for the possibility of treating them as theoretical constructs rather than as directly observable behavior. The scheme is exemplified in the research to be described in this paper.

The research started with a general interest in the mediating process and has become more and more concerned with how the process develops in children. This development has been studied in two inter-related ways. One way is primarily comparative. It consists of presenting a similar experimental situation to different species and to different age levels to study the uncontrolled changes that occur as a function of the differences among subjects. The other way employs the experimental method to discover and manipulate the variables that appear to be related to these "natural" developmental changes in order to determine how they come about and consequently render them subject to experimental control.

We have experimented in two areas that are generally conceded to be part of that area variously called cognitive process, thinking, or problem solution. One of the areas is *concept formation* or *abstraction*. The other is *inference*, defined as the spontaneous integration of discretely acquired habits to solve a problem. These processes have been reduced to some very simple operations in order to study them at their inception in young children. The operations are so simple that there may be some disagreement about their continuity with the high level process that they presume to study. The prepared reply to such potential objection is that there is no known way of reliably determining, on an a priori basis, the proper level of analysis for scientific research. It is only by its fruits that we shall know it.

CONCEPT FORMATION

The experimental paradigm used in the investigation of concept formation is based on procedures developed by Buss (1953) and Kendler and D'Amato (1955). It consists essentially of studying mediation by means of the transfer demonstrated from an initial to a subsequent discrimination. The initial discrimination presents stimuli that differ simultaneously on at least two dimensions, only one of which is relevant. After criterion is reached, another discrimination is presented that utilizes the same or similar stimuli but requires a shift in response. One type of shift, called a *reversal shift*, requires the subject to continue to respond to the previously relevant dimension but in an opposite way. In another type of shift, called a *nonreversal shift*, the subject is required to respond to the previously irrelevant dimension. For example, if a subject is initially trained on stimuli that differ simultaneously in brightness (black vs. white) and size (large vs. small) by being rewarded for responses to black regardless of size, a reversal shift would consist of learning to respond to white, and a nonreversal shift would consist of learning to respond to small. Comparisons between these two types of shifts are of particular interest because theories based on single-unit versus mediated S-R connections yield opposed predictions about their relative efficiency. A single-unit theory assumes a direct association between the external stimulus and the overt response and would predict a reversal shift to be more difficult than a nonreversal shift. This is because reversal shift requires the replacement of a response that has previously been consistently reinforced with a response that has previously been consistently extinguished. In a nonreversal shift previous training has reinforced responses to the newly positive and negative stimuli equally often. Strengthening one of these associations does not require as much extinction of its competitor as in a reversal shift and should, therefore, be acquired more easily. Kelleher (1956) confirmed the prediction that, for rats, a reversal shift was more difficult than a nonreversal shift.

A theory that includes a mediating link (or links) between the external stimulus and the overt response leads to a different prediction. The mediating link is conceived of as a perceptual or verbal response, often covert, to the relevant dimension, which produces cues that elicit the overt response. In a reversal shift, the initial dimension maintains its relevance, hence, so does the mediated response. Only the overt response needs to be changed, and since the experimental situation provides only one alternative overt response, the problem presents no great difficulty. In a nonreversal shift the previously acquired mediation is no longer relevant, consequently both the mediating and the overt response must be replaced, making the task more difficult than a reversal shift. It is therefore to be expected that for subjects who mediate, a reversal shift will be acquired more easily than a nonreversal shift. Experiments by Buss (1953), Kendler and D'Amato (1955), and Harrow and Friedman (1958), using a more complex variation of the reversal-nonreversal technique with college students, confirmed the prediction of the mediational analysis. Unlike rats, college students learn a reversal shift more easily than a nonreversal shift.

This discontinuity between rats and adult humans led to two investigations with young children to determine whether their behavior, in this type of situation, was more consistent with the single-unit or the mediational formulation. The results suggested that children between 3 and 4 years of age respond predominantly in the single unit manner (Kendler, Kendler, and Wells [1960]) and that children between 5 and 7 years of age divide about evenly, with half mediating and half not (Kendler and Kendler [1959]). What seemed to be implied was a developmental process in which very young children's behavior is governed by a relatively primitive, single-unit S-R process. Increasing maturity leads to increase in the proportion of children whose performance is determined by some mediating system of responses.

A recent investigation of the shift behavior of children from five age levels (3, 4, 6, 8, and 10 years) provided a direct test of these developmental implications (Kendler

et al. [1962]). Previous procedures were modified to allow each subject to choose whether or not he would behave mediationally. This was accomplished in the following way. For their initial discrimination (series I) the children were presented, in random alternation, with two pairs of stimulus cards. One pair consisted of a large black square (LB) and a small white square (SW). The other pair consisted of a large white square (LW) and a small black square (SB). Each concept (L, B, S, W) was correct for one fourth of the subjects.

For the purpose of illustration let us take a child for whom black was the correct concept and size was irrelevant. For him all responses to SB or LB were rewarded with a marble. If he responded to SW or LW, he had to return a marble to the experimenter. After he reached the criterion of nine out of ten successive correct responses, a second discrimination (series II) was presented that involved only one of the stimulus pairs, e.g., LB and SW, and the reward pattern was reversed. Now only responses to SW were rewarded, and he was again run to a criterion of nine out of ten successive correct responses. The child could reach criterion in this series by responding to the whiteness, in which case he was categorized as a *reversal* subject since he was responding in a reverse way to the original concept. Such a child is, by virtue of the previous analysis, presumed to have made relevant mediating responses in the first discrimination which either led to other relevant mediators or continued to be relevant in the second discrimination, thus requiring a shift only in the overt response.

A child could also reach criterion in series II by responding to the smallness of SW. Such a choice would be expected from nonmediators since during Series I responses to small were rewarded half of the time, while responses to whiteness were never rewarded. Such a child would, therefore, respond more readily to a stimulus from the previously irrelevant dimension (S) than to the incorrect stimulus of the previously relevant dimension (W) and would consequently be categorized as a nonreversal subject.

The last possibility is that the child learned to respond to both the smallness and the whiteness. A single-unit analysis would predict this result for nonmediating children who take a relatively long time to learn series II since each reinforcement should increase the habit strength of both stimulus components. As the trials increase, the difference in the excitatory strengths of white and small should decrease and ultimately disappear. Such children, for reasons that will soon be clear, were categorized as *inconsistent*.

In order to determine on which of the three possible bases series II was learned, it was followed immediately by a third series. During this last series both pairs of stimuli were again shown in random alternation. The pair that had not been used in series II, which is LW and SB in our illustration, served as the test pair. With this pair the child could respond either to the whiteness or to the smallness but not to both simultaneously. The test pair was presented ten times and either choice was rewarded. On the basis of his choices to this pair the child was classified as one of the three categories just described. The function of the other pair, which maintained its previous reinforcement pattern, was to keep the child responding as he did in series II.

The results for each category are presented in Figure 9-1. The prediction, based on theoretical analysis and previous results, was that the percentage of children who reversed (mediated) would be below 50 between the ages of 3 and 4 (Kendler, Kendler, and Wells [1960]), rise to about 50 between 5 and 7 (Kendler and Kendler [1959]), and then continue to increase with increasing age until some relatively high asymptote was reached. The results, which are in good agreement with the prediction, serve to confirm the general developmental implications of previous studies.

It was expected, of course, that the percentage of nonmediators would decrease with age. There seemed no a priori reason for making a discrimination between the nonreversal and inconsistent children, and so the decrease was expected in both categories. The results show a sharp and steady decrease for the inconsistent category. There was, however, no perceptible trend in the nonreversal group.

Despite the need for explanation of the performance of the nonreversal group, to which we shall return presently, it seems reasonable to conclude that the results of this experiment bear out the implication that there is a transition in the course of human development from unmediated, single-unit behavior to mediated behavior, at least with reference to size and brightness concepts. They also suggest that the proportion of children who have made this transition increases in a gradual and lawful manner. It remains for further research to determine whether the same or similar relationships will obtain with other concepts.

In addition to these results there were some *ad hoc* observations about the verbal behavior of the children that provide interesting suggestions about the nature of the mediation process and its development. These verbalizations should not be regarded as demonstrative of confirmed relationships. They should be regarded as empirically derived suggestions that require further experimental verification.

After the children had completed series III, they were shown the stimulus pair used in series II and asked a series of questions to find out whether they could or would give a correct verbal report of what they had been doing and whether there would be any relationship between this after-the-act verbal behavior and mediated choices in series III. Table 9-4 presents these results arranged in three categories that are illustrated as follows. If a child had been responding to brightness in the test pair and described the "winner" as white (or black), he was grouped with those who *verbalized the correct dimension*. If he said "the square

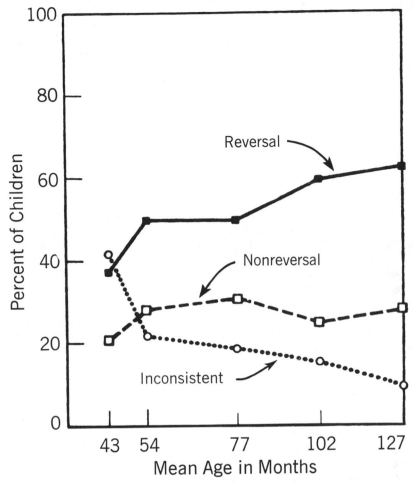

FIGURE 9-1. *Percentage of children in each choice category as a function of chronological age.*

TABLE 9-4

Percentage of Subjects Giving Various Descriptions as a Function of Their Choices in Series III

Kind of choice	Verbalized correct dimension	Verbalized incorrect dimension	No relevant verbalization
Reversal	84.8	7.6	7.6
Nonreversal	66.7	25.6	7.7
Inconsistent	57.7°		42.3

° If the behavior was categorized as inconsistent neither dimension could be considered correct. Therefore, mentions of either dimension were combined and placed between the two columns to indicate their special character.

one" or "that one," or merely pointed without saying anything at all, he was placed with the *no relevant verbalization* group.

Despite the pressure on the child to respond generated by *E*'s persistent questions, with the stimulus cards in full view, 42 per cent of the inconsistent children failed to produce any relevant verbalization. If verbalization is important for the mediating process, then it would follow that nonmediators would be relatively inarticulate. By the same token, mediating (reversal) children should produce a relatively large proportion of verbal comment that was relevant to their previous performance. The data in Table 9-4 support this expectation. If the pattern is clear for the reversal and inconsistent children, the nonreversal children present more complications. Two statements may be made about this group. First, an overwhelming proportion produced descriptions of the stimuli in terms of at least one of the manipulation dimensions. The proportion for the nonreversal group was just as large as that for the reversal group, suggesting that, under pressure to do so, the nonmediators could verbally describe the stimuli as well as the mediators. However, the verbalizations of nonreversal children were less frequently relevant to their previous behavior than were those of reversal children.

One tentative way to tie these observations together, and simultaneously throw further light on the fact that the proportion of nonreversal children did not decrease with age, is to propose that reversal, nonreversal, and inconsistent choice behavior represent a three-stage hierarchy of development. Reversal choice reflects the highest level where covert verbal responses occur during training and mediate choice behavior. Nonreversal choice constitutes an intermediate level, at which covert verbal responses can occur and sometimes do, but either occur rather late in the learning or they do not necessarily or readily mediate choice behavior. The most primitive level is characterized by little or no covert response

and is manifested in inconsistent choice behavior. With increasing CA more and more children reach the highest level (i.e., reversal) and fewer and fewer are left at the lowest level (i.e., inconsistent), but at each age tested the proportion in transition between the two extreme levels (i.e., nonreversals) tends to be constant.

Such an analysis would lead to the expectation that the proportion of children who verbalized correctly would increase with age; the proportion of children whose verbalizations were absent or irrelevant would decrease with age; and the incorrect dimension category would not change. Figure 9-2 presents the verbalization data in terms of chronological age. The data demonstrate considerable correspondence between expectation and results and show a striking similarity to the choice behavior presented in Figure 9-1, a similarity that occurs despite the fact that the children who comprise each set of parallel developmental trends are not identical. For example, the "verbalized-correct-dimensions" results of Figure 9-2, which parallel the "reversal-choice" trend of Figure 9-1, included 67 per cent of the nonreversal children as well as 85 per cent of the reversal children. Thus, although these results do not point to a perfect relationship between verbal and choice behavior, the similarity of trends certainly suggests that the development of the mediational process is intimately related to the development of the ability to relate words to actions.

There is one more suggestive result yielded by the verbalization data that may help to explain (a) the high proportion of nonreversal children who verbalized correctly, (b) why the reversal results approached such a low asymptote, and (c) the lack of a decrease in the nonreversal category even at the ripe old age of 10. Some children described the "winner" accurately by mentioning both dimensions, e.g., "The big, white one." When this tendency was sorted out by age, it was found that the percentage of children who accurately

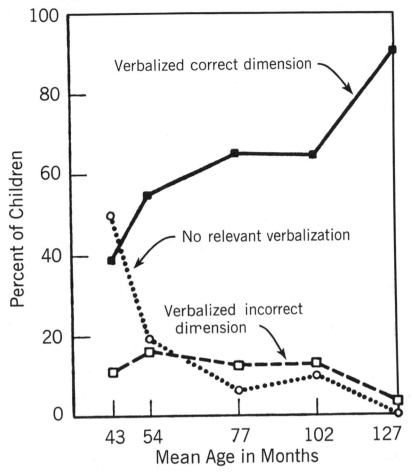

FIGURE 9-2. *Percentage of children in each verbalization category as a function of chronological age.*

described *both dimensions* was zero at age 3 and increased gradually to 25 at age 10, implying, reasonably enough, that there is a developmental aspect to the number of simultaneous mediating responses a child can handle. It also implies that at the upper age levels a nonreversal response to situations as simple as series II may not necessarily denote a primitive process. Instead it may represent the ability to integrate more than one mediating response. This is another way of saying that the task may have been too easy for the older children and that consequently they complicated it for themselves. It may be that the failure of the reversal curve to rise above 62 per cent and the nonreversal curve to drop below 28 per cent at age 10 is due to a perennial difficulty in developmental research: devising one task that is easy enough for the lower end of the scale and yet difficult enough to pose the proper challenge at the upper end. Although in the present instance the task was clearly capable of differentiating among the various age levels tested, it may be that the differences at the upper age levels were attenuated.

Thus far, the data derived from a comparative type of analysis show a measurable transition from a lower to a higher level behavioral process as a function of increasing chronological age. They also suggest that this development is somehow related to language. The relationship is probably not simple. Even the youngest children had a vocabulary sufficient for describing the simple concepts used. Moreover, one of the early experiments had demonstrated that with simple instructions all of the children could interpose relevant verbal comment between the presentation of the stimuli and their overt choice. It is clear that, if the overt behavior of the younger children is not influenced by mediating verbal discriminators, it is not because they are incapable of making these responses. This leaves two alternatives. One is that, although they are capable of doing so, they nevertheless do not, in the ordinary course of events, make such responses. The other is that they do make some verbal responses, but these responses, for some reason, do not serve as mediators. In order to explore some of these issues another experiment was performed which manipulated overt verbal mediation to ascertain its effect on the reversal shift behavior of 4- and 7-year-old children. Note that, while this study has developmental implications, it is more experimental in nature.

The same stimuli were used as in the study previously described, but they were presented differently. The initial discrimination used only one pair of discriminanda, thus rendering both stimulus dimensions relevant. Under these circumstances a child could be required to describe the correct stimulus according to either one of its two components. For example, if LB was correct, the child could be instructed to use either "large" or "black" to describe the correct stimulus. In the second discrimination both pair of stimuli were presented and all children learned a reversal shift. Only one dimension was relevant. For some children the reversal was on the size dimension, and for some it was on the brightness

dimension. In this way the verbalization during the initial discrimination was rendered relevant or irrelevant according to the experimental group to which the child had been randomly assigned. For example, if the child had learned to describe the correct stimulus (LB) as "large," he would be rewarded in the second discrimination for response to SB and SW (small) if he was in the relevant group. If he was in the irrelevant group, he was rewarded for responses to SW and LW (white). A control group with no verbalization completed the design.

The first question to be asked is whether such overt verbalization, intervening between stimulus and response, affects the acquisition of the reversal shift. The answer is clear: it does. For both age groups relevant verbalization produced significantly faster shifts than irrelevant verbalization. These results add credence to the mediating response model used to explain reversal-nonreversal shift behavior. They also provide a technique for exploring the interaction between verbal and other developmental variables.

Another question this research was designed to answer was whether the utilization of verbal mediators differs with age as has been suggested by Luria (1957). That is, will the difference between the reversal shift behavior of younger and older children be reduced or eliminated when both are provided with the same verbal response, or is there another ingredient, associated with development, which is necessary before words exercise control over overt behavior?

Table 9-5 presents the results analyzed separately for each age group. It can be seen that the effects were somewhat different for the two age levels. As expected, when there was no verbalization the 4-year-olds took significantly more trials to reverse than the 7-year-olds. Relevant verbalization did not facilitate the shift for the older children, presumably because they did not require instruction about verbalization to supply relevant mediation. They were able to supply it themselves. The responsiveness

TABLE 9-5

Mean Number of Trials to Criterion on Reversal
Shift for Each Verbalization Condition at
Two Age Levels

	Verbalization Condition		
	Relevant	Irrelevant	None
4 years	16.1	30.4	22.2
7 years	8.3	35.6	8.8

of the older children to verbal labels is seen, however, in the sharp increase in learning difficulty produced by irrelevant verbalization.

The 4-year-olds, on the other hand, profited from relevant verbalization and, like the older children, were hindered by irrelevant verbalization. This suggests that, although they are not likely to supply their own mediators, they can use their own words in this capacity when language responses are required. Although the results suggest an interesting interaction between verbalization and age, the implied interaction, as assessed by analysis of variance, fell short of statistical significance ($.10 > p > .05$). The definitive study of such interaction remains to be done.

Although it is clear that we have much to learn, some general conclusions can be drawn from these several studies. In this simple situation, which straddles the boundary between discrimination learning and concept formation, it seems that the single-unit S-R model adequately explains the behavior of the majority of children below 5 or 6 years of age. It does not explain the behavior of the majority of the older children. Invoking the theoretical construct of the mediating response can account for the more mature behavior within the S-R framework. This approach has the advantage of providing for continuity between the laws governing the behavior of younger and older children, since it attributes the observed developmental changes to a new and important system of responses, probably bound

up with the development of language, rather than to a different set of behavioral laws. It is not sufficient, however, to point to an explanatory mechanism. After recognizing its potential it becomes necessary to show when and how it functions. The study of mediating responses in children can provide information about the nature and development of mediating processes at their source. Such information can serve to enlarge the scope of behavior theory until it can encompass human problem solving.

INFERENCE

Although it cannot be attributed to any preliminary strategy, our research on inference falls into a logical format resembling that of the research on concept formation. The phenomenon we have called *inference* bears considerable resemblance to Kohler's "insight" (1925) and Maier's "reasoning" (1929). Initially we sought to convert an experimental paradigm into a research vehicle for studying problem solving in very young children. The paradigm was adapted from that of Hull (1935, 1952) in his analysis of the behavior of Maier's reasoning rats. Subjects are trained on three separate behavior segments, each of which presents a distinctive stimulus, requires a different response, and yields a different reward. Two of these segments, designated as A-B and X-Y, lead to subgoals. The third segment, B-G, leads to the major goal. After being trained on each of these segments individually, the subject is presented with a test trial in which only the A-B and X-Y segments are available to him and he is motivated to get the major goal. The solution to this problem is to link the behavior segments by responding to A to require B and then use B to get G. The X-Y segment serves as a control against which to assess the inferential behavior. For example, in our most recent study we used an apparatus with three horizontally arranged panels, one for each segment. For some children, the

A-B segment consisted of pressing a button on the right hand panel to obtain a glass marble. The X-Y segment consisted of pressing a button on the left hand panel to obtain a steel ballbearing. The B-G segment consisted of dropping a marble into a hole in the center panel which yielded a fairy tale charm. During the preliminary training on B-G, the subject was provided with a marble and a ballbearing, but only the marble would work. In the test situation neither was provided; instead all of the panels were opened and the child was told that if he did what he was supposed to he could get the charm. Solution consisted of pressing A to get the marble and then dropping the marble into B to get the charm. For half of the children the A-B segment was on the right, and for half it was on the left. Similarly, for half of the children the marble was the B subgoal, and for half it was the ballbearing (in which case only the ballbearing would operate the B-G segment).

In a somewhat comparable but more loosely controlled experimental situation, Maier found that rats were capable of inference (1929). As far back as 1935, Hull, who accepted this datum, was so impressed with the necessity for a behavior theory to explain such a phenomenon that he set out to provide his own explanation. Hull suggested that during the acquisition of each segment of behavior, not only was the overt S-R connection strengthened, but the subject also acquired an anticipatory goal response (r_g) appropriate to the goal object. This r_g worked backward until stimuli that marked the beginning of the segment became capable of evoking it. The stimulus properties associated with the distinctive r_g for the major goal thus became connected with the A-B segment; they did not become associated with the X-Y segment. Since more connections have been associated with the response to A, and since these response tendencies summate, the subject should, when presented with a choice between A and X, while motivated for G, choose the former. Once A is responded to, it produces

B, which in turn leads to the response necessary to produce G, by virtue of previous training. Thus, the habit segments were supposed to become linked to produce inferential behavior.

It is characteristic of Hull's explanations that they generate many deductions, several of which he made explicit. There was one readily testable and fundamental implication that he did not enumerate: inference should occur more readily when the order of training consists of presenting B-G before A-B, since this order maximizes the conditions for the associations between A and the r_g of the major goal.

The assembly of habit segments can also be viewed as an exercise in chaining. Skinner's formulation (1938) points out that in setting up a chain of behavior it is usually most efficient to start with the last link, in this case B-G. In that way the discriminative stimulus (B), through its association with the goal stimulus (G), acquires secondary reinforcing powers, which can serve to strengthen the A-B link. Since Y acquires no such additional secondary reinforcing capacity, the X-Y link should not be able to compete successfully with the A-B link. This analysis should engender the same prediction as was derived from Hull, namely that the optimum order would be that in which B-G precedes A-B.

Notice that both of these explanations are developed to account for the presumably demonstrated capacity of the rat to infer and consequently contain no response mechanism not available to that species.

Our initial interest in inferential behavior was to test the prediction about order using children as subjects. Before this could be done it was necessary to devise suitable experimental techniques. In the course of this search it was found that, given sufficiently simple segments, some nursery school children could infer (Kendler and Kendler [1956]) and this kind of inference was, like simple associative learning, influenced by reinforcement and motivation variables (Kendler et al. [1958]). More recently a study was completed that expressly tested the effect of order of presentation of the several segments on inferential behavior in preschool children (35 to 65 months) (Kendler and Kendler [1961]). The findings showed that there was *no order effect.* This study used a somewhat more complex procedure than the earlier ones and drew its sample from a lower socioeconomic level. Under these conditions, there was very little inferential behavior, and the little there was did not seem to be readily accounted for by the associative principles proposed by Hull.

The data were somewhat difficult to reconcile with the theoretical superstructure underlying the Hullian account and with Maier's data about the rat's capacity in this area. But after the study had been completed, an article by Koronakos (1959) appeared in the literature. He used the Hullian paradigm to study inferential behavior in rats. What he found began to help us see our results as part of a familiar pattern. After initial training when the rats were presented with the A or X choice, they chose one as often as the other. There was no evidence that rats could, in this carefully controlled situation, combine the habit segments spontaneously to attain the major goal.

It is now beginning to look as though inference, like reversal shift, may be a process that is not readily available to lower phylogenetic species and perhaps not to young children. Inference may be another developmental process with ontogenetic as well as phylogenetic implications. The last study to be described undertook to explore this possibility. All of the results have not yet been analyzed, and no statistical significances have yet been computed; nevertheless, some of the findings are sufficiently cogent to warrant presentation now.

This study compared the behavior of 64 kindergarten children (5 to 6 years old) with 64 third grade children (8 to 10 years old) on the inference task. When confronted with the test situation, only 50 per cent of the younger children as compared with 72 per cent of the older children chose to respond to A (the inferential choice). Furthermore, of the children who made the initial A choice only 12 per cent of the younger children and 67 per cent of the older children went on to complete the inferential sequence to obtain the major goal with no unnecessary steps.

This seems to be rather clear evidence that, in this situation, the capacity to combine independently acquired habit segments is present in very few youngsters below about 6 years of age. But among the third graders there were many more who plainly displayed such integrative capacity. Moreover, there is indication from other aspects of this experiment that the response of the two age levels to the connecting stimulus (B) is quite different. For the younger children it is necessary to have B in order to make the integrative response. For a substantial proportion of the older children the final integration is *more* dependent on self-produced cues than on the external stimulus B. Apparently the occurrence of inference, like the occurrence of reversal shift, is dependent on a system of covert mediating responses which occurs more readily in older than younger children. It seems that the experimental study of inferential behavior in children may provide another useful vehicle for examining the development of the covert response system underlying the higher mental processes.

CONCLUSIONS

Some interesting developmental changes occurring between early and middle childhood have emerged from applying an S-R learning theory approach to problem solving in children. Analyses of these changes in terms of a very broad conception of behavior theory has shown that the behavior of very young children is dependent on environmental cues, with which relatively simple S-R connections are formed and to which the laws of learning derived from simpler species are applicable. Older children's behavior, if it is to be dealt with in an S-R framework, must be conceptualized in terms of chains of responses in which some of the links are or become covert. It is proposed that a combined developmental-experimental approach can provide an understanding of how this transition occurs by studying it at its inception.

REFERENCES

Buss, A. H. Rigidity as a function of reversal and nonreversal shifts in the learning of successive discriminations. *J. exp. Psychol.*, 1953, **45**, 75–81.

Harrow, M., and G. B. Friedman. Comparing reversal and nonreversal shifts in concept formation with partial reinforcement controlled. *J. exp. Psychol.*, 1958, **55**, 592–597.

Hull, C. L. The mechanism of the assembly of behavior segments in novel combinations suitable for problem solution. *Psychol. Rev.*, 1935, **42**, 219–245.

———. *A behavior system.* New Haven, Conn.: Yale University Press, 1952.

Kelleher, R. T. Discrimination learning as a function of reversal and nonreversal shifts. *J. exp. Psychol.*, 1956, **51**, 379–384.

Kendler, H. H., and M. F. D'Amato. A comparison of reversal shifts and nonreversal shifts in human concept formation behavior. *J. exp. Psychol.*, 1955, **49**, 165–174.

———, and T. S. Kendler. Inferential behavior in preschool children. *J. exp. Psychol.*, 1956, **51**, 311–314.

———, ———, S. S. Plisskoff, and M. F. D'Amato. Inferential behavior in children: I. The influ-

ence of reinforcement and incentive motivation. *J. exp. Psychol.*, 1958, **55**, 207–212.

Kendler, T. S., and H. H. Kendler. Reversal and nonreversal shifts in kindergarten children. *J. exp. Psychol.*, 1959, **58**, 56–60.

——— and ———. Inferential behavior in children: II. The Influence of order of presentation. *J. exp. Psychol.*, 1961, **61**, 442–448.

———, ———, and B. Learnard. Mediated responses to size and brightness as a function of age. *Amer. J. Psychol.*, 1962, **75**, 571–586.

———, ———, and D. Wells. Reversal and nonreversal shifts in nursery school children. *J. comp. physiol. Psychol.*, 1960, **53**, 83–87.

Kohler, W. *The mentality of apes.* New York: Harcourt, 1925.

Koronakos, C. Inferential learning in rats: The problem-solving assembly of behavior segments. *J. comp. physiol. Psychol.*, 1959, **52**, 231–235.

Luria, A. R. The role of language in the formation of temporary connections. In B. Simon (Ed.), *Psychology in the Soviet Union.* Stanford, Calif.: Stanford University Press, 1957.

Maier, N. R. F. Reasoning in white rats. *Comp. Psychol. Monogr.*, 1929, No. 9.

Skinner, B. F. *The behavior of organisms.* New York: Appleton, 1938.

A Study of the Effects of Verbalization on Problem Solving

ROBERT M. GAGNÉ

ERNEST C. SMITH, Jr.

Scattered throughout the literature on problem solving are occasional studies which are interpreted as indicating that acts of verbalizing during problem solving result in lessened problem solving effectiveness. While most investigators of such behavior may be inclined to expect a facilitating effect of "transfer of principles" to a final

Reprinted with the permission of the senior author and the publisher from the article of the same title, *Journal of Experimental Psychology*, 1962, **63**, 12–18.

performance, studies have sometimes cast doubt upon the generality of such a finding, particularly in those instances where the principles are stated verbally.

Katona (1940), for example, found that a method which involved teaching verbal principles in solving matchstick problems to be less effective than a method of teaching by example. In a more recent study, Haslerud and Meyers (1958) found an experimental treatment in which verbally-stated principles of solution of cryptograms were given to Ss to be less effective for solution of new cryptograms than was a treatment in which Ss were required to discover solutions for themselves. Other findings supportive of this sort of conclusion are cited by Haslerud and Meyers (Hendrix, 1947) which suggest the superiority for transfer of "not-verbalizing" vs. "verbalizing" by Ss themselves, in solving mathematical problems. In another study using matchstick problems, Corman (1957) failed to find significant differences in performance among groups given various amounts and kinds of verbal instructions.

Results like these contrast markedly with those of an older study by Ewert and Lambert (1932), which used as a problem the task of transferring discs graduated in size from one circle to another in a triangular configuration of three circles. In successive tasks, different numbers of discs (from three through eight) are placed in Circle No. 1, arranged in order of size with the largest at the bottom. The problem is to transfer the discs from Circle 1 to Circle 2 in the least possible number of moves, moving one at a time. One of the experimental groups in this study was given only instructions about the rules of the game; a second group was encouraged to try to find a general principle for solution; a third was given a verbally-stated principle of solution; while a fourth was given a principle plus a demonstration of the correct method with three discs. A large difference was found in the performance of groups who were given a verbally-stated principle of solution and the performance of groups who were not.

The three-circle problem is fairly difficult, and one can spend much time and many moves before discovering a principle which is truly general. Perhaps the reason for the striking contrast between the results of Ewert and Lambert (1932) and those of more modern investigators resides simply in this fact. To a participant in the problem, it seems natural indeed that his performance should improve once he knows the principle—improve not only on the problem he has attempted, but on others of a similar type. It will

perhaps take more than one additional study to explicate these contrasting results.

It was our intention in the present experiment to make a further exploration into the effects of verbalizing on problem solving performance. We were interested particularly in the kind of verbalizing done by S himself during attempts to solve the problem, rather than by E.

Presumably, verbal principles provided in instructions must be repeated (perhaps to himself) by S, if they are to be effective. If we let S discover his own principles, in his own words, but require that he verbalize them, will this facilitate or interfere with problem solving? Marks (1951), for example, found no significant effects of providing Ss with a typed list of principles ("elements of the problem"), but a high correlation (.83) between performance and vocalization by Ss during solution. We were also interested in seeing whether we could establish the differences in performance suggested (but not confirmed) by Ewert and Lambert's (1932) results, of the effects of instructions to find and formulate verbally a general principle.

We chose to investigate these questions by measuring performance on a standard series of three-circle tasks of the sort employed by Ewert and Lambert, transfer to a final six-disc task of this type, and the adequacy with which Ss could make verbal formulations of general principles. Specifically, the experiment compared the performance of groups of Ss who solved two-, three-, four-, and five-disc problems successively, under four conditions representing combinations of two treatment variables: (a) a requirement to state verbally a reason for each move at the time it was made; and (b) instructions to search for a general principle which could be stated verbally after the tasks were solved.

METHOD

MATERIALS. The three-circle problem described by Ewert and Lambert (1932) was represented by three circles of 5 in. in diameter, drawn on a piece of stiff white paper, with their centers at the apexes of an equilateral triangle of side 7 in., and labeled A, B, and C. The discs were made of $\frac{3}{32}$ in.-aluminum, numbered 1 through 6, and graduated in diameter from $\frac{3}{4}$ in. to 2 in. A set of discs (two to six) is placed in Circle A, graduated with the largest at the bottom, and the problem is to move them all to Circle B so that they will be in the same order, in the smallest possible number of moves. Only one disc at a time may be moved, and it is never permitted to put a larger diameter disc on top of one with a smaller diameter. Under these rules, the fewest number of moves required (with any number n of discs) is $2^n - 1$.

The kind of principle which reduces this problem to a routine is the following: "If the number of discs is odd, move first to the circle to which you want to go eventually; if even, move first away from this circle. Continue by moving discs with odd numbers always in a clockwise direction, and the discs with even numbers always in a counterclockwise direction." There are, however, a number of other ways of formulating the second part of this principle, which are equally effective, although requiring more words.

SUBJECTS. The Ss were 28 boys in Grades 9 and 10, who were assigned randomly to four experimental groups. Their ages were 14–15 yr., and their IQs were all above 110. They had volunteered to participate in studies of learning, but were paid an amount equivalent to prevailing rates of odd-job work. Each S was questioned closely to determine that he had no previous acquaintance with the problem, and was not used in the experiment if he had.

PROCEDURE. First, each S was shown the materials and given instructions about the rules of the game. The three-disc and the four-disc problem were then administered in succession, and each was carried to final solution (i.e., getting all discs in Circle B in the proper order). The S was told in each case what the minimal number of moves was. If he decided he had made a wrong move, he was permitted to go back to an earlier point in the solution, or to the beginning. The E made a count of all moves. The purpose of this exercise was to give all Ss equal acquaintance with the problem, and also to provide data on equivalence of the groups.

Following this initial test, each S was assigned randomly to one of four conditions, each containing 7 Ss, as follows:

Group V-SS (Verbalizing, Solution Set) was instructed to state aloud why they were making each individual move at the time they made it. In addition, these Ss were instructed to try to think of a general rule by means of which they could tell someone how to solve these problems, which was to be solicited afterwards by E. Group V (Verbalizing, No Solution Set) was required to verbalize a reason for each move, but was not instructed to try to formulate a general rule for solution. Group SS (No Verbalizing, Solution Set) was not required to verbalize, but was instructed to try to formulate a rule. Group No (No Verbalizing, No Solution Set) was simply told of the problem to be presented and its ground rules, with no additional instructions.

With these instructions, Ss were kept at the task until they achieved a single final solution for two, three, four, and five discs in succession. One-minute rest periods were interposed between successive tasks. Number of moves was counted in each case. Of course, the making of moves was slower for those Ss who were required to verbalize, usually to the point of slight annoyance. Following this learning session, after approximately 3 min. rest, all Ss were presented the six-disc task as a final test. They were told that their time to solution would be measured (with a stop watch), as well as the number of moves taken. No verbalizing was required.

RECORDING. For the initial test (using three and four discs), E simply kept a record of the number of moves made by each S.

During administration of the main experimental treatments (two, three, four, and five discs) number of moves was recorded. For those groups instructed to verbalize each move, E recorded on a prepared record sheet a brief phrase indicating the verbal statement made by each S. No attempt was made to make exact verbatim reproductions of what S said. Whenever an unusual reason was given, however, E attempted to record its meaning fully.

On the final test, E recorded the number of moves and the time required to achieve solution. After the final test was concluded, each S was asked to give a rule or rules for doing the problem with any number of discs, as if he were telling it to a person ignorant of the solution. The E recorded these verbally stated principles.

RESULTS

Initial Test

The means and SDs for number of moves made by each of the four groups on the initial test composed of tasks with three and four discs were as follows: V-SS: $M = 26.4$, $SD = 4.5$; V:$M = 28.6$, $SD = 3.7$; SS:$M = 26.6$, $SD = 3.6$; No:$M = 27.9$, $SD = 4.9$. These results appeared to insure an acceptable degree of comparability ($F = .70$, $df = 3/24$; $P > .05$).

Practice Session

Mean performance curves for the four groups of the experiment are shown in Figure 9-3. These depict mean number of moves in excess of the minimum for the problems with two, three, four, and five

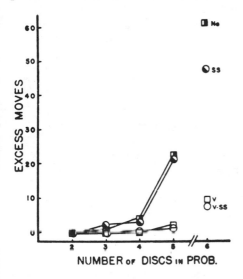

FIGURE 9-3. *Performance curves showing moves in excess of minimum required for successively administered problems of two, three, four, and five discs for the four groups of the experiment. (Values are shown for the final six-disc problem as a terminal point.)*

discs administered in sequence. The same measure on the final test is also shown for each group as a terminal point.

It may readily be seen that a difference among the groups, associated with the Verbalization variable, began to appear as early as the three-disc practice, and showed itself as an ever-widening difference thereafter. On the other hand, no differences of consequence appear in the performances of groups differentially treated with respect to a Solution Set, i.e., being told to look for a principle to be stated verbally. These apparent trends of the data were confirmed by an analysis of variance of the data for Trial 5. Since heterogeneity of variance was found in the raw data, they were transformed to logarithms. In this state, the null hypothesis regarding differences in variances could be rejected. An analysis of variance on these transformed data indicated significant treatment effects ($F = 6.67$, $df = 3/18$; $P < .01$). When t tests were applied to the pairs of differences between means these were found to be significant at less than the .01 level for each of the verbalization groups vs. each of the nonverbalization groups.

In contrast, neither of the pairs of groups differentiated by the presence or absence of the SS instructions yield means which are significantly different from each other. Verbalization made a significant difference, Solution Set instructions made none.

VERBALIZATION DURING PRACTICE. The verbalization done by Ss who were instructed to give a reason for every move tended to fall into certain standard categories, with rare exceptions. There were those which were oriented toward *single* moves, like (a) "only possible move"; (b) "just to try it"; or (c) "don't know" (this one was quite infrequent). Then there were those which anticipated to the extent of two moves, such as (a) "to get at the larger disc"; (b) "to free up a space." There were also instances of reasons which apparently anticipated *sequences* of moves. One of the relatively frequent ones was (*a*) "move as with a three-disc sequence"; also in this category should perhaps come (*b*) "If disc is odd-numbered, move to circle B," and (*c*) "if disc is even-numbered, move to circle C." Finally there were some expressions of truly *general* principles, such as (*a*) "move odd-numbered discs in the clockwise direction," and (*b*) "move even-numbered discs in the counterclockwise direction."

On the whole, the content of these "reasons" was by no means startling. It was not particularly surprising, considering the results of earlier investigators of thinking, that this form of thinking out loud was not very revealing about the nature of internal processes. A close examination of these data did not enable us to invent a method of relating specific types of verbal response to specific stages of the problem, except for the fact that the more general principles tended to occur later in practice than did the less general ones.

Final Task Performance

Mean number of moves in excess of minimum, and mean times (min.) to solution, for each of the four groups of the experiment on the final six-disc task are shown in Table 9-6. Here it can be seen that under standard conditions for all the groups, the differences in moves which appeared on the five-disc task are even greater on the six-disc task. Again the variances are markedly different between the verbalization and nonverbalization pairs of groups. A logarithmic transformation was found to make possible the assumption of homogeneity of variance. An analysis of variance performed on these transformed data confirmed significant treatment effects ($F = 9.13$, $df = 3/18$; $P < .01$). Application of t tests to differences between individual means indicated significance at the .01 level for comparisons of the verbalization and nonverbalization groups. Differences between means for Groups SS and No, and Groups V-SS and V, are not significant.

TABLE 9-6

Means and *SD*s for Number of Moves in Excess of Minimum, and for Time of Performance, on the Final Six-Disc Task for the Four Groups

Measure	Groups			
	V-SS ($N = 7$)	V ($N = 7$)	SS ($N = 7$)	No ($N = 7$)
Moves in excess of minimum				
Mean	7.9	9.3	48.1	61.7
SD	8.6	7.9	34.8	40.2
Time (min.)				
Mean	4.2	3.8	10.1	10.0
SD	2.2	2.0	4.1	5.5

An entirely similar set of comparisons exists with the means of time to solve, shown in Table 9-6. Here the F test for the total data is significant at lower than the .05 level ($F = 4.90$, $df = 3/18$). The t test indicates significance of differences of means associated with the contrast of verbalization vs. no verbalization (V-SS vs. SS; V-SS vs. No; V vs. SS; V vs. No) at better than the .05 level. Other differences in means are not significant.

Stating the Verbal Principle

Records of statements made by Ss in response to the instruction to state verbally how to solve these problems were examined by the 2 Es independently, and rated "Inadequate," "Partial," or "Complete." The following agreements were made beforehand: "Inadequate" was to mean any principle which was incorrect, irrelevant, or so fragmentary that it would be of no aid to anyone in finding solutions. "Partial" meant one of the two major parts of the principle, concerned with starting (move odd-numbered disc to the goal circle, etc.) or with procedure during solution (even numbers move clockwise, etc.) "Complete" meant both of these major parts.

With these criteria, it was quite easy to

TABLE 9-7

Number of Inadequate, Partial, and Complete
Verbal Principles Stated by Ss in Each Group

Group	N	Number of instances of principles judged as:		
		Inadequate	Partial	Complete
V-SS	7	0	3	4
V	7	0	5	2
SS	7	1	6	0
No	7	6	1	0

classify the principles the Ss stated, and
there were no differences in judgment
of the 2 Es. These results are shown in
Table 9-7.

Considering first the dichotomy Inadequate vs. Partial or Complete, the Fisher
exact probability test was applied to comparisons of the experimental treatments.
The probability of the observed contrasts
between V-SS and No, and between V and
No were found to be .002; between SS and
No, .014. All other comparisons yielded high
probability values. So far as being able to
state even *partial* verbal principles, Group
No is significantly poorer than those who
verbalized; for those who did not verbalize,
there is a significant effect of instructions to
look for a general principle. Second, the
dichotomy Inadequate or Partial vs. Complete was considered by this same method.
Here the only low probabilities were .036
between Groups V-SS and SS and also
Groups V-SS and No. The group required to
verbalize as well as to try to formulate a
verbal principle, was thus found to be superior to Groups SS and No in the formulation of *complete* verbal principles. It would
appear that verbalizing during practice is
the most important factor accounting for
this difference.

DISCUSSION

Our results indicate that requiring individuals to verbalize while practicing the
three-circle problem is a condition which is
significantly related to superior performance
in problem solving, which begins to show
itself during practice with two-, three-,
four-, and five-disc tasks, and is maintained
on a final six-disc task. There is a strong
suggestion also, that verbalizing is the most
important factor at work in producing a
greater number of individuals who can, at
the close of practice, state fully adequate
verbal principles of task solution.

Instructions to try to formulate verbal
principles for solution of these tasks appear
to have no effect on performance of the
task, and also an insignificant effect (by
themselves) in producing a greater frequency of fully adequate principles. They
do, however, produce more verbal principles which are at least partially adequate,
than is the case when they are omitted. It
will be apparent in interpreting these results
that we cannot be certain how great a contrast in "set to look for solution" was actually achieved by the instructions used. After
all, the noninstructed groups as well as the
instructed ones underwent an initial period
of testing on the three- and four-disc tasks,
and may have generated in themselves a set
to look for a general solution.

Surely the most striking finding is the
effect of verbalization by the Ss during
practice. Such verbalization is of course
very different from that which may result
from providing Ss with verbally stated principles of solution, as was done in the studies
of Ewert and Lambert (1932) and Haslerud
and Meyers (1958). Whatever principles
were used by the individuals in the present
experiment, they must have been discovered
by the Ss themselves. In this respect, at
least, the present findings are not inconsistent with those of Haslerud and Meyers, nor
with other results indicating the effectiveness of self-discovered principles for problem solving (e.g., Gagné and Brown, 1961).

It is perhaps of some importance to
emphasize that the individuals who were
required to verbalize also took more time
to make successive moves. We cannot tell
from these data, of course, whether this

more deliberate pacing of the task may have had some effects on the performance. The additional time between moves, however, was "filled" time, taken up entirely with the act of verbalization. Thus it would not be reasonable to suppose that the verbalization groups had any greater opportunity than did the nonverbalization groups for the deliberate rehearsal and recall of successful and unsuccessful moves. Verbalization is the most obvious variable at work; if other events are contributing to the results because of their association with time differences, it is not immediately apparent what they are.

As we pointed out, the content of the verbalizing during practice was fairly pedestrian and to some extent routine, so that it could be readily categorized. What then accounts for its effect on problem solving? In answering this question, we have no theory to call upon. It would appear that requiring verbalization somehow "forced the Ss to think." In other words, this treatment may have had the effect of constantly prodding the Ss to think of new reasons for their moves, particularly since they may have gotten a little tired of giving "the same old reasons" over again. This conception of the treatment would assign it a role similar to that of instructions to think of new word associates, as in the studies of Maltzman, Simon, Raskin, and Licht (1960). But this is a speculation which obviously does not come directly from present data. It would, however, be an interesting route for follow-up studies to take; namely, testing whether instructions to "think of new reasons," to be stated verbally, would have a facilitative effect on the solution of a task like that used here.

SUMMARY

A study was conducted to determine the effects of (*a*) requiring Ss to verbalize during practice, and (*b*) instructions to find a general principle to be stated verbally, on problem solving performance. The three-

circle task described by Ewert and Lambert (1932) was used. The Ss were 28 ninth and tenth grade boys, divided randomly into four groups of 7 each. Following the initial test on tasks with three and four discs, Ss were assigned to four groups given different treatments representing combinations of the two experimental variables. The practice session consisted of two-, three-, four-, and five-disc tasks administered successively. Records were kept of the verbalizing, for those groups who engaged in it, and of numbe   moves to achieve solution, for all groups. Following this, a final task using six discs was administered to all Ss under standdard conditions, and a record was made of number of moves as well as time to solution.

Significant differences were found between the scores of those groups who were required to verbalize and those who were not, in terms of number of moves. Similar differences based on time scores were found in the contrast between verbalization and nonverbalization groups. Differences between other pairs of groups were not significant.

Comparisons of success in stating verbal principles applicable to the solution of three-circle problems were made among judged categories of Inadequate, Partial, and Complete, for all groups. A significant difference was obtained between verbalizing and nonverbalizing groups, and one which favored the "instructed" groups when the dichotomy Inadequate or Partial vs. Complete was tested.

The results appear to indicate that requiring Ss to verbalize during practice has the effect of making them think of new reasons for their moves, and thus facilitates both the discovery of general principles and their employment in solving successive problems.

REFERENCES

Corman, B. R. The effect of varying amounts and kinds of information as guidance in problem solving. *Psychol. Monogr.*, 1957, **71**, No. 2 (Whole No. 431).

Ewert, P. H., and J. F. Lambert. Part II: The effect of verbal instructions upon the formation of a concept. *J. gen. Psychol.*, 1932, **6**, 400–413.

Gagné, R. M., and L. T. Brown. Some factors in the programing of conceptual learning. *J. exp. Psychol.*, 1961, **62**, 313–321.

Haslerud, G. M., and S. Meyers. The transfer value of given and individually derived princi-

ples. *J. educ. Psychol.*, 1958, **49**, 293–298.

Hendrix, G. A new clue to transfer of training. *Elem. Sch. J.*, 1947, **48**, 197–208.

Katona, G. *Organizing and memorizing.* New York: Columbia University Press, 1940.

Maltzman, I., S. Simon, D. Raskin, and L. Licht. Experimental studies in the training of originality. *Psychol. Monogr.*, 1960, **74**, No. 6 (Whole No. 493).

Marks, M. R. Problem solving as a function of the situation. *J. exp. Psychol.*, 1951, **41**, 74–80.

Instruction in Language
and Thought: There May Be
a Will without a Way

_____ 10

INTRODUCTION

We often confuse a heightened awareness of our problems with the amount of knowledge we have to solve them. More Americans today than ever before are aware of the problems of instruction. The methodology of teaching, once reserved for reflection and study in the group discussions and group projects of schools and colleges of education and banned from the halls and the parlors of the literati, has now become interesting and salable newspaper and magazine copy and conversational grist for everyone. American business now, more actively than profitably, is engaged in the creation and sale of wares that do more to salve the consciences of American parents than to educate their children.

The more sobering side of this story is that our desire is far greater than our knowledge of how to improve instruction. Teaching is a complex of activity, and we lack knowledge of the essential components. As with any complex human behavior, its final analysis and enlightened practice must rest on basic research on behavioral processes, which themselves are only dimly understood. Only recently, in fact, has there been lively interest in constructing teaching models that have heuristic value for research on teaching (Gage, 1963; McDonald, 1965). These models are highly speculative, and some of them will be very difficult to reduce to experimental testing. None seems to include all the organismic, behavioral, social, and even cultural dimensions of teaching. Indeed, a teaching model that attempted to embrace all the major classes of variables would be more a philosophical reflection than a serious program of research. Models that promise to produce the best research (we scarcely dare promise improved practice at this time) are obviously incomplete descriptions of teaching, and yet they are the most operational and testable models we have (Gage, 1963, pages 94–141).

Educational researchers are also discovering that they cannot disingenuously look to psychology for their guiding cues and principles. With the advent of programed instruction, educational researchers have discovered that they may even contribute a technique or two to psychological research. Research on teaching is discovering that rather straightforward applications of S-R learning theory, including both classical and operant conditioning, do not necessarily result in successful teaching techniques or programs (Gagné, 1962). The problem of applying laboratory findings to educational settings is resolved by research and not by heady extrapolation (Melton, 1959). Reinforcement, for example, may be a fairly precise operation in the experimental animal chamber. In the classroom, and even in the skill-learning experiment, it is an entirely mysterious mixture of motivation, feedback, and reward (Annet, in De Cecco, 1964). Consequently, the somewhat unexpected resurgence of the romance between educational psychology and the psychology of learning in the shape of programed instruction is undergoing a sobering reappraisal (De Cecco, 1964).

The rapprochement between the psychology of learning and educational psychology and the invention of programed instruction as a technique for research on teaching at least have impressed on educational researchers the need for theoretical and methodological rigor. Too often in the past, education research contained more moral sactimony than rigor, and more propaganda than empirical conviction. The rapprochement has been eminently successful if educational research has learned only to define in operational terms independent and dependent variables and to accept the construction of theory as its primary purpose. For educators to lament that such rigor is purchased at the price of relevance forces on them the responsibility of demonstrating that any worth-while educational research, either rigorous or relevant, is possible at this time.

It may be well for research on instruction to abandon the usual dichotomy between "pure" and "applied" research (Melton, 1959). There is not so much knowledge in the behavioral sciences that educational researchers should resist the invention of new techniques, models, and theories. The collection of research in this anthology may well indicate that even the research on language and productive thought may be premature. Language and thought, however, are obviously central to teaching. Educational researchers must therefore remain particularly aware of all theoretical and empirical developments in the study of complex human processes and, where possible, base their research on laboratory findings. Frequently, however, they may find themselves contributing to "basic" research as they explore problems of instruction and school learning.

The articles in this chapter, especially those concerned with the teaching of concepts, discovery learning and teaching, and the teaching of thought and inquiry, may be significant if not always successful attempts to undertake important educational research. Research on the teaching of language, both the native tongue and foreign languages, may be somewhat less impressive in its contribution to theories of teaching, but its accomplishments are at least sound [Carroll, 1960, Chapter 10]. Linguistics may make its contribution to education not directly through the modification of teaching practice but indirectly in enabling us to understand the higher mental processes that must be employed and developed in all school learning.

The articles on the teaching of conceptual thinking (Carroll, Kersh, Wittrock, Taba, Elzey, and Suchman) either implicitly or explicitly emphasize the importance of *sequencing* learning experiences. Sequencing is an example of a variable that probably should receive more attention in research on instruction than in laboratory research on learning. Carroll [1964, Chapter 10] states that failure to learn concepts can be frequently attributed to inadequate mastery of prerequisite concepts. The design of knowledge hierarchies assures the establishment of the necessary prerequisite behaviors (Gagné, 1962). Kersh and Wittrock, in considering how discovery teaching may depart from directive teaching technique and programed instruction, allude to the ordering of experiences that either the teacher or student must provide. Taba and Elzey, using Piaget's concepts of assimilation and accommodation [Piaget, Chapter 7], discuss the strategies teachers should adopt in moving from one level to another level of thought. Finally, Suchman describes his "inquiry training" as a sequence of stages.

The solutions that these investigators suggest for the problem of teaching conceptual thinking vary more than their formulation of the problem. Carroll, unlike the others, discusses the importance of the *deductive* teaching of concepts. Deductive teaching presents concepts by definition and description. It is the favored classroom procedure. Most of the research, however, has been on inductive teaching. Carroll observes that concept learning involves both induction and deduction. In reviewing laboratory research on concept teaching he reminds us that the concepts taught in the schools are considerably more complex than those taught in the laboratory. This complexity alone makes sequencing an important teaching variable.

Kersh and Wittrock have developed a very useful scheme for classifying teaching methods along a continuum of greater or lesser teacher participation in the learning process. This classification enables us to fit degrees of inductive and deductive teaching into a single dimension. In their broad but operational view of teaching methodology they include the nature of the learning task, the student's level of motivation and skill, and the provision for practice and reinforcement. "Discovery teaching" has rapidly become a modern educational nostrum. The discussion and conceptualization of Kersh and Wittrock introduce the concreteness and precision we have needed.

The instructional methodologies of Taba, Elzey, and Suchman are primarily inductive. In terms of Kersh and Wittrock they may be described as "guided discovery." Guided discovery is an explicit concern of Taba and Elzey, who are investigating types of instructional intervention or "teaching strategies." The intervention is designed to "stimulate productive and creative thought," what is later described as "inductive discovery." With the more rigorous definition of dependent variables it may be quite possible to utilize conventional experimental design in an operational test of competing teaching strategies.

Suchman also does not phrase his research in terms of particular educational outcomes. His purpose is to teach children how "to formulate hypotheses, to test them through a verbal form of controlled experimentation, and to interpret results." He employs the subject matter of science and, in effect, he teaches in some general way "scientific thinking." His method is more one of learning by asking questions than one of learning by discovery. In the approach of Taba and Elzey, the teacher asks the questions. The children must make their own inferences. The method should teach the child not only the particular concept or principle (if he makes the correct inferences) but also an "inquiry process." Inquiry training, according to Suchman, should supplement rather than replace other teaching methods. As yet his research program has not specified the conditions under which it should be used, in terms of task, student, and time variables.

The teaching of foreign languages to American school children has become part of the public educational debate. Instruction in foreign language is a popular research and essay topic (Pimsleur, 1957; Pickrel et al., 1958; Sapon and Carroll, 1958; Rocklyn and Moren, 1960; Carroll, 1963). In his provocative article Carroll outlines some of the problems that the adoption of this policy may raise. There is the question of *who* should be taught foreign languages, because we know that there is a significant difference in aptitude for learning other languages. There is some question about the assumption that children learn foreign languages better and more easily than do adults. This latter question is part of an even larger one: will the student be a better educated person on his graduation from college if he begins the study of foreign language in elementary school? Also, what is the value of the study of any one language for the later study of another? For the answers to these and other questions, Carroll notes our almost complete lack of scientific evidence. There are also the very thorny questions about language instruction, especially if we decide to teach foreign languages to children of average language aptitude. Even the invention of the language laboratory has not removed the need for time and patience in both teacher and student in the learning of a foreign language.

Politzer (1960) believes that effort (or "assiduity") should bring its own rewards in achievement. Teachers are too often in the embarrassing position of assigning average and poor grades to students who have invested saintly persistence in the course work. The language laboratory, according to Politzer, may now allow the language teacher to reward *both* effort and achievement with distinguished grades. Politzer is assuming that the language laboratory is an effective teaching device. As with Taba and Elzey, the accent is on the instructional conditions that benefit students of average as well as superior ability. In the context of this anthology the language laboratory with its emphasis on "audio-lingualism" as opposed to grammar translation, is an application of structural linguistics and psycholinguistics (Scherer and Wertheimer, 1964). Finally, Zais (1963) reports an interesting study that applied linguistic concepts to the teaching of punctuation. As in the audio-lingual foreign language programs, the emphasis is on the translation of speech into reading and writing.

REFERENCES

Annet, J. *Role of knowledge of results in learning: A survey.* Technical Report NAVTRA-DEVCEN. Port Washington: U.S. Naval Training Device Center. (Also in De Cecco, 1964.)

Carroll, J. B. Research on teaching foreign languages. In N. L. Gage (Ed.), *Handbook of research on teaching.* Chicago: Rand McNally, 1963.

De Cecco, J. P. Educational technology: Theory and practice. In J. P. De Cecco (Ed.), *Educational technology.* New York: Holt, Rinehart and Winston, 1964. Pp. 10–12.

Gage, N. L. (Ed.) *Handbook of research on teaching.* Chicago: Rand McNally, 1963.

Gagné, R. M. The acquisition of knowledge. *Psychol. Rev.*, 1962, **69**, 355–365. (Also in De Cecco, 1964.)

McDonald, F. J. *Educational psychology.* (2d ed.) Belmont, Calif.: Wadsworth, 1965. Chap. 2.

Melton, A. W. The science of learning and the technology of instruction. *Harvard Educ. Rev.*, 1959, **29**, 96–106.

Pickrel, G., C. Neidt, and R. Gibson. Tape recordings are used by seventh grade students in Westside Junior-Senior High School, Omaha, Nebraska. *Nat. Ass. Sec. School Principals' Bull.*, 1958, **42**, Pt. 1 (No. 234), 81–93.

Pimsleur, P. Experimental design in the language field. *Mod. Lang. Forum*, 1957, **42**, 157–163.

Politzer, R. L. Assiduity and achievement. *Mod. Lang. J.*, 1960, 14–16.

Rocklyn, E. H., and R. I. A. Moren. A feasibility study of a machine-taught oral-aural Russian language course. *Amer. Psychol.*, 1960, **15**, 423.

Sapon, S. M., and J. B. Carroll. Discriminative perception of speech sounds as a function of native language. *Gen. Linguistics*, 1958, 3, 62–72.

Scherer, G. A. C., and M. Wertheimer. *A psychoanalytic experiment in foreign-language teaching.* New York: McGraw-Hill, 1964.

Zais, R. S. The linguistic characteristics of punctuation symbols and the teaching of punctuation skills. *English J.*, 1963, **52**, 677–681.

Words, Meanings, and Concepts: Part II. Concept Teaching and Learning

JOHN B. CARROLL

I suspect that anyone who has examined the concept formation literature with the hope of finding something of value for the teaching of concepts in school has had cause for some puzzlement and disappointment, because however fascinating this literature may be, as it wends its way through the detailed problems posed by the methodology itself, its relevance to the learning of concepts in the various school subjects is a bit obscure.

Let us look at the major differences between concept learning in school and in the laboratory.

1. One of the major differences is in the nature of the concepts themselves. A new concept learned in school is usually a genuinely "new" concept rather than an artificial combination of familiar attributes (like the concept "three blue squares" such as might be taught in a psychological experiment).

2. New concepts learned in school depend on attributes which themselves represent difficult concepts. In more general terms, concepts learned in school often depend upon a network of related or prerequisite concepts. One cannot very well learn the concept of derivative, in the calculus, until one has mastered a rather elaborate structure of prerequisite concepts (e.g., slope, change of slope, algebraic function, etc.). Further, the attributes on which school-learned concepts depend are frequently verbal, depending on elements of meaning that cannot easily be represented in terms of simple sensory qualities as used in concept formation experiments.

3. Many of the more difficult concepts of school learning are of a relational rather than a conjunctive character; they deal with the relations among attributes rather than their combined presence or absence. Concept formation experiments have thus far revealed little about the acquisition of relational concepts.

4. An important element in school learning is the memory problem involved in the proper matching of words and concepts. Thus, the problems of paired-associate memory are added to those of concept learning itself. For example, a student in biology or social studies has to learn not only a large number of new concepts, but also a large number of unfamiliar, strange-looking words to be attached to these concepts. The rate at which new concepts can be introduced is probably limited, just as the rate at which foreign language words can be acquired is limited.

5. The most critical difference between school concept learning and concept learning in psychological experiments is that the former is for the most part deductive and the latter is generally inductive. It would be relatively rare to find a concept taught in school by the procedure of showing a student a series of positive and negative

Reprinted with the permission of the author and the publisher from the article of the same title, *Harvard Educational Review*, 1964, 34, No. 2, 191–202.

instances, labeled as such, and asking him to induce the nature of the concept with no further aid. Such instances could be found, of course; perhaps they would exemplify a pure "discovery method," and perhaps there should be more use of this method than is the case. The fact is that a pure discovery method is seldom used, because it is rather slow and inefficient. Even if a teaching procedure incorporates "discovery" elements, it is likely to be combined with deductive elements. The concept to be taught is described verbally—perhaps by a rule or definition—and the student is expected to attain the concept by learning to make correct identification of positive and negative instances. For example, he is told what an "indirect object" is and then is given practice in identifying the indirect objects (positive instances) among other words (negative instances). Many simple concepts can be taught by a wholly deductive procedure. For most students, the dictionary definition of *tarn* will be a sufficient stimulus for attainment of the concept. On the other hand, it is well known that purely deductive, verbal procedures are frequently insufficient to help learners attain concepts. Concept formation experimentation would be more relevant to school learning problems if it could give more attention to examining the role of verbalization and other deductive procedures in concept attainment.

Nevertheless, there are certain similarities between concept attainment in school and concept formation in psychological experiments. These arise chiefly from the fact that not every concept is learned *solely* in a formalized, prearranged school setting. The school environment is in many ways continuous with the out-of-school environment; concepts are learned partly in school, partly out of school. The process whereby the elementary concepts of a language are learned closely parallels that of the psychological concept formation experiment. A child learns the concept "dog" not by having the concept described to him but by learning to restrict his usage of the word *dog* to instances regarded as positive by the speech community. In this process there are many false responses—either false positives (calling a non-dog a dog) or false negatives (believing a dog to be a non-instance), before an appropriate series of reinforcements produces correct concept attainment. Similar phenomena occur with concepts in the school curriculum. A child who has been told that his cousins visiting him from Peoria are "tourists" may not realize that tourists do not need to be relatives, and when he is told that the Germans who have settled in his town are "immigrants," he may believe that all foreigners visiting his town are immigrants. Concept formation experiments yield information as to the range and variety of instances that have to be furnished for efficient and correct concept formation in the absence of formal instruction.

But if the foregoing statement is true, concept formation studies should also yield insights as to what information has to be furnished for *deductive* concept formation, e.g., from a formal definition. Obviously, a formal definition is successful only to the extent that it correctly identifies and describes all the criterial attributes that are likely to be relevant for a concept, and to the extent that it communicates the proper values and relationships of these to the learner. The burden is both on the definition itself and on the learner. A student may fail to learn the concept *tarn* from the definition previously cited either because it omits some essential criterial attribute (e.g., that a tarn must contain *water* rather than, say, *oil* or *lava*), or because the student fails to comprehend the meaning of its elements (for example, how small is "small"?).

What is actually going on in most school learning of concepts is a process that combines in some way deductive and inductive features.

Descriptions and definitions provide the deductive elements of the process. The several parts of a description or definition specify the attributes and relationships that are criterial for the concept. The order in which these specifications are arranged in the description and presented to the student may have something to do with the ease of concept attainment, particularly in the case of complex concepts with many attributes and complex interrelationships (like the case of *tort* discussed below). As yet we have no well-founded generalizations about the order in which the criterial attributes for a concept should be presented.

At the same time, inductive procedures entail the citing of positive and negative instances of the concept. We know from concept attainment research that learning is facilitated more by positive than by negative instances, even though the "information" conveyed by these instances is the same in a given experimental context. But in real-life concept learning, the number of dimensions that may possibly be relevant is less limited; the function of positive instances is as much to show *which* dimensions are relevant as it is to show what values of them are critical. We may speculate that the real value of what we are calling inductive procedures in concept learning is to afford the learner an opportunity to test his understanding of and memory for the elements of verbal descriptions and definitions. This testing may even involve the construction and testing of alternative hypotheses.

For example, consider the following verbal statement of what a "paradigm" (for research on teaching) is:

Paradigms are models, patterns, or schemata. Paradigms are not theories; they are rather ways of thinking or patterns for research that, when carried out, can lead to the development of theory.[1]

As a verbal statement, this is hardly adequate; fortunately, Gage proceeds to exhibit a number of positive instances of "para-digms" by which his readers can test out their notions of what this concept might be. Many readers will still have difficulty, however, because he fails to exhibit *negative* instances of paradigms.

What is needed, eventually, is a scientific "rhetoric" for the teaching of concepts —assembled not only from the traditional rhetoric of exposition but also from whatever scientific experiments on concept teaching can tell us. We will be better off, however, if concept-attainment studies begin to give attention to the manner in which real-life, non-artificial concepts can be taught most efficiently—presumably by combination of both deductive and inductive procedures.

ILLUSTRATIONS OF CONCEPT TEACHING PROBLEMS

To suggest the kinds of problems that arise in the teaching of concepts or that might be investigated through formal research, I propose to analyze a small number of concepts of various types, at several levels of difficulty.

Tourist versus Immigrant

A fourth grade teacher reported difficulty in getting her pupils to understand and contrast the meanings of the words *tourist* and *immigrant*. Neither word appears in Dale and Eichholz's[2] list of words known by at least sixty-seven per cent of children in the fourth grade, although *tour* (as a sight-seeing trip) was known by seventy per cent. In the sixth-grade list, *immigrant* was known by seventy per cent and *tourist* by seventy-seven per cent; the figures are

---

[1] N. L. Gage, "Paradigms for Research on Teaching." *Handbook of Research on Teaching,* ed. N. L. Gage (Chicago: Rand McNally, 1963), 94–141.

[2] Edgar Dale and Gerhard Eichholz, *Children's Knowledge of Words* (Columbus: Bureau of Educational Research and Service, Ohio State University, 1960).

ninety-seven per cent (for *immigration*) and ninety-six per cent (for *tourist*) in the 8th-grade list.

To an adult, the differentiation between the concepts designated by *tourist* and *immigrant* looks almost trivially simple. Aside from the sheer memory problem in learning and differentiating the words themselves, what are the sources of confusion for the child? In specific cases, a tourist and an immigrant might have many common characteristics: both might be from a foreign country, or at least from some distance away from the local community; both might be of obviously non-native culture because of dress, complexion, speech, and behavior; both might be doing what would appear to be "sight-seeing," though possibly for different purposes. The differences between a tourist and an immigrant might not be very apparent, being primarily differences of motivation. Indeed, a tourist might become an immigrant overnight, just by deciding to be one.

As we have seen, there is a sense in which the concept-attainment experimental literature is relevant to the child's problem in learning the meanings of the words *tourist* and *immigrant*. If the child is presented with various instances of people who are either tourists or immigrants, properly labeled as such, but with no further explanation, it will be the child's task to figure out what attributes or characteristics are relevant to the differentiation of these concepts. This might occur either in school or outside of school. Most likely the instances of tourists and immigrants will be relatively sporadic over time, and the instances may not vary in such a way as to show what attributes are truly relevant. For example, all the tourists may be obviously American whereas all the immigrants may be obviously Mexican, let us say. The tourists may all be well-dressed, the immigrants poorly dressed, and so on. If the natural environment is like a grand concept-formation experiment, it may take the child a long time to attain the concepts *tourist* and *immigrant;* indeed, the environment may

not be as informative as the usual experimenter, since the child may not always be informed, or reliably informed, as to the correctness of his guesses. No wonder a child might form the concept that a tourist is any well-dressed person who drives a station-wagon with an out-of-state license plate!

The purpose of teaching is to short-cut this capricious process of concept attainment within the natural environment. Through the use of language, there should be relatively little difficulty in explaining to a child that an immigrant is one who moves from one country or region to another in order to change his permanent residence, while a tourist is one who travels around for pleasure without changing his permanent residence. One can use simple explanations like: "He's going to stay here, have his home here. . ." or "He's just traveling around for the fun of it while he's on vacation, and someday he'll get back home." There should be no difficulty, at any rate, if the child has already mastered certain prerequisite concepts. Among these prerequisite concepts would be: the concept of home or permanent residence and all that it implies; the concept of the division of world territory into different countries and those in turn into regions; and the concept of traveling for pleasure or curiosity. It is very likely that the child who is having trouble understanding the concept of tourist vs. the concept of immigrant has not got clearly in mind these prerequisite notions that constitute, in fact, the criterial attributes upon which the distinction hangs.

Alternatively, a child might be having trouble because he has not dispensed with irrelevant aspect of these concepts: he might think that a tourist has to be always an American, whereas an immigrant must be a foreigner, because he has seen *American* tourists and *foreign* immigrants, no *American* immigrants nor *foreign* tourists. The ingenious teacher will think of the possible misunderstandings that could arise through the influence of irrelevant attributes of tourists and immigrants.

Time

K. C. Friedman[3] pointed out that elementary school children have much trouble with various time concepts. A child sees no incongruity, for example, in saying, "My older brother was born a long time ago." According to Friedman, it was not until Grade VI that all children in his school could state the date or list the months in perfect order. They had difficulty, he reports, in forming a concept of the "time line" and then in recognizing the placement of various historical events on such a time line. It is easy to see why the child would have these difficulties; even as adults it is difficult for us to appreciate the significance of the fantastically long periods implied by geological time. It should be noted that our concept of a time line is essentially a *spatial* concept whereby we translate temporal succession in terms of spatial order and distances. For a child, times does not flow in a straight line nor in any other particular direction, unless it is around the clock, in a circular or spiral dimension! How can the child form a concept of time and its units? Is time a class of experiences? Does it have criterial attributes? The paradigms of concept-formation experiments do not seem to apply here readily. But let us examine the situation more closely. How can the child have experiences of time and generate the concept of a time line? Certainly there can be experiences of intervals of time—watching a second hand of a clock move through the second-markings, or experiencing the succession of night and day, noticing the change of seasons or waiting for the end of the school year. Moving from one time period to another could be likened to moving from one square of a sidewalk to the next. It should be an easy transition to thinking of the time line as a sidewalk of infinite extent in both directions—toward the past and toward the future. Marking off the days on the calendar and naming the days and months should help to reinforce this cognitive structure. Extrapolation of the time line is like generalizing these time experiences to all possible such experiences.

One of the difficulties comes, presumably, from the fact that the far reaches of the past and the future cannot be immediately experienced, and one immediately has trouble if one attempts to show a time line that includes historical events in the distant past along with a representation of the relationship between today, yesterday, and the day before yesterday. (Incidentally, it is hard to believe Pistor's[4] claim that young children cannot tell the difference between the present and the past, in view of the fact that they can correctly use the present tenses of verbs in simple situations.) Time lines of different scales must be used, and the concept of scale will itself be hard for children to understand unless it is carefully explained—perhaps by showing maps of the immediate environment in different scales. Only after such ideas have been mastered will it be possible for the child to have any appreciation of such concepts as *year, century, 1492* (as a date), *B.C., generation. Generation* and *eon*, by the way, would have to be introduced as somewhat flexible, arbitrary units of time, as contrasted with fixed, measureable units such as *year* and *century*.

Quantitative Expressions like "many," "few," "average"

Ernest Horn[5] pointed out that certain quantitative concepts like *many, few,* and *average* are often so difficult that children do not give reasonable interpretations of them. It is very likely that the source of the difficulty is that children tend not to be able to think in relative terms. Children

---

[3] Kopple C. Friedman, "Time Concepts of Elementary-school Children," *Elem. Sch. J.*, XLIV (1944), 337–342.

[4] Frederick Pistor, "Measuring the Time Concepts of Children," *J. Educ. Res.*, XXX (1939), 293–300.

[5] Ernest Horn, *Methods of Instruction in Social Studies* (New York: Scribner, 1937).

(and perhaps their teachers) would like to be able to assign definite ranges of numbers for such words as *many, few, average, a sizable amount,* etc., when actually they are all relative terms. There has even been a psychological experiment to demonstrate this: Helson, Dworkin, and Michels[6] showed that adult subjects will consistently give different meanings to a word like "few" when it is put in different contexts. For example, "few" meant about twelve per cent on the average, in relation to 100 people, whereas it meant four per cent, on the average, in relation to 1,728,583 people.

In teaching a child these relational concepts the problem would be to exhibit or describe numerous instances in which the absolute base varies but in which the actual numbers of quantities meant would at the same time vary sufficiently to give the impression that these words do not indicate anything like exact amounts. It should be pointed out that 100 things might be "many" in some situations and "few" in others. The use of "average" in such a context as "There was an average number of people in church today" can be taught by drawing attention to its relation to the probable extremes of the numbers of people that might be in church, generalizing the concept to other situations like "I caught an average number of fish today." This might lead to the introduction of the average as a statistic or number that gives information about the "central tendency" of some frequency distribution. It may help to use an unfamiliar or unusual context to bring out this concept in sharp relief. For example, I like to illustrate the utility of the statistical mean or arithmetic average by asking students to imagine that the first space men to reach Mars discover human-like creatures there whose average height is —and this is where the mean becomes really informative—3 inches!

The basic concept of the mean arises in the context of experiences in which there is a plurality of objects measured in some common way. As a first approximation, as far as a child is concerned, the average is a number that is roughly halfway between the highest and lowest measurements encountered, and in some way "typical" of these measurements. Only at some later stage does the child need to learn that the mean is a number that can be computed by a formula and that it has certain properties.

Longitude

It is difficult to understand why E. B. Wesley[7] says that concepts related to the sphericity of the earth, like latitude and longitude, are not easily taught to the average child before Grades VI and VII. Wesley was writing before the advent of the space age when every child knows about space capsules traveling around the globe. Though it may still be difficult to get a child to see how the flatness of his immediate environment is only apparent and that the immediate environment corresponds to just a small area on the globe, it can certainly be done, well before Grade VI, through suitable demonstrational techniques. Having established the sphericity of the earth, one should be able to teach latitude and longitude as concepts involved in specifying locations on the globe. Their introduction should properly be preceded by simpler cases in which one uses a system of coordinates to specify location—e.g., equally spaced and numbered horizontal and vertical lines drawn on a blackboard with a game to locate letters placed at intersection of lines, a map of one's town or city in which marginal coordinates are given to help locate given streets or places of interest, and finally a Mercator projection map of the world with coordinates of latitude and

[6]Harry Helson, Robert S. Dworkin and Walter C. Michels, "Quantitative Denotations of Common Terms as a Function of Background," *Amer. J. Psychol.,* LXIX (1956), 194–208.

[7]E. B. Wesley and Mary A. Adams, *Teaching Social Studies in Elementary Schools* (Rev. ed.: Boston: D. C. Heath, 1952), p. 307.

longitude. Children exposed to the "new math" with its number lines and coordinates should have no trouble with this. Then let us show children by easy stages how a Mercator projection corresponds to the surface of the Earth (certainly an actual globe marked off with latitude and longitude should be used), then how it is necessary to select a particular line (that passes through the Greenwich Observatory) as the vertical coordinate from which to measure, and how the circumference of the earth is marked off in degrees—180° West and 180° East from the Greenwich meridian.

The object is to build for the child a vivid experience of the framework or cognitive structure within which the concept of longitude is defined. The further complications introduced by the use of other kinds of world projections or by the use of regional or even local maps could then be explored. Easily-obtained U.S. Geological Survey maps of one's locality would concretize the meanings of further concepts, e.g., the division of degrees into minutes and seconds, and the fact that a degree of longitude will gradually shrink in length as one moves northward from the equator.

Tort

The concept of *tort* is very likely to be unfamiliar or at least vague to the average reader. Even a dictionary definition[8] may not help much in deciding whether arson, breach of contract, malicious prosecution, or libel are positive instances of torts. The case method used in many law schools, whereby students examine many positive and negative instances of torts in order to learn what they are, is somewhat analogous to a concept formation experiment of the purely inductive variety.

[8]The *American College Dictionary* defines *tort* as "a civil wrong (other than a breach of contract or trust) such as the law requires compensation for in damages; typically, a willful or negligent injury to a plaintiff's person, property, or reputation."

A study[9] of the various laws and decisions relating to torts yields the following approximate and tentative characterization of the concept as having both conjunctive and disjunctive aspects:

$$\text{TORT} = (A + B + C + D + E + F + G + H)$$
$$(I + J) (K) (-L) (-M) (-N) (-O)$$

where

> A = battery
> B = false imprisonment
> C = malicious prosecution
> D = trespass to land
> E = interference to chattels
> F = interference with advantageous relations
> G = misrepresentation
> H = defamation
> I = malicious intent
> J = negligence
> K = causal nexus
> L = consent
> M = privilege
> N = reasonable risk by plaintiff
> O = breach of contract

Within a parenthesis, terms joined by the sign + are mutually disjunctive attributes; a minus sign (−) within a parenthesis signifies "absence of"; the full content of each parenthesis is conjunctive with the content of every other parenthesis. Thus, we can read the formula as follows: "A tort is a battery, a false imprisonment, a malicious prosecution, a trespass to land, . . . , or a defamatory act which is done either with malicious intent or negligently which exhibits a causal nexus with the injury claimed by the plaintiff, *and* which is done without the plaintiff's consent, *or* without privilege on the part of the defendant, *or* without a reasonable risk by the plaintiff, *or* which is not a breach of contract."

Thus, *tort* turns out to be a concept very much on the same order as *tourist*—a collocation of criterial attributes with both

[9]For helping me in my treatment of the concepts of *tort* and *mass* I am indebted to my student, Mr. Edward A. Dubois.

conjunctive and disjunctive features. Deciding whether an act is a tort requires that one check each feature of a situation against what can be put in the form of a formula (as done above). Presumably, a person presented with a properly organized series of positive and negative instances of torts could induce the concept, provided he also understood such prerequisite concepts as *battery, misrepresentation,* etc.

Mass versus Weight

One of the more difficult concepts to teach in elementary physics is that of *mass.* What kind of concept is it and how can one learn it and experience it? How can it be distinguished from the concept of weight? Actually, if we ignore certain subtle questions about mass, such as that of whether inertial and gravitational mass are demonstrably identical, the concept of mass is not as difficult as it might seem; the real difficulty is to teach the sense in which it is different from weight. In fact, weight is perhaps the more difficult concept, because the weight of an object can vary to the point that it can become "weightless."

The concept of mass, one would think, ought to develop for the learner (be he a child or an adult) in much the same way that concepts of other properties of the physical world develop—analogously, that is, to concepts of color, number, and volume. For mass is a property of objects that differentiates them in our experience: there are objects with great mass (like the earth, or a large boulder) and there are objects with small mass (like a feather or a pin or the air in a small bottle), and our experiences of objects with respect to mass can differ enormously, particularly in our proprioceptive senses. Further, mass is a property of objects that is *conserved* regardless of whether the object is in motion or at rest; conservation of mass is learned through experience just as conservation of other properties is learned. Even the physical

definition of mass as that property of things which accounts for the relative amount of force which has to be applied to produce a certain amount of acceleration is perceived in common-sense terms as the property of objects that determines the amount of force or effort that one would have to exert to move or lift it. The well-known "size-weight" illusion (in which, for example, we exert an undue amount of effort to lift or push some large but relatively light object) illustrates the fact that our perceptions of an object typically include some impression of its mass. The physical operation of measuring mass by determining the ratio of force to acceleration is an operational extension of the kind of behavior we exhibit when we see how much force it will take to move a heavy trunk.

The real trouble comes in the fact that we are too prone to equate mass with weight, mainly because equal masses also have equal weights when compared by means of a balance, or when measured with a spring balance at the same point on the earth's surface (at least, at the same distance from the earth's center). If we were more easily able to experience the fact that the weight of an object of given mass changes as acceleration due to gravity changes—for example by going to the moon and observing the "weight" of objects there, or by experiencing "weightlessness" in an orbital flight around the earth, weight and mass might be just as easy to distinguish as size and mass. Since such experiences would be rather hard to come by, to put it mildly, we have to be content with the imaginal representation of weight as a *variable* property of objects that really depends upon a relation between the gravitational force exerted on an object and its mass (actually, the product of these two). A child might be made to understand how objects of different masses could have equal "weight"—a relatively large object on the moon and a relatively small one on the earth, for example, as measured by a spring balance which is sensitive to the pull of gravity; or how an object of constant mass would have different weights at different distances from the earth (the pull of gravity thus varying). We would have to conclude that weight, properly speaking, is a relational concept that can only be understood when the total framework in which weight can be defined is described. Mass, on the other hand, is a concept that corresponds much more directly to immediate perceptions of reality.

It will be noted that the teaching of mass and weight concepts involves several prerequisite concepts—e.g., the pull of gravity, the relation between the mass of an object like the earth or the moon and the gravitational force it exerts, and the concept of acceleration. The pull exerted by a magnet could be used for illustrating certain aspects of the concept of gravitational force; a large magnet and a small magnet could represent the respective gravitational pulls of earth and moon; the concept of acceleration can be introduced verbally as "how fast something gets started" and later as an accelerating curve of velocity.

Without really meaning to do so, this discussion of mass and weight has turned out to be a consideration of how such concepts might be taught at relatively early stages—say, somewhere in the elementary school. Nevertheless, some of the same teaching techniques might not be amiss even at high school or college levels. At these levels the chief problem is to give meaning to mathematical formulas such as

$$mass = \frac{force}{acceleration}$$

The implication of this formula, that mass is constant for a given object, can be illustrated by showing with actual physical materials that as force is increased, acceleration is increased proportionately. The effect of increasing mass could be shown by demonstrating that acceleration (roughly indicated by distance traveled against friction) under a constant force diminishes. To a large extent, such experiments can be considered as yielding in precise mathe-

matical terms the relationships that are perceived in every-day experience and that lead to our intuitive understanding of such a concept as mass.

Above all, it should be noted that *mass* is a relational concept, a constant property of objects that reveals itself through the relation between the forces applied to the object and the resultant acceleration. Negative instances can only be properties of objects like weight, size, etc., that are not revealed in this way.

SUMMARY

The basic concern of this paper has been with the teaching of concepts and the relevance of psychological and psycholinguistic theory and experimentation in guiding such teaching.

It has been necessary, first, to point out that concepts are essentially nonlinguistic (or perhaps better, *a*linguistic) because they are classes of experience which the individual comes to recognize as such, whether or not he is prompted or directed by symbolic language phenomena. Because the experiences of individuals tend to be in many respects similar, their concepts are also similar, and through various processes of learning and socialization these concepts come to be associated with words. The "meanings" of words are the socially-standardized concepts with which they are associated. One of the problems in teaching concepts is that of teaching the associations between words and concepts, and this is analogous to a paired associate learning task.

At the same time, new concepts can be taught. One procedure can be called inductive: it consists of presenting an individual with an appropriate series of positive and negative instances of a concept, labeled as such, and allowing him to infer the nature of the concept by noticing invariant features or attributes. This is the procedure followed in the usual concept formation experiment: although our present knowledge allows us to specify several *necessary* conditions for the formation of a concept, we still do not know what conditions are *sufficient*.

Another procedure for concept teaching may be called deductive, and it tends to be the favored procedure in school learning (and, in fact, in all expository prose). It is the technique of presenting concepts by verbal definition or description. This technique has received relatively little attention in psychological experimentation, but it seems to parallel inductive concept attainment in the sense that verbal descriptions are specifications of criterial attributes that can enable the individual to shortcut the process of hypothesis, discovery, and testing that typically occurs in the inductive

concept-attainment procedure. Nevertheless, it is not known how relevant our knowledge of critical factors in inductive concept formation is for the guidance of deductive teaching procedures.

It is pointed out, however, that the efficient learning of concepts in school probably involves both inductive and deductive procedures. An analysis of typical concepts of the sort taught in school shows that they do indeed follow the models studied in psychological experimentation, but that they are more likely to involve complex relationships among prerequisite concepts. The difficulties that learners have in attaining a concept are likely to be due to their inadequate mastery of prerequisite concepts and to errors made by the teacher in presenting in proper sequence the information intrinsic to the definition of the concept.

Learning by Discovery: An Interpretation of Recent Research

BERT Y. KER

MERLIN C. WITTROCK

The teaching method frequently labeled the discovery method is not new but is very much in the forefront of attention in education today. This observation is supported

Reprinted with the permission of the senior author and the publisher from the article of the same title, *Journal of Teacher Education*, 1962, 13, 461–468.

[1]M. Beberman, *An emergency program of secondary school mathematics* (Cambridge, Massachusetts: Harvard University Press, 1958).
    R. B. Davis, "Madison Project of Syracuse University," *Mathematics Teacher* 53: 571–575;

by the substantial curriculum efforts in mathematics and science and by the programmatic research endeavors on cognition,[1] not to mention the numerous inde-

November 1960.
    J. R. Suchman, "Inquiry Training: Building Skills for Autonomous Discovery," *Merrill-Palmer Quarterly of Behavior and Development* 7: 147–169; 1961.
    G. Finlay, "Secondary School Physics: The Physical Science Study Committee," *American Journal of Physics* 28: 286–293; March 1960.

pendent efforts by researchers over the country.[2] In the opinion of the authors of this review, present interest in learning by discovery more than rivals that which centers around the new technology of programmed instruction.

The literature on learning by discovery dates back many years but is limited in this present review to the research studies published or reported since 1955. There is a break of approximately six years prior to 1955 during which very little research activity is evident, and afterwards a rash of publications appear which bear directly on the topic. Also, many studies of problem solving, thinking, and other complex processes related to discovery were ruled out because they were not conducted in the context of learning.

As is the case with defining programmed instruction, it is difficult to find a clear definition of discovery. In the research literature, the term "discovery" frequently describes a learner's goal-directed behavior when he is forced to complete a learning task without help from the teacher. Hereafter, in this article discovery is described in the same way. If the learner completes the task with little or no help, he is said to have learned by discovery. The most significant teaching variable is the amount of guidance or direction provided by the teacher during the discovery process. In practice, considerable help from the teacher may be provided and still the learner may be said to have learned by discovery, but in such instances the process is usually qualified and called guided discovery. As the amount of help from the teacher increases, it is said that opportunities for discovery decrease and the learner may rely more on rote processes.

Actually, the terms "discovery" and "rote" are probably not polar terms at all. It may be more correct to confine the one

term, discovery, to that phase in learning which precedes the learner's making the response desired by the teacher for the first time (the problem-solving stage) and the other, rote learning, to the phase which follows when the learner is memorizing or acquiring increasing skill.

It should be noted that the above definition is stated in operational terms, i.e., it states how the teacher operates with the learner or the conditions under which the learner operates during discovery. The definition does *not* infer anything about the learner's sensations or perceptions during or at the point of discovery.[3] When the learner first makes the required response with little or no help from the teacher he may or may not have experienced "insight," and he may or may not understand. Also, he may have been acquiring some other skills quite incidentally in the discovery process. Similarly, even after first making the required response, when the learner is memorizing it or practicing it, he may still ascertain something new (to him) about that which he is practicing.

COMPARISON OF LEARNING TASKS

It is becoming increasingly more evident that the somewhat inconsistent findings by researchers in recent years may actually reflect different learning outcomes resulting from two or three quite different processes of learning by discovery. We can no longer

---

[2] *Harvard Center for Cognitive Studies: Annual Report.* (Cambridge, Massachusetts: Harvard University, 1961).

[3] This is not to say that the term "discovery" refers to something other than covert behavior. The authors prefer to think that discovery is a type of covert behavior which is most likely to *occur* prior to the learner's first acceptable response, but which may actually occur at any time during the learning process. Although the term defies rigorous definition, even in operational terms, it should not be used to characterize stimuli presented to the learner, as in the "discovery method." Also, "discovery phase" should not be construed to refer to an interval of time, per se.

speak of the discovery method in general terms and make all-encompassing claims about it any more than we can speak of the auto-instructional method now as if it were one technique.

In this article, an attempt is made to look at the learner's task—what he was required to discover and under what circumstances—in each of the recent research studies and to infer what the learner might have learned in addition to the measured outcome. From this perspective it can be shown that the apparently different findings of some of the more recent studies are actually highly consistent and that it is possible to make some new interpretations of the research findings.

Formal Phases in the Learning Process

In the diagram in Figure 10-1, the line represents the learning process from start to finish. For convenience, the letter symbols are used to designate formal steps in the sequence. Formal steps in learning are determined by the teacher. Between A and B there is what might be called the discovery phase. Point B marks the point at which the learner first makes the required response, with or without help from the teacher.

Starting at B in the learning process, the learner is memorizing or acquiring increasing skill in using whatever was ascertained at B. He could be learning to transfer to new situations, to make discriminations, or to increase the rate of his responses.

Point C designates the end of formal practice, after which the teacher no longer has direct control over the learning process. Formal testing may begin at C. If the first test is at C, it would be called a test of immediate recall or a learning test. If

another test is given after some designated time interval, the test would occur at D in the learning process.

Not all learning involves the entire sequence A through C. In typing, for instance, the student typically is started at B, as if there is very little to discover in learning to typewrite. The teaching of typewriting assumes that the student already has acquired certain fundamental skills and can begin by practicing the use of these skills in a new context. In teaching mathematics, however, it is often assumed that the student may have to work for some time on a problem before he learns the principle involved, or, we might say, "discovers" the solution. In this case the learning process may be said to start at A.

In the previous discussion it may have been suggested that the learner does not practice during the discovery phase. Actually, it is not a matter of practice or no practice, but rather what is practiced and reinforced, how and to what extent. During the problem-solving or trial-and-error process which characterizes discovery learning, the learner may try to apply a principle to examples in order to verify his solution. This may constitute "practice" of the sort that may be restricted formally to the post-discovery phase. Even more likely, during discovery the learner may be practicing other behaviors called "employing search models," "seeking relationships," and "shifting approaches."

Exactly what is practiced and how the reinforcement is schedules during discovery or afterwards cannot be indicated in the diagram, but the amount of practice can be, to some extent. Extensive practice will be indicated hereafter by a solid line, and when comparisons are made between experimental groups, less extensive practice will be indicated by a dotted line.

FIGURE 10-1. *Formal phases in the learning process*

Discovery:	A_____B		C	(Post-experimental practice)	D	(Test for B)
Guided D:	A _ _ _ _ _ _ _ B		C		D	(Test for B)
Directed:		B_____C			D	(Test for B)

FIGURE 10-2. *Kersh's experiment (1958)*

Typically, in experiments on discovery, learning tasks are used which may either be started at A or at B. In other words, the learner may be required to discover the answer for himself or he may be told the answer and then be given practice in using it. Requiring the student to begin at A is described as learning by discovery, and starting at B is described as directed learning or learning by reception. As implied earlier, typically there is an intermediate type of learning described as guided discovery which starts the learner at A but provides some guidance from the teacher during the discovery phase.

Kersh's Experiment

Consider now some of the more recent studies in terms of the diagram. Kersh[4] employed an arithmetic task in an experiment which compared groups of college students taught by the three methods described above. The procedure may be diagrammed as in Figure 10-2.

This diagram shows that one group, the Discovery Group, was required to discover the arithmetic rules for itself without help from the experimenter. This extensive discovery experience is indicated by the solid line from A to B. No formal practice was required after the rules were discovered at B. Instead, the formal learning period was terminated at C with a test of immediate recall. However, subjects in the discovery group tended to continue practicing the

[4] B. Y. Kersh, "The Adequacy of 'Meaning' As an Explanation for the Superiority of Learning by Independent Discovery," *Journal of Educational Psychology* 49: 282–292; October 1958.

rules or to continue their efforts to discover the rules after the formal learning period had terminated.

The Guided Discovery Group was also required to discover the rules but was given some help in the form of clues in its efforts to discover them. The fact that help was given during the discovery process is indicated by the dotted line from A to B in the diagram. In every other respect, this group was treated as the Discovery Group was, but there was no evidence of post-experimental practice with the Guided Discovery Group.

The third group, the Directed Group, was told the rules outright and given some examples for practice. Learning started at B and terminated at C.

All three groups were retested approximately one month later (D) for their ability to remember the rules and apply them in the solution of appropriate examples. In other words, they were tested on whatever was acquired at B.

From the diagram, it would be predicted that at the end of the learning period (C) the Directed Group would be superior to the other two groups in ability to apply the rules to solve specific addition problems because of the practice in this activity during learning. This is what Kersh found. In fact, some of the individuals in the Discovery Group failed completely to discover the rules during the time allowed.

However, after one month, the tables were turned. On the test given at D, the Discovery Group was superior to both of the other groups. Presumably, the superior performance of the Discovery Group reflected the post-experimental practice. Individuals in the Discovery Group probably were motivated to continue their

Discovery: A ——————— B — — — — — C   D   (Test for B and A-B Transfer)

Guided D: A — — — — — B ——————— C   D   (Test for B and A-B Transfer)

Directed: B — — — — — C   D   (Test for B and A-B Transfer)

FIGURE 10-3.   *Kittell's experiment (1957)*

efforts to learn the rules and to practice the rules after the formal learning period. In another experiment, Kersh[5] substantiated this interpretation.

Kittell's Experiment

By way of contrast, Kittell[6] reported an experiment which employed a word task with sixth-grade subjects. The various treatments are shown in the diagram in Figure 10-3. The Discovery Group (Kittell's Minimum Direction Group) was given examples of the principles involved in the word task with directions indicating only that there was a principle involved. If the principle was discovered early enough, some practice in applying it was possible. The Guided Discovery Group (Intermediate Direction) was given the same directions and a statement of the general rule so that actually it had only a limited discovery experience, if any. Finally, the Directed Group (Maximum Direction) was told not only the principle but also the answer to each of the examples. The Directed Group had a relatively restricted practice opportunity, consequently.

The diagram of Kittell's experiment indicates that the Discovery Group actually had little opportunity to practice the application of the general principles because the task proved to be very difficult for the sixth-grade youngsters. They discovered, on the average, less than three principles out of fifteen in addition to those measured on a pre-test. The dotted line from B to C indicates this lack of practice. In the case of the Guided Discovery Group the dotted line from A to B indicates little practice in discovery of the principles, and the solid line from B to C suggests extensive formal practice in applying them. The Directed Group had no discovery experience and limited formal practice in applying the general principles involved.

The post-test measured the learners' ability to apply the principles and to discover new principles from new examples. In effect they were tested on what was acquired at B and on their ability to transfer discovery skills learned during discovery (A-B) or elsewhere.

In view of the formal practice provided the Guided Discovery Group, it may be expected that this group would be superior to the other groups in applying the principles. Kittell's findings do indicate this. From the solid line between A and B, it may be predicted that the Discovery Group would be superior to the other groups in discovering new principles from new examples. Instead, Kittell's findings indicate that the Guided Discovery Group was also superior in this respect. However, when one recalls that the Discovery Group learned less than three of the fifteen principles, it is not difficult to understand Kittell's findings. In effect, their discovery behavior may have been extinguished rather than reinforced.

[5] B. Y. Kersh, "The Motivating Effect of Learning by Discovery," *Journal of Educational Psychology* 53: 65–71; 1962.

[6] J. E. Kittell, "An Experimental Study of the Effect of External Direction During Learning on Transfer and Retention of Principles," *Journal of Educational Psychology* 48: 391–405; November 1957.

The Gagné and Brown Experiment

The last experiment to be discussed is diagrammed in Figure 10-4. Using an arithmetic task similar to that used in the Kersh

Discovery: A —————————— B   C (Test for A-B Transfer)

Guided D: A _ _ _ _ _ _ _ B   C (Test for A-B Transfer)

Directed: B —————————— C (Test for A-B Transfer)

FIGURE 10-4. *Gagné and Brown's experiment (1961)*

experiment, Gagné and Brown[7] constructed three self-instructional programs designed to teach in the three modes discussed previously. Each group was instructed in the basic mathematical concepts and notations involved. The Discovery Group was then required to discover the rules for several different problem series. The Discovery Group had no formal practice in the application of the rules. In the Guided Discovery Group, the learner was carried rather systematically through a series of steps leading to his own formulation of the general rule. Again, no formal practice on specific examples of the rules was provided. The Directed Group (Rule and Example) was told the rules and then was given formal practice in the application of each rule to a series of examples.

The test in the Gagné and Brown experiment came almost immediately after the end of the formal learning period. The test measured only the learner's ability to discover new rules from different problem series. As such, it was a transfer test of discovery skill, *not* a test of recall or application of rules. The average time and the number of hints required to discover the new rules were used to compare the teaching treatments.

From the diagram of the Gagné and Brown experiment, it may be predicted that the Discovery Group would be superior on the transfer test, followed, in turn, by the Guided Discovery Group and the Directed Group. The findings indicate that the Guided Discovery Group was slightly superior to the Discovery Group but both dis-

covery groups were definitely superior to the Directed Group.

Although the Gagné and Brown experiment does not provide data on retention of rules learned, it may be predicted that on a retention test the Directed Group would perform most effectively, since this group had had the most practice in the application of the rules.

A comparison of the diagrams of the three experiments will reveal one finding which is not easily explained in terms of the relative amount of practice. In Kersh's experiment the Discovery Group engaged in post-experimental practice, and this finding was not reported by either of the other two researchers. Gagné and Brown did not allow much time for such practice, but there were approximately twenty-four hours during which their subjects could have engaged in post-experimental practice. Presumably the findings of both Gagné and Brown and Kittell would have been influenced by the extra practice, had it occurred.

One explanation for the unique finding in Kersh's study becomes evident when one examines the learning process in each case and infers what was learned in addition to the particular rules or principles involved.

In the Kersh experiment, reinforcement was provided intermittently for discovering, per se. The experimenter gave support and encouragement regardless of the learner's success or failure. In the Kittell experiment, reinforcement was provided regularly for providing answers to specific examples, and Gagné and Brown similarly reinforced only the correct response. The fact that Kersh's treatment fostered a kind of searching behavior explains the "motivating effects" of the discovery experience. The findings of the three experiments may actually be

[7]R. M. Gagné and L. T. Brown, "Some Factors in the Programming of Conceptual Learning," *Journal of Experimental Psychology* 62: 313–321; 1961.

reflecting different learning outcomes resulting from two quite different processes of learning by discovery.

In general these studies, along with the others cited below, suggest that learning by discovery is indeed many faceted. Answers to problems, general rules for solving problems, and even the motivation to continue learning may be acquired separately or in combination. Moreover, it is often possible to predict, from a careful analysis of the practice and reinforcement schedules involved in discovery learning, which facets will be acquired. Also, it is probable that more facets may be acquired simultaneously under conditions of discovery (guided or not) than when learning is highly directed.

Other Experiments

The three experiments discussed above have been analyzed in detail because they are considered typical of the more recent experiments. It is felt that a detailed report and analysis of the other studies recently reported would not alter or contribute to the present interpretation. Therefore, the other recently published experiments are briefly summarized below. The reader is invited to skip ahead to the next section if the brief reviews are of little interest at this time.

Craig[8] tested the equivalents to the Discovery and Guided Discovery Groups. As would be predicted from what was practiced and reinforced, Craig found that the Guided Discovery Group was superior on a retention test. On a transfer test, no significant difference was found between the groups.

Haslerud and Meyers[9] found that when codes are discovered solely from concrete instances, as contrasted with a procedure of giving specific directions on decoding, the directed procedure is better on original learning, but there is no significant difference on a later transfer test. Since only one group of subjects was employed in their experimental design, each learner had equal practice in discovering codes and in applying them. The lack of difference on the transfer test is consistent with the practice and reinforcement schedules. Haslerud and Meyers, however, interpret their results to indicate strong support for the notion that derived principles transfer more readily than do principles which are given.

Forgus and Schwartz[10] compared three groups in the learning of a code based on a principle. Learning the principle made the memorization of the code much simpler. Their results on a retention and transfer test indicated that learning the principle by either the "discovery" or "guided discovery" techniques was superior to rote learning.

Soon to be published by Wittrock is a study which also employed a coding task.[11] Consistent with Kittell's findings, Wittrock reports that on the test of initial learning, the Directed and Guided Discovery (Intermediate Direction) Groups were superior to the discovery groups. On the test of retention and transfer, the Guided Discovery Group proved superior to the other groups.

COMPARISON OF
TEACHING TECHNIQUES

What do these findings mean to the teacher? It is evident that one can learn

---

[8] R. C. Craig, "Directed Versus Independent Discovery of Established Relations," *Journal of Educational Psychology* 47: 223–234; April 1956.

[9] G. M. Haslerud and Shirley Meyers, "The Transfer Value of Given and Individually Derived Principles," *Journal of Educational Psychology* 49: 293–298; 1958.

[10] R. H. Forgus and R. J. Schwartz, "Efficient Retention and Transfer as Affected by Learning Method," *Journal of Psychology* 43: 135–139; 1957.

[11] M. C. Wittrock, *Mediation Theory Applied to Discovery Learning: Cueing and Prompting Mediated Responses.* (Mimeographed report, 1962)

different things by the process labeled "discovery." Therefore, to talk intelligently about discovery methods of teaching or learning, one must state his desired outcome or teaching objective.

The comments which follow bear only upon those tasks which can be either discovered or memorized. Also, it is presumed that whatever the objective, it is desirable to achieve the goal as rapidly as possible, all other things being equal.

Even within the context of such tasks the teacher's goal may be more or less specific. The teacher may be satisfied to have the learners memorize rules and learn to apply them for purposes of a particular project or activity. At the other extreme, a teacher may use a particular exercise as a means of teaching the children techniques for discovering new rules from different examples or as a means of stimulating their interest in a particular area of study.

For the goal of teaching specific aspects of subject matter—aspects which could be either memorized or discovered—it is clear that the process which was described as "directed learning" is the most efficient. Generally speaking, a teacher should not employ highly directed techniques if she wishes to develop long-term retention and transfer effects. However, the directed procedure does not necessarily produce learning outcomes which are short-lived. Retention and transfer effects primarily reflect the practice and reinforcement schedules.

With organized bodies of information, very often the teacher is most interested in teaching the organizational framework itself. Usually this framework is in the form of principles, rules, generalizations, and conceptual schemes. If so, the research evidence suggests the intermediate direction or guided discovery techniques. It makes little difference, apparently, whether the rule or principle is discovered or is taught directly, provided the learner is reinforced for effective practice in using the rule or principle. Organizational schemes, however, often need to be understood through the establishment of relationships between new and previous learning. When the learner lacks the necessary background of information and is not motivated, generally it is more effective to establish such relationships by using techniques of guided discovery rather than more or less directed techniques. The important thing is that the new learnings are established in relationship to previous learning. Provided the learner has the related knowledge and willingness to assimilate the material, the directed technique may be equally effective and more efficient than guided discovery.

Very often the teacher has as his objective techniques of discovery, per se. The actual subject matter involved may be of secondary importance. The purpose of the learning experience is to exercise and to reinforce the learner in what may be called "searching behavior"—strategies of problem solving, divergent as opposed to convergent thinking, flexibility in thinking—in essence, the characteristics of what is often labeled "the creative person." With such objectives, discovery or guided discovery techniques are most appropriate. However, if the task is so difficult that the learner does not succeed in discovering the relationships which he is supposed to discover, there will be little opportunity for reinforcement of that very process which is being taught. It is most important that the learner have success experiences when learning by discovery.

It has become increasingly apparent that the learners' attitudes towards a subject matter area may be as important as what he learns in the cognitive sense. If a student is highly interested in a subject, he is likely to continue to learn. Under appropriate conditions of practice and reinforcement, the discovery technique will foster favorable attitudes and interests. It is interesting and challenging for students to discover, particularly if their efforts are successful, or at least occasionally so. The opposite effect may result when their efforts never or almost never meet with success. Also, there is reason to believe that an intermittent or irregular pattern of success may be more effective than a regular pattern in maintaining interest.

SUMMARY

Consistent throughout the recent research, as interpreted above, is evidence that the discovery method is effective for what it requires the learner to do and for what is reinforced during learning. The learner may acquire more effective ways of problem solving through the discovery process than through another process simply because he has an opportunity to practice different techniques and because his more

effective techniques are reinforced. Similarly, the learner may become more proficient in applying rules through the directed process of teaching simply because, through formal practice, he has more opportunity for effective practice and reinforcement than otherwise. Guided discovery seems to offer a happy medium between independent discovery and highly directed learning. Some of the efficiency of directed learning is maintained along with the benefits of the discovery process, specifically, motivation and problem-solving skill.

Learning is a complex process. It cannot be explained solely in terms of practice and reinforcement. However, these two concepts are powerful and do enable us to understand much of what a student learns by discovery.

Teaching Strategies

and Thought Processes

HILDA TABA

FREEMAN F. ELZEY

The development of critical thinking has figured as an important objective of education for a long time. Yet, the implementation of this objective in curriculum construction and teaching has been sporadic and ineffective for a variety of reasons.

First, thinking has been treated as a global process. Consequently, the problem of defining thinking is still before us, as is the need to identify its specific elements, especially in terms which are helpful to planning effective teaching strategies. In a

jungle of definitions, thinking has meant anything that goes on in the head, from daydreaming to creating a concept of relativity. Neither has knowledge of the development of thinking been too adequate. While Piaget has spent his lifetime in studying the development of thinking and has produced a quantity of reports, until re-

Reprinted with the permission of the senior author and the publisher from the article of the same title, *Teachers College Record*, 1964, **65**, 524–534.

cently, his work received scant attention in the United States.

Implementation of thinking as an educational objective has also been handicapped by several questionable assumptions. One rather widely accepted assumption is that reflective thinking cannot take place until a sufficient body of factual information is accumulated. Teaching which follows this assumption stresses factual coverage and burdens the memory with unorganized and, therefore, rather perishable information.

An opposite, but equally unproductive, assumption is that thought is an automatic by-product of studying certain subjects and of assimilating the end-products of disciplined thought. Some subjects are assumed to have this power independently of how they are taught or learned. Inherently, memorizing mathematical formulae or the steps in mathematical processes is assumed to be better training than memorizing cake recipes, even though both may be learned in the same manner and call for the same mental process—rote memory.

The combination of these factors has prevented the focusing of attention on the development of teaching strategies designed to stimulate productive and creative thought. The curriculum is seldom organized to focus on active discovery and the use of abstract ideas. Classroom learning experiences are not usually designed to provide a cumulative sequence in the maturation of thought which is at once psychologically sound and logically valid.

All this has contributed to considerable underachievement in the mastery of autonomous and disciplined thought processes. Hence, a rather frequent criticism of current teaching-learning procedures is that they tend to cultivate passive mastery instead of an active discovery of ideas—a tendency to follow "recipes" in solving problems instead of analyzing them and searching for generalizations with which to organize the needed facts and to plan an attack on them (Bartlett, 1958; Buswell and Hersch, 1956).

COGNITION REVISITED

Recently, there has been a renewed interest in the study of cognitive processes in general and thinking in particular. For example, Bartlett (1958) and Rokeach (1960) have been concerned with open and closed thought. Getzels and Jackson's study (1962) of creativity and Gallagher's study (1961) of productive thinking employed the classification of divergent and convergent styles of thought. Sigel (1961) has been interested in the relationship of the styles of organizing and labelling to personality dynamics.

The difficulty with such studies is that the findings about general cognitive styles fail to shed light on the processes by which these styles are acquired. Consequently, the data cannot be translated into guidelines for more effective teaching.

The study of thinking in elementary school children, on which this paper is based, set out to examine the processes of thought in the classroom in terms which are capable of shedding a light on the learning and teaching of certain cognitive skills in the school setting. The fundamental assumption was that thought consists of specific, describable processes which are subject to training, not in some category of powers which are inherent in the individual. Therefore, the study sought to create categories for analyzing thought which described learnable, and therefore also teachable, processes of thought. Specific processes in three cognitive tasks were identified: (1) concept formation, (2) the making of inferences and the induction of generalizations from interpretations of specific data, and (3) the application of generalizations to explain new phenomena and to predict the consequences of certain events and conditions. Critical thinking *per se* was excluded because the curriculum offered meager opportunities for its development.

The study was also conducted under conditions which presumably offered optimal conditions for the training of thought processes. First, the 20 elementary classrooms involved followed a social studies curriculum which centered on a series of basic ideas and was organized for an inductive discovery and development of these ideas. In addition, the curriculum outline also included a planned sequence of learning experiences designed to enhance the development of generalizations and their application to solving problems (1959). [See Contra Costa in References.]

Finally, the design for the study provided for special training of the teachers in the analysis of thought processes and in devising effective teaching strategies for their development. In other words, the study proposed to explore thinking under conditions which included the twin impact of the curriculum and of specified teaching methods.

THE THEORETICAL FRAMEWORK

The study, as well as the curriculum which provided the context for it, and the training of teachers were based on several concepts regarding the nature of thought and its development. First among these was the idea that the maturation of thought follows an evolutionary sequence in which the simpler mental operations form a basis for the creation of the increasingly more complex and abstract mental structures. For example, the learning experiences in the curriculum outlines were arranged so that each preceding step developed skills and cognitive operations which constituted a prerequisite for the next more complex or more abstract mental operations. The cycle of these operations usually began with the analysis of a concrete instance of the general idea on which the unit was centered and ended with the formulation of the idea and its application to new problems and situations (*Contra Costa*, 1959; Taba, 1962).

The exploration of the logical structure of the three cognitive tasks with which the study was concerned revealed another, more specific series of hierarchically ordered sequences of thought processes. For example, the sequence in concept formation begins with enumeration of concrete items, such as listing the differences one would expect to encounter when traveling in Latin America. The next step is that of grouping these items on some conscious basis, such as deciding the basis on which to group together "climate," "weather," and "altitude." The process ends with labeling or classifications, such as deciding to subsume a group of items under "standards of living." These steps constitute a necessary sequence in the sense that each preceding step is a prerequisite for mastering the next one. Underlying the steps are still other cognitive processes, such as differentiation of certain properties of phenomena or events with some degree of precision and an ability to abstract common elements and to determine the basis on which to group and label them.

In a similar manner, the logic of interpreting information and making inferences involves the assimilation of specific points of information, followed by relating several points to each other and making inferences or generalizations which go beyond that which is explicitly given.

The process involved in applying known facts and principles is a bit more complex, involving as it does divergent lines of prediction as well as the hierarchies of leaps in each according to the distance, ranging from the most immediate consequences to the most remote—such as predicting that water will bring grass, in comparison to predicting that the presence of water will cause nomads to cease to be nomads and turn to building cities.

The logic of the sequential steps in this process is not entirely clear. This unclarity is reflected in the rating scheme used. Obviously, the individual must draw upon his memory for the relevant information to form any predictions at all. But he must also relate this information to the requirements of the situation and to construct the parameters of conditions necessary for the predicted consequences to occur. This process entails both the construction of chains of consequences, such as water → growing crops → settling down → building cities, and the perception of the logical relationships between the conditions and consequences. The chief point about the sequences in the development of thinking is that a deficiency in mastering the first step, such as the analysis of concrete instances, leads to incapacity to function on the level of the final step, such as the formulation of generalizations. The chief task of teaching, then, is to determine the order of learning tasks and to pace each step appropriately. This is a crucial point in the formulation of teaching strategies, and one against which current teaching methods commit the greatest errors.

COGNITIVE COMMERCE

The concept that the cognitive operations are an active transaction between the individual and his environment or the material was another idea which influenced the design both of the curriculum and of the study. Children inevitably build mental schemes with which to organize the information they encounter. The quality of the learning experiences determines the degree of productivity of these schemes. All learning experiences teach what Harlow (1949) calls "sets to learn." Depending on the teaching strategies employed, children may learn to look for the structure of the problems set by the learning tasks or for arbitrary procedures. They may acquire a disposition to search for relationships and patterns among ideas and facts, or to look for single "right answers."

When the teaching strategies pay little attention to creating models for thinking, children tend to acquire faulty or unproductive conceptual schemes with which to organize information or to solve problems. For example, procedures such as asking students to name the important cities in the Balkans, without revealing the criterion for

importance or without developing such a criterion with the class, leave students no alternative but to guess what the teacher wants or to recollect what the book said about the matter. Repeated experiences of this sort cause students to adopt irrational, unproductive, and arbitrary models of thinking and a dependence on memory rather than on judgment or inference.

Burton (1952) cites an extreme example of an irrational or mechanical model or schema. He describes an elementary school child who made good grades in arithmetic because she "came up" with the right answers. When asked how she decided when to use which process, she explained her method as follows: "I know what to do by looking at the examples. If there are only two numbers I subtract. If there are lots of numbers, I add. If there are just two numbers and one is smaller than the other, then it is a hard problem. I divide to see if it comes out even, but if it doesn't, I multiply." Evidently this child had built a scheme to fit the manner of presentation of problems in the arithmetic book. By applying the scheme, she was also learning an unproductive model of thinking or a "set" which excluded understanding the structure of the problems.

The idea of thought as an active organization of mental processes underscores the importance of addressing teaching strategies to the development of autonomy and productivity. Effective teaching is seen as consisting primarily of what we get out of the children instead of what we put into them (Sigel, 1961). In other words, helping students to develop a basis for and a method by which to judge the importance of cities may be of greater value than their simply knowing which cities are important.

Of special relevance is the idea that thought matures through a progressive and active organization and reorganization of conceptual structures. The individual fits the information he receives at any moment into the conceptual scheme he already possesses. When the requirements of the situation do not fit his current scheme, however, the individual is forced to alter it or to extend it to accommodate new information. Piaget (1947) calls this fitting process "assimilation" and the process of alteration "accommodation."

This process suggests a teaching strategy which includes a rotation of learning tasks, calling for the assimilation of new information into the existing conceptual scheme with information that requires an extension and reorganization of the scheme (Hunt, 1961). Prolonged assimilation of facts without a corresponding reshaping of the conceptual schemes with which to organize them is bound to retard the maturation of thought. On the other hand, a premature leap into a more complex or a higher level of thought is likely to immobilize mental activity and cause reversion to rote learning or, at any rate, to a lower level of thought. Students need a sufficient amount of assimilation to have the "stuff" to think with. But they need equally a challenge to stretch their modes of thinking and their conceptual schemes. An appropriate transition from one to the other demands a proper match between the current level and that which is required. Determining the proper match is perhaps one of the most difficult tasks in teaching and constitutes in effect, a new concept of readiness and pacing. This task is complicated by the fact that the mastery of abstract communications, such as language and number, often masks the actual level of thinking. Verbalization may deceive the teacher and lead him to assume that thinking is more advanced than it is and, hence, to pushing the child's verbal habits of learning beyond his level of thinking (Peel, 1960).

REASONABLE HOPES

It seems reasonable to assume that, given an adequate analysis of the learning processes involved in certain important cognitive tasks, and teaching strategies which

effectively implemented the principles of sequence, of active mental organization, and of adequate rotation of assimilation and accommodation, it should be possible for all students to achieve higher levels of cognitive operation than seems possible under current teaching. Furthermore, it is not beyond possibility that by far the most important individual differences may be found in the amount of concrete thinking an individual needs before formal thought can emerge. This difference may distinguish the slow but capable learner from one who is incapable of abstract thought. It is not beyond possibility, therefore, that many slow learners can achieve a high level of abstract thought, provided that they have the opportunity to examine a greater number of concrete instances than the teaching process typically allows. The employment of teaching strategies which are scientifically designed for the development of cognitive skills may make it possible to develop cognitive processes at a much higher level and in a greater number of students.

This rationale set certain requirements for the methodology of studying the development of thought processes in the classroom. It required, first, securing records of classroom transactions. Second, it required a multidimensional analysis of these transactions in terms of what the teacher does, of what the responses of the students are, and of the product of the interaction.

Four discussions were taped in each of the 20 classrooms. Because the curriculum outline projected learning activities, it was possible to place each taping at a point in a sequence at which a specified cognitive task of concern to the study occurred. The first taping was made during the very first class session in which enumeration, grouping, and classification was the chief task. The next two tapings recorded discussions involving interpreting data and formulating inferences from them: one an interpretation of a film, and another at a point at which students reported information from preceding research, compared and contrasted their data, and attempted to express their findings in generalizations. These tapings were taken at the midyear. The final taping, at the end of the year, was of discussions involving application of previously learned knowledge to predicting consequences from described hypothetical conditions.

UNITS AND SCORES

One problem in analyzing classroom transactions for the purpose of describing thought processes is to decide on units of analysis which are at once capable of being scored accurately and which express sensible units of thought. In this study, the time sampling was discarded in favor of a "thought unit." "Thought unit" was defined as a remark or series of remarks expressing a more or less complete idea, serving a specified function, and classifiable according to a level of thought. It is, therefore, possible for one word or an entire paragraph to be designated as a "thought unit." For example, the word "cement," when it occurs in the process of enumerating materials for building houses, is considered a thought unit. So is a paragraph, such as "The people in the other country do not have electric saws and things that the men in this country use to build houses. The children help chop the wood and can do a lot of things to help build the houses. But the children over here cannot do very many things because of the danger."

In order to describe simultaneously the teaching acts and the levels of thinking of students, the verbal transactions were "scored" by three different "ratings." The first is that of *designation*. It describes the source of the thought unit—whether it emanated from the teacher or from the student and whether the person is giving or seeking information. The code symbols for designation are *child gives* (CG), *child seeks* (CS), *teacher gives* (TG), and *teacher seeks* (TS).

The rating of *function* describes how a thought unit functions in the context of discussion. When applied to remarks or questions by teachers, these ratings may be used to describe teaching strategies which affect the subsequent thought of children.

Two large groups of function ratings may be distinguished: (1) questions or statements made by the teacher or the students which are psychological or managerial in their function and unrelated to the logic of the content. Statements of this type include those that express agreement (A), approval (AP), disagreement (D), disapproval (Dp), management (M), and reiteration (R). (2) The second group includes teacher or student statements which function to give direction to discussions, but which at the same time can be rated according to the logic of content. Such ratings include focusing (F), refocusing (F2), change of focus (FC), deviating from focus (Fd), controlling thought (C), extending thought on the same level (X), and lifting called to a higher level (L).

The third rating, called *levels of thought*, describes both the student's and the teacher's verbal behavior by specifying the logical quality and the level of thought expressed. A separate rating scheme was developed for each of the three cognitive tasks. For each of these tasks, categories were established which represent the hierarchical levels of thought, according to their level of abstraction and complexity. These categories refer to the specific thought processes which need to be mastered in a sequential order, because performing on the preceding level is a prerequisite to being able to perform on the next. Thus, the rating scheme represents the developmental sequence for each cognitive task. In addition, within each category, distinctions were made between the irrelevant, the disconnected, and the related information or content.

The rating scheme used for designating the levels of thought for each of the cognitive tasks is as follows:

Cognitive task: Grouping and labeling[1] (giving or seeking)

10 specific or general information outside of focus

11 specific or general information within focus

12 specific or general information with qualifications

30 grouping information without basis

31 grouping information with implicit basis

32 grouping information with explicit basis

40 categorizing information without basis

41 categorizing information with implicit relationships between items

42 categorizing information with explicit relationships between items

Cognitive task: interpreting information and making inferences (giving or seeking)

10 specific or general information outside of focus

11 specific or general information within focus

12 specific or general information with qualifications and relationships

50 specific reason or explanation that does not relate to the information

51 specific reason or explanation that relates or organizes the information

52 specific reason or explanation that states how it relates or organizes the information

60 irrelevant or incorrect inference which is derived from information

61 relevant inference which is derived from information

62 relevant inference which is derived from information and expresses a cause and effect relationship, explanation, consequence or contrast

70 relationship between information which implies an irrelevant or incorrect principle or generalization

71 relationship between information which implies a principle or generalization

[1]Categories in the 20 series were originally reserved for "general information" but were later combined with the 10 series.

72 principle or generalization which is derived from information

Cognitive task: predicting consequences (giving or seeking)

90 correcting the cause or condition

Establishing parameter information

100 relevant information

101 relevant information for establishing the total parameter (if-then) or for a particular hypothesis or prediction

102 relevant information for the total parameter or any particular prediction with appropriate explanation

Establishing parameters of conditions

110 irrelevant or untenable condition for the total parameter or for the particular prediction or hypothesis

111 relevant condition without connecting it with relevant information

112 relevant condition and information and establishing logical connection between them

Prediction:

Level one, immediate consequences

Level two, remote consequences

120–220 incorrect or out of focus prediction

121–221 prediction with no elaboration

122–222 prediction accompanied by explanation, qualification, differentiation, comparison, or contrast

123–223 prediction accompanied by a stated or implied principle

In determining the level at which to rate a particular thought unit, it was necessary to consider the context in which the thought unit occurs. For example, the statement, "a hammer, because you can drive large nails with it," may be rated as "specific information with qualifying statement" if it is offered in response to the task of naming tools used in building a house; it merely gives additional information about the hammer and does not constitute a reason for naming "hammer." If the focus is on identification of tools most useful to primitive people, however, the same response would be rated as "relevant inference derived from information," because the phrase is an explicit reason for naming "hammer."

FUNCTION AND LEVEL

In describing the effect of teaching strategy on thought levels, four groups of function rating are especially important: focusing (F), extending the thought on the same level (X), lifting thought to a higher level (L), and controlling thought (C). Focusing establishes both the topic and the particular angle for its treatment. It sets the cognitive task. For example, the statement by the teacher, "If the desert had all the water it needed, what would happen?" establishes the central focus for discussion and calls for prediction of consequences.

The coding system also specifies the shifts in subject matter (change of focus), the degree to which the teacher finds it necessary to bring the discussion back to the original topic (refocus), and the number of times that the discussion wanders from the subject (deviation from focus).

A statement of the teacher or a child is coded as extension of thought (X) when it gives or seeks additional information or provides elaboration and clarification on an already established level. The following example illustrates a series of extensions on the level of providing specific information:

(1)	C	Malobi took the money home with her	CG 11
(2)	T	What did Malobi do with the money?	TS 11
(3)	C	She saved it.	CG 11X
(4)	C	She put it underground.	CG 11X
(5)	C	She put sticks and tin over it.	CG 11X
(6)	C	Before she did that, she put it in a little pot.	CG 11X

A thought unit is functioning to lift the level of thought whenever the teacher or child seeks or gives information that shifts thought to a higher level than had previously been established. In the following example, the teacher attempts to lift the level of thought from giving information to explanation:

(1)	C	They carried things in baskets on their heads.	CG 11
(2)	T	Explain why.	TS 61L
(3)	C	I suppose they can carry more things that way.	CG 61L

A question may function to extend the thought in one context and to lift it in another, as illustrated in the following example:

(1)	C	They were working fast on the house.	CG 11
(2)	T	Why?	TS 51L
(3)	C	They wanted to get the house done before the rain came.	CG 51L
(4)	T	Why?	TS 51X
(5)	C	Because unless it is finished, the rain will destroy it.	CG 52X

The inquiry on line two is rated as teacher seeking to lift the level of thought from the established level of giving specific information to the level of inference. The child's response provides the reason on the level sought by the teacher. The same inquiry on line four and the child's response on line five function to extend the thought because the level at which the question is asked has already been established.

Controlling of thought occurs when the teacher performs a cognitive task that students should be induced to do. This is the case when the teacher gives a category for classification, an inference in interpretation, or a prediction in the task of applying principles.

STRATEGIC PATTERNS

As elements of teaching strategy, the frequencies of these functions may represent either effective or ineffective teaching strategies. For example, frequent shifts in focus may be needed at some points in the discussion to introduce sufficient information to form a basis for comparison and generalization. Other tasks may require that the discussion remain on one focus long enough to provide full treatment of the subject before proceeding to another, higher level of thought process. Frequent refocusing may indicate a faulty handling of the sequence in thought processes, which results in the necessity for constantly having to bring the children back to the focus.

This multiple coding scheme makes it possible to depict the flow of the classroom discussion by charting the sequences of transactions between the teacher and the children, the changes in the level of thought during the discussion, and the effect of these strategies upon the level and the direction of thought. The flow of thought can be reconstructed even though the specific content of the discussion is not given.[2] For example, an empirical sequence of thought may, when translated from the code, be read as *child gives specific information, teacher seeks an extension of that information, child provides the requested extension, teacher seeks to lift the level of thought from the "information" level to the "reason" level, child provides a reason as requested by the teacher,* and *teacher gives approval to the child.* In a similar manner, any sequence of ratings can be reconstructed from the observationally developed flow charts.

When the flow charts identify individual children, then one can describe the characteristic modes and levels of thought of particular pupils, such as a tendency to operate only on the level of concrete information or on the level of inference and generalization, the tendency to remain focused or to stray from the focus, to give relevant or irrelevant information, etc. It also permits the accounting of the fre-

[2] Charts based on empirical observation will be published later as a part of the report to the US Office of Education of a study of "Thinking in Elementary School Children" (Project No. 1574).

quencies of the various thought patterns which prevail in the classroom group and the discrepancies between what the teacher seeks and how the children respond.

Data of this sort depict the various strategies which teachers may employ and their consequences. For example, when the teacher attempts to raise the level of thought very early in the discussion, this typically results in the children's returning to a lower level and in their inability to sustain discussion at the higher levels of thought. On the other hand, a strategy representing an effective pacing of shifting the thought onto higher levels seems to follow a characteristic course. The level of seeking information is sustained for a considerable time during the first portion of the discussion. Grouping is requested only after a large amount of information has been accumulated. The result is that in a fairly brief period, children transcend from grouping to labeling and then to providing reasons for labeling and to inferences.

Other strategic patterns that have been empirically identified include the teacher's repeated attempts to steer discussion to the inferential level without permitting the development of a body of needed information; in such a case, the children repeatedly return to the information level. Or when there is a constant change of focus, the children's thought alternates between several levels, is not sustained at the higher level, and gradually stabilizes on the most primitive one.

SOME IMPLICATIONS

This multidimensional analysis of classroom transactions has several advantages. First, by combining the description of the teacher's acts in terms of their explicit functions with the assessment of the logical quality of student responses, it is possible to evaluate the impact of the teacher's behavior in terms of its productivity. This addition of the dimension of the logical quality of the content of thought carries the analysis of classroom transactions a step beyond what has been available to date. Most current studies of classroom transactions concentrate more or less exclusively on the analysis of the psychological functions of teaching acts (Flanders, 1960; Hughes et al., 1959). This emphasis has evoked the criticism that teaching is explained and controlled exclusively in terms of psychological principles and that the logic of teaching and of its product in learning is overlooked (Smith, 1950).

A further advantage lies in the fact that, in addition to describing the impact of teaching exclusively in terms of the frequencies of specific acts, this scheme permits studying the cumulative impact of certain patterns or combinations of acts, including their pacing. It is at this point that a transfer is made from the study of teaching acts to the study of teaching strategies. Flanders [See References] has taken a step in this direction by describing the points of shift in the nature of teaching acts.

Finally, the scheme permits the examination of the effect of teaching strategies in terms of a measurable change in a specified outcome—levels of thinking in this case—and thus frees the study of teaching from the necessity of inferring the effect from the assumed consequences of the frequencies of certain types of teacher behavior. A preliminary analysis of the typescripts of classroom discussion reveals an enormous influence of teacher behavior on the thinking of students. This impact is exercised in a variety of ways: by the nature of the questions asked, what the teacher gives to the students or seeks from them, the timing of these acts in the total sequence, which ideas are picked up for elaboration and which are passed over, points at which approval and disapproval are given, etc. For example, the focus which the teacher sets determines which points students can explore and establishes the models for thought they can practice. Of great importance is

the sequence of mental operations called for and the appropriateness of this sequence to developing productive thought models.

It seems clear, further, that the level of thinking attained is influenced not only by the nature of the single act by a teacher just preceding a given response. The level of thought attained seems to be determined by the whole pattern of transactions: the particular combination of focusing, extending, and lifting; the timing of these acts; the length of time spent on a particular focus, such as exploring specific descriptive information before examining causes or attempting explanation; the distance between the mental operations of the students at the moment from the level required by the teacher, and the points at which the teacher seeks information from students and gives it. These combinations, not merely the frequencies alone, constitute a teaching strategy.

Only a casual identification of these strategies is available at the moment of writing this article. The variations in the patterns are too numerous to permit analysis by ordinary means. The staff, in cooperation with experts in computer programing, has developed a high-speed computer program designed to aid in accounting for these patterns. Such a computer program should permit the identification of the elements and the cumulative patterns of strategies associated with high and low performance.[3]

The findings so far suggest that if the acquisition of skills in autonomous thinking is to be a realistic objective, a much more thorough study of and experimentation with the appropriate teaching strategies and their impact on the development of thinking is called for. As Flanders [see references] suggests, any step in the direction of specifying productive teaching strategies should lead to a more adequate understanding of the connection between teachers'

[3] Such a computer program has been devised by P. J. Stone and M. S. Smith as a general sequence analyzer, planned to identify recurrent patterns in a list of events.

behavior and student response. A scientific mapping of such strategies should also add considerably to the developing theory of instruction, and especially to our under-

standing of the conditions which maximize the development of higher mental processes on the part of all students, not only the intellectual elite.

REFERENCES

Bartlett, F. E. *Thinking: An experimental and social study.* New York: Basic Books, 1958.

Burton, W. N. *The guidance of learning activities.* New York: Appleton, 1952.

Buswell, G. T., and B. Y. Hersch. *Patterns of solving problems.* Berkeley: University of California Press, 1956.

Contra Costa County Social Studies Units, Grades 1–6. Pleasant Hill, Calif.: Contra Costa County Schools, 1959.

Flanders, N. A. Teacher influence, pupil attitudes, and achievement. Pre-publication manuscript of a proposed research monograph for the U.S. Office of Education, Cooperative Research Branch, Washington, D.C., 1960.

————. Some relationships between teacher influence, pupil attitudes, and achievement. Ditto MS of a chapter submitted to the AASA, the NTBA, and the NEA Classroom Teachers Division. No date.

Gallagher, J. J., Mary Jane Aschner, Joyce M. Perry, and S. S. Afaar. A system for classifying thought processes in the content of classroom verbal interaction. Ditto MS. Urbana,:

Institute for Research on Exceptional Children, University of Illinois, 1961.

Getzels, J. W., and P. Jackson. *Creativity and intelligence.* New York: Wiley, 1962.

Guilford, J. P. Basic conceptual problems in the psychology of thinking. *Ann. New York Acad. Sci.*, 1961, **91**, 9–19.

Harlow, H. F. The formation of learning sets. *Psychol. Rev.*, 1949, **56**, 51–60.

Hughes, Marie, et al. Development of the means for the assessment of the quality of teaching in elementary school. Salt Lake City: University of Utah, 1959. (Mimeo.)

Hunt, J. McV. *Experience and Intelligence.* New York: Ronald, 1961.

Peel, E. A. *The pupil's thinking.* London: Oldbourne, 1960.

Piaget, J. *The psychology of intelligence.* London: Routledge, 1947.

Rokeach, M. *The open and closed mind.* New York: Basic Books, 1960.

Sigel, I. Cognitive style and personality dynamics. Interim report, Merrill-Palmer Institute, 1961.

Smith, B. O. Concept of teaching. *Teachers Coll. Rec.*, 1950, **61**, 229–241.

Taba, Hilda. *Curriculum development: Theory and practice.* New York: Harcourt, 1962.

Inquiry Training
in the Elementary School

J. RICHARD SUCHMAN

Skills of scientific inquiry are being taught to elementary school children at the University of Illinois through the use of motion pictures and verbal "experimentation." For the past three years, a research project known as the Illinois Studies in

Inquiry Training has been experimenting with the teaching of strategies and tactics of scientific inquiry to children who learn

Reprinted with the permission of the author and the publisher from the article of the same title, *Science Teacher*, 1960, **27**, 42–47.

to apply them in question-and-answer investigations. Short films of physics demonstrations pose problems of cause and effect. The children learn to attack these problems with questions by which they gather data and perform imaginary experiments. The teacher provides the answers to the questions.

A portion of a typical session would go something like this: (The children have been shown a film of the "Ball and Ring" demonstration.)

> PUPIL: Were the ball and ring at room temperature to begin with?
> TEACHER: Yes.
> PUPIL: And the ball would go through the ring at first?
> TEACHER: Yes.
> PUPIL: After the ball was held over the fire it did *not* go through the ring, right?
> TEACHER: Yes.
> PUPIL: If the ring had been heated instead of the ball, would the results have been the same?
> TEACHER: No.
> PUPIL: If both had been heated would the ball have gone through then?
> TEACHER: That all depends.
> PUPIL: If they had both been heated to the same temperature would the ball have gone through?
> TEACHER: Yes.
> PUPIL: Would the ball be the same size after it was heated as it was before?
> TEACHER: No.
> PUPIL: Could the same experiment have been done if the ball and ring were made out of some other metal?
> TEACHER: Yes.

Such questioning continues for about thirty minutes as the children gather data, identify variables and determine their relevancy to the problem, and formulate hypotheses of cause and effect which they test experimentally. No data are given that the children do not obtain through observation or from the teacher's "yes" or "no" answers to their highly structured questions.

To these children and others who are inquiring into the causes of physical phenomena, science is the discovery of new relationships. Children sometimes discover by accident; and sometimes "discovery" is carefully contrived by a skillful teacher. Whichever way it occurs, children are typically thrilled by the sudden new insights, and the learning that results has deep roots. But if we are going to teach the child how to discover meaningful patterns independently and consistently in a highly complex environment, we must teach him how to probe aggressively, systematically, and objectively, and how to reason productively with the obtained data. In other words, we must teach him the skills of inquiry.

OBJECTIVES

Inquiry training is designed to supplement the ordinary science classroom activities. It gives the child a plan of operation that will help him to discover causal factors of physical change through his own initiative and control, and not to depend on the explanations and interpretations of teachers or other knowledgeable adults. He learns to formulate hypotheses, to test them through a verbal form of controlled experimentation, and to interpret the results. In a nutshell, the program is aimed at making pupils more *independent, systematic, empirical,* and *inductive* in their approach to problems of science.

THE STRATEGY OF INQUIRY

The children are given a general three-stage plan to guide them in their investigations and help them develop a logical, systematic approach. Each stage has its own goal and a set of tactics helpful in attaining it.

Stage I. Episode Analysis

GOAL. The identification, verification, and measurement of the parameters of the problem.

In order to perform the operations of this stage, the child must learn to use a set of categories to describe and analyze each episode. Taken together, these categories form a logical system in which each element has an established relationship to the others. The episode-analysis categories are as follows:

1. *Objects:* Objects are the easiest elements for the children to recognize. Familiar objects that are clearly visible pose no problems. The chief difficulty is identifying *all* the objects, whether or not they are visible, familiar, or seemingly unimportant. Included in this category are *systems,* two or more objects combined to form a functional unit. As such they have certain properties that the objects do not possess separately. Water is an object; a beaker is an object. A beaker of water may be regarded as a system.

2. *Properties:* Properties relate to both objects and systems. A property of an object is its predisposition to behave a certain way under a given set of conditions. Properties may be identified through experimentation. By placing an object under varying conditions and observing the resulting changes, a person can determine as many of its properties as he may desire. The identification of objects by their properties is generally more useful than identification by name.

3. *Conditions:* Conditions pertain to the state of objects or systems. While the identity of an object remains constant, its conditions may change. Conditions are identified by observation or measurement.

4. *Events:* Events are defined as changes in the conditions of objects or systems. If an object moves, evaporates, expands, or merely gets hotter, an event has taken place. Events are the consequences of changing the conditions of objects or systems. The type or amount of change that is necessary to produce a given event is a function of the properties of the objects and systems involved.

Using a question-asking strategy to obtain the kinds of information defined by this system of descriptive categories, the child can collect and organize data which provide grist for the mill of inductive investigations.

Episode analysis involves a number of tactical operations. Careful observation must be supplemented by instrumentation and measurement. Many parameters or condition changes are not directly observable, yet may be critical factors in the causation of an event. If the child confines his attention to those variables which are striking or obvious, he is bound to overlook many highly significant dimensions. A thorough and orderly assessment of the objects, conditions, and events of an episode increases the probability of gathering all of the significant data.

One problem is that people tend to perceive new events and situations as total patterns (Gestalts) unless they have a specific set to analyze and a system of categories on which to base an analysis. Total perceptions may be superficial and misleading, causing children to make false analogies to similar total patterns. It is typical, for example, for children to conclude that a bimetallic strip is melting when it is held in a horizontal position over a flame so that it bends downward. The total pattern of this episode is identical to others in which a heated object melts. Yet a careful analysis would reveal the fact that the melting point of the metals is never even approached when the bending occurs.

Stage II. Determination of Relevance

GOAL. The identification of the conditions that are necessary and sufficient to produce the events of the episode.

Not all the parameters identified in Stage I are critical. Often many can be changed without altering the events of the episode. The process of determining criticalness is accomplished through experimentation. Various conditions and objects are changed, one at a time, through a series of controlled verbal experiments. The effects of these changes on the events of the episode are noted. Obviously, only when critical conditions are changed, will events change. Thus, experimentally, the child can determine the relevant variables. This is strictly an empirical solution to the problem of causation. It brings the child halfway to the ultimate goal of understanding the causation of events. More complete comprehension includes the recognition of the events as necessary consequences of universal principles that make a certain set of conditions necessary and sufficient. Stage III is devoted to the search for these principles.

Stage III. *Education of Relations*

GOAL. The formulation and testing of theoretical constructs or rules that express the relationships among the variables of the observed physical event.

During this phase, experimentation is still the principal tool of inquiry, but each experiment is designed as a critical test of some hypothetical construct. Obviously, the scope of operations must extend well beyond the domain of the original event. This stage demands a higher degree of conceptual sophistication, flexibility, and imagination than the others. The problem of designing an unequivocal test for an hypothesis can be as taxing as formulating the hypothesis itself. The child sees his objective as the discovery of rules that express the relationship between variables. He learns that the value of any rule he constructs is a function of (1) its validity within a specified realm of applicability and (2) the scope of this realm.

THE METHOD OF INQUIRY TRAINING

During the past three years the inquiry-training program has evolved into a somewhat structured pedagogical procedure. At the fifth-grade level, ten seems to be the optimum group size. With classes of thirty or more, the remaining children serve as nonparticipating observers who have an important evaluative role. Rotation permits all children to participate in turn. The training sessions are about one hour long and thus far have been held at weekly intervals, although we now believe that more frequent intervals and shorter sessions would be desirable.

Practice, corrective feedback, and exposition are incorporated into each training session. While they are generally applied in a regular sequence, a degree of flexibility in their use in maintained. A typical training session is organized in the following way.

Presenting the Problem

A silent motion picture of a physics demonstration provides the problem episode. Typical of the demonstrations used is the "Collapsing Varnish Can."[1] As any teacher of science knows, children who do not have well-developed, operative concepts of atmospheric pressure and condensation are exceedingly perplexed by this demonstration. In producing the current series of stimulus films—40 demonstrations in all—we tried to capitalize on this perplexity to provide an intrinsic motivation for inquiry. Our technique is predicated on the belief that the drive to "find out why" can surpass in sustained motivational power almost any other classroom incentive.

In addition to their motivational function, the films pose cause-and-effect problems in very specific terms. They make available some parameters and suggest areas where important additional parameters might be sampled. In short, the films provide a portion of empirical experience which the child must then relate to his conceptual systems. To the extent that these systems are not sufficiently developed to

[1] The condensation of water vapor inside a corked varnish can reduces the inside pressure and permits the can to be crushed by the atmospheric pressure.

accommodate the experience, he must expand and strengthen them through inquiry until he is capable of explaining the episode.

The Practice Session

Immediately upon seeing the film, the children begin the inquiry process. All probes are verbal, originate from the children, and must be so phrased as to be answerable by "yes" or "no." Keeping the inquiry at the verbal level permits the teacher and the rest of the group to keep track of most of the information the children are obtaining. The questions must originate from the children because the selection and design of questions are as much a part of inquiry as the interpretation one makes of the answers. The questions must be answerable by "yes" or "no" because in this way only can the child be discouraged from transferring control of the process to the teacher. "Yes" or "no" questions are hypotheses. The teacher in answering merely establishes the tenability of the hypothesis. If the children were permitted to ask, "Why did the can collapse?" the responsibility for selecting the kind of information to be supplied next would be on the shoulders of the teacher. The children would thus be relinquishing their roles as inquirers by returning to the traditional dependent role of obedient listeners and memorizers. This would inhibit the occurrence of inquiry behavior.

The children have two types of questions available to them as information-gathering tools. In identifying parameters in Stage I they may simply ask questions of verification. Since the film provides stimuli that are one step removed from firsthand experience, the children have recourse to verification questions to confirm or test their hunches as to the identity of objects and their conditions at any given time during the episode. They may also need to check the specifics of the observed events, e.g., what happened when. As indicated previously, adequate verification and identification of parameters is an essential first step.

The second type of probe is the experimental question. The child states a set of conditions and postulates a resulting event. The question is answered by the teacher in terms of whether the postulated event will or will not be the result. If the conditions of the experiment are not complete or clear enough to permit the teacher to give an unequivocal answer, he may say, "That all depends" or "Tell me more." Either of these answers tells the child that his experiment has not been sufficiently controlled. Presumably every experimental question is a test or part of a test of an unstated hypothesis. If the child suspects that the cork in the varnish can was a necessary condition for the collapse of the can, he might ask, "If the cork had not been placed in the mouth of the can before the can was cooled, would the same result have occurred?" The teacher's answer of "no" supports the hypothesis that the corking of the can is a necessary condition and tends also to lend support to an hypothesis that the can must be kept airtight while it is being cooled. *But the child must make these inferences himself from the empirical data he obtains.* He cannot test his hypotheses *directly*, even if such questions are phrased as "yes"-"no" questions. If the child had asked, "Does the cork have anything to do with the collapsing of the can?" the teacher does not answer the question. Such a query tends to tap the *teacher's* understanding of the relationships involved. The child is asking the teacher to make certain inferences *for him* and in so doing is relinquishing some of his own responsibility in the inquiry process. Such questions are frequently asked by children, even after they have been trained for several months. The standard response by the teacher is, "What could you do to find that out for yourself?" This retort, without the slightest note of admonition, puts the responsibility right back where it belongs.

The Critique

Generally the inquiry session is terminated by either the achievement of the objectives, the inability of the children to proceed without further conceptual development, or the expiration of time. The latter is usually the case. Following the inquiry session is the "critique," a period in which the strategy and tactics of the group are reviewed and evaluated by the teacher, the nonparticipating members of the class, and the members of the participating group itself. It has been our practice to tape record each inquiry session and utilize the tapes as a point of departure. But we now feel that this is not entirely necessary, particularly if the critique immediately follows the inquiry session. Immediate "feedback" has long been recognized by psychologists as an important condition for effective reinforcement. Some comments and suggestions by the teacher are best made during the course of the inquiry session itself. If this practice is followed to excess, however, the children may be distracted too often from the physics problem at hand. This may impair their efficiency in this work.

The principal function of the critique is to correct weaknesses in the inquiry of the children and to build up a repertoire of tactics that will increase their accuracy and productivity. At times, the critique becomes something like a lecture-discussion in which the teacher may be trying to help the group conceptualize the general design of inquiry strategy. Sometimes special recordings of model inquiry sessions are played. These provide clear examples of the strategies and tactics that the teacher wants the children to utilize.

The critique is indispensable; when it is

eliminated morale slips and inquiry becomes progressively worse.

CONCLUSIONS

Preliminary analysis of the results of three pilot studies suggests the following conclusions about inquiry training.

The inquiry skills of fifth-grade children can be improved over a fifteen-week period as a result of the methods described herein. Most of the children who receive training become more productive in their design and use of verification and experimentation. They develop a fairly consistent strategy which they can transfer to new problem situations. They make fewer untested assumptions; they formulate and test more hypotheses; and they perform more controlled vs. uncontrolled experiments in the course of their inquiry.

The children have little apparent desire to improve their inquiry skills per se. The chief motivating force is the desire to comprehend the causation of the observed episodes. An explanation by the teacher might satisfy this desire, but in the absence of such explanations the children accept inquiry as a means to their goal. Whenever inquiry is not directly related to the satisfaction of their need to "find out why," they show little interest in the strategies and tactics being discussed. Thus methods for constant improvement are desirable.

Our final conclusion for the present is that inquiry skills cannot be successfully taught to this age group as an isolated content area. The major focus in elementary science education should remain the *content* rather than the *methods* of science. Inquiry training and abundant opportunities to attain new concepts *through* inquiry, however, seem to produce increments in the understanding of content as well as an important new grasp of the scientific method and proficiency in its use.

Wanted: A Research Basis for Educational Policy on Foreign Language Teaching

JOHN B. CARROLL

Any observer of the national scene today cannot fail to have noticed the ever-increasing tide of statements by people both in high and low places concerning the need for more and better foreign language teaching in America. What is interesting is that seemingly many shades of educational opinion—from the arch-conservative Bestors and Rickovers to the more liberal Woodrings and Conants—are united in favoring more foreign language teaching. The cry has been taken up in governmental quarters, right up to the White House, and we now have on the books the National Defense Education Act of 1958, which authorizes the expenditure of considerable government funds to support foreign language teaching and research. Happily, enabled by generous appropriations by the Congress, the United States Office of Education has for the past year been energetically moving to carry out the provisions of this Act—among them, the provisions relating to the support of foreign language teaching. It has granted funds to numerous institutions to establish centers for language research, to conduct institutes for foreign language teachers, and to make various studies concerning foreign languages, their teaching, and their rôle in American life. In addition, it has provided public schools and colleges with funds for the construction of language laboratories and the purchase of equipment and materials for language teaching.

I do not think there is much doubt that more Americans should acquire more kinds of competence with more foreign languages, and if all the statements being made and actions being taken will help produce this competence, we can look forward to congratulating ourselves. What concerns me is that with regard to many of the specific recommendations which have been made, there is almost a complete lack of research evidence on which one can rely in order to provide either support or refutation. We do not have an adequate basis in empirical research for answering such important questions as: *who* should be taught foreign languages? at what age or grade levels should children begin the study of foreign languages? how long should they study foreign languages? what objectives and methods should be emphasized in the teaching? However sympathetic we may be to the recommendations, they are often based on assumptions about which the most charitable thing to say is that they have not been proved. For example, it is widely assumed that children can learn foreign languages faster than adolescents and adults, and this is used as one justification for recommending the introduction of foreign languages in the elementary school. I am not sure that this assumption is correct; below, I will briefly consider the scanty evidence bearing

Reprinted with the permission of the author and publisher from the article of the same title, *Harvard Educational Review*, 1960, 30, 128–140. Revised from an address given at the Department of Romance Languages, University of Massachusetts, April 3, 1959.

on it and discuss the consequences for educational practice.

What I wish to point out, therefore, is the need for a research basis for the formation of educational policy concerning foreign language instruction. Such a policy does not have to be an official "line" or attitude which might be adopted by an organization or group. It means simply a series of propositions about foreign language learning and teaching which would be buttressed by reason and research, and which American citizens could use with confidence in forming opinions and making decisions concerning the place of foreign language teaching in the schools and its proper conduct.

In seeming to raise questions about foreign language teaching, I would not want these remarks to be used for the justification of any slackening of effort in this important area of the work of the schools. The urgency of our national situation calls for anything we can do, at all educational levels, to raise the level of foreign language competence in America, but in the meantime let us know what we are doing and let us find out how we can do it better—this is the practical application of research. The research itself, I assure you, can range from the most theoretical research in psychology and linguistics to the most crassly practical compilation of nose-count statistics. For theoretical psychologists, I cannot think of any more complex and intriguing problem than that of investigating the processes by which an individual learns a second language—i.e., learns to respond to referents with symbolic responses other than those which he originally learned to make to them. For applied linguists there is, at the other end of the spectrum, the problem of adapting linguistic analysis to the making of texts, workbooks, taped lessons, and other materials to facilitate optimal learning. For applied psychologists and educational statisticans there are problems of measurement and the analysis of student aptitude, motivation, and achievement.

The first of a number of problems which

I consider important in the framing of educational policy on foreign language teaching is that of *who* should be taught foreign languages. Phrased in this way, this is a hard question to answer. It implies, of course, that there is to be some selectivity in the teaching of foreign languages—that not everybody "should" study foreign languages. The use of the word *should* implies that there exist generally accepted standards or values by which one could judge whether the study of a foreign language would be a suitable educational activity for an individual. I am not sure that either of these implications is justified; a full discussion of them would take us deep into educational philosophy. All I can do here is to state the relevant findings from empirical research and mention the gaps which remain in our knowledge. One thing of which I am reasonably well convinced from research findings[1] is that people differ among themselves greatly in the ease and facility with which they can learn foreign languages. The differences are so great, in fact, that in situations where money is to be invested in the special intensive training of adult personnel in a foreign language—as in military forces, foreign missionary organizations, and business corporations operating in foreign countries—only about one-third to one-half of typical samples of candidates have sufficient measured language aptitude to make this training economically worthwhile; that is, the chances

[1] The chief findings from my own program of research on the measurement of foreign language aptitude are presented in the *Manual* for the *Modern Language Aptitude Test*, by John B. Carroll and Stanley M. Sapon (New York: The Psychological Corporation, 1959). See also: John B. Carroll, "A Factor Analysis of Two Foreign Language Aptitude Batteries," *Journal of General Psychology*, LIX (1958), pp. 3–19; John B. Carroll, "Use of The Modern Language Aptitude Test in Secondary Schools," *National Council on Measurements Used in Education*, Sixteenth Yearbook (1959), pp. 155–159; John B. Carroll, "The Prediction of Success in Intensive Foreign Language Training" (prepared for a symposium on Training Research, University of Pittsburgh, February, 1960).

are too high that the remainder will fail the drastically accelerated training which has to be given in these special circumstances. The results also suggest that for a certain percentage of college students—perhaps as high as 10 to 15 per cent, the chances of eventually learning a language to the point of practical usefulness are so small as to call into question the desirability of maintaining absolutely rigid language requirements in colleges and universities. Differences in what we may call foreign language aptitude are observable not only in adults and in college student populations, but also in elementary school children and in high school students. Furthermore, at all levels the differences show considerable independence from differences in general intelligence. For example, several years ago I gave tests of foreign language aptitude to "gifted" children in grades 3, 4, 5, and 6 in Cleveland, Ohio, where the famous "Cleveland Plan" of foreign language instruction for talented children has been in effect for many years. The average IQ of these children was approximately 125, but the interesting thing was that even these children varied considerably in their rate of foreign language learning, and that this rate was predicted better by special foreign language aptitude tests than by intelligence ratings.

These facts need to be taken into account by those who have urged, as James B. Conant does,[2] that foreign language instruction be reserved for the top 15 per cent of our youth in the high schools. Mr. Conant has implied that those of lesser ability— the next 25 per cent, say,—will have considerable trouble with foreign languages. My results suggest some modification of this view. There are many extremely talented students in the schools who will still have trouble with languages, and there are many students of only moderate general ability who could succeed quite well in foreign languages; the potential failures in both

these groups can be detected to a very useful extent by means of appropriate aptitude tests. Of course, it remains to be determined whether some special method of teaching can reach students of low foreign language aptitude and pull them up to a level comparable to that of high aptitude students taught by more usual methods. There is already some suggestion in some preliminary work I have done that the use of semiautomatic presentation and reinforcement devices (the so-called "teaching machines") may in some cases make it possible for low aptitude students to learn almost as well as high-aptitude students. This was the case, for example, in an experiment with the use of a tape-recorder and correlated worksheets programmed to teach students to read the Arabic alphabet at the outset of a course in Classical Arabic. Whether the same phenomenon would be noted in other phases of language instruction, only further investigation can tell. It is to be noted, in any event, that research on foreign language learning is a very complicated business: one cannot pay attention to a single variable like foreign language aptitude (and actually this variable is complex) without considering its interaction with other variables such as the method of teaching, the age of the subject, his motivation, and many others, and this is at least one reason why a fundamental understanding of the process of foreign language learning is badly needed.

The question of the age of the learner has already been noted, and I have aired my concern about the assumption that children learn foreign languages better and faster than adults. Recently[3] reviewed evidence bearing on this assumption suggests that except for one important aspect, children who have already learned their native language do not learn foreign languages any better and faster than adults. If anything, children may be slower. The impor-

[2] James B. Conant, *The American High School Today* (New York: McGraw-Hill, 1959), p. 58.

[3] John B. Carroll, "Teaching Foreign Languages to Children: What Research Shows," *National Elementary Principal*, (May, 1960).

tant way in which children seem to have an advantage over adults or even adolescents is the ease with which they can learn a native-like *pronunciation* of the foreign language—without the extensive pronunciation drills and phonetic explanations which older people seem to need in order to achieve acceptable pronunciation. The most salient and first noticed feature of a person's performance in speaking a foreign language is his pronunciation or "accent"; thus, when children are observed speaking a foreign language their good pronunciation is likely to give the false impression that they are equally capable in other aspects of performance. This, at any rate, is a possible explanation for the widespread notion that children learn foreign languages more readily than older people. Aside from this, however, it is probable that given equal time, aptitude, and motivation adults can learn to speak foreign languages with at least the same amount of ease or difficulty that children experience. We tend to forget the fact that thousands or even millions of adults have learned to speak, understand, read, and write foreign languages without undue difficulty, albeit with considerable expenditure of time and effort. It is a mistake to recommend foreign language study in the elementary school solely on the ground that children are quicker foreign language learners—all the more so because this ground is partly erroneous.

There could be other grounds for urging foreign language study in early years of schooling, but the research evidence supporting these grounds is even less clear than it is for the considerations discussed in the preceding paragraph. One of these is the argument that early foreign language study gives the child a better appreciation and understanding of foreign culture. Another is the argument that early foreign language study facilitates later language learning by giving the child confidence, before he has had time to build up apprehension and negative feelings, that he can learn to speak a foreign language and that learning a for-

eign language can be pleasant. Whatever we may think of these arguments, there is need for research evidence to help us examine their merits.

We can make the problem of when to start foreign language teaching very difficult by asking the following question: Other things being equal, will a student be a better educated person at his graduation from college if he has learned a foreign language *in his elementary school experience* than if he has not? The question will doubtlessly have different answers depending on whether the student continues to practice and use his knowledge of the foreign language through the high school and college years, and also depending on whether he takes up the study of still other languages in those years. The answer to the question will then depend on whether there is indeed any transfer effect of the early language instruction on further language study, as claimed. One study[4] which sought to measure long-term effects of elementary school foreign language instruction found that high school students with previous foreign language training tended to get slightly better marks than their controls in the *first* high school language course they entered, but were barely able to maintain superiority in subsequent courses. But it is difficult to draw positive conclusions from this study because it gives us no information about the nature of the pre-high school instruction or the extent of student achievement in it. Perhaps the relative failure of the elementary language instruction to produce savings in the high school program lay in poor planning for transitions between various stages of learning. If we are to have programs of foreign languages in the elementary schools we must provide what the school people call "articulation" with later stages of instruction—that is, we must allow

[4] J. Justman and M. L. Nass, "The High School Achievement of Pupils Who Were and Were Not Introduced to a Foreign Language in Elementary School *Modern Language Journal,* XL (1956), pp. 120–123.

the student to pass naturally to more advanced levels of content as he moves up the educational ladder. If we start the child learning a foreign language in the elementary school, this may mean that a great deal of advance planning of curriculum is necessary, particularly if we expect the child to continue to be well motivated and to see meaning and challenge in foreign language study up through the secondary school years and beyond. From the point of view of research, however, one is forced to ask the question: if we wish to produce a specified degree of foreign language competence at the point of high-school graduation, say, is it indeed most efficient to start the child in the elementary grades, just in terms of the sheer amount of the students' time and without consideration of the teaching force and other facilities that this requires? In the present state of ignorance about rates of learning at different ages, it is not possible to give even educated guesses as to the answer to this question. Perhaps it would be more efficient to concentrate efforts at the junior high school level, or perhaps the use of intensive summer courses at the senior high school level would constitute an equally effective program. With the present efflorescence of foreign language programs at various levels of schooling, it would be tragic if nobody bothered to try to investigate the questions being raised here.

One of the most acute problems relating to the formation of educational policy on foreign language instruction is that of the value of the study of any one language for the subsequent study of another. Is it true, as many have claimed, that learning one language makes the learning of other languages easier? Before we try to answer this question, let us see why it is important. It seems obvious that the national interest requires that our citizens be able to acquire competence in a variety of languages—and not necessarily the languages which are customarily taught in our schools. With all due respect to the merits of the French, Spanish, and German languages, and their

literatures, it is a bit parochial to think that these are the only languages likely to be of crucial importance in our dealings on the international scene. If anything, we should be putting more stress on Russian, Arabic, and Chinese. But there will always be other languages which some Americans will desire to learn at relatively short notice. One net result of public education should be to equip language students with techniques of language learning. Instruction in foreign languages should exemplify the best methods of language learning—methods which the individual can call on when he has to learn a new language under his own auspices, if need be.

With the question put in this light, I can say that there is no directly relevant scientific evidence about the efficiency of language instruction in teaching people how to learn new languages. (We must rule out anecdotal evidence because we have no control or knowledge of the various critical factors.) We do not know whether present methods of teaching languages have any effect on subsequent language learning. Situations will undoubtedly arise, in the coming years, when this kind of problem can be investigated properly. In the meantime, I will cite one bit of evidence on the relevance of experience in language learning: on several occasions I have found that even after taking account of language aptitude (i.e., controlling it statistically), the number of years of experience in studying foreign languages is a significant predictor of success in further language courses. On the whole, the notion that language learning has transfer value for new language learning receives support, but it seems reasonable to qualify this statement with one caution: it must be language learning that stems from a kind of instruction which will produce transfer.

In some of his public addresses, Mr. Conant has chosen an apt metaphor when he says that the widespread practice of requiring only two years of foreign language study for high school students is like stopping our drills before striking oil. He recommends that high school students who show requisite ability to study foreign languages at all should be urged to study a foreign language for four years. This recommendation is based on the testimony of foreign language teachers to the effect that two years of academic study in typical high school courses is far short of the time required to achieve anything like a desirable degree of mastery. In addition to the testimony of foreign language teachers, we could look at the results of standardized achievement examinations, which would likewise show, I think, that students do not learn a satisfactory amount after two years. We need, in fact, to compile large amounts of data on how much students actually accomplish in foreign language learning. Just as an oil-drilling engineer can tell you such facts about oil production as the number of barrels a day expected, the probable lifetime of a well, and so forth, we need to amass statistics about expected rates of language learning. I would call these studies *parametric* studies, because they seek to define the *parameters* of the language learning process. Such studies would allow us to state, given a person with a specified degree of language aptitude, how long would be necessary (in terms of hours of instruction) to bring him to a given degree of competence in a foreign language. If you visit the language school of the Foreign Service Institute of the Department of State, you will find posted on a wall a chart which purports to tell how many months of *intensive* (full-time) study it will take a person of high, medium, or low aptitude to learn a language like Russian or Hindi, or a language like Chinese, Japanese, or Korean. We are told, for instance, that it will take 12 months for the average person to learn to speak Mandarin Chinese. These figures, I reiterate, are for *intensive* language training and cannot be immediately translated into statistics applicable to the high school or college situation. But we need statistics like these for the high school and college

situations, and even for the elementary school.

These parametric studies will require good techniques of measurement. We must have better ways than we have now of testing and specifying the amounts and varieties of competence with a language which an individual can demonstrate.

To round out the picture given by such parametric studies, it would also be useful to get some notion of the retention and relearning curves. How rapidly does language competence decline and how readily can there be relearning? What are the best and most efficient techniques of maintaining competence or refreshing knowledge? In our language teaching, even if we train a student long enough for him to "strike oil," we allow him to pour most of it down the drain in the sense that we fail to provide opportunities for maintaining the refreshing knowledge. A national educational policy for foreign language instruction might well recommend conversation clubs, refresher courses, pen pal clubs, or other devices to encourage people to keep language competence alive.

Thus far we have concerned ourselves chiefly with the background considerations which might lead us to recommend who should be taught languages, when, and for how long. We have not yet mentioned the *how* of language teaching.

What *is* the "state of the art" in language teaching? Occasionally I am tempted to say that we have already perfected the art of language teaching and that the investigation of ways to improve it is largely in the nature of a mop-up operation. As you can imagine, this is intended only as a provocative overstatement of the case, but there is some truth in it. Without swallowing all the stories of "miracles" wrought by the "Army" method in World War II (remember, it was an "Army" method solely because the Army had wisely appealed to descriptive linguists to help in developing a method), let us observe that the Army method, and methods like it or derived from it, *have* produced thousands of competent speakers of foreign languages. Given aptitude on the part of the learner, enough time, semiprivate instruction, reasonably well-designed texts and learning materials, and above all, a will to learn, a person can, without too much difficulty, learn a language to the point of practical usefulness. The rub comes when there is not enough aptitude, less than adequate motivation, not enough time, a dearth of appropriate learning materials, or circumstances requiring large instructional groups.

This is where foreign language teaching most needs scientific help, and even the best known methods in vogue today could doubtless be improved by experimental research. From the standpoint of educational policy, we need to do whatever can be done to make language teaching more effective. But even before we start thinking about how to do that, there are some mountainous problems concerning what our objectives in language teaching ought to be and how they can be best approached.

For example, under what conditions will we aim for a command of the spoken language, and under what conditions will we be satisfied with a reading knowledge? This problem has been debated up and down the halls of academe for the last fifty years, but one cannot find a sufficient amount of objective research evidence which would enable us to make a sound judgment in any particular case. The dilemma is this: linguists have been claiming that even if you want only to learn to read a language—to keep up with foreign scientific literature, for example—you should learn the language initially as a *spoken* language, on the ground that language is primarily a matter of speech and only secondarily a matter of writing. There is much attraction and even subtlety in this claim, for there seems to be an inherent correctness in the notion that reading is most facile when it is founded on deep-rooted habits of talking and listening. But it is hard to see why a person could not learn to read a foreign language, even quite

fluently, without more than a first acquaintance with the spoken forms, and there are plenty of anecdotal cases which apparently support such a claim. Let us then put the matter to experimental test: to what extent does learning to speak and understand a language facilitate reading the language, and is it economical of time, effort, and facilities to adopt an approach through speaking and listening when one desires only a reading knowledge? This is truly a question for which we ought to have an answer based on empirical research, for it is one which generations of students, especially graduate students, have asked when faced with various kinds of language requirements. It is a particularly vexing question for teachers of the so-called dead languages: should Latin be taught by the direct method? To ask a collateral question, what are the best methods of acquiring solely a reading knowledge of a foreign language? In our zeal to improve methods of imparting a command of the spoken language let us not overlook this secondary but important question. I am not at all convinced that we know the answer, for one can think of many possibilities for improving the methods of teaching a reading knowledge. For example, one could try to exploit the capabilities of films, programmed teaching machines, and "trots" produced by mechanical translation machines. We must also determine the extent to which prior learning to read accelerates or, under certain conditions, possibly retards indefinitely the later acquisition of the spoken language.

Generally, however, we assume that command of the spoken language is the prime objective in any case. Certainly it is the prime objective for anyone who expects to go abroad as a tourist, a businessman, or foreign service officer. What are the main research issues concerning the teaching of the spoken language?

Above all, we must settle the question of the utility of the "language laboratory." The language laboratory—which is really no more a laboratory than a music practice room or a gymnasium—has been widely accepted by foreign language teachers who wish to emphasize audio-lingual training. The few holdouts (aside from those who would like language laboratories but who cannot avail themselves of necessary funds) are those who have enough time in the classroom or a sufficient pool of native informants to give the auditory stimulation and practice which can otherwise come about through the use of the electro-mechanical aids found in the language laboratory. The need of this auditory stimulation and practice is commonly accepted. Trying to teach a spoken foreign language without it would be like trying to teach musical appreciation solely from printed musical scores. The question of the utility of the language laboratory, therefore, is simply one of finding the most practical and efficacious methods of presenting auditory stimulation and of encouraging and directing oral practice.

The language laboratory probably would win hands down if the use of a language laboratory were compared with a teaching situation in which there was a complete lack of attention to auditory training—at least, if the criterion of success were to be ability to comprehend the spoken language, as measured, say, by the listening comprehension tests now available through the Educational Testing Service.

There are undoubtedly many questions of detail concerning the use of language laboratory equipment. The gadget is not everything; one must find out how to use the gadget and what to teach by it. Conceivably, almost as much could be done with simple phonograph records, which the student is allowed to take home and play to himself, as with the more elaborate two-channel set-ups which can be found in some language laboratories. Only a carefully controlled laboratory experiment will tell us the answer to this question, and it takes effort and patience to conduct such experiments. One could experiment with other comparisons, such as the effect of enabling the student to listen to his own repetitions

of the voice on the tape, or of enabling the student to receive a constant feedback of his own voice. The details of mechanical arrangements will probably be less important, however, than what is presented for the student to learn and in what sequence it is presented.

One of the complaints most frequently voiced about contemporary foreign language learning methods is that drill, drill, and more drill deadens the interest of the student. But it is significant that one does not hear this complaint universally. Some foreign language teachers seem to have been able to organize their instructional methods and materials so that the student's intelligence is not insulted, and so that there is sufficient variety of drill activities to prevent the setting in of monotony and lack of interest. Bright and apt students recognize the need for drill and repetition (if it is of the right sort) and even go so far as to complain if there are not sufficient opportunities for drill. Nevertheless, we are still faced with the fact that language study, even at its best, requires time and patience. Some have called for what they term a "breakthrough" in methods of language teaching, and have looked to the possibilities of special electro-mechanical teaching devices which would not only present stimuli for learning but also tell the student whether his answers are right or not. "Teaching machines" have already proved feasible and, on the whole, successful in other areas, such as the teaching of spelling, arithmetic, physics, and psychology; why not in foreign languages? As I have intimated above, teaching machines may have the effect of reducing the effect of individual differences in aptitude.

To a limited extent, the tape and magnetic disc recorders now used in language laboratories are "teaching machines"; they present stimuli, and their presentations can be correlated with visual displays. Furthermore, it is usually possible for the student to determine immediately from the presentations whether his answer is correct or not. They fall short of being full-fledged teaching machines largely because of what I would call a lack of two-way linkage between teaching device and student; even if the student fails to make any response at all, the machine plays on. The next step in research with teaching devices in foreign language teaching is to investigate ways of remedying this deficiency. In some ways, this is a large order, because with present technology it is virtually impossible to build a machine that will recognize and evaluate a spoken phoneme or word. Nevertheless, I believe it would be possible to exploit the possibilities of teaching devices with correlated visual and auditory displays and with arrangements that would in some way necessitate active (and correct) response on the part of the student in order to allow the machine to advance to the next item of instruction.

Whether the use of "teaching machines" will represent any kind of "breakthrough" in foreign language teaching remains to be seen. Psychologists who have worked with teaching machines modulate their enthusiasm for them with reports of the great efforts needed to "program" instructional content, its grading and manner of presentation. The materials presented in language laboratories require nearly as much attention to "programming" as do the more advanced semi-automatic teaching devices.

The problem of the equipment needed for foreign language teaching is of no small importance, but of even greater moment is the question of the adequacy of presently available methods and materials. I suggested above that foreign language teaching methods may already be in a high state of perfection. Granted that highly effective methods exist—though only in certain quarters and in the hands of a few teachers— the methods represented in the literally millions of foreign language textbooks in the hands of high school and college students are nevertheless highly suspect from the standpoint of current thinking in the

psychology of language. Open almost every textbook and you get the impression that learning a foreign language is a matter of learning a translation code; witness the vocabulary lists with English glosses, translation exercises, and the like. There are some who view this situation with alarm. As a researcher, I would only want to raise the question of whether so liberal a use of the native language in textbooks is a good thing. One could cite psychological theory which suggests that it is not, and that this incessant use of the native language as a "key" to the foreign code is one of the major faults found in foreign language teaching in this country. We seem to be finding that people can learn foreign languages in two fundamentally different ways.[5] The "compound" bilingual, the theory says, learns a foreign language symbol as an equivalent to a native language symbol, and thus must use his native language as a mediating system when he uses a foreign language. The "coordinate" bilingual, on the other hand, is much more facile because he learns the foreign language system as a completely independent system of symbols for the referents in the world around him. Much of our language teaching may tend to produce the former type of bilingualism, which is presumably less desirable than the latter type. But we need much more evidence to judge this question.

These are only illustrations of the many crucial problems which await decision based on research. At the same time, we already have a sufficient number of answers to give assurance that if an energetic and imaginative program of experimental research is undertaken, it will eventually be possible to frame a sound educational policy on the teaching of foreign languages to Americans.

[5] See, for example, W. E. Lambert, J. Havelka, and C. Crosby, "The Influence of Language-Acquisition Contexts on Bilingualism," *Journal of Abnormal and Social Psychology*, LVI (1958), pp. 239–244.

Index of Names

Index of Subjects